THE COMPLETE BOOK OF
GARDENING

David,

with best wishes

from

mum, & Hugh

July 20ᵗʰ 1961.

(To help those green fingers!)

HIPPEASTRUM
EQUESTRE
BARBADOS LILY

From a painting by Emily Sartain

E. SARTAIN

THE COMPLETE BOOK OF
GARDENING

J. COUTTS, A.H.R.H.S., V.M.H.
(FORMERLY CURATOR)

A. OSBORN

&

A. EDWARDS

(FORMERLY ASSISTANT CURATORS)

OF THE

ROYAL BOTANIC GARDENS, KEW

Revised and Edited by G. H. Preston, F.L.S. (Assistant Curator)
of the Royal Botanic Gardens, Kew

---

16 COLOUR PLATES
SEVERAL HUNDRED PHOTOGRAPHS
AND DIAGRAMS

WARD, LOCK & CO., LIMITED

LONDON, MELBOURNE AND JOHANNESBURG

MADE IN ENGLAND

Printed in Great Britain by
EBENEZER BAYLIS AND SON, LTD., THE TRINITY PRESS, WORCESTER, AND LONDON

PREFACE

By reason of their positions at the Royal Botanic Gardens, Kew, the authors and the editor are exceptionally qualified to write a really practical, comprehensive, and up-to-date book covering all phases of gardening, for their joint knowledge of gardening matters is unique and essentially practical. A glance through the pages of the book will show how ably they have carried out their task.

They have set out to write a plain, straightforward book of instruction that tells in simple language, in which technical and botanical terms are reduced to a minimum, how to plan and make a modern garden and how to maintain it. The work embodies the very latest horticultural practice, and recommends the most recently introduced and really desirable varieties of flowers, shrubs, vegetables and fruit trees; at the same time, the old favourites are still conceded the positions they deserve.

Modern nomenclature and classification of many plants has called for considerable changes and rearrangement, for example, Arum Lily is no longer Richardia, it is Zantedeschia; the Flowering Crabs are no longer to be found under Pyrus, they are now classified under Malus, etc. etc. Such changes, although essential to an up-to-date book, can prove confusing to the gardener who persists in calling his Montbretia, Montbretia, when it is now classified as Tritonia, and so to obviate confusion we have left in both text and index cross-references from old names which have now been changed or altered in any way.

The first aim of the authors and the editor has been to ensure accuracy and up-to-dateness, secondly they have striven for comprehensiveness, and the publishers feel confident that the book will prove of the greatest value to gardeners, whether tyros or "old hands", for from their own extended experience the authors and the editor have been able to judge of the points upon which the readers will be most likely to require advice. Especially have they shown just How and When the various operations should be carried out.

The work is thoroughly practical and in it will be found answers to all questions likely to puzzle the amateur and beginner. Because a gardening volume is essentially a book of reference, it should be as handy in form as possible and the information it imparts should be quickly and easily accessible; for this reason a complete index has been added, popular and botanical names have been carefully cross-referenced, and where changes in classification have taken place, these are cross-referenced with the old names; the work has, as far as possible, been arranged alphabetically, and much of the matter is in the form of lists and tables, so that the book might well be called a veritable *Gardening at a Glance*.

The first few chapters describe the general principles of gardening— Laying out the Garden, Making Beds, Paths and Lawns, Soil Improvement, Manuring and Propagation. Next follow chapters on subjects such as the Herbaceous Border, Bedding Schemes, Bulb Planting, the Rock Garden, the Wall and Paved Gardens, and the Water and Bog Gardens. In the A.B.C. of Plants will be found the detailed culture of well over 700 different genera; annuals, biennials, perennials, bulbs, shrubs, climbers, ferns, greenhouse plants, etc.—how and when to propagate them, soils and situations most suited to them, and lists of the best species and varieties to grow, showing their height, colour of flowers and times of blooming. The detailed culture of all fruit, vegetables and salads is described in the same practical and comprehensive manner, and in the chapter on the Greenhouse, are instructions for the care of tender plants, together with lists of plants that will make a show in the house throughout the year.

It will be seen that every branch and phase of gardening has been considered in detail. Moreover, the common mistake of assuming that the reader has at least some knowledge of the point in question has been avoided, the subjects being treated lucidly, fully, yet concisely. The man with very little experience will, therefore, find the book invaluable, while, owing to its wide scope, accuracy and detailed instructions, it will be exceptionally useful even to the expert.

The authoritative information, together with the 16 colour plates and 64 photographic illustrations, depicting accurately the chief garden operations and enabling the reader to identify with certainty nearly 200 flowers, shrubs, fruit and vegetables, make this the *standard authority of the day*.

THE EDITOR.

Warwick House,
116, Baker Street,
London, W.1

CONTENTS

CONTENTS (*continued*)

8

COLOUR PLATES

ILLUSTRATIONS

ILLUSTRATIONS (*continued*)

Note.—The Publishers are indebted to Messrs. Gibbs Box Ltd. for their assistance in allowing many of the photographs used in this volume to be taken at their nurseries.

DIAGRAMS IN THE TEXT

13

DIAGRAMS IN THE TEXT

CHAPTER 1

PLANNING THE GARDEN

The man who sets out to make a garden for himself is on the way to experience, at their fullest, many joys: that of creation, of exciting discovery, and of self-expression which, we are assured, is the true end of life. If he has unlimited scope from the beginning; if he takes over from nature, so to speak, the cultivation of his particular patch and has, moreover, a free hand in the selection of that patch, he is as much to be envied as the adventurer who sets out upon a voyage of discovery. Many of the elements which go to the make-up of such an enterprise have their parallel in the making of a garden. Once it is established, his garden will afford him an absorbing interest which will last him through life and increase proportionately with the devotion he gives it.

THE GARDEN PLAN

The wise gardener will stand out against the seductions of any prevailing fashion, and will refuse to follow it merely because it is the fashion. In his selection of a site for the garden, and in his adaptation of that site, he may follow certain authentic rules; but in the actual designing and stocking of that site he must take into account all kinds of eventualities that no former prescription can possibly provide for. Ask one man to design a garden, and he will draw up a plan on paper, or dogmatically expound his principles, with little or no regard for the situation in which the garden is to be made. He will treat the problem as though site and soil and atmosphere and situation were of so little account that their consideration would be superfluous. One might just as well expect to design a successful costume without knowing the sex, age, proportions, or type of the wearer.

The actual design and embellishment of a garden must of necessity be governed by the character and formation of the ground at the gardener's disposal.

SOIL AND SITUATION

Few people have an unlimited choice in the matter of locality in which to build their house and garden, but even though that scope be somewhat circumspect, there are many things still to be taken into account. It is obvious, for example, that the various suburbs of even a small town differ very much in climate, in density of atmosphere, and in convenience, so that in choosing a site for a garden each of these factors should be duly con-

15

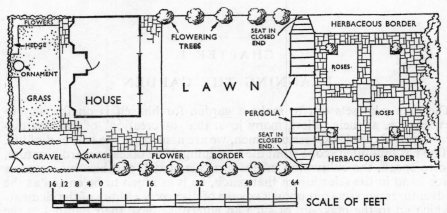

FLOWERS

HEDGE

ORNAMENT

GRASS

HOUSE

FLOWERING TREES

SEAT IN CLOSED END

L A W N

PERGOLA

SEAT IN CLOSED END

HERBACEOUS BORDER

ROSES

ROSES

HERBACEOUS BORDER

GRAVEL   **GARAGE**   **FLOWER   BORDER**

16 12 8 4 0   16   32   48   64

SCALE OF FEET

FIG. 1. SUGGESTED LAY-OUT FOR A SMALL RECTANGULAR GARDEN

sidered. One side of a town is likely to present more advantageous features from the gardener's point of view than another, apart from the nature of its soil. The direction of the prevailing wind, to take only one example, dictates not only the steps he must take to shelter his crops, but also the presence or otherwise of smoke and fogs. It is clear that if the prevailing winter wind is a south-westerly one, then the garden situated in a north-easterly suburb will be more liable to smoke and fog than one which stands to windward of the town. It is wisest to select a site upon slightly rising ground which is not so high as to be difficult of access or to suffer from exposure. Fogs are more prevalent in valleys and low-lying hollows; and in valleys, too, owing to the slower evaporation, spring frosts persist until later into the year than they do on rising ground, and autumn frosts begin much earlier.

With the actual neighbourhood fixed upon, consideration should be given to the nature of the soil which covers it. For both building and horti-cultural purposes such soil should be light and rather spongy in texture. Heavy, sluggish, and impervious soils make gardening a very unprofitable business. They are not only difficult to work, but in wet weather become cold and greasy, hold the water, and promote the ill-health and decay of plant and vegetable alike; while in hot, dry weather, evaporation from them takes place so speedily that the surface cakes together and cracks, and the tender roots in consequence are starved. The atmosphere about such land remains cold and moist all the winter, making the house built upon it damp and unhealthy, while the labour involved to produce even the smallest satisfactory results in the garden is out of all proportion to that which would produce the same or indeed infinitely greater results from a garden whose surface and subsoil are lighter and more pervious.

16

From a Painting by Beatrice Parsons

PLATE 2   *MAYTIME IN A SMALL HERTFORDSHIRE GARDEN*

The most desirable kind of land, then, for gardening purposes, is that which is light in substance and fairly loose in texture. Such soil does not become water-logged, and so the necessity for extensive artificial drainage is obviated.

In examining the nature of the soil, due regard must be given to the sub-soil. This should consist either of chalk, loose gravel, or coarse sand. If the surface soil is shallow, a substratum of clay or close, unyielding gravel soon has its blighting effect upon the larger-growing plants.

Given, then, these good qualities of surface and subsoil, the whole art of simple gardening consists really in thoughtful adaptation, in thinking out a scheme which will make the most of the natural facilities of the site. For example, the actual laying-out of the garden determines to a great extent the amount of labour necessary to keep it neat and flourishing.

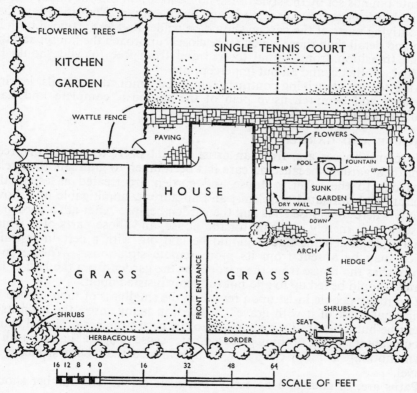

FIG. 2. PLAN FOR A GARDEN OF MODERATE SIZE, WHEN THE
HOUSE IS IN THE CENTRE OF THE PLOT

In the case of a very small garden it is sometimes a mistaken enterprise to devote much time or space to vegetables. As a rule, they can be bought for less than it costs the amateur to grow them.

AVOID OVERCROWDING

While bareness should be avoided, the other extreme of planting the garden too generously with trees and shrubs is also a great mistake. Snugness and seclusion are two very desirable qualities in a garden, but they should be achieved without too dear a sacrifice of air and sunshine. The garden as a whole should seem compact without in any way presenting a cramped appearance; and this desirable effect is most easily obtained by preserving a unity between its successive and varying features. The range of such variety in the different parts of a garden should lie between the definite bounds set by the style of the house itself, on the one hand, and by the paddock or surrounding landscape on the other. That is to say, that the outlying parts of the garden should be wilder and less artificial both in plan and detail than those which more closely approach the house; and the actual transition from formal to free and from free to wild should be gradual, synthetic, and all but imperceptible.

All attempts at striking contrasts should be confined to details, leaving the large and comprehensive plan of the garden a complete and harmonious whole.

HOUSE AND GARDEN

So many houses are, from an artistic point of view, utterly divorced from their gardens because no care has been taken to graduate their relations one to the other. House and garden are treated as essentially separate and unrelated problems, and an abrupt, unmitigable line shows exactly where the house ends and the garden begins. After all, a garden in most cases is merely a setting for the house, and those parts of it which actually approach the house should be laid out with a certain restraint which may be absent from its more remote situations. Whether one approaches the house from the garden, or the garden from the house, the change should be led up to and not suddenly insisted upon.

Too many people insist upon revealing the smallness of their garden by laying out most of it with gravel. Indeed, in many cases, the lawn itself might be but a decorative appendage to the bare stretches of gravel which circumvent it. While nothing gives a greater sense of space than breadth of lawn, nothing is more cramping in appearance than bare stretches of gravel.

Paths are, of course, a necessity, but their extent and number should be restricted purely to necessity.

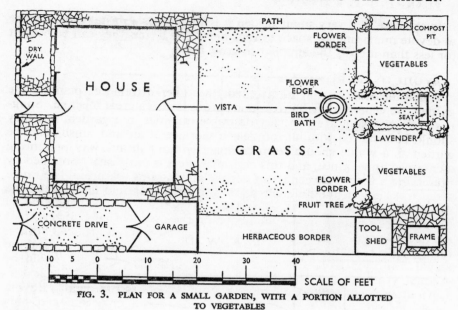

FIG. 3. PLAN FOR A SMALL GARDEN, WITH A PORTION ALLOTTED
TO VEGETABLES

THE LAWN

The lawn should often be the chief feature of the small garden, even at a sacrifice of flowers. It is a permanent beauty, the hardiest of perennials, the most capable of adaptation and, from every point of view, offers the most rewarding prospect. It is both useful and ornamental, far more decorative—if imaginatively treated—than any amount of prim flower-beds, while at the same time lending itself to an infinitude of practical uses (*see* Chapter 8).

MAKING USE OF NATURAL FEATURES

Nothing is to be more deprecated than the habit of mere paper planning, that is, of drawing up a hard and fast disposition of the garden without practical reference to the site itself, and of forcing extremes of fashion upon an uncongenial locality. From all of which it must not be understood that any particular style of gardening—the formal, the natural, and so on—is condemned as such. Certain situations demand a formal, even as others call for a freer, treatment. The character of the site and its architectural and rural surroundings should give the general lines upon which the plan should be formed. Many people insist upon making a clean sweep of everything with which nature has already endowed the proposed site. Such drastic treatment is almost always a great mistake. In the case of such

19

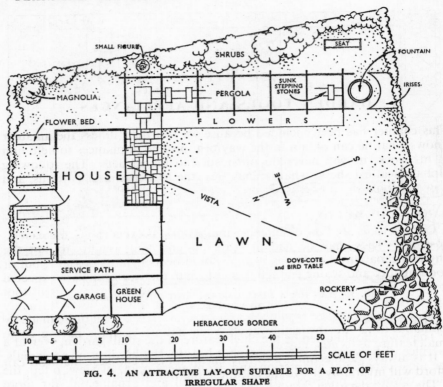

FIG. 4. AN ATTRACTIVE LAY-OUT SUITABLE FOR A PLOT OF
IRREGULAR SHAPE

natural features as trees, clumps of shrubs, etc., thought should be given
to decide how far these original tenants can be utilized in the gardener's
scheme.

HOW TO COMMENCE THE WORK

The actual spade work should not be embarked upon until the plan of
the garden is complete in every important detail, its boundaries fenced,
and the walks and leading features decided upon. For it is here, in the early
stage of carrying out a plan in practice, that the proper methods must be
understood and followed.

CHAPTER 2

GARDEN TOOLS AND APPLIANCES

This chapter has been included because we feel that, unless the amateur knows what he can obtain in the way of tools and appliances to help him in his work, he will never do full justice to his garden. The following alphabetical list shows what he may buy, the best sizes and patterns, and how the tools should be used.

SIZE AND WEIGHT

Garden tools are now designed to make work as expeditious and easy as possible. They may be had in sizes, designs, and weights to suit the physical capabilities of the user, and should be as light as possible, but of good quality and strong enough to stand up to the work they are expected to accomplish. Much better results can be obtained by using a light tool correctly than by trying to handle a tool that is too heavy. With many tools the patterns made by different makers vary greatly; all those made by reputable firms are invariably good, each pattern perhaps having some small feature to its advantage.

It is always false economy to buy cheap tools. The best that you can afford will invariably prove the cheapest and most profitable in the end.

The essential garden tools are the spade, the fork, and the hoe. But there are many others which render work less arduous and encourage good results, and are a necessity in any but the smallest gardens.

CARE OF TOOLS

Tools must always be kept clean and all unpainted metal work should be dried on old pieces of sacking immediately after use and should then be rubbed over with an oily rag to keep off rust. If kept bright and clean, they will not only last longer, but will do their work in a more satisfactory manner.

Each tool should have its own allotted position in the shed, and, where possible, should be hung up on a large nail or hook. It is surprising in how small a space tools can be stored, if carefully arranged, and provided each tool is replaced as soon as it is finished with. The tool-shed need not be a large one, in fact, it can quite well be combined with the potting-shed; this must, however, be rainproof, and if possible, damp-proof. Such tools as billhooks, the scythe, and similar sharp and dangerous instruments should always be kept well out of the reach of children and domestic animals.

CULTIVATORS

Hand-drawn Cultivator

The cultivator, or drag, is a type of hoe, and has three or five steel prongs some nine inches long, in place of the blade. It is used for breaking up the soil among growing crops. The handle is usually from 4 to 5 feet long. In some types, one or two of the prongs are removable, or the spacing between them is adjustable, so that the size of the tool may be adapted to the distance between the rows of plants. In other types the centre teeth are removable, so that the tool may be used to work between two rows at a time. The cultivator is used on light friable soil through which it is quickly dragged.

Wheeled Cultivator

This is an excellent implement where much work has to be done. It usually has either one or two wheels, and handles similar to those of a plough. Hoes, cultivator prongs, rake, or a small plough shear can be used as required. This machine is quite easy to push along between the drills.

Motor Cultivator

In this machine a motor drives the wheels on which it runs, and at the same time operates a rotary sleeve upon which tines, or prongs, are mounted. In one operation this machine ploughs, harrows, rolls, and disc-harrows the soil, and is a most useful appliance where a large area of ground has to be worked. There are several types available.

DAISY FORKS

A good daisy rake will remove all flowers as they come out, but the only plan to clear a lawn effectually of these disagreeable weeds is to take them out with the daisy fork wherever they are found. This handy little tool is made in different forms, or rather with handles of different lengths, but the principle is the same in all. A short form of the fork consists of an iron shaft, about ½ an inch square, set in a wooden handle. The extremity of the iron is formed into a cleft fork, which is thrust into the ground so as to take the daisy plant between the prongs or tines. An iron ring which is attached to the iron is pressed against the ground, and acts as a fulcrum on which the cleft end is raised when the handle is pressed downwards. The raising of the cleft end lifts the daisy out of the ground. It is sometimes used to remove dandelions and docks, but it is not so effectual for these weeds, which have long tap-roots firmly secured in the ground and which generally break when an attempt is made to lift them.

The best tool for removing all stout tap-rooted weeds is a carpenter's chisel, with a blade about 1½ to 2 inches wide.

All weeds are more easily removed in wet weather.

DAISY RAKES

A daisy rake is very easily made. First of all, a thin plate of iron is obtained and cut into broad teeth along one edge; the iron should be just so thick as not to bend easily to pressure or any resistance. Two slips of ash are then cut out, each being of the same length as the iron and about ¾ inch in thickness and 2 inches wide. These are bevelled towards the inner edge—the upper one but slightly and the other to the thickness of a ¼ inch. The iron is placed between them, and the two pieces of wood and the iron are all firmly fastened together by stout screws or rivets. A five-foot handle is then put into the rake.

Holes should be drilled through the iron plate to admit of the passage of the rivets and handle. The teeth of the rake, which should number about sixteen, should be bent slightly upwards, or, in other words, slightly curved.

DIBBLES OR DIBBERS

This is an indispensable tool in any garden. It is used for transplanting most plants that are grown in seed-beds originally and then planted out at regular and wider intervals. The dibble may be described as a short piece of rounded wood, terminated by a blunt point at one end, and with a handle like that of a spade at the other, in fact any broken fork or spade can be cut down to any length and utilized as a dibber.

The pointed end is thrust into the earth and the root of the plant placed in the hole, the earth then being brought round it by two or three thrusts of the dibble into the soil at a short distance from the plant.

The dibber should not be used for planting bulbs or anything having a "ball" of roots.

EDGING TOOLS

Lawns and beds cannot be kept in good order without the frequent use of edging irons, otherwise known as turf or verge cutters, and edging shears. The latter, as the name implies, are used for shearing off the long grass that grows on the edge of the turf. A turfing iron is an instrument that is used for cutting turf to be taken up in rolls from grass land for the purpose of laying down on lawns. In the simplest form of turfing-iron, a stick or handle, bent at the end so that the horizontal part may rest flat on the turf when held by the operator, has a coulter-shaped knife or cutting iron inserted close to the bend. When pushed along in front of the work-man, the blade cuts the turf in a line of any length, and to the required thickness, usually about 1½ to 2 inches. It is useful only for cutting turf to

23

lay down on lawns. The ordinary tool for cutting the edges of lawns, often known as the grass plot knife, consists of a crescent-shaped blade, 7 to 9 inches in length, with an iron socket in the centre into which the handle is fixed. The manner of using it is obvious.

FORKS

This tool is as indispensable as the spade. It is handled in much the same manner as the spade, the only difference being that the handle, usually between 30 and 36 inches in length, is inserted into a socket proceeding upwards from the centre of the head of the fork and does not enter the top of the blade as in the spade. For gardening purposes, forks are made with three, four or five prongs or tines. For digging and trenching, a fork with four prongs is the most suitable. The lower part of each prong should be of steel, and the upper part and the tread and socket of the best scrap iron, while the prongs of all forks used for digging and trenching should be slightly curved, and are best made square and tapering if to be used for work in heavy soil; while for light soil they are more suitable if flat. The prongs are about 9 to 10 inches in length and almost straight. The whole tool should be nearly straight so that it can be inserted perpendicularly into the soil. This fork will serve for all ordinary purposes, but for trenching and breaking up ground at some little depth a fork with stronger and broader prongs should be used.

Border or Lady's Fork

This fork is a tool with slight prongs, square above and pointed at the extremity, and is similar in structure to the ordinary digging fork, but much smaller. It is useful for border work in stirring the surface of soil to the depth of two or three inches, an operation which is commonly known as "pointing".

Hand or Weeding Fork

This handy and useful form of fork is supplied either with a handle some 15 inches long or with a short handle of only 5 inches. Either kind may be used with one hand. The prongs are broad and pointed. These forks will be found useful and serviceable for weeding in the rock garden, in transplanting border plants and in working the surface of the soil in borders in which growing plants stand closely together—too closely, in fact, for the safe use of the border fork and for weeding. They are also handy for taking up asparagus and other roots that are not too large for removal by such means.

HEDGE CLIPPERS

(*See* Shears.) Full instructions in regard to the clipping of hedges will be found in Chapter 10.

HOES

The special use of the hoe is for cleaning purposes, though it is also serviceable in loosening and stirring the surface of the soil amid growing crops, as well as for destroying weeds. Hoes are of many forms, but they may be broadly classified as draw-hoes and thrust-hoes. As these names imply, the draw-hoe is pulled towards the operator and the thrust-hoe is pushed from him. Hoes are generally made with sockets into which a handle of ash or pine is inserted, and when the shank of the socket is long enough, it is secured to the handle with a rivet. The handle of a hoe should be from 4 to 6 ft. in length. The handles of draw-hoes are generally shorter than those of thrust-hoes.

Draw-Hoe

The chief varieties of draw-hoes are the short-necked hoe; the long-necked hoe; the swan-necked or Bury hoe, so-called from the bent formation of the part of the neck between the blade and the socket; and the triangular hoe. The swan-necked is an excellent type of draw-hoe and is employed mostly for heavy work, earthing up potatoes, celery, etc. A tool with a 6-inch blade is universally useful. The triangular form of hoe is convenient for cutting up weeds, as its corners are sharper than those of the hoes with square blades; it is also used for drawing out seed drills. In some hoes there are several adjustable blades of varying widths, it being possible to use each separately on the same handle.

Thrust-Hoe

There are several varieties of the thrust-hoe. The Dutch hoe, or scuffle, as it is sometimes called, consists of a sharp and comparatively narrow blade, some four inches long, attached to a socket by two arms which spring from the lower end of the latter, and are fastened at their extremities to the blade, one on each side. The blade of the hoe, being thus attached, forms an angle of about 30 degrees with the handle, and by this means is almost parallel to the surface of the soil when in use. The edge is thrust into the earth with a pushing motion and cuts up the weeds, which, with the surface soil, pass through the aperture between the arms. It is especially useful on light soils. In the best patterns the actual blade is of steel, and, therefore, keeps sharp.

Spud

This consists of a stiff, narrow, spade-like blade about 2 to 3 inches wide with a wide socket to admit of its attachment to a long handle. It is used for cutting up docks, dandelions, thistles, and other weeds, for thinning-out onions and similar crops, and for loosening the soil between plants in rows. There is another form with a horn proceeding from the upper left-hand

25

corner of the blade. This projection is utilized as a hook for pulling up weeds or hooking down any tangled growth, etc. All kinds of hoes, except the swan-necked, the triangular hoe, and the spud, are made in sizes ranging from 3 to 10 inches, measuring along the edge of the blade, increasing by one inch from the smallest to the largest. The smallest size of swan-necked hoe is four inches; the largest size of triangular hoe is eight inches, the former going up to 10 inches, the latter commencing at three inches.

Spuds are made in three sizes, namely, 2-inch, 2½-inch, and 3-inch. Short-neck, long-neck and swan-neck hoes are also made with blades having a curved or crescent-shaped edge, in which case they are called half-moon hoes.

HOSES

This is an appliance that is subjected to a large amount of wear-and-tear, and often receives very little care. In buying a hose, therefore, it always pays to choose one of the best quality, even if the first cost is somewhat higher. Hoses may be of rubber or plastic.

The rubber hose is made of one or more thicknesses of canvas, which keep it rigid and strengthen it, and is lined inside and out with rubber to prevent water and grit from injuring the canvas. The type most generally encountered is that with the smooth rubber surface, but as the hose has to stand a good deal of dragging about over rough ground, the outer surface is often ribbed or else bound round with spiral coils of wire, which protect it and give it the name of "armoured hose." The most useful sizes are half, three-quarters, or one inch in diameter.

Hose-piping is sold in lengths of 60 or 120 feet, or may be bought by the yard, and should be able to withstand a water pressure of some 200 lbs. to the square inch.

The hose should not be left about in the hot sun, and must be emptied of all water after use. In winter, and when not likely to be in use for some time, it must be rolled up on a special hose reel and stored under cover, taking care that all water is emptied out.

Hose Fittings

These, among others, comprise the rose and jet, usually of brass. There must, of course, be a tap to turn the jet off. Another necessary fitting is the union connecting the tube or hose with the water-tap. This is a metal fitting, lined with rubber, into which the tap fits closely and is kept in position by a grip, so that no water can leak from the union. This is for use on taps that are not threaded on the end. A hose coupling consists of two ribbed metal tubes on to which are fitted the ends of the lengths of hose to be joined, and secured in position by copper wire; one fitting has a female thread, the other a male thread on a ring that can revolve independently, but which still remains attached to its fitting. By screwing this male thread on to the female, a watertight junction is effected. They can be obtained to fit any diameter of hose.

Hose Reels

These are essential if the tubing is to last any length of time. There are several patterns obtainable. Perhaps the simplest and most popular is the reel which consists merely of a steel or iron frame made up of two circular pieces side by side, and about ten inches apart, these are joined together by metal bands upon which the hose or tubing is wound as the reel is rolled along the ground, parallel to and over the hose.

MEASURING RODS AND TAPES

A measuring rod should be used to ensure regular planting; it consists of a rod of wood about nine feet in length and one and a half inches square, marked off in regular gradations, such as 3, 6, 9, 12, 15, and 18 inches.

Measuring Tapes

Tape measures that roll up into strong leather cases will be found most useful in the garden. The lengths usually sold are 6 feet, 9 feet and 12 feet; or 50 feet, 66 feet and 100 feet.

MOWING MACHINES

There are many good mowing machines on the market, all designed on one of two principles, and ranging in size from very light models that cut a strip of grass eight inches in width and which can easily be pushed by a woman, to the heavy machines with iron rollers driven by a motor, and which cut a width of a yard or more at a time. In between these is a range of machines both for hand and motor propulsion. The models are classified according to the width of grass that they cut, the measurement increasing by two inches in each model, from the little 8-inch machine up to the big 54-inch motor-mower. Push or hand mowers rarely have a cutting cylinder of more than 24 inches in width; in many, the handles are adjustable to suit the user, while in others the parts are made of stamped metal for lightness sake. The smaller machines, which cut a strip from 8 to 12 inches in width, meet all the requirements of the little garden, and are also useful in the large garden for cutting edgings and banks. The heavier roller-machines are steadier and cut the lawn more evenly, and of course, cover the ground in much less time, though they are considerably heavier to work. It will be quite as much as one man can do to manage a 12-inch roller machine, while a 20-inch roller model will require two men to work it.

27

Machines of all sizes work on much the same principle; the revolving cutting-blades are driven by cogs on the side wheels that carry the smaller models, and by cogs or a chain-drive, often running in an oil bath, from the iron rollers that support the bigger machines, which have no side wheels. The revolving blades just touch a stationary lower knife. When these knives are too far apart, the grass is not cut, but if they are over close, the machine works so stiffly that it can hardly be pushed. Most of the newer machines have ball-bearings, in the drive, and also in the rotary cylinder carrying the cutting blades, and these run very smoothly if kept clean and well oiled. There should be 5 to 7 of these revolving blades; where there are only three or four—as on some cheap models—ridges will be left on the lawn, especially if the ground is at all uneven. The blades must be of hardened, tempered steel. In the machines with iron rollers, adjustment is made by moving the revolving cutters up or down after loosening a nut on each side, or in some machines simply by operating a hand-wheel; in the wheeled machines, however, it is the stationary lower blade that has to be adjusted, the revolving blades remaining fixed. Care must be taken that the adjustment is even and that the blades are the same height from the ground each side, otherwise the grass will be cut unevenly; it is likewise essential to see that the nuts are re-tightened after adjustment. Where a chain-drive is used, the chain must be kept at the correct adjustment; this is effected by loosening two screws—one on either side—and by moving the iron roller either backwards or forwards in grooves, thus tightening or loosening the chain. There is also a small wooden roller at the rear in light machines, and in front on the heavier roller types, which, by being set higher or lower, regulates the length at which the grass is cut. A collector, or grass box, is fitted to all models save, perhaps, the very smallest, and in view of the labour it saves, it should always be used, except in very dry, hot weather. With certain machines a roller is supplied with spikes, which loosen and throw up moss into the grass box as the machine progresses, and also raise long grasses and bents so that the blades can cut them out.

The mower cannot be expected to cut grass that has been allowed to get too long; this must first be cut with a scythe.

Motor Mower

Although the motor mower is designed on the same lines as the hand mower as far as its cutting apparatus is concerned, a few words as to its particular characteristics will not be out of place. Most makers manufacture machines ranging in size from that which cuts a strip 16 inches wide, to the heavy pattern that has a cutting-cylinder 54 inches in width.

The 24 to 36 inch machines, with engines of up to 4½ horse-power, are useful in large gardens; the largest of this range being especially suitable

28

where the lawns are undulating. The weight of the heavier models enables them to combine the duties of mower and roller. A mower with a cutting cylinder 22 inches wide and a motor of 2 to 3 horse-power will cut as much as five or more acres in a day, and for lawns of some two acres in extent, where a two-man machine would otherwise be required, a motor mower with a cutting-cylinder of 20 inches width will be adequate.

Most models have a clutch, which throws the cutting cylinder in and out of action, the machine can, therefore, be used solely as a roller and can be run about the garden without fear of damage to the blades. A kick-starter is also a useful fitting. The controls are operated from the handles, and on some machines the grass is automatically removed from the grass-box while the mower is in motion, this saves many stops when a large area is being cut. In the larger models, the rollers are divided into two or three sections, as in the better class garden rollers, to facilitate turning and to avoid marking the lawn when the ground is soft. In large gardens and sports grounds, where there are large stretches of grass, triple mowers are used.

RAKES

The rake is a tool that is extremely useful when sowing seed. It is not so much required in the flower garden as in the vegetable garden where its use is necessary to bring the surface of the soil to some uniformity of fineness and to draw the earth over seed that has been newly sown either in drills or in patches. It is also used for drawing weeds, stones, etc., together into a heap prior to removal.

The rake itself consists of a straight flat bar of iron, from 6 to 16 inches in length and from half-an-inch to three-quarters-of-an-inch wide, in which steel teeth about $2\frac{1}{2}$ inches in length and resembling pointed nails, are riveted at right angles to the under surface of the bar. Some cheap makes have the teeth stamped out of a metal sheet; these, however, should not be bought, as they usually bend after a little use.

The teeth are usually slightly curved, but sometimes they are straight, and sometimes, instead of being like a cylindrical curved peg they are flat and as wide as the bar of the rake, but set in the bar with the width of the tooth transversely to the bar. The teeth of rakes are generally one inch apart, and the rakes are made in sizes containing from 4 to 12 teeth in light rakes, and from 4 to 25 teeth in strong and extra stout ones. A rake with 12 teeth makes an excellent all-round instrument. The handle is usually of ash and is 5 to 6 feet in length.

ROLLERS

Ordinary garden rollers are of two kinds, single cylinder and double cylinder. They vary in size from 14 inches in diameter and 14 inches in width, and weighing just over a hundredweight, up to the larger model, 30 inches wide and weighing some eight hundredweight. The double cylinder type (with self-oiling bearings), is by far the most useful. The best types are made with balance handles. *See* also *Mowers* (*motor*).

RUBBISH DESTRUCTOR

This is usually made in the form of a round cast-iron stove about twenty inches in diameter and some thirty inches in height. The rubbish is inserted in a trap in the top of the stove, which is usually portable. A brick rubbish incinerator may be built, if preferred, but this is more expensive.

SCYTHES

Since the introduction of the mowing machine, the scythe is comparatively little used, and is regarded rather as an agricultural instrument than as a gardener's tool. But even now, there are times when its use on a lawn is necessary, and that is when the grass has been allowed to grow to too great a length to permit the use of the mowing machine. There are now several types of mechanically driven scythes available. They are easy to operate even in a small garden.

SECATEURS

This is an instrument for branch pruning. In most patterns the blades are parrot-billed, are both falciform or curved, and the edge of each is bevelled in the opposite direction, so that the flat parts of the blade may work smoothly one on the other. Secateurs are sometimes made with a movable centre, and sometimes one blade is hooked while the edge of the other is convex or rounded in form from heel to point. When formed in this way, the cut that is made is cleaner than when both edges are straight or curved inwards.

SHEARS

Garden shears are made on the principle of scissors, but are much larger and heavier, the blades being thick at the back and bevelled thence to the edge, which is perfectly straight from heel to point in most kinds, such as the "rolcut" type, while in other types they are curved convexly or concavely, in order to give greater cutting power. There are two chief types of shears: one is the common garden shears, used for all ordinary purposes of clipping grass and hedges; the other is employed for trimming the edges of lawns, beds, verges, etc., and is furnished with long handles, some 36 inches in length, so that the necessity of stooping on the part of the operator is entirely obviated. In many patterns, the blades can be adjusted to the required angle, so that they may also be used as surface-cutting shears. Mechanically operated shears for hedge trimming, etc., are now becoming very popular.

SIEVES

The garden sieve is used for sifting mould and other ingredients of the compost to render them fine enough for potting seedlings and cuttings; for sifting stones and gravel, in which case a stronger and wider mesh is necessary; and, in some cases, for sorting seeds. Sieves have their meshes made of strong iron wire $\frac{1}{8}$, $\frac{1}{4}$, $\frac{1}{2}$, $\frac{3}{4}$, or 1 inch apart and are known respectively as sieves of $\frac{1}{8}$, $\frac{1}{4}$, $\frac{1}{2}$, $\frac{3}{4}$, or 1 inch mesh. The round frame is usually made of good strong oak, and is 14 or 20 inches in diameter and 3 to 4 inches deep.

SPADES

This indispensable tool is a straight broad blade, usually of hammered steel, rectangular in form, attached to a handle, some 28 inches in length, of tough ash, the upper end of which is in the form of a D, or fitted with a transverse bar, like the head of a crutch. The D form is the more convenient for digging. The blade is hollow at the top, for the reception of the lower end of the handle, and from it run, in an upward direction, two straps, one in front and the other behind, that are fitted to the handle and secured to it by rivets. The space between the front and back part of the blade is covered with a narrow iron plate, called "the tread," which affords support for the foot of the operator when it is pressed on the blade in order to force it into the soil. The transverse bar of the D-shaped handle is apt to split, as the grain runs transversely in its length. It should, therefore, be strengthened by boring a hole of small diameter through it, into which is inserted a piece of iron wire, riveted over a small plate at each end. The blade should be set almost straight on the handle, so that it may be driven perpendicularly into the soil. All the best spades are made in this way.

There are many different varieties of spade for trenching and digging, distinguished by some slight peculiarity of construction. The gardener's spade is made with a broad, straight edge, because this form is better calculated to hold and lift masses of earth and to penetrate equally all over the bottom of the trench, than would a pointed tool. Spades suitable for the gardener's use are made in four sizes, numbered, 1, 2, 3, and 4, proceeding from the smallest to the largest. Of these, Nos. 2 and 3 are useful sizes for amateurs.

For working in soggy clay and stiff, adhesive soil, a spade with a hollow or slightly curved blade is preferable, and for cutting drainage trenches a spade with a very narrow blade is used. The spade is a short implement, and although excellent for digging and turning over ground, it is by no means so handy for loading a barrow with earth, or for throwing earth from one spot to another, as is a shovel, which is not so familiar an object as the spade. Spades are invaluable on very heavy soils that have to be actually cut when being dug, or for use on very light soils. If the spade becomes blunt through digging on heavy and stony soils, the use of a file on the cutting surface will soon rectify matters.

Rustless steel spades are more expensive than the ordinary type, but are very efficient and nice to use.

SPRINKLERS

These are mechanical appliances that are attached to the hose and used to throw water in an even and gentle manner over lawn or garden beds in dry weather. They aim at making the spray as nearly like natural rain as possible. In many types the pressure of the water keeps them in operation, it being merely necessary to connect them to the hose and turn on the tap. The nozzles must be adjusted to suit the water pressure available. There are several types on sale, but all are very similar in their working.

SYRINGES

A garden syringe is an indispensable weapon in the garden. Without it no effective fight can be waged against insect pests, etc. It should be strongly made and have two or three interchangeable nozzles. These require overhauling every now and then, for they are liable to become choked by grit and dirt. The syringe should always be well rinsed out with clean water after it has been used for any solution containing a chemical.

TROWELS

These are tools that no gardener can possibly do without, as they are frequently required in planting and transplanting operations. Garden trowels are classified as "light," "strong," and "best," and are made in sizes of 5, 6, 7, and 8 inches in length. In transplanting small seedling plants and cuttings, the utility of the trowel is great, for a hole may first be made in the soil with it for reception of the plant, and the plant lifted bodily, with soil and roots undisturbed, and gently deposited in the hole. It is also invaluable for planting bulbs.

WATERING-POTS

Watering-cans are an important part of the gardener's outfit. The principle of the water-can is the same in every case, but the forms differ slightly and the work for which the can is needed must decide the question of size, weight, shape, metal, and rose required.

A can should be lighter for greenhouse and indoor work than for general garden purposes, as in these cases it is frequently necessary to reach plants above the operator's head. Cans for this work have long spouts and are specially constructed for the work they are expected to accomplish.

Watering-cans should always be hung up or stood upside down when not in use, so that they may dry.

PLATE 1 Gardening tools which, reading from *top* to *bottom* and *left* to *right*, are Dutch hoe, cultivator, draw hoe, French furrower, broad-tined cultivator, mattock and fork, lawn rake, border or edge trimmers and grass trimmers.

PLATE 2 When digging (1) keep the spade upright, (2) do not lean right over the work, (3) never take too large a spit and (4) always get well down to the work.

WHEEL-BARROWS

A good, strong wheel-barrow is essential in a garden, and is used chiefly for the carriage and transfer of mould, manure, and garden produce. They are made either entirely of wood (oak, ash, or elm), or of galvanized iron mounted either on pneumatic rubber tyres or wrought-iron wheels and framework.

The most usual sizes are 30 by 26 inches, and 28 by 23 inches. The back of the barrow is best formed by a movable slide working between fillets nailed on to the insides of the walls of the barrow so as to form grooves for the reception of the slide.

The capacity of the barrow for light stuff in the form of litter, leaves, and grass may be increased by having raves in the form of a light wooden frame, 6 to 9 inches deep, to fit over the top. This should be just large enough to slip over the outside of the barrow and should be held in place by buttons at the side or by thumbscrews. If made flush with the sides, it can be secured by hooks and eyes. An occasional coat of paint will preserve the wood of the barrow. It should be kept under cover, and a drop of oil should from time to time be applied to the bearings. Some of the metal barrows have a close-fitting cover; these are useful for standing in the yard, near the back door, so that rubbish may be shot straight into them.

CHAPTER 3

THE PRINCIPAL GARDEN OPERATIONS

HOW AND WHEN THEY SHOULD BE DONE

Even if the reader knows just what should be done at certain times of the year, he may not always be quite sure of the best way of doing it. For instance, he may be told to "blanch" his celery, or to "mulch" his peas in dry weather, or to "trench" the vegetable garden. If he is not certain what this means or how and when to do it, a glance at this chapter will set his mind at rest, for in it all the principal garden operations are described in detail.

Banding (*See* Grease-banding against Winter Moths, page 532.)

BLANCHING VEGETABLES

Several vegetables require blanching to be made tender and to have the green colouring matter and in some cases bitterness removed from them—celery, leeks, seakale, cardoons, chicory, endives, lettuces require it. The first two of these are blanched by the process of earthing-up, which is dealt with on page 36. Seakale is blanched under pots prepared for this purpose, and covered over with litter, sand, ashes, leaves, or it may be grown in the dark, in a shed, cellar, or under the greenhouse staging with sacks or other material to keep out the light.

The best plan with endive is to place over each plant, when full-grown, a large tile or slate, which will effectually exclude all light. With lettuces there is no better plan than tying.

(*See also the culture of the individual plants Chapter 35.*)

DIGGING (SINGLE)

Single digging is one of the most important of garden operations. In digging with the fork, little can be done beyond breaking and turning over the ground and reducing the clods thus turned up. In digging with the spade the soil can be transferred more readily from one position to another. Shallow digging is of very little value, and to enable the soil to be deeply worked, the spade should be inserted in as nearly an upright position as possible. The digger should stand well over his spade, and must not try to dig out more than 5 to 6 inches of soil each time—that is

34

to say in width—he must always dig to the full depth of the spade. The first thing to be done is to mark the ground out into strips each some 10 feet wide, if trenches longer than this are dug, it will be found difficult to keep the soil level. Next take out a trench about a spade deep and a spade wide, or, in other words, about 12 inches in depth, the same in width, and the full width of the strip. The sides of this trench must be cut straight and square, and all loose earth must be removed from the bottom, which must be flat and even. The soil from this trench should be removed to the other end of the ground to be dug over. Another trench of the same size is now taken out, and the soil is transferred into the first trench and is left as rough as possible, thus exposing as large a surface as may be to the action of the weather during the winter months. This process is carried on until the whole ground has been dug over and the last trench taken out is filled with the soil taken from the first trench.

Digging should be completed before the soil becomes too wet. If left over-late, the ground may become quite unworkable and the digging may have to be deferred until the early spring—a very bad policy, as the soil is thereby deprived of the beneficial action of air, rain, and frost through the long winter. Digging when the soil is very wet does more harm than good, for the earth becomes trodden down and compressed and loses all its porosity, which is the very characteristic that digging is meant to increase. Two-thirds of the cultivated soil in a garden should be dug over each year; the other third should be bastard trenched (*See below*).

In digging, all roots of perennial weeds should be carefully picked out, but vegetable stems and leaves and all annual weeds can be dug in as manure, provided they are deeply buried. In manuring during digging, the manure should be thrown with the fork along the bottom of the trench, and the earth from the next trench must be thrown on top of it (*See also* Double Digging, below, and Trenching, p. 45).

"DOUBLE DIGGING" OR "BASTARD TRENCHING"

Trenching to three spades' depth, as described in the article on *Trenching*, is not often performed, as unless the top-soil is very deep and good there is always the danger of bringing dead, useless subsoil to the top. On only moderately deep ground bastard trenching, that is, to two spades' depth, is usually adopted. The process is the same, except that the second spit is not removed but is broken up in the same way as the third spit in trenching proper. The top spit of the second portion of ground is not wheeled away, but is placed over the second spit in the first trench. Bastard trenching does not, of course, take so long as trenching proper; it should be possible to cover the same area in three-quarters of the time necessary for trenching to three spades' depth.

All cultivated land must be bastard trenched every third year at least, at which time ample farmyard manure should be worked in a spade's depth below the surface.

Grassland to be broken up for cultivation must always be double-dug, the turf being chopped up and buried under the top-spit.

Ground that has been bastard trenched in autumn or early winter must again be "single dug" preparatory to planting in the spring, to break down the clods.

EARTHING-UP VEGETABLES

A term employed to describe the drawing up of the soil about the stems or stalks of any growing plant, as, for example, peas, beans, potatoes, celery, leeks, and many other plants. It induces the growth of rootlets from the stem in some cases, and affords greater shelter for the roots. In the case of the potato, it facilitates the formation of tubers, which are found below and around the bottom part of the haulm and near the surface. If these are exposed to the light and air, they turn green and become unfit for food. This operation is desirable also to draw up the soil round the stalks of cabbages of all kinds. (*See also* Blanching.)

MULCHING

This operation, which saves much watering in dry weather, consists in spreading a 3-inch layer of half-decayed stable manure, well-decayed vegetable refuse, leaf-mould, coconut fibre, hop manure, or other material over the soil occupied by the roots of plants, especially those which have been recently transplanted, and in times of drought watering thoroughly before the mulch is laid down. The mulch will then prevent the water from evaporating too quickly. During very dry weather, the lawn may also be well watered in the evening, the following day the mower is run over without the grass-box; the cut grass will act as a mulch and preserve the moisture. Rain falling or water applied on a mulch soaks through and carries nourishment through to the roots and thus performs an additional service. Where a mulch of manure or other matter is unsightly and unpleasant, as on some flower borders, coconut fibre can be used as the mulch itself or can be sifted over to hide the mulch used. A mulch is of little benefit unless it is at least 3 inches in thickness, but if deeper it is liable to make the roots too cold. After a time the material used may be forked into the soil; a new mulch should then be applied. It is, however, seldom necessary to apply more than one mulch during the season.

A mulch should be very retentive of moisture; certain mulches are more suitable to one soil than to another. For instance, rich loamy or clayey soils are best mulched with well-decayed leaf-mould, freshly mown grass, or with well-rotted horse manure; on light sandy soils, a mulch of vegetable matter should always be well-decayed, and cow or pig manure should be used in preference to horse manure. The mulch must not be placed close up to the stems of the plants, as it is apt to damage them and cause them to rot, besides it is the finer roots that benefit by the mulching and these are often to be found a considerable way out from the stem.

A word of caution is, however, necessary, for there are several materials that should not be used as mulches; some because they soon "cake" and form a hard crust, others because of chemical properties they impart to the soil, or because they encourage insect pests. The following are a few substances that should *not* be used: mud from the bottom of ponds and streams, road-sweepings, pine needles, and newly fallen leaves. Such materials as soot and wood ashes should not be employed, as they soon sink into the soil and are useless.

Mulching is usually carried out during the months of May, June, and July; it should not be confused with top-dressing (*which see*), which only aims at providing nourishment for the roots, and does not prevent evaporation in hot weather. Every newly-planted tree, and all wall fruit trees should have a mulching of some sort spread around them. Plants whose roots lie near the surface of the soil, such as beans, cauliflowers, peas, and raspberries, are those that suffer first in a drought, and these are the ones that most require mulching. With plants of this nature, a mulch is put down in the spring; with other plants many gardeners wait until the drought has arrived. Where mulching is impossible, hoeing will go a long way towards making up for it.

NAILING UP CLIMBERS

This is a rather difficult operation, for nails are, as a rule, by no means ornamental, and the less they show the better. The gardener's skill must be exerted to conceal his nails and shreds as much as possible. For use in brick or stonework, cast-iron nails are best, for these will pierce very hard substances without bending. Cloth list or shreds of old cloth are generally used; but strips of leather or black tape are preferred by some, under the supposition that they not only have a neater appearance, but afford less harbour for insects. The shreds vary from $\frac{1}{2}$ to $\frac{3}{4}$ of an inch in width and from 4 to 6 inches in length, according to the size of the twig or branch on which they are to be used. Fruit-trees should be nailed close in to the wall, but ornamental shrubs, etc., should be merely fastened in for support.

PLANTING

Unless well planted, the tree, shrub, vegetable, or flower cannot thrive. Firm planting is essential in almost all cases; another vital matter is the preparation of the soil and the site for planting.

Detailed instructions will be found in the chapters on *Bedding Plants, The Herbaceous Border, Climbing Plants, Ornamental and Flowering Shrubs and Trees, Fruit, Bulbs, Vegetables,* and *Potting,* etc.

37

"POINTING" THE BORDERS

This consists in thrusting the garden fork some 5 or 6 inches into the soil, which is lifted and turned over. The process is useful in beds and borders filled with plants whose roots run near the surface and where it would be harmful to dig to a spade's depth. By pointing, manure is worked into the herbaceous and shrub borders in the autumn, the manure being first laid evenly over the surface, and then worked in around the plants. The surface of a bed or border is usually pointed over when it has become unduly caked and hard.

PROTECTION FROM WIND, FROST AND SUN

Wind

If the garden is very much exposed to certain prevalent winds, belts of trees or dense-growing shrubs must be planted to break its force, and to protect the tenderer plants in the borders. (*See chapters on* Hedges, page 93, *and* Trees and Shrubs, page 177.) Where the garden is walled, this protection is, of course, not needed, for the walls, as well as helping to ripen the fruit, protect other plants particularly tender ones grown on them, and provide a most efficient protection against wind. For protecting early spring flowers, such as tulips, in very exposed positions, temporary screens of coarse canvas, scrim, or coconut matting can be erected on poles 3 to 4 feet high, or straw or wattle hurdles may be used to break the force of the wind. If branches of fir or other evergreens are available, these can be stuck into the ground on the windward side of the plants.

Frost

Against cold weather and frosts individual protection for the more tender plants will be required, and there are many ways of affording this, varying with the nature of the plant. In exposed localities dwarf roses, especially teas, are best protected by a small mound, 2 to 3 inches in height, of clean dry straw, bracken, coconut fibre, or some similar material, heaped round them, or by several inches of soil drawn up round the stem. The taller roses, standards, and half-standards should have dry bracken fronds tied in amongst their heads. The ordinary garden mat is the most useful thing for tying round other tender shrubs and for covering frames during hard weather. It may be tied into a cone shape and supported on small sticks like a "wigwam" over small plants, or spread over trees trained against walls. The more tender herbaceous perennials in the open borders may, in severe winters, need protection from frost. The means by which this is supplied is described in the chapter on The Herbaceous Border, Chapter 16. The great thing is to keep the plants dry during cold weather; it is when a plant gets wet and is subsequently frozen that the damage occurs. In the early spring protection is chiefly needed for the blossoms of early flowering fruit trees, such as the peach and apricot, during the period when there is risk of night frosts. This is best given by means of cheap calico, netting, or garden tiffany suspended by means of hooks or rings attached to nails in the wall.

Sun

Many plants in the greenhouse will need shading from the sun during the summer months, and the reader is referred to the chapter on The Greenhouse, where this is fully discussed.

Where individual blooms in the open require shading from the sun, or protecting from the weather, the gardener may either make or purchase a cone-shaped shade of calico from 6 to 12 inches in diameter, stiffened and supported by a galvanized wire frame-work and mounted by a clip on a wooden stake so that it can be moved up and down until at the right height to give the necessary protection. Such a shade is especially useful for protecting roses from the sun and thus enabling them to keep their colour. Where sweet peas for exhibition have to be protected, these individual shades are not practicable, and in this case large strips of cheap calico, canvas, or scrim, should be arranged on poles over the rows of peas to protect the blooms from the sun.

STAKING AND TYING-UP PLANTS

As the plants in the beds and borders begin to grow, all that attain a height of over, say, 2½ feet, and many more of a less robust nature, will require staking, otherwise wind and rain will soon break them down. Rather than use one large stake, to which all the stems of the plant are tied in a tight bush, quite spoiling its natural shrubbiness and contour, it is better to support each of the stronger shoots of the plant with a separate stick and so preserve the natural contour of the plant. Bamboo canes are excellent for this work.

Time will, however, rarely be available for this treatment to be given to smaller plants; with these it will usually suffice if three or four sticks are driven in around the plant and bass or string is tied from stick to stick to support the flower stems. The stakes should slope slightly outwards and away from the plant and the string must not be drawn too tight. This is a good method of supporting plants with delicate stems that would be damaged if individually tied to stakes. As an alternative method, a stake may be driven into the ground at the centre of the plant and the chief stems can be tied to this with bass, not so that they are drawn tightly round the stake, but so that they may assume their natural positions. The smaller stems can in turn be looped to those already attached to the stake. Where there are rows of plants, stakes can be set close in on both sides of the rows and at intervals of from 6 to 10 feet, string or wire can then be

39

stretched from stake to stake at the height at which it will best support the plants; as they grow it may be necessary to add another line of wire or string above the first one.

Staking should always be done so that the plants retain their natural form and habit, and the stakes should be hidden as much as possible, and are best placed behind the stems and foliage. Where natural branches and twigs of hazel or birch, which are the least unsightly, are not used, the stakes should be stained green or brown. Stakes will be very unsightly if allowed to overtop the flower stems; they should, on an average, be three-quarters of the length of the stem to be supported, excluding, of course, the portion of the stake thrust into the ground. It must not, however, be forgotten that this refers to staking the mature stalk, and that when supporting young flower-spikes, allowance must be made for growth.

The Stakes

As to the materials used for staking most annuals and all plants with fine branching stems, natural twiggy branches of hazel or birch, as usually employed for supporting peas, are hard to beat and are not used enough. They afford excellent support, eliminate the need for a large amount of tying, and encourage a natural habit of growth. Straighter, taller, and larger-stemmed plants require bamboo or prepared wooden stakes. Bamboo canes, if very tall, should be thick and firm at the base, but tapering and supple at the top to allow the flower stem to sway somewhat in the wind. If staked too firmly, tall-stemmed plants will have their blooms damaged by the wind and rain—they should be able to give slightly to the wind. Prepared wooden stakes, generally of rounded deal, are best stained green or brown to make them less visible. The larger stakes, like those used for supporting dahlias or roses, should be treated with paint, creosote, tar, or some other preservative; they will then last several years, if carefully stored during the winter. The lower part that is placed in the ground will be more durable if charred before it is tarred. Sticks of many different sizes will be needed, and a varied stock should always be kept at hand.

For staking pot plants, small wooden sticks, the prunings of fruit trees, or wires, will be found most suitable.

Tying Materials

The material used for tying naturally varies with the plant and the weather conditions to which it will be subjected. For trees in the open, tarred cord of thickness to suit the size of the trees is used. Perennial border plants are tied up with soft tarred string if it is to last for more than a season. For annuals in the open, for most greenhouse plants, for all tying, in fact, that need not last for more than a year, raffia or bass, worsted, or soft string, will be found most suitable.

40

Whatever the method of staking adopted, the material should always be first tied securely round the stake and then looped round the stem sufficiently tightly to hold it in position, but not tightly enough to cut into the bark or stem, due allowance being made for the future growth of the branches. Tight tying will stop the circulation of the sap, will be the cause of poor blooms, and will ultimately kill the branch. Stems should be so tied that they maintain their natural distances apart; if bunched tightly together, they will be deprived of a large amount of sun and air and will suffer heavily in consequence.

Staking Vegetables

Beans and peas, of course, require staking, and the reader is referred to the paragraphs devoted to these plants in the chapter on *Vegetable Growing*. For these, stakes of hazel, birch, or beech, are those generally used. They should be inserted in the ground close to the seedlings, so that the young plants can easily get hold of them at an early stage, and they should lean slightly outwards at the top to furnish ample space for the heads of the plants, which grow luxuriantly and need all possible sun and air to conduce to prolific bearing. In the case of peas, small additional twigs a foot or two high are set close to the seedlings to give them an early start to their climbing, for if the seedlings can find no support, the stems will fall back on to the ground, become bent, and the flow of sap will be retarded, and the plants will never wholly recover.

For peas stakes five to six feet high will serve. Beans need a height of eight or more feet, they are often run up on strings supported by a wooden frame or on strings nailed to a fence. Peas can also be grown on large-meshed wire netting supported on stout wooden stakes.

(*See* Staking and Tying in the chapter on *Fruit Growing*, and *Training Plants* in this chapter.)

SWEEPING

Of all the brooms for sweeping lawns and walks the best is the old-fashioned birch besom with the long natural twigs. If skilfully used, this will pick up all odds and ends, and disturb the surface as little as may be. When sweeping up fallen leaves or light rubbish, the user should always work in the same direction as the wind is blowing. The latter will then prove a help instead of a hindrance.

TIDYING-UP

The primary object of tidying-up may be to keep the garden neat and tidy, but it has such beneficial effects upon the plants that it may be said to be essential in the garden, even if the primary object is not considered. Firstly, the collecting and burning of waste materials, such as dead leaves

41

and twigs, does much to stop the propagation of fungoid diseases and insect pests. Secondly, the hoeing and pointing-in of the soil does untold good. These processes, together with the benefits they confer, are fully explained in other paragraphs in this chapter.

Removal of Dead Blooms

But it is more with the removal of dead shoots after flowering and the picking off of dead flowers and seed-pods that we have to deal here. Many think that these things are done purely to make the beds appear tidier; this is certainly a useful function, but the main reason is a far more important one. To reproduce its species is the foremost aim of every plant, and as a rule once this has been ensured, the plant ceases to bear more flowers, and in the case of an annual, dies down altogether. For this reason, all annuals should have their dead blooms and seed-pods picked off as soon as possible, to encourage the production of fresh flowers; this will greatly extend the period of blooming. With early-flowering herbaceous perennials, such as delphiniums and lupins, the same process should be carried out, except that the whole of the stem supporting the dead blooms should be cut away; this will enable the plants to put forth a second crop of bloom in the early autumn.

Trimming Back and Cutting Down

About mid-summer, or slightly later, it will be found that border plants will require additional treatment to that mentioned above. Many of them will have grown unwieldy and may be suffocating less vigorous plants; these must be trimmed back with a sharp knife to keep them within bounds. Plants of a trailing and creeping nature will require pegging down to lead them into the way they should go and to make them cover their allotted space. (*See* the paragraph entitled *Staking and Tying-up* in this chapter.)

TOP-DRESSING

Although some mulches are at the same time top-dressings, these two preparations are applied for entirely different purposes. Mulches are used primarily to prevent over-rapid evaporation and to keep the roots warm or cool; the aim of the top-dressing is to enrich the soil and furnish new food for the roots.

Most of the organic manures and artificial fertilizers mentioned in the chapter on *Manures* may be used as top-dressings; those most generally employed for this purpose are: bonemeal, kainit, leaf-mould, old lawn mowings, old hot-bed manure, nitrate of soda, sulphate of ammonia, superphosphate of lime, and wood-ashes. For flower-beds and borders, a dressing of 75 per cent. old hot-bed manure, or if this cannot be obtained, the same proportion of well-decayed farmyard manure, and 25 per cent. leaf-mould, or other well-rotted vegetable matter is excellent. Rock plants will need an additional 25 per cent. of leaf-mould and a liberal sprinkling of coarse sharp sand; granite or limestone chippings may also be used. The reader is referred to the table showing *When and How to Apply Manures*, p. 61, and to the sections on *Manuring Vegetables*, Chapter 35, and *Fruit Tree Manuring*, Chapter 39, where the manures, either organic or artificial, most suitable to each fruit or vegetable are shown together with the amount to give and the season of application.

Top-dressings are used to augment the plant food supplied by the manure dug in at planting time or when it is not feasible to disturb plants so that manure may be dug in, as in the case of the herbaceous border or the rock garden. They are usually employed in spring or early summer, or in the autumn, the coarser organic manures are generally applied in even layers an inch to two thick and are then forked into the soil. Artificial fertilizers are usually very fine in texture and must be well raked into the soil and then watered.

Pot Plants

In the case of pot plants that occupy the same pot for some time, the top inch or two of soil may be removed so that a fresh top-dressing of compost may be added, usually without any stimulant, or in the case of plants known to be "gross-feeders" sufficient room is left in the pot at potting time to enable one or more top-dressings of fresh soil and fertilizer to be given as the roots fill the old soil and seek nourishment on the surface. Where stimulants are required, one of the artificial fertilizers will be found more suitable than the more bulky organic manures, and is best applied in three or four dressings at intervals.

Top-Dressing for the Lawn (*See* Chapter 8).

TRAINING

This is necessary in the case of flowers, climbers, and ornamental shrubs to help to produce the greater number of really good blooms; to keep the plants neat and within bounds; and, as far as possible, to make them cover a required space while still retaining a natural habit of growth and appearance. The nature of each plant must be carefully studied before the training is undertaken, as it is obviously folly to trim off in autumn and winter shoots of a shrub that should flower on these branches the following summer. The habits and growth of each plant are described in the paragraphs dealing individually with them (Chapter 34), and the reader is advised to glance at these before starting to train his plants. (*See also* Pruning and Training Shrubs, Chapter 18.)

Fruit and vegetables are, of course, trained and pruned with a view to quality and quantity in production. (*See* Training *and* Pruning *in the chapter on* Fruit Growing.)

Ornamental trees and fruit trees should be carefully trained from the outset; it is very difficult to recast the shape of a tree badly trained or neglected when young. Keep the tree well-balanced by trimming and lopping equally on both sides, and where it is necessary to let in more air, cut out a complete branch here and there rather than shorten a number. A clean straight stem should always be encouraged, and the supporting stakes (*see* Staking Fruit Trees, Chapter 39) must be inserted where necessary.

On Walls

A brick wall is by no means improved by having a mass of nails driven into it; other means of supporting a climber are, therefore, often used. Wires can be stretched horizontally in staples across the wall at intervals of, say, 18 inches, and to these the climbers are loosely tied by means of tarred string. A better plan, however, is to make a wooden trellis, with square meshes, which can be fastened against the wall, the climber being tied to this. Climbers should be trained regularly and must not be allowed to run rampant. If neglected, the stems will become weak and will be unable to support the heads in future years. Especially is it necessary to cut back the growths of young and newly planted climbers to encourage the formation of strong, sturdy stems; it is wise to cut all new growth on young climbers back by two-thirds each year.

(*See also* Staking and Tying, *and* Nailing *in this chapter*.)

TRANSPLANTING

Most of the remarks on planting in this chapter refer equally well to the process of transplanting.

In transplanting—whatever the subject may be—the great thing is to keep the roots out of the ground for as short a time as possible, and for this reason, when transplanting trees and large plants, it is advisable to prepare the sites and dig the holes they are to occupy in advance. Keep the roots "heeled-in" if possible, but if they *must* remain out of the soil for some little time, moisten and cover them with litter and matting to keep them from the frost and from becoming dried up, as once the small fibrous roots dry up, they perish and the plant must form new ones before it can again take up nourishment from the soil. It, therefore, takes a long time to become established and receives a severe check. If the roots have become dry, soak them well before planting. The "ball" of earth round the roots should be kept intact, although this is not feasible in the case of large shrubs and trees, in view of the weight of the soil to be moved.

Every care must be taken not to damage the roots. Seedlings should not be roughly pulled up with the hand, a trowel or hand-fork should be used; herbaceous plants and small shrubs are best lifted by inserting two garden forks to their full depth vertically one on each side and close into the plant, and then levering the handles gently downwards and away from the plant. This method will lift the plant from the soil with the roots intact. Large shrubs and trees are a more difficult matter; the best way is to dig a trench round the tree and from 2 to 3 feet from it, then to dig inwards towards the tree until the roots are reached, next dig downwards under the tree and it will be found possible to remove it without much damage to the roots. Trees and shrubs should be planted firmly, and well watered after transplanting. If the weather becomes dry before they are thoroughly established, evergreens should have their foliage thoroughly syringed every evening as long as the drought lasts.

The method of setting the plants in their new sites is fully described in the chapters devoted to the various kinds of plants.

(*See also* Thinning and Transplanting *in the chapter on* Propagation.)

TRENCHING

The immediate object of trenching is to deepen the soil and prepare the subsoil to nourish the fibres of deep-rooting plants. The subsoil is not

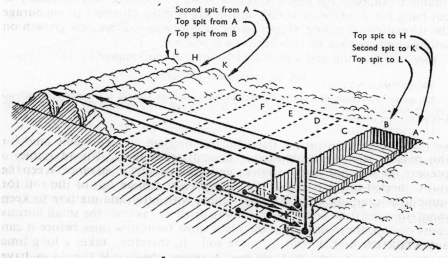

FIG. 5. TRENCHING—COMMENCEMENT

The top spit of trench *A* is wheeled away to *H* and the second spit to *K*; the top spit of the second trench *B* to *L*. The second spit of *B* replaces the second spit of *A*, and the second spit of *C* that of *B*; the top spit of *C* replacing that of *A*, and so on.

brought to the surface. The operation is commenced by digging a trench 2 to 2½ feet wide and a foot deep, throwing out the top-spit, and wheeling it to the farther end of the bed. The second spit is treated in the same manner, if the trenching is to be three spades deep. This done, the bottom of the trench is dug over to the full depth of the fork, well broken up, and is left level. The top-spit of a second portion of the ground is now removed and placed alongside the top-spit from the first trench, and the second spit of this portion is dug up and placed roughly over the bottom of the first trench. The first spit of a third portion is now removed and placed in as large masses as possible over the second spit in the first trench; the bottom of the second trench is then dug up in the same manner

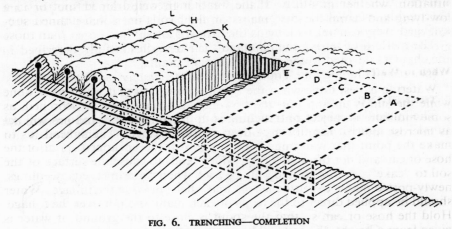

FIG. 6. TRENCHING—COMPLETION

K (the second spit from A) replaces the second spit of the last trench; H (the top spit from A) the top spit of the last trench but one; and L (the top spit from B) takes the place of the top spit of the last trench.

as the first, and so on till the whole is finished. Heavy soils are best trenched in the autumn, throwing the soil up in ridges, thus exposing a large surface to the action of frost and air during the winter. Treated in this way, the ridges should in the spring break down to a fine tilth. Light soils may be trenched in the early winter, or dug at almost any time, as required.

WATERING

Rainwater is by far the best for plants, as the carbonic acid and the nitrates that it contains make it a soil fertilizer. Even pump water, apparently clear, is often far too hard to be suitable for watering plants, but this hardness may be removed by keeping it in shallow tanks and exposed to the air for some time before use. Plants under glass should always be watered from tanks kept at the same temperature as the plants are growing in; therefore, some vessel must always be kept in the house. Nothing does greater mischief to plants than the continued chilling of them with water of lower temperature than the atmosphere they are in.

Water supplied by pipe from the main is not usually so cold as well-water, but it is often equally hard. If possible, it should be stored in a tank, exposed to the air for at least twenty-four hours to soften it, and to raise it to the required temperature before use.

It is impossible to make hard and fast rules for watering, for many points have to be considered. First, the nature of the plants; then their situation, whether in sun or shade, on a high well-drained spot or in a low-lying and damp locality; plants on light soils on a well-drained sub-soil, such as gravel or chalk, will suffer from drought far sooner than those growing on heavy loams with retentive clay beneath them.

When to Water

Watering is best done when the sun has gone down; if watering is done while the sun is up and hot, the flowers and foliage may be scorched, as some moisture is sure to find its way on to them, and the globules will act as microscopes to magnify the power of the sun's rays. This leads us to make the point that watering is best done with the uncapped spout of the hose or can and not through a rose, which tends to cause the surface of the soil to "cake". A rose should only be used when watering seeds, seedlings, newly-potted plants to settle the soil, and when spraying the foliage. Water should be applied direct to the roots of each plant and not over the foliage. Hold the hose or can so that the spout is close to the ground; if water is given from a height, the soil will be much disturbed or washed away.

Watering in the Open

Watering in the open should never be undertaken until it is apparent that it is essential. When commenced it must be done generously and sufficient must be given thoroughly to moisten the top 30 inches of the soil; this takes a good deal more water and longer than most people imagine. A little water over the surface merely chills the soil, and draws the roots to the surface, where they are quickly scorched unless water is frequently given. This, however, soon "cakes" the surface, and prevents the air from penetrating to the roots. It pays to give a thorough watering once a week rather than a daily sprinkling. Constant hoeing, or mulching (*see* p. 36), will eliminate the need for frequent watering. If a bed is thoroughly forked up and is then well watered one evening, and mulched the following morning with well-rotted dung, decayed vegetable material, or coconut fibre refuse, or well hoed—the latter is, of course, not so

47

effective—it will require little further moisture for some considerable time.

Plants to Watch

There are several classes of plants that are often overlooked as far as the question of watering goes, and among these are: pot-plants stood out in the open during the summer; a large surface of the soil is exposed to the air and heat, so that the compost quickly becomes dry and needs frequent attention, unless the pots are "plunged" in the soil, in ashes, or in coconut fibre; the leaves of evergreens prevent all save quite a small amount of rain from reaching the roots even in winter when other plants receive a good store of moisture; in the same way climbers, shrubs, and trees trained on a wall often suffer during the summer, unless watered and mulched, as the position of the wall will frequently prevent the plants from receiving moisture.

Newly-Potted Plants

In watering newly-potted plants, it is important that the whole of the soil shall be thoroughly and evenly moistened all through. This can only be accomplished by filling up two or three times with water, or by a thorough soaking provided by immersing the pot to above the brim in a pail of water and then standing it to drain in the shade. This process of watering is especially useful in the case of hard-wooded plants, such as azaleas, deutzias, heaths, and myrtles, which have fine fibrous roots and are very firmly potted in light sandy soil or peat. If at any time allowed to become too dry, the inner "ball" round the roots will not readily absorb water, and this will flow round the "ball" leaving it unmoistened, although the surface soil may seem to be sufficiently damp. Such plants will need a thorough soaking, and to prevent them from getting into such a state it is a wise policy to immerse them in a pail of water for five or ten minutes every week or ten days. No fear need be entertained of over-watering; if the plants have been rightly potted (*see chapter on* Potting, p. 127), all surplus water, beyond what the soil can conveniently retain, will drain away. Irregular watering is frequently the cause of failure in plant-culture, even with experienced growers.

Water each individual plant as it requires it. Because one plant in a batch needs water does not mean that all are too dry. Plants in full growth and coming into bloom always require more water than plants past their prime and "going-off". It is of immense importance to bear in mind that the lower the temperature in which greenhouse plants are placed, the less *water* they require, and *vice versâ*. Cold, which stimulates man's digestive organs to the utmost, paralyses those of plants in the exact ratio of its intensity. Hence the necessity of a more stinted supply of water in cold weather.

PLATE 3 Making a compost. *Top*, ingredients in visual proportions which, reading left to right, are (in dishes) superphosphate, lime, hoof and horn and potash, and (in heaps) loam, peat and sand. The ingredients can be either mixed (centre) by hand or with a trowel. *Bottom*, filling and firming down in seed-box.

PLATE 4

SOWING SEED IN BOXES

The seed should be sprinkled evenly on the firmed-down soil (*top left*) and a thin layer of sifted soil added to the top (*top right*).

The boxes should be placed in the greenhouse with a sheet of glass (*above*) placed over each to retain moisture. Brown paper (*right*) can be used to exclude light until the seeds germinate when it should be removed.

Plants should never be watered overhead when in bloom or in cold weather, or, rather, while they are in a cold atmosphere; and never, except to wash off dust, should those having a soft or woolly foliage be so treated. On the other hand, some plants, such as azaleas, myrtles, heaths, and others with hard leaves, may be plentifully syringed, or watered overhead from a fine rose in warm weather, especially when in full growth, or in order to soften the bark and encourage the formation of new shoots. Syringing should not be overdone as it tends to weaken the plants; if a moist atmosphere is required, this is better obtained by keeping the walls and floor well damped rather than by excessive overhead watering. The best time to syringe is in the early morning before the sun is up and again after the sun has lost its strength in the late afternoon and after the house has been closed. (*See also* Watering *in the chapter on* The Greenhouse, Watering Seeds *in the chapter on* Propagation, *and* Watering the Lawn, p. 83).

Other gardening operations will be found under the chapters and paragraphs devoted to those subjects, for example:

In the chapter on PROPAGATION	*In the chapter on* FRUIT-GROWING	*In the chapter on* DISEASES AND PESTS
Budding	Disbudding	Grease Banding
Cuttings	Fertilizing	Spraying
Division of Roots	Gathering Fruit	
Germination of Seed	Pruning, Root-Pruning	*In the chapter on*
Grafting	Storing Fruit	SOIL IMPROVEMENT
Hardening-off	Thinning Fruit	Fumigation of Soils
Layering		Sterilization of Soils
Leaf-Cuttings	*In the chapter on*	
Pricking-out	THE GREENHOUSE	*In the chapter on*
Ringing	Damping-down	THE LAWN
Root-Cuttings	Fumigation, Stoking-up	Edging the Lawn
Sowing	Syringing	Feeding the Lawn
Thinning-out	Ventilating	Mowing, Rolling

Special chapters are devoted to such subjects as:—

Bedding-out	Levelling Land	Potting
Draining Land	Manuring	Weeding
Forcing	Path-making	

CHAPTER 4

SOIL IMPROVEMENT

CLASSIFICATION OF SOILS

Soils are composed of two great groups of compounds: namely, inorganic matter, i.e. material derived from the decay of rocks; and organic matter i.e. material derived from the decay of vegetable and animal matter. The organic matter is termed humus.

Practically all soils contain sand, clay, limestone, and humus, but in very differing proportions. The preponderating ingredient determines the nature of the soil. Thus:—

Calcareous soils contain upwards of 20 per cent. of lime in their composition. They are formed largely of lime with clay, loam or sand, and humus in very small proportion.

Clay soils contain 50 per cent. of stiff unctuous clay. They are composed chiefly of clay with a little sand, and are lacking in lime and humus.

Loamy soils are soils in which the proportion of clay varies from 20 to 40 per cent. sand and various kinds of alluvium making up the remainder, with a little lime and humus. When the loam contains a large proportion of sand, it is known as *Sandy Loam*; when it contains a large proportion of lime, it is called a *Calcareous Loam*.

Gravel loam and chalk loam are loams in which there is a considerable proportion of gravel and chalk respectively.

Marly soils are the *débris* of limestone rock decomposed and reduced to a paste. They contain from 5 to 20 per cent. of carbonate of lime, and humus is found in them. They are distinguished as *Argillaceous*, *Loamy*, and *Sandy* Marls, according to the predominance in their composition of clay, loam, or sand.

Peaty soils, or vegetable mould, the richest of all garden soils, contain from 5 to 12 per cent. of humus, that is, decomposed vegetable and animal matter. *Peat* and *Bog Soil* is composed of fibrous insoluble vegetable matter, mixed with sand and humus.

Sandy soils contain 80 per cent., or thereabouts, of *silica*, that is, the crumbling *débris* of granite or sandstone rock. In other words, they consist chiefly of sand, with a little clay and lime, and a small proportion of humus.

50

A loose open soil shifts beneath the feet, and does not adhere to the boots; a clay, or heavy soil, impedes walking and clings to the boots. A clay soil, especially when wet, can be moulded in the hand; a loose soil will pass through the fingers. The texture of a soil can be told by rubbing between the fingers. If it has a greasy or soapy feeling, it is a clay soil; if gritty, a sandy soil.

IS THE SOIL GOOD OR POOR?

A good soil is indicated by—

Gentle slopes; strong woodlands, but no birch or fir; good strong hedges; rich green pasturage, with an abundance of white clover; deep soil, of a good brown or reddish colour; and strong healthy weeds. Oak trees and cowslips grow on clay soils.

A poor soil is indicated by—

Prevalence of birch, larch and fir trees; stunted hedges and trees; sedges plentiful; thin soil, wet and spongy; and the presence of various weeds, such as quaking grass, Yorkshire fog, broom, heath, bracken, and moss. Birches, alders and cotton-grass grow on wet and marshy land.

THE IDEAL GARDEN SOIL

The perfect soil for general garden use should be composed of the various elements in the following proportions: $\frac{1}{12}$ lime, $\frac{1}{6}$ humus, $\frac{1}{4}$ clay, and $\frac{1}{2}$ sand. Soil containing constituents in these ratios will rarely be found, but many loams will not be far from the ideal, and a little judicious improvement will, in many cases, furnish a compost in which most plants will thrive beyond expectation.

Wherever facilities are available for improving the soil by the addition of other constituents as clay, sand, lime, or humus (which must be well decayed), these should be evenly spread over the soil in autumn and then be dug in in the spring.

IMPROVEMENT OF THE SOIL

To some extent different soils naturally need different treatment if they are to be rendered fertile, but there are certain general principles which are more or less applicable to all. In relation to a plant's life the soil can be considered from various standpoints. In the first place, it furnishes a root-hold by means of which the plant is able to fix itself in space. Then, again, it acts as a storehouse from which the plant absorbs, as required, the greater part of the nourishment on which its continued life depends. Clearly, therefore, we must see to it that if our garden soil is to be fertile, it must be of such a texture as shall be compatible with the healthy life and development of the roots and rootlets, and shall contain within reach of those rootlets in an assimilable form the necessary food elements for

51

the plant's growth, and a sufficient supply of moisture at all seasons to present those elements in a dissolved form for absorption.

DRAINING THE SOIL

Water-logged soil will not allow the continued life of the majority of plants. Very sandy soil so unretentive of moisture as rarely to contain enough water for dissolving plant foods is equally hopeless. What most plants require is a soil which, while efficiently drained and containing within a few feet of the surface no body of stagnant water, shall yet be of such a texture and shall include a sufficient proportion of organic material as to retain for an appreciable time a moderate degree of water. If the soil is naturally very heavy, that is to say, if it consists very largely of clay, and especially if it rests at a comparatively shallow depth below the surface on an almost impervious layer, it is almost certain to be more or less water-logged. And it is necessary in such a case to dig it deeply and to provide adequate drainage, in bad cases by means of pipes, in less bad cases by means of stones and broken bricks, and at the same time to lighten the upper layers of the soil by the addition of sand, leaf-mould, organic manures such as stable manure, and the like (*see chapter on* Drainage, p. 64). In a similar way very light, sandy soils should be improved by the liberal addition of clay, fibrous loam such as is obtained from the top-spit of meadow land, leaf-mould, and cow or pig manure. These latter, which, in the case of the heavy soils, serve to keep open the clay which would tend otherwise to form a solid block, help, in the case of sandy soils, to bind them together, and enable them to retain a greatly increased volume of water.

In the case of practically all soils, one of the first things to do, over and above such special measures as have been suggested above, is to trench the ground or to dig it deeply. The processes of trenching, though extremely simple, are not always well understood by amateur gardeners. They essentially aim at the breaking-up of the soil.

For the methods of digging, *see* Chapter 3, The Principal Garden Operations, p. 34.

FUMIGATION AND STERILIZATION
Fumigating the Soil

Newly-broken land is nearly always infested with wire-worms, leather-jackets, and other pests, and a dressing with some soil fumigant such as naphthalene or carbide refuse is invariably necessary before successful crops can be obtained.

Soils that have been under cultivation for some time also frequently become pest-ridden. The presence of these pests is indicated by the poorness of crops, and by the weak and sickly state of individual plants whose roots are perhaps attacked.

It is in the autumn that most of these pests will be present in the soil; at this time not only those that dwell in the earth all the year round will be found, but those that descend from plants and trees to pass the winter in the soil can also be here destroyed at this period, if properly treated.

For this reason soil fumigants should be used in the autumn or early winter; another reason for application at this time is that seeds and plants cannot be inserted until most of the fumigants have laid in the soil for at least three months, or they will be damaged. Use the fumigants in December at the latest, therefore, so that crops may be sown in March. Where bushes and herbaceous perennials are left standing in or near the soil to be treated, naphthalene will be found the safest fumigant to use, as it can be employed with impunity quite near the stems of plants. Other chemicals must be kept well away from the roots.

Most of the chemicals used are very poisonous and give off gases when exposed to the air and moisture. The fumigant should be applied to the surface of the soil either as a powder or a liquid, as the case may be, and must be dug in at once so that the fumes may be retained in the soil, as they are the chief agencies in destroying the pests. Fumigants left lying about on the surface of the soil, for one day even, soon lose their strength and efficiency.

Sterilization

This process consists in burning, or heating the soil to such a degree that all pests and seeds of weeds are destroyed and plant growth is stimulated. Sterilization cannot, save the process of burning to be described later, be applied to any great extent to ground in the open, and is generally confined to soil used in pots and the borders of glass houses.

Plants in sterilized soil will at first be slow in growth, as numbers of the bacteria which promote this are destroyed with the pests. Those remaining, however, are free from the influence of pests and quickly multiply, so that after a time the growth of the plants becomes surprisingly vigorous and rapid. There are several methods of effecting this sterilization; that by which the largest area can most easily be treated is by:—

Burning.—In this method, all available combustible garden refuse, such as straw, hard and fibrous vegetable matter, and leaves are collected and spread evenly over the soil to be treated. This refuse is set fire to and encouraged to smoulder, rather than to burn fast, so that the process of burning is spread over the longest possible period. This method is best pursued in the late autumn or early winter, at which time the pests will be nearest the surface of the soil. Apart from the sterilization effected by the heat, the ashes will greatly benefit the soil.

Where small quantities of soil are to be treated other methods can be adopted.

53

(1) *Baking.*—Here the soil is placed in a shovel, or is spread thinly on a metal sheet or tray over an open fire, and is heated uniformly to 212° F. and maintained at that temperature for some considerable time. The moisture in the soil will evaporate in steam, but the soil must be removed from the fire before actual smoke appears. After baking, the soil should be well mixed and allowed to remain for four to five weeks before it is used.

For satisfactory baking the soil must be in a suitable condition, a porous well-drained soil baking better than a heavy clay soil.

Another method of baking the soil is to insert red-hot bricks in it. Sufficient bricks must be used to heat the soil adequately, or they must be re-heated and moved about in the compost until every corner has been sterilized.

(2) *Steaming.*—This undoubtedly is the best and most effective method of sterilizing soil. It consists of passing quantities of steam into the soil until the temperature rises to 212° F. The success of sterilizing depends upon being able to maintain this temperature uniformly. There are several well-known methods in operation as used in greenhouses by private and commercial growers, viz., the "small grid", the "Harrow", the "Tray" and the "Spike" methods. For those that require only a small but effective outfit, portable steam sterilizing plants can be obtained to take anything from a bushel of soil upwards. Some gardeners prefer to make their own plant. A wooden box is constructed with several parallel pipes 1 inch in diameter, running at intervals across the bottom; these pipes are riddled with small holes. The box is filled with soil and covered over with a wooden top or sacking so as to retain the steam which is forced along the pipes and up through the soil until it is heated to a temperature of 210° to 212° F. This temperature should be maintained for about twenty to thirty minutes. The pressure of steam should be about 70 lb. to the square inch. After the soil has been allowed to cool it must be removed and a fresh quantity added.

(3) *Scalding.*—When this method is adopted, the pots filled with compost ready for planting have boiling water poured over them until the soil is thoroughly heated all through. They are then well drained and allowed to cool before planting. Should a larger quantity of soil require treatment, put it in a wooden box and proceed as described for single pots. The process should be lengthened considerably in order that the larger quantity of soil may be thoroughly sterilized.

A better method, perhaps, is to stand a pail full of the soil in a bath of boiling water and to leave it there until the soil is thoroughly heated through and through; a fire must be kept burning under the bath or the water will cool before sterilization is complete.

On a larger scale in the open, fumigation is, of course, always preferable to sterilization.

Soil Fumigants

Chemical	Rate of Application	Remarks
Carbide Refuse .	15 oz. per square yard	Applied as powder. Useful for small pests.
Carbolic Acid . .	Mix 2 oz. concentrated acid with each gallon of water. Apply 25 gallons of mixture to each square rod of soil—⅚ of a gallon to the square yard.	Applied as liquid from watering-can. Poison; all liquid should therefore, be used up.
Formaline	Mix 2 oz. with each gallon of water. Apply 25 gallons of mixture to each square rod of soil—⅚ of a gallon to the square yard	Stir the mixture just before application and use in can. Containers of formaline should be opened in open air, or the operator may be gassed. It is advisable to use a gas-mask during application.
Naphthalene . .	3–4 oz. per square yard	Store in air-tight containers. Harmless to plants.
Salt	12½ oz. per square yard	Effective for pests at surface only.
Soot	12½ oz. per square yard	Should be fresh. Must not touch leaves of plants. Effective for pests at surface only.

NOTE.—30¼ square yards = 1 square rod. 1 oz. per square yard is equal to 2 lb. per square rod or 2¾ cwt. to the acre.

CHAPTER 5

MANURES: ORGANIC AND ARTIFICIAL

In the first place, manures are a source of actual food elements, which they directly contribute to the plants' necessities, and secondly—and this is true particularly of so-called organic manures, such as farmyard manure—by reason of the fermentation which takes place in the manure, chemical changes are brought about in the surrounding soil which liberate materials required by the plants.

ORGANIC MANURES

It is because it fulfils both these functions that farmyard manure, or its equivalent, is so specially valuable.

Not only does it directly add to the soil constituents needed for the healthy life of plants, but also through the fermentation which it undergoes, and the acids produced thereby, it liberates from the soil itself plant foods which would not otherwise be available.

By its texture, and by the gases produced in the process of its fermentation, moreover, it tends to lighten the soil and keep its texture open. For similar reasons there is considerable value in such manurial substances as leaves, lawn cuttings, vegetable refuse, fish guano, and seaweed.

All organic waste, indeed, has some manurial value. It is very great in the case of such substances as cow manure, fowl manure, pig manure, sheep manure, and night soil. Wood-ashes and soot are also useful, the former largely on account of the potash it contains, the latter on account of its ammonia.

Natural Manure the Best

Whenever possible, natural, rather than artificial manure, should be employed in the garden. The rubbish-heap, composed of turf parings, soft vegetable matter, and clearings of the garden, forms a compost which puts heart into the land. Artificial manures are to the land what stimulants or tonics are to the human being, useful for a season, but imparting no lasting and enduring benefit, and incapable of rendering the soil fit to keep up a sustained effort over a considerable period of time. Artificial manures, useful as they may be for the crop that immediately follows on their introduction, are soon exhausted, and leave no traces of their influence if not constantly renewed.

56

In its dissolution the contents of the rubbish heap adds to the humus, or vegetable mould, which forms so essential a part of fertile soils and supplies, or is the means of supplying, all growing plants with the food that is so absolutely necessary to their growth and well-being.

The Compost Heap

The gardener who is anxious to secure bumper crops should always have at hand:—

All the leaves which can be got together, except those in the shrubberies which should be dug in.

A heap of clean grit.

A heap of silver sand.

A heap of coarse sand.

A heap of farmyard manure.

A stack of turfy peat.

All the waste of the garden should also be placed where it may rot, for it is a capital dressing.

The scourings of ditches, organic kitchen waste, decayed short grass, half-rotten leaves, all soft vegetable matter, soot, and every bit of solid manure that can be got, should be collected and well mixed together, and allowed to rot thoroughly before being applied as manure to the soil in the late autumn or early winter. If turned two or three times, the heap will decompose without getting too hot or becoming mildewed. After turning, the heap should again be pressed firm, and occasionally sprayed with water or liquid manure or sprinkled with sulphate of ammonia to assist decomposition. The matter should remain in the stack for at least six months; if left for longer, it should be covered with a layer of six inches of earth. The compost should be applied to the soil at the rate of 15 lb. to the square yard, and must be well dug in in the autumn or winter, or forked in at planting time in spring, or later when the plants are growing.

A Warning

The compost of the rubbish heap *must* have reached a sufficient stage of decomposition before it is mingled with the soil. In the suburbs of large towns, where ground is valuable and space limited, it often happens that kitchen gardens are severely overtaxed, through a prevailing notion that good cultivation and abundant manuring make up for lack of room. This is true to a certain extent, but it has its limits, for instances are not wanting to show that serious results are traceable to this cause. The ground gets filled with insects, undecomposed manure is worked into the soil after each crop—it is trenched in, dug in, or laid on the surface as mulch sometimes—and all manner of half-rotted rubbish and garden refuse is trenched

57

in two or three feet deep. The result is obvious, for where decomposition takes place, many agencies hasten the work; insects are bred in vast numbers, club root and canker are prevalent, and good gardening becomes impossible.

The remedy for this state of things is either a copious dressing with unslaked lime, burning the soil, or the substitution of new soil, if the surface-parings of a pasture are conveniently obtainable. But prevention is better than cure.

ARTIFICIAL MANURES

It is, however, not always convenient to obtain a sufficiency of stable or farmyard and organic manure for the requirements of one's garden. In such cases resort must be had to various so-called artificial manures, most of which provide plant food in a highly concentrated form. These, for the most part, have but little effect—at any rate directly—on the structure or chemical activity of the soil itself. They add no humus to the soil and do not affect the tilth, and for this reason, if for no other, they cannot entirely replace organic manures.

The three elements which it is generally necessary to add to soil in the form of manure if crops, whether vegetable, fruit or flowers, are to be raised year after year on the same ground, are phosphates, potash, and nitrogen. And it must be remembered that these have not only to be added to the soil, but to be added in such a form that they are, or readily become, soluble and so capable of being absorbed by the finer rootlets of the growing plants.

NITROGENOUS MANURES

The most expensive of these elements is nitrogen, that is to say, nitrogen in a form available for plant food. Apart from guano and other mixed elements manures, the most useful nitrogenous manures are *nitrate of soda* and *sulphate of ammonia*, the latter should be applied early in the spring at the rate of 1 oz. to the square yard. The former is often applied at the rate of ½ oz. to the square yard as a top-dressing during the growing season. *Nitrate of potash* is also good, but is much more expensive. In well-drained soils certain bacteria exist, especially round the roots of leguminous plants such as peas, beans, and clover, which, by their activity, collect nitrates from the air and add them to the soil. Thus it is often possible to furnish a soil with both humus and nitrates by growing a crop of clover and lucerne and digging it in. Nitrogenous manures act very rapidly and appreciable growth is often visible a few days after application. The plants become noticeably greener and more vigorous. Nitrates must, however, not be added to excess, or rank growth will follow, accompanied by lack of flowers and fruit and susceptibility to attack by fungoid diseases.

POTASH MANURES

These help the development of sugar and starch in seeds, tubers, and fruit, and improve the colour and size of the blooms. Of potash manures, *kainit* is, on the whole, the cheapest and most useful; it should be dug well into the soil at the rate of $1\frac{1}{4}$ oz. to the square yard early in spring. On heavy soils, *sulphate of potash* applied at the rate of $\frac{3}{4}$ oz. to the square yard in early spring is also valuable. A simple way of providing potash for a small plot of ground is to add wood ashes and the ashes from burnt weeds in generous quantities.

PHOSPHATIC MANURES

These assist the correct development of the plant, its fruit or seed, and its roots. The three commonest forms of phosphatic manure are *superphosphate of lime*, *dissolved bones*, and *basic slag*. Superphosphate is the quickest acting, whilst basic slag is the cheapest, slowest acting, and therefore most enduring. It is best applied in autumn. Superphosphate is usually applied just before the plants are mature at the rate of $2\frac{1}{2}$ oz. to the square yard, and should be thoroughly mixed with the top 4 inches of the soil.

Basic slag is a chemical manure much used of late years, consisting largely of lime, phosphoric acid, and various iron oxides. It contains other constituents as well as these, but in small proportions. Its effects are much those of superphosphate, but almost twice the quantity is required to produce a given result. It does not succeed mixed with ammonia salts, as it sets free the ammonia and wastes valuable material, but is useful with nitrates. It is most useful on medium or heavy soils which are deficient in lime, or are too wet and stiff; but to obtain the full advantage the soil must already be fairly well provided with organic matter.

As a manure it is good for flowering shrubs, roses, fruit trees, lawns, and pastures. It should be applied and dug well in in the autumn at the rate of $7\frac{1}{2}$ oz. to the square yard.

Phosphates encourage the formation of fibrous roots, cause earlier development of the plants, and counteract rank, sappy growth caused by an excess of nitrogen in the soil. They should be applied every third year.

Where chemical manures are applied to trees and plants which have made full root growth, so that the soil is filled with roots, the best plan in order to avoid injury to the plants, is to scatter the manure where it is required, and then lightly to "point it in" with a small fork, only placing the manure just under the surface of the ground. In this way the manure is protected from loss by wind or rain, while the delicate roots of growing plants are not liable to suffer, as they are bound to do if the manure is dug in with a spade.

59

REQUIREMENTS OF DIFFERENT CROPS AND SOILS

Different crops have naturally different manurial requirements. Thus potatoes and tomatoes, for example, have special need of potash, whilst leguminous plants, such as peas and beans, and certain roots such as turnips, are particularly influenced by the addition of phosphates.

The requirements of each soil can only be ascertained after individual consideration, experiment, and possibly analysis. But there are certain rough rules. Farmyard manure in reasonable quantities improves almost all soils, heavy or light. It is usually unnecessary to add potash to clay soils, and usually advisable to add it to sandy soils. At the same time, it may be necessary in order to liberate the potash in the clay soil, to add lime. Gravelly and sandy soils are nearly always deficient in nitrogen, and are much less retentive of manures generally. Soils that are peaty, or that have become sour from excessive humus from constant year-by-year manuring with organic manure, are much improved by the addition of quicklime applied frequently in small doses and dug in at once.

Then again, different manures in each class differ in their action; nitrate of soda, for instance, works more rapidly than sulphate of ammonia. Some fertilizers suit one crop, others another. The requirements of both soil and crops must be studied when applying manures. (*See* Manuring Vegetables, Chapter 35, and Fruit, Chapter 39.)

Amount of Manure Required

As some guide to the amount of various manures to apply in average cases, we may say that it is safe, as a rule, to add to a square-yard of ground needing that particular manure, $1\frac{1}{4}$ oz. of kainit or $\frac{3}{4}$ oz. of sulphate of potash, $2\frac{1}{2}$ oz. of superphosphate, 2 oz. of dissolved bones, $2\frac{1}{2}$ oz. of steamed bone flour, 6 to $7\frac{1}{2}$ oz. of basic slag, 1 oz. of guano, a good dressing of stable manure, 5 oz. of fowl manure, $\frac{1}{2}$ oz. of nitrate of soda, 1 oz. of sulphate of ammonia.

The fertilizers must be spread evenly over the soil and must be crushed fine and be free from lumps, so that every inch of soil receives its proportion of the fertilizer. If this is not done, parts of the ground will receive an excess amount, which may kill the plants. The manure should be well worked in.

When to Apply the Various Manures

Slow-acting manures, such as bonemeal, basic slag, farmyard and poultry manure, are best applied while the digging is being done in the autumn and early winter. Quicker-acting fertilizers, as dissolved bones, kainit, nitrate of soda, sulphate of ammonia, sulphate of potash, must be applied in the spring or when the crops are growing.

HOW AND WHEN TO APPLY MANURES

SHOWING THE SOILS TO WHICH THEY ARE MOST SUITABLE AND THE TIME AND QUANTITY
TO APPLY

NOTE.—A dressing of 1 oz. per square yard is equal to 2 lb. to the square rod, or 2¾ cwt. per acre.

Manure	Soil to which best Suited	When to Apply	Rate per Sq. Yard	Remarks
Ammonia, Nitrate of .	Any	Growing Season	1 oz.	Fruit and Vegetables
Ammonia, Phosphate of Ammonia, Sulphate of	Clay and Chalk	Spring and Early Summer	1 oz.	Cabbage Tribe, Cucumbers, etc. Never on soil deficient in Lime.
Basic Slag . . .	Heavy or Light	Autumn (Heavy) Spring (Light)	7½ oz.	Best for slow-growing plants. Do not use on Chalk or Sand.
Blood, Dried . . .	Any	Growing Season	3 oz.	Good for Flower and Vegetables.
Bonemeal . . .	Light	Autumn	2½ oz.	Excellent for Lawn, Fruit, Shrubs and Herbaceous Plants.
Bones, Dissolved . .	Chalk	Spring or Summer as Top-dressing	2 oz.	Never on soil deficient in Lime. Good for all plants.
Farmyard Manure . .	(Horse) Heavy (Cow) Light	Autumn or Winter Spring	A good dressing	All crops.
Fish Meal . . .	Light or Medium	Autumn and Winter	1½ oz.	Good for nearly all plants, especially Potatoes, Turnips, etc.
Guano	Any	Growing Season	1 oz.	Never on soil deficient in Lime.
Hop Manure . . .	Clay, Chalk, Gravel and Sand	Autumn	15 oz.	Good for all Fruit Trees, Shrubs and Herbaceous Plants.
Horn Shavings, Feathers, Hair, etc. .	Any	Autumn	7½ oz.	Useful only for slow-growing plants.
Kainit Salts . .	Heavy or Light	Autumn (Heavy) Spring (Light)	1¼ oz.	All Vegetables and Fruit.

Manure	Soil to which best Suited	When to Apply	Rate per Sq. Yard	Remarks
Leaf Mould . . .	Heavy Clay	Winter or Early Spring	A good dressing	Adds Humus to the soil.
Lime, Nitrate of . .	Any	Growing Season	1 oz.	Especially good for Cabbage Tribe, suitable all crops.
Lime Sulphate of, .	Clay or Medium	Spring or Early Summer	6 oz.	Fruit and Vegetables.
Nitrate of Potash .	Any	Spring	1 oz.	All plants.
Nitrate of Soda .	Light and Dry	Spring or Early Summer	½ oz.	Helps on leaf growth in cold weather or after pest attack.
Potash, Muriate of .	Light and Medium	Spring or Early Summer	1½ oz.	Fruit and Vegetables.
Potash, Phosphate of .	Light	Spring or Early Summer	1¼ oz.	All Flowers and Vegetables, and all Fruit under glass.
Potash, Sulphate of .	Light or Heavy	Spring or Early Summer	¾ oz.	All Flowers; Asparagus, Carrots, Cauliflowers, Onions, Potatoes.
Poultry Manure .	Any	Growing Crops or Autumn	5 oz.	All plants, especially Root Crops.
Salt	Light	Spring or Early Summer	1 oz.	Salt-loving plants such as Asparagus, Beet, Cabbage, Leeks, Onions, etc.
Seaweed (fresh) .	Light	Spring to Autumn	A good dressing	All salt-loving plants as above.
Soot	Sandy or Light	Summer	Dust heavily	All young plants.
Superphosphate of Lime	Medium or Light	Autumn (Medium) Spring (Light)	2½ oz.	Never on soil deficient in Lime.
Vegetable Ashes .	Any	Spring	5 oz.	Beans, Carrots, Onions, Peas, Potatoes, etc.
Vegetable Refuse .	Medium to Light	Winter	A good dressing	Adds Humus to the soil.
Wood Ashes . .	Heavy and Rich	Autumn or as Top-dressing	5 oz.	Excellent for Beans, Carrots, Onions, etc.
Wool Waste (Shoddy) .	Any	Winter	7 oz.	Slow-growing crops. Manurial value lasts over 3 years.

THE USES OF LIME

The nitrates, phosphates, and potash supplied by manures are quite inaccessible to plants in a soil deficient in lime. Lime, too, assists the bacteria which render organic matter in the soil available to crops, and is itself an essential plant food. It makes heavy soils more porous and, therefore, better drained and warmer, cleanses the soil of insect and fungoid pests, and sweetens sour soil, which has become deficient in lime.

On soil naturally deficient in lime, heather, gorse and bracken will be found to flourish. The first sign that cultivated land is becoming sour, that is, deficient in lime, is the prevalence of "club-root" or "finger-and-toe" disease among cruciferous crops such as turnips. In sour soil crops become weakly, are unable to resist the attacks of disease and insect pests, and are prone to wither long before they attain maturity. When soil has thus become sour, the state should be rectified as soon as possible by the application of lime at the rate of 10 oz. to the square yard, the dressing being repeated every 4 to 5 years. If the soil is not sour, but merely deficient in lime, dressings equal in amount to those shown in the table below will be sufficient. Lime must never be applied at the same time as farmyard manure. When applied it should be perfectly dry and powdered as finely as possible, must be evenly dusted over the ground, and immediately well pricked into the top 3 to 4 inches of the soil, which must also be dry. Whether the lime is applied in the form of slaked lime or carbonate of lime, depends on the nature of the soil, and the time of the year.

The following table will show the forms calculated to prove most effective under the various conditions prevailing.

Form of Lime	Nature of Soil	When to Apply	Amounts to Apply	Remarks
Slaked Lime .	Heavy	Before ground is dug over in autumn or winter, unless soil is manured. In the latter case apply 3 weeks before sowing in spring.	6 oz. per sq. yard	Use immediately after slaking. Useless on Light Soils.
Carbonate of Lime . .	Light and Sandy	Three weeks before sowing, at any season. Will not hurt if applied at sowing time or while seedlings are growing.	10 oz. per sq. yard	Useless on Heavy Soils.

CHAPTER 6

DRAINING AND LEVELLING THE LAND

WHEN IS ARTIFICIAL DRAINAGE NECESSARY?

Good drainage is of vital importance. A badly drained garden is unpleasant to work in and has but little attraction for him who wishes to wander peacefully, or to rest contentedly. Besides, nothing save marsh plants will thrive in it.

Whether garden land requires draining or not depends on the type of soil and on the situation. If the land has a good slope, artificial drainage will probably be unnecessary, and there is rarely any need to drain lands with gravelly, sandy, or stony subsoils. Where this consists of a stiff clay, and in low-lying situations, artificial drainage is almost always essential. The following are two simple tests for ascertaining whether drainage is required. In winter dig a hole 3 to 3½ feet deep; if water percolates quickly into the cavity, the land must be drained. Soil where the water hangs about in pools on the surface for more than a couple of hours after the cessation of heavy rain will also require attention.

TRENCHING DRAINS THE LAND

There are some lands that have a thin stratum of material impermeable to water some 18 inches below the surface. It is obvious that such lands cannot be drained by a system of land-drains and trenches, for the water, over the greater part of the surface, would not be able to percolate into the drains. It is here that trenching shows up in its true value. By digging to a depth of 2 to 3 feet over the whole surface the hard crust is thoroughly broken up and the water from the top-soil is enabled to sink down through it. This in all probability, will be found to provide adequate drainage; if it does not, pipe- or trench-drainage must be installed.

DRAINAGE IN SMALL GARDENS

This is often a very difficult problem—at least the carrying away of the surplus water is no easy matter, for the natural slope is probably towards a neighbour's garden, and the small garden rarely has a ditch into which the drains can be carried. Pipe-drainage is also a somewhat expensive and laborious matter; the cost and difficulties, therefore, often lead to the small garden not being drained at all, which is, of course, the worst possible

64

PIUS XI   DORIA   DEUIL DU ROI ALBERT

PLATE 3 *D A H L I A S*

MDE. F. BRAEME   WILLY DEN OUDEN

SATAN   REEDLEY

policy, for nothing save a few sickly-looking specimens will thrive in saturated and water-logged land. Some attempt must, therefore be made at drainage, where necessary, and when cost makes the use of pipes prohibitive, quite efficient drainage can be effected by cutting parallel trenches about 3 feet deep and 1 foot wide across the ground to be drained. Into the bottom of these trenches should be thrown 9 inches of broken bricks, old rubble, and ballast—in fact any hard material that will keep the soil open and allow the water to percolate through. Brushwood and heather may be used, but are not so lasting as clinkers and rubble. Over this drainage material place turves bottom-side-up to prevent the finer soil from silting through and clogging up the drainage. The remaining 18 inches or so should be filled in with the excavated soil; this must not be rammed down, but should be allowed to sink naturally, otherwise the drain will be rendered useless and might as well not be there.

These drains must either empty themselves into a ditch that will carry off the water, or, where this is not possible, a large sump must be dug in the lowest part of the garden and filled in with drainage material in the same way as the drains. Into this the water will flow and be gradually dissipated through the soil.

LAYING OUT THE DRAINS

There are various ways of laying out the drains, according to the configuration of the surface. If the ground has a clay sub-soil and has a uniform slope, as is often the case with garden ground, it will be sufficient to lay parallel lines of 2 or 3 inch pipes at a distance of from 15 to 20 feet apart, provided always that pipes are used in making the drains. When the land slopes slightly on either side to a depression in the middle, a main drain of 3 or 4 inch pipes should be laid along this depression from the head to the outfall, and lateral drains of 3 inch pipes should enter the main drain and connect with it by junction-sockets and elbow-joints. No precise directions can be given in this matter, for the construction and disposition of the drains must in every case depend on the nature of the soil and the contour of the surface. The depth, too, will also depend upon circumstances, but a main drain will vary in depth from $2\frac{1}{2}$ feet to $4\frac{1}{2}$ feet, being shallowest at the head and deepest at the outfall. The depth of lateral drains will,

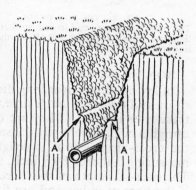

FIG. 7. SECTION OF A DRAIN
Drains are best dug V-shaped, as shown in the above diagram. At the bottom, along the narrowest part below the shoulders *A*, are placed the pipes end to end.

65

of course, be affected by that of the main drain. All lateral drains should enter a main drain obliquely and not at right angles, and the fall should be greater where the lateral approaches the main drain than at any other portion of its course. From 15 feet to 20 feet should be allowed between the feeders to a main drain on clay soils. The fall of a main drain should never be less than 1 in 200.

LAYING DOWN THE DRAIN-PIPES

Sometimes the drain-pipes are laid with collars, that is, short pieces of piping sufficiently large to receive the ends of two pipes, thus keeping them firmly in their place. In other cases the pipes are joined together by bands of tempered clay, which answer very well, but when this method is adopted, the upper sides of the pipes should be perforated with holes for the reception of the water, so that the solid junction of the pipes is no detriment. It is not usual, however, to do more than lay the pipes end to end in a straight line, or just fit the end of one pipe into the socket made for its reception at the end of the pipe that comes next to it, if pipes of this construction are used. In this case no clay or cement must be used to bind the pipes together, but at the junction

FIG. 8. THE PIPE DRAIN
The pipes are placed end to end, so that they lie fitted closely together and all evenly at a uniform angle.

of any feeder with a main drain the union should be carefully made by clay or cement where permanent drainage is expected. A straight-edge and spirit level should always be used to ensure that the pipes are laid truly. This will save many clogged or ineffective drains in the future years.

BONING RODS

In laying drains over long distances where a straight-edge would be too short and take too much time, boning rods are used. There are three of these rods in a set. They are constructed on the lines of a T-square, the uprights being essentially the same length, i.e. 3 feet 6 inches or 4 feet, and the cross-piece 1 foot in length. The material should be white wood measuring 3 inches by $\frac{3}{4}$ inch, the joint being morticed to ensure security. The over-all length of the three must be the same. In use they are simple, if the pegs at either end are fixed, i.e. pegs to the required depth of the pipes, for by holding erect a boning rod on either peg, it is easy to find the correct depth for intermediate pegs by merely sighting across the top of one and just catching a glimpse of the ridge on the other. The intermediate pegs should be driven in so that when the third boning rod is held erect on them, the upper edges of the three cross-pieces are in line when sighted across from either end. Similarly if two pegs are put in level with the straight-edge and spirit-level, one may get a third by sighting across the two already in. To obtain sufficient fall, knock in this end peg to allow for drop, and put in the intermediates as described above.

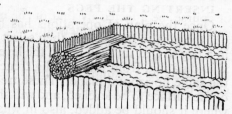

FIG. 9.   THE BUSH DRAIN
In this type of drain brushwood, laid length-wise, is used in place of pipes.

COVERING THE PIPES

Cover the pipes for a few inches with rough porous rubbish or broken crockery, heather, gorse, or any such material, and the drains will be effective and permanent; this is especially necessary in heavy clay soils. An excellent plan is to lay down soles or flat tiles, and on these to set half-pipes or bridge-pipes, which are of a tunnel shape; the rough stuff is then laid over these, and the trench is filled in with earth, which should not be rammed or trodden very tight, but merely allowed to settle. (*See also* Draining the Lawn, p. 74, *and* Draining Paths, p. 88.)

LEVELLING

In view of the work entailed and the cost, levelling should not be under-taken on anything but a very small scale, unless the scheme has been care-fully considered and the site very thoroughly reconnoitred with reference to the probable effect on the drainage system. Where the surface is raised, there will be little need for hesitation, but when the levelling consists largely in excavating a considerable portion of the soil in the lower part of the garden, the site, if the soil is heavy and retentive clay, may quite pos-sibly become waterlogged and may require extensive draining, which may not be easy in comparatively low-lying sections of the garden. As levelling is to a great extent carried out in the autumn and winter, the gardener may not have long to wait for a few heavy showers of rain, which will soon prove what drainage, if any, is necessary.

A number of flat-headed pegs, a garden line, a rake, a heavy roller, a spirit level, a straight-edge at least 10 feet long, and a set of boning-rods will be re-quired.

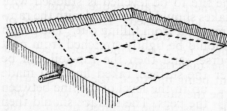

FIG. 10.   DRAINING THE TENNIS COURT
The above diagram shows "the herring-bone" system of laying drains. The dotted lines indicate the laterals running into the main drain.

67

INSERTING THE PEGS

Once the plan of operations has been decided, commence by staking out the area to be levelled, then select one corner as a starting-point, drive in a peg so that its head lies at the level to be worked to, and, if the ground is undulating, from this peg dig trenches, the bottoms of which are all in the same horizontal plane. These trenches should radiate over the whole of the surface to be levelled, and will show where soil must be cut away and where it should be added, also in what quantities. In these trenches start driving in pegs 6 to 9 feet apart, so that the heads of all of them are exactly level with the top of the first peg in the corner whence a start was made. To make sure that the pegs are level, the straight-edge is laid across from peg to peg, and the last inserted peg is knocked in until the bubble of the spirit-level resting on the straight-edge is in the centre of its run. Where a depression is to be filled in, or where the slope is even, there is no need to dig these "trial" trenches, for the lie of the ground is obvious and the pegs can be put in at once, still working from one guiding peg.

REMOVING THE SOIL

If the slope is considerable, such rough masses of materials as can be got out of the higher portion of the ground should be piled in a line along the lower end so as to furnish something in the shape of a containing wall to hold in the earth afterwards thrown into the intervening space. If there are no stones or rough earth that can be utilized, a few rows of short stakes may be driven in to sustain the earth, which must be dug out and thrown if the distance is short enough, or wheeled if it is too far to throw, until the hollow has been filled, and all the earth removed from the higher portion. Before the so-called rough levelling is commenced however, all the top-soil should be removed and stacked clear of the field of operations, otherwise the subsoil will, in some places, get thrown on top of the top-soil, in other parts the subsoil will be left uncovered.

As the earth is gradually cut away, more pegs can be driven in, all with their heads on the same level, until the site to be levelled is studded with pegs. The earth thrown between the stakes should be rammed with the rammer to give consistency to it and to prevent it from falling out. The rough levelling completed, the garden-line should be tightly stretched from post to post—from the very tops, of course—and then the top-soil can be brought back and spread evenly over the surface, raked fine and made up to the level of the line between the pegs. The surface should then be rolled firm. When the soil has settled sufficiently, trial must be made by means of a level, to see that the surface is true.

FIG. 11. MOVING THE SOIL

CHAPTER 7

MAKING THE BEDS AND BORDERS

The planning and construction of the beds and borders in a garden is a matter deserving the closest attention, and it must always be borne in mind that the first aim is not that the bed itself shall be beautiful in shape but that it shall be so constructed and situated that it will display the flowers planted in it to the best advantage. The more simple the shape the better it will, as a rule, fulfil its purpose, and will at the same time be all the more easy to construct, plant, and keep in order. Elaborate geometrical designs have, except in the more formal Dutch and French gardens, gone right out of fashion. Many of these older designs had sharp-pointed extremities, which were very awkward to plant and care for; the most useful shapes are circles, ellipses, squares, and rectangles. Rectilinear beds are generally used in the more formal parts of the garden, near the house, as they best harmonize with the straight lines of the architecture. If beds are laid out on the lawn, they should be so placed that their longer sides run parallel with those of a neighbouring straight path, or with the edge of the lawn, and must be so designed and situated that the lawn-mower can operate easily; grass verges or walks between beds should never be less than 18 inches or 2 feet wide, otherwise even a small machine will have difficulty in cutting them well. Except when they are permanently to accommodate shade-loving plants, the beds should be so placed that they are open to the sun, but should at the same time have shelter from cold or strong winds.

MARKING OUT BEDS WITH CURVED SIDES
Ellipses or Ovals

The chief point to bear in mind concerning these, is that the length must always correspond with the width. In cases where both the length and the breadth are given, the easiest way to proceed is as follows: Mark out a line, AB, Fig. 12, equal to the given length, and another CD equal to the given breadth and bisecting AB at right angles at E, itself being also bisected by AB in the same point E. Now take a distance or radius equal to half the length of the ellipse in this case equal to AE or BE—and with this radius, from the points C and D as centres, describe the dotted arcs shown in the figure which cut each other and the line AB in F and G. Drive two stout stakes into the ground at F and G, and having taken a piece of cord with a loop at each end equal in length to AB, slip one loop over F and the other over G, and then, tightening the cord to the utmost with a stick or iron stake, extend the cord till it touches the point A, and keeping it tight, trace the curved line ACBDA, which is the ellipse required.

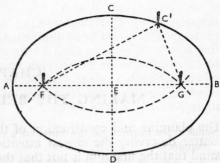

FIG. 12. MAKING AN ELLIPTICAL BED

In case the reader has forgotten how to erect one line perpendicular to another, it will be as well to explain the very simple process by which this may be done. In Fig. 13, let AB be a straight line to which it is required to erect a perpendicular at C. Take any point D in CA and make CE equal to CD, thus getting two points in AB, one on each side of C where the perpendicular is to be erected and equidistant from it. Then from E as centre and with the distance ED as radius describe the arc DF, and from D as centre and with the distance DE as radius describe the arc EF. From F, the point in which the arcs DF and EF intersect, draw the straight line FC to C; FC will be perpendicular to AB. By continuing the arcs to intersect in G, and joining F and G, a straight line FG is obtained, which passes through AB at right angles to it.

Spirals

In the following paragraphs we describe the best ways of forming curved spiral lines.

(1) To form a spiral with spacing: make a circle around the centre of your intended spiral, as great in circumference as you intend the breadth of your border to be. Place pegs close together round the circumference of this circle, and tie one end of a garden line to one of them; then, taking the other end in your hand, go out to the point where you intend the spiral to begin, and, as you walk round, holding the line stretched tight, you will mark out the figure required.

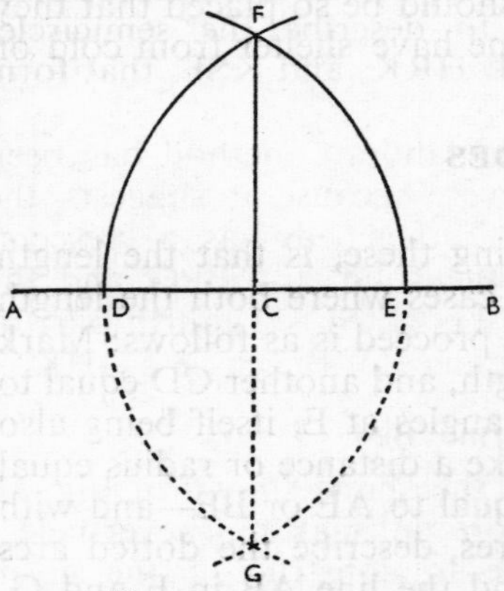

(2) To form a spiral line where the border is narrower towards the centre, like the shell of a snail; make a circle as before, and instead of driving in the pegs upright, let them form a cone; or instead of pegs use a large flower pot turned upside down, and,

FIG. 13. ERECTING ONE LINE PERPENDICULAR TO ANOTHER

70

if necessary, a smaller one also placed upside-down over it. Measure the radius of your spiral, and wind that length of line round the cone in such a manner as to correspond with the varying breadth of your intended border. Now, by unwinding the line, commence making the figure, starting at the centre.

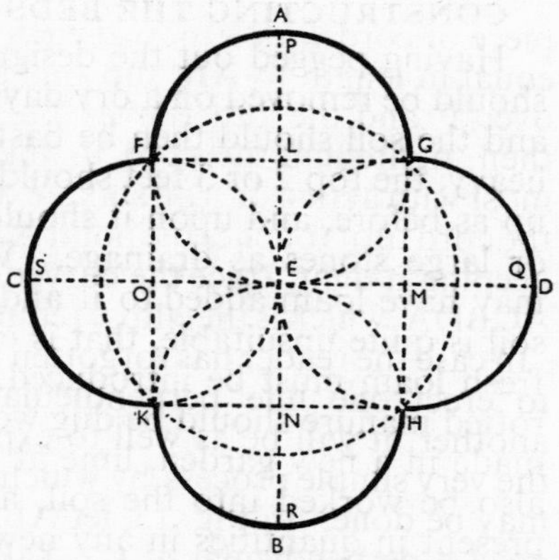

Semicircles Formed on the Sides of a Square

To make this bed the first thing is to lay out two straight lines, AB, CD, as in Fig. 14, intersecting each other at right angles at E. Then from E as centre, with any length of radius that may be

FIG. 14. BEDS FORMED BY THE USE OF CIRCLES, SEMI-CIRCLES, AND SQUARES.

determined upon, describe the circle FGHK. In this circle inscribe a square, FGHK, and from the points L, M, N, O, in which the sides of the square intersect the straight lines AB, CD, describe the arcs FPG, GQH, HRK, KSF. A bed of the shape shown in the diagram by the solid arcs of circles will then be formed, consisting of four semi-circles described on the four sides of a square. The simplest method of actual construction is to lay out a square first of all, as FGHK, next to bisect the four sides of the square in the points L, M, N, O, and from these points as centres to describe the semicircles FPG, GQH, HRK, and KSF, that form the bed.

The more elaborate method has been given however, because it suggests the formation of other beds—as a crescent, formed by the solid arc FPG and the dotted arc FG, which is a fourth part of the circumference of the circle FGHK.

The Serpentine Bed

A bed of the shape shown in Fig. 15 is a little more unusual, but nevertheless quite simple to construct if the given details are carefully followed.

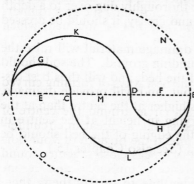

FIG. 15. MAKING THE SERPENTINE BED.

Divide *AB*, the length of the bed, into three equal parts in the points *C* and *D*; subdivide *AC* and *DB* each into two equal parts in the points *E* and *F*. From *E* and *F* as centres, with radii *EA* and *FB*, the semi-circles *AGC* and *BHD* are described, and from *C* and *D* as centres, with radii *CA* and *DB*, the semi-circles *AKD BLC* are described, completing the outline of the bed. Divide *AB* into two equal parts at *M* and with *M* as centre and radius *AM* describe circle *ANBO*, thus forming a pear-shaped bed *AGCLBO*.

CONSTRUCTING THE BEDS

Having pegged out the design to the required size and shape, the turf should be removed on a dry day with a turfing-iron in turves 2 inches deep, and the soil should then be bastard-trenched, *see* p. 35. If the soil is very heavy, the top 2 or 3 feet should be removed, the subsoil should be broken up as before, and upon it should be placed 5 to 6 inches of broken bricks or large stones as drainage. When the top-soil is moderately good, it may have loam added to it and can then be returned to the bed, or if the soil is quite unsuitable, that is clayey or stony, all should be removed and fresh loam must be introduced. In either case a liberal dressing of well-rotted manure should be dug well into the top-soil. If these beds are being made in a new garden, lime at the rate of 14 oz. per square yard, should also be worked into the soil, as insect pests and fungi are certain to be present in quantities in any newly-broken grass-land.

Each autumn the beds should be dressed with manure, as bedding plants are, as a whole, voracious feeders, like a rich soil, and soon exhaust it when spring and summer bedders are, as is usually the case, grown in the same bed. If manuring cannot be carried out in the autumn, it should be done in April or May when the summer-bedding is put in. Every three or four years the soil should be thoroughly dug over to a depth of two spades, and if it appears at all sour and greasy, it should be dressed with lime.

The addition of new soil, manure, and drainage material will raise the bed somewhat above the level of the surrounding ground. The soil should be made to slope neatly up to the centre of the bed, and will thus best display plants of equal height when bedded out, and will provide drainage. A bed 4 feet wide should be about 4 inches higher at the centre than at the edges; beds of other sizes, of course, varying in height at the centre in proportion to their width. If on a lawn, the edging of the bed should be neatly trimmed round with an edging-iron. (*See* also Chapter 15.)

CHAPTER 8

THE LAWN: ITS CONSTRUCTION AND UPKEEP

HOW TO LAY DOWN THE LAWN

Most people will agree that the lawn is the most important feature in a garden. The largest country seat has its expanse of well-kept lawns; a tiny plot of grass should, if possible, grace even the smallest backgarden. Grass, when well tended and trimmed, is perennially green and gives us a vivid and pleasing patch of colour in the depth of winter when the garden is looking at its drabbest. Every garden, therefore, should have its lawn. It should be properly constructed and well looked after; a weedy, mossy, ill-drained lawn is an eyesore and should not be tolerated, for with care and the expenditure of a little money the worst of lawns can be made presentable.

But to make a lawn takes a considerable time. It is possible to obtain a covering of grass in a single season, but anything that could reasonably be called a lawn is a work of years. Of course, a grass plot on which one may walk almost at once may be prepared by transplanting blocks of turf from a neighbouring field, common or hillside, and rolling it into place. But more and more gardeners have come to the conclusion that a perfect lawn of uniform colour and even surface, free from plantain and other weeds, can only be obtained by careful preparation of the soil, and by sowing carefully selected grass seed mixture.

The seeded lawn is cheaper than one laid down with good turves, but cannot be used—as a tennis-court for instance—during the first year after sowing as the turved lawn can be.

SITUATION AND SITE

Where there is any choice of situation a northern aspect is to be preferred to a southern one, especially where the water supply is limited. A fairly moist soil is, indeed, essential to a good lawn, though it is equally necessary that the soil should be well-drained, and must not remain soft and spongy for long after a shower of rain. Deep drainage is not necessary, seeing that the roots of grasses do not penetrate far below the surface; but on heavy clay, pipe-drains are usually necessary, and a 4- to 5-inch layer of ashes must be placed immediately below the top-soil, which should be from 6 to 9 inches in thickness. Whatever the nature of the soil, the

73

whole surface should be trenched over to a depth of 18 inches to 2 feet, the best soil being kept on top. A point to remember is that the final dressing of soil over the drains must be much poorer than that covering other parts, otherwise the grass will grow better and greener over the drains than elsewhere, and a patchy lawn will result. (*See chapter on* Draining and Levelling Land, p. 64.)

LEVELLING

It is more than likely that it will be necessary to level the lawn; this is, of course, essential in the case of the tennis-lawn. Levelling should be commenced as early as possible so that the land may have ample time to settle before the sowing or turfing is done. Unless the soil is very porous a lawn should not be dead level, or the water may hang on it after rain; even a tennis-court should be from 4 to 3 inches higher on one side than the other; this will not be apparent and will in no way affect the play. Where levelling is necessary, however, the reader is referred to the chapter on Draining and Levelling, page 64, where the detailed instructions for this operation are given.

PREPARING THE TOP-SOIL

The soil itself should be a good fibrous loam, rich in humus, the ordinary soil excavated in making the foundations of a house, which it is often desired to employ for a lawn, being altogether unsuitable. Where good soil, from 18 inches to 2 feet in depth, is not already *in situ*, it should be obtained, and used to replace, at any rate, the top foot of the existing earth. A deep root-run like this will assist the drainage of the lawn and will prevent the grass from becoming scorched up in hot, dry weather. In introducing soil from outside it is, however, important to remember that it is likely to contain the seeds of many weeds which would be fatal to a satisfactory lawn. A certain time should, therefore, be allowed to elapse, in order to afford opportunity for these seeds to germinate, and the resulting weeds to be destroyed before any grass seed is sown. As an alternative the introduced soil may be burned, and then enriched with a liberal dressing of manure.

If it is impossible for fresh mould to be introduced, the top-soil, if heavy, must be well broken up, weeds and stones must be removed, and with the soil should be incorporated plenty of finely sifted ashes or coarse sand and grit to render the soil porous and to enable the roots to work through it.

If the soil is too light, some well-decayed manure and leaf-mould should be added until the top 10 inches of the compost consists of one part of these ingredients to four parts of soil. In any event, a good dressing of farmyard manure, say twenty cart-loads to the acre, should be incorporated

74

with the top-spit of soil and should not lie more than 4 inches below the surface.

Where lime is found to be lacking, powdered lime must be dug in at the rate of 6 oz. to the square yard. If this preparation is made in the autumn, the ground should be allowed to lie fallow through the winter. In the spring the surface should be again carefully tested for level with a straight-edge and spirit-level, so that any inequalities may be made up; the upper 4 inches of the soil is then made as fine as possible by repeated rakings and thorough rollings, until the surface is so firm that it scarcely shows the mark of a foot when trodden on and is entirely devoid of stones and weed-free.

SOWING THE SEED

Seed can be sown either early in April or about the end of August or the beginning of September. Spring-sown seed will take between a fort-night and three weeks to germinate, but in the autumn—the better time to sow—the soil is warm and the seed may be expected to show above the ground in a week or ten days. Seed should be sown on a day when there is no wind and when the soil is dry enough not to stick to the feet or the rake, and great evenness should be aimed at, two sowings being made at right angles to one another. This even distribution of seed is best obtained by marking the lawn out into squares whose sides are from a yard to 2 yards in length.

The seed, which should have been mixed with twice its quantity of fine mould, is then divided into as many portions as there are squares so that each square may receive an equal amount of seed.

Quantity of Seed to Sow

From 2 oz. to 4 oz. per square yard is the quantity of seed to sow, and special seed should be obtained for the purpose from a first-rate firm of seedsmen. No economy should be attempted in this important matter, as the seed must be good; and it is difficult to sow too thickly, for the thicker the sowing the less chance weeds will have of growing through, and the young seedlings, when closely massed together, are not so liable to damage by frost or scorching sun. When autumn sowing is practised, the lawn should, if possible, be drained, levelled, and should have the surface prepared in spring. Then if the soil is thoroughly and consistently weeded throughout the summer, there should be an absolutely weed-free seed bed for sowing in August or September.

When sowing a lawn, care should be taken to see that the seed sown is suitable for the soil, the situation, and for the use to which the lawn is to be put. Grasses vary just as other plants do in their tastes and require-ments, and careful selection will do much to secure the establishment of a permanently satisfactory lawn.

75

GRASS SEEDS FOR DIFFERENT SITUATIONS

The following list will enable the reader to choose seed suitable for sowing on a lawn in practically any situation that he is likely to encounter. All reliable firms will, however, supply a mixture suitable for any particular class of soil.

GENERAL USE:
> *Festuca tenuifolia*
> *Cynosurus cristatus*
> *Poa nemoralis var. sempervirens*
> *Poa pratensis*
> *Poa trivialis*

LIGHT SOIL:
> *Cynosurus cristatus*
> *Festuca longifolia (duriuscula)*
> *Festuca tenuifolia*
> *Festuca rubra*
> *Poa pratensis*

DRY SOIL:
> *Festuca rubra*

POOR AND SHALLOW SOIL:
> *Festuca longifolia (duriuscula)*

UNDER TREES OR MOIST, SHADY SITUATIONS:
> *Poa trivialis*

TOWN GARDENS:
> *Poa annua*
> *Poa nemoralis*

SPORTS GROUNDS:
> *Festuca rubra*

NEAR SEA:
> *Festuca rubra*

Care after Sowing

A very light raking is then desirable, just cover with a ¼ of an inch of finely sifted soil, and afterwards the ground should be rolled over, lengthwise and across, provided the soil is not damp enough to stick to the roller. To protect the seeds from the birds, black cotton should be stretched on short sticks, or old netting can be thrown over small tree branches spread over the seeded surface. As soon as the grass is an inch or so high, roll it with a light wooden roller—in fine, dry weather—and when it has grown to 2 to 3 inches above the ground, weeds must be removed and regular cutting with the scythe and rolling must be begun. A top-dressing of an ounce of guano to the square yard will help on the young grass. The scythe must continue to be used for several months until the grass is sufficiently secure in the ground to bear the mowing machine, which has a tendency to pull young grass up by the roots.

It should be possible to use the mower in June, but the blades must be raised an inch above the normal level for the first two or three cuttings. That is to say, the grass should be cut so that it is from 1 to 2 inches in length, instead of the ½ to ¾ of an inch necessary for well established and mature grass.

LAWNS FROM TURF

The turves laid down should be of good quality, that is to say, the texture of the grass must be fine and the turves moderately weed-free. Turves of coarse grass and full of weeds will give endless trouble and never make a good lawn. If really good turf cannot be obtained, it is far better to sow seed. Cumberland turf is among the best, but the cost of the carriage makes it expensive and out of reach of most pockets. The best possible turves, however, should be obtained and all the largest weeds should be carefully removed before laying them down.

Preparing the Ground

In preparing a piece of ground for turfing, the soil should be well dug to a depth of about 9 inches and a light dressing of well-rotted manure may with advantage be incorporated with it. The ground should then be well rolled and levelled, any hollows being filled with soil and again rolled. Immediately before the turves are laid down, the top ½ inch of the soil should be raked up so that the roots of the grass may work into it and bind the turf to the soil. The turves are usually cut 3 feet long, 1 foot wide, and 1½ or 2 inches thick, and rolled. In this form they are easily torn and will require to be very carefully laid if the lawn is to be level and even. Turves 1 foot square and the same thickness as the above are often used, for they are far more easy to handle and give much better results. They should be placed turf side down in a wooden frame or gauge-box 1½ inches deep, made so that they lie tightly in position. A two-handed knife with a long curved blade, or an old scythe, is then passed straight across the frame to cut off any inequalities, so that the turf shall be exactly 1½ inches thick all through. Generally speaking, however, this is only necessary for bowling greens and tennis-courts. If the turves are not to be laid down immediately, they should be kept in a sheltered position out of the sun. They should not, however, be stacked for longer than is necessary, and should be laid down while the grass is still green and bright in colour. When put down, they should be fitted very close together, should be laid diagonally across the lawn, and must be "bonded" as bricks are in a wall; that is to say, the junction between two in one row must come opposite the middle of a turf in the rows before and after it. Finely-sifted soil must be worked in to fill the crevices, and the turf should at once be watered well and then thoroughly and evenly pounded with the turf-beater. It should then be rolled, a spirit-level and straight-edge being used to ensure evenness. Water should be given daily for some time, and rolling both across and up and down the lawn with a light roller should be very frequent, provided the soil is not too wet. A dressing, ½ an inch thick, of fine sharp sand, after the rolling has been completed, will be found to improve the texture of the grass and should be well-brushed in. Turves may be laid in fine weather, either in spring or autumn, the latter being, perhaps, the better time. Turf must never be laid later in the spring than April, otherwise it is liable to suffer from drought. For the first three weeks the grass should be cut twice a week with the scythe, after that time it should be cut at least once a week with the machine, being rolled after each cutting during the first year. Lawns laid down in turf wear better than a seeded lawn during the first two or three years.

CARE OF THE LAWN

In the autumn, the lawn should be well swept and raked to drag out all possible moss, weeds, and dead grass. It should then be rolled with a spiked roller, or the prongs of a garden fork should be thrust perpendicularly into the turf to a depth of 6 inches, to aerate the soil and help to surface-drain it through the winter. The holes made by the fork should not be more than 3 to 4 inches apart, and should stud the whole surface of the lawn. If the grass, from the nature of the soil, is inclined to grow rank and coarse, it will be much improved by a good dressing early in February of clean sharp sand all over it; should it, on the other hand, have a tendency to scald and burn up, it will receive great benefit from a dressing of equal parts of leaf-mould and fibrous loam together with a sprinkling of good guano, soot, or finely-powdered hornmeal. The loam must be free of fungi, the eggs of insect pests, and of the seeds of weeds; if there is room, this may be ensured by spreading out the soil for six months or so before use, so that any seeds may have time to germinate. A sprinkling of napthalene will invariably dispose of insect pests.

MOWING THE GRASS

The two methods of lawn-mowing—mowing by machine and with the scythe—are best done at different times in the day. The mechanical lawn-mower works best and most quickly when the grass is dry, but for cutting with the scythe the early morning, when the dew is still on the grass, is the best and easiest time. In the cool of the morning the grass is fuller of moisture and stiffer in the stem, thus standing up more firmly against the scythe. The exact times of the year at which mowing should be commenced and ended vary, of course, with the seasons, but as a general rule mowing is necessary from March until the middle of November. The lawn should be well swept before the first mowing of the season to clear it of all stones, twigs, and worm casts that would otherwise injure the machine. Mowing should be commenced as soon as the ground will stand it, and the grass, unless newly sown, should not be allowed to grow so long that the first cutting has to be by the scythe. In spring and autumn it will be sufficient to mow the lawn once in ten days; in summer it will be necessary once a week and even twice a week when the weather is warm and showery.

In very hot, dry weather, the knives should be raised and the collecting-box should be left off so that the cut grass may act as a mulch to the roots. If during the winter the weather is very mild, the grass may start growing, and should it become over 2 inches in length, the mower should be run over it if the ground is firm enough, otherwise the grass will tend to become thin and straggly.

ROLLING THE LAWN

Great mistakes are made in rolling, and lawns otherwise in excellent condition are often ruined through ignorance of the proper methods of doing this. The roller should be used periodically from September to May, when the lawn is not too wet and sodden; if rolled with a heavy roller when in the latter condition, a hard crust is formed on the surface, surface-drainage is impeded, and the air is prevented from reaching the roots of the grass. Roll, therefore, when the lawn is rather on the dry side, and not directly after rain, and remember that two rollings with a light roller are far more beneficial than one with a heavy roller. Rolling is intended to keep the surface even and to spread the roots of the grass, but it is *not* intended, and *cannot* make the lawn level; this should have been done when the lawn was laid down. Never, therefore, use a heavy roller in wet weather.

Rolling should be more frequent on a newly laid lawn than on an older one, when a few rollings in the early autumn and another three or four in the spring, just before mowing commences, should be sufficient. The roller should never be used directly after frost; allow the turf to become thoroughly thawed out before either rolling or even walking on the grass.

CARE OF THE EDGINGS

These should be kept neat, and must be cut regularly with the edging shears; if they are neglected, an edging-iron has to be used. This implement requires great skill in its manipulation and often results, in amateur hands, in ragged and uneven edges. Do not, therefore, neglect the edgings. During the summer the edgings may, in places, be trodden down; in autumn, therefore, as soon as the ground becomes softer, a spade should be driven under them to raise them to the correct level.

FEEDING THE LAWN

No lawn, however good the soil, can go on looking its best year after year unless it receives an occasional stimulant in one form or another. In the natural state the grass remains long, and in the autumn dies down to form plant-food in the soil. This natural process does not occur in the lawn, as the grass is cut weekly, if not more often, and the cuttings are caught in the cutting-box and removed from the lawn, which is thus deprived of nourishment.

Lawns must, therefore, be fed at least every two or three years or the grass will become weak and thin and will gradually give place to moss and weeds, which are always ready to force their way even into the best-kept lawn. The grass should, for this reason, be carefully watched, and when it becomes off-colour, it should be dressed three or four times in one season with intervals of three weeks between the feedings. Little and often should be the motto in dressing the lawn. Too heavy a dressing at one time may scorch up the grass, and it must be remembered that the fertilizer must be chosen to suit the condition of the grass and the nature of the soil. Fertilizers must not be applied indiscriminately; a chemical good for one lawn may ruin another. All fertilizers are best applied in showery weather and the lawn should afterwards be well brushed with a hard birch broom to work the dressing well into the roots. If no rain is likely, give the lawn a good soaking with the sprinkler or the hose. Mix the fertilizers with twice the quantity of finely sifted loam if dressing a lawn on a sandy and rather poor soil, and with the same amount of sand when working on a clay soil: this makes even distribution of the fertilizer more easy. Stimulants such as sulphate of ammonia are, as a rule, applied at any time from April to September, two or three dressings being applied during that period. (For rates to apply the various fertilizers *see* table, p. 81.) Dressings of freshly-slaked lime or powdered chalk, used to sweeten a sour soil and to keep down moss, can be given in November or December, at the rate of 10 oz. to the square yard. These dressings should not be rolled into the lawn, as they would form a hard covering and would exclude air from the roots. They must not be allowed to lie about on the lawn, but must be raked and swept backwards and forwards, first in one direction and then in another, with a stiff broom, so that they are worked well down into the roots, and any dressing left lying on the surface after three weeks or so should be cleared away before a subsequent one is put on. If farmyard manure is used as a dressing, it must be well-decayed, finely sieved, and must not be applied too thickly or it will smother and kill the fine grass. It should be mixed with twice its bulk of finely-sieved loam, which must be absolutely weed-free.

About twenty-five barrow-loads would be required for a full-size tennis-lawn, and should be applied in December or January. Any dressing remaining in March or early April should be swept off the lawn, as it will hinder the growth of young grass.

Many advise the use of road-sweepings, but these are, in most cases, undesirable, since they are bound to contain the seeds of weeds, in addition to being contaminated with tar and oil in these days when most of the roads are tarred.

80

PLATE 5

CONSTRUCTION OF A CRAZY-
PAVING PATH

Mark out the course of the path and fit the
wooden frame (*left*) to the markings by means
of wooden battens. Remove the soil within
the frame to the appropriate depth (see p. 87).

Fill the excavation with rubble consisting of
largish stones and/or clinker (*right*) to about
one-third or one-half the depth.

Cement may be mixed in with the rubble to
make a really sound foundation (*left*).

Firm down the foundation evenly and solidly
with a rammer (*right*).

PLATE 6

CONSTRUCTION OF A CRAZY-PAVING PATH
(continued)

After the foundation has been well rammed add the cement and level off with a rake (*right*) ; the cement level should be just below the top of the frame.

Fit the pieces of crazy paving by bedding into the cement (*left*). The pieces should be carefully selected for shape and small pieces avoided whenever possible.

Use a trowel to level off the stones and, in the case of thin pieces, use it to add more cement (*right*).

The final operation is pointing the pieces (*left*), again using a trowel, with a stronger mixture of cement. It is advisable to allow the cement plenty of time to dry before using the path.

Fertilizers and Dressings for the Lawn

State of Lawn	Nature of Soil	Fertilizer or Top-Dressing Required	Amount to Apply per Square Yard	When to Apply	Remarks
Grass Poor and Weak	Light	Sulphate of Potash, or Kainit	1 oz.	March	
Grass Poor and Weak	Heavy	Bone Meal, or equal parts of Bone Meal and Superphosphate of Lime	2 oz.	October or February	Bone Meal should not be used too freely as it encourages the growth of clover. Superphosphate is more suitable to a medium soil than to a heavy clay and is best applied in autumn, but never on soils deficient in lime.
Grass Poor and Weak	Damp and Sour	Slaked Lime (fresh), or Pulverized Chalk	10 oz.	November or December	This dressing sweetens the soil. Ten days after application thrust the prongs of the fork vertically 6 in. into the surface, all over, to let the air into the soil.
Grass Rank and Coarse	Heavy	Clean, Sharp Sand (well-screened Sea or River Sand is best, never use soft-binding Sand)	Dressing ½ in. Thick	Early February	The compost should be very finely sifted. If well-sieved the compost soon works down into the roots and allows the fine grass to grow.
Grass Scorched	Light Sandy or Gravelly	Equal parts of well-sieved fibrous Loam and Leaf-mould with a sprinkling of good guano, soot or hornmeal finely powdered	Dressing ½ in. Thick	February	
Grass Scorched	Heavy	Nitrate of Soda	½ oz.	March	Discourages clover, but encourages growth of grass in cold weather.
Young Seedling Grass	Any	Guano	1 oz.	May	Never apply guano on soils deficient in lime.
Lawn, Mossy	Any	Soot	Sufficient just to Blacken Grass	October and November Before rain if possible	The soot should have been exposed to the atmosphere for 6 months before application. Encourages growth of young grass. Wood ashes applied in December also help towards the elimination of moss.

Dressings for Killing Weeds on Lawns

Type of Weed	Dressing to be Used	Quantity applied per square yard	When to Apply	Remarks
Clover	Nitrate of Soda *or* Anti-clover Mixture	½ oz. ⎫ ¾ oz. ⎬	March. Repeat Dressing in 3 weeks' time	Besides discouraging clover, this fertilizer encourages the growth of grass in cold weather. Clover may also be raked out and is weakened by very close cutting with the machine in dry weather. Most seedsmen sell a special anti-clover mixture with full directions on the container.
Daisies	3 parts Ammonium Sulphate, 1 part Sulphate of Iron, and 30 parts Fine, Sharp Sand *or*	2½ oz.	September in Dry Weather, with a Second Dressing early in April	Mix the ingredients of this lawn-sand thoroughly together.
	Weed-killer	A Drop in Heart of Each Weed	Spring or Autumn	Apply on a dry, still day.
Dandelions	Weed-killer or Carbolic Acid (1 oz. to a gallon of water) in a weed-killer ejector or on a skewer	A Drop in Heart of Each Weed	October and November	Pierce the heart of each weed and apply weed-killer.
Moss	2 parts Kainit to 3 parts Superphosphate of Lime *or*	2½ oz.	January	Give this dressing two or three years running.
	Sulphate of Iron	¼ oz.	October	Rake out all possible moss before applying the weed-killer, which must be mixed with twenty times its bulk of sand or fine mould and well raked into the surface. Ten days after application again rake out all dead moss.
Plantains	*See Daisies*			

There are now various proprietary selective Weed Killers on the market which are exceptionally good if carefully used according to the makers' instructions.

WATERING THE LAWN

Water should never be applied unless necessary. To begin with, grass seed should not be watered after sowing, and the established lawn should not receive water until a long drought makes this necessary, as once begun, watering must be continued, at least once a week, as long as the dry weather lasts. Watering seems to encourage the increase of weeds and clover rather than grass; at the same time grass seems to stand dry weather better than the weeds. Brown, scorched and apparently dead grass recovers remarkably quickly after a shower or two of rain, and as the weeds do not make so quick a recovery, many lawns are greatly benefited by a drought, if the burnt-up appearance can be countenanced for a short time. If the drought becomes serious, and the top-soil is thin and sandy, watering may be essential, and must then be applied liberally by means of the garden hose or sprinkler. The ideal way is to apply water through a fine spray over a long period, so that it can permeate several inches into the ground, rather than to flood the area in a short time by using a coarse nozzle; in the latter case the water soon runs off, much of it being of little value to the grass.

When mowing the lawn, during the period that water must be applied, the machine should be run over the grass the day after watering, and the collecting-box should be left off so that the cut grass may form a mulch to preserve the moisture at the roots.

WEEDING THE LAWN

Before regular mowing commences, it will be well to go over all grass and carefully remove all rank and unsightly weeds, such as daisies, plantains and dandelions. There is only one way of doing this thoroughly, and that is to stretch two garden lines across the lawn parallel to each other and from 3 to 4 feet apart, and to work steadily along between these lines until every weed is out. The worker should have a bucket of fine soil with which grass seed has been mixed, and should fill up any large holes left by the removal of the weeds. He must ram the soil down hard, so that a cup or depression is not left when the soil settles, and should roll each strip thoroughly as soon as weeding has been completed. This can be done at any time in autumn or spring, provided it is possible to get on the lawn without damaging it: the autumn is perhaps the better time, as the grass has longer to recover before the following summer.

REMOVING WORMS FROM THE LAWN

There is a very general opinion that worms are beneficial to the lawn, in that the burrowings provide natural drainage. This may to some extent be true, but they do far more harm than good; they make the surface muddy and soft to walk upon, the grass becomes weakly and easily wears

83

out if much used, and their evil-smelling casts, with which they cover the ground in autumn, winter, and spring, stifle fine grass and encourage the growth of coarse grasses and weeds. Worm casts should always be swept off the lawn before the roller is used—never roll them in. On an ordinary lawn as many as one thousand worms to the square yard may be found. Every effort must, therefore, be made to exterminate them.

The only way to get rid of worms on a lawn is to use a worm-killing solution. A ready-made mixture can be obtained from any seedsman; full instructions for use are sent with the mixture and these should be closely followed.

Watering the soil with potassium permanganate at the rate of $\frac{1}{2}$ oz. to the gallon of water can be very effective.

IMPROVING OLD AND NEGLECTED LAWNS

Where a lawn has in the first place been badly laid, or when it has been very much neglected, it is frequently the wiser and cheaper policy to have it up and relay it altogether. The old turves, if stacked grass-side down with a layer of soil between each turf, will after a time form an excellent heap of potting compost. It is wisest not to dig this old turf into the top-soil, as is sometimes advised, for some of the perennial weeds are sure to find their way to the surface and into the new turf. When the case is not so serious, however, much may be done to improve the lawn, if the following instructions are followed.

Where a lawn has become poor and exhausted, it is a good plan in October to mow it closely and remove weeds such as plantains, dandelions and docks, by means of a daisy lifter. Mossy parts should be watered through a watering pot with a rose with a solution of 2 lb. of iron sulphate to 4 gallons of water to every thirty square yards. The mossy area should again be watered with this liquid in three days' time, after which the moss can easily be raked and swept away. Next top-dress with an inch or two of equal parts of wood ashes, pulverized fibrous loam and well-rotted stable manure, or with one of the artificial fertilizers mentioned on page 81. If, however, the soil is tested, and lime is found to be lacking, this dressing must be deferred until the following spring and carbonate of lime or powdered chalk at the rate of 10 oz. to the square yard should be evenly sprinkled over the soil in November or December. In February or March, when the lime has been thoroughly absorbed, the stimulants mentioned above should be applied. A little good soil should then be added, and sown at the rate of 1 oz. to the square yard with good lawn-grass seed to suit the soil and to match that already there.

Seed should, of course, be sown thickly where the turf is somewhat thin and worn and lightly in other parts. Rake the seed well in and keep the roller frequently at work.

84

Bare Patches

Bare patches caused by hard wear and tear, as on a tennis-court, are best treated by having new turves inserted, care being taken to secure turf of a similar texture and grass, and to allow ½ an inch or so for settlement. More than the actually worn portion should be cut away so that the join between the new and old turf shall be vigorous and healthy. The new turf may be taken from a less used part of the lawn, the empty space being levelled up with fine soil and seeded. (*See* Lawns from Turf.) Where there are small hollows or bumps, the turf should be turned back so that soil may be removed or added to bring the surface to the required level. This work is best done in autumn, for the grass has then more time to become established.

INSECTS INJURIOUS TO THE LAWN

The Cranefly, commonly known as the Daddy-long-legs, can be a very destructive pest in lawns, golf-courses, etc., particularly where heavy infestations occur.

They are to be found chiefly in moist soils feeding on the roots of grass, while they will attack the roots of other plants.

When fully fed the leather jacket, as it is commonly known, turns into a pupa and remains in the soil until the adult cranefly emerges. Just prior to this, the pupa forces its way up to the surface and sticks one end out of the soil. From that end the fly emerges. This usually takes place about dusk during late summer, therefore where lawns have been attacked, thorough rolling every evening will destroy a considerable number before they emerge and lay their eggs.

Other controls against this pest. Apply a dressing of naphthalene at the rate of 2-3 oz. per square yard. The use of a poison bait such as Paris Green and bran is very effective.

CHAPTER 9

HOW TO CONSTRUCT PATHS AND EDGINGS

Paths, rightly planned and constructed, can be made to add interest to a garden; they may themselves even become beautiful, if the art of path-making is understood. At any rate, they are, in most cases, a necessity and the enjoyment of a garden is greatly increased, as also is its utility, by the provision of good and well-kept paths. The essentials of a good path are that it shall be in appearance harmonious with the rest of the garden, and that it shall afford a dry surface in wet weather. Cement, concrete, ashes, brick-dust, and asphalt are sometimes employed for the purpose; but, speaking generally, we may say that the three most suitable surfaces for garden paths are afforded by gravel, bricks, and broken paving stones.

It will be sufficient to describe the construction of the gravel path, the crazy path, and the grass walk. Save for the different materials used, the principles of construction are the same for the ash, brick, concrete, or asphalt path, as those described for gravel paths.

How Broad should the Path be?

A path must never be less than 2 feet in width, even if it is of quite secondary importance. A good average width is 4 feet; this allows for the easy passage of the barrow and other garden implements, and for two people to walk abreast; an amenity often overlooked. Paths may be made much wider than this, but it should be remembered that the broader the path, the more difficult and expensive will be its upkeep; short paths should not be made too wide. Entrance drives and tracks which must bear motor traffic should be 8 feet wide, at least; usually rather more.

Convexity and Height of Path

Perfect dryness is of the utmost importance in paths, for they should be clean and accessible in all weathers and at all seasons. Although some say that paths should be sunk below the general ground level, and others above it, yet walks as a rule look best on a level with the surface of the surrounding beds or grass. When thus constructed, paths must be sunk two inches at the edge, in order to leave this height of verge, which never ought to be exceeded in garden paths. The paths themselves should be nearly flat, two inches being sufficient convexity for a ten-foot walk. The wider the walk, the smaller is the permissible proportionate rise in the centre.

86

CONSTRUCTING THE PATH
Excavation and Drainage

Let the path be well designed and carefully made; if so constructed, it will last many years, and will not only serve its purpose as a means of communication, but will also be a great help in draining the garden.

Whether it will be necessary to lay a pipe-drain or not depends upon the nature of the soil and the lie of the land. In light, porous soils the rough stones, bricks, or clinkers used as a foundation will provide sufficient drainage, but in heavy, retentive clays a pipe-drain will invariably be advisable; this may run directly below the centre of the path, or else on either side of the path; on the lower side when the path is on a side slope, and always at the lowest point below the clinker or brick foundation, and resting on a firm base. Where there is any doubt as to the porosity of the soil, always lay a drain. As has been said above, a single drain down the centre or down one side will be found adequate for ordinary paths of 4 feet in width; but paths wider than this and drives should have drains down each side. The pipes used for draining should be 3 or 4 inches in diameter and must be laid from $1\frac{1}{2}$ to 2 feet deep, according to the nature of the soil and the width of the path. (*See chapter on* Draining Land, p. 64.) The drains must slope gently towards the outlet, which may be into a garden main drain or into a ditch or pond. The pipes being in position, cover them with 12 to 15 inches of broken bricks or rough stones through which the water can trickle.

Putting down the Foundations

The chief thing to be done in every case is to provide a solid, but yet porous substratum, which will afford sufficient support to the materials of which the upper part of the walk, or rather its surface, is made, and yet allow of the rapid passing away of the water that may fall on the path in the form of rain. Of course, we are now supposing that the walk is to be made in the ordinary way, and coated—if a road, with broken stones, technically called "metalling"—and if a garden path, with gravel.

THE GRAVEL PATH

The course of the path or road must first be marked out with stakes, and the surface soil removed to the depth of 9 to 18 inches, if there is no lack of materials to

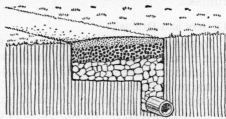

FIG. 16. THE GRAVEL PATH.
Over the drain is placed 6-9 inches of coarse clinker or rubble, rammed firm. Over this is laid 4 to 6 inches of coarse gravel, and on top of this again 2 inches of gravel "hoggin".

87

fill it; the wider the path the deeper the excavation necessary. The nature of the soil also affects the depth of excavation: in heavy clay at least 18 inches should be removed, in light soil 9 inches to a foot will suffice. There is a point that must be stressed here, and that is the importance of eradicating all perennial weeds, especially those with long creeping roots, from the soil at the bottom and sides of the path. If this is not done, all kinds of weeds will soon make their appearance through the new path, and will be very difficult to get rid of. Weed-killer *will* kill these perennial weeds, but it takes three or four years to effect a thorough clearance. From one-third to one-half the depth of the excavation must now be filled up with rough stones, brickbats, clinkers from the brickfields, slag and scoriæ from the iron-works, or any coarse, hard rubbish that can be gathered together. The greater part of the remainder must then be filled up with coarse gravel, shingle, etc., which may be mixed with a little earth to give consistency to the whole, and finally coated with gravel to the depth of 2 or 3 inches, which must be raked level and be constantly rolled with a heavy garden roller until the path is hard and solid. The gravel must not be made too wet or it will adhere to the roller, and any large stones should be screened out of the gravel and used in the foundation. The correct level for the crown of the path can be marked by wooden pegs driven in to the right depth. (*See* Levelling, p. 68.) Allow the path to set for a few days before using it and then fill up any hollows with gravel and roll again. Gravel taken from the beach should not be used if another kind is obtainable, as it does not bind and always remains loose. If, however, it must be used, mix a quarter part of clean dry clay with the gravel before it is laid; when moistened, the mixture will bind well. Supposing, as is sometimes the case, that the ground is of a loose, porous character, or wet and marshy, and, therefore, not calculated to afford a solid basis for the pathway, it is then a good plan to make the trench deeper, and to lay brushwood at the bottom before throwing in the rough rubbish.

Gutters and Drainage

In some cases it is desirable to have a solid facing to a garden path so that it may be impervious to rain, and in this case it is of importance that the surface of the walk shall be rounded—higher in the centre, and sloping down on either side. The water will escape into the earth or turf by which the walk is bordered, or, if desired, gutters can be made to carry the water to a tank formed for its reception in some part of the garden. The gutters may either be moulded in the material of which the path is made or they may be constructed below the surface, like a drain, and hidden from view. In this case catch-pits with iron gratings should be made on each side of the path at distances of about 30 feet apart. In no case, however, should

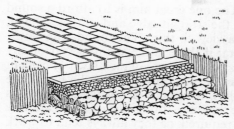

FIG. 17. THE BRICK PATH

Here the foundations are made as for the gravel path, but in place of the top layer of hoggin is a layer of mortar in which the bricks are set.

these gratings communicate directly with the drains, as the sand soon chokes them up. They should consist of a well, formed of brick, a foot or 18 inches square, and of sufficient depth to leave a space of 1 foot or 18 inches (for a 4-foot path) below the level of the drain, which should be directly below the grating and at the top of the pit. This allows ample space for collecting the sediment. The main drain, into which these side drains empty, usually runs down the centre of the path.

Where the path lies on a steep slope, a heavy shower of rain may soon cause havoc with the gravel, the surface water rushing down and ploughing great furrows in the path. This can be prevented by constructing brick, tile, or cement gutters, 6 inches to a foot in width, down both sides of the path, and by inserting catch-pits at regular intervals.

Large bricks or pieces of rock placed in the gutter just below the catch pits will do much to impede the rush of water and will enable the drains to carry it off more easily.

Another way of getting over this "washing-out" trouble is to mix cement with the gravel when laying it down in the proportion of six parts of gravel to one of cement. Add water and mix until the consistency of a thick paste is obtained, then immediately lay the mixture down over the path, flatten out with the back of the spade, and level off with a lath of wood or with the back of a rake, and allow it to set thoroughly.

CRAZY PAVING

Crazy paving must be well and evenly laid, otherwise it is very unpleasant to walk on and will always be giving trouble because of the loosening and rising of the stones. In the initial stages of construction the procedure is the same as for a gravel path, that is to say, the same remarks apply as to drainage, and the foundation of large stones or broken bricks is laid down in the same way, but need not be quite so deep;the same may be said of the

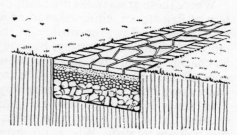

FIG. 18. CRAZY PAVING

For crazy paving the foundations are the same as for the gravel path, but they need not be quite so deep, and in place of the gravel "hoggin" is a 1 to 2-inch layer of sand or fine ashes in which the paving is set.

89

layer of clinkers or smaller stones. The one great aim is to afford a sound and level surface for the paving, and the straight-edge and spirit-level will, therefore, be constantly in use with a view to this. The foundations must be rammed and rolled absolutely firm; if there is the slightest fear of any settlement in the base, as may well happen in clay, an inch layer of cement in which to lay the paving had better be put down. Over the hard core spread a 2-inch layer of sand or ashes, if cement is not used; make this quite level and then lay down the paving, fitting the pieces carefully together so that small pieces are not required, as they always tend to work loose and twist one's ankle. No crevices of much more than an inch in width should be left between the stones or the path will be uncomfortable to walk on and will not remain firm. Where there is likely to be much traffic, the main stones, and all those at the sides of the walk, should be set in mortar. This will tie the whole together and keep it firm. Fill the interstices with sandy loam, so that rock plants, such as saxifrages, thymes, etc., may be planted. (*See* The Paved Garden, p. 203).

GRASS WALKS AND VERGES

Grass walks running between gay borders are a delight, but ought never to be depended upon as much-used routes to or from any given place. When of great length, and 12 or 18 feet wide, they are most imposing. They should never be less than 2 feet in width, otherwise there will be difficulty in handling the mowing machine; rather should their breadth be well over 6 feet; the wider they are, within reason of course, the more imposing they will be. Where there is likely to be much traffic on grass walks, their foundations should be formed and drained as if for gravel, but it will be more satisfactory to make good gravel walks for the general traffic, and to reserve the grass walks for occasional use only, their beauty providing ample justification for their existence.

Where these grass walks are desirable and likely to be much used, a single row of flag-stones, either edge to edge or some 2 feet apart, sunk in level with, or just below, the surface of the turf, will not only make the walk more substantial and lasting, but will also, in many cases, greatly enhance its charm. Equally pleasing and more useful, because the borders can be approached in wet weather, will be two paved walks, 18 inches to 2 feet wide, down both sides of the grass way.

In newly laid-out gardens the grass walks are usually formed of the existing turf, and it is surprising what consistent weeding, rolling and cutting will accomplish. Where, however, the walks are to be sown, a variety of seed that will stand much wear should be chosen. If the barrow is to be used on grass walks in winter, boards must be laid down to prevent the wheel from sinking into and ruining the turf.

For details as to upkeep of grass walks, *see* Chapter 8.

EDGINGS: FORMAL AND INFORMAL

Edgings to paths resolve themselves broadly into two classifications—formal and informal. As formal we include edgings of stone, bricks, tiles, and wood; also grass verges, and miniature hedges of box. Edgings made of plants (*see* list, p. 92) are, of course, informal. Where suitable stones can be obtained, the most interesting borders of all are afforded by irregular blocks of stone with alpines growing between and over them. The stones must never project more than 6 inches from the border.

Formal Edgings

Below are brief descriptions of the best formal edgings.

Tiles.—This word seems to conjure up the exceedingly ugly borders of fancy tiles seen in some gardens. A tile border, however, need not be ugly; it should be severely plain and nondescript in colour, and must never attract the eye, its function being utility, pure and simple. The tiles must be firmly set in the soil and should be even and regular. Some have hollow heads through which canes or wires may be inserted to keep the tiles straight and in line. To lay the tiles, dig a straight-sided trench to the required depth and with its bottom cut level with the incline of the surface of the path. On the inner (border) side of the trench place a long and straight board and against it set the tiles evenly. Now fill in the earth and gravel on the path side of the tiles, ram it very firm, then remove the board, fill the space with soil, and firm the tiles from that side.

Bricks.—Bricks make excellent border edgings, but they must be of a good hard variety; those that will crumble under the action of frost, when lying in the damp ground, are worse than useless and soon become ragged and unsightly. The bricks should be laid on edge, that is to say, with one of the shorter sides in the ground, and sloping slightly inwards towards the border and away from the path. If they are set vertically, or incline outwards over the path, they are more liable to be damaged by the passage of the barrow or roller. Nearly half the brick should be buried in the soil, or it may be set in a 2-inch layer of mortar, when only one-third of the brick need be below the surface level.

Concrete.—This makes a good edging, and is easily constructed. Two boards of wood one-half to an inch in thickness, a foot high, and of any length, are set up 4 inches apart, with 6 inches of their height covered by the soil. The earth between them is excavated to the full 12-inch depth of the boards, which are held firm and upright by stout pegs driven into the soil on the outer sides and nailed into the boards. A series of boards of similar size are laid in this way, in line, where the edging is required. The concrete (*see* p. 207) is now mixed and the space between the boards is filled up, the top being made flat and neat with a trowel. When the concrete has set (four to five days), the boards should be removed and a neat

91

permanent edging will remain. An iron rod is often laid in the centre of the concrete edging, while in the course of construction, to reinforce it.

Wood.—Wood edgings are neat and last a considerable time if creosoted or tarred. They should be made of planks 1 inch thick and 6 to 9 inches wide. Half the width should lie in the soil, and they must be kept firm and upright by strong wooden pegs, about 2 inches square and some 2 feet in length, driven in on the inner (border) side till they are flush with the top of the board. The pegs should be inserted about every yard, and should be fixed to the planks with long galvanized iron nails.

Grass Edgings or verges are the neatest and most pleasing of all the formal edgings. They entail a good deal of labour if they are to be kept properly trimmed and cut, but if the time can be spent on them, they will repay the gardener for it. They are out of place in the small garden and should only be used as edgings to large beds or borders, as they must be at least 2 feet wide to enable the mower to work properly on them. If they are too small to be conveniently cut with the mower, the gardener must then have ample time and patience to spare, to keep them in anything like good order.

A Selection of Edging Plants

NOTE.—For details as to Colour, Height, Season of Flowering and Culture, *see* the ABC of Plants, page 255.

Achillea umbellata (H.P.)	Dianthus (Pinks)	Myosotis, Royal Blue (For-get-Me-Not) (H.P.)
Ageratum Houstonianum (H.H.A.)	D. squarrosus, etc. (H.P.)	Nepeta Faassenii (H.P.)
Alyssum saxatile var. com-pactum (H.P.)	Dryas octopetala (H.P.)	Phlox subulata vars. (H.P.)
	Erica darleyensis, E. vagans and E. carnea (H.S.)	Polyanthus vars. (H.P.)
Antirrhinums (dwarf, vars.) (H.P.)	Genista pilosa (H.P.)	Portulaca grandiflora (H.H.A.)
Arabis caucasica var. fl.-pl. (H.P.)	Geranium (dwarf species) (H.P.)	Primulas Juliana and vars. (H.P.)
Aubrieta deltoides vars. (H.P.)	Geum (dwarf species and vars) (H.P.)	Reseda odorata (Mignon-ette) (H.A.)
Bellis perennis vars. (H.P.)	Gypsophila repens (H.P.)	Saponaria ocymoides (H.P.)
Brunnera macrophylla (H.P.)	Hypericum olympicum (H.S.)	Saxifraga (dwarf vars.) (H.P.)
Campanula (dwarf, species) (H.P.)	Iberis sempervirens (H.P.)	Silene pendula compacta (H.A.)
Cerastium Biebersteinii (H.P.)	Lavendula spica (H.S.)	
	Linum salsaloides (H.P.)	Tagetes (Dwarf vars.) (H.H.A.)
Cheiranthus Allionii (Siberian Wallflower) (H.P.)	Lithospermum diffusum (Heavenly Blue) (H.P.)	Tropæolum majus vars. (Dwarf Nasturtium) (H.A.)
	Lobelia Erinus vars. (H.H.A.)	
Cotyledon Purpusii (H.H.P.)	Lysimachia nummularia. (Creeping Jenny) (H.P.).	Verbena (hybrid vars.) (H.H.A.)
Dianthus deltoides (H.P.)	Malcomia maritima (Vir-ginia Stock) (H.A.)	Zephyranthes candida (H.P)

NOTE.—H.A. = Hardy Annual; H.H.A. = Half-hardy Annual; H.P. = Hardy Perennial; H.H.P. = Half-hardy Perennial; H.S. = Hardy Shrub.

CHAPTER 10

HEDGES, FENCES AND WALLS

HEDGES

Until quite recently it was the custom to plant the inevitable and monotonous privet or laurel, but of late years it has been realized that there are better subjects for the hedge. Of deciduous hedges, the beech, horn-beam, cherry plum, and quickthorn are the most general, while the cypress *Cupressus macrocarpa*, *Lonicera nitida*, holly, *Thuja plicata* and yew all make excellent evergreen hedges.

Considering its importance very little forethought is given, as a general rule, to the choosing and planting of a hedge, which can do much to make or mar the garden.

THE USES OF THE HEDGE

Whether the hedge is required as a shelter from the wind, as a screen, as a barrier, or purely as an ornament, are points which must be taken into consideration, and shrubs suited to the soil and aspect should be chosen. Evergreens like holly, laurel, or yew, and leafy, quick-growing deciduous shrubs like the elder or privet, are excellent for shelter from cold winds. As a screen, cypress, holly, laurel, Lonicera nitida, or yew are undoubtedly the best; while flowering shrubs such as Berberis stenophylla and B. Dar-winii, guelder rose, double gorse, flowering currant, lilac, or Viburnum Tinus, make an excellent ornamental hedge. Nothing is so suitable for a barrier as beech, hornbeam, cherry, plum, or quickthorn.

FORMING THE HEDGE

In forming any hedge, it is, of course, necessary to take into considera-tion the aspect, the quality of the soil, and many other particulars. All plants will not suit all climates, all situations, and all soils. It is wise, therefore, to consider that though there are many ornamental plants and shrubs that will make good hedges, it is not all of these that may choose to flourish where we wish our hedge to grow. As a general rule, the knife may be used unsparingly on all things suitable for hedges, and the hedge itself will be greatly improved by its use. All hedges, but especially those that bear the shears or clippers, should be cut upwards to a narrow ridge, for by this means the lower part, not being overshadowed by the upper, will be kept thick, and the lower part of the hedge will last sound much longer. After they have been planted several years, hedges of most materials require to be cut down, frequently the soil renovated, and, perhaps, new plants introduced. This necessity, however, is very generally the result of neglect in early years, for where proper care has been bestowed and annual pruning given, hedges will last for very many years.

FLOWERING SHRUBS AS HEDGE PLANTS

Many flowering shrubs make excellent informal hedges. The best of these are Berberis Darwinii, B. stenophylla, the flowering currant, Chænomeles lagenaria, double gorse, guelder rose, lilac, and the shrubby honeysuckles. The hedge need not necessarily be composed entirely of one species; a very ornamental hedge, sections of which will be in blossom almost the entire year through if the plants are carefully selected, can be made up of various species of flowering shrubs. Evergreens may be interspersed among the flowering shrubs, and the hedge will be all the firmer if a thorn or a cherry plum is inserted fairly frequently as a stiffener. The Sweet Briar and the Penzance Briars make a splendid hedge.

HOW TO PLANT

Many seem to think that a hedge will grow anywhere and however it is planted; but it must be borne in mind that a hedge, once planted, is usually in position for many years, and that if it is to do well, every care should be taken in its planting. A strip of ground 3 feet wide, in which the hedge is to be planted, should be trenched to a depth of at least 2 feet, and vegetable refuse, leaf-mould, and well-decayed manure should be forked in. Most hedge shrubs are best planted when from 2 to 3 feet in height, they then more easily establish themselves, are easier to train, and are also cheaper. The larger the shrub the more care necessary in planting. With the exception of the quicker or larger-growing shrubs, such as the evergreen oak or the cupressus, most hedge shrubs are best planted out 10 to 15 inches apart; if a very thick hedge is required two rows may be planted some ten inches apart, the plants, as before, being 10 to 15 inches apart in the rows, but planted so that those of one row come opposite the middle of the gaps between those in the other row thus: · . · . ·

TIME FOR PLANTING

Hedges of deciduous shrubs are, with few exceptions, best planted in November. The earth then is still warm and the roots get hold of the soil almost immediately. Such work, however, may be carried out during open weather until March. Avoid frosty periods and cold piercing winds. Evergreens require more care in planting, as the leaves continue functioning even in midwinter. The second half of September and October or April

94

and early May are the periods when the conditions are usually the most favourable.

Long tap roots should always be shortened back before planting, and to ensure bushy plants, in the case of deciduous shrubs, 6 to 10 inches must be trimmed from the top of the newly-planted hedge when the buds begin to swell in spring. Evergreens are best cut back at planting time. Water well after putting the shrubs in, and once a week in dry weather until the roots are established. Should a very dry season follow, syringe the foliage of evergreens every evening if the plants do not appear to be thriving. In late April or early May, during its first year, the hedge should be well watered and then mulched with a 2- to 3-inch layer of equal parts of well-decayed manure and leaf-mould. Severe frosts during the first winter after planting will probably raise the bushes somewhat from the soil. After frosts, therefore, newly-planted shrubs should be firmed back with the foot. We refer the reader to the *chapter on* Shrubs, page 177, and to the *table of* Shrubs for Hedges, page 97, where will be found a wide choice of hedge shrubs, together with details as to the planting, and the manner of pruning and trimming.

For individual cultural details and particulars as to species and varieties, *see* Chapter 34.

PRUNING AND CLIPPING HEDGES

Most hedges are best trimmed twice a year, in May and again in August or September; few shrubs will make much growth after the autumn trimming and will remain tidy all the winter.

Hedge-clipping is not an easy matter for the amateur, and only the man with a very "straight eye" can trim successfully without some guidance in the form of a string stretched taut horizontally and at the required height.

All hedges, especially evergreen hedges, are best cut to a point pyramidically; for if the top is allowed to overhang the bottom, the lower shoots will invariably die off. If carefully trimmed, they may also be cut square at the top, as is necessary in the rose garden and some of the more formal parts of the garden, but the top must not overhang the bottom. With hollies and laurels use the knife in pruning, to avoid the rusty appearance of the withering of half-cut leaves. Privet, box, thorn, and all small-leaved shrubs may be clipped with the garden shears. With such plants as Berberis stenophylla, clipping should take the form of pruning, if bloom is desired. This should be done immediately after flowering, when all the coarse shoots and old flowering wood may be cut back to the required length.

In winter the hedge and the soil round it should be thoroughly cleaned; all dead wood should be cut out and any brambles and climbers should be removed. The weeds must be taken out from the hedge bottom and the soil should be turned up. Where insect pests and disease have been prevalent, the hedge should be sprayed in the early spring, with a caustic soda solution, which must not be too strong in the case of flowering shrubs, or the blossom may be damaged.

NEGLECTED HEDGES

Few things afford stronger indications of the necessity of renovation in a garden than the state of the evergreens and hedges. These are so easily and so insensibly allowed to grow wild, and are so seriously injured by want of care and the proper use of the knife, that neglect cannot go on very long without its ill consequences becoming manifest. Portugal laurels (*Prunus lusitanica*) and many other evergreens may be cut in; but with the common laurel (*Prunus Laurocerasus*) it is a saving of time to cut it down at once. Privet (*Ligustrum ovalifolium* and *L. vulgare*) and holly hedges (*Ilex Aquifolium*) which from years of neglect are found to be occupying too much space, must be cut in.

The former may often be cut down with advantage to within a few inches of the ground, and the latter cut close on all sides to the main branches. This drastic cutting back is best done in April.

HEDGES IN THE SMALL GARDEN

Although hedges are delightful and useful features in a garden, too many should not be planted in a small garden, as they take up a deal of room, and make a great demand upon the soil.

BANKS

A narrow bank with steep sides covered with turf, and planted along the top, say, with bush-roses at intervals of about 4 ft., and dwarf plants on either side along the intervals, is always pleasing, either as a border to a lawn or bowling-green, or as a division between one portion of a garden and another, and is often far preferable to a wall. A substratum of rough stuff should be piled on the ground on either side, to afford support to the earth that forms the interior of the mound. Against the exterior, earth should be thrown up and beaten flat with a spade, to afford a better lodgment for the turf, with which the sides must be covered. An angle of 30 deg. will be found convenient for the slope of the sides of such a bank as this, but it may be less if desired. When placed in position, the turf should be well watered and beaten, and then left alone until the grass has rooted into the earth beneath.

Banks of Roses

Grass banks, however, are very difficult to keep tidy, they are not easily cut with a scythe, or with a mowing machine, unless the slope is only slight. Far better is it to plant them with rambler roses such as Albertine,

PLATE 7 Methods of watering. Seed boxes should be immersed in water (*top left*) lettuces at ground level (*top right*) and beans watered from overhead (*bottom left*). Watering the greenhouse floor (*bottom right*) is a good means of maintaining humidity.

PLATE 8
FLOWERING SHRUBS

Top left. *Cornus nuttallii* (Tree Cornel), *top right, Cistus laurifolius* (Rock Rose) and *centre left, Viburnum opulus* (Guelder Rose).

Bottom right, Clematis jackmannii and *bottom left, Spiraea vanhouttei.*

SHRUBS SUITABLE FOR HEDGES

NOTE.—For Times of Flowering, Colour of Blooms, and Cultural Details, *see* the ABC of Plants, page 255.

Name	Common Name	Average Height in Feet or Form of Hedge and Time in Years to Make Good Hedge	Height in Ins. at which to Plant	Number of Rows	Distance in Inches between Plants	Distance in Inches between Rows	When to Trim
Berberis Darwinii (E)	Barberry	5 ft.; 6 yrs.	20	1 or 2	15	15	Shorten long shoots after flowering
B. stenophylla (E)	Barberry	5 ft.; 5 yrs.	18–24	1 or 2	18–24	18	
Chamæcyparis Lawsoniana (E)	Cypress	7 ft.; 7 yrs.	12–24	1	20	—	April, trim with knife
Chænomeles lagenaria (D)	Japanese Quince	6 ft.; 6 yrs.	18–24	1 or 2	18–24	18	Shorten after flowers
Cotoneaster Simonsii (E)	Rockspray	5 ft; 5 yrs.	18–24	1 or 2	18	18	August or February
Cratægus monogyna (D)	Hawthorn or May	6 ft.; 8 yrs.	12–20	2	6	15	April and August
Cupressus macrocarpa (E)	Cypress	9 ft.; fast grower	12–20	1	25	—	May and Aug., twice yearly
Cytisus albus, etc. (D)	Broom	6 ft.; 5 yrs.	12	2	15	—	June
Euonymus japonicus (E)	Japanese Spindle Tree	6 ft.; 6 yrs.	12–18	1	24	—	Trim April and August
Fagus sylvatica (D)	Beech	Tall; 6 yrs.	18–30	2	10	20	August
Forsythia intermedia vars. (D)	Golden Bell	8 ft.; 6 yrs.	12–18	1	12–18	—	Cut well back in May
Fuchsia Riccartonii (D)	Fuchsia	5 ft.; 6 yrs.	12–18	1	12	—	February or March
Hebe (Veronica) Traversii (E)	Speedwell	3 ft.; 6 yrs.	12–18	1	18	—	Little necessary
Ilex Aquifolium (E)	Holly	Thick Hedge. Slow grower	15	1 or 2	12	12	May and August
Lavendula spica (E)	Lavender	2–3 ft.; 5 yrs.	12	1	12	—	After flowers
Ligustrum ovalifolium (E)	Privet (Oval-leaved)	Screen. Fast grower	20	2	10	15	Whenever straggly
Ligustrum o. aureo-variegatum (E)	Privet (Golden)	4 ft. Fast grower	20	2	10	15	April and August
Lonicera fragrantissima (D)	Honeysuckle Shrubby	4 ft.; 5 yrs.	18	1	12	—	April, shorten long growths
Lonicera nitida (E)	ditto	5 ft.; 5 yrs.	12–18	1	12–18	—	June-August
Olearia Haastii (E)	N. Zealand Daisy Bush	4 ft.; 5 yrs.	12–18	1	12–15	—	Trim straggly shoots
Osmanthus ilicifolia (E)		8 ft.; 5 yrs.	9–12	1	18–24	—	August
Prunus Laurocerasus var. pyramidalis (E)	Laurel	6 ft.; 5 yrs.	20	1	24	—	May and Sept., with knife
Prunus cerasifera (D)	Cherry Plum	Boundary; 6 yrs.	20–40	2	6	15	June
Ribes sanguineum (D)	Flowering Currant	5 ft.; 4 yrs.	18–24	1	18	—	Shorten after flowers
Rosa rubiginosa and Penzance Briars (D)	Sweet Briar	6 ft.; 4 yrs.	30	1	24	—	March and August
Tamarix gallica (D)	Tamarisk	6 ft.; 5 yrs.	24	2	12–15	18	February
Taxus baccata (E)	Yew	5–10 ft.;	30–60	1	24	—	May and Aug.
Thuja plicata (syn. gigantea) etc. (E)	Thuja	As background; fast	30	1	18–20	—	April to September
Ulex europæus fl. plenus. (E)	Double Gorse	5 ft.; 6 yrs.	12–18	2	20	25	Trim after flowering
Viburnum Tinus (E)	Laurustinus	5 ft.; 5 yrs.	12–20	1	18	—	Spring

NOTE.—D = Deciduous; E = Evergreen.

C.B.G.—G

Emile Gray, Excelsa, New Dawn, Paul's Scarlet, and similar varieties. The plants should be put in from four to five feet apart and the varieties which make long growths may be pegged down.

Banks of Stone and Rockwork

The rock bank is an excellent feature, and if planted with trailing or climbing plants or rock plants, affords one of the best means of supporting ground on a higher level. *See the chapters on the* Rock Garden *and the* Wall Garden.

Banks of Flowering Shrubs

These banks are useful, if not too steep, in that they do not entail much upkeep, save occasional hoeing, trimming now and again, and an annual turning of the soil. Rhododendrons are suitable where the slope is slight, and where these and azaleas are used, a mulching of well-rotted leaves is all that is required; it being better not to fork over the soil round these shrubs, for rhododendrons are surface feeders and the roots would be harmed. Other eminently suitable subjects include Berberis species, some of the more brightly berried Cotoneaster species, Spiræas, Symphoricarpus, and rose species.

FENCES

Forms of Fences

Fences may be constructed of various materials and many patterns.

Close Wooden Fencing.—If privacy is desired, close-boarded oak fencing should be used. This type is strong and will last a considerable time. Split oak makes a more durable fence than sawn oak. The usual heights are from $3\frac{1}{2}$ to 7 feet. Fir, larch, pine, or deal, are sometimes used in lieu of oak. They are, of course, by no means so durable, and should be creosoted to preserve them from the weather.

Wattle Hurdles make effective and quite artistic fences; they are easy to set up and are comparatively cheap. As a shelter from the wind they are hard to beat, and have the great advantage of being easily removed, if required in another position.

Split Chestnut Fencing, in which the palings are wired together with strong strands of wire so that there is an interval of about 3 inches between each, makes an efficient and economical fencing, although it affords no shelter from the weather and no privacy. It forms a useful boundary fence of a temporary nature; and is itself quite durable as a protection to a newly-planted hedge. The fencing is stretched to posts some 10 feet apart. The footings of these posts should be charred and tarred.

Rustic Fences are much used to separate one part of the garden from another. They can be made of hazel, larch, spruce, and indeed of any

98

young trees. The bark should always be left on, and the more numerous and rougher the knots, the more rustic the fence will be. The bars of rustic trellis-work should be slightly notched one into another at the points at which they cross, so that they may have a better bearing one against another and a firmer holding than round sticks could possibly have if nailed together without notching.

Wire Netting.—There are many patterns and sizes of this "rabbit-netting" to choose from, and the size of the mesh and the strength of the wire used should be regulated by the purpose to which the netting is to be put. The closer the mesh of the netting, the higher in proportion will be the cost; do not, therefore, use netting with an unnecessarily small mesh. Wire netting lasts quite well, but cannot be called very lovely. It is stretched on posts planted on an average 10 feet apart, and where it is required to turn rabbits, 9 inches of netting should be buried beneath the turf, 3 inches of which is turned out in the direction from which the onslaught is expected. Straining-posts will be needed every 100 feet and, of course, at each corner. Link Fencing of different heights and mesh, can be treated as the wire netting and is much more durable.

Iron Palings form a very durable fence. There are two favourite types: the park fencing, usually with three horizontal bars supported by uprights every 3 or 4 feet; or upright iron-spiked palings, 4 inches apart and held in position by two horizontal bars, one at the top, the other at the bottom. The latter type is more useful for keeping off intruders, but is rather more ugly than the park fencing. These palings require painting periodically to keep them in good condition.

WALLS

The Kitchen Garden

Garden walls have long been a subject for discussion, and will probably always remain so; like everything else connected with gardening, they depend on local circumstances. The walls which would be suitable for a moderate-sized kitchen garden, in a flat or thickly-wooded country, would be very unsuitable for a loftier site, on the side of a hill, or in an open, undulating country; while a plot of small extent, enclosed by walls 14 or 16 feet high, would be inadmissible both on artistic and physiological grounds. On the first, the walls would appear prison-like; on the second, they would exclude the air, which is essential to the growth of plants.

A walled garden is usually designed as a parallelogram and not as a square. Besides the fact that the former shape is more pleasing, there is also the utilitarian reason that north and south walls are more useful than east and west walls and are, therefore, made longer. In addition, owing to the fact that the power of the sun in these colder latitudes is greatest an hour or so after noon, the south wall of a garden is generally so situated that the sun strikes it fully about 1 p.m. (ordinary time); that is to say, the wall faces slightly west of south.

Height of Walls in the Kitchen Garden

It is considered by most gardeners that for small gardens 8-feet walls are suitable, provided the trees on them are planted so far apart as to admit of full horizontal expansion. For gardens of larger size, 10-feet walls, and for an extensive garden 12, and even 14 feet, will not be too great. Where an acre of ground, on a gentle slope, in the form of a parallelogram, is enclosed, a north wall might well be 14 feet high, and the east, west, and south walls only 10 feet; if the slope of the ground is considerable, the difference may be less. In gardens of greater extent—enclosures of four acres for instance—the walls may be higher, but in no instances more than 18 feet high for a north wall, 15 feet for east and west walls, and 12 feet for a south wall. (*See also* Training Fruit Trees, Chapter 39.)

Preservation and Radiation of Heat

But besides the protection it affords, the properly constructed garden wall has other important duties. The wall and its coping prevent the radiation of heat. During the heat of the day it absorbs the sun's rays, and, in common with all heated bodies, it radiates its heat in a ratio proportionate to the square of its distance; so that if an object placed a foot from the wall receives 1 deg. of heat from it, at 1 inch it will receive heat equal to 144 degrees. The reflection, also, of all unabsorbed rays striking the surface of the wall greatly increases the temperature of the air in immediate contact with it. Besides this power of absorbing heat, moisture is also absorbed, both from rain and from the atmosphere, and, with the heat, is given out by radiation, tempering the atmosphere during the night. A wall is thus, in every sense, a source of protection; and it is of considerable importance that its height and form, as well as its workmanship and materials, should be well considered.

Walls in the Flower Garden

Walls are occasionally introduced into flower gardens, either for the shelter they afford in bleak localities, their architectural effect near houses, or for the culture of the more tender plants in the open air. They should seldom be more than 10 or less than 6 feet high. It would be worth going a hundred miles to see a wall 6 feet high and 50 yards long, covered with a collection of tea roses in full bloom. If the wall were mounted with a coping projecting 4 inches, so constructed as to prevent the drip of water, and the roses were slightly covered in winter with spruce branches, and sheltered with canvas from early spring frosts, such a sight might well be realized. (*See also* Climbing Plants, p. 187, *and* Wall Gardening, p. 200.)

PLATE 9   Sowing in the open. Peg out line and hoe drills (*top left*) and plant seed (*top right*).
Cover drills with soil using wooden rake (*below*).

PLATE 10 Transplanting cabbage plants using a line and dibber. If the soil is known to be infested by " clubroot " then dip the roots of the plant in calomel.

CHAPTER 11

METHODS OF PROPAGATION

There are several methods by which plants may be propagated; they may be raised from seed; cuttings may be taken; they can be layered; with a great number, especially herbaceous perennials, the roots may be divided, of some, root-cuttings can be secured; a few can be propagated by leaf-cuttings; while others, mostly fruit trees, roses and many trees and shrubs, are propagated by budding or grafting. In this chapter we describe in detail the various processes.

PLANTS FROM SEED

Generally speaking, seeds retain full vitality for one or two years only in ordinary circumstances. From this we gather it is better to sow seeds as soon as convenient after ripening or in the spring of the following year.

A large number of seeds which are sown in autumn usually germinate quicker, often making better plants than those sown in spring. This is an advantage, particularly in districts where there are favourable climatic conditions, but in other less favourable parts of the country, particularly in the industrial districts where fog is prevalent, spring sowing is to be preferred.

Preserving and Storing Seeds

Seeds should be carefully collected and put in paper packets, bags or boxes together with their names. Avoid where possible gathering seeds or seed pods when wet, as there is the danger of them rotting. Care should be taken to see that they are stored in a cool dry place with an even temperature and a good circulation of air.

Do not leave the seeds in their pods any longer than is necessary for after a time the pods dry up and draw both moisture and vitality from the seeds. In most cases the seeds drop out as soon as they are ripe, and it is therefore advisable to gather the pods before this happens, but on no account should seeds be collected before they are ripe, otherwise very few kinds will germinate when sown because they are not properly matured. This is a very important point to bear in mind.

After cleaning they can be stored until required in tins with tightly fitting lids, in thoroughly clean glass bottles if kept in the dark, or in glazed paper impermeable to moisture.

Soft absorbent paper is bad, as the seeds will either dry and shrivel up, or if kept in too moist a place, will get damp and mouldy.

Weather for Sowing

Never sow in a cold, wet soil. Wait until the ground has dried sufficiently and until the weather really bids fair to be mild. It is false economy to sow before one feels sure of the weather, just on the off-chance of getting an extra early crop. Dry weather should therefore be chosen, for seed sowing, and if seed can be sown just before a gentle shower, or when the weather is likely to be showery, so much the better. Of course there is a proper time for sowing for every kind of seed (*see* Chapter 34), but this cannot be specified in a series of general instructions which apply equally to all. The smaller the seed, the finer should be the soil in which it is grown. The soil in which seed is sown should be tolerably dry—dry enough to crumble lightly when worked with the hand. It must not clot together in a pasty mass. Place or position—whether in the open air or under protection—also forms an important factor with regard to time.

SOWING UNDER GLASS

The less hardy plants must be raised under glass in seed pans or boxes, being sown in John Innes seed compost or a mixture of two-thirds good loam and one-third leaf-mould, together with a good sprinkling of sharp silver sand. The compost should be sieved through a quarter-inch mesh and the soil for covering the seeds through a sieve even finer. Mix the compost thoroughly, press it gently into the pot or box, and make a level surface just below the rim of the pot. The seed pans or boxes should be drained by means of "crocks" or broken pots, an inch of crocks being required in a box or pot 5 inches in depth. Earthenware pots or pans are preferable, as the earthenware keeps the soil more evenly moist than does the wooden box. The seeds must be sown thinly in February or March, being watered afterwards, not with a can, but by the pots or pans being immersed nearly to their brims, the water being in this way able to soak up from the bottom. Set the seed pans in a frame or greenhouse in moderate but steady heat (about 60 deg. F.). A sheet of glass should be placed over the boxes, the glass in turn being covered with a sheet of brown paper to keep out the light. Each day the glass must be lifted so that the condensation may be wiped off, otherwise the seeds will be kept too moist. No further water need, as a rule, be given until the seeds have germinated. As soon as the seeds are up (in about three weeks' time, this varies according to the type of seeds), the glass and paper may be removed, and the boxes must be lifted by gradual steps up to within 6 inches of the lights of the house. If the box is left some distance from the glass, weak straggling seedlings will result. In warm weather it is wise to water the seedlings in the evening, but in the colder weather the watering must be done before lunch time or there may be a danger of the seedlings "damping off", *see also* Chapter 31 on The Greenhouse.

Sowing in a Frame

The seeds may be sown in a frame in exactly the same way as described for sowing in pans or boxes. The frame should be in a sheltered position, for it is essential to ventilate as much as possible when the weather is sunny and calm.

Pricking-off the Seedlings

When the seedlings are large enough to handle readily, they must be pricked-off and transplanted into boxes containing John Innes Potting Compost or a mixture of 3 parts loam, 2 parts peat and 1 part sand with a little lime and fertilizer, being set from 1 to 3 inches apart so that the leaves do not touch. After this they should again be put in position some 6 inches from the lights. When pricking-off, the wooden label should be inserted in the soil an inch or so from the seedling, whose roots may then be gently levered up without damage—never should seedlings be pulled up between the finger and thumb, as this will sorely damage the roots. The seedlings should be planted so that the first pair of leaves show just above the soil. They must be planted firmly and should have the soil pressed lightly down round the roots and stems, though care must be taken not to injure any part of the seedling. A thin dibble about the size of a pencil should be used to make the holes for the seedlings, and these must not be made too deep, otherwise the roots of the seedlings will not reach the bottom, and the air-pockets left under them will wither their roots. Do not "firm" the seedlings by pressing the earth round the stems with the fingers, but use the dibble, inserting it into the soil, in three or four places round the seedlings, about half an inch from them, and to the same depth as when preparing the holes. This will firm the soil all round the seedlings, right down to the bottom of the roots; the fingers would only press in the top and the roots would be left loose in the soil. Strongly-growing seedlings can be potted up at once, the process of pricking-off being unnecessary. In the case of seeds that germinate irregularly, the first batch of seedlings should be pricked-off as soon as they can be handled, and the seed boxes should then be replaced so that the remaining seeds may germinate.

Such treatment is necessary with plants like the anemone, auricula, polyanthus and other primulas. After pricking-off, keep the young seedlings in a close atmosphere and shade them from the sun for a few days until they are established.

Hardening-off and Planting-out

In March or April the seedlings should be transplanted into the cold frame, which should contain soil similar to that in the seed boxes. There they are hardened-off by being gradually allowed more and more air until they are planted out very firmly in the reserve garden in May or early June. Annuals will, of course, be placed in their flowering position, some prefer to be sown direct in their flowering site.

Protection in Winter

Half-hardy biennial and perennial seedlings, however, will require protection during the coming winter, and in early October must be lifted, then replanted close together in light sandy soil in boxes, to be stored in the greenhouse in a temperature of about 50 deg. F., or in a cold frame. As much air as possible should be given when the weather is fine and dry to prevent the plants from "damping-off". Should there be any signs of this, every opportunity should be taken of thoroughly ventilating on dry warm days, the soil being sprinkled very finely with powdered charcoal, or better still, water with "Cheshunt Compound". This can be obtained from any horticultural stores in powdered form complete with directions on how to use it. In the following May the biennials should be set out in their flowering positions, and the perennials must again be placed in the reserve garden. Half-hardy perennials will require protection during each winter, and will again have to be lifted in October, and wintered under glass. It is as well to look at the thermometer the last thing at night and to cover the lights with sacking if the frost is likely to be severe. These mats should not be removed too early in the morning.

Half-hardy perennials or biennials can, of course, be sown in the open in May or June and wintered as stated above. The seeds of hardy plants are frequently sown under glass to procure early and sturdy plants for bedding-out in the spring.

SOWING IN THE OPEN
Preparing the Seed-Bed

The seed-beds for tender and choice plants should be sheltered from the north and east. The soil should be made as fine as possible, first by breaking up the lumps with a fork and then by raking it thoroughly until the earth is well pulverized. It should contain 10 per cent to 20 per cent of sand—this will make it porous and will enable the air to penetrate freely through it. If the soil is not made fine in this way, many of the seeds will fall down in between the clods and will not germinate. Those that do come up have their tiny roots parched, as there will be no fine soil through which they can work and so obtain nourishment and moisture. Too rich a soil must not be used, for the seedlings would become tall and straggly,

104

instead of short and sturdy, which is the ideal at which to aim. The bed must be pressed down firmly and left to settle for a few days before seeding. Water the bed thoroughly, if dry, and sow the seed thinly in drills running north and south, if possible, and from 6 to 12 inches apart (for times, depth to sow, and distances apart for the different flowers, vegetables, etc., *see* Chapters 34 *and* 36). Sowing in drills is much better than the "broadcast" method, in which the seed is scattered over the entire surface of the seed-bed. It saves seed and makes the sowing and weeding more easy. Thick sowing means that the seedlings will get drawn up and will be sickly; thin sowing secures short, sturdy seedlings, and also reduces the danger of "Damping off".

How Deep to Sow

Cover the seeds lightly with fine, sandy soil. The depth of covering required depends on the size of the seed. Minute seeds need hardly anything over them, a mere sprinkling of sand is sufficient; medium-sized seeds must have a covering a little less than half an inch thick; and large seeds, such as those of the iris or pæony, and also those like the seeds of the anemone and phlox, which quite often do not germinate the first year after sowing, can do with $\frac{1}{2}$ to 1 inch of soil over them. Few seeds require a covering of more than 1 inch in thickness. Seeds may be sown slightly deeper out of doors than under glass, as the rain is liable to wash out any with too sparse a covering. A good rule is to cover the seeds with a layer of earth twice their own thickness. Do not pat down the soil after the seeds have been planted. Seeds sown in heavy soil must not be placed so deep as those planted in sandy loam, while in a sandy soil a covering of nearly twice that given in a heavy soil will be required. Do not plant the seeds too deep, however, as if so planted and they ever reach the surface at all, they will have used up most of their strength and energy and will make weak, straggly seedlings.

Should the soil of the seed-bed be very dry, the seeds must be soaked overnight in warm water.

Watering and Protection from Birds

Should the weather be dry, as soon as the seeds have been covered, give them a good watering from a can with a fine rose; the rose must be very fine or the seeds may be uncovered and washed away. Keep the soil uniformly moist, but not too wet; over-watering causes the seeds to rot and is the most frequent cause of failure. A few strands of black cotton, supported on small sticks, should be stretched across the bed to keep the birds away. If, before planting, the larger seeds are steeped in a weak solution of paraffin, or rolled in red lead, neither mice nor birds will trouble much about them. Care should be taken to see that the seeds are not left in the paraffin any length of time, otherwise failure to germinate may occur, particularly with small seed.

Thinning Out and Transplanting

In a month or so the seedlings should be about 2 inches high and will be large enough to be handled between finger and thumb and pricked-off. This should always be done at the earliest possible moment. Delay in thinning and transplanting means that the seedlings become drawn-up and weakly, and when they are eventually moved, the fibrous roots may be torn and the seedlings will take much longer to become established. They will, in fact, never make such sturdy plants as those transplanted at the right time. In order that the roots shall not be torn, the seed-bed should be watered the evening before the day on which thinning is to take place. The seedlings should be raised from the seed-bed by means of a small fork, each seedling may then be separated from its neighbours without any damage to its roots, and should be planted very firmly, by means of a small trowel, in a hole just large enough to receive the roots without cramping them or doubling them up, and care must be taken not to leave an air-pocket below the roots or they will soon be parched. Sturdy seedlings should be transplanted about ten inches apart; smaller ones 6 inches apart. If, as in the case of carrots or onions, the seedlings are to be thinned and not transplanted, the fork is not used to raise them, but the unwanted seedlings are pulled up between the finger and thumb, a finger of the other hand being pressed upon the soil to keep the roots of the other seedlings in place. The soil should be firmly pressed back around those seedlings left in the seed-bed or they will be likely to die off. If transplanting is done in the evening, the seedlings will have the cool night in which to recover, and will not be so liable to be scorched as when transplanted in the heat of the day. The reserve garden into which the seeds are transplanted must possess a sunny aspect, should have been well dug and the soil, if poor, will be all the better for having had good, well-rotted manure mixed with the top 3 inches, and must be dressed with just sufficient soot to blacken the surface in order to ward off slugs. A further dressing of vegetable ashes will help to lighten the soil and furnish nourishment for the seedlings. In dry weather the reserve bed should be well watered the day before it is to receive the seedlings, but it must not be made too wet, as the seedlings will not grow if it is made to "cake". The bed should be again watered after the transplanting has been done. If transplanting can be carried out in showery weather, so much the better.

When to Apply Manure

In dry weather, the seedlings should be watered (but not when the hot sun is on them) and the bed must be well hoed. Tepid water is far more

106

congenial to them than cold water from the tap or a deep tank, and provided the soil is fairly rich, the seedlings should receive no manure until they approach maturity. A dressing of sootwater is a sufficient stimulant, and a protection from slugs.

Protection During Winter

In warm and sheltered districts the young seedlings of hardy plants may be left in the open all winter (annuals will, of course, have attained maturity, flowered, and died down), but in colder districts it is safer to winter them in a frame, where they should be placed in October. Light, sandy soil and a southerly aspect best suit most seedlings. As much air as possible should be given, but care must be taken to exclude frost and damp.

In November of the second season or in March of the third year the plants can be put out in their permanent positions; tender plants receiving protection during the second winter as afforded in the first. Slugs are the great enemy of young seedlings and some good soil fumigant should be used to keep these at bay. *See* page 529.

DIVISION OF ROOTS

Plants are best divided in October and November, or in March and April. The clumps should be lifted with their roots as entire as possible, that is, with a good "ball" of earth round the fibres. This is done by inserting two forks vertically downwards, one on either side of the plant with their backs facing each other, and then by levering the clump and its roots gently upwards. When the plant has been lifted, don't, as is so often done, use a spade to cut the roots apart, but carefully divide the plant up into as many crowns as possible by means of a sharp knife; this will do the minimum injury to the roots. The strong new outer crowns are those that should be retained and replanted; the old inner roots being removed. The stems that have already borne flowers should be cut away from the new crowns, so that only the young and vigorous shoots from the base remain. Replant as described in the chapter on *The Herbaceous Border*.

PROPAGATION BY OFFSETS

Offsets afford yet another means of propagation suitable to many herbaceous perennials and to many rock plants. These offsets are growths forming young crowns round the older central crown, and may be carefully separated from the parent crown complete with some roots when large enough and can be potted up into small pots or transplanted in the open. About a month after the plant has flowered will be found the best time to accomplish this.

RAISING PLANTS FROM CUTTINGS

Preparing the Cuttings

Cuttings should be taken of shoots that have ripened or which are beginning to ripen, because in wood which is attaining or has attained maturity the callus so necessary to root formation is more readily induced to show itself. The side shoots of plants, low down on the stem, are the best for cuttings, and should be taken when the sap is in full motion, because its return by the bark tends to form the callus, or ring, of granular matter from which the roots proceed. The leaves of a cutting must never be cut off, except in so far as may be necessary at its base in order that it may be inserted in the soil. The foliage is the lungs of the plant, and if it is cut, the sap that it contains will be lost to the cutting and prevented from passing downwards to form the callus. Cuttings of plants that are difficult to strike may frequently be induced to do so if a ring is made round them, or if a piece of string is tied round them for a short time before they are taken from the parent plant. The downward flow of the sap is arrested by the tightened ligature and a swelling is caused, which forms a callus from which roots are soon emitted. The cutting must be severed from the parent plant just below the ring or band, and the callus formed should be covered when the cutting is inserted in the soil.

In taking cuttings, strong, sturdy shoots varying from 3 to 12 inches in length should be removed from the plant, with a very sharp knife, by a clean, straight cut just below a joint. If it is possible to take a "heel" or small wedge-shaped portion of the old wood and bark with it, so much the better, and it is then not essential to cut immediately below a joint. The joint need not necessarily be the junction of two stems; it may equally well be the "eye" from which a pair of leaves has sprung. When no "heel" is taken, the cut must be especially clean and just below a joint, but the joint itself must be left intact; n fact, about an eighth of an inch of wood should be left below the joint. The "heel", from which all ragged edges should be trimmed, when placed in contact with the ground, provides a larger surface on which roots can form. The length of cuttings is decided by the distance between the joints; when these are, say, an inch apart, the cuttings must be 12 inches long and over half this length must be buried in the soil. Where the distance between joints is less, the cuttings may be shorter, but all hard-wooded cuttings should have at least 6 inches in the ground, and all cuttings must be inserted right to the bottom of the hole prepared for them.

Cuttings of Hard-Wooded and Soft-Wooded Plants

Cuttings of hard-wooded shrubs, such as the heath or myrtle, are more difficult to strike than those of soft-wooded plants, such as the geranium, and for this reason on hard-wooded cuttings the "eyes" on the part of

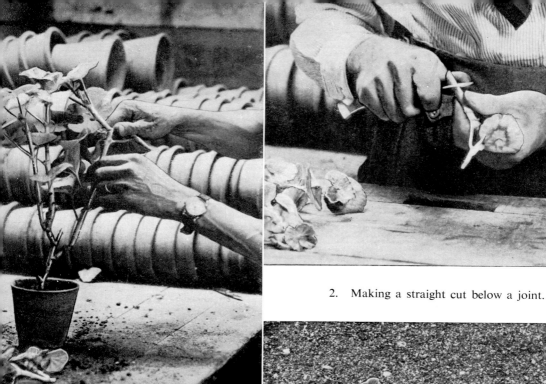

2. Making a straight cut below a joint.

1. Cutting a healthy side shoot from an old plant

3. Comparison between an untrimmed and trimmed cutting.

4. Bedding four cuttings to a depth of about $1\frac{1}{2}$ in. in a 4 in. pot filled with light sandy soil.

PLATE 11

PELARGONIUMS
PROPAGATION

PLATE 12 Young growths of Carnation for propagation ; *right*, a rooted cutting.

the stem that will be placed underground should be carefully cut out. This will encourage the formation of roots at these places. Cuttings of free-growing hardy plants, such as the gooseberry, and the willow, strike freely without care or attention after being inserted in the soil. The position for all cuttings should, of course, be sheltered and shaded from full sun, and although not necessary with hardy plants, most cuttings when planted in the open do better if covered by a hand light until the roots have formed. The less hardy and less vigorous plants should be struck in pots or boxes in a cold frame or under hand lights, while the more delicate still require artificial heat or the bottom-heat of a propagating box. It may be taken as a general rule that cuttings of soft-wooded plants require more heat than those of hard-wooded plants. "Soft" cuttings, as a rule, should not be struck in the open, for, apart from a little heat being desirable, the wind and sun would dry the moisture from their leaves and the roots would never form. A glass covering is, therefore, necessary. Cuttings of soft-wooded plants, such as the geranium, strike best when they have not too much foliage to bear, and should have the stems shortened to two or three joints beneath the point from which the foliage springs. Never make the cuttings longer than necessary. In the case of the less hardy plants, the soil should be stored in a warm greenhouse for a few days before the cuttings are inserted, and rooting will be more certain and prompt if the cuttings are watered with lukewarm water.

Hollow-stemmed Plants

There are several plants like the pansy or the honeysuckle whose stems, when mature, are hollow and useless for ordinary cuttings. In such cases the young shoots must be struck, or with the honeysuckle both ends of the cutting may be inserted in the soil. There are other plants, such as dahlias and lupins, whose cuttings must be taken at the junction of the stems and the roots. These require a glass covering.

Greenhouse Plants

Cuttings of nearly all the less hardy and greenhouse plants require a propagating case, placed over the hot-water pipes. With the more hardy kinds no artificial heat is needed, except that provided by the glass, but the soil must be kept uniformly warm and moist.

Shrub Cuttings

Shrub cuttings may be taken at three distinct periods: firstly in autumn when the wood has hardened and is quite mature; secondly in September or August when the shoots have half-matured; and thirdly when the shoots are beginning to ripen in early summer. The last time is, perhaps, the best of the three. With many of the hardier shrubs, the cuttings may be struck

109

in sandy soil in a sheltered bed in the open (*see* Chapter 18), provided the wood is fully ripe. Half-matured cuttings, even of hardy shrubs, must, however, be treated like those of the less hardy natures and be struck under glass. Cuttings of hardy evergreen shrubs are also best struck under glass, not because they need heat, but because a close, steady, and fairly moist atmosphere is required. (*See* Propagation of Shrubs, p. 181).

When cuttings are struck in pots or boxes, the latter should be well drained by an inch layer of crocks at the bottom, and must be clean. If they are dirty, the mould will be likely to stick to them when the cuttings are turned out for transplanting and the tender new root fibres may be torn.

Preparing the Compost

Coarse sand is, perhaps, the best medium in which to strike cuttings. A light soil through which the air can pass freely is essential to the well-being of all cuttings. That aeration is necessary is proved by the fact that cuttings will strike readily in coconut fibre, a material that is extremely pervious to air and which retains moisture for a considerable period. Powdered charcoal also forms a good medium. Perhaps the free access of air through the excellent drainage in such a position is the reason why cuttings root more freely when placed close to the side of the pot.

A good compost for striking the cuttings of most plants can be made by mixing equal quantities of leaf-mould and well-sieved loam and by adding to this a good proportion of coarse sand, and then sieving the whole through a quarter-inch mesh. It is always well to sprinkle the surface of the soil which is to receive the cuttings with a layer of coarse sand about 1 inch thick, so that when the dibble is pressed down to form the hole for the cutting, some of the sand will trickle into it and be ready to encourage the production of roots. The sand keeps the soil porous and prevents the base of the cutting from rotting. The soil should be firmed down and the slips inserted at least 1½ inches apart. They must not be placed too close together, otherwise they may "damp-off". Press the earth well down round the cuttings, as they will not root if standing loosely in the soil. If the cuttings can be fairly easily pulled up, it may be taken as an indication that they are not planted sufficiently firmly.

Setting the Cuttings in the Soil

As has been said, cuttings strike more readily when placed at the side of a pot, than when inserted in its centre. Of ordinary plants about seven cuttings can be placed in a 4-inch pot. No cutting should be set too deeply, but as in the case of seeds, the depth will depend mainly on the size of the cutting. A good general rule is to set about two-thirds of the length of hard-wooded cuttings in the soil, with soft-wooded cuttings only one-third or one-half should be inserted. Leaves should not be permitted to touch the soil; if they do, they will "damp-off". Water well after insertion.

When using pots or boxes, it is better, but not necessary, to sink these nearly to their brims in ashes or coconut fibre. This will keep the soil at an even temperature. Whether the cuttings are covered by plates of glass, glass bells, or the lights of a frame, the condensation must be wiped off each morning. Once the cuttings have struck, ventilation must be given whenever possible, and decaying leaves must be removed to avoid any possibility of "damping-off". The great thing is to keep the soil at the same temperature as the surrounding air.

Shade and Ventilation

Too much light, air, water, heat, or cold are alike injurious to cuttings freshly inserted under glass. A close, equable temperature and a moderate degree of moisture should be maintained until the cuttings have "rooted". This condition is best attained by covering them with a bell glass or hand-light, and by shading them from the hot midday sun, if not placed in a shady position. Once they have struck, which will be in about three weeks, the cuttings should be gradually given more ventilation and hardened-off until they can be potted up singly for the greenhouse, or planted out into the open.

Transplanting and Potting off

Soft-wooded cuttings soon form roots, and can often be potted-off within a few weeks; cuttings of hard-wooded shrubs, however, take root less quickly and should not be disturbed for at least a year (sometimes 18 months) after being struck. To give the cuttings ample room to grow they are usually planted at least 6 inches from each other in rows 10 inches to a foot apart.

Rooting Cuttings with the aid of Chemical Stimulants

In recent years, a number of chemical substances have been discovered which have the property of stimulating the formation of roots on stem cuttings. The physiological action of these substances, which are mostly complex organic acids or salts derived from them, in some ways resembles that of the hormones that occur naturally in plants and animals. For this reason they are sometimes referred to as *plant hormones*. This description is misleading, however, because most of those that are commonly used by gardeners are synthesized by purely chemical methods, and are not known to occur naturally in plants at all. It is, therefore, more satisfactory to refer to these chemical stimulants as plant growth substances. It so happens that one of the earliest growth substances to be

111

discovered was shown to be identical with a naturally occurring plant hormone, and this circumstance has led to much misunderstanding amongst gardeners concerning the true nature of these chemicals.

Chemical root stimulants can be applied to cuttings in several distinct ways. The most familiar and efficacious method is to insert the bases of the cuttings, to a depth of an inch or two, in a very diluted solution of the growth substance in water, usually for a period of seventeen to twenty-four hours. During this time a leafy cutting in a well ventilated place will generally take up sufficient of the growth substance to stimulate the formation of roots. The cuttings are then rinsed in water and subsequently inserted in sand or any other suitable rooting medium in the usual way. Alternatively the growth substance is mixed with a fine powder, in which the previously moistened basal ends of the cuttings are inserted, momentarily, before the cuttings are placed in the rooting medium. This method has the advantage of being quick and easy to perform, but, unfortunately, it is usually less effective than the solution method described above. Other special methods of application have also been tried, but these are not likely to be of much value to the amateur gardener.

Plant growth substances, when pure, have the form of fine powders or crystals. It cannot be too strongly emphasized, however, that they must be applied to the cuttings in a very diluted form, for, although they stimulate root formation when applied at the correct strength, they are actually very poisonous to plants when more concentrated. So great a degree of accuracy is required when making up solutions of the pure powder that this operation cannot be performed without access to a delicate chemical balance. It is for this reason that a number of manufacturers have come to the aid of gardeners by putting plant growth substances on the market under proprietary names. The proprietary substances are in the form of liquids, powders, or tabloids which have only to be mixed with, or dissolved in, water, according to the maker's instructions, before they are ready for use, so they can readily be employed even by those gardeners whose knowledge of chemistry is limited.

When correctly applied, growth substances will stimulate the formation of roots on cuttings of many different species and varieties. It must be remembered, however, that each kind of plant requires its own special concentration of the chemical, and an appropriate duration of treatment, if optimum results are to be obtained. For this reason the maker's instructions must be followed with the utmost care. There are, unfortunately, many species that will not respond to the growth substances that are at present on the market, and this important fact seriously limits the extent to which they can be usefully employed. Then again, leafless, hardwood cuttings seldom respond to treatment. The reasons for these failures are not, at present, fully understood, but further investigations by chemists

112

PLATE 4 *Above, VERONICA GENTIANOIDES; Below, DRY WALL IN SUMMER*

gardeners, and botanists may eventually lead to some improvement. Meanwhile the use of chemical root stimulants can be commended to all those who are interested in propagation by cuttings, for considerable improvement in the ease and certainty with which many species can be rooted will inevitably follow if the substances are applied intelligently to those plants that are known to respond.

LAYERING

This is an easy and very sure method of propagation, usually effected about July, though it may be satisfactorily carried out at any season of the year. It consists in the production of roots on one or more of the lower shoots of the plant to be reproduced. An upward cut, just below a joint, is made in the layer or shoot; the incision passes from the underside through to the centre of the shoot, and is from about 1 inch to 3 inches in length, according to the size and nature of the plant to be propagated.

The aim is to produce a "tongue" of bark and wood that can be wedged open and pegged down into the soil; the more the tongue is kept open when placed in contact with the earth, the better the chances of rooting.

The shoots chosen for layering must be perfectly healthy, and should be semi-matured. It is usual to layer several shoots at a time, and when the cuts have been made, as described above, the earth all round the plant is stirred up to a depth of 3 inches and the layers are pegged down firmly, so that the open tongues come well in contact with the soil. Little mounds of earth some 6 inches high are then piled up over the layers, which are pressed firmly down into the earth, and well watered.

An addition of coarse sand to the soil (often in the proportion of 50 per cent of its volume) as in the case of cuttings, helps the layers to root. The outer end of the shoot, beyond the cut, should be turned upwards to check the flow of the sap, and all buds not required to form shoots in the new plant should be removed. When the layers have rooted firmly, they may be cut away from the parent plant, being potted up or planted out, preferably in autumn. The layers of soft-wooded plants, such as the carnation, will be found to root in six weeks or so, shrubs like the laurel or veronica will take two or three months to form roots; while with hardwooded shrubs, like the daphne, magnolia or rhododendron, it will be a year or more.

PROPAGATION BY RUNNERS

This is, perhaps, the most simple method of propagation, though only possible with certain plants, namely those that throw out long, thin stems or runners which grow out over the surface of the ground. The strawberry is a well-known example of the runner-producing plant. At intervals along the stems will be found joints, and wherever one of these joints comes in contact with the soil and so remains for some time, roots form and foliage is thrown up.

To assist in this method of propagation, the earth should be stirred up to a depth of 2 or 3 inches, all round the plant and the runners must be firmly pegged down into it at the required number of joints. Young roots will form and after a few weeks they will be strong enough to support the new plant, which may be cut away from its parent, and potted up or transplanted. A better method, but one entailing a little more work, is to sink to their brims pots of good sandy soil exactly under the joints of the runners and to peg the latter down firmly to the soil in the pots. This operation provides an easier way of transplanting.

ROOT-CUTTINGS

This is another and easy method of propagation eminently suitable in the case of plants with fleshy roots or those that sucker freely. If the roots of plants of this nature are examined in the early spring, they will be found to be covered with small, whitish knobs or shoots; these are the "eyes" from which the new growth will spring. Cuttings of these roots from 2 to 8 inches in length, in accordance with the virility of the plant, and each having an "eye", are taken. They are planted 1 inch deep and 8 inches apart in light sandy soil in partial shade, or in a cold frame with a warm, close atmosphere. The cuttings are inserted vertically with that part of the root which was nearest the stem uppermost.

In propagating plants whose roots are fleshy, but rather more fibrous in nature, the larger root-stems should be cut away from the crowns with as many of the smaller fibrous roots as possible adhering, and should be planted as advised above, but should be left intact and not be cut up into small pieces.

In the case of plants whose roots creep horizontally just below the surface of the soil, cut the roots into pieces from 1 to 6 inches in length, each piece having an "eye" or bud from which shoots can spring, and plant them horizontally at the same depth as they were before being dug up.

The root-cuttings will require frequent watering during the following few months, and will be benefited by the occasional application of a little weak manure water. It is essential to keep the surface of the soil loose. The cuttings can be planted out in the autumn or in the following March or April.

PROPAGATION BY LEAF-CUTTINGS

Propagation by leaf-cuttings is a very interesting method not often resorted to, and then only in the case of plants with succulent or thick spongy leaves, and soft veins. A healthy leaf is taken and planted, stalk downwards, and with the leaf proper just clear of the soil, in a propagating case in equal parts of sandy loam and leaf-mould. Roots will soon form and a young plant will grow from them. Examples of plants which can be treated in this manner are, saintpaulia, ramonda, and haberlea. In the case of a large and thick leaf, the veins on the back may be slit at their junctions. The stalk is then planted in sandy soil, and the whole leaf is pinned firmly backside-down, so that it cannot move, on to the soil in the propagating case (temperature 70 deg. F.), and allowed plenty of moisture, though the bed must be well-drained and should not be permitted to become stagnant, or the leaves will rot. In a short time plants will grow wherever the veins have been slit. The little plants can be transplanted or potted up as soon as they have roots strong enough to support them.

This method, which may be resorted to at any season when fully-matured leaves are available, is particularly suitable in the case of such plants as the achimenes, begonia, and the gloxinia.

RINGING

Hard-wooded plants which are difficult to propagate by other methods may be increased by a process known as ringing, and which consists

in removing a small narrow ring of bark all round the stem, in the place in which the formation of roots is desired. Care must be taken not to cut deeply into the stem—indeed, it is better to peel off the outer bark only, and not to cut into the inner wood at all; no hindrance is then offered to the ascent of the sap. A callus is formed on the upper edge of the ring, and this thickens as time goes on, and ultimately emits roots. Branches and trailing stems operated on in this way should be firmly pegged down, and earth should be drawn over the incision. Layers should be brought into as erect a position as possible, and they may be shortened back. (*See also* Layering, page 113.)

BUDDING. 1.
FIG. 19. (*Left*) A rose shoot suitable for providing buds. It must have borne a flower.
FIG. 20. (*Right*) The shoot after the leaves have been cut off; only the base of the leaf stem is left.

BUDDING

Budding is resorted to as a means of improving or altering the nature of the fruit and flowers borne by a given tree, and it is based on the same principles as those which govern grafting (page 119). It is superior to the

115

latter inasmuch as it produces a more perfect union, a proportionately larger surface of the inner bark coming in contact with that of the stock. In budding no wood at all is left on the bud employed, only the bud itself and a surrounding surface of bark being left on the "bud" when prepared.

Preparing the Bud

In this operation, unlike grafting, the bud and stock are prepared on the spot, not beforehand, and a time should be chosen when the sap is rising freely both in stock and bud. The tree should be looked over, and the best shoot selected for the cutting of the buds. If they are not to be used at once, the shoots should be put in water, or the bark will dry slightly and be more difficult to work. In the case of a rose, a suitable shoot for furnishing the buds may be selected by trying it with the finger, which should be gently rubbed over the prickles. If these fall off easily, the shoot is in a fit condition.

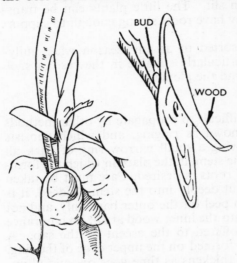

BUD

WOOD

BUDDING. 2.

FIG. 21. (*Left*) Cutting the bud out of the shoot.
FIG. 22. (*Right*) Separating the wood from the bark

Choosing the Buds

In selecting the buds, particularly in the case of fruit trees, care must be taken to make sure that the buds are wood buds, from which a shoot will start, and not fruit buds, which will not make wood. These two kinds of bud are more easily distinguished in some kinds of trees than in others, but as a general rule it may be taken that the wood buds are more pointed than are the fruit buds. The buds of some fruit trees, most usually in dry seasons, are troublesome to peel away from their wood, the wood very frequently pulling out the middle of the bud with it, as described on p. 117. When this is very marked, it is a good plan to pierce the wood just behind the bud with the point of the knife, so as actually to cut it away from the bud at that point, before beginning to peel it from the bark. The shoots selected for budding, whether for fruit or rose-trees, should be plump, firm, and well-ripened. Watery shoots or buds are valueless.

A good well-matured shoot of current year's growth having been chosen, the leaves should all be removed from it close to the leaf-stalk, only a piece of the latter being left on. If the leaves are left on, they will draw and pass out the moisture from the bark and the bud, causing the latter to shrink. With a sharp knife the bud is then cut out of the wood, the knife making a curve behind it, leaving the bud midway on a thin strip of bark and wood. The knife should enter the wood some half an inch above the bud, and come out an equal distance below it, leaving a piece of bark of the shape of a long shield, whence the name of "shield-budding" sometimes given to the operation. The woody part

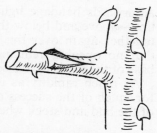

FIG. 23. BUDDING. 3. Cut in side shoot of standard rose ready for budding.

of this must now be removed, and in order to do this, the piece is held by the leaf-stalk and bud, while the bark is started away from the wood at the top end with the tip of the knife, and is then given a sharp pull, when the bark should peel cleanly off the slip of wood. Occasionally, and generally when the bud is too forward when cut, the wood, when it pulls away, will leave a small hole in the bark behind the bud, as if it had pulled out a little bit of the inside of the bud with it. When this has occurred the bud is spoilt, and will shrivel and die before it has time to build up new cells. Such a bud should be thrown away and a fresh one, less developed, taken.

Preparing the Stock

The bud being ready, the stock must next be dealt with. A clean, smooth spot on the stem is chosen, and with the budding knife a cut about $1\frac{1}{2}$ inches long is made, only just sufficient pressure to pierce the bark without penetrating the wood beneath being employed. At the top of this a cross-cut half an inch long should be made with equal care, the bark on either side of the first cut then being raised from the wood by means of the blade of the knife, or its thin handle, slipped in between bark and

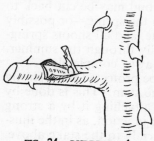

FIG. 24. BUDDING. 4. The bud inserted and the bark cut off level.

wood. The point of the "shield" containing the bud is then inserted at the cross-cut, and is gently pushed down under the bark until the bud is well down below the level of the cross-cut. The easiest way to do this is to hold the shield between the finger and thumb of the left hand, by the leaf-stalk, while holding the bark open with the knife held in the other hand. When the bud is well down, the projecting tip of the shield should be cut off with a cut exactly on a level with the cross-cut in the stock, so that the tip of the shield fits inside the bark.

117

Afterwards bandage lightly with soft material—raffia, worsted, or matting—above and below the eye, bringing the lips of the bark of the stock together again over the bud by means of the ligature in such manner that no opening remains between them. Above all, take care that the base of the eye is in free contact with the bark of the stock.

As much rapidity as is consistent with thoroughness should be used, for much of the success of the operation depends on the moist condition of the bud and stock when brought into contact.

Time for Budding

A spell of showery or dull weather should be chosen for the operation of budding, as then the bark separates freely and easily from the wood,

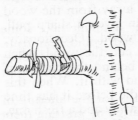

FIG. 25. BUDDING. 5. The bandage applied to bud inserted in side shoot of standard.

but if the year is very dry and hot, the stocks to be budded should be given a good soaking of water for a day or two before the operation. The best time for budding is between the early part of July and the end of September, and if the buds do not start until the next spring, so much the better. New wood of the current year's growth is usually the best for budding upon, but young growths up to two or three years may be used, if otherwise more suitable. Fruit trees are best budded in July and August, while roses do best if budded between the middle of July and early September.

After-care for the Bud

After the budding process is completed, the stock should be left untouched, neither leaves nor any other part being cut away until about November, when the binding must also be cut to allow the stock to grow. At this time the top of the stem which bears the bud may be cut back to about 3 inches above it. When the bud shoots in the spring—or possibly before—this three inches should be reduced to one, and all shoots springing from the stock should be cut away periodically through the summer. In autumn the "snag" above the bud may be cut away completely.

When the buds begin to grow, they require to be protected from strong winds; otherwise they would be detached from the stem. This is done by driving a stake (Fig. 27) firmly into the ground, attaching it by a strong cord to the stem of the stock above and below the junction, as in the illustration, and tying the shoot of the young scion firmly to the stake above, protecting it by a bandage of hay or other substance, to prevent the bark being injured.

GRAFTING

Grafting has been spoken of as "ennobling", the branch which is transferred being spoken of as the "scion", and the tree to which it is attached as the "stock". The scion becomes, as it were, parasitic upon the stock, and by carefully removing all branches which spring from the stock below the point of union, gardeners are enabled to divert to the scion all the energy produced by the roots of the stock. It is only possible to graft a scion on to a stock of a nearly-allied species. Thus quinces, apples, pears, and medlars can all be mutually grafted on to one another, so also can plums, peaches, apricots, and almonds, but it would be impossible to graft an apple on to an oak or a plum on to a willow.

PURPOSES OF GRAFTING

Alteration of Habit

Much valuable time may be saved by grafting; it might take some fifteen or twenty years before a tree raised from seed would bear fruit, whereas by grafting, fruit might be had in three or four years. Better results are also obtained by grafting a tree on to a stock and roots other than its own.

Another purpose for which grafting is employed is for the altering of the habit of a tree. Thus, pears and apples are dwarfed by grafting them respectively on the quince and the paradise stock, and dwarfed weeping trees are converted into tall standards, by attaching a scion from the weeping variety to a tree with a tall, upright trunk.

Restoration and Development

Grafting is also occasionally employed to bring about the development of flowers or fruit from parts of a tree otherwise lacking in them. Sometimes, again, it is made use of for the purpose of restoring an exhausted tree; and lastly it is employed to bring together on one stock the two sexes of monœcious plants—that is to say, plants which bear their male and female flowers on different trees—and so to facilitate their fertilization and consequent fructification.

Times for Grafting

In order to effect a successful union by grafting, it is necessary that the sap shall be flowing in the portions of the wood used for the operation, and it is therefore possible to graft in the open between the first signs of growth in the buds at the beginning of spring until about midsummer, when the sap has risen fully. The greenhouse propagating case, with slight bottom-heat, is of great assistance in grafting evergreen shrubs like the rhododendron and choice or delicate trees and shrubs, including hamamelis mollis and the hybrid brooms. It is very desirable to pot up

119

the stocks in autumn in order to have them well established in pots before grafting. Better still, allow the stocks which are to be used for grafting a whole twelve months in which to make plenty of root, and so get established by the following spring. With more root action available the flow of sap will be greater and help the stock and the scion to grow together much quicker. Under glass the time for grafting is somewhat earlier, the operation being possible any time from January to March, and again from July to September. The time for grafting trees will, therefore, vary with the time of their breaking into leaf; those kinds which bud early being the first to be dealt with. Plums are generally the first to be ready in late March, next come quinces and pears, followed by cherries and apples in this order; but as the time of leafing varies with certain varieties, the order is not without exceptions. To ascertain whether the stock is ready for grafting, the bark should be slit, and if it is easily raised to expose the polished surface of the wood beneath, the stock is ready. If the bark tends to tear, the stock must be left for a week or so longer.

Preparing the Scions

Grafting needs a certain amount of previous preparation. The stock or tree which is to receive the graft should be cut back or beheaded at about the end of January. Where the frosts are still very hard, it is well to defer the operation till the weather loosens a little, but no risk must be run of movement having begun in the sap. The object of the preparation of the grafts and scions beforehand is that the last year's ripened sap shall still be in them, to supply life to the severed scion until union has been effected, and to this end the scions, which must be well ripened one-year-old wood and taken from prolific and healthy trees only, should be cut in winter before there is any chance of movement, and while the buds are still absolutely dormant. Grafting must be carried out when the scion is in the same state of vegetation as the intended stock. It is necessary, therefore, where the grafts selected are in a more advanced state of vegetation, to detach them from the parent stems and to lay them with their stems three parts buried in moist soil under a north wall until stocks and grafts are in a similar state. In this position the grafts will remain stationary while the stocks are advancing. When the weather is so mild as to appear likely to cause movement of the sap, the scions should be pulled up occasionally, and left exposed to the air for a little while in order to check growth. The scions should be cut at about the same time as the stock is cut off.

Cutting off the Stock

This process consists in removing from the stocks, which should be three-year-old plants, planted at least a year before grafting, all the side

120

branches together with the tops, and cutting down the main stock to just above a bud within about 7 or 8 inches of the soil. Where older plants are used as stocks, as in the case of grafting, on mature trees, these should be cut back throughout to within from 3 to 6 feet from the stock, according to the size of the tree. Enough wood should always be left to allow for removal of a further portion, as this will be necessary when the actual grafting is proceeded with. If this cutting back is not done until the actual time of grafting, the junction is seldom so good, and where the trees employed are stone-fruit trees—particularly liable to this accident—gumming is very likely to result, with consequent weakening of the trees. Stocks to be used as standards must be allowed to grow to the height required. The time of grafting varies according to the stock used. It should be ascertained with accuracy that the sap is really rising, and it is better for that reason to be a little too late than too early, when there is a chance that it has not yet begun to move. Usually May will be found the best time for grafting on mature trees, and April for those only in their third year.

Suitability of the Stock for the Soil

In the selection of a suitable stock, attention should be paid not only to the readiness with which connection is able to be established between the scion and the stock, but to the soil in which the trees are to be grown. Thus, for example, in light soil, plums grown on their own roots rarely do well, but when grafted on the peach they usually thrive. *Vice versa*, peaches on their own roots rarely do well in heavy soils, and may often be made to succeed by grafting them on the plum. Again, on chalky soil, where the peach usually does badly, it can often be made to grow and fruit by grafting it on the plum. It is certain, also, that in some cases the flavour of fruit can be modified by the stock on which the variety is grafted. For some years now research work has revealed the importance of using the right type of stock for various fruit trees if the best results are to be obtained, *see* Fruit Culture, Chapters 39 and 40.

THE PRINCIPLE OF GRAFTING

Except when standard or half standard trees are to be formed, the stock should be grafted, as in the case of budding, as near to the ground as possible. To effect a union, the inner edges of the inner bark of the two parts must meet and remain in contact, this inner layer of bark being the only portion of the wood that is capable of uniting. The process consists in cutting the bark of the two portions so that this inner layer shall be in contact when the two pieces are pressed together, and in keeping them together and excluding air, which might dry the tissues, by means of wax or clay and raffia.

121

Materials and Tools

When grafting is to be undertaken, all materials should be got in readiness beforehand. The stocks and grafts should be prepared and at hand, together with a few tools such as a strong knife for cutting back the stocks, a saw, chisel, mallet, a small knife with a narrow blade for fine operations, raffia or soft string for tying, and the wax or clay required. The clay needs careful preparation, and should be obtained some weeks before it is required for use, being beaten up into the consistency of mortar with water. This moistening and beating should be repeated every day for a fortnight, and a day before it is to be used it should be mixed with one-third of its own bulk of cow manure and about the same amount of hay. The hay should be cut up into lengths of about 3 inches, being thoroughly mixed into the other ingredients. It will prevent the clay from cracking off as it hardens, and will also materially assist in keeping it moist.

It is simpler for the amateur to buy a good grafting wax than to prepare it for himself, and he is advised to obtain some such good cold grafting wax as Mastic l'Homme Lefort, an excellent French cold wax. There are many other types now to be obtained from any horticultural sundriesman in tins of convenient sizes. A good substitute for grafting wax is the quick-drying varnish called "knotting". This is very quickly dry, and is impervious to wet and weather. It is applied with a brush over the part to be protected.

FORMS OF GRAFTING

Whip- or Tongue-Grafting

The method of grafting employed depends largely on the size and other conditions of stock and scion. Where the stock is a young one, and about the size of the finger, the kind known as tongue-grafting is the most suitable. With this method of grafting, the stock must be more advanced in its state of growth than the scion. The scion is prepared by taking a well-ripened one-year-old shoot some 6 inches long, and selecting a place on it where two good buds come on opposite sides of the shoot, one a little higher than the other. Beginning just below the upper of the buds, make a clean cut at one sweep through the wood in a downward slope, coming out just below the lower bud. It is essential that there should be a good bud just above the cut at each end. Now, beginning at the top of the cut just under the top bud, with a perfectly sharp knife cut a hollow curve in the wood, sloping the cut from the inner end of the curve down in a straight line to the tip of the cut by the lower bud. The bottom of the shoot, seen sideways, should now have a section like the letter J turned upside down. It is important that these cuts should be made firmly and without unevenness, otherwise the scion will not fit closely to the stock,

122

and its chance of a perfect union will be lessened. Having prepared the scion, attention should be turned to the stock. This, as will be remembered, was cut back late in January to about 8 inches from the ground. Remove all side growth from the base and selecting a good smooth place about 3 or 4 inches from the surface of the ground, cut the stock cleanly off just above a good healthy bud. This bud's chief function will be to draw up the sap into the top of the cut parts while they are healing together, just as do the buds on the scion, but while the latter are allowed to grow and, indeed, become the real tree, the former should not be permitted to outlive its utility, and when perfect union has taken place, it should only be allowed to grow two or three leaves, and then should be stopped out. Having cut down the stock, its top should be carefully measured against the scion, and cut in a curve corresponding with the curve on the scion. Where the scion has a long "tail", the tail of the "J" shape, a strip of wood and bark should be peeled from the side of the stock, with the greatest care to adjust it, so that the stock and scion, when placed together, may fit with accuracy. The tail of the scion will be found to fit on to the peeled strip of the outside of the stock, though, owing to the different angle of the section, a narrow strip of the inner bark of the stock will show round the edge of the scion when applied. The important thing to arrive at is that the cut surfaces of the inner bark of both stock and scion shall touch as much as possible. If it is found impossible to make these layers of bark meet on both edges, make them meet perfectly on the one.

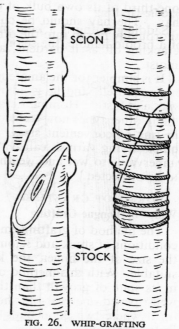

FIG. 26. WHIP-GRAFTING

The tail of the scion should not in any case come below the end of the peeled piece of the stock, if anything it should err very slightly on the other side.

When both scion and stock fit perfectly, a further security should be obtained by making a small upward cut in the tail of the scion, in order to obtain a slip projecting towards the stock. In the stock itself, opposite this slip, should be made an incision into which the slip will exactly fit, thus holding stock and scion together during the operations of tying and covering with wax. This slip should be thin, or it may cause the junction to bulge, and the scion to be pushed away from the stock. When these two

123

latter are fitted closely together, and it is found that their layers of inner bark are fitting closely and neatly, the junction should be made firm by tying with raffia, woollen thread, or soft string; the ligature being made firm enough to prevent movement, but not tight enough to prevent the proper circulation of the sap beneath the bark.

The last process is the secure covering of the whole junction—scion, stock, and ligature—with grafting wax or clay—and the graft is complete. The label should always be attached to the stock, not to the scion, as otherwise there would be an added risk of the scion being caught accidentally and pulled off before a union has been effected.

Saddle-Grafting

Saddle-grafting is a kind much used for stocks of about the thickness of a broom-handle, the scion in this case being about the same thickness as the stock and cut with two tails, the one below the upper bud being shorter than that below the lower bud. The whole of the inner part of the wood below the buds is removed, and at the top the cuts are ended by a cross-cut beginning just behind the upper bud and sloping slightly upwards. The scion will now have two tails of unequal length, the shorter one having a bud at its upper extremity, and the longer one having a bud midway up its length. The stock should then be taken, and its top cut to slope slightly, at an angle corresponding with that of the cross-cut of the scion. A slip should be peeled corresponding with the long tail of the scion, and the latter laid over the stock, saddle-wise, the long tail fitting its peeled slip, and the top angle of the stock fitting into the top angle of the cross-cut. The short tail of the scion will be found to cross the top of the stock and project a little. A slip should be cut off the side of the stock to fit this projecting piece of the tail, which should then be bent down on to it, and the graft is ready for tying and waxing. This system has the advantage that the scion unites on both sides of the stock, and is therefore not so liable to an accidental break during the healing process.

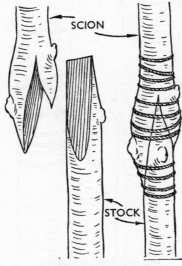

FIG. 27. SADDLE-GRAFTING

These methods of grafting are both employed for young stocks, but others must be used in the case of mature trees, where the branches are usually too large for either of the systems described—Cleft-grafting,

Stub-grafting, and Side-grafting. The first system is not to be recommended, as it results in a crack being left right across the top of the stock, in which rain, insects, and fungi are apt to lodge and injure the tree.

Frameworking

This is another way of dealing with established trees especially when they are well-grown and healthy, and the object is simply to substitute a more suitable variety. Unlike top-working where the tree is headed back and grafted on the larger limbs, this method uses the existing framework and quickly refurnishes the tree with the new variety. A large number of scions are required. They should be fairly long, having 6 to 8 buds and are set sloping along the branches. A tree so treated can generally be brought back to full cropping within three years. There are several methods of frameworking, the most usual being:

Stub Grafting

Small laterals and spurs are cut away but those that are suitably placed and have a diameter of 1 inch or more are retained. The scions are prepared with a wedge-shaped base, one side of the wedge being slightly longer than the other. A cut is then made in the upper surface of the lateral to be grafted about $\frac{1}{2}$ inch from its junction with a branch, just deep enough to reach half-way through the lateral. The lateral is next bent down to open the cut and the scion inserted with the long side of the wedge underneath, care being taken to make sure that the bark of both scion and lateral meet on one side at least. The graft is sealed with wax and the lateral released and cut off just beyond the point of grafting.

Side Grafting

The scions are prepared as above and set in the sides of the branches at suitable intervals at an angle of about 20° and sealed.

Inverted L Grafting

All laterals and spurs are removed leaving the main branches of the framework. The scions are prepared by cutting one side about $1\frac{1}{2}$ inches long and the other about $\frac{1}{2}$ inch long and removing a small thin slice from the base of both sides of the cut. The branch to be grafted is cut in two directions, one cut sloping downwards, the other sloping upwards, the two making an angle of 120° to 150°. The scion is inserted in the 7-shaped slit and nailed in position with a gimp pin.

After-Care of the Graft

In May the grafts should have begun to make growth, and if this is

125

the case, the clay or grafting wax should be removed so that the binding may be undone before it "throttles" the new growth, which it will do if left in position. If the graft is not yet secure, the binding must be replaced, but more loosely. The clay or wax must not be replaced. The graft should also be supported by a stake firmly bound to the stock. Laterals that form on a graft should be pinched off to encourage a good straight single shoot from the graft, and any shoots forming on the stock below the point of grafting must be rubbed off, once they have served their purpose in drawing sap up to the graft.

The wax may be found difficult of removal and in such a case care is required in order to get it off without damaging the junction. It is best done by placing a block of wood or some other firm thing on one side of the lump of wax, and then lightly hitting the other side with a hammer, no unnecessary force being employed. The wax will crack off, and may be removed with ease.

126

CHAPTER 1

POTTING AND RE-POTTING

THE POTTING SHED

To every greenhouse of sufficient size a potting shed should be attached. It should be quite near so as to be handy, and in order that the more delicate plants shall not be harmed by a long journey through the cold air when taken from the house to be potted-up. The shed must be roomy and above all should have ample head-room. The door must be wide enough to admit the hand barrow, for it greatly increases labour if materials have to be handled more than is absolutely necessary. Another important point in designing the potting shed is, if possible, to avoid any steps; these are very awkward obstacles when pots are being carried about. Lighting is another important question. Side windows in the two shorter ends of the shed are, perhaps, best; this leaves one of the longer sides intact for the bench with shelves above and below it, and the other side for the door and yet more shelves and cupboards. If possible, arrangements should be made for a headlight in the roof directly over the bench and artificial light is invaluable for working in winter. The hot water system from the greenhouse boiler should be carried into the shed, not only for the comfort of the gardener, but in order that composts may be dried and warmed.

The Bench

The shed should be furnished with a shelf or stage of suitable height on which plants can be potted or repotted, as the case may be, before removal to the greenhouse. This should be large and strong enough to hold sufficient potting soil to complete a good batch of plants, before it is again necessary to mix more compost, and must be of sufficient height to obviate stooping. In a potting shed it is convenient to place bins below the shelf or stage to contain a sufficient supply of potting materials for immediate use: silver sand, peat, loam, coconut fibre, crocks, etc.

HOW TO POT UP

CLEANING THE POTS

Pots that have been used should always be washed, otherwise any disease or fungus present in the old potting soil will be transferred to the

127

next inhabitant of the pot. Besides, a dirty pot will not be porous, as it should be, to allow the air to permeate the soil. Even new pots should be put in water for at least half an hour, for a dry pot will draw away the moisture from the potting soil. The pot, however, must not be actually *wet* when used, as this would be almost as bad as using a dirty pot, for the soil and eventually the roots, would stick to it. For the winter, always store pots in a dry, frost-proof place: if they are dry, the frost will not hurt them; if they are wet, however, when the frost comes, it is almost certain that many of them will be ruined.

PREPARING THE POTTING SOIL

When it is considered that the compost is the medium whereby the roots receive nutrition, water, and air, it will be realized what an important part it plays in the life of the plant, and for this reason every effort should be made to provide the compost best suited to the needs of each plant. In our *Alphabetical List of Flowering Plants*, Chapter 34, details as to the most suitable individual composts are given.

When potting-up, it is just as easy to include two, three, or even more ingredients in the compost, provided certain arrangements are made, as it is to use plain loam.

The most usual ingredients of potting composts are: loam, which generally forms the greater part; leaf-mould, or if this is unobtainable any of the forms of peat-moss which are obtainable; sand; old mortar rubble; well-rotted manure; and charcoal. The gardener should have small heaps of these handy on his potting bench, or in the bins below it.

MIXING THE COMPOST

If the gardener has not the time or inclination to prepare his own potting composts, he may purchase them quite cheaply already mixed, according to the formula of the John Innes Horticultural Institution. These composts are specially suited to the needs of most plants and can easily be modified for any particular requirements. Lime-hating plants such as rhododendrons and heaths must, of course, be potted in lime-free composts of peat and sand.

The potting soil must be moderately moist, that is to say, if a handful is taken up and gripped firmly, it should become moulded to the shape of the hand, but at the same time it should be dry enough to crumble as soon as it is disturbed. If too dry it should be watered, but should be allowed at least a day in which to absorb the moisture, otherwise the compost will be patchy and not evenly moist all through. Mix the ingredients well together, but do not sieve the compost; this would rob it of much of its plant food and most of its porosity, large lumps must of course be broken up. Only for seeds and cuttings should the compost be sieved, and in this

128

PLATE 13 Repotting a chrysanthemum plant. *Top left*, tapping the plant from the pot, *top right*, example of a root-bound plant, *bottom left*, placing the plant in a larger pot and *bottom right*, firming the plant into the pot.

PLATE 14 *Top left*, correct method of staking and tying a chrysanthemum plant and *right*, incorrect method. At the recommended time chrysanthemums must be stopped, i.e., the centre shoot pinched out. *Bottom left*, unstopped plant and *right*, stopped.

case through a quarter-inch mesh. Young plants with fine fibrous roots need a compost much finer in texture than do mature and vigorous plants being potted-on into their final pots.

As has been said before, the proportions in which the various ingredients are added to the compost vary in accordance with the requirements of individual plants, but the following may be taken as a suitable compost for the general run of soft-wooded plants.

$\frac{1}{2}$ part Fibrous Loam. $\frac{1}{8}$ part Well-rotted Manure.
$\frac{1}{4}$ part Leaf-mould or $\frac{1}{8}$ part Coarse Silver Sand.
     Peat Moss.

The compost should be stored in the potting shed, and where greenhouse subjects are to be potted-up, the compost should be kept in the warm house for at least twenty-four hours previously to potting, if possible.

TIME FOR POTTING AND RE-POTTING

The time at which a plant should be re-potted depends on whether the "ball" is to be broken up, as for instance when a plant from the open ground is to be potted-up or when a plant has to be re-potted because the soil is old and sour, or whether the "ball" is to be left practically intact as when a growing plant is to be "shifted" into a slightly larger pot. In the latter case, the operation can be performed at any time when the plant is in fairly active growth, as the roots will at once go ahead and take possession of the new soil. Where the "ball" is to be broken up, however, re-potting can only be undertaken just as the roots are beginning to come into active growth, at which time they will be able to penetrate the new compost. If the "ball" were broken up when the roots were not in their most vigorous state, the young root-matter could not fail to be badly damaged and in consequence would be unable to recuperate in sufficient time to penetrate the fresh compost before the "resting" period set in, and the new soil would become sour before it could be occupied.

During the growing season, a plant or two of each batch of a similar kind, whether they are biennials being grown on for greenhouse use, soft-wooded perennials, or hard-wooded plants, should be turned out of their pots so that it may be seen whether re-potting is necessary. As soon as the roots begin to wind round the sides of the pot, a larger one should at once be given unless the "resting" season is approaching, when potting should be held over till the plants again become active. They make most growth in April and May and again in August and September. The best time to re-pot, therefore, is just before this growth commences, that is to say, about March and again in August and early September. March is the better time at which to re-pot established plants, as growth in spring is more vigorous than in autumn.

THE SIZE OF THE POT

Pots are generally made in what are termed "casts"—that is to say, a certain quantity of clay is taken, from which one pot is made, or two, four, six, eight, twelve, sixteen, twenty-four, thirty-two, forty-eight, sixty, or eighty; and pots are, therefore, known to gardeners as ones, twos, fours, etc., according to the number of pots made from a single cast.

The following table shows the inside measurements of the pot-sizes in general use.

Sizes.	Diam. Top in Ins.		Depth in Ins.	Sizes.	Diam. Top in Ins.		Depth in Ins.
Thimbles .	. 2	...	2	Sixteens .	. 9½	...	9
Thumbs .	. 2½	...	2½	Twelves .	. 11½	...	10
Sixties .	. 3	...	3½	Eights .	. 12	...	11
Fifty-fours .	. 4	...	4	Sixes .	. 13	...	12
Forty-eights .	. 4½	...	5	Fours .	. 15	...	13
Thirty-twos .	. 6	...	6	Twos .	. 18	...	14
Twenty-fours .	. 8½	...	8	Ones .	. 20	...	16

It is always advisable to put a plant into a pot slightly too small rather than too large. Unless the plant is very pot-bound, or is required to grow very quickly (as in the case of many young and growing plants), put the plant back in the same sized pot if possible. Many gardeners like to have 1 inch of soil between the "ball" and the sides of the pot.

It is fatal to try to save work or to force a plant on by putting a small subject into a pot too large for it. The small roots will be unable to make use of all the moisture and plant food in the soil; this hangs about in the compost and it is a long time before any fresh air is able to enter, so that the soil becomes clammy and finally sour. For this reason pot-up into small pots, re-potting frequently as the plants grow and the roots become pot-bound. It is rarely necessary to move a plant into a pot more than two, at the most three, sizes larger than the old one. As soft-wooded plants are, as a rule, vigorous growers, they may usually be put into proportionately larger pots than slower-growing hard-wooded plants.

DRAINING THE POT

In potting it is always necessary to make provision for the escape of surplus water—that is to say, water which, when given to the plant in the pot, cannot be retained by the soil in which it grows. For the purpose of providing drainage, every gardener keeps by him a store of fragments of broken pots and saucers, oyster shells, and even pieces of soft brick. The oyster shell is useful for placing over the hole at the bottom of the pot, and surrounding this and above it may be placed small pieces of broken pots, technically called "crocks". For cuttings, which are not intended to remain in the pot for any length of time after they have rooted, a single piece of crock, convex side uppermost, is sufficient, but when the time of tenancy is likely to be prolonged to months, and perhaps even years, it is necessary

130

to fill one-sixth, and in some cases as much as one-fourth, of the entire depth of the pot with broken potsherds. If possible, it is desirable to give a conical form to the crocking placed in the pot.

Small round pieces of perforated zinc can now be obtained and placed singly over the hole of the pot before crocking, this will prevent worms and many other insects from coming up through the bottom of the pot into the compost.

FILLING IN THE POTTING COMPOST

The pot being crocked, some gardeners like to place a little moss or coconut fibre, or even a few leaves, over the crocks before putting in the soil. This prevents the interstices between the crocks from being choked by the finer particles of earth that may be carried down from time to time during the process of watering. There is, however, no absolute need to do this, as the very presence of the shells and potsherds at the bottom of the pot secures the escape of the surplus water.

The crocking being done and a little coarse soil thrown over them, some fine mould should be put in and shaken together by gently knocking the edge of the bottom of the pot against the potting-bench, or by striking the sides of the pot gently with the hand. This soil at the bottom of the pot should be just sufficient to lift the plant so that the top of the "ball", when set in the new pot, is within 1½ inches of the rim—when firmly planted and covered with ½ to 1 inch of new soil, it should be 1 inch below the rim in a large pot and ½ inch in a small one.

REMOVING THE OLD POT

The most suitable times for re-potting the various kinds of plants will be found in the individual articles in the Alphabetical List of Flowering Plants, Chapter 34.

The plants to be re-potted should, if necessary, be watered an hour or so before the work is to take place so that the "ball" of earth round the roots may be just moderately moist; if too wet the fibrous roots may be torn; if over-dry the small roots will find great difficulty in becoming established in the new compost. Now turn the pot upside-down, placing first and second finger of the left hand so that the stem lies between them while the palm and fingers lie across the top edges of the pot, and grasp the bottom of the pot, which is now uppermost, with the right hand. Next tap the rim of the pot gently on the edge of the potting-bench, and the roots and soil will come out complete, being supported by the left hand, as the pot is removed with the right. Care must be taken that the plant and soil do not drop from the pot. Should the plant "ball" not come out of the pot, the finger or a small blunt-headed stick should be inserted through the drainage hole at the bottom, and gentle pressure applied.

131

POTTING-UP THE PLANTS

Soft-wooded plants are not, as a general rule, kept in the pot for more than two or three seasons. It is, therefore, not necessary to remove all the old soil from the "ball", which can be kept intact. If it is necessary to give the plant an entire change of soil, the operation should be carried out as advised for re-potting, on the next page. We may assume here, however, that the "ball" is to be left intact.

The crocks, any sour soil and dead roots must be carefully removed so that the roots are not bruised, and some of the thickest roots should be drawn out from the "ball" with a pointed stick; these will establish themselves in the new soil round the sides of the larger pot. Now place the "ball" on the soil already in the pot so that the plant will be quite central, and pack the soil with the hand or potting stick between the "ball" and the sides of the pot, consolidating the earth by knocking the pot from time to time on the bench, and pressing the compost down round the sides with a potting stick, or the thumb, which is more convenient when dealing with the smaller sizes of pots. Press the new soil firmly about the collar of the plant with the thumbs. Keep the new soil *level* with the top of the old "ball". The collar should not be raised above the general level, but to depress it beneath is certain death to hard-wooded plants. All plants, however hardy, should be kept warm and moist for a few weeks after re-potting, especially if they have received a large shift.

Only remove from the "ball" that soil that is really sour; it is a mistake to disturb the roots when the soil is still fresh. If, however, the compost has become very sour, all the soil must be removed and the roots well washed through with luke-warm water, any dead or diseased parts being cut away.

POTTING-ON SEEDLINGS AND CUTTINGS

Cuttings and seedlings are best potted-up in the house in which they have hitherto been grown. They are delicate and if transferred to a cold draughty shed, may receive a set-back. Once established in their new pots, they can gradually be hardened off to stand the temperature of their new house.

The size of the pot to be used naturally depends on the kind and size of the plant, but as a general rule 3 or 4 inch pots are suitable for the first potting-up of seedlings that have previously been pricked-off into boxes, round the sides of the pots, or into thumb pots; the new pots should be just large enough to take the roots without their touching the sides; a larger pot will be needed with each shift as the plants grow. The size of the pot in which the plant is ultimately to be flowered bears closely upon the dimensions of the pot used for the first potting-up. If the ultimate pot is to be 8 inches in diameter, the first pot should usually be a 3½-inch one, the pot for the second shift being a 5-inch one. A 3-inch is generally large enough as a first pot when the eventual size is to be 6 inches, the intermediate shift being into a 4-inch pot. For the general run of biennials potted-on for greenhouse use, three pottings in all (excluding the seed or cutting boxes and the pricking-off) are all that the gardener can afford to give, though in some cases more frequent potting is beneficial, when possible. Perennials are potted-on as they increase in size and as they become pot-bound.

The procedure is the same as for the potting-up of maturer plants, but the stem of the seedling must be buried nearly up to the two small seed leaves or cotyledons. The young roots are very brittle and tender, so that the soil must not be pressed down with the thumbs and fingers as when potting maturer plants; the tapping of the pot on the bench and the watering afterwards should render the compost quite firm enough. Seedlings grown in boxes or close together in pots should be potted-off early before the roots begin to intertwine.

DEGREE OF FIRMNESS IN POTTING

With most plants it is desirable to pot firmly, not to ram the earth down hard, but sufficiently firm for the plant to offer resistance if slight pressure is applied to it to pull it upwards. The degree of firmness necessary varies with the age of the plant, the nature of the roots, and the character of the compost. Young plants of all kinds, whose roots will expand, need planting only moderately firmly, the soil being packed just tight enough to hold the plants in position; each potting must, however, be firmer than the previous one. When mature, fibrous-rooted plants should be planted very firmly, the more sandy the compost the firmer must the planting be. Plants with large fleshy roots require a much looser compost. Between these two extremes there are roots of varying sizes and characteristics, and in each case the gardener must use his discretion. Although it may be necessary to firm the soil firmly round the roots, do not pack the surface down hard or the air will be excluded. Lastly, never fill a pot with soil right up to the edge, but only to about half an inch below the edge of smaller pots, and 1 inch for larger pots. This should be done in order to afford sufficient room for watering. This must always be given through a fine rose directly after potting-up, so that the soil may settle round the roots, after which the plants should be kept rather dry in a close atmosphere for a week or so until established. Soft-wooded plants should also be shaded from the sun. Plants which are rather top-heavy, or whose roots do not grip the soil firmly, must be staked—the stick should be thin, but strong, and should be pushed into the compost down the side of the pot to avoid piercing and damaging the roots. (*See* Staking *and* Tying, p. 40, *and* Potting Bulbs, p. 174.)

133

CHAPTER 13

THE IMPORTANCE OF WEEDING

As a rule, gardeners do not begin weeding sufficiently early in the season. They give the weeds a start which they later find impossible to overtake. Weeding should be commenced in the early spring—about the beginning of April and must be continued all through the summer and autumn, even as late as the beginning of November; it being remembered that all weeds grow apace in warm weather after rain. Apart from their unsightliness, weeds do great damage in the garden, for they exclude the sun and air from the soil and deprive the more delicate cultivated plants of much needed nourishment and moisture. They also harbour and encourage insect pests and diseases.

WEEDING BEDS AND BORDERS

The hoe is undoubtedly the best implement with which to control weeds on beds, and if this is used early in the season and is kept in constant use, weeds will get little chance to multiply. By its aid annual weeds will be destroyed, and biennial and perennial weeds, owing to the frequent cutting down, will be so weakened that eventually they will die.

All weeds that have flowered or seeded, likewise all those with "runner" roots with "eyes" on them, which will grow again if they come into contact with the soil, must be burned, and must not be dug into the soil as vegetable manure. This latter procedure would surely spread the weeds; the ashes, however, may safely be used as a fertilizer. Other weeds can be put on the refuse heap and can later safely be used to manure the garden. In hot dry weather, if the weeding is done early in the day, this class of weed may be left lying on the soil to wither and die, but in damp weather and when the soil is wet, they must be removed to the rubbish heap, for there is danger of their again taking root.

Hand-weeding—gripping the weeds as near the soil as possible and twisting them out with as many of their roots as one can—must be resorted to where the plants are too close to permit of the use of the hoe. If this method is adopted shortly after a good shower of rain, many perennial weeds may be destroyed.

As weeds spread so readily, it is most necessary to keep all rough grass near the garden cut, especially before it has time to seed. The weeds in

134

grass-paths, grass-edgings, and on the lawn must also be kept well in check for the same reason; this also applies to all neighbouring banks and hedgerows, which must be kept clean and weed-free.

CLEANING THE PATHS

It is a mistake to hoe up weeds on paths. They may be banished temporarily in this way, but the turned-up gravel is in a more favourable condition for their increase later on. The best method of destroying weeds on paths is to apply one of the following weed-killers in spring and in fine weather after a good shower of rain. A thorough soaking should be given, and if no rain falls for a few days after, good results can be confidently expected.

In spraying the paths, care must be taken always not to treat areas covering the roots of edging plants or these will be poisoned, and no dogs or domestic animals should be allowed to use the paths for at least three days after the application of the weed-killer.

WEEDING THE LAWN

(*See chapter on* The Lawn, p. 83.)

SOLUTIONS FOR WEED-KILLING

(1) Salt 1 lb. in Hot Water 1 gallon.
(2) Copper Sulphate 1 lb. in Water 6 gallons.
(3) Sulphate of Iron 1 lb. in Water 2 gallons.
(4) Caustic Soda 1 lb. in Water 8 gallons.
(5) Carbolic Acid 1 lb. in Water 10 gallons.

The solutions should be thoroughly stirred and kept well mixed while in use, and must be applied through a fine rose. A galvanized can should be used, as the chemicals are not so likely to affect it. Do not allow the mixtures to touch the skin or clothes, and label all bottles or receptacles containing the solutions "*Poison*" and keep them locked away in a safe place.

Always use up *all* the solution, bearing in mind that it is poison; wash the can and mixing utensils thoroughly, and store the tin or bottle of weed-killer out of harm's way. One cannot be too careful.

Weed-killers can be purchased ready for use. This saves the trouble of having to mix one's own. Non-poisonous mixtures are obtainable and are to be preferred, while the use of new selective weed-killers, as they are termed, is rapidly becoming very popular for certain types of weeds.

CHAPTER 14

PLANNING AND PLANTING THE FLOWER GARDEN

The flower garden is usually situated within close range of the house, so that its beauties may be seen from the windows. On this account its plan should be formal and should not present too startling or scattered an effect.

We are only now beginning to break away from the cast-iron method of planning, a method which has survived the primness of outlook in which it originated, whose every line and form are severely geometrical and every colour crude and definite. The formalities of the Georgian age were tightened and cramped into the carpet and other artificial forms of bedding of the Victorian. The most intricate patterns were produced in flowers whose natural forms were clipped and stunted in the services of this most inartistic fashion, and their individual beauties were ignored. A comparison has only to be made between, say, one of the simple cottage gardens of Devonshire, aglow with flowers, and the most ambitious example of carpet bedding, for the utter inferiority of the latter to become apparent. We are beginning to tire of these wasteful and ugly extravagances, and to seek inspiration from more natural sources where pleasant and harmonious comparison prevails between colour and colour, and where beauty results from freedom rather than restriction of form.

HARMONY IN COLOUR

The flower garden is of necessity more obviously artificial than those parts of the garden where lawn and shrub and tree hold natural sway. For this reason its planning is more liable to be attended by mistakes from the artistic standpoint. The gardener cannot go far wrong in the arrangement of bush and lawn, but the management of large masses of bright colour is an altogether more difficult proposition and one which requires skill and a sense of beauty to produce a successful result. The beauties of a landscape view may be utterly spoiled by the sudden intrusion into its foreground of a profusion of bright flowers, and where no other position is possible for the flower garden than that which directly intervenes between such a view and the spectator, some arrangement should be made for screening the too obtrusive colour. Such a difficulty is not likely to occur in a town garden when the only view is usually restricted to the bricks and mortar of other houses.

136

SOIL AND ASPECT

Wherever it is possible the flower garden should have a southern or western aspect, which is sheltered from cold winds. Such shelter, whether natural or artificial, should be sufficient to protect quite tall-growing shrubs without excluding light and air. It is an almost hopeless enterprise to attempt very much in the way of flower culture in a soil that is heavy and impervious, or in an exposed situation, unless shrubs can be grown to afford shelter, and the impervious soil either replaced by one of light texture or so improved by the addition of some element such as sand, leaf-mould, lime, or chalk, that the tender roots may be able to penetrate it.

DRAINAGE

Drainage, too, is a very important consideration, and one which such a treatment of heavy soil as is recommended above makes doubly necessary. It will be obvious that if certain portions of the soil are broken and lightened, they become automatically drains for the heavier surrounding land, and all the surface water which such land is unable to absorb will just drain down into the beds that have been rendered pervious, turning them into a sort of natural reservoir. The foundation of such beds must, therefore, be constructed of such loose yet durable ingredients as will permit the accumulation of water to drain through. For this purpose, nothing is better than broken brick or flints, but even this precaution needs support from a drain which will collect and convey the surface water away. It will be seen, therefore, how essential it is that the land to be used for a flower garden shall be properly prepared before cultivation is begun.

CHOICE OF PLANTS

If care is exercised in the selection and planting of its stock, the flower garden can be kept, if not generously blooming, at least verdant through practically the whole year. How much more satisfactory is it when the flowers of each season appear in their ordered turn, and in passing give place automatically to a fresh crop, than when the efforts of the gardener are devoted to a fierce display of blooms, which, though they may make a wonderful show during the actual period of their blossoming, perish with the first frost in autumn, leaving no successors to grace the bare and unlovely soil. The garden in winter need by no means present the barren and disagreeable appearance it too often does.

ARRANGEMENT OF COLOUR AND FOLIAGE

Colour, again, is one of the chief considerations which should control the arrangement of the flower garden, and we would refer the reader to *the chapter on* Hardy Perennials and the Herbaceous Border (page 152), where we have devoted considerable space to colour grouping.

Foliage, too, plays a very important part in perfecting the colour scheme of the garden. It mitigates the clash of warring shades, assists the gradation of tint into tint, and provides by far the most effective background for the display of the garden's colour beauties. A much freer arrangement of colour may be followed, for instance, against a close background of shrubs than if the flowers are grouped together without such help. The most thoughtful planting may give utterly unsatisfactory results if the colour grouping of the flowers is ignored. It is always best to avoid too close and sharp contrasts of colour.

FRAGRANCE IN THE GARDEN

Fragrance, again, is a quality that needs no recommendation, since so many of our most beautiful flowers and shrubs have also the sweetest scents. Roses, lilies, stocks, and wallflowers, jasmine, honeysuckle, and sweet verbena, to mention but a few, are all flowers beautiful in themselves and in their odour, while rosemary, sweet briar, southernwood, laurel, bay, and myrtle combine equally charming qualities of scent and form.

BACKGROUNDS AND SETTINGS

An important consideration in the arrangement of the garden is that of form; that is, the selection of plants, beautiful in themselves and their arrangement singly or in groups, as backgrounds for smaller flowers, as screens, boundaries, and hedges. When one speaks of form in the matter of plants, one's mind turns instinctively to such outstanding examples as the cypress, whose telling silhouette is so beautiful a feature of the Italian landscape, to the tropical palm, to the poplar groves of France, and last but not least to the many beautiful varieties of English trees which at any season of the year present such lovely appearances.

Among the plants whose foliage is beautiful and whose presence in the garden is of the utmost value from the point of view of backgrounds, are the willow, the acacia, the asparagus, various specimens of bamboo, reeds, pampas grass, the cypress, cedar, yew, and fir, and a host of hardy evergreens and flowering shrubs. Such plants, indeed, lend themselves to a variety of decoration and practical purposes. The larger of them can be used as screens for unsightly corners, and to afford shelter to more delicate specimens; others to break up the monotony of a lawn and to maintain the beauty of the garden through even the most trying winters. Others again require no such practical warrant. Their mere beauty is sufficient reason in itself for their inclusion. The azalea, magnolia, rhododendron (in moderation), broom, Chænomeles lagenaria, to mention but a few whose flowering periods but crown their common life as elegant shrubs, should need no recommendation. In the use of evergreens discretion should be exercised, and their hardy and enduring qualities must not be favoured to the detriment of more valuable plants. In moderation their usefulness cannot be too highly praised, but it must be remembered that most evergreens are greedy feeders; their roots are voracious and spread very widely; and when, as is often the case, they are used to border flower beds, if planted there too generously or allowed to multiply unchecked, they impoverish the soil and weaken the chances of the flowers.

THE USE OF FLOWERING SHRUBS

The many varieties of beautiful flowering shrubs which grow well in this climate should appeal to the gardener for more than their purely outdoor qualities. Most people who have gardens like also to decorate their houses with flowers, and, in this connection, nothing lends itself more charmingly to indoor use than single sprays of some small flowering shrub.

As an immediate setting for the house, also, no form of planting is more satisfactory than groups of flowering evergreens. Here, above all other places in the garden, permanence is a quality to aim at, for this is the view which is most constantly in evidence. In winter weather it may, perhaps, be regretted but not deplored that the remoter places of the garden are not bright with flowers, but if the immediate view from the windows is equally barren then the dreariness of the whole garden will weigh more heavily. For this reason, then, the use of flowering evergreens near the house is recommended.

ANNUALS: HARDY AND HALF-HARDY

The class of plants which flower and fruit in the same year as that in which its seeds are sown, or, at any rate, complete the series of those processes within twelve months of the time of sowing, is known as that of Annuals. In the flower garden it includes some of the most beautiful, as well as undoubtedly the most easily grown of all those things which make up a typical English garden.

Hardy Annuals

Any ordinary garden soil is suitable for hardy annuals, and in fact for annuals generally. It does not require to be at all rich, since this encourages luxuriance of growth, which is incompatible with the production of flowers. Annuals do best, however, in light, sandy soil, and they should have this where possible, though not necessarily. Good drainage is essential.

In almost all cases it is wise to incorporate with the natural earth a very generous allowance of humus or of leaves or other decomposing vegetable matter which will help to create humus. In the process of decomposition of leaves or other organic matter, various acids and other products are created, and these tend to liberate from the mineral elements in the soil certain foods essential to the life of plants. Gases also are generated, which

139

help to keep the soil in a porous, spongy state, which is agreeable to the roots, and which assists in the maintenance of that moist condition so essential to healthy growth.

Very hardy annuals may be sown in autumn, not earlier than the last week in August, and not later, even in sheltered spots, than the last week in September. Autumn-sown plants, if they survive the winter's frosts, will bloom early in spring. The situation best suited for autumn sowing is one that is sheltered from strong and cutting winds, but free from shade and well exposed to the sun. Spring sowings for blooming in summer may be made at any time from the middle of March to the middle of April. Later sowings for flowering in autumn should be made from the middle of May to the middle of June. The different conditions and climates in the various districts make it impossible to give exact times and details.

To raise hardy annuals for transplanting, they may be sown in V-shaped drills about half an inch deep and 10 inches apart in the reserve garden or elsewhere, and removed when about half-grown to the position in which they are intended to flower. On an average, about 9 inches should be left between each plant. They should be firmly planted then well watered to fix the soil round the roots. The transplanting of annuals, unless very carefully done, is always attended with some danger. This may be obviated if they are raised in pots, from which they can be turned out without disturbing the roots. Alternatively, they may be sown on pieces of turf turned grass downwards, the seeds being covered with a thin coating of mould after they have been sprinkled thinly on the turf. Hardy annuals sown in spring, and some kinds sown in autumn, need no protection from the weather. (*See* Sowing Seed, p. 104, *and* Bedding Plants, p. 143.)

Half-hardy Annuals

The seeds should be sown in March or April in a mixture of loam, leaf-mould, well-decayed manure and silver sand in well-drained pots or pans, and should be sheltered in a frame, or else the pots should be plunged in moderate bottom-heat, such as a hot-bed that is gradually cooling. The temperature should not rise above 75° F. by day or fall below 55° at night. (*See* Sowing Seed, p. 102). Harden-off gradually and remove to flowering quarters about the middle of May, but delay the removal to the end of the month if the weather is cold and unfavourable.

HARDY AND HALF-HARDY BIENNIALS

The difference between annuals and biennials consists in their nature and habit only. The former grow flowers, yield seeds for their reproduction, and die in the same year; biennials, on the contrary, are sown and grow in the first year, but do not come to maturity until the second, when they flower, seed, and die.

Hardy Biennials

Hardy biennials may be sown at a later period of the year than annuals, that is to say in May, June, or July, sometimes in August, though not later than the middle or end of September, for plants sown at this time will bloom the following year as freely as those that have been sown at an earlier date. However, it is wise to sow as early as possible, for this enables the plants to become well-established before the colder weather sets in, and to ensure well-developed plants for flowering the following year. If a frame is available, early sowing is not so important, as the plants will continue development in the frame at a time when cold and bad weather would impede any growth in the open. Biennials should be raised in drills 8 to 10 inches apart in partially shaded beds in the reserve garden. As soon as they are tall enough to be handled, they should be thinned out to 6 inches apart or transplanted to the same distance between plants. Plant out in moderately good deeply-worked soil in their blooming quarters in the spring, or in October if planted in early summer and sufficiently grown.

Half-hardy Biennials

Half-hardy biennials should be sown in boxes from March to June. They should be protected during the winter in a frame or in the green-house, and should be planted out in their flowering positions the following spring, from April to June. (*See* Sowing Seed, p. 102.)

HARDY HERBACEOUS PERENNIALS

Of all sections of garden plants that of the Hardy Perennials is on the whole the most satisfying and the most interesting. Each individual plant comes to possess a certain character and certain associations of its own, which no annual and no tender transplanted flower of a season can ever own. Hardy perennial plants are those which possess a herbaceous character, for the most part dying down in the autumn and springing up fresh from the base in the spring. But many of them are evergreen or evergrey plants, furnishing beauty in winter as well as in summer time.

Hardy perennials have always been characteristic features of English gardens, and the majority of our old-fashioned flowers belong to this group. Moreover, they are the simplest of all to grow, and most of them yield beauty of form as well as of colour, whilst the greater number of fragrant flowers and fragrant leaves are yielded by them. At the same time, hardy perennials are by no means universally properly grown. Because they will grow almost anyhow, and almost anywhere, it is often thought sufficient to dig holes in the ground and put their roots therein. But in order that these plants may give their full measure of grace and beauty, considerable care and preparation is necessary. (*See also* the chapter on the Herbaceous Border, p. 152.)

A FEW OF THE BEST ANNUALS AND BIENNIALS

For Notes on Colour, Height, Season of Flowering, Culture, and the best Species and Varieties, *see* A.B.C. of Plants, page 255

Hardy Annuals

Alyssum maritimum
Calendula officinalis (Pot Marigold)
Centaurea Cyanus (Cornflower or Bluebottle)
Centaurea suaveolens (Sweet Sultan)
Clarkia elegans and vars. and C. pulchella
Collinsia bicolor
Convolvulus tricolor and vars.
Coreopsis tinctoria, etc.
Delphinium Gayanum, syn. Ajacis (Larkspur)
Eschscholzia californica (Californian Poppy)
Gaillardia Lorenziana picta
Gilia lutea, G. multicaulis and G. tricolor

Godetia Single and Double vars.
Gypsophila elegans
Helianthus annuus and H. cucumerifolius (Sunflower)
Iberis umbellatus (Candytuft)
Ipomœa purpurea
Lathyrus odoratus (Sweet Pea)
Lavatera trimestris
Limnanthes Douglasii
Linaria maroccana
Linum grandiflorum, var. rubrum
Lupinus hirsutus, L. luteus, L mutabilis (Lupins)
Malcomia maritima (Virginian Stock)
Malope grandiflora

Matthiola bicornis (Night-Scented Stock)
Nemophila insignis, N. Menziesii
Nigella damascena and N. hispanica (Love-in-a-Mist)
Papaver Rhœas (Shirley—Poppy) and P. somniferum and vars. (Opium Poppy)
Reseda odorata (Mignonette)
Salvia Horminum and vars.
Senecio elegans
Silene pendula compacta
Tropæolum aduncum (Canary Creeper)
T. majus (Climbing Nasturtium) [Nasturtium)
T. nanum and vars. (Dwarf

Half-Hardy Annuals

Ageratum Houstonianum
Alonsoa Warscewiczii
Amarantus caudatus (Love-lies-Bleeding)
Arctotis stœchadifolia, syn. grandis
Brachycome iberidifolia
Callistephus chinensis (China Aster)
Celosia cristata (Prince of Wales' Feathers or Cockscomb)
Cryophytum crystallinum (Ice Plant)
Dianthus Heddewigii and D. chinensis

Dimorphotheca aurantiaca
Gaillardia (Single and Double)
Helichrysum bracteatum, etc.
Helipterum Manglesii and roseum
Impatiens Balsamina
Kochia trichophila
Limonium Bonduellii, L. sinuata, L. Suworowii
Lobelia Erinus vars.
Matthiola annua (Ten-week Stock)
Nemesia strumosa vars.
Nicotiana affinis, N. Sanderæ (Tobacco Plant)

Petunia vars.
Phlox Drummondii and vars.
Portulaca grandiflora
Salpiglossis sinuata
Salvia carduacea and S. coccinea
Scabiosa atropurpurea
Schizanthus pinnatus, S. retusus
Tagetes erecta, T. patula vars. signata African and French Marigolds
Tropæolum aduncum (Canary Creeper)
Verbena vars.
Zinnia elegans

Biennials

Althæa rosea (Hollyhock)
Anchusa capensis
Campanula Medium (Canterbury Bells)
Campanula pyramidalis
Cheiranthus Cheiri (Wallflower)
Coreopsis grandiflora
Dianthus barbatus (Sweet William)

Digitalis purpurea (Foxglove)
Lavatera arborea
Lunaria biennis (Honesty)
Lychnis Flos-jovis (Rose Campion)
Matthiola (Intermediate Stock)
Matthiola (East Lothian Stock)

Matthiola incana (Giant or Brompton Stock)
Myosotis sylvatica (Forget-me-not)
Œnothera biennis (Evening Primrose)
Papaver nudicaule (Iceland Poppy)
Trachelium cæruleum
Verbascum species (Mullein)

NOTE.—Although some two or three of the species included in these lists are not actually biennials, in a true sense, they are most satisfactory when grown as such.

CHAPTER 15

SPRING AND SUMMER BEDDING PLANTS

Bedding-out has been criticized as stiff, old-fashioned and monotonous. There is, certainly, an unnecessary lack of variety if no imagination is used, and if the beds are filled year after year with pelargoniums (geraniums), calceolarias and lobelia. Although these are excellent plants, if used with discretion, and should never be forgotten, there are so many other beautiful flowers that may be included in the bedding schemes, and which, if tastily combined and laid out, will give brilliant masses of colour all through the summer.

It is now a common practice to use for this purpose such beautiful annuals as saponaria and myosotis (forget-me-not), or such hardy plants as pansies and violas. Still, the old term of "bedding plants" is commonly used to refer to certain half-hardy flowering plants which are grown under glass during the winter and spring, and are merely planted out during summer to be again lifted as soon as the hot months are over. Pelargoniums or geraniums, as they are commonly called, begonias, verbenas, petunias, calceolarias and lobelias are the plants most frequently grown in this way.

MANURING THE BEDS

As soon as the summer bedding is cleared away in the autumn, some well-rotted manure (old hot-bed manure is excellent), leaf-mould, and thoroughly decayed vegetable refuse should be forked into the beds to a depth of about 12 inches, this will draw the roots well down. If the beds are kept well cultivated, no other manuring should be necessary, with the exception of the application of some bonemeal or steamed bone flour, a dressing of which may be given every second year at the rate of 6 oz. to the square yard.

A sprinkling of lime should be applied every second year; this is specially important in gardens near large cities where the soil is usually acid from atmospheric deposits. The construction of the beds is fully described in Chapter 7.

COLOUR HARMONY IN BEDDING SCHEMES

Great care must be taken in the colour schemes so as to avoid clashing colours. The colours must harmonize or else the gardener must aim at

143

getting a contrast. Do not use too many colours, two, or at the most three, are best massed together; likewise only two or three kinds of flowers should be used in each bed. It is necessary, too, to remember the height and habit of the plants associated together; some make ideal carpet plants, others are excellent for use as the principal plants or for "dot" plants, while, a point sometimes forgotten, all subjects in a bedding-scheme must flower together.

Never overcrowd, as this leads to weak, straggly plants with poor and scarce blooms. No plant, unless very small, should be planted nearer than 6 inches to its neighbour, while the average-sized plants need to be some 10 to 15 inches apart.

Dot plants are placed about 3 feet apart, while edging plants are best set about 10 inches from the edge of the bed, otherwise they are liable to be damaged when the grass is cut.

For colour schemes we would refer the reader to the *Summer and Spring Bedding Schemes*, pp. 146–148, and to our remarks as to colour grouping in the chapter on *The Herbaceous Border*, page 152. The plants used must depend chiefly on individual taste and on the glass available to raise them.

As to the bedding designs they should be as simple as possible, especially in small beds, and should aim at providing masses of one colour rather than small patches of highly contrasting shades in a small bed. Where the plants themselves are very small, more complicated designs may be attempted.

Cannas or tall fuchsias make very striking "dot" plants in a large bed of begonias, as do standard heliotropes or kochias in a bed of salmon pink geraniums. Abutilons and plumbagoes also make excellent "dot" plants. Bear in mind the beauty of pale pink flowers thrown up by a groundwork of mauve, dark blue or purple; a group of dark blue or purple flowers if edged with yellow violas makes a most striking display. Beware of associating colours like magenta or pink with scarlet; these colours need very careful handling.

SUMMER BEDDING
When to Bed-out

Although it is unwise to bed-out too early, this does not mean that the preparation of the beds should be left until just before it is time to put the plants in. The beds should be prepared as soon as the spring bedding is over. All bulbs used in bedding schemes should be lifted and heeled in, in the reserve garden until the foliage has turned yellow. They should then be dried off and stored. If care is taken of them, they may be used for three or four years in succession without any appreciable deterioration in the blooms providing they are healthy and free from diseases. The

PLATE 15 Layering carnations. *Top left*, preparing plant for layering, *right*, stripping the shoots, *bottom left*, cutting the stems and *right*, pinning the shoots into the soil ; layering is more fully dealt with on page 113.

PLATE 16 *Top left*, carnation carrying five buds and *right*, same plant after disbudding. *Bottom*, examples of good and bad calyx.

amateur is often worried as to what he should do with the spring bedding he takes out; should he save any of it or should he destroy it all? As space is usually a consideration, all plants that are easily raised from seed should be destroyed, but such perennials as arabis, bellis (daisies), erysimum, polyanthus, or violas should be divided into small plants and placed in the reserve garden where they will be shaded from the hottest rays of the sun and can be grown on for the next year's spring bedding.

After the beds have been dug over, they should be made thoroughly firm by treading, if the soil is light, and should then be raked over, the soil being drawn well up towards the centre of the bed. This will not only assist the drainage, but will display the plants to better advantage. In hot, dry situations the beds should be kept flat.

Antirrhinums, calceolarias, chrysanthemums (marguerites), and violas are among the most hardy of our summer bedding plants and a start can be made with these as soon as the beds have been cleared of the spring bedding. This will not only help to get the work forward at this busy time, but will give these plants time to become established before the hot weather comes.

Planting

Pot plants make better bedding subjects than those grown in boxes, as the roots are not so liable to be damaged when removed for bedding-out. In planting, use a trowel to scoop out just sufficient earth to make a hole to take the roots without crushing. Do not use a dibble as this is apt to make a hole so deep as to leave an air pocket under the roots, which will be parched and will also not have a hole wide enough to accommodate them.

Press the soil *very firmly* round the roots with the hands after planting, if this is not done the plants will be slow in becoming established and will be greatly handicapped. Should the weather be warm, bedding-out should be done in the late afternoon or in the evening, and after planting, the bed should receive a thorough soaking with warm water through a fine rose—which operation should be repeated daily for a week or so if the weather is very dry. In cases where the nights tend to be cold, water should not be applied through a rose, but a little should be given to the roots of each plant by means of a can with the rose removed. This will prevent possible chilling of the foliage and the consequent checking of growth, or even the death of the plants. Do not bed-out while the soil is very dry, either in the case of summer bedding or when planting the spring bedding. Give the bed a good soaking with water the evening previous to the planting, before the final raking down of the soil, and, as stated above, after the bedding-out has been completed. (*See* Mulching, p. 36; *and* Watering, p. 47.) Care must be taken to insert the plant to about the same depth as it stood in its pot or in the box. Keep the "ball" intact and plant so that the top of it is just half an inch below the ground level. If the plant is set in too low, there is the possibility of it "damping-off". Always remove the crocks at the bottom of the pot before the plants are bedded-out, otherwise the bed, in the course of time, will become littered with these bits of broken pot.

Care of the Bed

For the care of the bed during the summer—that is to say, weeding, removal of dead flowers, staking, etc.—we refer the reader to the *Care of the Herbaceous Border*, page 152.

COLOUR SCHEMES FOR BEDDING

NOTE.—For details as to Colour, Height, Time of Flowering and Culture, see the A.B.C. of Plants, page 255.

SUMMER BEDDING

Principal Plant	*Ground, Edging or Dot Plant*
Ageratum Houstonianum (Pale Blue)	... Geranium Madame Crousse (Rose-pink)
Ageratum Houstonianum Swanley Blue	... Alyssum maritimum minimum (White)
Antirrhinum nanum Carmine Queen	... Centaurea ragusina (candidissima)
(Rose) ...	(Silver Leaves)
Antirrhinum nanum Golden Queen	... Ageratum Houstonianum Swanley Blue
Antirrhinum nanum Bonfire	... Gladiolus Snowflake (White)
(Orange-flame)	
Antirrhinum nanum Enchantress (Pink)	... Browallia viscosa (Blue)
Antirrhinum nanum Prima Donna	... Gladiolus primulinus Souvenir
(Terra-cotta pink) ...	(Canary-yellow)
Antirrhinum nanum White Queen	... Gladiolus primulinus Vanessa
(White) ...	(Salmon-orange)
Begonia semperflorens Bonfire (Scarlet)	... Alyssum maritimum Little Dorrit
	(White)
Begonia semperflorens Bonfire (Scarlet)	... Artemisia arborescens (Silvery Leaves)
Begonia semperflorens Pink Profusion (Pink)	... Alyssum maritimum Little Dorrit (White)
Begonia semperflorens Prima Donna ,,	... Lobelia Erinus Celestial (Blue)
Begonia semperflorens Triumph (White)	... Lobelia Erinus Cambridge Blue
Begonia Bertinii nana (Scarlet)	... Albizzia lophantha (Green Foliage)
Begonia tuberous rooted vars. (Various)	... Alyssum maritimum Little Dorrit (White)
Calceolaria amplexicaulis (Pale Yellow)	... Delphinium grandiflorum Blue Butterfly
Calceolaria amplexicaulis (Pale Yellow)	... Verbena venosa (Rosy Purple)
Calceolaria Camden Hero (Brown)	... Phlox Drummondii nana Snowball
Calendula officinalis Orange Cockade	... Salvia patens (Blue)
Calendula officinalis Orange King	... Anchusa capensis (Blue)
Canna Fire Bird (Scarlet)	... Centaurea gymnocarpa (Silver Leaves)
Canna Van de Schoot (Yellow and Red)	... Salvia splendens Glory of Zurich
	(Scarlet)
Dahlia Coltness Gem (Scarlet)	... Viola White Swan (White)
Dahlia Ada (Yellow)	... Lobelia tenuior (Cobalt Blue)
Eucalyptus globulus (Silver-blue Leaves)	... Geranium Madame Kovalesky
	(Pelargonium) (Orange-red)
Fuchsia Ballet Girl (Red and White)	... Phlox Drummondii nana (Mixed vars.)
Fuchsia Madame Cornellison ,, ,,	... Begonia semperflorens luminosa (Red)
Fuchsia Thalia (Orange-red)	... Fuchsia Golden Treasure (Golden Leaves)

146

SUMMER BEDDING (continued)

Principal Plant		Ground, Edging or Dot Plant	
Geranium Paul Crampel (Pelargonium)	(Scarlet)	Abutilon Thompsonii	(Yellow and Green Leaves)
Geranium Paul Crampel (Pelargonium)	(Scarlet)	Centaurea ragusina var. compacta	(Silver Leaves)
Geranium Salmon Crampel	(Salmon)	Zea Mays gracillima variegata	
Geranium Madame Crousse	(Rose-pink)	Antirrhinum White Queen	(White)
Gladiolus Majuba	(Scarlet)	Antirrhinum nanum Golden Queen	
Gladiolus Prince of Wales	(Salmon-rose)	Stocks, East Lothian	(White)
Gladiolus Hopman's Glory	(Yellow)	Antirrhinum nanum Pink Gem	
Gladiolus Red Charm	(Rich Crimson)	Antirrhinum nanum Golden Queen	
Gladiolus Snowflake	(White)	Antirrhinum nanum Defiance	(Orange-flame)
Godetia Rosy Morn	(Coral-pink)	Dianthus chinensis Purity	(White)
Godetia Shell Pink		Viola Rolph	(Pale Blue)
Heliotropium peruvianum Lord Roberts	(Violet)	Calceolaria amplexicaulis	(Pale Yellow)
Heliotropium peruvianum Giant vars. „		Eucalyptus globulus	(Silver-blue Leaves)
Impatiens Holstii	(Scarlet)	Alyssum maritimum	(White)
Kochia trichophylla (Burning Bush)	„	Tagetes erecta nana Orange Prince	
Lobelia fulgens Huntsman	(Scarlet)	Chrysanthemum inodorum Bridal Robe	
Lobelia fulgens Queen Victoria	(Scarlet)	Antirrhinum White Beauty	(White)
Nicotiana Sanderæ	(Red)	Chrysanthemum frutescens (Marguerite)	(White)
Nicotiana sylvestris	(White)	Polygonum orientale	(Crimson)
Nigella damascena Miss Jekyll	(Blue)	Verbena Miss Willmott	(Rose)
Penstemon Mrs. Fulford	(Red)	Antirrhinum majus album	(White)
Penstemon Southgate Gem	(Carmine)	Phlox Drummondii compacta Snowball	
Petunia Countess of Ellesmere	(Rose)	Callistephus chinensis Comet	(White)
Petunia Silver Lilac	(Silvery Lilac)	Senecio leucostachys	(Silvery Leaves)
Phlox Drummondii (Rose and Pink Shades)		Gaura Lindheimeri	(White, tinted Red)
Plumbago capensis	(Blue)	Chrysanthemum frutescens (Marguerite)	(White)
Salvia patens	(Blue)	Stock Princess Alice	(White)
Salvia patens Cambridge Blue		Leucophyta Brownii	(Silvery Leaves)
Salvia splendens Harbinger	(Scarlet)	Limonium Bonduellii	(Yellow)
Scabiosa atropurpurea	(Mixed)	Helichrysum bracteatum	(Yellow and White)
Senecio Cineraria Diamond	(Grey Leaves)	Gladiolus America	(Lilac-rose)
Sutherlandia frutescens	(Orange-red)	Lobelia Erinus compacta alba	(White)
Tagetes erecta	(Orange)	Lobelia Erinus Sapphire	(Sapphire-blue)
Tagetes patula nana	(Yellow and Brown)	Zinnia elegans Dahlia-flowered	(Mixed)
Tagetes signata pumila	(Yellow)	Coreopsis tinctoria The Garnet	(Crimson-scarlet)
Trachymene cœrulea	(Light Blue)	Dahlia Shirley White	(White)
Tropæolum nanum Fireball	(Orange-scarlet)	Penstemon White Bedder	(White)
Tropæolum nanum Golden King	(Yellow)	Penstemon Pink Beauty	(Pink)
Verbena Mammoth Firefly	(Scarlet)	Antirrhinum majus Yellow King	
Verbena hybrida cœrulea	(Blue)	Fuchsia Mrs. Marshall	(Red and White)
Verbena venosa	(Rosy Purple)	Alyssum maritimum Little Dorrit	(White)
Verbena venosa	(Rosy Purple)	Artemisia Purshiana	
Zinnia elegans	(Scarlet and Yellow vars.)	Gazania longiscapa	(Golden Brown)
Zinnia elegans gigantea Dahlia-flowered	(Mixed)	Tagetes patula nana Legion of Honour	(Yellow and Brown)
Zinnea Haageana	(Orange-yellow)	Tropæolum nanum Feltham Beauty	(Scarlet).

COLOUR SCHEMES FOR BEDDING

NOTE.—For details as to Colour, Height, Time of Flowering and Culture, see the
A.B.C. of Plants, page 255

SPRING BEDDING

Principal Plant		*Ground, Edging or Dot Plant*	
Alyssum saxatile compactum	(Yellow)	... Wallflower Dwarf Blood Red	
Anemone His Excellency	(Scarlet)	... Tulip Cottage Bouton d'Or	(Yellow)
Anemone The Bride	(White)	... Tulip Darwin William Pitt	(Scarlet)
Anemone St. Brigid	(Mixed)	... Iris Spanish	(Mixed)
Cheiranthus Allionii	(Orange)	... Aubrieta deltoidea G. S. Baker	(Violet-blue)
Cheiranthus Allionii	(Orange)	... Myosotis alpestris Royal Blue	
Hyacinth City of Haarlem	(Yellow)	... Myosotis alpestris Victoria	(Blue)
Hyacinth Gertrude	(Rose-pink)	... Aubrieta deltoidea, var. Lavender	
Hyacinth Grand Maître	(Lavender-blue)	... Bellis perennis Mammoth White Daisy	
Hyacinth King of the Blues	(Dark Blue)	... Myosotis alpestris alba	(White)
Hyacinth Lady Derby	(Salmon-pink)	... Viola Primrose Dame	(Pale Yellow)
Hyacinth L'Innocence	(White)	... Primula (Polyanthus) var.	(Red)
Hyacinth La Victoire	(Rose red)	... Viola William Robb	(Lavender)
Hyacinth Queen of the Pinks		... Pansy Winter-flowering Ice King	
Hyacinth, Myosotis	(Pale Blue)	... Pansy Winter flowering Helios	(Yellow)
Iris Dutch	(Mixed)	... Violas, Blue, Yellow and White	
Iris Spanish	(Mixed)	... Violas, Blue, Yellow and White	
Muscari Heavenly Blue	(Blue)	... Tulip Early Prince de Ligne	(Yellow)
Narcissus Emperor	(Golden-yellow)	... Arabis caucasica (albida) fl. pl.	(White)
Narcissus Empress	(Yellow and White)	... Muscari Heavenly Blue	(Blue)
Narcissus Golden Spur	(Golden Yellow)	... Iberis sempervirens	(White)
Narcissus Lucifer	(White and Orange-red)	... Wallflower Orange Bedder	
Narcissus Seagull	(White)	... Myosotis dissitiflora Perfection	(Blue)
Primula (Polyanthus) var.	(White)	... Bellis perennis Mammoth Etna	(Red)
Primula (Polyanthus) var.	(Orange)	... Crocus Maximilian	(Azure-blue)
Primula (Polyanthus) var.	(Red)	... Viola White Swan	(White)
Tulip Brilliant Star (Early)	(Scarlet)	... Arabis caucasica (albida) variegata	(White)
Tulip Keizer Kroon (Early)	(Scarlet-yellow)	... Arabis caucasica (albida)	(White)
Tulip Mon Tresor (Early)	(Yellow)	... Viola Maggie Mott	(Mauve)
Tulip White Hawk (Early)	(White)	... Myosotis alpestris	(Royal Blue)
Tulip Early Van der Neer	(Plum-purple)	... Tulip Mon Tresor	(Yellow)
Tulip Early Vermilion Brilliant	(Scarlet)	... Pansy Winter-flowering Winter Sun	(Yellow)
Tulip Early Double El Toreador	(Orange-scarlet)	... Primula (Polyanthus) var.	(Yellow)
Tulip Early Double Couronne d'Or	(Orange and Yellow)	... Iberis sempervirens Little Gem	(White)
Tulip Early Double Snow Queen	(White)	... Chionodoxa Luciliæ	(Blue and White)
Tulip Early Double Van der Hoef	(Yellow)	... Myosotis alpestris Victoria	(Blue)
Tulip Darwin Bartigon	(Carmine-red)	... Wallflower Ivory White	(White)
Tulip Darwin Clara Butt	(Pink and Rose)	... Myosotis dissitiflora Perfection	(Sky)
Tulip Darwin La Tulipe Noire	(Maroon-black)	... Arabis caucasica (albida)	(White)
Tulip Darwin King Harold	(Blood-red)	... Iberis sempervirens	(White)
Tulip Darwin Orion	(Scarlet)	... Saxifraga Wallacei	(White)
Tulip Darwin Princess Elizabeth	(Rose)	... Silene pendula Bijou	(Salmon-rose)
Tulip Darwin Pride of Haarlem	(Cerise)	... Doronicum plantagineum	(Yellow)
Tulip Darwin Rev. Ewbank	(Heliotrope)	... Tulip Darwin Clara Butt	(Pink and Rose)
Tulip Darwin William Pitt	(Scarlet)	... Narcissus Leedsii White Lady	(White)
Tulip Breeder Bacchus	(Royal Purple)	... Wallflower Golden Monarch	
Tulip Breeder Don Pedro	(Red, shaded Mauve)	... Wallflower Primrose Dame	(Primrose)

148

SPRING BEDDING (*continued*)

Principal Plant		*Ground, Edging or Dot Plant*
Tulip Breeder Panorama	(Chestnut red) ...	Wallflower Ivory White
Tulip Cottage Bouton d'Or	(Golden) ...	Aubrieta deltoidea Carnival (Reddish Purple)
Tulip Cottage Ellen Willmott	(Primrose) ...	Veronica gentianoides (Violet-blue)
Tulip Cottage Inglescombe Pink	...	Tulip Cottage Arethusa (Primrose)
Tulip Cottage Inglescombe Scarlet	...	Wallflower Fire King (Orange-scarlet)
Tulip Cottage Picotee	(White and Rose) ...	Viola Kitty Bell (Lavender)
Viola Jersey Gem	(Purple) ...	Tulip Cottage Inglescombe Yellow
Wallflower Vulcan	(Crimson) ...	Tulip Cottage Orange King
Wallflower Ruby Gem	(Ruby-violet) ...	Tulip Breeder Yellow Perfection (Bronze-yellow).

SPRING BEDDING

Spring bedding requires much the same treatment as summer bedding. It should be done as early as possible, so that the plants may establish themselves before the severe weather sets in. Plant them, therefore, early in October, as soon as the summer bedding has been cleared away; this should be done immediately the flowers are over. The question of what plants to discard and what to save again arises. As summer bedding plants are nearly all either half-hardy or tender, they will require the protection of glass through the winter. The amount of glass available, therefore, usually largely decides the question. Glass space is always very valuable, and for this reason it would be folly to preserve any plants that can easily be raised from seed or from cuttings. Such plants as the following can, therefore, be thrown away: alyssums, antirrhinums, asters, calceolarias, coreopsis, gaillardias, geraniums, geums, heliotropes, lobelia, penstemons, petunias, stocks, and verbenas. These, however, must not be discarded until cuttings have been taken from them. Woody plants such as abutilons, fuchsias, standard heliotropes, hydrangeas and plumbagoes, also cannas, centaureas, cinerarias, and other foliage plants that take several years to grow to the most effective size should be taken up with as complete a ball of roots as possible and planted in suitably sized pots, the branches being trimmed if space is at a premium. If the branches are trimmed, the roots may also be reduced. Store the plants in a frost-proof frame or on shelves in the greenhouse and water them occasionally. Bulbous and tuberous-rooted plants such as begonias, dahlias and gladioli must, of course, be saved. (*See* paragraphs on individual plants, Chapter 34.)

Do not leave the bedding-out until the early spring when bloom is coming and the roots are not in a favourable condition to establish themselves. As soon as the summer bedding has been removed, dig over the bed to two spades' depth and manure it as described on page 35, then put in the plants that are to form the groundwork, and let them be just far enough apart so that, when grown, they will cover the surface of the bed. In the interstices between these insert the bulbs. (*See* Chapter 34, *and* chapter on Bulbs, p. 170.)

Plants for Spring Bedding

At one time bulbs were practically the only plants used by the gardener for spring bedding. This use of bulbs alone had many drawbacks. Firstly the beds were plain and bare all through the winter, then as soon as the bulbs had flowered, the beds would become untidy and uninteresting. To-day we use a groundwork of alyssum, arabis, aubrieta, bellis (daisies), myosotis, polyanthus, silenes, violas, wallflowers, and other dwarf hardy plants, through which the bulbs rise to form a mass of colour over a carpet that is chosen either to harmonize or contrast with them. This groundwork clothes the soil and looks neat all the winter and also keeps the bed tidier and interesting for some time after the bulbs have flowered. Spring bedding is thus rendered less formal and stiff, and the period of bloom is considerably extended. In addition, small shrubs and dwarf conifers are often used to relieve the bareness of the bed during the winter. These are best sunk into the bed in pots, they are then easily removed when the summer bedding has to be put in. The correct time to buy bulbs is in September. See that they are plump and firm, of good but not excessive size, and free from disease. No growth should be visible.

HOW TO BED OUT

Both with spring and summer bedding it is best to mark the positions of each plant by means of stakes and string, before a start is made with the actual planting.

If planting a round bed, a stake should be inserted at the exact centre and to this stake is attached a piece of string. By fixing a peg of wood successively at different distances down this string, the gardener can trace out circles of different diameter, on which the plants, still in their pots, should be spaced out evenly. The gardener can then see more or less how his scheme will look when planted, and the number of each kind of plant required to fill the bed.

In bedding-out small beds, most gardeners find it easiest to work from the edges inwards to the centre; in large beds, however, mark the centre accurately and work outwards from this, using a board to stand on so that the feet do not tread down the soil. If this plank can span the bed and rest on two or three bricks on each side, it will be raised above the bed and will save any pressure on the soil.

PLANTS FOR CARPET BEDDING

Carpet bedding consists in arranging masses of low, compact-growing plants with variously coloured leaves in such a manner as to form patterns. It is usual to arrange a background of plants of some one colour, and through this to run plants of other shades in masses, stripes or ribbons, so as to produce the artificial result desired. Among the commoner plants

150

used for this purpose are: Sempervivums of various colours (grey and green), Echeverias, Sedum glaucum (grey), Cerastium tomentosum (silver), Herniaria glabra (green) and Chrysanthemum Parthenium var. aureum (yellow).

PROPAGATION OF BEDDING PLANTS

It is advantageous to have bedding plants as well advanced as possible. Late and consequently undeveloped plants bear poor flowers. Sow the annuals in heat, if possible, in February, or in the open, if hardy, in March or April. Biennials should be sown from May to August and wintered under glass. Annuals, too, may be treated as biennials, sown in September, and wintered under glass.

Cuttings of most half-hardy plants such as pelargoniums and verbenas, are taken in July and August; ageratums, calceolarias, and salvias in September, and may be kept in the open till the end of September, when they must be wintered in a cold frame or better still near the glass in a greenhouse in slight heat. For cuttings to be taken in early spring, old stocks must be placed in gentle heat and induced to grow, then when sufficiently large, the young shoots may be taken off as cuttings, to be rooted also in gentle heat. (*See* Propagation, p. 108.) Begonias and similar tuberous-rooted plants need to be "started" in heat early in February and will then be ready for planting out with the other bedding plants at the end of May or early in June.

Hardening-Off

Never bring the plants straight out of the frame or warm house into the beds. Harden-off by giving gradually more and more air for three weeks to a month before the time for bedding-out, which is usually about the middle of May. Planting out without adequate hardening-off is responsible for much failure and usually results in checked growth, and consequently late and poor flowering, or often complete loss of the more tender plants.

For further information as to the propagation of bedding-plants, see the chapter on *Methods of Propagation*, page 101, and for cultural details peculiar to each species, see the A.B.C. of Plants, page 255. *See also* Making Beds and Borders, Chapter 7.

CHAPTER 16

HARDY PERENNIALS
AND THE HERBACEOUS BORDER

The herbaceous border entails very little labour as compared with the upkeep of beds filled with annuals or with the laying out of the more severe bedding designs. Once planted the herbaceous border lasts for many years, merely requiring weeding, staking, periodical division of the roots of the plants, occasional mulching, and forking over annually. For these reasons it is justly a popular feature of the garden, chiefly because of the glorious masses of colour it provides, which, if careful and skilful planting has been resorted to, may be had from early spring until November.

The width of the border must naturally vary according to the size of the garden and many other considerations. But where possible it should be not less than 4 feet wide, and if there is plenty of space, it should be at least double that width.

SOIL AND SITUATION OF THE BORDER

The herbaceous border may occupy almost any position in the garden, but the best results will be obtained if it faces due south and has some protection in the form of a wall or a hedge from the cold winds from the north and east, though care should be taken that the hedge is far enough away for its roots not to take nourishment from the flowers in the border. Much thought should be bestowed on the choice of a background, as it can make or mar the border. A wall or trellis covered with roses is good, so also is a wall planted with fruit trees, but the dark green background provided by a yew hedge is very hard to beat. Most perennials will grow in almost any soil, but a deep, rich, well-drained loam is preferred.

THE CONSTRUCTION OF THE BORDER

The ground intended to be devoted to this purpose should be thoroughly prepared in advance. This is even more important than in the case of beds for annuals or for tender plants, which will occupy the ground but for a single season. Let it be remembered that the carefully prepared and properly-planted border should not require thorough re-making or re-planting for several years to come for one of its chief charms consists in the "settled-down" appearance, only possible with plants that have occupied the same ground for some time.

152

The border may be prepared either in September or in early January. In the first case, the plants should be put in in October or November and in the second in February, March or April.

The ground should be well drained and then thoroughly trenched to a depth of 2 to 3 feet, care being taken not to bring any sour or heavy subsoil to the top. With the bottom spit should be mixed good stable manure when the soil is heavy, or cow or pig dung if the land should be light, while some substance such as the ashes of burnt vegetable matter, bonemeal, or basic slag should be added to the top-spit. If the soil is too light, it may be improved by the addition of leaf-mould and a little thoroughly pulverized clay. Should the earth prove very heavy, coarse sand and wood ashes will serve to lighten it. The border should be left for a month or so after trenching, in order that the soil may settle down.

GROUPING THE COLOURS

Now we come to colour grouping. This is, perhaps, the most difficult problem that has to be solved in the construction of the border. So much depends on the correct solution, and infinite pains will have to be expended in order that the best result may be obtained. Aim at large splashes of colour. Do not go out for contrasts, but let the tints merge gently from the one into the other, and with a gentle crescendo lead up from the paler shades to the most vivid colours.

Let us first of all plan our red group. Start with the pale pinks, next to them put the deeper shades, and so on until the most vivid and powerful reds are reached. From this zenith of colour work gradually back to the palest of pink. The purples, blues, and yellows can be treated in the same way as described for the reds. We cannot, however, place these groups up against one another indiscriminately or we should have hard lines and in places clashing colours, but we know that pink harmonizes delightfully with pale yellow, so we may join our red group to the yellow group. Similarly pink is exquisite alongside lilac, so we can link these up with our purple group, and our blue group with our yellows.

We should also remember that tints may be made to lead the one from the other so as to blend harmoniously. The yellows will run into orange, the orange through orange-scarlet to scarlet, and thence to the deepest crimson. Similarly through the pale blues we reach dark blue, then purple and down again through lilac to pale blue or lavender grey or white. Plants with ample green foliage must not be neglected, for nature uses green very liberally in her colour schemes. White, if not used to excess, is invaluable, for it will always help us out of difficulties, and it may be placed next to the strongest colours equally as well as against the palest. But if too much white is used, the border will look "patchy".

Many of the strong colours may be associated without going through a

153

gradation of their paler tints. Deep blue, or purple, for instance, blends well with gold, orange, or yellow, but care must be taken not to use any clashing colours in close proximity. The ultra vivid colours should be most carefully handled, as they strike the eye so quickly and are apt, if used too freely, to submerge the more delicate tints.

Do not fall into the common mistake of placing all the bright colours at the back and middle of the border, let there be some groups of vivid colouring well to the front. There are innumerable edging plants, such as aubrietas, dianthus (pinks), and saxifrages, that afford brilliant tints for this purpose. These groups of colour must not be bounded by hard straight lines. Each group must be irregular in shape and should merge gradually and imperceptibly into the group next to it.

HEIGHT GRADATION AND DISTANCE APART

Generally speaking, the taller-growing plants, such as the rudbeckia, sunflower, hollyhock, and delphinium, should be placed at the back of the border, and there should be a gentle gradation down through plants of medium height, as for examples, the phloxes, campanulas, and carnations, to the violas, daisies, silenes, and dwarfer species in front, but this procedure must not be adopted invariably or a stiff and severe effect will ensue, and the freedom and irregularity which are the chief charms of a herbaceous border will be lost. Here and there, clumps of the taller flowers should be grouped in outstanding positions well to the front of the border, and some low-growing and creeping plants should seem to find their way some way towards the back, at the base of the taller ones, so as to break up the general outline and to introduce some element of surprise, for a border loses much of its charm if it can all be seen at a glance from

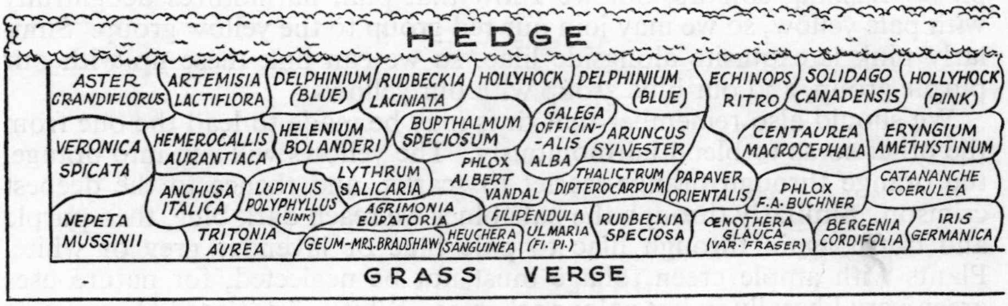

FIG. 28. PLAN OF

The above is a plan of a mixed border (100 by 12 feet), backed with a hedge and surrounded border, one must, however, intermix annuals, biennials, and bulbs. The planning is largely a should be carried out.

154

one end. The flowers should be planted in groups of from four or five to eight or nine of each kind in a clump, but not too closely together; the dwarfer the plants, the more in a group. It is one of the greatest mistakes to plant perennials singly in various parts of the border, for this gives a patchwork effect, which is not at all pleasing. The ideal to aim at is masses of striking, but well-harmonized colours.

The distances at which the crowns should be planted from one another depend on the height to which the plants may be expected to grow, and on their "bushiness". But as a guiding principle, it can be taken that the dwarfer kinds should be set about 8 inches apart, the medium sorts 15 inches apart, and the tallest kinds some 2 feet from one another. So far as space provision is concerned, the aim should be to show practically no bare earth during the period of active growth, and at the same time to avoid any overcrowding, for this interferes with individual development.

Each plant should be clearly labelled as it is planted, otherwise confusion either in the colour scheme or in the gradation of height will ensue.

ARRANGING A CONTINUITY OF BLOOM

In this we have a problem nearly as difficult as that provided by the colour scheme. Our aim is to secure a continuity of bloom from early spring until late in the autumn. Thus the plants we choose for the border must be not only brilliant in their colours, but should have as long as possible a period of bloom. If the border is wisely planned, there is no reason why there should not be plenty of colour to the end of October.

Bulbs such as the snowdrop, the crocus, the tulip, the scilla, the chionodoxa, and the anemone, and such early flowering plants as the alyssum, the anchusa, the aubrieta, and the earlier delphiniums, will provide a good

HERBACEOUS BORDER

by a grass verge. The plants included are mainly perennials. To get the best out of such a matter of personal taste, but the above diagram illustrates the manner in which the planting

155

show in spring. During May, June, and July, pæonies, lupins, delphiniums, irises, inulas, erigerons, antirrhinums, and many others will furnish all the colour needed. In August and September we have sweet peas, thalictrums, phloxes, sunflowers, penstemons, and antirrhinums, while gladioli, red hot pokers, aconitums, rudbeckias, dahlias, and chrysanthemums will carry on the bloom well to the end of October.

SCREENING AND REPLACING THE EARLY BLOOMS

The designer of the herbaceous border has still other things to think about. He must remember that by midsummer, or even before, the early-flowering plants will have finished blooming and will be beginning to look untidy however carefully dead flowers have been picked off. He must, therefore, endeavour to plant later-flowering and taller-growing flowers that, as they grow up, will screen these. This, however, is more difficult than it at first appears, for a plant that will grow tall enough totally to obscure the plant behind it, but not until that plant has flowered, must be chosen. It will not do to plant *any* later-flowering plant to replace an early bloomer, even though it grows to the correct height to continue the uniformity of the scheme and flowers at the right time, for it must be remembered that the substitute plant must also fulfil the requirements of the colour scheme; it being necessary to replace a yellow flower by a yellow one or by one whose flowers harmonize with those surrounding it.

Annuals may be used to fill vacant spaces, and for this purpose alyssum, asters, centaurea, clarkia, stocks and nemophila are hard to rival.

RAISING HERBACEOUS PERENNIALS

Herbaceous perennials may be propagated from seeds, cuttings, offsets, layers, and from root divisions. The last method is the most generally used. The use of seeds, however, is becoming increasingly popular, especially in the case of new species, although it is a somewhat lengthy process, as the plants in many instances do not attain to their best for three years. Seed is best sown in shallow drills 10 inches apart in the open in May or June, and the young seedlings must be transplanted to the reserve garden, and set ten inches apart, as soon as they are fit to be handled, and before they become drawn up and straggly. If preferred, seed may be raised in shallow boxes in a cold frame, the seedlings being later planted out in the reserve garden as advised for those sown in the open. First-year plants must not be allowed to flower at all; second-year plants may be permitted to bloom in moderation, but they must not be allowed to go to seed. In the chapter on The Propagation of Plants, p. 101, will be found full instructions for the various methods of propagation mentioned above, and in the A.B.C. of Plants, page 255, is shown the method most suitable to each plant, also the best time to propagate.

A FEW OF THE BEST HARDY HERBACEOUS PERENNIALS

NOTE.—For details as to Colour, Height, Season of Flowering, Culture, and the best Species and Varieties, *see* the A.B.C. of Plants, page 255.

Acanthus longifolius, A. mollis, and A. spinosus
Achillea clypeolata, A. filipendulina, A. Ptarmica fl. pl.
Aconitum Carmichaelii, japonicum, and A. Napellus
Adonis amurensis and A. vernalis
Agastache mexicana
Alstromeria aurantiaca, A. hæmantha var. rosea
Althæa rosea (Hollyhock)
Anchusa italica (Dropmore, Opal, and Pride of Dover)
Anemone alpina, A. apennina,
A. coronaria, A. fulgens, A. Hepatica, A. hybrida (japonica) and its varieties.
Anthemis tinctoria vars.
Anthericum Liliago
Aquilegia cœrulea
A. longissima
Armeria latifolia, A. plantaginea and varieties
Artemisia lactiflora
Asphodeline lutea
Asphodelus ramosus
Aster Amellus and vars.
Aster novæ-angliæ vars.
Aster novi-belgii and vars.
Astilbe Arendsii hybrids, A. Davidii
Aubrieta deltoidea vars.
Bellis perennis and vars.
Bergenia cordifolia
Bocconia (See Macleaya)
Boltonia asteroides and B. a. var. decurrens
Buphthalmum salicifolium
Campanula lactiflora, C. latifolia,
C. persicifolia and vars.
Catananche cœrulea and C. c., var. alba
Centaurea hypoleuca, and C. macrocephala
Centranthus. (*See* Kentranthus)
Cephalaria tatarica
Cheiranthus Cheiri "Wallflower"
Chelone Lyonii and C. obliqua

Chrysanthemum arcticum, C. coccineum, C. maximum, etc.
Cimicifuga cordifolia, C. racemosa
Coreopsis grandiflora, C. lanceolata
Corydalis nobilis
Delphinium (hybrids)
Dianthus barbatus (Sweet William)
D. Caryophyllus (Carnation)
D. plumarius, etc.
Dicentra Cucullaria, D. spectabilis
Dictamnus albus
Dodecatheon Hendersonii, D. Meadia, etc.
Doronicum plantagineum var. excelsum, etc.
Dracocephalum sibiricum
Echinacea purpurea
Echinops Ritro and others
Eremurus Bungei, E. Elwesii, E. Olgæ, etc.
Erigeron speciosus, etc.
Erodium Manescavii
Eryngium amethystinum, E. Oliverianum, etc.
Erysimum Perofskianum
Filipendula palmata etc.
Gaillardia grandiflora
Galega officinalis, G. patula and varieties
Gaura Lindheimeri
Geranium armenum, G. Endressii, G. ibericum and vars.
G. pratense
Geum Borisii, G. Bulgaricum, etc.
Gypsophila paniculata, G. p. var. fl. pl.
Hedysarum capitatum, H. coronarium, etc.
Helenium autumnale vars. H. Hoopesii
Helianthus mollis, H. rigidus vars.
Helleborus niger (Christmas Rose) H. orientalis vars.
Hemerocallis aurantiaca, H. flava, and hybrids

Heuchera sanguinea vars.
Horminum pyrenaicum
Hosta Fortunei, H. lancifolia and vars. H. Sieboldiana and H. plantaginea
Hypericum olympicum
Iberis sempervirens
Incarvillea Delavayi
Inula ensifolia, I. Hookeri and others
Iris germanica and vars.
Kentranthus ruber, etc.
Kniphofia Uvaria, K. Nelsonii, etc. and many garden vars.
Lathyrus grandiflorus, L. latifolius, etc.
Leptandra (Veronica) virginica
Ligularia clivorum L. Ledebourii, etc.
Linaria dalmatica, L. purpurea
Linum flavum, L. narbonense, L. perenne, etc.
Lobelia fulgens, L. cardinalis, L. syphylitica
Lupinus polyphyllus vars.
Lychnis chalcedonica
Lysimachia clethroides
Lythrum Salicaria and L. virgatum, etc.
Meconopsis cambrica
Macleaya cordata, M. microcarpa
Malva moschata
Mimulus luteus
Monarda didyma, M. fistulosa, etc.
Myosotis scorpioides
Nepeta Faassenii (Mussinii)
Œnothera glauca var. Fraseri and others
Pæonia lactiflora, etc.
Papaver orientale vars.
Penstemon barbatus gentianoides vars. and hybrids.
Phlox paniculata, P. decussata vars.
Physalis Franchetii, etc.
Physostegia virginiana Vivid
Polemonium cœruleum and varieties

157

A Few of the Best Hardy Herbaceous Perennials—cont.

Potentilla argyrophylla P. nepalensis var. minor P recta, etc.
Poterium obtusum
Primula elatior, P. vulgaris and many garden vars.
Rudbeckia laciniata, R. speciosa and many vars.
Salvia hæmatodes, S. superba
Saponaria officinalis, S. o. var. flore pleno, etc.

Saxifraga granulata fl. pl. S. umbrosa, and many garden varieties
Scabiosa caucasica vars.
Sedum spectabile and S. s. var. variegatum, etc.
Sidalcea candida, S. neo-mexicana, S. spicata, etc.
Smilacina racemosa
Solidago canadense
Stokesia cyanea, and S. c. var. alba

Thalictrum aquilegifolium, T. Delavayi, T. dipterocarpum
Trillium grandiflorum
Tradescantia virginiana and varieties
Trollius asiaticus, T. euroæus and varieties. T. pumilus
Veronica incana, V. spicata and V. longifolia
Viola, various garden vars.

WHEN AND HOW TO PLANT

As a general rule, the best time to plant the border is in October or November, but in the north and in very exposed positions, it is often advisable to defer the planting until March or April. The plants that bloom early should, if possible, be put in in the autumn so that the roots may get well-established before they have to bear the strain of flowering. This applies to such flowers as lupins and pæonies. Autumn planting is also advisable in light soils. In wet, cold soils, spring planting is best; if in a soil of this kind plants must be put in in the autumn, let it be done in September. Thick succulent-rooted plants are more apt to decay if planted in autumn; these should be spring-planted whenever possible.

In planting, holes should be dug of sufficient depth to allow the roots to be placed in without being doubled up, and wide enough to admit of the roots being well-spread out and covered with fine soil, which should be pressed firmly round the crowns. Firm planting is essential, and care must be taken that the crowns are not placed lower than ground level, as there is every possibility of their rotting off if this is done. The plants should be so inserted that the crowns are just on the surface of the soil. Some herbaceous plants, such as the anchusa and sunflower, are "tap-rooted", and these demand an extra deep hole for planting; otherwise their long roots will be bent up and prevented from penetrating deeply into the soil. When planting, study the habits of the roots, and allow them to follow what seems to be their natural course.

ATTENTION REQUIRED THROUGHOUT THE YEAR

Let us say that the border has been constructed and planted in the autumn. Through the winter little attention will be necessary, but it will be wise to cover the crowns of the less hardy perennials, such as kniphofias, lobelias, etc., with fibre or small mounds of ashes to protect them from hard frosts in case the weather should be too severe. In the winter, too, when there is little foliage and most pests are dormant, is the time to wage war on slugs and other pests infesting the borders. (*See* Chapter 42.)

158

In the early spring, weeds will have begun to grow, and a great deal of labour will be saved later on if these are kept down from the beginning. During the spring and summer it is necessary to keep the hoe busy, not only to keep down the weeds, but to keep the soil well turned and to conserve moisture in dry weather. When the buds are forming, the plants should be assisted by the application of a little artificial manure, applied just before rain, if possible. If no rain comes, the chemicals should be well hoed in. A suitable mixture is one of 1 part of sulphate of ammonia to 2 parts of nitrate of soda. This should be applied at the rate of 2 oz. to the square yard. If preferred, a top-dressing of two-thirds well-decayed stable manure and one-third leaf-mould may be given in spring.

During the very dry weather, the plants will benefit if watered about every other day. Dead flowers should be cut off at once, as this will prolong the period of bloom; once a plant is allowed to go to seed, it soon stops flowering. As the foliage of the plants dies and turns yellow, it must be cut down to within 3 inches of the ground. This keeps the border tidy and gives room to other plants. In November, when all flowers are over, every plant should be cut down like this and should be clearly labelled. Evergreen plants, such as red hot pokers, should, of course, not be cut down. At this time, or late in February, dig some well-decayed manure and leaf-mould in between the plants, but do not let the manure cover the crowns or they may rot off, and do not injure the roots.

RETRENCHING AND MANURING THE BORDER

About every three to four years the border will be all the better for a thorough retrenching and manuring. Many of the plants, too, will be getting over-bulky and will need dividing, partly because they will overcrowd less vigorous neighbours, and also for the reason that their flowers will have deteriorated both in size and colour. The border is best renewed in November, when all the plants, with the exception of such as pæonies, delphiniums, lilies, daffodils, and irises, should be removed, carefully labelled as to colour, height, species, etc., and laid aside in a warm and sheltered position. If they are to be left out of the border for more than a couple of days or so, they should be "heeled-in" in the reserve garden. Delphiniums and irises do best if lifted and divided every fourth or fifth year. The border must be thoroughly trenched, digging should be carried out as close as possible up to the plants left in position, and the subsoil should be well manured. If the soil is at all sour, it should be dressed with lime at the rate of 10 oz. to the square yard. The plants should be divided, the inner and older stems being discarded, and the outer and younger crowns being replanted in the same way as when the border was first made. This work may also be done in February or March. This is wiser in colder localities.

SOME PLANTS FOR THE BLUE HERBACEOUS BORDER

The reader must bear in mind when consulting the following table that seed of many of the plants is invariably sold (mixed colours), and that only by stipulating a special variety and colour, or by growing and preserving his own seed, will he be sure of obtaining the desired results. The table has been compiled with the object of making it easier to select plants suitable in height, and of the desired colour, for the front, middle, and back of the border. The times of flowering are added so that it is possible to arrange for a continuity of bloom throughout the season.

For further cultural details, see the lists of Half-hardy Annuals, Hardy Annuals, Hardy Herbaceous Perennials, and the A.B.C. section dealing with all the various Flowering Plants, Chapter 34.

Annuals

Botanical Name	Common Name	Height in Inches			Time of Flowering
		Up to 12	12 to 36	Over 36	
*Ageratum, Blue Star (Light) . .	Floss Flower	6–10	—	—	May to Sept.
Imperial Dwarf (Deep) . . .	Floss Flower	5	—	—	May to Sept.
Swanley Blue	Floss Flower	10	—	—	May to Sept.
*Anagallis arvensis, var. cœrulea . .	Pimpernel	6	—	—	All summer
Anchusa capensis (Alkanit). .		10	—	—	July
*Arctotis stœchadifolia, syn. grandis .		—	24	—	Summer
Asperula orientalis (Light) . . .	Woodruff	—	12	—	June to Sept.
*Brachycome iberidifolia Blue Star .	Swan River Daisy	10	—	—	All Summer
*Browallia elata (Purple blue) . .		12	—	—	July to Sept.
Callistephus chinensis	Asters	—	9–24	—	Autumn.
Charieis heterophylla	Cape Aster	6	—	—	June to Aug.
Centaurea Cyanus.	Cornflower or Blue-bottle	—	20	—	July to Oct.
Convolvulus tricolor		12	—	—	June to Sept.
Delphinium Gayanum, syn. Ajacis, vars	Larkspur	—	12–30	—	June to Sept.
Consolida vars	Larkspur	—	24–30	—	June to Sept.
* grandiflorum var. Blue Butterfly .	Larkspur	—	12–18	—	July to Oct.
Lathyrus odoratus (vars.) . . .	Sweet Peas	—	—	36–72	July to Oct.
Limonium sinuatum	Sea Lavender	—	18	—	June to Oct.
Linum usitatissimum	Common Flax	—	24	—	July to Oct.
*Lobelia Erinus vars. (Light and Dark)	Lobelia	6–12	—	—	July to Sept.
*Lobelia tenuior		12	—	—	July to Sept.
Lupinus Hartwegii	Lupins	—	24	—	June to Oct.
Lychnis (Viscaria) Cœli-rosa, var. cœrulea		12	—	—	June to Sept.
*Nemesia strumosa, Blue Gem . .		12	—	—	July to Sept.
Nemophila insignis (Sky-blue, White centre)	Californian Bluebell	3–12	—	—	July to Sept.
Nicandra physaloides	Apple of Peru	—	24	—	July to Sept.
Nigella damascena, var. Miss Jekyll .	Love-in-a-Mist	12	—	—	June to Sept.
*Nigella hispanica	Love-in-a-Mist	12	—	—	June to Sept.
Phacelia campanularia		9	—	—	June to Aug.
Salvia farinacea	Salvia	—	24–30	—	July to Oct.
Salvia Horminum, Bluebeard . .	Salvia	—	18	—	July to Sept.
Trachymene cœrulea	Lace-flower	—	12–30	—	July to Sept.
*Verbena (hybrid vars)	Verbena	—	12–24	—	Summer and Autumn.
*Violas (vars.)	Violas	6	—	—	Summer and Autumn.

NOTE.—* denotes half-hardy species.

160

From a painting by Beatrice Parsons

PLATE 5   *A JULY BORDER AT THE HEIGHT OF FLOWERING*

SOME PLANTS FOR THE BLUE HERBACEOUS BORDER

Perennials

Botanical Name	Common Name	Height in Inches			Time of Flowering
		Up to 12	12 to 36	Over 36	
Aconitum Carmichaelii and Napellus (Deep)	Monkshood	—	—	48–60	June to Oct.
Adenophora liliifolia	Gland Bellflower	—	12–36	—	June to Aug.
Anchusa italica (Dropmore, Opal and Pride of Dover)	Alkanet	—	—	36–50	June to Oct.
Anemone apennina	Anemone	9	—	—	March to May
Aquilegia cærulea	Columbine	—	12–18	—	May to July.
Aster Amellus Framfieldii	Michaelmas Daisies	—	24	—	Autumn.
King George	"	—	24	—	"
Ultramarine	"	—	24–30	—	"
Aster novi-belgii Blue Gown	"	—	—	48–55	"
Climax, Plenty	"	—	—	60	"
Little Boy Blue, The Sexton	"	—	24–30	—	"
Campanula carpatica, var.	Bell Flower	9	—	—	June to Sept.
lactiflora	"	—	—	48–62	June to Aug.
latifolia vars.	"	—	—	48	May to Oct.
persicifolia	"	—	24–30	—	May to Aug.
rotundifolia	Star Blue-bell	12	—	—	May to Oct.
Catananche cœrulea	Cupidone	—	30	—	July to Aug.
Centaurea montana	Knapweed	—	24–30	—	July and Aug.
Ceratostigma plumbaginoides	Lead Wort	9	—	—	Aug. to Oct.
Delphinium vars	Larkspur	—	—	60	July to Aug.
Echinops Ritro	Globe Thistle	—	36	—	Aug. and Sept.
Eryngium alpinum	Sea Holly	—	20–36	—	July to Sept.
amethystinum	"	—	24–30	—	July to Sept.
Bourgatii	"	—	24	—	Aug. to Oct.
planum	"	—	24	—	July to Sept.
Geranium grandiflorum, etc.	Crane's Bill	—	18	—	June to Aug.
Horminum pyrenaicum	Pyrenean Clary	10	—	—	June to Aug.
Iris germanica, vars.	Blue Flag	12	—	—	June.
Limonium Gmelinii and latifolium	Sea Lavender	—	12–24	—	June to Aug.
Linum narbonense		—	12–18	—	June to Aug.
Linum perenne	Perennial Flax	—	12–18	—	May to Oct.
Lithospermum diffusum (Heavenly Blue)	Gromwell	4	—	—	May to Sept.
Lobelia syphilitica	Lobelia	—	24	—	Summer.
Lupinus polyphyllus	Lupins	—	18–36	—	May to July.
Meconopsis betonicifolia		—	—	36–72	Summer.
Mertensia maritima	Oyster Plant	4	—	—	Summer.
Mertensia virginica		—	24	—	April to May.
Myosotis sylvatica (Royal)	Forget-me-Not	12	—	—	Spring and Summer.
Nepeta Faassenii (Mussinii)	Catmint	12	—	—	May to Oct.
Polemonium cœruleum	Jacob's Ladder	12	—	—	Summer.
Pulmonaria angustifolia var. azurea (Gentian Blue)	Lungwort	12	—	—	March.
Salvia pratensis	Meadow Sage	—	—	40	July to Sept.
Salvia uliginosa	Meadow Sage	—	—	48	July to Oct.
Scabiosa caucasica	Scabious	—	18–24	—	June to Sept.
Stokesia lævis	Stoke's Aster	9–12	—	—	Early Autumn.
Tradescantia virginiana	Spiderwort	—	18	—	June to Sept.
Veronica exaltata	Speedwell	—	—	40–48	June to Aug.
longifolia	"	12	—	—	July to Sept.

NOTE.—Shades such as purple, mauve, and lilac are frequently included in the Blue Border. We have compiled a separate list for these variations of blue. For bulbs and shrubs with blue flowers see the separate lists.

THE HERBACEOUS BORDER

SOME PLANTS FOR THE PURPLE, MAUVE, LILAC AND VIOLET HERBACEOUS BORDER

The reader must bear in mind when consulting the following table that seed of many of the plants is invariably sold (mixed colours), and that only by stipulating a special variety and colour, or by growing and preserving his own seed, will he be sure of obtaining the desired results.

The table has been compiled with the object of making it easier to select plants suitable in height, and of the desired colour, for the front, middle, and back of the border. The times of flowering are added so that it is possible to arrange for a continuity of bloom throughout the season.

For further cultural details, see the lists of Half-hardy Annuals, Hardy Annuals, Hardy Herbaceous Perennials, and the A.B.C. section dealing with all the various Flowering Plants, Chapter 34.

Annuals

Botanical Name	Common Name	Up to 12	12 to 36	Over 36	Time of Flowering
Alyssum maritimum, Lilac Queen (L)	Sweet Alyssum	6	—	—	Summer.
*Amarantus caudatus (P)	Love-lies-bleeding	—	12–36	—	July to Oct.
*Callistephus chinensis vars.	China Aster	9–12	12–24	—	Autumn.
Centaurea suaveolens (P)	Sweet Sultan	—	20	—	July to Oct.
Clarkia elegans (P)	Clarkia	—	24	—	July to Oct.
Clarkia pulchella fl. pl. (P)	Clarkia	—	18	—	July to Oct.
Collinsia bicolor (P)	Collin's Flower	12	—	—	May to July or July to Oct.
*Datura fastuosa (P)		—	30	—	July to Sept.
*Datura Tatula (Dp. L.)	Thorn Apple	—	24	—	July to Sept.
Delphiniums vars.	Larkspur	—	12–36	—	June to Sept.
Eucharidium Breweri (LP)		12	—	—	July to Sept.
Gilia tricolor (P)	Gilia	10	—	—	June to Oct.
Iberis umbellata (P)	Candytuft	12	—	—	July to Oct.
Lathyrus odoratus (vars.)	Sweet Pea	—	—	36–72	Aug. to Sept.
Limonium sinuatum (M)	Sea Lavender	—	16	—	July to Oct.
Linaria maroccana (P)	Toadflax	—	18	—	June to Oct.
Lupinus hirsutus (L)	Lupin	—	12–36	—	July to Oct.
Malcomia maritima (L)	Virginian Stock	8	—	—	July to Aug.
Matthiola bicornis (L)	Stock	12	—	—	June to Aug.
*Nemesia versicolor (M)	Nemesia	12	—	—	June to Sept.
Nigella damascena (P)	Love-in-a-mist	—	12–24	—	Summer and Autumn
*Petunia (vars.) (P)	Petunia	8–10	—	—	June to Aug.
Phacelia Whitlavia (P)		—	20	—	Summer and Autumn.
*Salpiglossis sinuata vars. (P)		12	—	—	Summer and Autumn.
*Salvia carduacea (L)		12	—	—	All Summer.
*Scabiosa atropurpurea (L)	Sweet Scabious	—	24–36	—	June to Sept.
*Schizanthus (vars.)	Butterfly Flower	—	18–48	—	June to Oct.
Senecio elegans (P)	Groundsel	12	12–20	—	Summer and Autumn.
*Verbena (vars.)	Verbena	—	12–24	—	All Summer.
*Viola (vars.)	Tufted Pansy	6	—	—	All Summer.
Xeranthemum annuum (P)	Immortelle or Everlasting Flower	12	—	—	July to Sept.

NOTE.—* denotes half-hardy species, and (R), (P), (L), (V) and (M) stand for red, purple, lilac, violet and mauve respectively. For bulbs and shrubs bearing flowers of these colours see the separate lists of Bulbs and Tubers, and of Flowering Shrubs and Trees.

SOME PLANTS FOR THE PURPLE, MAUVE, LILAC AND VIOLET HERBACEOUS BORDER (*continued*)

Perennials

Botanical Name		Common Name	Height in Inches			Time of Flowering
			Up to 12	12 to 36	Over 36	
Acanthus mollis	(L)	Bear's Breech	—	—	40	August.
Althæa rosea vars.		Hollyhock	—	—	72–120	Aug. to Sept.
Antirrhinum vars.		Snapdragon	—	12–36	—	Summer.
Aquilegia vulgaris vars.		Columbine	—	24	—	May to July.
Aster Amellus,		Michaelmas Daisy	—	24	—	Sept. to Oct.
Beauty of Ronsdorf	(LP)					
Amellus Framfieldii	(P)	,,	—	24	—	Sept. to Oct.
cordifolius elegans	(L)	,,	—	—	48	Sept. to Oct.
novæ-angliæ, Ryecroft Purple	(P)	,,	—	—	48	Sept. to Oct.
novi-belgii, Col. Durham	(M)	,,	—	24	—	Sept. to Oct.
novi-belgii, W. S. Churchill	(P)	,,	—	36–45	—	Sept. to Oct.
novi-belgii, Queen of Lilacs	(L)	,,	—	—	48	Sept. to Oct.
novi-belgii, The Archbishop	(P)	,,	—	24	—	Sept. to Oct.
Aubrieta deltoidea vars.		Rock Cress	4	—	—	April to June.
Campanula latifolia macrantha	(P)	Bellflower	—	36	—	June to July.
Chelone Lyonii and obliqua	(P)	Shellflower	—	30–36	—	Late summer.
Chrysanthemum decorative vars.		Chrysanthemum	—	36	—	Autumn.
Corydalis solida	(P)	Fumitory	9	—	—	May.
Delphinium vars.		Larkspur	—	—	36–72	July to Sept.
Dianthus barbatus	(P)	Sweet-william	—	18	—	Summer.
Caryophyllus	(M)	Carnation	—	18	—	Summer.
superbus	(L)	Pink	—	18	—	June and July.
Echinacea purpurea	(R)	Coneflower	—	36	—	Aug. and Sept.
Erigeron speciosus	(PL)	Fleabane	—	30	—	May to Oct.
Eupatorium purpureum	(P)	Hemp Agrimony	—	—	60	Aug. to Oct.
Geranium ibericum vars.	(P)	Crane's Bill	—	12–36	—	June to Sept.
Galega officinalis	(L)	Goat's Rue	—	30–36	—	July to Sept.
Hosta Sieboldiana	(L)	Plantain Lily	—	12–18	—	July to Aug.
Lactuca Bourgæi	(L)		—	—	50	July to Aug.
Limonium latifolia	(L)	Sea Lavender	—	24	—	July to Sept.
Linaria purpurea	(P)	Toadflax	—	12–24	—	June to Oct.
Lupinus polyphyllus vars.		Lupins	—	30–40	—	May to July.
Lythrum virgatum	(R)	Purple Loosestrife	—	36	—	Summer.
Nepeta Faassenii (Mussinii)	(L)	Catmint	12	—	—	May to Oct.
Phlox paniculata—						
var. Antonin Mercie	(L)	Phlox	—	30	—	July to Sept.
var. Iris	(V)	Phlox	—	30	—	July to Sept.
var. Dr. Charcot	(V)	Phlox	—	30	—	July to Sept.
var. Undine	(M)	Phlox	—	36	—	July to Sept.
var. Wm. Ramsay	(P)	Phlox	—	36	—	July to Sept.
Primula Beesiana	(P)	Primula	—	24–30	—	Early summer.
Primula denticulata	(L)	Primula	12	—	—	May to June.
Prunella grandiflora	(P)	Self-heal	6	—	—	Summer.
Scutellaria baicalensis	(P)	Skull-cap	12–15	—	—	May to Sept.
Stachys Betonica var. rosea	(P)	Betony	—	6–24	—	July to Aug.
Stachys grandiflora	(P)	Betony	—	12–18	—	May to July.
Thalictrum aquilegifolium	(P)	Meadow Rue	—	36	—	June to Sept.
Thalictrum dipterocarpum	(P)	,, ,,	—	—	48–72	July.
Verbascum phœniceum	(P)	Mullein	—	18	—	July and Sept.
Viola cornuta	(V)	Viola	6	—	—	Spring and Summer.

NOTE.—(R), (P), (L), (V) and (M) stand for red, purple, lilac, violet and mauve respectively. For bulbs and shrubs bearing flowers of these colours see the separate lists of Bulbs and Tubers, and of Flowering Shrubs and Trees.

SOME PLANTS FOR THE RED HERBACEOUS BORDER

The reader must bear in mind when consulting the following table that seed of many of the plants is invariably sold (mixed colours), and that only by stipulating a special variety and colour, or by growing and preserving his own seed, will he be sure of obtaining the desired results.

The table has been compiled with the object of making it easier to select plants suitable in height, and of the desired colour, for the front, middle, and back of the border. The times of flowering are added so that it is possible to arrange for a continuity of bloom throughout the season.

For further cultural details, see the lists of Half-hardy Annuals, Hardy Annuals, Hardy Herbaceous Perennials, and the A.B.C. section dealing with the various Flowering Plants, Chapter 34.

Annuals

Botanical Name	Common Name	Height in Inches			Time of Flowering
		Up to 12	12 to 36	Over 36	
*Alonsoa linifolia (Scarlet) . .	Mask Flower	—	18	—	July and Aug.
*Alonsoa Warscewiczii	Mask Flower	—	18	—	July and Aug.
Amarantus caudatus and hypochondriacus.	Love-lies-bleeding and Prince's feather	—	12–36	—	July to Oct.
*Anagallis grandiflora	Pimpernel	6	—	—	All Summer.
*Begonia semperflorens vars. .	Begonia	9–12	—	—	June to Sept.
Clarkia elegans (Crimson) . .	Clarkia	—	24	—	July to Oct.
*Cosmos bipinnatus (Crimson) . .	Mexican Aster	—	—	30–70	Summer and Autumn.
*Dianthus chinensis vars. . . .	Pink	9–12	—	—	July to Oct.
Emilia flammea (Orange-scarlet) .	Tassel Flower	—	12–18	—	July to Sept.
Gaillardia pulchella var. Lorenziana .	Blanket Flower	—	12–18	—	July to Oct.
Godetia vars.	Godetia	12	—	—	July to Oct.
Helichrysum bracteatum . . .	Everlastings	—	36	—	July to Oct.
Iberis umbellata	Candytuft	12	—	—	July to Oct.
Kochia trichophylla	Summer Cypress	—	30–36	—	Summer and Autumn.
Lathyrus odoratus vars. . . .	Sweet Pea	—	—	36–72	July to Oct.
Linum grandiflorum var. rubrum .	Carmine Flax	12	—	—	July to Oct.
Lupinus hybridus albus coccineus .	Lupin	—	24–30	—	July to Aug.
Lychnis Haageana	Lychnis	12	—	—	July to Sept.
Malcomia maritima	Virginian Stock	8	—	—	July to Oct.
Malope trifida	Mallow-wort	—	15–24	—	June to Oct.
*Martynia fragrans		12	—	—	July to Sept.
Matthiola annua vars.	Stocks	12	—	—	July to Aug.
*Nicotiana Sanderæ	Tobacco Plant	—	18–30	—	Aug. to Oct.
Papaver Rhœas vars., P. Pavoninum.	Poppy	—	24	—	June to Sept.
*Perilla nankinensis (Purple foliage) .		—	18–24	—	June to Oct.
*Phlox Drummondii	Phlox	12	—	—	June to Oct.
Polygonum orientale (Purple-rose) .	Persicaria	—	30–36	—	July to Oct.
*Portulaca grandiflora	Purslane	6	—	—	July to Sept.
Quamoclit cardinalis			Climber		July to Sept.
Quamoclit lobata			Climber		July to Oct.
Reseda odorata	Mignonette	9	—	—	July to Aug.
*Salpiglossis sinuata vars. . . .		—	18	—	July to Sept.
*Salvia coccinea	Scarlet Sage	—	18–24	—	June to Sept.
Saponaria calabrica (Rosy) . . .	Soapwort	6	—	—	June to Oct.
*Scabiosa atropurpurea	Sweet Scabious	—	24–36	—	All Summer.
*Schizanthus Grahamii, S. retusus .	Butterfly Flower	—	18–48	36–48	June to Sept.
Tropæolum majus and nanum vars. .	Nasturtium	12	—	—	July to Sept.
*Verbena (Scarlet and Crimson vars.).	Verbena	—	12–24	—	Summer and Autumn.

NOTE.—* denotes half-hardy species.

SOME PLANTS FOR THE RED HERBACEOUS BORDER (*continued*)

Perennials

Botanical Name	Common Name	Height in Inches			Time of Flowering
		Up to 12	12 to 36	Over 36	
Asclepias tuberosa	Butterfly Weed	12	—	—	July to Sept.
Althæa rosea	Hollyhocks	—	—	72–120	Aug. to Sept.
Alstromeria hæmantha	Peruvian Lily	—	30–36	—	May to Aug.
Anemone fulgens (Scarlet)	Anemone	6–12	—	—	May to June.
Antirrhinum majus vars.	Snapdragon	—	12–36	—	Summer.
Armeria latifolia	Giant Thrift	12	—	—	May to July.
Aster novæ-angliæ, Mrs. J. F. Rayner	Michaelmas Daisy	—	—	36–72	Sept. to Oct.
Aster novi-belgii, Red Rover	„	—	—	36–72	Sept. to Oct.
Aster novi-belgii Beechwood Challenger	„	—	—	36–72	Sept. to Oct.
Aster novi-belgii, The Cardinal	„	—	—	36–72	Sept. to Oct.
Astilbe Arendsii vars. Fanal and W. Reeves	Goat's Beard	—	12–24	—	May to Sept.
Aubrieta deltoidea var. Vindictive	Rock Cress	4	—	—	Spring.
Bellis perennis var. monstrosa	Daisy	6	—	—	April to June.
Cheiranthus Cheiri vars.	Wallflower	—	18–24	—	April to June
Chrysanthemum decorative vars. and coccineum vars.	Chrysanthemum	—	18–36	—	Autumn.
Delphinium cardinale	Larkspur	—	18–36	—	June to Aug.
Delphinium nudicaule	Larkspur	12	—	—	May and June.
Dianthus barbatus	Sweet-william	—	18	—	Summer.
Dianthus Caryophyllus	Carnation	—	18	—	Summer.
Dianthus plumarius	Pinks	8	—	—	June.
Dictamnus albus, var. purpureus	Burning Bush	—	30	—	June to Aug.
Echinacea purpurea	Coneflower	—	36	—	Aug. and Sept.
Erodium Manescavii (Purple)	Heron's-bill	—	12–18	—	Summer.
Filipendula palmata (Crimson)	Meadow Sweet	—	24	—	July and Aug.
Fuchsia Riccartonii	Fuchsia	—	36	—	Summer.
Gaillardia vars.	Blanket Flower	—	30	—	May to July.
Geranium armenum	Crane's Bill	6–12	12–36	—	June to Sept.
Geum coccineum, var. Mrs. Bradshaw (Bright), etc.	Avens	—	24	—	May to July.
Helenium cupreum	Sneezeweed	—	18–24	—	July to Sept.
Helenium Riverton Gem	Sneezeweed	—	—	36–40	July to Oct.
Heuchera sanguinea (Scarlet)	Alum Root	—	18	—	May to Sept.
Incarvillea Delavayi (Rosy)	Incarvillea	—	24	—	June to Aug.
Kentranthus ruber	Valerian	—	24	—	Summer.
Kniphofia uvaria vars.	Red Hot Pokers	—	—	48	June to Oct.
Lathyrus grandifolius (Rosy Red)	Perennial Sweet Pea	—	—	48–96	Summer.
Lobelia cardinalis (Crimson)	Cardinal Flower	—	24	—	Summer.
Lobelia fulgens (Scarlet)	Lobelia	—	30	—	Summer.
Lychnis chalcedonica (Scarlet)	Jerusalem Cross	—	30	—	June to Sept.
Lychnis fulgens (Scarlet)	Campion	6–12	—	—	June to Sept.
Mimulus cardinalis (Scarlet)	Monkey Flower	—	24	—	June and July.
Monarda didyma (Scarlet)	Bee's Balm	—	36	—	June to Sept.
Pæonia officinalis flore plena	Pæony	—	30	—	May.
Pæonia tenuifolia	„	—	30	—	May.
Papaver orientale vars.	Oriental Poppy	—	24–30	—	May and June.
Penstemons vars.	Beard Tongue	—	18–30	—	June to Oct.
Phlox paniculata vars. Blake Amos, Spitfire and New Bird	Flame Flower	—	15–30	—	July to Sept.
Polygonum amplexicaule	Knot Weed	—	24–30	—	July to Oct.
Potentilla atrosanguinea	Cinquefoil	—	24	—	June to Sept.
Saxifraga decipiens hybrids	Rockfoil	6	—	—	May.
Tradescantia virginica rubra	Spiderwort	—	20	—	June to Sept.

NOTE.—For bulbs and shrubs with red flowers, see the separate lists of Bulbs and Tubers, and of Trees and Shrubs.

PLANTS FOR THE PINK, ROSE AND SALMON HERBACEOUS BORDER

The reader must bear in mind when consulting the following table that seed of many of the plants is invariably sold (mixed colours), and that only by stipulating a special variety and colour, or by growing and preserving his own seed, will he be sure of obtaining the desired results. For further cultural details, see the lists of Half-hardy Annuals, Hardy Annuals, Hardy Herbaceous Perennials, and the A.B.C. section of Flowering Plants, Chapter 34.

Annuals

Botanical Name	Common Name	Height in Inches			Time of Flowering
		Up to 12	12 to 36	Over 36	
*Abronia umbellata (R-Pk)	Sand Verbena	6–12	—	—	Summer.
*Begonia semperflorens vars. (P)	Begonia	9–12	—	—	June to Sept.
Clarkia elegans (R and S)	Clarkia	—	24	—	July to Oct.
*Cosmos bipinnatus (P)	Mexican Aster	—	—	30–70	June to Oct.
Delphinium Gayanum, syn. Ajacis (P)	Larkspur	—	30	—	June to Sept.
*Dianthus vars. (P)	Pink	9–12	—	—	July to Oct.
Godetia vars. (P and S)	Godetia	—	12–24	—	July to Oct.
Iberis umbellata vars. (P)	Candytuft	12	—	—	July to Oct.
Impatiens Balsamina	Balsam	—	18	—	June to Aug.
Lathyrus odoratus vars.	Sweet Pea	—	—	36–72	July to Oct.
Lavatera trimestris vars. (R)	Mallow	—	30–36	36–60	July to Oct.
Limonium sinuatum, var. roseum (R)	Sea Lavender	—	18	—	June to Oct.
Lupinus subcarnosus	Lupin	—	12–36	36–48	June to Oct.
Malope trifida (R)	Mallow-wort	—	20	—	June to Oct.
Matthiola incana vars.	Stock	12	—	—	July and Aug.
*Nicotiana Sanderæ	Tobacco Plant	—	30	—	Late Summer.
Papaver Rhœas vars.	Poppy	—	24	—	June to Sept.
Petunia vars		12	—	—	June to Oct.
*Phlox Drummondii vars. (P)	Phlox	12	—	—	June to Oct.
Saponaria calabrica (P)	Soapwort	6	—	—	June to Sept.
*Schizanthus retusus (R)		—	—	18–48	June to Oct.
Senecio elegans (R, P and S)	Groundsel	—	12–20	—	July to Oct.
Tropæolum majus and minus vars	Nasturtium	12	—	—	Summer and Autumn.
*Verbena hybrida vars.	Verbena	—	12–24	—	
Xeranthemum annuum (R)	Immortelle	12	—	—	July to Sept.
*Zinnia elegans vars. (R)	Zinnia	12	—	—	July to Sept.

NOTE.—* denotes half-hardy species. (P), (R) and (S) signify pink, rose and salmon respectively.

Perennials

Botanical Name	Common Name	Height in Inches			Time of Flowering
		Up to 12	12 to 36	Over 36	
Acanthus latifolius, etc. (R)	Bear's breech	—	24	—	Summer.
Althæa rosea vars.	Hollyhock	—	—	72–120	Aug. to Sept.
Anemone Hepatica var. rosea (P)	Hepatica	6	—	—	March to May.
Anemone hybrida (japonica) (R)	Jap. Anemone	—	36	—	Aug. to Sept.
Antirrhinum vars.	Snapdragon	9–12	12–36	—	Summer.
Aster Amellus—					
General Pershing (P)	Michaelmas Daisy	—	24	—	Sept to Oct.
Jacqueline Genebrier (P)	,,	—	24–30	—	,,
Aster novæ-angliæ—					
Barr's Pink (P)	,,	—	36–48	—	,,
Lil Fardel (P)	,,	—	—	48–55	,,

PLANTS FOR THE PINK, ROSE AND SALMON HERBACEOUS BORDER (*contd.*)

Perennials

Botanical Name	Common Name	Up to 12	12 to 36	Over 36	Time of Flowering
Aster novi-belgii—					
Heather Glow (RP)	Michaelmas Daisy	—	36	—	Sept to Oct.
Prosperity (R)	,,	—	24–30	—	,,
Gay border Supreme (R)	,,	—	24–30	—	,,
Little Pink Lady (P)	,,	—	24–30	—	,,
Astilbe Arendsii vars. Rheinland (SP)	Spiræa	—	24–36	—	May to June.
Astilbe Meta Immink (P)	False Spiræa	—	24–36	—	May to June.
Aubrieta (Bridesmaid) (P)	Rock Cress	4	—	—	April to June.
Bellis perennis vars. monstrosa (P)	Daisy	6	—	—	April to June.
Bergenia crassifolia B. lingulata (P)	Rockfoil	10	—	—	May.
Centaurea dealbata (P)	Knapweed	—	24	—	July and Aug.
Chelone Lyonii (Rosy Purple)	Shellflower	—	—	40	July to Sept.
Chrysanthemum decorative vars.	Chrysanthemum	—	36	—	Autumn.
Corydalis solida (R)	Fumitory	9	—	—	May.
Dianthus barbatus vars. (P and S)	Sweet-william	—	18	—	Summer.
Dianthus Caryophyllus	Carnation	—	18	—	Summer.
Dicentra spectabilis (P)	Lyre Flower	—	24–30	—	May to July.
Eremurus Elwesianus (R)	King's Spear	—	—	96	June.
Eremurus robustus (P)	King's Spear	—	—	96	June.
Erigeron B. Ladhams (R)	Fleabane	—	24	—	May to Sept.
Gaura Lindheimeri (R)	Gaura	—	—	40	June to Oct.
Geranium Endressii (R)	Crane's Bill	12	—	—	May to Sept.
Gillenia trifoliata (R)		—	24	—	July to Aug.
Heuchera tiarelloides (P)	Alum Root	—	24	—	June to July.
Heuchera Zabeliana (R)	Alum Root	—	18	—	July to Oct.
Incarvillea Delavayi (R)	Incarvillea	—	12–24	—	June to Aug.
Kentranthus ruber	Valerian	—	24	—	Summer.
Lathyrus grandiflorus (R)	Perennial Pea	—	—	45–84	Summer.
Lavatera Olbia rosea (R)	Mallow	—	—	48–60	June to Aug.
Lupinus polyphyllus vars. (R)	Lupin	—	36	—	June to Oct.
Lychnis fulgens (S)	Campion	12	—	—	Summer.
Lychnis Viscaria fl. pl. (R)	Catchfly	9–12	—	—	June and July.
Lythrum Salicaria roseum (R)	Purple Loosestrife	—	—	36–48	July to Aug.
Malva Alcea fastigiata (P)	Mallow	—	36	—	July to Sept.
Malva moschata (R)	Marsh Mallow	—	30	—	Summer.
Pæonia officinalis vars. rosea	Peony	—	20–36	36–48	May to July.
Papaver oriental var. Mrs. Perry (SP)	Oriental Poppy	—	24–30	—	May and June.
Penstemon vars.	Beard Tongue	—	18	—	July to Oct.
Phlox paniculata vars. Salmon Glow, P. D. Williams (P), and Elizabeth Campbell (SP)	Phlox	12–18	24–30	36–40	July to Sept.
Phlox subulata vars. (P)	Moss Pink	4	—	—	Early Summer.
Polygonum campanulatum (P)	Knotweed	—	24–30	—	Autumn.
Potentilla Miss Willmott (P)	Cinquefoil	—	18	—	June to Sept.
Poterium obtusum (R)	Burnet	—	30	—	July to Sept.
Primula cortusoides (Rose)	Primula	10	—	—	June.
Saponaria officinalis (Rose)	Soapwort	—	12–18	—	July to Aug.
Saponaria ocymoides (R)	Soapwort	6	—	—	May to July.
Saxifraga decipiens hybrida (R)	Rockfoil	6	—	—	May and June.
Sedum Anacampseros (Pink)	Evergreen Orpine	10	—	—	Summer.
Sidalcea, Rosy Gem (R)	Sidalcea	—	30–36	—	June to Sept.
Stachys Betonica var. rosea (R)	Betony	—	12–18	—	May to July.
Thalictrum aquilegifolium	Meadow Rue	—	—	36–60	June to Sept.
Verbascum phœniceum (R)	Mullein	—	18	—	July to Sept.
Veronica longifolia rosea (R)	Speedwell	—	24–30	—	June to Aug.

NOTE.—(P), (R), (S) stand for pink, rose and salmon respectively. For bulbs and shrubs, see separate lists.

PLANTS FOR THE YELLOW HERBACEOUS BORDER

The reader must bear in mind when consulting the following table that seed of many of the plants is invariably sold (mixed colours), and that only by stipulating a special variety and colour, or by growing and preserving his own seed, will he be sure of obtaining the desired results. The table has been compiled with the object of making it easier to select plants suitable in height, and of the desired colour, for the front, middle, and back of the border. The times of flowering are added so that it is possible to arrange for a continuity of bloom throughout the season.

For further cultural details, see the lists of Half-hardy Annuals, Hardy Annuals, Hardy Herbaceous Perennials, and the A.B.C. section dealing with the various Flowering Plants, Chapter 34.

Annuals

Botanical Name	Common Name	Height in Inches			Time of Flowering
		Up to 12	12 to 36	Over 36	
Arnebia cornuta	Prophet Flower	12	—	—	July to Sept.
Calendula officinalis	Pot Marigold	—	18	—	June to Oct.
*Celosia plumosa aurea . . .	Prince of Wales' Feathers	—	20	—	August.
Centaurea suaveolens . .	Sweet Sultan	—	20	—	July to Oct.
Chrysanthemum coronarium (Golden Queen)	Chrysanthemum	12	—	—	July to Oct.
Chrysanthemum segetum vars. .	Chrysanthemum	12	—	—	July to Oct.
Coreopsis Drummondii . . .	Tickseed	12	—	—	July to Sept.
Erysimum Perofskianum . . .	Hedge Mustard	—	12-18	—	July to Oct.
Eschscholzia caespitosa, E. californica	Californian Poppy	9-12	—	—	Early Summer & July to Oct.
Helianthus annuus	Sunflower	—	18-36	36-90	July to Oct.
Helichrysum bracteatum (yellow var.)	Everlasting Flowers	—	36	—	July to Oct.
Hibiscus africanus	Mallow	—	24	—	July to Sept.
Layia elegans	Tidy Tips	10	—	—	July to Sept.
Leptosyne Stillmannii . . .		12	—	—	July to Sept.
Limnanthes Douglasii . . .		3-6	—	—	Summer.
*Limonium Bonduelli	Sea Lavender	12	—	—	Summer and Autumn.
Linaria Broussonetii . . .	Toadflax	—	12-18	—	July to Oct.
Lupinus luteus	Lupin	—	24	—	June to Oct.
Matthiola incana vars. . . .	Stock	12	—	—	July to Aug.
Mentzelia Lindleyi . . .		—	12-15	—	June to Oct.
Nemesia strumosa vars. . . .	Nemesia	9-12	—	—	July to Sept.
*Oxalis valdivensis	Wood Sorrel	8	—	—	Summer and Autumn.
Papaver nudicaule var. . . .	Iceland Poppy	12	—	—	July to Sept.
Platystemon californicus . .	Cream Cup	4	—	—	June to Aug.
Portulaca grandiflora, Yellow var. .	Rock Purslane	4	—	—	Aug. & Sept.
Reseda odorata (Golden) . . .	Mignonette	9	—	—	July to Aug.
Sphenogyne anthemoides, erithmifolia and pulchera		6-12	—	—	July to Aug.
*Tagetes erecta	African Marigold	—	20-30	—	Late Summer & Autumn.
*Tagetes patula	French Marigold	6-9	24	—	Late Summer & Autumn.
Tropæolum majus and nanum .	Nasturtium	12	—	—	July to Oct.
Venidium calendulaceum . .		9	—	—	July to Sept.
*Viola vars.	Tufted Pansy	6	—	—	All Summer.
*Waitzia aurea	Everlasting Flowers	—	18	—	July to Sept.
Zinnia elegans (Yellow and Orange)	Zinnia	—	18-24	—	} Summer and
Zinnia Haageana (Orange) . .	Zinnia	12	—	—	Autumn.

Note.—* denotes half-hardy species.

PLANTS FOR THE YELLOW HERBACEOUS BORDER (*continued*)
Perennials

Botanical Name	Common Name	Height in Inches			Time of Flowering
		Up to 12	12 to 36	Over 36	
Asclepias tuberosa (Orange) . .	Butterfly Weed	12	—	—	July to Sept.
Achillea filipendulina	Milfoil	—	—	36–40	July to Oct.
Adonis vernalis	Pheasant's Eye	10	—	—	Spring.
Althæa rosea	Hollyhock	—	—	72–120	Aug. to Sept.
Anemone various	Anemone	9–12	12–18	—	Summer.
Anthemis tinctoria Kelwayi. . .	Chamomile	—	24	—	June to Oct.
Antirrhinum majus vars. . . .	Snapdragon	9–12	12–36	—	Summer.
Aquilegia chrysantha and longissima	Columbine	—	30	—	May to July.
Asphodeline lutea	Asphodel	—	24–36	—	May to July.
Buphthalmum salicifolium . . .	Ox-eye	—	24	—	July to Sept.
Centaurea babylonica C. macrocephala	Knapweed	—	—	48–72	July to Aug.
Cephalaria tatarica		—	24–30	—	June to Aug.
Cheiranthus alpinus	Wallflower	6	—	—	Summer.
Cheiranthus Cheiri vars. . . .	Wallflower	—	18–24	—	April to June
Chrysanthemum vars.	Chrysanthemum	—	24–36	—	Autumn.
Coreopsis lanceolata	Tickseed	—	24–30	—	July to Sept.
Corydalis nobilis	Fumitory	9–12	—	—	May.
Delphinium sulphureum . . .	Larkspur	—	24–30	—	July to Aug.
Dianthus Caryophyllus . . .	Carnation	—	18	—	Summer.
Doronicum plantagineum . . .	Leopard's Bane	—	24–36	—	March-May.
Eremurus spectabilis	King's Spear	—	24	—	June.
Gaillardia grandiflora var. . . .	Blanket Flower	—	30	—	May to July.
Geum, Lady Stratheden, etc. . .	Avens	—	18–24	—	May to July.
Helenium autumnale, var. superbum,	Sneezeweed	—	20–30	—	July to Oct.
Helianthus multiflorus major . . } Perennial Sunflower		—	—	60	Aug. to Oct.
Helianthus rigidus vars. . . .		—	—	84	Aug. to Oct.
Heliopsis scabra		—	—	40–48	Aug. to Sept.
Hemerocallis flava and vars. . .	Day Lily	—	30	—	June to Aug.
Hypericum olympicum. . . .	St. John's Wort	10	—	—	June to Sept.
Inula grandiflora (Orange) . . .	Fleabane	—	18–24	—	July to Sept.
Iris aurea I. germanica vars., etc..	Iris	—	—	36–48	June to July.
Kniphofia Uvaria and Goldelse .	Red Hot Poker	—	30	—	June to Oct.
Ligularia clivorum, etc. . . .	Groundsel	—	—	48	July to Sept.
Linaria dalmatica	Toad Flax	—	30	—	June to Sept.
Linum flavum	Flax	10	—	—	Summer.
Lupinus arboreus	Tree Lupin	—	—	60	May to July.
Lysimachia vulgaris	Loosestrife	—	24–36	—	Summer.
Meconopsis cambrica	Welsh Poppy	12	—	—	Summer.
Mimulus moschatus	Musk	6	—	—	July to Oct.
Œnothera biennis	Evening Primrose	—	—	60	June to Sept.
Pæonia lutea, P. Mlokosewitchii .	Pæony	—	24–36	—	May to June.
Papaver nudicaule var.. . . .	Iceland Poppy	6–12	—	—	May to Sept.
Potentilla recta	Cinquefoil	—	24–30	—	June to Aug.
Primula helodoxa and luteola . .	Primula	12	—	—	May.
Rudbeckia speciosa	Cone Flower	—	24	—	July to Sept.
Rudbeckia laciniata fl. pl. . . .	Cone Flower	—	—	60	Aug. to Sept.
Solidago canadense, etc. . . .	Golden Rod	—	—	48–100	Aug. to Oct.
Solidaster luteus		—	24–30	—	July to Sept.
Thalictrum flavum	Meadow Rue	—	36	—	June to Sept.
Thalictrum glaucum	Meadow Rue	—	—	60	June to July.
Thermopsis montana	False Lupin	—	24–30	—	June and July.
Trollius europæus and Canary Bird	Globe Flower	12	—	—	May and June.
Verbascum longifolium, V. Lagurus .	Mullein	—	—	60–70	June to Sept.
Viola vars.	Viola	6	—	—	May to Nov.

NOTE.—For bulbs and shrubs with yellow flowers, see the separate lists.

CHAPTER 17

BULB CULTURE

Details of the special management of all the more important bulbs, such as crocus, hyacinth, daffodil, tulip, and gladiolus, are given under their respective headings. The general treatment of bulbs is much the same, however, and it will be sufficient for our present purpose to describe this broadly, any special points being discussed under their separate headings.

WHAT IS A BULB?

The term *bulb* is really applicable only to roots such as the hyacinth, which grows in successive coats superimposed one over the other, and the lily, which is formed of scales growing one over the other, as tiles are placed on the roof of a house. Bulbs following the formation of the hyacinth are said to be "tunicated" bulbs, and those following the formation of the lily are said to be "imbricated". From this it is evident that snowdrops, daffodils, etc., which are similar in construction to the hyacinth, and all that possess the scale-like formation of the lily are genuine bulbs. In a strict sense the crocus, the gladiolus, the cyclamen, and other fleshy roots of bulbous forms which have not the construction of either of the classes just described are not really bulbs. But having the exterior appearance of bulbs, they are commonly accepted as such. If the root, say, of a crocus is divided in any way, whether from top to bottom or transversely from side to side, it will be found that it is a fleshy root without any division whatever in the interior like the hyacinth, but consists of one mass throughout like the potato. It differs, however, from the potato in that the roots by which nourishment is drawn from the soil are sent forth anew each year from a ring or circular patch at the base of the bulb, and not from eyes, as in the potato, from which stalk and roots both proceed, the former in an upward direction and the latter downwards. Fleshy masses like the gladiolus and crocus are called *corms* to distinguish them from the tunicated bulb of the hyacinth and from the scaly bulb of the lily. Masses like the potato are called tubers.

BULBS IN BEDS AND BORDERS

The generality of bulbs are of the easiest cultivation, needing but to be planted in the early autumn at about two or three times their own depth, in reasonably good and light garden soil, with which a good amount of

170

leaf-mould has been mixed. They should be planted at a uniform depth, which, naturally, varies with the kind of bulb, and should not come into contact with recent manure. Good drainage is essential. If the soil is inclined to be at all heavy, it is desirable to lighten it by working in sand at and around each spot in which a clump of bulbs is to be placed. Bulbs, as a rule, should be planted deeply, rather than shallowly, especially crocuses, gladioli, and lilies, because the bulbs are then less likely to suffer from the effects of frost.

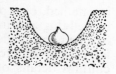

FIG. 29. CORRECT WAY OF PLANTING A BULB The hole for the bulb should be scraped out with a trowel—not made with a dibber.

Plant the bulbs as early in the autumn as possible, especially the spring-flowering ones. They then have ample time to develop their roots before the strain of flowering makes its demands on them. Early planting promotes larger blooms. It is advisable always to plant the bulbs with a trowel, and to press them firmly, but gently, into the earth before they are covered up. Never plant bulbs with a dibber; this makes a narrow "V"-shaped hole in which it is difficult to set the bulb straight and in which unless the soil is sandy, an air space, which will parch the roots, will be left.

Most bulbs, having been planted in suitable soil at a reasonable distance apart, may be allowed to remain for several years without being taken up, divided, and replanted. But there are certain exceptions. Tulips and hyacinths, for example, should be lifted when the leaves die down, being carefully dried, stored in a cool dry place, and replanted in October and September respectively.

Some Individual Requirements

Ranunculuses and anemones should be planted in fairly rich, deep soil early in February, being placed about three inches apart in drills five inches apart; the drills being made about three inches deep, an inch of soil being loosely spread along their bottoms, and the roots pressed therein. These bulbs should be taken up as soon as the leaves die down. Gladioli again should be lifted in autumn and planted in April. But, as a general rule, we may take it that the shorter time bulbs are out of the ground each year the better, and care should be exercised that the bulbs do not become excessively dry or warm; rather should they be kept *in a cool place* so long as they do not suffer from damp. Lilies of the valley should only be taken up at intervals of a few years. They should have beds to themselves, in a shady part of the garden, and each year the plants

FIG. 30. INCORRECT WAY OF PLANTING A BULB If the bulb is planted with a dibber, the inevitable air-space beneath the bulb will parch the roots.

171

in one bed, or a part of a bed, should be lifted and the crowns replanted in well-dug and moderately enriched soil. Nothing else should be grown in a bed occupied by these flowers. Of the lilies proper the number is very large, and different kinds call for special treatment. For individual cultural details of the various bulbs, *see* the A.B.C. of Plants, page 255.

Manure

Bonemeal is a good artificial manure for bulbs, and should be dusted round the bulbs at the rate of 2 oz. to the square yard and well forked in in February. An equal amount of superphosphate may, with advantage, be added at the same time.

Removing Withered Foliage

No attempt should be made to remove leaves or flower-stalks until they have withered and decayed to such an extent that they may be pulled away by a very slight effort. The long, sword-like leaves of crocuses, hyacinths, etc., should be allowed to remain until they are quite decayed. The dead flowers ought to be cut off just below the spike of bloom, unless it is wished to save the seed. This holds good for all bulbs that have a woody or strong flower stem.

Lifting and Storing the Bulbs

When the leaves have completely died away, but not before, bulbs may be taken up and allowed to dry. When the tops are dry and withered, they should be cut off an inch above the bulbs, and the roots should also be cut away. The bulbs should then be kept in a dry, dark, and frost-proof place, to which the air has free access, until the time for planting comes round again. This commences in September for hyacinths, etc., and ends in March or April for late-flowering varieties of the gladiolus, the period of planting being regulated in a degree by the period of flowering. When bulbs have to be lifted to make room for summer bedding before the foliage is dead or the bulbs fully matured, they should be "heeled-in" in a sunny position in the reserve garden and when quite matured should be lifted and stored.

Taking up the Bulbs

This, briefly, is the accepted creed with regard to the culture of bulbs, and for sale purposes it is absolutely necessary that bulbs shall be taken up when their leaves are withered and dried, so that transit from place to place may be effected when they are in this condition. They must be without tender and succulent rootlets; otherwise they will suffer injury by removal and carriage. But in the amateur's garden bulbs may be allowed to remain where they are from year's end to year's end, provided that the soil is suitable, the drainage sufficient, and that they are planted deeply. (*See individual cultural details in* Alphabetical List, chapter 34.) Bulbs have a tendency to rise to the surface, especially corms, for in the crocus and gladiolus, though not in the cyclamen, the new corms are formed every year on the top of the old corms which perish. The continuance of bulbs in the places in which they are first planted leads to the formation of splendid masses, from which rise glorious flower spikes.

Various spring bedding schemes for planting bulbs are given on page 148. Here will be found a list of dwarf plants that will form a suitable ground-work, and that will harmonize in colour with the bulbs.

BULBS GROWN IN THE GRASS

Most of our spring bulbs are far more beautiful when viewed in their natural surroundings among the grass and in the meadows, woodlands, or wild garden, than when planted, however naturally and artistically, in borders. Most of them, too, especially daffodils, crocuses, and scillas, do much better in this natural state than in beds or borders.

Do not plant them on lawns, as the grass cannot be cut until the leaves of the bulbs have turned yellow and dried up, which means an untidy lawn for a considerable period, and even when cut, one that suffers from the necessary neglect in spring and early summer. Another word of caution; do not plant daffodils in pastureland, they are poisonous to cattle.

Bulbs to be naturalized in grass are best planted in long, narrow, oval strips some 30 to 40 feet in length, shaped like patches of snow driven by the wind into long slender drifts on the ground. They should be scattered on the grass over an area shaped as above, so that they lie thicker towards the centre of the "drift", and should be planted with a trowel or bulb planter just where they fall. There should be no regular, well-defined margin to the "drift"; the edges should be indistinct and merging gradually into the surrounding grass.

August and September is the best planting time. Small bulbs, like the crocus and scilla, should be set some 3 inches apart, while daffodil bulbs should have about 10 inches between them. Bulbs that have been used for beds and borders are equally as good as new bulbs for naturalizing in grass, and should be replanted immediately after being lifted from the beds and while their foliage is still green and succulent. Although they will not carry the numbers of flowers that new bulbs would have done in their first year, they will soon recover and produce their blooms freely.

Some seven years at least, may be allowed to elapse before it is necessary to disturb naturalized bulbs, provided they receive an annual top-dressing of leaf-mould each autumn.

For bulbs most suitable for planting in grass, *see* p. 176.

173

BULBS GROWN IN POTS

These should be planted in autumn and the crowns should just appear above the surface of the soil, which must come up to within ¾ inch of the top of the pot. After planting, the pots should we well soaked in water and placed in the open on boards or slates, so that worms cannot get up into the soil. The pots should be surrounded and covered with a layer of 5 inches of fibre or ashes, which maintains equable conditions at the root, and does away with frequent watering. They should then be left alone for seven to nine weeks, until the roots will have formed and the tops have made an inch of growth, when they may be moved to a frame or a cold greenhouse, if the roots have made sufficient growth, and should be liberally supplied with water, but not saturated. The less forward plants should be put back in the ashes, and will furnish a succession of later blooms if brought into the greenhouse at successive intervals. The darkness encourages good root growth, which is so essential. Bulbs should never be forced on before their roots have developed sufficiently.

The pots must not be subjected to full light until two or three days after the covering of fibre has been removed, that is, until the pale yellow shoots have turned green. When this has happened, the pots should be placed close to the glass, and should be brought on gradually till the flower buds are well advanced, when liquid manure-water may be used and the plants forced on with moderate heat. A good compost consists of a mixture of equal parts of loam, leaf-mould, and well-rotted cow-manure, together with a little sand.

As to the number of bulbs that may be planted in a pot, this, of course, depends on the species of bulb and on the size of the pot used. Snow-drops, crocuses, and scilla may be planted so that they practically touch one another, that is, about nine bulbs in a 5-inch pot; larger bulbs, such as those of the daffodil and tulip, may be planted six in a 5-inch pot; while only three hyacinths should be grown in a 6-inch pot.

Depth to Plant

The bulbs of the daffodil, hyacinth, tulip, and similar flowers should be potted so that their tips are just above the surface of the soil; a few other bulbs should only be half-buried; while others, again, must be set one, three, or even more inches below the surface. Crocuses and scilla, for instance, should be just covered with soil. For the depth to plant each species of bulb, *see* the *Alphabetical List of Flowering Plants*, Chapter 34.

After forcing, which cannot be done for more than one year running, bulbs may be planted out in borders or used for naturalizing. They should be dried off and planted out in July or August. The year after forcing, the bloom may not be very fine, but in subsequent years a wealth of bloom will be provided.

BULBS GROWN IN FIBRE

When growing bulbs in this way in small numbers, it is obvious that it is false economy to buy any but the best bulbs for treatment. It is waste of time, labour, and space, to grow small weak plants, some of which may not flower at all. In ordering the bulbs, it is best to tell the people from whom they are procured that they are required for this form of culture, and they will select suitable bulbs. At the same time order the fibre, which will be found on experiment to be the best material for filling the bulb bowls. These latter should be simple in shape and colour, so that they will not distract attention from or clash with the flowers growing in them, and should be shallow, some 5 inches deep, and glazed. Porous bowls are not good. Mixed with the fibre will be found a certain proportion of lumps of charcoal, and a few of them should be placed at the bottom of the bowl. If the fibre is at all lumpy, pick it over and rub out the lumps between the fingers, then soak it for a day or so and drain it thoroughly until only a drop or two of water comes out when the fibre is squeezed in the hand. Then fill your bowls to a depth of about one-half for large bulbs, such as the narcissus and hyacinth; three-quarters for the smaller, such as crocuses and scillas. On this layer, which should not be pressed down too tightly, place your bulbs. If the bowl is very large, group them in small clumps, do not space them regularly over it; if it is small, the bulbs may nearly, but not quite touch. Then fill the bowl nearly to the top with the fibre, so that the extreme tips of the bulbs just show above it.

The bowls should be kept for the first six weeks in a dark place, preferably an airy one, and certainly not near a fire. A cool, airy cupboard or cellar will do. Once a week or so examine the bowls to see whether the fibre is dry, and if it shows signs of dryness plunge them in a tub or basin of lukewarm water, which should cover them completely. When the fibre is well soaked, take out the bowls and turn them carefully sideways, so that any superfluous water may drain off. While this is being done, care must be taken that the whole of the contents of the bowl do not fall out; the fibre should be supported by the open hand during the operation. The fibre should be just damp, never sodden. When the bulbs have made shoots about an inch long, the bowls should be brought out into the light, but they should not be exposed to full air and sunshine until the shoots have turned a healthy green. While this is happening, the bowls should be kept in a shady corner of the room. When the shoots are green, the more light and air they have the better, but when they are placed in a window they should always be removed to the middle of the room if there is the smallest likelihood of a frost during the night. It should also be remembered that the plants will naturally grow towards the light, so that to ensure good straight plants and flower stalks, the bowls should be turned each day. No manure should be used.

175

SOME OF THE BEST BULBS AND TUBERS

NOTE.—For Cultural Details, for Colour, Height, Season of Flowering and the best Species and Varieties, *see* the A.B.C. of Plants, page 255.

*Agapanthus orientalis
Allium species
Alstrœmeria aurantiaca
Amaryllis Belladonna
Anemone (tuberous vars.)
Antholyza paniculata
Begonia (tuberous vars.)
Brodiæa species
Bulbocodium vernum
Calochortus species
Camassia species
Chionodoxa Luciliæ and vars.
Colchicum species and vars.
Commelina cœlestis
Convallaria majalis
Corydalis solida
Crinum species
Crocus species and vars.
Cyclamen species
Dicentra spectabilis

Eranthis hyemalis
Erythronium species
Fritillaria species
Galanthus (Snowdrop) species.
Gladioli vars.
*Gloxinia vars.
*Habranthus pratensis
Hyacinth vars.
Iris vars.
*Ixia vars.
*Ixiolirion montanum
Lapeyrousia cruenta
Leucojum æstivum
Lilium species
*Mirabilis Jalapa
Muscari species and vars.
Narcissus vars.
Nerine sarniensis (Guernsey Lily)

Ornithogalum species
Oxalis species
Pancratium illyricum
Paradisia Liliastrum
*Phædranassa chloracea
Polygonatum multiflorum
Puschkinia scilloides
Ranunculus vars.
Schizostylis coccinea
Scilla species
*Sparaxis tricolor
Sternbergia lutea
Tigridia vars.
Trillium grandiflorum
Tritonia (Montbretia) vars.
Tulips vars.
*Vallota purpurea eximia
*Watsonia Meriana var. Ardernei
Zephyranthes candida

NOTE.—* denotes half-hardy bulbs or tubers only suitable for growing in the open in warm, sheltered situations or in the greenhouse. For Rock Garden subjects, see page 198.

For Growing in Pots or Pans

Achimenes vars.
Agapanthus orientalis
Allium neapolitanum
Brodiæa species
Calochortus species
Chionodoxa Luciliæ and vars.
Clivia miniata
Convallaria majalis
Crocus vars
Freesia species and vars.
Fritillaria meleagris, etc.
Galanthus (Snowdrop) species
Gladioli vars.

Hyacinthus azureus, H. orientalis vars. (Hyacinth)
Iris bulbous vars.
Ixia speciosa, etc.
Lachenalia species
Lapeyrousia cruenta
Lilium species
Mirabilis longiflora
Narcissus (various)
Nerine sarniensis (Guernsey Lily)
Ornithogalum arabicum
Oxalis Bowei
Polianthes tuberosa
Ranunculus asiaticus, etc.

Schizostylis coccinea
Scilla bifolia, S. peruviana, S. sibirica, S. præcox and S. verna
Sparaxis grandiflora and S. tricolor
Sternbergia lutea major
Tecophilæa cyanocrocus
Tigridia conchiflora and T. Pavonia
Trillium grandiflorum
Vallota (Scarborough Lily)
Watsonia Meriana var. Ardernei
Zephyranthes candida

For Naturalizing in Grass

Allium Moly
Anemone apennina
Chionodoxa Luciliæ
Colchicum autumnale and C. speciosum (Autumn Crocus)
Crocus vars.

Cyclamen species
Fritillaria species
Galanthus nivalis (Snowdrop)
Hyacinthus azureus
Leucojum æstivum and L. vernum

Muscari armeniacum
Narcissus vars.
Ornithogalum nutans
Scilla bifolia, S. sibirica, S. præcox and S. verna

CHAPTER 18

TREES AND SHRUBS FOR THE GARDEN

Shrubs are little bushy trees; that is to say, they are plants of varying sizes less than that of a tree, but with woody, branching stems. The distinction is purely artificial, but it has conveniences. This class of plants has been much abused in gardens. Shrubs have been used merely as fill-gaps and have been planted in crowded masses where no individual has room for proper development or the exhibition of its natural grace and form. Consequently the shrubbery has but too often been a mere shapeless green mass, devoid alike of grace and interest.

Yet, in almost every garden, shrubs have a very important part to play. As individual plants, often of considerable beauty, as providers of shade, as interesting backgrounds for smaller plants, as instruments for the division of the garden into its several parts, shrubs serve purposes the importance of which it is difficult to over-rate. The variety which is now available of flowering and of evergreen shrubs is enormous. Yet to look at many gardens, one would think that the privet, the laurel, the elder, the aucuba and the euonymus constituted the whole race.

Certain general rules are applicable to the cultivation of almost all shrubs, as indeed of other plants. In the first place, the ground should, in advance, be deeply dug or trenched to a depth of 2 feet, enriched with well-rotted old manure and leaf-mould, and sufficient space should be allowed to each individual plant for the free and full development of its own peculiar habit of growth. The turf within a radius of 3 to 4 feet round bushes planted on lawns should be permanently removed so that the earth may be cultivated, kept free of weed, and exposed to the air.

ARRANGEMENT OF THE SHRUBS

The arrangement of shrubs naturally varies according to the purpose which they are to fulfil. If they are to serve as individual specimens on a lawn or similar situation, clearly no "arrangement" is required. When planted in groups, it is usually desirable that several plants of a kind should be placed together, though even here full space should be allowed for each individual to develop. This grouping together of, say, three to half a dozen specimens is not only more effective than scattering single plants about indiscriminately, but it makes it easier to give each group of shrubs the special soil in which they thrive best. (For soils suitable to each species, *see* the Alphabetical List of Flowering Plants and Shrubs, Chapter 34.) The fact that we can have a continued sequence of bloom from flowering shrubs almost all through the year, provided they are carefully selected, is often overlooked. It is necessary, therefore, to select shrubs not only for the colour of their flowers, their suitability for their situation, but also for the time of year at which they flower. Care must be taken that specimens whose colours clash and which bloom simultaneously are not placed together. Associate shrubs whose blooms harmonize in colour and time of flowering, and allow the blooms of the specimens in flower to be set off and enhanced by the foliage of shrubs whose flowers are over or still to come. The stronger growers must be kept in check by periodical pruning, or they may overpower the more beautiful but perhaps less vigorous plants. When planting shrubs as backgrounds to borders, too great a regularity is usually to be avoided, and they should not present a straight forbidding line. Rather should they afford projections and bays, now pressing out into the border, now forming recesses in which vigorous plants from the border may find welcome shade and shelter. During the summer the soil round the shrubs should be kept well hoed, and should be forked over each winter, and where a shrub is seen to be doing badly or to be exhausted, well-decayed manure should be thoroughly worked into the soil round the roots.

HOW TO PLANT

As a general rule, plants of medium size for their kind should be planted rather than fully-grown specimens. They more readily take root and the proportion of losses is much smaller. While there is no hurry, and planting is done with an eye to an effect which is to be produced several years later, it is often wise to plant even younger bushes. In this case it is possible either to fill the space with small bushes and to remove a proportion when they become over-crowded, or each shrub may be allotted the full space it will require in later years, the bare soil in between being temporarily decorated by herbaceous plants. Provided there is no frost, and the soil is not too wet, deciduous shrubs may, however, be planted from November to March. Usually the best time to plant deciduous shrubs is during November or failing this in February and early March. Evergreens are best planted in September and early October, or in April and the beginning of May. Never plant evergreens in the depth of winter when their vitality is at the lowest, nor when cold, drying winds are prevalent. Plants that have been grown in pots may, of course, be planted out at almost any time during the year.

As the shrubs will probably occupy the same position for many years, it is essential that the ground shall be well prepared for them. The holes in which the bushes are to be planted should be of a sufficient diameter to

178

allow the roots to be laid out horizontally, and of such a depth that the main stems will be about half an inch lower in the ground than was previously the case, as shown by the mark on the stem. The bottom of the hole should be made moderately firm though not too hard, before placing the roots thereon. Any damaged roots are better cut off with a clean knife. The roots should be well spread out, and should then be covered with some fine soil, preferably from some old, spent hot-bed or similar source. This should be trodden firmly, as the work of covering-in proceeds. The hole should be filled in with the ordinary soil which has been previously removed from it and the ground then thoroughly soaked with water. It is often recommended, and it is good advice, that the roots of shrubs about to be planted should, if dry on being unpacked, be placed in a vessel of water for an hour or so before planting.

In the case of both deciduous and evergreen shrubs of any considerable size, it is usually wise, at the time of planting, to thin out and reduce the length of the branches by about one-third; this will somewhat relieve the strain put upon the roots, at this time themselves considerably reduced. Especially is this necessary in the case of evergreens. Never plant when the ground is sodden or during a spell of frosty weather.

For details as to how to plant, *see* Planting Fruit Trees, Chapter 39.

SHRUBS FOR TOWN GARDENS

One of the chief things to be borne in mind in the selection of shrubs and plants for town gardens is that it is necessary to select, as far as possible, those whose leaves are moderately smooth, or even glossy. The clogging of the pores by soot and smoke is a great danger to the town plant; and one which bears a leaf having a surface which does not catch the dirt, and is smooth enough to be washed clean by a fairly heavy shower or by a good dousing with a syringe or garden hose, has a far better chance of a healthy life than one without this advantage. This rule holds good especially in the case of the evergreen shrubs, which have to keep their leaves in working order throughout the smoky town winter season. As far as possible, therefore, choose shrubs for town use with glossy or smooth leaves. Some of the best are the evergreen Barberry, the Privet, Holly, Box, Aucuba, Cotoneaster, Cratægus and Pyracantha. *See* also list on p. 186.

COLOURED AUTUMN FOLIAGE

In planting trees and shrubs it is well worth while considering their appearance, not only in the spring and summer, but in the late autumn and winter also, for when the garden is at its most sombre, trees and shrubs may be made to provide notes of cheerful and striking colour. A useful selection of these trees and shrubs will be found listed on p. 186.

CONIFEROUS TREES

These are all handsome and graceful trees and among them will be found many species that may well be planted singly as specimen trees on the lawn. Among the best for this purpose are: *Abies homolepis, A. nobilis*, and *A. alba; Cedrus atlantica; Chamæcyparis Lawsoniana*, and *C. obtusa; Cupressus macrocarpa; Picea Abies, P. Smithiana*, and *P. pungens glauca; Pinus Griffithii (P. excelsa), P. nigra*, and *P. sylvestris; Pseudolarix amabilis; Pseudotsuga taxifolia; Sequoiadendron giganteum; Taxodium distichum; Thuja plicata* and *T. orientalis*; and *Tsuga Albertiana*.

HOW AND WHEN TO PRUNE SHRUBS

When to Prune

The time for pruning depends to some extent on the season of flowering, and the method is dependent upon whether the bloom is borne on the new or the old wood. Where the new shoots, that is to say those of the current year, bear the flowers, pruning may be done any time from October to February, as the flowers are usually borne in summer or early autumn. Where, however, the plants flower on the old wood, generally in late winter or spring, pruning is usually done in late spring or early summer directly after flowering, as it is of vital importance to give the plants as much time as possible to form and ripen new wood before the winter sets in, for on this wood the flowers will be borne the next spring. Many such plants, the earlier-flowering spiræas and the diervillas for example, are only thinned, the old flowering branches being removed and pruned sufficiently to keep them tidy and trim.

April is the best time to trim evergreens, except conifers, which are best trimmed in September or October. Conifers, however, except when grown as hedge-plants, are not usually pruned. When such conifers as the Cupressus or Tsuga are used as hedges, they can be pruned back as desired.

How to Prune

The aim of pruning is, firstly, to let air and light to the wood so as to ripen it and thus encourage bloom on flowering shrubs; secondly, to train the plant into shape and size required; and thirdly, to keep it tidy. There are also several ways of pruning, the most usual being the cutting back of the shoots. Side shoots are often "spurred" or cut right back, leaving only three or four buds; plants requiring this treatment are usually late flowerers, such as the *Buddleia*. Again, the strong main shoots may be "topped" or cut back by about one-third to encourage sturdy growth, or may be only just "tipped" to keep the plant tidy and the growth within bounds; at the same time all old and weak wood is cut out. Another method of pruning, often required, is the removal of the seed-heads from such plants as the Lilac and the Rhododendron. If these seed-heads are

180

allowed to remain in position, a poor crop of bloom will result in the following year. Disbudding, the removal of superfluous buds, is also looked upon as pruning, for it increases the size of the flowers.

Tender Shrubs

More or less tender shrubs grown in the open in sheltered positions should never be pruned in autumn. This would lay them open to attacks by frost. When necessary, they should be pruned in April, or even later as soon as the danger of severe frosts is past. The reader is referred to the *Alphabetical List of Flowering Plants and Shrubs*, Chapter 34, where full instructions for the pruning of each kind of shrub will be found. *See also* Pruning Fruit Trees, p. 461, and Clipping Hedges, p. 95.

PROPAGATION OF SHRUBS AND CLIMBERS

CUTTINGS

This is undoubtedly the most popular method of propagating shrubs. It provides larger plants in a much shorter time than most other means, and ensures that the new plants shall be true to type, which cannot always be relied upon when raising from seeds. This method is resorted to especially when propagating popular varieties and rare shrubs. Healthy shoots varying from 3 to 6 inches in length should be taken. During the spring, summer, and autumn most shrub cuttings may be struck in a close propagating frame in a greenhouse, preferably with slight bottom heat. A gritty sand provides a suitable medium for rooting most cuttings. During August and September a bed of sandy soil in a cold frame, or under handlights, cloches, or bell-glasses, provides a medium for rooting cuttings of brooms, double gorse, heaths, etc. During October and November cuttings of very many shrubs may be inserted in a sheltered border outside. These, as a rule, should be longer than the cuttings inserted under glass. They should average 9 to 12 inches in length, from one third to one half being inserted in the soil. The cuttings of most conifers and many evergreens require the protection and moist atmosphere that glass provides. (*See also* p. 109.) Cuttings inserted in the autumn remain inactive through the winter and do not usually form roots until the following spring. They must, therefore, not be disturbed until the next autumn, when they may be planted-out 12 to 18 inches apart in a nursery bed.

RAISING FROM SEED

When sowing seeds saved from the garden, they should not be gathered too early, but must be allowed ample time to ripen, and must be cleaned before being sown. The seeds of such trees as the chestnut, oak, walnut, and magnolia are oily in nature and, unless carefully stored in slightly

181

moist sand or fibre, are apt to shrivel. They are, therefore, best sown as soon as they are ripe, but the seeds of most other shrubs are better sown under glass, in well-drained boxes of sandy soil, in February or March, and when germinated and sufficiently high, should be thinned-out to 1½ inches to 2 inches apart; the less hardy kinds being hardened-off in a cold frame and the hardy kinds planted out in nursery beds in the open. The seeds of most shrubs and trees germinate in a month or two; some, however, like the rose and thorn, take a year and even more, unless sown straight from the trees. The seeds of most conifers must ripen in their cones on the trees for about a year, some require to hang for quite two years. When the cones have been gathered, they should be stored in a warm and dry place; the dryness opens the cones and the seeds are liberated and should be sown thinly in the open in March or April, being only just covered with fine sandy soil. Seeds from healthy trees only should be used. Transplant from the seed-beds to rows in the nursery garden as soon as the seedlings are large enough to handle. It is wise to shelter the young seedlings from the sun. It may be necessary where rabbits are troublesome to enclose the seed beds and nursery garden with wire netting.

PROPAGATION BY DIVISION OF ROOTS

All the so-called "tufted" shrubs, or those that throw out suckers from their crowns or base, may be propagated by division at the time of year when they are best transplanted. Examples are: Symphoricarpus (the Snowberry), Kerria, and Spiræa.

LAYERING

This is a most valuable method of increasing rare and uncommon shrubs, notably the magnolia, stewartia, hamamelis, and disanthus. In nurseries it is the method very largely employed to propagate lilacs, acers, azaleas, and many rhododendrons. No definite "best" time can be named for layering, but in the case of deciduous subjects, the work is more easily done when the shoots are leafless. The actual process of layering is to bury a portion of the branch without severing it from the parent plant until an independent root system is formed. The average length of the shoot may be from 6 to 18 inches, but it is often allowed to be longer, in the endeavour to obtain a good-sized specimen in a short time.

BUDDING AND GRAFTING

Budding is usually effected in the open in July and August. If the shrubs are grafted, it is usually effected by grafting under glass between January and early June, but many of them may be grafted in the open in April and May. The reader is advised to consult the *Alphabetical List of Flowering Plants and Shrubs*, Chapter 34. *See also* Propagation of Plants, p. 101.

A FEW OF THE BEST TREES AND SHRUBS FOR THE GARDEN

Hardy Flowering Trees and Shrubs

NOTE.—For Colour of Flowers, Time of Blooming, Heights, Cultural Details, and the best Species and Varieties, *see* Chapter 34.

Abelia triflora (D) and A. grandiflora (E)

Æsculus Pavia (D), A. parviflora (D) (Horse chestnuts)

*Ailanthus altissima (D)

†*Amelanchier canadensis

Andromeda polifolia (E)

*Arbutus Andrachne, A. Unedo (E)

*Aucuba japonica (E) *s*

Azalea vars. (E or D)

*Azara dentata, etc. (E)

*Berberis Darwinii (E), B. stenophylla (E), B. Wilsonæ (D)

Buddleia alternifolia (D), B. Davidii vars. (D)

Buxus sempervirens (E) *s*

Calluna vulgaris (E) *r*

Calycanthus floridus (D) *s*

Cassinia fulvida (E) *r*

Castanea sativa (D)

Catalpa bignonioides (D)

Ceanothus species (E)

Chænomeles lagenaria var. C. japonica (D) *w*

Chimonanthus præcox var. grandiflora (D) *w*

Chionanthus retusus (D) *s*

Choisya ternata (E) *s*

Cistus (Rock Rose) (E) *r*

†*Clerodendron trichotomum (D)

*Colutea arborescens (D)

*Cornus (D) *w, r, s*

†Cotinus Coggygria (Smoke Bush) (D)

*†Cotoneaster (E) or D) *r, s*

†*Cratægus Carrierei, C. monogyna (Thorn) (D)

Cytisus scoparius vars. and C. species (D or E) *r*

Dabœcia polifolia (E) *r*

*Daphne species (E or D) *r*

Deutzia species and var.(D)

Diervilla florida vars. and syriaca (Weigela) (D) *s*

†Enkianthus campanulatus (D)

Erica species (E) *r*

Escallonia species (E or D) *s*

Euonymus japonicus (E)

Exochorda grandiflora (D)

Forsythia intermedia suspensa (D) *s*

Fraxinus Ornus (D)

Fuchsia magellanica and var. Riccartonii (D)

Garrya elliptica (E) *w*

*†Gaultheria procumbens and G. Shallon (E) *r, s*

Genista cinerea (D), G. hispanica (D) *r*

Grevillea rosmarinifolia *r*

Halesia carolina (D)

Halimium lasianthum, H. formosum

†Hamamelis mollis (D) *w*

Hedera Helix (Ivy) (E) *s*

Hibiscus syriacus (D) *s*

Hydrangea macrophylla, H. paniculata (D) *s*

Hypericum patulum vars. (D) *s*

Itea virginica (D) *s*

Jamesia americana (D) *s*

Jasminum officinale (D), J. revolutum

Juglans regia (D)

Kalmia latifolia and others

Kerria japonica fl. pl. (D)

Laburnum (various) (D)

Laurus nobilis (E)

Lavendula spica (E)

Ledum latifolium (E) *r*

Leiophyllum buxifolium

*Leycesteria formosa (D) *s*

*Ligustrum (Privet) (E) *s*

†Liriodendron tulipifera

Lonicera americana etc. (D) (Honeysuckle)

Lupinus arboreus (D)

Magnolia species (E or D)

†*Malus Eleyi (D)

M. floribunda

Malus Scheideckeri

M. spectabilis Kaido

M. toringoides

Morus nigra (D)

Myrtus communis (E)

Olearia Haastii (E) *r, s*

Osmanthus Aquifolium

†Parrotia persica (D)

*Pernettya mucronata (E)

Philadelphus (Mock Orange) (D) *s* species and hybrids

*Phillyræa media (E) *s*

Pieris floribunda and P. japonica (E)

Prunus Amygdalus (D)

Prunus Avium fl. pl. (D)

P. cerasifera (Cherry Plum) (D)

P. Persica (Peach) (D)

P. serrulata vars. (Japanese Cherry)

*Pyracantha Lalandii (E)

Rhododendron (E)

†Ribes aureum, R. sanguineum (D) *s*

Robinia hispida (D)

Romneya Coulteri (D)

*Rosa Hugonis (D)

R. Moyesii

*†R. rugosa (D)

Rosmarinus officinalis (E)

Rubus ulmifolius fl. pl. (D) *s*

Salix babylonica (D)

*Sambucus canadensis maxima (E) *r*

Santolina Chamæcyparissus (D) *s*

*Skimmia japonica (E) *s*

Spartium junceum (E)

Spiræa species (D) *s, r*

Staphylea colchica (D) *s*

*Symphoricarpus racemosus laevigatus (D) *s*

Syringa vars. (Lilac) (D) *s*

Tamarix pentandra (syn. hispida æstivalis) (D)

Tilia dasystyla (D)

For meaning of key letters, see note at end of list on page 184.

Hardy Flowering Trees and Shrubs—cont.

Ulex europæus fl. pl. (E)
Hebe Traversii (Speedwell) (E) *r*

†*Viburnum Opulus var. sterile (D), tomentosum var. plicatum (D), V. Carlcephalum (E)
†*V. Tinus (E) *w, s*

Vinca major elegantissima (Periwinkle) (E) *s, r*
Weigela (*see* Diervilla)
Yucca gloriosa (E)
Y. recurvifolia (E)

NOTE.—* Denotes best Berry-bearing shrubs; † Coloured Foliage in Autumn; *w*, Winter-flowering Shrubs; *r*, Shrubs for the Rock garden; and *s*, Shrubs that will grow in the shade. E = Evergreen; D = Deciduous.

Winter-flowering Shrubs

Arctostaphylos Manzanita
Berberis japonica
Chaenomeles lagenaria,
C. japonica
Chimonanthus præcox grandiflora
Clematis calycina
C. cirrhosa
Cornus Mas
Cratægus monogyna præcox
Daphne Mezereum autumnalis
Erica carnea
E. darleyensis

Garrya elliptica
Hammamelis mollis and H. virginiana
Jasminum nudiflorum
Lonicera Standishii
L. fragrantissima
Prunus subhirtella autumnalis
Rhododendron Christmas Cheer, dauricum sempervirens, emasculum, George Cunningham, mucronulatum, etc.
Ulex nanus
Viburnum Tinus (Laurustinus).

NOTE—For Colour of Flowers, Time of Blooming, Heights to which they grow, and full cultural details *see* The Alphabetical List of Flowering Plants and Shrubs, Chapter 34.

Large Specimen Deciduous Trees

Acer saccharinum (Silver Maple)
A. macrophyllum (Oregon Maple)
A. rubrum (Red Maple)
Æsculus carnea (Red Chestnut)
A. Hippocastanum (Horse Chestnut)
A. indica (Indian Chestnut)
Ailanthus altissima (Tree of Heaven)
Alnus cordata (Alder)
Betula papyrifera (Paper Birch)
Carpinus Betulus (Hornbeam)
Carya cordiformis (Bitter Nut)
Castanea sativa (Spanish Chestnut)
Catalpa bignonioides (Indian Bean)
C. speciosa (Western Catalpa)
Corylus Colurna (Constantinople Nut)
Davidia Vilmoriniana (Chinese Dove Tree)
Fagus sylvatica (Beech)
F. s. purpurea (Copper Beech)
Fraxinus americana (White Ash)
F. excelsior (Ash)
F. Ornus (Manna Ash)
Ginkgo biloba (Maidenhair Tree)
Juglans nigra (Black Walnut)
Liquidambar styraciflua (Sweet Gum)

Liriodendron Tulipifera (Tulip Tree)
Nyssa sylvatica (Tupelo)
Platanus acerifolia (London Plane)
P. orientalis (Oriental Plane)
Populus canescens (Grey Poplar)
P. trichocarpa (Black Cottonwood)
Quercus castaneæfolia (Chestnut-leaved Oak)
Q. Cerris (Turkey Oak)
Q. coccinea splendens (Scarlet Oak)
Q. Lucombeana (Lucombe Oak)
Q. robur (Common Oak)
Q. rubra (Red Oak)
Q. sessiliflora (Durmast Oak)
Robinia Pseudacacia (False Acacia)
Salix Salamonii (Hybrid Willow)
Sophora japonica
Tilia dasystyla (Lime)
T. petiolaris (Pendent Silver Lime)
Ulmus campestris Louis van Houtte (Golden Elm)
U. montana (Wych Elm).
U. nitens (Smooth-leaved Elm)
U. stricta Wheatleyi
Zelkova crenata.

Fastigiate or Upright-branched Trees

Æsculus Hippocastanum pyramidalis
    (Horse Chestnut)
Betula verrucosa (alba) fastigiata (Birch)
Carpinus Betulus columnaris (Hornbeam)
C. Betulus pyramidalis
Cephalotaxus pedunculata fastigiata
Chamæcyparis Lawsoniana erecta viridis
Cratægus monogyna stricta (Thorn or May)
Cupressus sempervirens fastigiata
Fagus sylvatica fastigiata (Dawyck Beech)
Juniperus communis hibernica
    (Irish Juniper)

Liriodendron Tulipifera fastigiata
    (Tulip Tree)
Populus alba pyramidalis (White Poplar)
P. nigra italica (Lombardy Poplar)
Quercus robur fastigiata (Oak)
Robinia Pseudacacia fastigiata (False Acacia)
Sorbus pinnatifida fastigiata
Taxus baccata fastigiata (Irish Yew)
T. baccata fastigiata aurea (Golden Irish Yew)
Thuja plicata pyramidalis
Ulmus montana fastigiata (Wych Elm)
U. stricta Wheatleyi (Wheatley's Elm).

Dwarf Trees and Shrubs for the Rock Garden

Abies balsamea hudsonia
Berberis Darwinii nana
Buxus sempervirens rosmarinifolia
Cedrus Libani nana
Cephalotaxus drupacea prostrata
Chamæcyparis Lawsoniana var. Fletcheri
C. Lawsoniana nana
C. obtusa ericoides
C. obtusa nana
C. obtusa tetragona minima
C. pisifera ericoides
C. pisifera nana
Juniperus chinensis globosa
J. communis compressa
J. communis echiniformis
J. communis nana
J. communis prostrata
J. pachyphlæa
Picea Abies Clanbrassiliana
P. Abies conica elegans
P. Abies Gregoryana

Picea Abies humilis
P. Abies pumila
P. Abies pygmæa
P. Abies reflexa
P. Abies tabuliformis
P. glauca, var. Albertiana conica
Pinus sylvestris pumila
Pseudotsuga taxifolia nana
Rhododendron ferrugineum
R. calostrotum
R. chryseum
R. impeditum
R. intricatum
R. rupicola
R. sanguineum
R. Williamsianum
Ribes aureum pumilum
Taxus baccata nana
T. cuspidata nana
Thuja orientalis compacta.
Thujopsis dolabrata nana

NOTE.—For Colour of Flowers, Time of Blooming, Heights to which they grow, and full cultural details *see* The Alphabetical List of Flowering Plants and Shrubs, Chapter 34.

Pendulous or Weeping Trees

Betula verrucosa (alba) pendula (Birch)
B. v. purpurea pendula (Purple Birch)
B. v. Youngii (Young's Weeping Birch)
Cratægus monogyna pendula (Thorn or May)
Fagus sylvatica pendula (Beech)
F. s. purpurea pendula (Copper Beech)
Fraxinus excelsior pendula (Ash)
Ilex Aquifolium pendula (Holly)
I. A. argentea pendula (Silver Holly)
I. A. aurea pendula (Golden Holly)
Morus alba pendula (White Mulberry)

Populus tremula pendula (Aspen)
P. tremuloides pendula (Parasol de Julien)
Prunus Mahaleb pendula (St. Lucie Cherry)
P. subhirtella pendula (Japanese Cherry)
Quercus robur pendula (Oak)
Salix babylonica (Willow)
S. Caprea pendula (Goat Willow)
S. vitellina pendula
Sorbus Aucuparia pendula (Mountain Ash)
Ulmus montana pendula (Wych Elm)
U. nitens pendula.

185

TREES AND SHRUBS

Conifers

Cedrus atlantica pendula (Atlas Cedar)
C. Deodara pendula (Deodar)
Chamæcyparis Lawsoniana pendula (Lawson Cypress)
Picea Abies pendula (Spruce)

Picea Morinda (Himalayan Spruce)
Sequoiadendron giganteum var. pendulum
Taxus baccata pendula
Thuja orientalis pendula
Tsuga canadensis pendula

Evergreen Trees

(Excluding Conifers)

Arbutus Menziesii and A. Unedo
Ilex Aquifolium varieties
Laurus nobilis
Magnolia grandiflora

Quercus densiflorus and Q. Ilex
Q. Lucombeana
Q. Suber
Umbellularia californica.

Evergreen Shrubs

Arundinaria Murielæ, A. nitida
Aucuba japonica
Berberis Darwinii
B. stenophylla
Buxus sempervirens vars.
Choisya ternata
Cistus cyprius
C. laurifolius
Cotoneaster buxifolia
C. Franchetii
C. microphylla
C. pannosa
C. salicifolia, and C. turbinata
Elæagnus pungens
Erica alpina
Escallonia edinensis, E. Ingramii
Euonymus japonicus vars.
Fatsia japonica
Garrya elliptica
Gaultheria Shallon

Hebe Traversii
Kalmia latifolia
Ligustrum lucidum
Mahonia Aquifolium
Olearia Haastii
Osmanthus Aquifolium
Phyllostachys Castillonis, P. nigra, P. viridi-glaucescens
Phillyrea decora
P. latifolia
Pieris floribunda
P. japonica
Prunus Laurocerasus (Cherry Laurel)
P. lusitanica (Portugal Laurel)
Pyracantha coccinea and vars. Lalandii and Rogersiana
Rhododendrons (many species and varieties)
Rosmarinus officinalis (Rosemary)
Viburnum Tinus
Yucca gloriosa
Y. recurvifolia

Coloured and Variegated-leaved Shrubs

Arundinaria Fortunei variegata
Aucuba japonica
Berberis vulgaris purpurea
Buxus sempervirens argentea
Cornus alba sibirica variegata
C. alba Spæthii
C. Mas variegata
Corylus maxima atropurpurea
Cotinus Coggygria purpurea
Diervilia florida purpurea
D. florida variegata
Elæagnus pungens aureo-picta
Euonymus japonicus aureo-pictus

Kerria japonica variegata
Ligustrum ovalifolium aureum
Lonicera japonica aureo-reticulata
Neillia opulifolia lutea
Osmanthus Aquifolium variegatus
Pieris japonica variegata
Prunus cerasifera Pissardii
Rhamnus alaternus variegata
Ribes alpina foliis aureis
Sambucus nigra folius aureis
S. nigra variegata
Santolina Chamæcyparissus

186

CHAPTER 19

CLIMBING PLANTS: SHRUBBY, PERENNIAL AND ANNUAL

Climbing plants have their place in almost every garden. Even the smallest cottage or villa garden calls for sweet peas, honeysuckle, rambling rose, and clematis or jasmine, whilst in gardens of larger size, climbing plants should form one of the most interesting and most decorative features. The beauty of the English hedgerow is in large part attributable to those beautiful climbing plants which are native to our country. Traveller's joy and honeysuckle, ivy and bryony, all in due season garland the copse and hedge. In our gardens, wall, trellis, and arch, overhung with the lovely climbers which are now available, may be among the loveliest features.

Climbing plants are often given but crude treatment, yet if they are to thrive and be truly luxuriant and beautiful, it is scarcely possible to spend too much attention in the preparing and enriching of the soil in which their roots are to grow.

SELECTING THE POSITION

Nearly all creepers do better if the air can circulate freely round their stems and shoots, but this does not mean that they enjoy cold draughts from the north or east. Most climbers will thrive better on a wooden trellis, provided it is sheltered from these cold blasts, than they will against a brick wall which throws back the sun's rays and is apt to scorch them. Many of less hardy nature, of course, demand the shelter of a wall and several require that this wall shall also face south to catch all available sunlight and warmth. In Chapter 34 we have pointed out the preference as to aspect shown by each.

HOW TO PLANT

A creeper must not be planted with its roots right up against a wall, the stem should be placed some 6 to 9 inches from the wall, so that the roots may receive adequate air and moisture. In dry weather, a good watering should be given periodically to all wall plants, even though correctly planted with their roots some way from the wall. The creosote or paint used on the wooden supports of a pergola may be very harmful if it comes into contact with the roots, and this is another reason why the climber should not be planted too close to its support.

The hole to receive the roots must be dug two feet deep and about three feet wide. The soil at the bottom should be well loosened and with it should be mixed stable manure, decayed leaf-mould or vegetable refuse; over this must be placed a layer of mould some six inches in thickness, to prevent the roots from coming into direct contact with the manure. The soil that has been taken from the hole, if too heavy, should be lightened by the addition of sandy loam, well-rotted stable manure, ashes of garden rubbish and leaf-mould; should it be too light, it can be improved by mixing heavy loam, a little pig or cow manure and leaf-mould with it.

In planting climbers that have been grown in pots, the outer roots should be spread out carefully, but the "ball" of earth around the roots should be as little disturbed as possible. They should then be planted to about the same depth as was previously the case; that is to say, the top of the ball of earth should be only just covered with fresh soil. The soil about them should be firmly pressed or trodden in. In the case of non-potted plants, the roots should be well spread out, and the soil firmly pressed about them as before. The necessary supports should be at once afforded, and the plants attached thereto. Except in wet weather, water should at once be given and continued at intervals as required.

WHEN TO PLANT

Planting may be done at any time during the winter or spring, provided the ground is not too wet and that there is not a frost. It is, however, best to plant as early in the autumn as possible, so that the plants may become established and be better able to withstand inclement weather.

Deciduous climbers can be planted at any time between the falling of the leaves and early April of the next year, and evergreens during September and October or April and May, or if in pots, whenever soil and weather conditions permit from October to April. Allow as large a "ball" of earth as possible to remain round the roots while replanting—this is especially applicable to evergreens—and do not permit the roots to be exposed to cold, dry winds, to the hot sun or to frost. As much of the fine roots as possible should be carefully taken up when transplanting. If the roots have been damaged, the injured parts must be cut away before planting, and should the parts trimmed be very thick, the cut surfaces should be painted with coal tar, to prevent "bleeding". Where it has been necessary to cut away a considerable part of the roots, a proportionate amount of branches should also be sacrificed, so that the roots shall not have undue top-growth to nourish.

A good mulching in spring of well-rotted manure about an inch or so deep after a thorough watering, will assist the plants to become established, and will help to keep the soil moist through the summer. *See also* the instructions for planting shrubs in Chapter 18.

188

TRAINING AND NAILING UP

For growing climbing plants other than those which, like ivy, attach themselves by means of roots against walls, wooden trellis, is on the whole, the most satisfactory framework. Stretched galvanized wires form another convenient support for such plants. Or, again, plants may be attached to the walls by nails and shreds of cloth, or by patent nails with soft metal tops which can be twisted round the stems. Iron or other metal is too subject to changes of temperature to make good supports for climbing plants.

Pergolas and arches should be of as simple a construction as possible, larch poles with joining crosspieces being as satisfactory for the purpose as any. The long, straggling growths of such climbers as the clematis or the honeysuckle should be periodically disentangled and should be trained in to cover the required space. *See also* the paragraph on p. 43.

PRUNING

Pruning should generally take place in February. In the case of plants which flower on the old wood, little pruning is required, but superfluous, weak, and straggling shoots may with advantage be removed. On the other hand, plants which bear their flowers on the young wood, may be cut back to within two or three eyes of the old wood or, in some cases, to within six inches of the ground in November for spring flowers, or a little less severely in spring for autumn blooming. *See also* the section on pruning Trees and Shrubs, p. 180.

Full cultural details of the climbers mentioned in this chapter are given in Chapter 34; and for propagating *see* Chapter 18 on Trees and Shrubs.

ANNUAL CLIMBERS

The most valuable of our garden climbing plants are perennials, but annuals also furnish us with a number of beautiful climbers which, by their quick growth and easy culture, are often of the greatest value.

A FEW OF THE BEST CLIMBING PLANTS

For Cultural Details, and for Colour of Flowers, Time of Flowering, Height, and the best Species and Varieties, *see* the A.B.C. of Plants, page 255.

Annual

*Calonyction aculeatum (Moon Flower)
*Cobæa scandens (grown as annual)
*Cucurbita vars. (Gourd)
Humulus japonicus

*Ipomœa purpurea (Morning Glory) [Pea]
Lathyrus odoratus (Sweet
*Quamoclit coccinea, Q. lobata, Q. pennata (Cypress Vine)

*Tropæolum aduncum (Canary Creeper)
T. majus (Climbing Nasturtium)

For Perennials and Shrubby Wall Plants, *see* page 190.

Climbing and Other Perennial and Shrubby Wall Plants

Ampelopsis. (*See* Partheno-
  cissus)
Aristolochia macrophylla
  [Syn. A. Sipho], S.W.
Azara microphylla (Warm,
  sheltered), S.
*Berberidopsis corallina
  (Southern Counties
  only), S.W.
Calycanthus occidentalis,
  S.W.
*Campsis grandiflora
  (Trumpet Flower)
C. radicans
*Carpentaria californica
  (Southern Counties), S.
Ceanothus dentatus, S. [S.
C. var. Gloire de Versailles,
C. rigidus
*C. Veitchianus, S.
Celastrus scandens, N.E.
Chaenomeles lagenaria
  vars., C. japonica, E.W.
Chimonanthus præcox
  (Winter Sweet), S.W.
*Choisya ternata, S.
Clematis flammula, E.W.
C. florida vars., E.W.
C. Jackmanni vars., E.W.
C. lanuginosa vars., E.W.
C. montana vars., N.E.W.
C. patens vars., E.W.
C. Vitalba (Traveller's Joy),
  N.E.W.
C. Viticella vars., E.W.
Cotoneaster horizontalis,
  N.E.
C. Henryana, N.E.W.
Cratægus Pyracantha. *See*
  Pyracantha coccinea,
  N.E.
*Eccremocarpus scaber, S.
  (Treat as an annual)

Escallonia exoniensis, S.
E. langleyensis, S.
E. macrantha, S.
E. montevidensis, S.
Forsythia suspensa, S.W.
Garrya elliptica, N.E.W.
Hedera dentata, N.
H. Helix (Common Ivy)
Humulus Lupulus aureus
  (Golden Hop)
*Hydrangea petiolaris
  (Scandens), N.W.
Jasminum nudiflorum,
  N.E.W.
J. officinale, W.E.
J. primulinum, S.W.
J. revolutum, S.W.E.
Kerria japonica var. fl pl.,
  S.W.
Lathyrus grandiflorus,
  S.W.
L. latifolius (Everlasting
  Pea), S.W.
Lonicera Caprifolium, E.
L. japonica flexuosa, N.E.
L. japonica aureo reticu-
  lata, N.E.
L. Periclymenum, N.E.
L. P. belgica (Early Dutch),
  N.E.
L. P. serotina (Late Dutch),
  N.E.
L. sempervirens (Trumpet
  Honeysuckle), N.E.
Lycium chinense
Magnolia denudata, W.
M. grandiflora, S.W.
M. Soulangeana
Mutisia decurrens (Shel-
  tered), S.W.
Myrtus communis, S.
M. lusitanica tarentina,
  S.

Parthenocissus Henryana
  (Sheltered), S.
P. quinquefolia [syn. Am-
  pelopsis hederacea],
  (Virginia Creeper),
  N.S.E.W.
P. tricuspidata,
  var. Veitchii (syn. Am-
  pelopsis Veitchii),
  N.S.E.W.
Passiflora cærulea (Passion
  Flower), S.W.
P. c. Constance Elliott
Polygonum baldschuani-
  cum
Pyracantha angustifolia,
  N.S.E.W.
P. coccinea (Fire Thorn)
P. c. Lalandii, N.S.E.W.
Rosa. *See* Roses, p. 386
Rubus laciniatus (Parsley
  leaved Blackberry)
R. thyrsoideus fl. pl. (Db.-
  flowered Blackberry)
R. ulmifolius var. bellidi-
  florus
*Solanum crispum, S.W.
*S. jasminoides (Sheltered),
  S.W.
Trachelospermum jasmin-
  oides
Tropæolum speciosum
  (Flame Nasturtium), N.
Vitis Coignetiæ (Crimson
  Glory Vine), S.
V. vinifera purpurea
  (Claret-leaved Vine),
  S.W.
Wisteria multijuga, S. or
  S.W.
W. m. alba, S. or S.W.
W. sinensis, S. or S.W.
W. s. alba, S. or S.W.

NOTE.—N.S.E. or W. indicates the most suitable position, e.g. Wall facing North, South, East or West. * Denotes Half-hardy.

CHAPTER 20

THE ROCK GARDEN

There are few features in the garden that provide such a variety of interests in so little space as a well-planned and carefully planted rock garden. The smallest plot may contain a rock garden which will house a representative and charming collection of alpines including those native to this country, but, on the other hand, there are few features in the ordinary garden that are so neglected and so ill-understood.

FUNCTION OF THE ROCK GARDEN

It must be remembered that the chief function of the rock garden is to provide the plants grown in it with the conditions similar to those existing in their natural haunts. The alpines and high alpines are the most typical of all rock plants and are mostly natives of the high mountain crags and screes.

The ideal rock garden, therefore, should, as far as possible, provide the soil and climatic conditions pertaining in these regions. Though such a state of affairs is far beyond our reach we can at least work in that direction.

But it should be remembered too that were it not for the wonderful adaptability of these small plants, our efforts would meet with very little success.

During the short alpine summer, these little plants are subjected to fierce and baking sun; many of them, therefore, have thick leaves covered with down or hair to protect them from its shrivelling rays. The roots, too, at this time need ample moisture, and this is provided by the melting of the snows on the mountain tops, whence it permeates through the scree of the moraine (*see* The Moraine Garden, p. 196). In winter, this downy foliage, which rots very rapidly if there is excessive moisture overhead or round the crowns of the plants, is protected by a blanket of snow until summer again comes round.

It is obvious, therefore, that the two most important, indeed essential requirements of alpine plants, especially high alpines, are ample drainage for the soil in which they grow and protection from damp in winter. The former can be obtained with a little care during the construction of the rock garden (*see* p. 192), and the latter essential can be provided by the use of panes of glass and hand-lights (*see* p. 196).

191

LAY-OUT AND CONSTRUCTION

The chief uses of the rocks and stones in a rock garden are to provide coolness for the roots and to store up moisture in crevices for the use of the plants. But the idea that rock plants grow best in practically nothing but rock is a mistaken one. A generous allowance of good soil between, amongst, and beneath the stones is essential for the healthy growth of the plants.

As the function of the rocks is to provide shelter for roots, it is clearly useless to plant slabs of rock or stone perpendicularly in the soil. No protection is afforded in this way: the roots cannot get beneath them, and they do not preserve any moisture.

Large masses of stone, two or more feet in length, should be used, where possible, and should be sunk well and firmly in the earth in a slightly slanting direction—tilted backwards, not forwards, so that the rain may trickle down to the roots of the plants.

If the rocks lean forward, over the plants, the roots will be sheltered from the rain and probably parched. Although the visible portions of the rocks in the garden should be as pleasing as may be to the eye, and should all slant in the same direction to represent a natural outcrop or stratum of stone, it should never be forgotten that they are not put there for the sake of picturesque effect, but to protect the roots of the plants growing among them. The slopes of the mounds in which the boulders are set must not be too steep and should be as natural in appearance as possible; there should be miniature ranges and mountain peaks, and dividing them valleys into which spurs from the hills project. Winding paths, 18 inches to 2 feet in width, with stepping stones, should be cut through these gorges so that every part of the rock garden is easily accessible. A broader path, of course, being a necessity in large rock gardens, especially in public gardens.

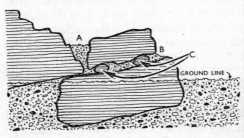

FIG. 31. MAKING CREVICES BETWEEN THE ROCKS
A shows a vertical crevice; *B* a horizontal fissure. The small stones *C C* provide space for soil between the rocks.

The pockets in which the alpines are to be planted should be irregular in shape and may vary from a few inches in diameter to as many feet across.

They must be from a foot to 18 inches in depth, and so constructed that the soil will not wash out of them. If there is any chance of the soil in the pockets becoming sodden, clinker and rubble drainage must be provided, although on an average well-drained site this should not be necessary.

192

DREAM GIRL

SONNY BOY

PLATE 6 *GLADIOLI*

FORERUNNER

J. B. PRIESTLEY

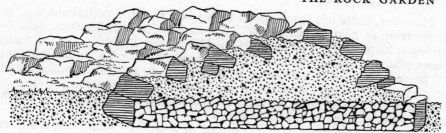

FIG. 32. CONSTRUCTING THE ROCK GARDEN

The rocks should be set at a uniform angle to simulate the strata of a natural outcrop of rock; they should tilt slightly backwards and the higher rocks must not overhang those below them, or no moisture will find its way into the horizontal fissures. The brick or rubble drainage is clearly shown.

SITUATION AND SUITABLE STONE

As regards the situation of the rock garden, it should, where possible, have an open, sunny position, preferably facing all aspects, for the benefit of various plants, and away from walls and overhanging trees. The latter will prevent the circulation of fresh air so necessary to alpine plants and in addition, the roots will soon find their way into the soil provided for the rock plants, and rob it of nourishment, while the drip off the branches can have a bad effect on the plants. The rock garden always looks best where it has not to bear contrast with any formal arrangement of garden or shrubbery; a wild and "natural-looking" site, and, where possible, one where the natural rock of the district crops up here and there, is the most favourable, when there is choice. In making the garden, the stone of the district should always be used if it can, but any stone will do, except, perhaps, the very crumbling slates or magnesian limestone. Two of the best are weathered limestone and sandstone. In localities with a small rainfall, a rough, porous sandstone is to be desired; whilst in the wetter regions, on the west coast, a harder stone, such as limestone, is perhaps more suitable, giving a quick drainage, the former, being porous, is more retentive of moisture. It is essential that there shall be no spaces and hollows under and around the stones, and that the earth shall be well bedded round them. If this is not done, the air within the hollow spaces will dry up the soil and drain the moisture from the roots of the plants. while the stones may also subside and upset the general effect.

PREPARATION OF THE SOIL

The great majority of alpines and rock plants like a rich soil containing a large portion of coarse sand or grit, leaf-mould and other decayed vegetable matter. As a whole these plants are not faddy as to soil and most thrive well in the compost mentioned above.

However, there are some which thrive best in a soil containing a large proportion of peat or leaf mould, such as Meconopsis, Shortias, Schizocodon soldanelloides, and many of the Himalayan Primulas. In the main these plants belong to regions where they are afforded a certain amount of protection by dwarf-growing Rhododendrons and other bushes, and so prefer a fairly humid position in our garden. Such a position is, perhaps, best attained by reserving for them a small valley, similar to that in which the moraine is constructed. (*See* p. 196.)

For soil, supply them with a compost of a $\frac{1}{2}$-part rough peat, a $\frac{1}{4}$-part granite chips, and a $\frac{1}{4}$-part of well decayed leaves and loam, except where other compost is recommended in the chapter devoted to the Alphabetical List of Flowering Plants and Shrubs. (*See* Chapter 34.)

Plant the dwarf Rhododendrons and Azaleas, leaving sufficient space for the smaller plants to obtain light and air, the shrubby plants merely affording protection against parching sun and retaining in the surrounding atmosphere the humidity necessary for the growth of this type. If this sort of shrub protection cannot be given, then choose a site in the rock garden which is shaded from the hot midday sun by rocks. Most of these peat-loving plants like a cool, moist, well-drained soil and they do not object to the early morning or the late afternoon sun.

Alpine plants in their native habitat receive a yearly top-dressing of vegetable matter from the material carried down by the melting snows, and alpines in a rock garden are all the better for a top-dressing artificially applied in imitation of this natural process.

Where rock plants are studied in their natural conditions, it will be found that in most cases, the soil around the roots is completely covered by the stalks and leaves, each plant touching its neighbours, and that practically no soil is left exposed. This arrangement is of the greatest use to the plants, as by preventing the exposure of the soil to the action of sun and wind, its natural moisture is preserved. For this reason we should provide this protection as far as is possible. This is, however, rather difficult to do at first, for while the plants are still small and most need protection, they are unable to cover the surface of the ground, and to plant them closer together would merely mean starving and overcrowding them. In such a case, the best thing to do is to cover the intermediate surface of the soil with a layer of chips of stone, small enough to be easily pushed aside by a shoot, but sufficient to prevent the over-drying of the earth.

HOW TO PLANT

Rock plants should be planted out either in the spring or in the early autumn, but not later than September or early October, since the roots make but little growth after that time, and the plant is liable to be washed out of the earth by heavy rain, or lifted from the soil by the action of the frost. However, in and around our larger cities, spring is the more satisfactory planting time, the plants then having the summer in front of them to get established before the rigours of fog and smoke overtake them. If care is taken, however, all alpines can be planted out at any time between early April and the end of September. Plants from pots may, of course, be planted at any time, providing the weather is neither too dry nor too wet.

When planting in a crevice, it is essential that there shall be no air-pocket at the bottom; this would drain all moisture from the roots and may cause them to shrivel. To avoid this, first ram plenty of good, gritty soil well into the crevice and make sure that the bottom is well filled, then scrape out some of the soil at the top and set the plant in firmly, pressing the soil well down round the roots, and fix it in tightly by means of a smaller wedge of stone. Care should be taken that shade lovers like Ourisias and Shortias are given congenial situations such as a sheltered position at the base of a rock facing north or east, while sun-loving plants such as Alyssum, Arabis, Onosma, should be planted in crevices or on ledges where they can hang over and furnish the face of the rocks, while on the flat parts and damp low-lying situations Gentians, Primulas of the candilabra types and all the more luscious of the moisture-loving plants will thrive.

When planting out do not overcrowd but allow plenty of room for the plants to grow and spread.

SUMMER WORK IN THE ROCK GARDEN

All through the summer months, the rock garden must be periodically weeded and all dead flower heads should be cut away, except for those plants of which seed is required. Water the choicer species during dry spells, and in May top-dress with a thin layer of sandy loam and leaf-mould. By July, most of the plants will have borne the best of their bloom, and many of the most vigorous will now be pushing forth new growth and will commence to overcrowd the less rampageous inmates. These plants, including the shrubby subjects, should, therefore, be trimmed back and at the same time the older portions of the plants and all dead stems and foliage should be removed. Do not trim the plants back too evenly; endeavour rather to foster the wild and natural appearance of the rock garden.

CARE OF PLANTS IN WINTER

Silver foliage plants and others whose leaves are covered with fluff or down are, when in their natural haunts, usually protected from frost and damp during the winter by a coat of snow. When they are grown out of

195

doors in this country, they must, therefore, be given a covering of glass during the winter months. When the plant is a small one nestling in a crevice between the rocks, it is often possible to cover it with a sheet of glass resting on the surrounding rocks, but when this cannot be done, four pieces of stiff galvanized wire should be inserted firmly in the ground and bent over at the top to hold the glass plate securely in position over the plant.

If the weather is especially severe or the plant very delicate, four other pieces of glass may be set in the soil and supported by the wires so as to form four walls protecting the plant. Sufficient space between the glass roof and the tops of the four walls should be left for adequate ventilation—but not enough to admit the rain or snow—or the plant will be liable to damp-off. The frost will often raise the plants from the soil, especially those planted the previous autumn. In spring, therefore, each plant should be carefully scrutinized, and if necessary, gently pressed down into the soil.

RAISING ROCK PLANTS

Rock plants may be increased by seed sown as soon as ripe or failing this in early spring. Sow in pots and raise under glass. Some germinate better if the pots are plunged out of doors where they are exposed to all weathers and in spring removed to a warm house or frame. Propagate also by cuttings or division of the roots in April or September. For some people it is better to raise Alpines from cuttings and division rather than from seeds.

If seedlings are raised from a plant which is a variety or of hybrid origin the chances are that they may not come true to the original plant. In such cases increase by means of cuttings, division or root cuttings. (*See* Methods of Propagation, Chapter 11.)

THE MORAINE GARDEN

Many of the more fastidious of the alpines will not prosper in the ordinary rock garden. The plants to which we refer grow on mountain slopes covered with loose stones, where the melting of the snow during summer provides them with plenty of ice-cold water and where a blanket of snow protects them during the winter. The conditions we have to endeavour to reproduce are, therefore, adequate moisture for the roots in summer, good drainage, and protection from damp in winter.

Construction of the Moraine

An ideal and natural position for the moraine would be at the lower end of a valley between two rocky spurs, the gorge gradually expanding into a flat bed of scree with occasional boulders strewn over it. To make

PLATE 17   The rock garden above is an excellent example of what can be done with a sloping site.   Below is a rock garden combined with a small lake.

H. & V. Joel

Saxifrage Aizoon

Oxalis enneaphylla

PLATE 18

Phlox Douglasii

Iris innominata

the moraine, dig out about 2½ feet of the soil and make the bottom of the basin or trench slope slightly towards the front; the slope must not be too steep or the moraine will become over dry in summer. The lower 10 inches of this basin must be made water-tight by means of puddling with clay or by means of cement. Make an outlet in front, which when closed keeps about 10 inches of water, but not more, in the lowest part of the basin, while when the outlet is open, none at all remains. Now cover the bottom of the trench with about 10 inches of rubble, stones, or any material that will afford good drainage. Above this place another 3 inches or so of smaller stones roughly 1 inch in diameter; these will fill the gaps between the larger stones and prevent the small grit above from sinking through and blocking the drainage. The hollow must then be filled up with a mixture of stone chips and gravel, good loam, leaf-mould, and small stone chips similar to those used in frosty weather for sprinkling on wood-paved roads. Cover this, again, with a two-inch layer of chips. Granite or limestone chips are excellent and easily obtained; flint chips should not be used as they do not conserve moisture. Place a few boulders in the moraine, in order to break up the surface and to give the plants some protection.

A natural trickle of water may be led into the top of the moraine, or sufficient moisture given from a watering can each day to cause an over-flow from the outlet at the bottom. From November to May when no additional moisture is needed, the outlet should be left open. Many plants that have proved failures in the rock garden proper will, on trans-plantation to the moraine, flourish.

GROWING ALPINES UNDER GLASS

There are some choice alpines that cannot be cultivated in the open to the best advantage in our uncertain climate. To say that they are choice does not necessarily mean that they are delicate, but that the blooms of many are apt to be spoilt by inclement weather, and it is to these subjects that the alpine house affords protection while they are in bloom; it will also prolong their season of flowering. Most of the inmates can be brought on in pans sunk to their rims in ashes in the open or in frames until they are about to flower, when they should be transferred to the alpine house to be removed again to the open when they have flowered. After the beginning of October, all the plants should be housed in a frost-proof frame and must be removed to the house as the blooms become visible. The alpine house does not require artificial heating, and is best of the low span-roofed type, of light structure enabling the plants to get the maximum amount of light with full ventilation on both sides and top, so situated that it runs north and south. For management, *see* The Cold House, p. 238.

Compost and Potting

Two-thirds fibrous loam and leaf-mould with one-third coarse, gritty sand makes an excellent compost for most plants grown in the alpine house. Many of the finer saxifrages like a little splintered limestone in their soil. Individual tastes must be studied as far as possible. Pot-up in pans from 6 to 9 inches in diameter and about 5 inches deep, and because ample drainage is required, place 1 to 2 inches of broken crocks in the bottom of the pans for plants like Androsaces and Saxifrages. For plants of a more vigorous nature and for bulbs, 1 inch of crocks will suffice. Re-potting is only needed every second or third year. The stagings are as a rule covered with a 2-inch layer of shingle or ashes. Some authorities suggest that alpine plants do better on stages constructed of 2-inch by ¾-inch spars of wood (preferably teak), set from ¾ to 1½ inches apart, so that the air may pass freely up through the stage and around the plants.

CHOICE OF PLANTS

When making a selection of plants for the rock garden, there are several points to be borne in mind. The first is that we should aim at having bloom over the longest possible period of the year. In this connection, some of the smaller-growing bulbs which bloom in the winter and early spring are invaluable, while those later autumn-flowering alpines, such as *Astilbe simplicifolia*, *Saxifraga Fortunei*, and *Zauschneria californica*, furnish colour long after the great majority have finished blooming.

Some of the stronger growers soon over-run the rock garden and smother other plants less luxuriant, perhaps, but more beautiful and useful. These vigorous growers must be limited in number and sternly cut back and kept in check. To add interest to the rock garden, as many of the various genera as possible should be selected, but the garden must never be overcrowded. Bulbs are often overlooked. This should not be, for few sights are more lovely than some of the smaller-growing bulbs blooming above a carpeting of Acæna microphylla, Arenaria balearica, or other dwarf trailer. For a selection *see* list below.

Bulbs for the Rock Garden

Allium azureum, A. Bee-sianum, A. cœruleum, A. cyaneum, A. Moly, A. narcissiflorum, etc.	Chionodoxa Luciliæ	Leucojum æstivum and L. vernum
	Colchicum autumnale etc.	
	Crocus species	Muscari armeniacum, M. botryoides
	Cyclamen coum, C. euro-pæum, C. neapolitanum	
Anemone blanda and vars. A. hortensis var. fulgens, A. nemorosa vars.	Eranthis hyemalis	Narcissus Bulbocodium, N. cyclamineus. N. minimus and N. triandrus
	Erythronium species	
Brodiæa species	Fritillaria species	Puschkinia scilloides
Bulbocodium vernum	Galanthus (Snowdrop)	Scilla bifolia, S. peruviana, S. præcox, S. sibirica, etc.
Calochortus Howellii, C. pulchellus, C. venustus	Hyacinthus azureus	Tulipa species
	Iris species	

198

SOME OF THE BEST ROCK PLANTS

NOTE.—For details as to Colour, Height, Season of Flowering, Culture and the best Species and Varieties, *see* the A.B.C. of Plants, page 255. Those plants that will grow in the shade are marked*; those suitable for the Moraine Garden are marked †.

*Acæna Buchananii, A. microphylla, A. novæ-zelandiæ
†Achillea clavenæ, A. rupestris, A. tomentosa
Adonis vernalis
†Æthionema pulchellum
Alyssum montanum, A. saxatile var. citrinum
†Androsace lanuginosa, A. sarmentosa
*†Anemone Hepatica, A. Pulsatilla
Anthyllis montana var. atrorubens
*Aquilegia glandulosa
Arabis caucasica fl. pl., A. muralis rosea
*Arenaria Ledebouriana, A. montana, A. tetraquetra
†Armeria cæspitosa
*Brunnera macrophylla
*†Campanula carpatica, C. cochlearifolia, C. Portenschlagiana
Cerastium tomentosum
Ceratostigma plumbaginoides
Codonopsis clematidea
Corydalis cheilanthifolia
Cotyledon oppositifolia
*Cyclamen (Hardy species and vars.)

Cytisus kewensis and C. Beanii
†Dianthus alpinus, etc.
Dodecatheon Hendersonii, etc.
†Draba species
Dryas octopetala
†Edraianthus serpyllifolius
Erica carnea (Heath)
†Erodium species
Erysimum rupestre
Gaultheria procumbens
Genista sagittalis
†*Gentiana species
Geum species
Gypsophila repens
*Haberlea rhodopensis
Helianthemum (Sun Rose)
Heuchera sanguinea vars.
†Hypericum species
*Iberis species
*Iris (Dwarf Bearded, Hybrid, and Bulbous)
†Lewisia Tweedyi, etc.
†Linaria alpina
Linum species
Lithospermum diffusum, L. intermedium
Lychnis alpina (Campion)
Macrotomia echioides
Meconopsis species
Megapterum (Œnothera) missouriense
†*Mertensia primuloides

†Morisia monantha (hypogœa)
Nierembergia rivularis
†*Omphalodes Luciliæ, O. verna, etc.
†Onosma albo-roseum, O. echioides
*Ourisia coccinea
Oxalis adenophylla, O. enneaphylla
†Papaver alpinum
Penstemon Scouleri and others
Phlox adsurgens, P. ovata, P. subulata vars.
Polygonum vaccinifolium
†Potentilla species
†*Primula species
*Ramonda Myconi
†*Ranunculus alpestris
*Roscœa cautleoides
Saponaria ocymoides
†*Saxifraga species and vars.
†Scutellaria orientalis
Sedum species
Sempervivum species and hybrids
Silene dwarf species
Soldanella alpina, etc.
Thymus species
*Viola species
Wahlenbergia species
†*Waldsteinia siberica
Zauschneria californica

NOTE.—In addition to the flowers named in this list there are many dwarf annuals which, though not rock plants in the true sense, deserve a position in the rock garden. Many ferns are also suitable. For dwarf shrubs for the rock garden, *see* list of Shrubs and Trees.

CHAPTER 21

THE "DRY" WALL

Nine times out of ten, when laying out a garden on a piece of sloping ground, one will be confronted with the problem of what to do with the banks, which of necessity will be formed. They are usually made into grass slopes, which are difficult to keep well trimmed, and are consequently apt to look untidy if labour is at a premium. Alternatively, they may be planted with shrubs or may be covered with some such trailing plant as ivy or periwinkle.

There is, however, a far better solution to the problem; the unwanted bank may be converted into a wall garden bright with colour and full of interest during the greater part of the year.

CONSTRUCTING THE "DRY" WALL

The "dry" wall, as it is called, consists of stones, usually sandstone or limestone, from 2 to 8 inches in thickness, of any size within reason, rectangular and more or less untrimmed. Stones are better than bricks as they provide cooler and moister root-beds for the wall plants. They should be bonded, that is laid in layers, so that the lateral extremities of a stone lie over the centres of the two stones in the row immediately below it. This structure serves to keep the wall secure and firm. The stones are best when their upper surfaces are flat, or even cupped, and when placed in position, they should be inclined slightly backwards so that they are lower at the back than at the front; the rain will then be collected and drained into the soil at the back of the wall to furnish moisture for the roots.

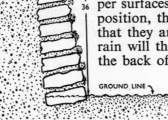

FIG. 33. CONSTRUCTING THE "DRY" WALL

The wall should incline slightly backward, at an angle of about 1 in 6 from bottom to top; that is, in a wall 3 feet high, the base will project 6 inches beyond the top.

No cement is used, but fine earth is rammed firmly into the crevices between the stones, sufficient soil being added to keep the stones about an inch apart, vertically. This soil must be rammed well into the back of the wall so that there is soil from the very front to the earth supporting the wall at the back. The soil should be well "firmed" after each row of stones has been laid, and

200

no "air-pockets" must be left in the crevices, otherwise the roots of the plant will be dried up.

PREPARING THE SOIL

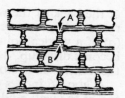

A mixture of good loam, decayed cow manure, and leaf-mould makes the best compost for the wall garden. The first essential is to make a good foundation for the wall. This should be about 10 inches deep and a shade wider than the base of the wall. Here, ram the soil well down till a solid footing is provided. Now lay the first layer of stones, using the largest available, and place them so that their upper sides form one straight horizontal line. If the stones are of moderate size, the gaps left laterally between them may be about 3 inches; the smaller the stones, the smaller the gaps between them. Next pack the crevices between the stones very tightly with the compost of good loam, leaf-mould, and decayed cow manure. On this is placed the next layer of stone, properly bonded as explained already, and the process is repeated until the wall has reached the required height. If a stone is occasionally inserted lengthwise from back to front, the wall will be all the more secure. The wall should not be built exactly vertical, but the top should incline slightly back at an angle of about 1 in 6; that is to say, in a wall 4 feet high the base will project 8 inches further forward than the top.

FIG. 34. HOW TO PLANT THE "DRY" WALL A plant should never be placed at the *top*, (*a*) of a vertical joint between the stones; it should be set in the crevice (*b*), at the *bottom* of a vertical fissure

The top of the wall is best left flat so that the rain may soak through to the roots beneath.

PLANTING

It is, of course, easiest to plant the wall as it is constructed, the roots may then be spread out as they should be, and be well covered with soil. The best way to do this is first to plunge the roots into a puddle of soil and water. This greatly helps in establishing the plants, especially in dry weather.

It is, of course, possible to plant the wall when complete, but the result is not so satisfactory. March and April, when root growth is very vigorous, are the best months in which to construct and plant the wall garden.

Seed may be sown in the crevices in spring. The best way to do this is to mix the seeds with a little well-sieved, moist sandy soil and to press it into the chink in the wall. A small piece of moss inserted into the crevice will keep the seed moist and will prevent it from being dislodged.

In planting, every effort should be made to insert the plants with their roots well spread out, and so that they may penetrate well into the soil

201

at the back of the wall. A little well-rotted cow manure inserted with the roots will prove beneficial. A plant should never be placed at the *top* (*a*) of a vertical joint between the stones, its roots would then be likely to become dried up. Rather should it be planted in the crevice (*b*) just above the centre of a stone, *see* Fig. 34.

A good 6 inches of compost should be firmly rammed down on to the top of the wall, and in this soil, at intervals, should be placed large stones. These will help to keep the soil in place and will furnish moist, cool sites for the roots of such plants as rock roses, wallflowers, snapdragons, sedums, and saxifrages—all ideal plants with which to crown the wall.

SOME PLANTS FOR THE "DRY" WALL

NOTE.—For Cultural Details and for Colour, Height, and Time of Flowering, *see* the A.B.C. of Plants, page 255.

*Acæna adscendens, A. Buchananii and A. microphylla
Acantholimon glumaceum
Achillea. *See* list of rock plants
Æthionema grandiflorum
Alyssum alpestre, A. saxatile and its vars.
Amarcus Dictamnus, A. pulcher
Androsace primuloides and vars.
Antirrhinum various
Aquilegia species
Arabis androsacea and A. caucasica fl. pl.
*Arenaria balearica
Armeria corsica, A. maritima and its vars.
Asperula Gussonii
Astragalus danicus
Aubrieta vars.
Campanula cæspitosa, C. fragilis, C. Portenschlagiana
Cerastium tomentosum
Cheiranthus vars. (Wallflower)
*Corydalis lutea

*Cotyledon Umbilicus
Dianthus alpinus, D. cæsius, D. deltoides, D. plumaris
Erigeron mucronatus
*Erinus alpinus
Eriogonum flavum, E. subalpinum
Erodium macradenum
Gypsophila prostrata and G. repens
Helianthemum vars.
Helichrysum bellidioides
Heliosperma alpestre [Syn. Silene]
Hypericum fragile and H. polyphyllum
Iberis sempervirens
Kentranthus ruber
Lavauxia acaulis [syn. Œnothera]
Leontopodium alpinum
Lewisia species
*Linaria alpina and L. Cymbalaria
Linum alpinum, L. salsoloides
Lithospermum graminifolium

Megapterium missouriense (Syn. Œnothera)
Minuartia laricifolia (Arenaria)
Morisia monantha (hypogæa)
Nepeta Faassenii (Mussinii)
Onosma albo-roseum, O. tauricum
Penstemon Menziesii, P. Scouleri
Phlox amœna, P. subulata vars.
Phyteuma comosum
Polygonum affine
*Primula Allionii, P. Auricula, and P. viscosa
*Ramonda Myconi
Santolina incana
Saponaria cæspitosa and S. ocymoides
*Saxifraga species
Sedum species
Sempervivum species var.
Silene Schafta
Teucrium Polium
Thymus serpyllum coccineus
Tunica Saxifraga
Veronica Guthrieana
Zauschneria californica

NOTE.—Those plants suitable for growing in the shade are marked *.

CHAPTER 22

THE PAVED GARDEN

It is, indeed, pleasing to note that those responsible for designing and laying out gardens have recently made great efforts to obtain effects, both as regards form and colour grouping, similar to those which nature herself so unfailingly accomplishes. Thus we see the reason for the present popularity of the wild garden, the rock garden, and the modern paved garden, all of which aim at providing as natural as possible a setting for so many delightful flowers which, either singly or in masses, are only seen at their best when grown as nature intended that they should be.

The paved garden consists of a path or any area, of whatever size and shape, covered with "crazy" paving or flagstones, in the crevices between which dwarf rock plants and creepers are planted or, better still, are allowed to seed naturally.

CONSTRUCTION

The most suitable position for the paved garden is in connection with the rock garden, the bog garden, or the water garden.

The site must, of course, be well drained; in fact, the foundations should be constructed in the same way as those of any ordinary pathway. Over this base is placed a layer of sand and soil some three to six inches in thickness, and on this the flags are laid in an irregular pattern and so that there are gaps of some one to two inches between the stones. (*See* Crazy Paving, p. 89.) As to the stones used, the majority should not be less than about ten inches in diameter, otherwise, the paving will have a patchy appearance.

Stones rectangular in shape are invariably best for paths, but for covering square, circular, and oval spaces the flags may be of any shape and size, provided they are not too regular. The spaces between the stones should be filled with good loamy soil mixed with an eighth part old mortar, and in this will be inserted the plants in small groups or in isolated tufts. A selection of plants suitable to this purpose will be found on p. 204.

SUITABLE PLANTS

In making the paved garden, however, it must not be thought that to plant naturally is to plant without order or reason. Nature is severely orderly in her workings and everything has its allotted place. Only certain plants are, therefore, suitable to the paved garden; these are dwarf in nature and many of them will thrive although trodden on and walked over to a considerable degree, for it must be remembered that the prime reason for a path is its utility as a means of progress. A limited number of plants only, therefore, must be planted in the interstices of the paving and these must appear to have seeded naturally from surrounding borders or from the rock garden, and must in no way impede the pedestrian, although the paved garden should not be subject to constant traffic. More paved gardens are spoiled by indiscriminate and excessive planting than by any other cause. If rock-work of any kind forms the boundary to the path or the paved garden, allow the plants covering it to encroach a little way, and in an irregular manner, over the flagstones. This informality will add a touch of harmony and will help to erase the traces of the handiwork of man.

SOME PLANTS FOR THE PAVED GARDEN

NOTE.—For Cultural Details and for Colour, Height, and Time of Flowering, *see* the A.B.C. of Plants, page 255.

*Acæna Buchananii, A. microphylla and A. myriophylla
Achillea rupestris and A. tomentosa
Alyssum montanum
Antennaria dioica and A. d., var. tomentosa
Anthyllis montana
Arabis bellidifolia variegata
*Arenaria balearica
Armeria maritima
Aubrieta vars.
Bellium minutum
Calamintha alpina
Campanula cæspitosa, C. cochleariifolia, C. garganica, C. Portenschlagiana
Cerastium arvense and C. tomentosum

*Corydalis lutea
Dianthus deltoides and ceasius
Dryas octopetala
*Erinus alpinus vars.
Erodium chamædryoides
Geranium Pylzowianum
Globularia cordifolia
Gypsophila cerastioides, G. repens
Helianthemum vars.
Herniaria glabra
Hutchinsia alpina
Hypericum nummularium and H. reptans
*Linaria alpina, L. repens
Lippia nodiflora
Lotus corniculatus fl. pl.
*Mazus Pumilio, M. radicans
*Mentha Requienii
*Mimulus radicans

Minuartia laricifolia
Morisia monantha (hypogœa)
Oxalis corniculata var. atropurpurea and O. Acetosella rosea
Paronychia argentea and P. serpyllifolia
Penstemon Menziesii
Potentilla alba and nitida
Saponaria ocymoides
Saxifraga species and vars.
Sedum acre, S. album, S. anglicum
Sempervivum montanum and S. tectorum
Silene acaulis
Thymus Serpyllum and T. S. var. lanuginosus
Tunica Saxifraga
Veronica alpina, V. repens
*Viola cornuta

NOTE.—Those plants suitable for growing in the shade are marked *.

PLATE 19   A dry wall makes an attractive addition to a garden.   After the initial laying out and planting it requires hardly any close attention.

H. & V. Joel

PLATE 20   Top left, Sagittaria japonica plena and top right, Nymphaea (Blue Beauty).   Below, a medium-size water garden with rockery and dry wall.

CHAPTER 23

THE WATER GARDEN

When we speak of the water garden, we mean a garden of plants growing actually in water or in the saturated ground adjacent to water where the soil is periodically submerged.

Few features in a garden are more attractive and interesting than the water garden.

The pond selected for the water garden can be large or small, it may be constructed in part of a river, or a tiny stream may afford the water supply. It is, however, useless to attempt water gardening unless a continuous supply of water, the year through, is available. A very small supply, even a trickle artificially laid on, will suffice, provided it is continuous, but a water garden which is liable to dry up in the summer is a source of disappointment.

A low-lying piece of land should be selected, preferably one where a natural depression already exists. One should look down on the plants; it should not be necessary to have to look up at them, as is sometimes the case when the water garden is constructed of artificial tanks. The pond—assuming that one does not already exist—should be made about 3 feet in depth at the deepest point.

DESIGNING THE POND OR STREAM

We should first of all consider the situation of the artificial water garden, and remember that the aim is to construct it in harmony with its surroundings as nearly as possible. Let the water garden, therefore, occupy the lowest-lying part of the ground, and to assist in this striving for harmony, the water garden may often be advantageously associated with the wild garden, or the rock garden. Size can be made to suit requirements and the surrounding conditions, providing the water is deep enough to grow plants.

Shape is dependent upon space available and the other features of the garden; naturalness must be the aim, and it should be remembered that a series of sharp and erratic curves will never produce a pleasing and natural outline.

The design must be simple; and although curves may be used, of course, they must be long, sweeping, and natural. On the other hand, not a single curve need come into the picture; the severely simple square or rectangular

205

pool has a charm all its own. In such cases, the garden becomes more formal, the pool may well be bordered by a paved walk, and in the crevices between the stones may grow small wall or rock plants. Where the more informal shape has been chosen, the grass may be allowed to clothe the gently sloping banks right down to the water's edge, and bog- and marsh-loving plants can be planted from the brink of the pond or stream up to the higher slopes.

DEPTH OF WATER

Few water plants, except very strong growers, which are better excluded even from the moderately large water garden, require a greater depth of water than $2\frac{1}{2}$ to 3 feet. To allow for the thickness of the pond lining and for the inclusion of soil to nourish the roots, it is necessary to excavate to a depth of somewhat over 3 feet. The actual walls of the pond itself are best cut perpendicularly if concrete is to be used (they must be left sloping if the pond is to be "puddled" with clay), but the earth should be thrown well back several feet from the pond so that the banks, on which the bog and marsh plants are to grow, may slope very gently right down to the water's edge.

Now as to the impervious lining to keep the water in the pond. There are three materials that can be used, puddled clay, bricks and mortar, or concrete and cement.

We would recommend the last as being the easiest to work and the most lasting.

Where the sub-soil consists of a stiff, sticky, impervious clay, puddling, provided it is well done and is carried to a depth of from 8 to 10 inches, is a cheaper and equally successful process.

EXCAVATING THE POND

It must be remembered that all constructional work will have to be hidden and that a permanently moist margin of soil some 2 to 3 feet wide round the pond to accommodate marsh plants will be desirable. It will, therefore, be necessary to excavate to a width sufficient to allow for this; that is to say, supposing it has been decided that the pond shall be 10 feet wide, a hole 3 feet deep all over and 16 feet wide will have to be dug. This allows for a $2\frac{1}{2}$ foot margin of moist earth, as well as 6 inches for the thickness of the wall on each side, if concrete is used.

The concrete at the bottom of the pond need not be more than 5 inches in thickness.

When the excavation is complete, all loose soil must be dug out and the bottom made thoroughly firm by pounding with a heavy beater. If the soil over which the concrete is to be laid is left loose, it may shrink away and cause the concrete to crack.

206

MIXING THE CONCRETE

Concrete is a mixture of cement, sand, gravel, broken stones, brick rubbish or similar materials in varying proportions. A useful mixture consists of one part of cement, two parts of sand, and five parts of gravel, broken stone, or brick. Whilst still in the dry state, the materials should be turned over two or three times. The heap is then wetted with water poured over it from a large water-pot fitted with a fine rose, and the whole mixed by again turning it over once or twice, so that the materials may be thoroughly amalgamated.

CONSTRUCTING THE POND

When well mixed and in a semi-liquid condition, place a layer of concrete 6 to 9 inches thick over the bottom of the pond and work it well with

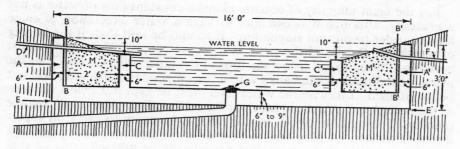

FIG. 35. MAKING THE LILY POND

A and *A'* are walls of concrete 6 inches thick; *C* and *C'* are also of concrete and of the same thickness, but are 10 inches shorter than the outer walls. *B* to *B'* shows the overall width of the pond; *M* and *M'* are pockets of saturated soil for bog plants; *D* is the inflow pipe; *E.E'* corners with hard core underneath and *F* the overflow. The plug *G* enables the pond to be emptied and cleaned.

the trowel or shovel before smoothing it down firmly; next build a retaining wall of boards parallel to the earth walls, but 6 inches nearer the centre of the pond. The gap between the wood and the earth sides, when filled up with concrete, will form the two walls A and A'. The supporting boards B'B' and BB are, of course, not removed until the concrete is thoroughly dry.

Now construct the two inner walls C and C', each 2½ feet from the outer retaining walls, but 10 inches shorter than them. Every 2 or 3 feet along the bottom construct small bridges six inches high by means of pipes or slates sufficiently large to allow the water to pass freely and also to drain the soil when emptying the pond. Always make sure that the joint be-

207

tween the base and the wall is clear of soil that may have worked its way over the surface. This is best ensured by scrubbing the surface with a coarse brush and water. It is most necessary also to work the concrete in the walls well to prevent their being porous.

An inflow pipe D and an outlet pipe F should be inserted before the concrete work is completed. As soon as the concrete is quite dry, it should be roughed over, wetted, and then thoroughly worked over with cement-wash, 2 inches in thickness, care being taken to see that the corners E and E' are perfectly watertight. A word of warning may here be given —it is unwise, apart from the shade cast and the dead leaves and twigs that will fall into the water, to construct a pond under or near trees, for their roots run a considerable distance underground, and are in time likely to crack the concrete unless it is very strong.

THE WATER SUPPLY

For the great majority of aquatic plants a constant flow of water is not a necessity, although it is essential to have a water circulation of some kind in order to prevent stagnation. It should be said that, if the border of marsh plants around the pond is to prove successful, the water must never be allowed to fall below the tops of the inner walls C and C', or the marshy conditions of the banks within the outer containing walls will not be maintained. Likewise the water level must be kept just below the tops of the walls A and A', or too much of the surrounding ground will become marshy. The outflow pipe F is, therefore, a necessity to carry off super-fluous rainwater. A plug and outflow G at the bottom of the pond is a useful feature, the water may then periodically be drained away so that the pond can be cleaned and rearranged.

PREPARATION FOR PLANTING

When the concrete is thoroughly dry, the spaces M and M' between the retaining walls A and C and A' and C' are filled with a compost of loam and peat, or loam and leaf-mould, placed on a 6-inch layer of broken bricks or clinkers to provide drainage. The soil may then be banked up so that the tops of the walls A and A' are covered with soil and hidden from sight. The surrounding ground should slope up gently from this point, so that turf may, in places, run right down to the water's edge whence the water and marsh plants may best be surveyed.

At other points, rocks may be firmly cemented on the tops of the walls A and A', and sometimes just below the water level. These shelves under the water will form ledges on which aquatics can be planted, and the rocks, which can be built up as miniature cliffs on one side of the pond, will present an excellent contrast to the smooth turf running down to the water's edge on the other.

208

STATEN ISLAND

WABASH

PLATE 7 *I R I S*

FIRE DANCE

ST. MARY

In the moist pockets M and M' are planted the bog or marsh plants, those requiring 4 to 6 inches of water over their crowns being placed under water lower down the bank, while a shade higher up the moist shelf should be grouped those plants flourishing on cool, moist, swampy banks. The bottom of the pond should be covered with fine soil some 12 inches deep.

HOW TO PLANT

The best method of planting water plants in a pond or lake is in pans, small tubs or flat baskets, in which the plants are placed in fibrous loam and a little well-decayed cow-manure, the pans or baskets then being gently lowered into the water in the desired situation. A layer of enriched mud should cover the bottom of the pond, the baskets resting in this so that the roots of the plants can work out and ramble at will.

The margin of the pond should be clothed with such plants as spread out on the surface of the water, while rooting in the firm soil at the water's edge. Among these are the water forget-me-not, *Myosotis scorpioides*, *Calla palustris*, and *Veronica Beccabunga*. These, prettily grouped, will clothe the margin, while beyond them the taller-growing plants, such as irises and spiræas, with the sedges, grasses, and rushes, thrive on the slightly swampy banks.

Many of the ferns love such a situation as this, among them the beautiful *Osmunda regalis*.

CARE OF THE WATER GARDEN

Once planted, many aquatic and marsh plants are better if left undisturbed, and only lifted and replanted when they appear to be unhealthy and ailing. Others, however, are much like hardy perennials in their requirements and thrive best if lifted, divided, and replaced every third or fourth spring, or when they appear overcrowded. Some of the water lilies make tremendous leaf growth and consequently little bloom, cover the surface of the water, and prevent the sun's rays

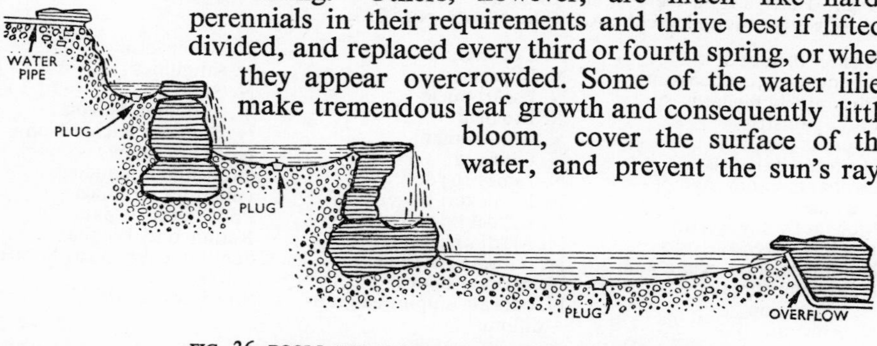

FIG. 36. POOLS AND WATERFALLS IN THE ROCK GARDEN
The rocks forming the pools in the above diagram must be set in cement to keep the structure firm; the pools are of concrete and lined with cement. A continuous trickle, artificially fed if necessary, will keep the miniature falls running.

from warming it; a function so essential to most aquatics, especially the nymphæas or water lilies. This strong growth must be periodically cut away, and the roots should be divided if necessary.

Blanket Weed

Many people are troubled with an objectionable slimy green growth called Blanket weed. This covers the surface of the water in hot, dry weather, usually in spring and summer. It may be disposed of by adding 4 oz. of copper sulphate or 1 oz. of potassium permanganate to each 25,000 gallons of water contained in the pond. A second application should be made in a week's time, should the first be unsuccessful. This will harm neither plants nor fish.

NOTE.—To obtain the capacity of a pond, multiply the length, breadth and average depth in feet, then multiply by 6 and this will give the approximate number of gallons of water contained in the pond.

PROPAGATION OF AQUATIC PLANTS

Aquatic plants, as they are termed, are propagated, some by seed and some by division of the roots, which is best carried out in early spring just before growth commences. The seeds, when sown, must be placed under water. In other respects they require the same general treatment as other herbaceous plants.

(*See also* the Alphabetical List of Plants, Chapter 34, for the culture of individual aquatics.)

A SELECTION OF PLANTS FOR THE WATER GARDEN

NOTE.—For Cultural Details, and notes as to Colour, Height, Time of Flowering, and depth of water required, *see* the A.B.C. of Plants, page 255.

Alisma Plantago
*Aponogeton distachyum
Butomus umbellatus
Calla palustris
Cyperus longus
Hottonia palustris
Limnanthemum nymph-
 æoides
Menyanthes trifoliata
Nuphar advena
Nymphæa alba plenissima
N. atropurpurea
N. Attraction
N. Aurora

N. Colossea
N. Ellisiana
N. Escarboucle
N. Frœbelii
N. Gladstoniana
N. Gloriosa
N. James Brydon
N. Laydekeri fulgens
N. Laydekeri purpurata
N. Marliacea vars.
N. odorata maxima
N. odorata minor
N. odorata sulphurea gran-
 diflora

N. Robinsonii
N. sanguinea
N. Sunrise
N. tetragona helvola
N. tuberosa Richardsonii
N. W. B. Shaw
Orontium aquaticum
Peltandra virginica
Pontederia cordata
Ranunculus Lingua
Sagittaria japonica, S. lati
 folia
Stratiotes aloides

NOTE.—Those plants suitable for growing in the shade are marked *.

CHAPTER 24

THE MARSH OR BOG GARDEN

Although its presence is to be desired, for the overflow can be used to feed the marsh, a pond is not an essential feature of the bog garden. It is vital, however, that the soil of the marsh garden shall be kept in a moist, swampy state through the whole year. The site of the bog garden must, naturally be low-lying, and where the surface drainage will naturally collect. If the subsoil is of sticky clay, a mere trickle of water will keep the ground in a sufficiently moist condition. Should the subsoil be light and well drained, a certain amount of excavation will be necessary.

CONSTRUCTION

Dig out about two feet of the top soil and introduce a little clay to form a basis, over this spread a five-inch bed of rubble or large stones, and then a layer of coarse soil. Now fill the hollow, almost to the level of the surrounding land, with a compost of half loam and half leaf-mould or peat.

Unless a natural flow of water is available, an artificial trickle, just sufficient to keep the bog swampy, must be introduced. Because bog plants should never suffer from drought, the marsh garden should be kept quite moist, but on the other hand must not become stagnant, and it is for this reason that slight bottom drainage is introduced. The bog should never be more than two feet in depth, its extent, of course, will depend on the space available and upon taste.

Paths of rough stones or bricks should be made through the bog, and over these should be placed flat stepping-stones, in order to make every part of the bog accessible.

SELECTING THE PLANTS

As will be seen from our list, which shows a few good marsh plants, there is no scarcity in this direction. Almost any moisture-loving plant may be used, so may all the subjects that are usually to be found at the margins of streams and ponds, even some of those which at times have six or more inches of water over their crowns; in fact, all plants growing freely in shallow water may also be grown in the bog garden. Be careful not to overcrowd the plants, rather group together three to five plants of the same kind, leave a space, and again plant a clump of subjects of different colour, type, and height. This irregularity and variety will please the eye, which would tend to become surfeited by a mass of the same colour, size, and form. The actual marsh plants selected will depend upon the layout and size of the garden. The natural surroundings must also be very carefully considered. If the area is restricted, greater variety and beauty can be obtained by the use of small-growing species; while among extensive surroundings full rein may be given to the freer-growing plants, many of which are invaluable as a background where space permits. It is always necessary, however, to bear in mind the size to which the plants will grow in time, and to arrange them accordingly.

Only a sound knowledge of the habits and rate of growth of the plants introduced and a clear visualization of the picture one is endeavouring to produce can ensure success in this exceedingly difficult matter of planting for future effect. The novice will certainly find it no easy matter, but he will soon learn by experience. The most usual fault is over-crowding, and he will be wise if he will make up his mind to avoid this at any cost. Let him study the plants in their native haunts, and then, when planting them, endeavour to give them as natural a site as possible. If he will "follow nature" as closely as circumstances permit, he will stand a good chance of making a charming and realistic marsh garden.

SOME PLANTS FOR THE MARSH GARDEN

Acorus Calamus and A. C. var. variegatus
Anagallis tenella
Aruncus sylvester
Arundinaria (Bamboo) species
Arundo Donax
Astilbe species and hybrids
Caltha palustris fl. pl.
Caltha polypetala
Cardamine pratensis fl. pl.
Cimicifuga racemosa
Cypripedium reginea
Dodecatheon Media
Filipendula palmata
Gentiana Pneumonanthe, G. asclepiadea, etc.
Geum rivale
Gunnera manicata and G. chilensis

Helonias bullata
Hemerocallis vars.
Heracleum villosum
*Hosta species and vars.
Iris aurea, I. fulva, I. Kæmpferi, I. Monnieri, I. Monspur, I. orientalis, I. Pseudacorus, I. sibirica vars.
*Leucojum æstivum
Ligularia clivorum
Lysimachia clethroides, L. Nummularia
Lythrum Salicaria roseum
*Mimulus cardinalis, etc.
Osmunda regalis
Parnassia palustris
Peltiphyllum peltatum
Petasites fragrans, P. japonicus

Phormium tenax
*Pinguicula vulgaris
Polygonatum multiflorum
*Primula Beesiana, P. Buleyana, P. Florindæ, P. japonica, P. Juliæ, P. rosea grandiflora, P. sikkimensis, P. vulgaris, etc.
Ranunculus aconitifolius
Rodgersia æsculifolia and R. tabularis
Sarracenia purpurea
Saxifraga Hirculus, S. pennsylvanica
Scirpus lacustris
Thalictrum species
Trollius species and vars.
Typha angustifolia and T. minima

Note.—Those plants marked * will grow in the shade.

CHAPTER 25

FERNS

Ferns can always be distinguished from other plants by two characteristics. Firstly, their young fronds are curled up tightly and gradually unroll as they grow, till the whole leaf is flat and visible. Secondly, they bear, generally on the back of their fronds, lines or masses of very small capsules (sporangia) filled with spores that look like fine brown powder. These are the "spores" from which the young ferns grow.

The great variety found among ferns, both as regards size, appearance, and the conditions under which they flourish, makes them one of the most useful of plants to the gardener. They are found all over the world, and vary in size from the tiny moss-like specimens found on the walls and in rock crevices to the gigantic tree ferns of the New World. There used to be an idea that ferns would only do really well in a warm temperature, but this has been found untrue even of many of the exotic kinds. Of course, our own hardy ferns provide a wonderful variety of beautiful kinds, but there are many foreigners which will succeed equally well out of doors in our climate.

Ferns generally may be grown among other plants in the rock garden; they can be planted in masses in some cool and shaded spot in the marsh garden; or some place may be devoted to them alone, and most charming fern gardens may be made in parts of the garden where nothing else flourishes, for most of the hardy ferns are shade lovers and need practically no sunlight.

HARDY FERNS
Habits and Requirements

Hardy ferns, as a general rule, like a sheltered and shady position, away from drying winds, where their roots can get at plenty of water. Although they must not have direct sunlight they must have plenty of air and light, or they will become drawn up and weakly. Where they grow naturally, they are accustomed to a certain amount of protection from the frost, provided by their own dead fronds. When grown in the garden, therefore, the dead leaves should not be cut away in autumn, but should be allowed to remain until after the frosts of the following spring. Wild ferns also get a good supply of water during the winter months whilst they are dormant.

These conditions should be imitated as closely as may be possible in the garden.

Ferns like a deep loam, with a good deal of leaf-mould, peat, and some coarse sand in it, and although kept moist, it should be well-drained. There are just a few which will flourish in boggy and marshy places, but even these prefer their water supply to be in the form of a running stream or moving pool. In planting ferns together, they should be arranged with a certain amount of care, that the evergreen and deciduous kinds may be fairly distributed.

For propagation, *see* Greenhouse Ferns, p. 215.

GREENHOUSE FERNS

The position of the fernhouse should be exactly opposite to that of the greenhouse—that is to say, it should front to the north, north-east, or north-west.

Atmosphere and Temperature

Nearly all the half-hardy ferns may be grown in a greenhouse unheated in the summer, but slight artificial heat is necessary to keep the temperature to about 40 deg. F. in winter. Tender ferns, of course, need a temperature on a winter's night of at least 60 deg. F. and must, therefore, be grown in the warm house.

Ferns at all times, and especially in summer, need a moist atmosphere and should be shaded from the direct rays of the sun. From October until April most varieties are more or less dormant, and at this time require to be kept cooler than during their period of growth in summer and also considerably drier at the roots, although no ferns should ever be allowed to become "dust-dry". The atmosphere, too, should be less humid at this period.

Ventilation.

Ventilation in the fernhouse needs careful attention and should be attended to as advised for the greenhouse, p. 231.

Potting

Spring, just when the new growth is starting, is the best time for this. For most ferns two parts fibrous loam, and the remaining part composed of well-sieved rotted manure, sifted leaf-mould or peat, coarse sand, and some powdered charcoal forms an excellent compost.

For information as to pot sizes, how to pot, and treatment after potting, *see* Chapter 12, in which all aspects of potting and re-potting plants are thoroughly discussed.

Watering

It is essential that all ferns should be watered regularly and on no account should they be allowed to become dry at the roots.

During spring and summer when the ferns are making new fronds, the atmosphere in the house must be kept fairly moist, by keeping the staging and floors of the house damp, while on hot days a light spray overhead with a very fine syringe is beneficial, except in the case of such types that have any trace of farina or powder on the fronds.

THE PROPAGATION OF FERNS

Spores

Ferns may be increased by several methods, the most general is by means of "spores" which are contained in small capsules (sporangia), usually on the underside of the fronds. When these capsules are ripe, that is just before they are ready to burst, the fronds should be picked and wrapped in smooth, white paper. If these are undone after a day or so, the paper will be found to be covered with fine, brown dust, which looks like brown pollen, and is composed of millions of tiny "spores". The spores are sown in the same way as seeds (*see* Sowing Seed under Glass, p. 102), but the compost used, e.g. equal parts of loam, peat, leaf-mould, and sand, must be first sterilized with boiling water (*see* p. 54), and then allowed to cool. When sown, the pans should be stood in a saucer of water in a shady place and should have a pane of glass placed over the top of each, for it is fatal to let pans get dry. Ferns may be propagated by spores at any time, but preferably in March or July.

Division of Roots

This method is best carried out in March or April, at which time the ferns are planted out. (*See* Division of Roots, p. 107.)

Trailing Roots

This is the simplest of all methods, and consists in cutting off an inch or so of the tuberous rhizome of such ferns as the polypody, and potting it up. The root must, of course, have a frond sprouting from it.

Minute Plants on Fronds

On Shield-ferns and some others, there appear from time to time small replicas of the parent plant. The frond bearing these may be pegged down on pots of sandy soil standing by the side of the parent plant or may be cut off and pegged down on to shallow boxes or pots filled with light, sandy, well-sieved, and smooth soil. The little plants will soon root, when they can be cut apart and potted-up. A close, moist atmosphere will encourage rooting.

FERNS

SOME HARDY FERNS

Adiantum pedatum (Hardy Maidenhair), D.
Asplenium Adiantum-nigrum (Black Maidenhair-Spleenwort), E.
A. fontanum (Smooth Rock Spleenwort), E.
A. Ruta-muraria (Wall Rue), E.
A. septentrionale (Forked Spleenwort), E.
A. Trichomanes (Maidenhair Spleenwort), E.
A. viride (Green Spleenwort), E.
Athyrium Filix-fœmina vars. (Lady Fern), cristatum, depauperatum, multifurcatum, plumosum elegans, and pulcherrimum, D.
Blechnum spicant B. orientale (Hard Fern), B. penna marina (Alpine Hard Fern) E.
Cryptogramme (syn. Allosorus) crispa (Mountain Parsley Fern), E.
Cystopteris fragilis (Alpine Bladder Fern), D.

Cystopteris bulbifera and C. montana (Mountain Bladder Fern), D.
Dryopteris æmulum (Hay-scented Fern), E.
D. Filix-mas (Common Male Fern), D.
D. Linnæana (Oak Fern), D.
D. Oreopteris, D. O. vars. cristatum gracile, and ramo-coronans (Mountain Buckler Fern), E.
D. Phegopteris (Beech Fern), D.
D. remota and D. rigida (Remote, and Rigid Buckler Ferns), D.
D. Robertiana, E.
D. spinulosa, D. s. var. grandiceps, D. s. var. lepidotum, and D. Goldiænum (Broad Buckler Fern), E. and D. Thelypteris (Prickly, and Marsh Buckler Ferns), E.
Lastrea. See Dryopteris
Onoclea sensibilis (Sensitive Fern) D.

Osmunda regalis (Royal Fern), O. regalis cristata, D.
Phyllitis Scolopendrium (Hart's Tongue), E.
P. S. var. crispum (Frilled Hart's Tongue), E.
P. S. Kelwayii (Tasselled Hart's Tongue), E.
Polypodium vulgare (Common Polypody), E.
P. v. cambricum (Welsh Polypody), E.
P. v. var. cornubiense (Cornish Polypody), E.
P. v. var. semilacerum (Irish Polypody), E.
Polystichum acrostichoides (Christmas Fern), D.
P. aculeatum (Hard Shield Fern), E.
P. aculeatum cristatum (Soft Prickly Shield Fern), E., and P. a. plumosum
P. Lonchitis (Holly Fern), E.
Pteridium aquilinum (Bracken), D.
Woodsia alpina and W. ilvensis D.

SOME STOVE AND COOL GREENHOUSE FERNS

Adiantum æthiopicum, A. Capillus Veneris and vars., A. cuneatum and vars., A. formosum, A. Moorei, A. tenerum and A. farleyense, etc. (Maidenhair Fern)
Anemia Phyllitidis and A. rotundifolia (Flowering Fern)
Asplenium biforme, A. bulbiferum, A. caudatum, A. Nidus, etc. (Spleenwort)
Blechnum brasiliense, B. gibbum (Deer Fern), B. Moorei, and B. occidentale
Camptosorus rhizophyllus
Ceropteris calomelanos and var. chrysophylla, etc. (Gold and Silver Ferns)
Cyathea medullaris (Tree Fern)

Cyclophorus Lingua
Cyrtomium caryotideum, C. falcatum (Shield Fern)
Davallia bullata, D. canariensis, D. elegans, D. solida var. fijiensis, etc. (Hare's Foot Fern)
Doodia aspera and D. media
Dryopteris decomposita, D. parasitica, D. patens, etc. (Buckler Fern)
Hemitelia capensis
Leptopteris superba (Filmy Fern)
Nephrolepis cordifolia and var. compacta, N. exaltata, and N. e. var. elegantissima (Ladder Fern)
Onychium japonicum
Osmunda regalis (Royal Fern) vars. japonica and corymbifera, O. palustris

Pellæa cordata, P. hastata, and P. rotundifolia (Cliff Brake Fern)
Phyllitis rhizophyllum
Platycerium bifurcatum, P. grande (Elk's Horn)
Polypodium appendiculatum, P. aureum vars. glaucum, & Mayi, P. subauriculatum (Polypody or Oak Fern)
Polystichum cristatum
Pteris cretica and vars albolineata, Alexandræ and cristata, P. internata, P. longifolia quadriaurita var. argyræa, P. serrulata and var. cristata (Ribbon Fern)
Todea barbara (Crape Fern)
Trichomanes radicans (Killarney Fern)
Woodwardia radicans vars. orientalis, and plumosa

NOTE.—Although most ferns can be raised from spores, the numerous varieties of some of the species are not likely to come true when so raised, and should, therefore, be increased by division. D denotes Deciduous; E, Evergreen.

216

CHAPTER 26

ORNAMENTAL GRASSES

It is scarcely possible to overestimate the decorative qualities of ornamental grasses. Some are exceedingly graceful, others remarkably neat and compact in growth. There are some again, very curious in form; while others are stately and majestic in appearance. The graceful and curious are best suited for planting in the border or wild garden, while the neat, compact-growing kinds make beautiful subjects for the rock garden. By the side of streams and ponds the larger-growing species make handsome specimens.

In spite of the utility, and the ease with which most of them may be grown, ornamental grasses are not used in gardens to anything like the extent that they should be.

Many of the species may be gathered and dried, when they are useful for winter decoration.

TALL-GROWING GRASSES

First, let us consider those splendid importations from the River Plate, *Cortaderia Selloana* [*C. argentea*] (Pampas-grass), and *C. conspicua* (Silvery Reed-grass from New Zealand). In severe winters these should have some dry, strawy litter thrown over them, and a few spruce boughs or evergreen shrubs stuck round to prevent the litter from blowing away.

The Pampas-grass is decidedly the king of all grasses, and deserves a place in every garden. As the centre group of a *grassery*, an isolated lawn specimen, or placed in a shady dell, near rocks or water, it finds a congenial home.

A rich alluvial soil, at least three feet deep, abundance of space to unfold its large, graceful leaves, and throw up its flower-stems, an unlimited supply of water, and shelter from strong winds, are all the conditions it demands. It can be raised from seed, and with liberal treatment seedlings will flower in their third or fourth year. By sowing thinly in February or March in pots, and planting out in prepared beds in May, almost a season may be gained in the growth of the plants. It can also be rapidly increased by division in spring.

Plants that have been thus divided are more tender than others, and will require more protection and a stake to keep them firm until they are thoroughly established.

ORNAMENTAL GRASSES

A companion grass to this, with broad-striped foliage and large, feathery flowers, is the *Erianthus Ravennæ*, the Woolly Beard Grass, growing to four or more feet in height. Other tall-growing grasses are: *Arundo Donax*; and a beautiful, little-known kind, *Glyceria maxima var. variegata*. The Tussock Grass (*Deschampsia cæspitosa*) and some of the common reeds and rushes also form beautiful features when used in connection with these.

ANNUAL GRASSES

Among the annual grasses we have several varieties of *Zea Mays* (Maize), which has a most pleasing effect when planted among other subjects. These are half-hardy annuals, and should be sown in gentle heat, being pushed rapidly forward so as to secure strong plants for planting out in May.

The remarkably pretty Millet Grass, *Milium effusum*, charming Love Grasses (*Eragrostis multiflora*, and *E. ægyptiaca*), and the several species of *Briza*, or Quaking Grass, especially *B. maxima* and *B. minor*, should be sown either in pots or in a rather sheltered site out of doors.

Other beautiful annual grasses are: *Agrostis tenuis* (Bent Grass), and *A. pulchella*; *Bromus brizæformis; Desmazeria sicula*, whose branches rival in beauty the deciduous cypress; *Hordeum jubatum* (Crested Barley Grass); and *Lagurus ovatus*, the Hare's Tail Grass. *Rhynchelytrum repens* (Natal Grass) is also useful, and, like all other annual grasses, should be raised from seed.

Last but by no means least there is *Mibora minima*, a pretty miniature grass which grows no higher than one to two inches.

PERENNIALS

The Feather Grasses, *Stipa arundinacea*, and *Stipa pennata*, *S. Calamagrostis* and *S. splendens*, along with *Miscanthus japonicus*, *M. sacchariflorus*, *M. sinensis*, and the varieties of the last named, *M. s. variegatus* and *M. s. zebrinus*, are all most useful for mixing with other flowers, and very elegant in themselves, all reach a height of 3 to 5 feet, with the exception of *M. sacchariflorus* which will grow to 10 feet in a suitable situation. The smallest Feather Grass almost rivals the *Festuca glauca* for edgings. The handsome silver foliage of the *Festuca* contrasts beautifully with red gravel paths. The flower-stems require cutting off in summer. The Buffalo-Grass, *Tripsacum dactyloides*, and the Lyme-Grass, *Elymus arenarius*, are two other kinds well worth growing.

CULTURE OF GRASSES

As has been said already, ornamental grasses will grow in any ordinary soil with very little care from the gardener.

Annuals

The hardy annuals are best sown where they have to grow, the seed being put in in April, or in May in colder localities. Except in cold, damp soils and in exposed districts, most hardy annuals are all the better if treated as biennials and sown in July or August where they are to grow. Half-hardy annuals are sown under glass in a temperature of from 60 deg. to 70 deg. F., hardened off in May, and planted out in June; or they can be sown the middle of May where they are to grow.

Perennials

Hardy perennials are sown in a nursery bed of fine soil in the open in May and June, and are transplanted to their permanent positions in October; half-hardy species being sown under glass in March, to be planted out in the open in the next October, while some of the more difficult ones are best raised in a frame and kept in pots during the winter. All grasses sown where they are to grow must be thinned when from two to three inches high, if bushy plants are to result. Almost all species thrive in good, well-drained loam, in a sunny, open position. In cold, damp situations, it is frequently necessary to treat many of the perennials as annuals and to raise fresh plants each year. Perennial grasses are also propagated by division of roots either in April or October, at which times they may also be transplanted.

CUTTING AND DRYING FOR WINTER USE

Apart from their beauty as rock, marsh, and wild garden plants, many ornamental grasses, when correctly dried, can be used effectively to fill the flower vases, or at least to supplement the cut flowers, during the period of shortage of blooms through the winter months. They must, however, be cut at the right time, usually between June and the end of August, and must be correctly dried; otherwise they quickly assume a sickly, dull colour, and the seeds soon drop.

In cutting, which must be done before the heads are fully out, and while the grass is still green, the stalks should be kept as long as possible. The grasses should be tied up in bunches preferably hung upside down and dried in a cool, airy place. Gathering must take place in fine weather and when the grass is quite dry.

219

CHAPTER 27

THE WILD GARDEN

The wild garden must be free and natural in its character; it must have none of the formality and neatness so essential to some other parts of the garden. The flowers of the wild garden must not be those that have been increased in size and varied in colour by the horticulturist, rather must they resemble their relations of the hedgerows, and the manner of their planting and grouping must be as if executed by nature herself.

Plants chosen for a wooded part of the wild garden must be those that will thrive in the shade or partial shade and under the drip of trees. They must also be able to withstand a certain amount of drought during the summer, as the trees themselves consume a great deal of moisture from the soil and, when in leaf, prevent much rain from reaching the soil. Woodland plants, therefore, usually have bulbs or thick tuberous roots, by means of which they are able to store up moisture and nutrition. The blue-bell is a good example of a woodland plant.

The plants selected for either wild or woodland gardens must be those that require little attention, no tying or staking; they must be those that will flourish in the soil the garden provides, and must be thoroughly hardy and suitable to the climate in which they have to grow, year in year out. It is chiefly to the bulbous and perennial plants and hardy shrubs that we look for subjects for the wild garden, for there should be a minimum of annual replanting, and very little trenching and digging of the soil, once the plants have been inserted, and there should be no need for protection during the winter, except in rare instances with plants of special value. It may, of course, become necessary from time to time to divide some of the crowns of the more vigorous growing species.

A point too often overlooked in choosing plants for the wild garden, is that they shall be as little as possible subject to such pests as slugs and caterpillars. Some plants are exceptionally free from pests, and these should be selected.

The most usual mistake made in planting is to include too many specimens; only a few should be scattered about naturally, and these, if suitable to their surroundings, will rapidly spread and gorgeous masses of colour and foliage will result. Study the individuals, and plant those loving partial shade round the edges of copses or in open glades. Shade-lovers may be set further in the woods, while those thriving in full sun should be kept

220

well in the open. It must be remembered that even the shade-lovers also require plenty of air and light.

With regard to naturalizing bulbs in grass, we would refer the reader to page 173, in our chapter on bulbs, where this fascinating subject is fully treated.

The following list, although by no means complete, as suitable subjects are almost innumerable, will give a very fair idea of plants that will look at home and which will thrive in the wild garden.

A FEW PLANTS SUITABLE FOR THE WILD GARDEN

NOTE.—For Cultural Details and notes on Colour, Height, and Time of Flowering, also the best Species and Varieties, *see* the A.B.C. of Plants, page 255.

Achillea filipendula
*Anemone apennina
Anemone hybrida vars.
*Aquilegia (Columbine) species
*Artemisia lactiflora
Aruncus sylvester
Arundinaria species (Bamboo)
Asperula odorata
*Astilbe Davidii
Brunnera macrophylla
Buphthalmum speciosum
Camellia japonica vars.
Campanula lactiflora
Centaurea babylonica
Clematis species and vars.
Convallaria majalis (Lily-of-the-Valley)
*Crocus species
*Cyclamen species
*Digitalis purpurea (Foxglove)
Doronicum plantagineum
*Epilobium angustifolium
*Eranthis hyemalis
Eryngium bromeliæfolium and E. pandanifolium
*Fritillarias imperialis and Meleagris
*Galanthus nivalis and other species (Snowdrops)

Galega officinalis and G. patula
Galtonia candicans
Gentiana asclepiadea
*Gunnera manicata
*Hedera Helix (Ivy)
Helianthus (Sunflower)
Hydrangea paniculata and var. grandiflora
Impatiens glandulifera
Iris fœtidissima and I. germanica
Kalmia latifolia
Kniphofia species and vars. (Red-hot Poker)
*Leucojum æstivum and L. vernum
Ligularia clivorum
Lilium croceum, L. giganteum, L. Hansonii, L. Martagon, L. pardalinum, L. pyrenaicum, and L. regale
Lunaria annua (Honesty)
Lupinus polyphyllus
*Meconopsis cambrica, M. betonicifolia (M. Baileyi)
Monarda didyma
Montbretia. (*See* Tritonia)
Myosotis pyrenaica and M. dissitiflora
Narcissus vars.
Œnothera biennis

Pæonia lactiflora vars. P. officinalis vars.
Phormium tenax
Polygonatum multiflorum (Solomon's Seal)
Polygonum campanulatum cuspidatum, P. molle, P. polystachyum
*Primula vulgaris (Primrose), P. Beesiana, P. Bulleyana, P. japonica, P. officinalis, P. sikkimensis, etc.
Rheum Alexandræ, R. Emodii and R. officinale
Rhododendron species and vars. [etc.
Rosa Moyesii, R. rugosa,
*Scilla nonscripta (Bluebell)
*Sibthorpia europæa
*Solidago canadensis, etc.
Thalictrum aquilegifolium, T. Delavayi
Tritonia Pottsii vars.
Tulips vars.
Valeriana officinalis
Verbascum phlomoides and V. pulverulentum
*Viburnum Opulus
*Vinca major and minor
Viola odorata (Violet)
*Woodwardia radicans (*see* Ferns)

See also List of Hardy Ferns, page 216, also Chapter 26, Ornamental Grasses.

NOTE.—The plants marked * will grow in the shade.

221

CHAPTER 28

THE TOWN GARDEN

It is frequently imagined that it is next to impossible to grow flowers successfully in a city or town garden, but this is far from being the truth. It is not at all a difficult task to maintain a succession of flowering plants throughout the greater part of the year, but, of course, only those plants must be selected that are known to be able to withstand the murky atmosphere to which they will be subjected. Soot is an excellent stimulant to vegetation when applied as a top-dressing or incorporated with the soil; it is highly deleterious when deposited on the leaves, stalks, and stems of growing plants. The breathing apparatus of all plants is on their leaves; if these are covered with soot, the plants are bound to suffer from a restriction of their means of respiration. The question as to what plants to grow becomes still more difficult to decide in those districts in which there are chemical works, since air impregnated with chemical fumes is particularly baneful to all plant life.

CARE OF THE TOWN GARDEN

Every garden, no matter where it may be situated, may be beautified. Under the most adverse conditions, but with plenty of light, grass will always be found to thrive excellently, if given a dressing of bonemeal spring and autumn and an occasional application of special lawn manure. Regular cutting and rolling are essentials in maintaining a good lawn, and once the grass is healthy, weeds and moss will have little chance to spread. Unsightly walls may be covered in the first place with trellis, and over this may be trained Ivies, Virginian Creepers, Jasmine, and Rose Gloire de Dijon and others. These will all prosper anywhere. One of the chief points to be remembered is that copious watering and syringing after a hot day is essential in the town garden. The harmful effect of soot and poisonous fumes in the atmosphere can be nullified to a great extent by a constant use of the syringe or watering can, to wash the foliage in the absence of rain. The soot and other solid matter deposited on the ground should be forked over at least once every year. If the soil is sour, as it is almost sure to be when it has not been treated for some time, lime should be dug in at the rate of 5 oz. to the square yard to sweeten it. If this is done, these impurities will prove a source of blessing rather than the reverse. Hoeing, too, should be far more frequent than in country

222

gardens, and poor soil should be replaced by loam, well-rotted manure and decayed garden refuse. In a town garden it is the more necessary to wage constant war on slugs and garden pests, as their ravages, once commenced, are deadly in the extreme. The town gardener will be wise to grown mainly hardy perennials and flowering shrubs and not to go in too much for the more tender bedding plants, which have to be renewed each year.

FLOWERS ALL THE YEAR ROUND

As an indication of what can be accomplished, even in the smallest town garden, the following rotation of plants is suggested. Other flowers, which will be found in the appended list, can also be grown.

For a winter flower the Christmas Rose is the best. This does well in a smoky atmosphere and brightens the garden considerably during the dull days of winter. Snowdrops can follow, since these bloom freely, while their place can be taken later by the crocus and tulip. These bulbs should be planted in good sized patches in October, and will make a fine show in March and April, especially if mixed with the common primrose. Virginian Stock can be sown round the patches of crocus in March, the latter affording the young stocks a certain amount of protection from wind and frost. Wallflowers can always be relied upon to make a particularly brave and colourful show.

Daffodils and Narcissus can follow, both proving adaptable to such surroundings. The yellow alyssum blooms at the same time; this should be struck from cuttings or raised from seed and kept in a cold frame throughout the winter. The rocket may come next, followed by daisies and pansies. The calceolaria always does well and will flower all the summer. These plants should be treated in the same way as the alyssum; that is to say, kept in a cold frame over the winter. Intermediate Stocks, too, will flower for a long period, if brought through the cold months in the same way, and planted out in March or early April. Scarlet pelargoniums (geraniums) can be depended upon to thrive well; therefore, these, too, should find a place in the town garden. If planted in March in a strong loam with the addition of leaf-mould and a little rotten dung, gladioli are excellent for the borders.

OTHER SUITABLE FLOWERS

Ageratum Houstonianum does very well. Cuttings planted early in September will keep in good condition through the winter. Verbenas flower profusely all the summer, but require care to keep through the winter. The dark Clove Carnation is very hardy and flowers beautifully. The Sweet-William, Lupin, Scabious, Antirrhinum, Polyanthus, Lychnis (Agrostemma) coronaria, Foxglove, and Lily of the Valley all do remarkably well. The Mimulus is a famous town flower. Nearly all the common hardy annuals may be recommended, especially branching Larkspur, Calendula, Collinsia bicolor, Phlox Drummondii, Lupinus, Coreopsis, etc. There are numbers of herbaceous plants that do very well, such as the Michaelmas Daisy (Aster), Double Sunflower, Sea-lavender (Limonium latifolium), and all hardy plants of this class. The varieties of the common English ferns thrive very well in shady parts, if watered every day in hot, dry weather. Dahlias do exceedingly well if well supplied with water, and carefully thinned as they advance in size. They ought to be planted very early in the spring, to get early bloom; as they are not required in September, the Chrysanthemum taking their place.

SHRUBS AND TREES FOR THE TOWN GARDEN

Many flowering and ornamental shrubs, especially several of those lately imported from the East, do quite well in town gardens. The Lilac blooms freely and does well as a screen, since it shows a little green in the summer. Aucuba japonica is the best tall evergreen in sheltered places. The euonymus does very well in smoke, and retains its foliage. Daphne Mezereum, and the white variety, do well, and flower freely. The two best rhododendrons for permanent planting in town gardens are Cunningham's White and Cunningham's Blush.

Dwarf roses, especially the free-flowering Hybrid Tea sorts, are amenable to culture in the town garden, provided the soil is suitable.

Do not plant too many privet hedges, they deplete the surrounding soil of much of its goodness. Berberis, Thorns, or Lilacs, make far more beautiful and satisfactory hedges and thrive in the town garden.

As regards forest-trees nothing does so well as the London Plane, *see* also list, p. 225.

PLANTS SUITABLE FOR THE TOWN GARDEN

For Notes on Colour, Height, Season of Flowering, Culture, etc., *see* the A.B.C. of Plants, page 255.

Annuals

Alyssum maritimum
Calendula officinalis vars.
Callistephus chinensis (China Asters)
Chrysanthemum tricolor
Clarkia elegans
Collinsia bicolor
Coreopsis tinctoria and C. Drummondii
Eschscholzia californica
Godetia vars
Gypsophila elegans

Helichrysum bracteatum
Lathyrus odoratus (Sweet Peas)
Lupinus mutabilis
Malcomia maritime (Virginian Stock)
Matthiola bicornis (Night-scented Stock)
Nemophilia insignis
Nigella damascena and N. hispanica (Love-in-a-Mist)

Papaver Rhœas vars. (Poppies)
Phlox Drummondii
Reseda odorata (Mignonette)
Salpiglossis sinuata
Scabious atro-purpurea
Tagetes patula
Tropæolum majus and minus (Nasturtium)
Zinnia elegans

224

PLANTS SUITABLE FOR THE TOWN GARDEN (*continued*)

Herbaceous Perennials

Achillea species
Aconitum Napellus
Althæa rosea vars. (Hollyhock)
Alyssum saxatile
Anchusa italica vars.
Anemone hybrida (japonica)
Antirrhinum (Snapdragon)
Aquilegia vars. (Columbine)
Arabis caucasica and fl. pl.
Armeria latifolia
Aster (Michaelmas Daisy)
Aubrieta deltoides vars.
Auricula hybrids
Bellis perennis vars. (Daisies)
Bergenia cordifolia
Boltonia asteroides
Campanula species
Cerastium tomentosum
Cheiranthus Cheiri (Wallflowers)
Chrysanthemum vars.
Coreopsis grandiflora
Dahlia (many vars.)
Delphinium (many vars)
Digitalis purpurea (Foxglove)

Doronicum plantagineum
Erigeron speciosus superbus
Gaillardia grandiflora
Galega officinalis, etc.
Geum Mrs. Bradshaw
Gypsophila paniculata
Helenium autumnale, vars. Riverton Gem and superbum, H. Bolanderi, H. cupreum
Helianthus rigidus and H. multiflorus vars.
Helleborus niger
Hemerocallis vars.
Heuchera sanguinea
Hieracium aurantiacum
Hosta species
Iberis sempervirens (Candytuft)
Iris germanica vars., etc.
Kniphofia (Red-hot Poker) species and vars.
Limonium latifolium
Lupinus polyphyllus (hybrids)
Lychnis chalcedonica and coronaria

Lysimachia Nummularia (Creeping Jenny)
Macleaya cordata
Malva moschata
Monarda didyma
Nepeta Faassenii (Musinii)
Œnothera biennis
Pæonia vars.
Papaver orientale vars.
Penstemon vars.
Phlox paniculata vars.
Potentilla vars.
Primula auricula vars.
Primula vulgaris (Primrose)
Rudbeckia laciniata fl. pl. R. speciosa
Saxifraga hypnoides, S. umbrosa, etc.
Scabiosa caucasica
Sedum spectabile
Sempervivum species
Solidago species
Statice (*see* Limonium)
Thalictrum aquilegifolium
Tradescantia virginiana
Veronica spicata
Viola vars.

Antirrhinums and Penstemons should be grown and treated as annuals, sowing the seeds in a greenhouse each year in early spring.

Bulbs and Tubers

Allium Moly and A. neapolitanum
Amaryllis Belladonna
Brodiaea (Ipheion) uniflora
Chionodoxa Luciliæ
Convallaria majalis (Lily of the Valley)
Crocus species and vars.
Fritillaria imperialis

Gladiolus vars.
Galanthus nivalis (Snowdrop)
Galtonia candicans
Iris Xiphium vars. (Spanish) I. xiphioides vars. (English)
Leucojum vernum

Lilium candidum, L. regale, L. testaceum, L. tigrinum, etc.
Narcissus (includes Daffodils) vars.
Muscari botryoides and other species
Scilla hispanica
Tulips vars.

Shrubs and Trees

Acer Pseudo-Platanus
Amelanchier canadensis
Aucuba japonica
Azaleas (some vars.)
Berberis vulgaris
Clematis Jackmanii
Cotoneaster frigida, etc.
Cratægus orientalis, etc.

Daphne Mezereum
Euonymus japonicus
Hedera Helix (Ivy)
Hypericum calycinum
Ilex Aquifolium (Holly)
Jasminum nudiflorum and J. officinalis
Olearia Haastii
Platanus acerifolia

Philadelphus various
Prunus Avium fl. pl. P. Hizakura, etc.
Rhododendrons vars.
Robinia Pseud-Acacia
Syringa vulgaris vars. (Lilac)
Viburnum Opulus sterile, V. Tinus, etc.

CHAPTER 29

WINDOW BOXES

There is one form of gardening from which not even the humblest tenement-dweller is entirely excluded. Fortunately, there is no one who has not even a window, and whoever has a window may have a window box.

It is good, though pathetic, to see how even under the most seemingly hopeless conditions afforded by the slums of our great cities, the love of gardening persists and manifests itself; and the passer-by may see even in the gloomiest of city streets, bits of healthy greenery and even blazes of colour decorating the windows.

Given somewhat more favourable surroundings, the possibilities of window gardening are considerable. If proper care is taken, if the soil is of suitable composition, and replaced or replenished every few months, there are few hardy plants which cannot be grown in this way. For it should not be thought that the only plants suitable for window boxes are the Marguerites, Scarlet Zonal and Ivy-leaved Pelargoniums (Geraniums), and Blue Lobelias—beautiful enough in themselves—which one sees with monotonous reiteration.

The list of plants tabulated on page 228 will show at a glance what a varied selection of plants are available.

PRINCIPLES OF WINDOW GARDENING

The essential principles of gardening are the same everywhere—that is to say, a good depth of soil with drainage in the bottom is necesssary for the healthy growth of nearly all plants, so that the window box should, certainly, not be less than nine or ten inches in depth. The soil should be of good texture—neither too heavy nor too sandy—and it should contain a reasonable amount of humus, or decomposed vegetable matter. For most plants, therefore, the soil of our window boxes should consist of fibrous loam, with which about one sixth of its volume of leaf-mould, well-decayed manure, and coarse sand has been mixed. A mulch of peat moss can be placed over the surface of the soil, so that heavy rain shall not splash the soil up and dirty the windows.

At regular intervals, the soil should be forked over lightly to loosen it and admit the air, and once a fortnight through the summer, the plants should be given a dose of weak liquid manure.

226

PLANTING

As soon as the crocks have been covered with sufficient coarse soil to lift the "balls" to the correct height when they are placed in the box, the plants should be put in position before any further soil is added. The dwarf and trailing subjects are best placed well up to the front edge of the box; if this is done, the taller kinds which come at the back can be kept well away from the windows and there will be ample room to wield the watering-can and the fork.

When all the plants are in position, fill in the soil, and press it firmly round the roots.

As in potting, a space of one half to an inch in depth must be left between the surface of the soil and the top of the box for the easy application of water and mulches.

TRAINING THE PLANTS

When training is required, it should be done neatly and unobtrusively, thin and pointed sticks and very fine fibres of raffia or soft twine being used. Anything like stiffness or formality should be avoided. The same may be said about pruning. Cut out any shoots that interfere with the symmetrical outline of the plant. More may be done, however, by timely disbudding than by cutting.

Faded and dead flowers should always be picked off at once. Only by careful and continuous attention of this kind can the period of flowering be extended.

BEST ASPECT FOR INDIVIDUAL PLANTS

Of the plants that are suitable for various aspects little need be said. The difference in aspect does not affect the plants nearly so much as might be imagined, but it may be taken as a rule that a sunny aspect is best for all flowering plants, except in the hot summer months, when they keep in bloom much longer if kept in the shade. It is possible, however, to have blinds fixed to a south window, by which the plants may be shaded or not at pleasure. (*See* also list, p. 228).

Hardy ferns make excellent subjects for the summer decoration of rather dark windows; in the winter their places may be taken by small shrubs.

The reader is advised to consult the following list of Window Plants when making his selection. Here he will find indicated plants suitable for any required aspect, whether in sun or shade. The most suitable soil for each, together with its colour, height, season of flowering, and method of propagation will also be found in practically every case in the Alphabetical List of Flowering Plants, Chapter 34.

PLANTS FOR WINDOW BOXES

For Notes on Colour, Height, Season of Flowering, Culture, etc., *see* the A.B.C. of Plants, page 255.

Abutilon Thomsonii, S. [S.
Ageratum Houstonianum,
Albizzia lophantha
Aloysia. *See* Lippia
Alyssum maritimum and A. saxatile, S.
*Anemone coronaria, S.E. and W.
Antirrhinum (Snapdragon) S.E. and W.
Arabis caucasica fl. pl., S.
Asparagus Sprengeri, S.
*Aspidium angulare many vars.), N.E.
Aubrieta deltoides vars.
*Aucuba japonica (small plants), N.E.
*Begonias (Tuberous and Fibrous-rooted), S.E. and W.
Bellis perennis (Daisy), S.E. and W.
Buxus sempervirens (Box) (small plants), N.E. and W.
Calceolarias vars. (Shrubby), S.E. and W.
Calendula officinalis, S.
Campanula carpatica, S.E. and W., C. fragilis and C. isophylla, S.E. and W.
Centaurea Cyanus (Cornflower), S.E. and W.
Chamæcyparis Lawsoniana · var Fletcheri (Shrub)
Cheiranthus Cheiri (Wallflower)
Cheiranthus Allioni, S.
Chionodoxa Luciliæ and C. L. sardensis, S.E. and W.
Chrysanthemums (Border), N.S.E. and W.
Clarkia elegans, S.E. and W.
Collinsia bicolor, S.
*Convallaria majalis (Lily of the Valley), N.E.
Convolvulus tricolor, S.
Coreopsis grandiflora, S.
Coreopsis tinctoria (dwarf vars. only), S.
Cotyledon glauca, S.
Crocus, S.E. and W.
Cryophytum crystallinum S.

Cytisus fragrans. S.
Dahlias (dwarf) Mignon, S.
Dianthus Caryophyllus (Carnations) S.
Dianthus vars. (Pinks), S.E. and W. [S.
Dorotheanthus gramineus,
*Erythronium species (Dog's Tooth Violet), S.
Fatsia japonica, N.E. and W.
Felicia amelloides, S.
*Ferns (Hardy or Half-hardy), N.E. and W.
*Fuchsias vars. and species, S.E. and W.
Galanthus nivalis (Snowdrops), S.E. and W.
Gazania Pavonia and G. splendens, S.
Geum coccineum and G. Heldreichii, E. and W.
Gypsophila elegans, S.E. and W.
Hedera Helix (Ivy), N.
Heliotropium peruvianum vars. (Cherry Pie), S.
Hyacinthus orientalis (Hyacinth), S.E. and W.
Hydrangea macrophylla vars., S.E. and W.
Iberis sempervirens (Candytuft), S.
Impatiens Balsamina (Balsam), S.
Ipomæa purpurea, S.
Lavendula spica (dwarf vars.) (Lavender), S.E. and W.
Lippia citriodora (Lemon Plant), S.
Lobelia Erinus vars., N.E. and W.
*Lysimachia Nummularia, E. and W.
Matthiola annua (Ten-week Stock), S.E. and W.
*Mimulus moschatus (Musk), N.S.E. and W.
Muscaria conicum (Grape Hyacinth), S.E. and W.
*Myosotis dissitiflora and M. alpestris, E. and W.

Myrtus communis (Myrtle), S. [W.
*Narcissus vars., S.E. and Pansies. *See* Violas
Pelargoniums Zonal vars. and Ivy-leaved, S.
Penstemon vars., S. [S.
Petunia (single and double),
Phlox Drummondii and P. subulata vars., S.W.
*Polyanthus, S.E. and W.
*Primula Auricula hybrids (Auricula), N.E. and W.
Primula vulgaris vars. (Coloured Primrose), S.E. and W.
Reseda odorata (Mignonette), S.E. and W.
Roses (Dwarf Polyantha), S.E. and W.
    Climbing vars. may be grown in tubs, boxes, or large pots, and trained.
Saxifraga vars., N.S.E. and W. [Especially S. umbrosa (London Pride)]
Scabiosa atropurpurea, dwarf var., S.E. and W.
Scilla sibirica, S. bifolia, and S. hispanica, S.E. and W.
Sedum spectabile, N.S.E. and W.
Silene pendula vars., E. and W.
Skimmia japonica and Fortunei (Shrub. Small plants), S.E. and W.
Tropæolum majus and minus vars. (Nasturtium), S.E. and W.
Tulips vars., S.E. and W.
Verbena hybrida, S.
Veronica rupestris, S.E. and W.
Viburnum Tinus (Laurustinus) (Small plants), S.E. and W.
*Vinca major and minor (Periwinkle), N.S.E. and W.
Violas (Pansies), N.E. and W.

NOTE.—The aspects for which the plants are most suitable are indicated after each name. All except those indicated with * like a sunny position, the latter, however, prefer shade.

PLATE 21

GREENHOUSE CUCUMBERS

Left, young cucumber plant climbing up wire in greenhouse ; when the main stem has reached the roof it should be stopped.

Left, young cucumbers forming on the laterals which have been trained along the guide wires. *Above*, the cucumber on right foreground is ready for harvesting ; malformed cucumbers should always be removed at once.

PLATE 22

PREPARING AND PLANTING
A HERBACEOUS BORDER
IN A VIRGIN SITE

After selecting the site for the propose
herbaceous border and marking the are,
proceed as follows : *top*, excavate ar
manure the marked area ; *centr*
cover over the manure with a layer
soil ; *bottom left*, lay out the plants
the desired plan ; *bottom right*, pla
and mark the area as shown.

CHAPTER 30

ROOM PLANTS

Room plants are so generally used, and so deservedly popular, that it seems time that their cultivation and care were more widely studied. Most people who keep a plant or two in their rooms have little or no knowledge of their needs, and so long as the plants have water at stated intervals, cannot understand why they frequently wither and die off leaf by leaf. Now, plants living in an ordinary sitting-room are living under what are to them highly artificial conditions, and care and watchfulness are needed if they are to adapt themselves to these conditions, and flourish as they do in their natural surroundings. First, perhaps, of the necessities to a room plant, is an ample supply of fresh air, though this must not be supplied in the form of a draught. More room plants die of draughts than of anything else, though frost is also a danger. The presence of a valued pot plant in a living-room is often the cause of good health in its owners, as the fresh air which it needs is equally necessary to human beings, and without its presence would often be excluded.

A pot plant should never be left between open door and open window, especially in a time of drying winds. It is through draughts that most of the hall plants perish.

POSITION IN THE ROOM

The best place for a room plant is in the window, where the maximum of light and sun are obtainable, but in cold weather the plants should be moved from the window at night and placed in a corner sheltered from draughts, further protected if necessary by a light screen covered with tiffany or newspapers, if any severe degree of cold is expected.

Dust is another of the powerful enemies of room plants. Anyone who knows anything of the structure of plants will realize that the pores in the leaves, fulfilling as they do the functions of the lungs in the human body, must never be allowed to become clogged with dust. It is through these pores that the plant breathes and perspires, and the little apertures must always be in a condition to work freely. This is best ensured by careful washing or spraying. Where the character of the foliage renders it possible, as in the case of palms, aspidistras, indiarubber plants, and all plants with thick textured leaves, actual sponging with a soft sponge and warm water two or three times a week, the frequency varying with the degree of dust present in the room, should be carried out. Rain water should be used, and not cold.

Most of the plants usually grown in rooms will thrive well in a soil composed of two parts of a fibrous loam to one part each of sand and leaf-mould. The cactuses like a good proportion of broken brick rubble, sometimes as much as one-half of the whole, added to their mixture, while the heaths will do best if peat is substituted for the leaf-mould. All the ferns enjoy a large proportion of peat. (*See* also Potting, p. 132.)

WATERING ROOM PLANTS

Watering must be carefully regulated to the needs of the plant, and good drainage is most essential. If the drainage is not absolutely free, the soil will become waterlogged and sour: conditions under which no plant will thrive. (*See* also Watering, page 46, *and* Watering Under Glass, page 240.)

BUYING PLANTS

In buying plants for use in rooms, it is always well worth while to get good plants from a good grower. The difference in price is trivial in the long run, and care is wasted upon a sickly, ill-grown plant, forced for the market, the kind that are mostly dealt in by the travelling hawker.

PLANTS THAT WILL THRIVE IN A ROOM

Although almost any greenhouse plant may be brought indoors and used for decorating a room, so long as it is returned periodically to the greenhouse to recuperate, the following is a list of plants which may be grown continuously in rooms, withstanding the effects of gas, fires and dust.

Adiantum Capillus-Veneris (Maidenhair Fern)
Aporacactus flagelliformis (Rat-tail Cactus)
Araucaria excelsa (Norfolk Island Pine) [Palm]
Aspidistra lurida (Parlour
Asplenium bulbiferum (Carrot-leaved Fern)
Begonia Rex
B. weltoniensis
*Campanula isophylla and var. alba (Hanging Bell-flower)

*Clivia miniata
Cocos Weddelliana
Cordyline stricta, small
Cyperus alternifolius
Cyrtomium falcatum
Dracæna stricta (Cordyline) (Small)
Davallia canariensis (Hare's Foot Fern)
Epiphyllum (Flowering Cactus)
Fatsia japonica
Ficus elastica (India-rubber Plant)

Howea Forsteriana
Livistonia australis (Fan Palm)
*Oxalis cernua and O. floribunda
Phœnix Rœbelinii
Platycerium bifurcatum
Pteris cretica (Ribbon Fern)
P. serrulata
P. tremula
Saxifraga sarmentosa
*Vallota purpurea (Scarboro Lily).

NOTE.—* indicates flowering plants. In addition to these, there are, of course, numerous bulbs which may be utilized for indoor decoration.

CHAPTER 31

THE GREENHOUSE

It is by no means necessary to have an imposing array of greenhouses in order to derive pleasure from gardening under glass. The smallest back-yard greenhouse will give a lot of profit and entertainment if it is well used. The fact that flowers and beautiful foliage can be had all the year round, together with a constant supply of pot plants for the house during the dark winter months, is alone worth the trouble of looking after the greenhouse, to say nothing of the pleasure of the work itself.

Many small greenhouses fail through over-ambition on the part of their owner. He wants to be able to grow at the same time and in the same house a quantity of plants with quite different requirements as regards temperature, moisture, and ventilation. He has not a large amount of space at his disposal, so that he overcrowds his plants and dwarfs his specimens in consequence. Plants, like people, cannot stand crowded conditions. It is a far better plan to select carefully the several species that require much the same treatment and to grow only such a number of these as will ensure that they each have sufficient room to develop fully.

ASPECT AND SITE OF THE HOUSE

If the greenhouse can be placed only in a shaded corner of the garden, it is clearly hopeless to attempt to grow plants and flowers that need much sunshine. It is better to devote the space to growing ferns, to which shade is not only not harmful, but absolutely necessary. If the greenhouse is to be used for fruit and flowers, it should stand in full sunlight. Daylight and shelter from north and east winds are essentials.

The greenhouse may be built in either of two shapes; the span-roof, where the roof has two equal sized and equally sloping sides, or the lean-to, where the roof slopes down in one plane from one side, or from a wall. Span-roof houses are best placed with the gable ends north and south; the light and heat from the sun can be better regulated in this way, and the houses require less attention. If one end of the house touches a wall, it should be the north end. Lean-to houses are best and most econo-mical when built with their highest side against a wall. This gives stability and cheapness together. Needless to say, the wall should not come on the sunny side of the house, or the latter will only be useful for shade-loving plants and ferns. There is an intermediate form of roof known as the hip-span, which is built with one slope of the roof very much shorter than the other, and is very useful for building against a wall too low to support a lean-to. Lean-to and hip-roof houses can be built with any aspect from south to west, the east being the worst of all, and a north being best for a certain kind of ferns.

ARRANGEMENT OF THE STAGING

In the span-roofed house the plants get the light from both sides, and therefore, grow a good shape. In the lean-to, however, the light falls on them from one side only; it is, therefore, necessary to turn the plants now and again.

The arrangements of the staging or support for the plants may vary. In a large house of the span-roof type where there is a good width, say 15 feet, the plants always look best arranged with a central staging some 4 feet wide running down the middle of the house, and two narrower stagings about 3 feet wide along the sides. This leaves room for two 2½-foot paths between the stagings. Plants are displayed admirably by this arrangement, but it is only possible in a good-sized house. Smaller span-roofs are inconvenient to fit up in this way, as when the stagings run only along the sides, it is necessary that the tallest plants shall be placed towards the middle of the house, and therefore, nearest the path, an unfortunate arrangement from the point of view of appearance, for the bigger plants hide the smaller ones nearer the outside. Lean-to houses are best arranged with a narrow staging on the outer and lower side, and a wide and high one on the other side, the path lying between the two. Where the house is a fair height at the back, the staging should be built well up it, for the sake of the health of the plants as well as for their looks, as otherwise the back plants would be too far from the glass to thrive well.

MATERIAL FOR THE STAGING

Plants do best when stood on a solid bed filled up with ashes and clinkers or even sandy soil: such beds always retain a natural moisture. Failing this, the best material for staging is provided by slabs of slate. These never become absolutely dry and so keep the bottoms of the pots from drying up too much. The slates should be covered with a layer of shingle or pea gravel. The usual strips of wood, with an inch or so between each strip, of which most ordinary greenhouse stagings are composed are not good. They permit far too free a circulation of air and heat round the pots, and by over-drying the latter, cause the root tips to wither up.

Slate slabs are costly, however, and the initial expense is prohibitive to many people, for whom the best substitute is a series of substantial wooden boards like small benches, or sheets of corrugated iron. A narrow strip of flat beading, an inch or so deep, should be nailed round the edges

232

of these boards and the shallow box thus produced should be filled with ashes, shingle, or some other absorbent material. Staging over pipes should touch the wall at the back so that it will protect the plants standing on it from direct heat.

THE HEATING SYSTEM

The method of heating greenhouses is, in its details, still a matter for individual opinion, but it is generally recognized in this country that the hot-water system is the best and least dangerous method. The fitting of a system of hot-water pipes requires considerable care and experience, and unless he is himself qualified to supervise the work, the reader is advised to put the work in the hands of a reliable firm.

The Hot Water Pipes

In fitting in a system of hot-water pipes, there are several simple points to be borne in mind. As I have said elsewhere, the boiler should be set in a shed outside and below the level of the house, firstly, because it is more economical of heat, and secondly, because this position will facilitate the next condition, which is a good level rise of the piping of 1 in 80 from the boiler to the highest point where the feed tank is situated. This cistern must always be kept filled. It is fatal to the efficient circulation of the hot water in the pipe for the latter to dip and rise again. Within reasonable limits, the greater the rise in the piping the better the circulation, and at the highest point of the system an air-tap should be provided to allow of the escape of any air that may get into the pipes. Without this escape, the "air-lock" would check the circulation. The upper system of pipes should be connected with the boiler fairly high up, the under set—the return pipes —being placed nearly at the bottom.

Size of the Boiler

It is well to err on the side of over size in buying your boiler. Small boilers may give a good deal of trouble, and require far more attention than do larger ones. The amount of piping required varies with the desired maximum heat of the house. The usual allowance is one foot of four-inch piping to every thirty cubic feet of space in the house, but a small margin had better be allowed over and above this for the small greenhouse, and for the amateur. This length of piping includes both "flow" and "return" pipes. It will maintain a temperature of at least 45 deg. F., which is quite sufficient for the cool house. If a house of the same cubic capacity is to be used as a warm house, the piping would have to maintain a temperature of at least 55 deg. F., and would have to be increased in length by six feet for every thirty cubic feet of space in the house, and in proportion for any additional heat required in a house of equal cubic capacity. Four-inch

233

piping should always be used, for pipes of smaller diameter lose their heat rapidly, and should the fire go out in cold weather, the small pipes will not long sustain the temperature of the house. Where the house is divided into two compartments, it is advisable to arrange the piping so that the section nearer the fire may be kept about 10 degrees warmer than the other. Although a new boiler and a brand-new system of piping may do all that it is supposed to do, it will be found, as it ages, that it will require more and more attention if the necessary heat is to be maintained. It is better to overdo it a little at first in the matter of the size of the boiler and the length of the piping and to feel safe about it. Far easier is it to keep down the temperature by using the ventilators than to raise it to the very fullest capacity of your piping. Likewise, it is far less expensive to keep a slightly larger system of pipes moderately warm than a smaller system at top heat which will be necessary to heat a house too large for the system. If possible, soft or rain water should be used in the hot-water apparatus, as hard water is apt to deposit lime.

Painting the Pipes

A small but important point to be considered in fixing the piping is the painting of the pipes to prevent them from rusting. Brunswick black is often used for this purpose, and while excellent in many ways, having a good glossy surface and being fairly lasting, it is a dangerous thing to use in a house full of plants. While it is drying, and especially when the pipes are hot, this varnish paint gives off powerful fumes, which will injure tender plants, so that it is only suitable for applying when the house is new or empty. A good and harmless paint may be made of boiled linseed oil, a little "dryers", and vegetable black. This will smell a little while drying, but its fumes are harmless. The oil is an important constituent and should be of the best kind.

Tar should never be used on pipes. Cleanliness of the flues and boiler is a matter often neglected.

A maximum and minimum thermometer is indispensable in the greenhouse, as otherwise the faults made in heating on the previous night cannot be remedied.

FUELS: COAL, COKE, OIL OR GAS

Gas, oil, coal, and coke are all used for heating greenhouses, and each has its own good points. The most popular fuels, however, are coal (the hard anthracite kind) and coke. Between the two there is not much to choose, the coke being a little duller in its fire, but nothing to make one hesitate to use it. In the case of small, upright boilers, coke *must* be used, the anthracite being unsuitable, and the fuel must be broken into pieces of the size of a walnut before being burnt.

234

How to Light the Fire

To light the fire, open the ash-tray door, pull out the damper and lay the fire with paper or shavings, dry wood, and some small coal as for a house fire, then close the fire-door. Light it, and put on a little more coal as the fire burns up, then add the anthracite or coke and anthracite. Close the ash-tray door, and regulate the draught by means of the damper. When the pipes are hot enough, push the damper in further to check the draught; if this does not regulate the fire sufficiently, open the fire-door a little. The more the latter is opened, the less the draught. The fire should remain thus until more heat is wanted in the late afternoon or evening when the final stoking up is given. For the last stoking before leaving the fire for the night, the bars of the furnace should be raked thoroughly clear and the hot coke or anthracite raked down together. The furnace should then be filled with anthracite or with coke which has been slightly moistened and mixed with breeze or slack. The door of the ash-tray should be opened, the fire-door closed, and the damper drawn out. The fire will now burn up, and if properly stoked, should go well till next morning. When the fire has burnt up, open the fire-door and leave it so during the night. Should the night be cold and windy, push the damper almost right in, and nearly close the ash-tray door, but if there is no wind, the damper should be half-way in, and the ash-tray door half open. In the morning, close the fire-door, pull out the damper, and open the ash-tray door, then rake out the clinkers after the fire has been stirred and had time to burn up a little. It may then be banked up to burn through the day. The slow-burning smokeless anthracite that is used in slow combustion stoves is good for the heating of large boilers, being, from the point of view of economy, perhaps, a little better than coke.

Oil Heaters

Oil stoves will do well for heating small boilers, and will accomplish it at a cost slightly higher than that of the necessary amount of coke. They require very little attention.

In using an oil heater for the boiler, perfect cleanliness is essential if the lamp is to burn well and give no trouble. The wicks should be quite dry and clean when inserted, and short pieces should be used and renewed at intervals. The wicks absorb a great deal of dirt, and when long strips are left for months in the oil reservoirs, they become quite choked with dirt and do not draw well. When first lighting the wicks, turn them up about an inch and moisten the ends with oil. Next, turn them down to about half an inch, and let them burn until they go out, this ensuring an absolutely even end. Do not light the lamp immediately the reservoir is filled, but allow time for the wicks to become thoroughly saturated with the oil. Adjust the height of the flame by turning the lamp higher than you

235

require it, and then slowly lowering it to the desired height. If the reverse is done, there is always a danger that the flame will increase after it has been, as one imagines, raised to exactly the right point. Never cut the tops of the wicks when trimming the lamps, but wipe them off level with a piece of soft paper or an oily rag. The level is kept by turning the wicks down nearly to the bottom, and wiping gently away to the level of the socket. If kept clean and level-wicked, the lamps will never smoke.

In oil-heated hot-water systems, upright boilers, connected by the hot-water pipes to another vertical tank of similar size, are usually employed. The oil tank will hold a supply sufficient for some twenty hours continuous burning.

Gas Heaters

Gas heating is very little trouble, but, on the other hand, it is undoubtedly expensive. There is not much to be said about it, except that the burners should never be placed inside the house, as there are few things more injurious to plants than the fumes of gas. Great care is necessary in the preparations made with gas heaters for the carrying off of the fumes. They require most careful arrangements of draughts and exits, and the risk of something going wrong is great. Gas-heating should be arranged to work from outside the wall of the house.

Electric Heating

This method has been used in a few instances but so far it has proved too costly to be done on a large scale. In a small house it may be successfully employed and can be thermostatically controlled. For raising early salad crops heating the soil by means of cables has proved satisfactory.

TEMPERATURES OF THE HOUSES

It is not possible to give any definite figures for the temperature of the greenhouse. This must of necessity vary with the plants grown, and instructions in this matter will be found under the headings of the different plants. Greenhouses are, however, roughly divided into hot, warm or intermediate, cool, and cold houses, and as a rough guide the following may be taken as the mean temperatures of the first three:

HOT HOUSE	Summer	Day	. . .	70° to 85° F.
		Night	. . .	65° to 75° F.
	Winter	Day	. . .	65° to 75° F.
		Night	. . .	60° to 70° F.
(INTERMEDIATE) WARM HOUSE	Summer	Day	. . .	65° to 75° F.
		Night	. . .	60° to 70° F.
	Winter	Day	. . .	60° to 70° F.
		Night	. . .	55° to 65° F.
COOL HOUSE	Summer	Day	. . .	60° to 65° F.
		Night	. . .	55° to 60° F.
	Winter	Day	. . .	55° to 65° F.
		Night	. . .	45° to 50° F.

236

Crittal

designs of
greenhouse
tructed of
and glass
ow becoming
popular.

Whitehouse

PLATE 23
GREEN-
HOUSES
←

Medium - size
greenhouse with
heated frames in-
corporated with
structure.

Two designs of
small greenhouse
constructed of
wood and glass.

↓

Bolton & Paul

PLATE 24 *Above*, effective shelving made up of corrugated iron covered with a layer of ashes. *Below*, plants being hardened-off in frames in two stages.

The temperature should never be allowed to fall below these lower figures in any of the artificially heated houses, and if in summer the temperature rises during the sunny part of the day, the house must at once be ventilated when the indicated maximum has been reached. Overheating weakens the plants and encourages the incubation of insect pests.

The amateur is very prone to give too much heat in winter at a time when most plants are resting. Forcing them at this period will weaken them and impair the beauty and quantity of their flowers. Exposure to the open air and sun matures the wood and strengthens all plants. All except the more tender greenhouse plants should, therefore, be kept in the open from the end of May until early in September, having first been hardened-off for a fortnight in a cold frame and then shaded from the strong sun for their first ten days in the open. On returning the plants to the greenhouse before the first frost, very free ventilation must be given. The plants are not usually taken out of their pots, but the latter should be plunged to their rims into beds, preferably not of earth, but of ashes or fibre, which will keep them well-drained and prevent worms from entering and attacking the roots.

THE HOT HOUSE

In winter the night temperature of the hot house should never fall below 65 deg. F., while the day temperature in summer should range between 70 deg. and 85 deg. F.

THE INTERMEDIATE (WARM) HOUSE

The intermediate, or warm, greenhouse requires a 55 deg. F. night temperature, and a 65 deg. F. day one all the colder part of the year, and from 65 deg. to 75 deg. of heat during the day all the summer and spring. This will be found warm enough to grow all the plants that the amateur is likely to handle. Houses heated above this point are troublesome to deal with, and a discussion on their management would require a special volume to itself.

The warm greenhouse will give the amateur a very wide choice, for many of the plants that have been included amongst those grown in the cold and cool houses can also be had in perfection in the slightly warmer house. This house also allows of very much greater scope in the matter of forced and out-of-season flowers.

The list on page 243 will provide an ample choice of plants for the intermediate house.

THE COOL HOUSE

The cool house will need artificial heat during the colder periods of the year only. Between October and March, a day temperature of 55 deg. F., with a night temperature of 45 deg. F., is necessary. During April and May, in a normal year, a temperature five degrees above that of the outer air, both night and day, will be enough. The cool house provides a home for a very large number of tender and half-hardy plants, and will be found the best all-round house for the amateur to manage. Few of the plants grown in it are delicate enough to be much injured by a variation of a degree or two in the temperature, although they are all too tender to stand in the open air. Many of the plants which thrive in this house are hardy in the summer months out-of-doors, but none of them can withstand the rigours of winter in the open and need the protection of glass.

THE UNHEATED OR COLD GREENHOUSE

This house depends solely on the heat of the sun for its warmth. Thus its temperature varies enormously at different times of the year. It requires no artificial heat even in winter. It must, however, be remembered that glass of itself will not keep out frost and the plants selected for the cold house must necessarily be hardy and able to stand a few degrees of frost. Much may be done by placing sacking and canvas over the glass to keep frost from the more tender plants and such hardy plants as bloom too early in the season to withstand the frost in the open.

Ventilation.—The cold house must have ample ventilation, but care must be taken to exclude all draughts. On warm summer nights, the ventilators may be kept open all night; in cooler and damper weather, it is best to ventilate thoroughly in the morning and to close the ventilators soon after lunch. This will conserve some of the heat of the day and will help to prevent "damping-off". The great thing is to avoid extremes of temperature, especially in the spring. *See* ventilation, p. 239. For shading, the roller type of blind is best, as these may be pulled down as protection against frosts on winter nights.

Watering.—Watering requires a good deal of care, and is best done in the morning. The foliage and atmosphere will then have time to dry somewhat before the cold night air can cause "damping-off". This applies especially to watering in autumn, winter, and spring; in summer, the watering may be done in the evening. In hot weather plants may be sprayed overhead and the paths and staging damped, as advised for the warm house, but this should be done with caution and only in the hottest periods, for the majority of cold house subjects are not lovers of a damp and humid atmosphere. *See* list of plants, page 244.

SHADING FROM THE SUN

During the summer, from about March to the end of September, the house will require shading from the strongest sunshine, or there is great risk of the plants being scorched and dried-up. No definite dates or hours when shading should be commenced, can be given, as everything depends upon the weather prevailing. The cool house, however, usually needs shading from about the end of March, and should be shaded each day as soon as the direct rays fall on the house. The blinds may be removed as soon as the rays are passed. The plants in the warm house can do with more sun and heat. Let the rays play for half an hour or so on this house before shading it, and remove the shading about half an hour before the sun's rays leave the glass, in order that the heat of the house may be maintained. Protection from the direct rays of the sun only should be provided. Where constant attention can be given, an arrangement of roller blinds is, of course, the best, as the amount of light can be better regulated, and the blinds can be left up on dull and sunless days. Where, however, as is often the case, the greenhouse must of necessity be left to look after itself for a good part of the day, some other plan must be adopted. The simplest, and on the whole the most satisfactory, method is to wash the glass over with a mixture of whiting and milk. It is far better to risk losing a little sun than to court damage from scorching. The whiting is easily washed off when cloudy weather sets in.

HEAT REGULATION AND VENTILATION

Upon the proper ventilation and regulation of the heat and moisture of the greenhouse, much of its success depends. It is very easy to kill, or at least gravely to injure, all, or nearly all, the plants in a house by injudicious opening or closing of all ventilators. Only in summer, when the temperature is too high, should top and side ventilators be opened simultaneously and then only in moderation, for a chilly draught between the two openings may cripple the less hardy plants. Only ventilators on the side opposite to that from which the wind is blowing should be opened, except in summer, when a mild wind can do little harm, provided a draught is not caused.

The amount of air admitted, of course, depends on the nature of the plants. Young, growing plants and seedlings require a warm and moist atmosphere, while plants in bloom require the air to be drier; the moisture would, in many cases, injure the bloom. Where there is ample top ventilation, there is far less need of side ventilation as well. Indeed, many experts now discontinue the use of side ventilators altogether, as they are held to make the atmosphere over-dry. In cases in which this dryness is desired, as it may be in a few houses built for particular plants, bottom ventilation may be employed by means of small sliding shutters placed in the side of the house and below the hot-water pipes. This latter position will ensure the slight warming of the air as it passes over the pipes and before it circulates in the house.

The leaves of plants, both under glass and out of doors, though most frequently the former, are liable to become scorched, in certain conditions, just as if they had been held before a fire. Dry heat and lack of sufficient moisture produce this effect, and the young leaves of vines and other greenhouse plants are often badly damaged. It is most important that the temperature of the house shall be carefully watched, especially in the morning, for the sun will often come out suddenly with surprising power, and unless the ventilation is regulated in time, the heat will become intense. In order to avoid the risk of scorching, the ventilators, in mild weather, should be opened early, beginning with a little opening, which is gradually increased as the sun becomes more powerful, and reversing the process towards evening as the temperature falls. Violent changes of temperature are as harmful to plants as to people, and the sudden check given to foliage which is in a state of great heat and transpiration on the sudden lowering of the temperature of the surrounding atmosphere will almost certainly give rise to mildew. If this occurs, dry flowers of sulphur should be sprinkled over the plants affected.

WATERING

Plants will need most water in the spring and summer, because the air is then drier, and because the plant is in full activity and is using up water at a great rate. Water at least once a day, sometimes twice, will be needed at this season, and it is permissible in very hot, dry weather to stand moisture-loving plants in saucers of water. Dormant plants and freshly-potted plants are best kept rather dry until growth begins. A watering once or twice a week will suffice for most plants in winter time; the soil must, however, be prevented from becoming dust-dry. In the greenhouse, watering is often as useful for keeping the air in a proper state of moisture as for anything else, and in hot weather, the walls, staging, and floor, should be frequently syringed. When the air is very hot and dry, the floor may with advantage be absolutely swilled with water, which will evaporate into the air and keep it moist. This is better than too much overhead watering with a rose, which tends to produce weak, insipid foliage.

In the summer, the watering of the plants themselves should be done when the sun's heat is at its lowest, early in the morning or in the early evening, but in spring, late autumn, and in winter, it is essential to water in the morning so that excessive moisture may have drained off before the evening, otherwise, there is great liability to "damping-off". Plants should never be allowed to become so dry as to droop, as this may cause irreparable damage; but if this has occurred, the whole plant, pot and all, should be stood in water deep enough to cover the pot. When thoroughly soaked, it should not at once be replaced on the staging but should be put in the shade for an hour or two to recover. Nearly all plants, and especially those that have not recently been repotted, will be the better for a watering with liquid manure every ten days while the buds are forming. The manure

240

PLATE 8 *LILIUM AURATUM*
The Golden-rayed or Japanese Lily
(From a painting by Emily Sartain)

water must be discontinued as soon as the flowers are out. *See also Watering*, p. 46.

Damping-Off

The disease known to gardeners as "damping-off" is due to the attacks of a fungus which causes the stems to decay and is very deadly to seedling plants. As its name implies, it is largely helped by damp, either in the soil or in the air, too thick sowing, too frequent watering, over-shading, and insufficient air and light all being the predisposing causes among the seed beds. The seedlings first go a bad, pale colour, then droop over, the attack of the fungus first touching the stem at or just above the soil line. As soon as these signs are noticed, the affected seedlings should be at once removed and burned, the healthy seedlings being transferred to fresh soil, which should have been previously watered with Cheshunt compound. This is made by mixing two parts by weight of copper sulphate and eleven parts of ammonium carbonate. The ammonium carbonate, which must be fresh, is reduced to a fine powder, by crushing. It should then be mixed with the powdered copper sulphate and stored before use for twenty-four hours in a tightly-corked glass or stone jar. The solution is prepared by dissolving one ounce of the dry mixture in a little hot water and adding to it two gallons of water.

If all soil used for seed sowing is thoroughly watered with this solution, damping-off will not be likely to occur. Where this disease has been allowed to gain ground, the whole of the seedlings in a pan will be found to be covered with the white thread-like mycelium of the fungus. The same patch of soil should not be used for the identical purpose in the following year, as the spores of the fungus survive in it throughout the winter.

CONTROL OF INSECT PESTS AND FUNGI

Cleanliness inside the greenhouse is most essential. Every dead leaf and withered stem left about is a hiding-place for insects and the breeding-ground of fungi. We create artificial conditions within our greenhouses, where the balance of nature is destroyed and the natural enemies of insect life cannot enter, so that unless we take their place in the thinning-out of superfluous insects, we shall soon be over-run. Aphides, thrips, red spiders, mealy bugs, scale insects, and woodlice are the chief pests met with here. The manner of countering them is shown in the chapter on *Diseases and Pests*, where fumigation is described. Keeping every corner of the house and the stem of every plant as clean and free from rubbish as possible will do a great deal to control the increase of insect pests. As a remedial measure, where red spider is found, spray infested plants at regular intervals with either one of the white oil emulsions or one of the new synthetic acaricides, but white oils must not be used on glaucous foliage plants, such as carnations. Spray these with potassium sulphide and soft soap, or fumigate with naphthalene Grade 16. For thrips, greenfly, leaf hoppers and mealy bug, fumigate at regular intervals with hydrogen cyanide or nicotine. Spraying the undersides of the leaves with nicotine and soft soap is just as effective.

Fumigating with nicotine should only be used where the plants in the house are full grown. It is often too strong a remedy for young and tender plants. One of the nicotine compounds that can be vaporized, is one of the best and safest methods of fumigating greenhouses. Tiny plants and seedlings may be dipped bodily into a weak solution of the insecticide.

All evergreen foliage plants in the greenhouse should have a frequent wash with warm rain-water and a little soap, applied either with a small sponge, where the leaves are large, or with the syringe where they are too small for this treatment. On each occasion, the plants should be finished off with a rinsing of clean warm rain water. The soap and water will remove all insects, and the process of sponging will keep the pores open and the plant in health. Pots should always be kept clean, no moss being allowed to grow on their surfaces. The greenhouse should be thoroughly turned out once or twice a year, when the plants are least active; all fibre, shingle, or such material should be replaced, all woodwork and glass being thoroughly washed with soap and hot water.

PROPAGATION

Propagating Frame

A propagating frame is a most useful adjunct to the greenhouse, both for the purpose implied in its name and for bringing on plants and bulbs required for forcing and for greenhouse decoration. It saves a great deal of room in the house, as well as giving a home to all kinds of plants, cuttings, and seedlings which do not help the attractive appearance of the house. The frame, for instance, is very useful in the case of forced tulips, lilies of the valley, narcissus, and other plants of the same habit. These may be left in the frame until the flowers begin to show, and should then be brought into the house and placed close to the glass. As the flowers attain their full beauty, they should have a warmer and warmer spot until they have reached their finest state, when removal to a cooler place will help to prolong their period of flowering. *See also* Chapter 11.

Propagating Box

For raising seedlings, propagating cuttings, and such purposes, a box within the greenhouse is very useful where a house cannot be set aside for this alone. This box may either be a fixture, in which case it should be built in such a position as to include within it some portion of the heating pipes, or it may be movable, if space is an object, so that it may be cleared

242

out of the house when not wanted. Where the pipes are built in, they should be covered with a good depth of coconut fibre, the pots or boxes containing the plants being plunged in the fibre.

The propagating box will need watching carefully while it is in use. The glass should have a sheet of paper thrown over it to shield newly-inserted cuttings and seeds from the sun, and this paper should be kept in position until the cuttings have rooted, probably in about three weeks, or until the seeds have germinated. All decayed leaves must be frequently removed, as they encourage "damping-off", and the condensation should be wiped off the glass every morning.

It may be here stated that the cuttings or seeds of nearly all cool house plants should be placed under glass in a temperature of 50 deg. to 60 deg. F. Warm house plants require a propagating temperature of from 65 deg. to 75 deg. F. For special cultural details of individual plants *see* Chapter 34, and the chapter on the Methods of Propagation, Chapter 11.

A SELECTION OF PLANTS FOR THE GREENHOUSE

NOTE.—For Cultural Details, for Colour of Flowers, Time of Blooming, Height, and the best Species and Varieties, *see* the A.B.C. of Plants, page 255.

The Warm House
Summer Temperature, 60°-75° F. ; Winter Temperature, 55°-70° F.

FLOWERING IN EARLY SPRING

Acacia armata (Mimosa)
Azalea mollis
Camellia japonica and vars.
Cineraria all types
Convallaria majalis
Carnations
  (Perpetual Flowering)
Cytisus canariensis
Diervilla florida
Erica hyemalis
Freesia refracta, alba, etc.

Kerria japonica fl. pl.
Laburnum anagyroides
Lachenalia Nelsonii and N. tricolor
Malus floribunda atrosan-guinea, M. purpurea, M. spectabilis
Olearia stellulata
Philadelphus Lemoinei
Primula obconica, P. mala-coides, P. stellata

Prunus serrulata, P. triloba fl. pl.
Pyrus. *See* Malus
Ribes aureum
Ribes sanguineum and vars.
Spiræa Van Houttei
Syringa vulgaris (Lilac) vars.
Viburnum tomentosum, var. plicatum (Japanese Snow-ball Tree)
Wisteria sinensis

FLOWERING IN LATE SPRING

Calceolaria herbeobrida
Cineraria all types
Deutzia gracilis
Dicentra spectabilis

Eupatorium Purpusii
Hippeastrum equestre hy-brids
Kalmia polifolia

Lilium longiflorum
Pelargonium zonal and regal vars.

FLOWERING IN SUMMER

Abutilon Thompsonii
Achimenes vars.
Agapanthus umbellatus
Begonia species and vars.
Campanula isophylla
Campanula pyramidalis
Canna indica and hybrids
Celsia Arcturus
Cobæa scandens
Cotyledon glauca

Crinum Powellii and C. Moorei
Dianthus (Malmaison Car-nation)
Fuchsia species and vars.
Gloxinia hybrida
Heliotropium peruvianum and vars.
Hydrangea macrophylla
Impatiens Balsamina
Lilium auratum

Lilium speciosum
Lippia citriodora
Mimulus moschatus
Nerium Oleander
Oxalis species   [vars.
Pelargonium zonal and regal
Petunia violacea
Plumbago capensis
Schizanthus retusus and hy-brid strains
Verbena hybrida

243

A SELECTION OF PLANTS FOR THE GREENHOUSE

The Warm House—*continued*.

Summer Temperature, 60°–75° F.; Winter Temperature, 55°–70° F.

FLOWERING IN AUTUMN

Begonia species and tuberous rooted
Bouvardia Humboldtii and garden hybrids
Chrysanthemum indicum and large decorative types

Nerine Bowdenii, N. Fothergillii and vars.
Polianthes tuberosa
Reseda odorata (Mignonette)

Salvia rutilans, S. involucrata var. Bethelii, S. leucantha, S. patens, and S. splendens varieties
Streptocarpus hybrids
Vallota purpurea (Scarborough Lily)

FLOWERING IN WINTER

Abutilon insigne
Begonia (Fibrous-rooted)
Bouvardia Humboldtii, B. jasminiflora
Chrysanthemum indicum decorative types
Cineraria all types
Cotyledon coccinea, C. fulgens
Cyclamen persicum

Daphne odora
Erica hyemalis, E. melanthera, etc.
Euphorbia fulgens, E. pulcherrima (Poinsettia)
Freesia refracta, alba
Narcissus Tazetta and vars. (Paper Whites)
Pelargonium zonal vars.

Primula malacoides, P. sinensis, P. stellata
Richardia. *See* Zantedeschia
Solanum Capsicastrum (Winter Cherry)
Sparmannia africana
Tropæolum Lobbianum
Zantedeschia æthiopica (Arum Lily)

FLOWERING ALMOST ALL THE YEAR ROUND

Abutilon species and vars.
Begonia semperflorens
Carnations, *see* Dianthus
Cassia corymbosa
Chrysanthemum frutescens
Dianthus (Perpetual-flowering Carnation)

Felicia amelloides
Jasminum grandiflorum
Lapageria rosea and var. alba
Pelargonium quercifolium (Geranium, Oak-leaved)

Pelargonium zonal types
Primula obconica
Reseda odorata (Mignonette)
Solanum jasminoides

NOTE.—Cuttings and seeds of nearly all warm greenhouse plants should be placed under glass in a temperature of 50° F. Light, sandy, well-drained soil is essential. *See* notes on propagation under glass, Chapter 11.

All shrubs that have been forced on in a warm house must be carefully pruned after flowering. They must be forced only alternate years.

The Cold House

FLOWERING PLANTS

Aquilegia cærulea
Astilbe japonica
Begonia (tuberous vars.)
B. semperflorens vars.
Calceolaria shrubby types
Campanula pyramidalis
Chrysanthemum large decorative types
Clarkia elegans
Convallaria majalis
Dianthus Heddewigii

Dicentra spectabilis
Fuchsias species and vars.
Godetia grandiflora and vars.
Lobelia cardinalis
Matthiola annua and vars. (Intermediate Stock)
Myosotis sylvatica
Pelargoniums
Phlox divaricata

Polygonatum multiflorum
Primula vulgaris (Primrose)
P. Auricula hybrids
P. variabilis (Polyanthus)
P. stellata
Schizanthus retusus and other types
Trollius asiaticus
T. europæus
Viola odorata (Violet)

A SELECTION OF PLANTS FOR THE GREENHOUSE

The Cold House—*continued.*

BULBS AND TUBEROUS-ROOTED PLANTS

Anemone blanda
A. fulgens
*Chionodoxa Luciliæ, var. sardensis
Crinum Moorei and C. Powellii
*Crocus vernus vars.
*Cyclamen coum
C. europæum
*C. neapolitanum
Erythronium Dens canis
*Fritillaria aurea
F. Meleagris [drop]
Galanthus nivalis (Snow-

Galtonia candicans (Cape Hyacinth)
Hosta species
Hyacinthus orientalis
Iris alata
I. reticulata and vars.
*Iris unguicularis
Ixia
Kniphofia Macowani
Lilium auratum
L. candidum
L. pumilum
L. regale
L. speciosum

Lilium tigrinum
*Muscari botryoides
*Narcissus Bulbocodium
*Narcissus cyclamineus
*N. minimus
Ornithogalum arabicum
*Scilla sibirica
Trillium grandiflorum
Tritonia crocosmæflora (Montbretia)
Tulip vars.
Watsonia Meriana var. Ardernei

* Denotes bulbs suitable for culture in the Alpine House. All small bulbs are best grown in shallow pans 5 to 6 inches in diameter; not in pots.

FLOWERING SHRUBS

Azalea mollis
Berberis Darwinii
Camellia japonica and vars.
Ceanothus rigidus
Chænomeles japonica
Choisya ternata
Clematis Jackmanii
Cytisus kewensis (Broom)
Daphne Cneorum
Deutzia gracilis

Deutzia Lemoinei
Erica carnea
E. mediterranea
Forsythia intermedia var. spectabilis
F. suspensa
Hydrangea macrophylla vars.
Jasminum nudiflorum
Magnolia stellata

Pernettya mucronata
Prunus japonica fl. pl.
Prunus nanus
Ribes sanguineum
Spiræa arguta
Syringa vulgaris (Lilac)
Veronica speciosa
Viburnum Tinus (Laurustinus)
Wisteria sinensis

Greenhouse Foliage Plants

(*See* also chapter on Ferns, and paragraph on Palms, page 365.)

*Acanthus mollis, var. latifolius
*A. spinosus
Agave americana
Aloe variegata
Araucaria excelsa
Asparagus plumosus nanus
A. Sprengeri
*A. verticillatus
Aspidistra lurida
*Aucuba japonica
Begonia Rex
Canna (many vars.)
Centaurea gymnocarpa
*C. ragusina
Chlorophytum elatum var. variegatum

Chrysalidocarpus lutescens
*Cineraria maritima
Cocos Weddelliana
Coleus Blumei vars.
Cordyline australis
Cotyledon glauca
Echeveria secunda glauca
Eucalyptus maculata, var. citriodora
E. globulus
*Eugenia buxifolia
Fatsia japonica
Ficus elastica
Hosta Sieboldiana
Howea Belmoreana
Iresine vars.

Liriope Muscari variegata
Oplismenus hirtellus
Pandanus Veitchii
Perilla nankinensis
Phœnix sylvestris
Pyrethrum aureum
Rhopalostylis Bauerii
Ricinus communis
Salvia argentea
Selaginella uncinata
Solanum Capicastrum
*Thalictrum adiantifolium
Trachycarpus excelsa
Yucca filamentosa
Zea Mays var. quadricolor

NOTE.—Plants marked with an * require no artificial heat in winter.

CHAPTER 32

FRAMES AND HOT-BEDS

THE COLD FRAME

To be of lasting utility, a frame should be well-made and of good materials. The woodwork should receive at least three coats of paint, and the glass should be well-bedded in putty; this will ensure its being rain-proof and will help to exclude the frost.

SPAN-ROOFED FRAMES

Span-roof frames are excellent, as the lights can be opened on either side, and it is, therefore, possible to ventilate, whatever the direction of the wind. There is no need to turn the plants in this type of frame, for the light enters from all sides and the plants grow symmetrically. Its greater height also enables taller plants, such as azaleas, fuchsias, and heliotropes, to be accommodated under the centre of the span. When seed-boxes or rooted cuttings have to be housed, a wooden staging can be used to keep them up near the glass. The span-roof frame should be placed so as to run north and south; either side then gets its share of sun. It is an advantage to have the frame small enough to be portable, so that it can be given any situation to suit the plants temporarily grown in it.

LEAN-TO FRAMES

Lean-to frames must face due south, so that they may get full sun, unless shade and a low temperature are necessary, when the frames should face north. Where there is a greenhouse, advantage should be taken of it to place the frame against one of its sides. The hot-water pipes may then be carried into the frame, if so desired.

THE FOUNDATION OF THE FRAME

The substance used to form the bed of the frame will depend upon the uses to which it is to be put. If pots or boxes are to be kept in it, a dry and hard bottom of ashes or shingle, some 3 inches deep, is admirable. This will keep out worms and other pests and will afford good drainage. If a seed-bed is made, support the four corners of the frame with bricks, place a layer of leaves at the bottom, and cover it with 6 inches of well-sieved compost consisting of loam, leaf-mould, and sand. Make the bed firm

246

and sprinkle the surface fairly liberally with coarse sand. (*See* Making a Seedbed, p. 104.) Most gardeners prefer to raise seedlings either in pots or boxes. For this purpose boxes about 20 inches by 10 inches and 3 to 4 inches deep will be

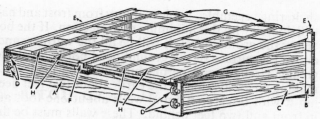

FIG. 37. THE TWO-LIGHT FRAME

A and *B* represent front and back respectively; *D* and *D* are mortices, tenons and pegs holding the frame together. The lights slide up and down on rebated ledges *E*, *E* and *F*. *H H* are flat iron bars which strengthen the lights; *G G* are iron handles.

found very handy. For transplanting the seedlings, or for larger plants, boxes 30 by 12 inches and from 8 to 9 inches deep will be found the most suitable.

If the seed is to be sown in a bed in the frame, it should be set in rows 4 to 5 inches apart. This enables the gardener to hand-weed between the drills before the weeds grow large enough to choke the young seedlings. The bed must, in any case, be made up so that the surface is not more than 6 to 9 inches from the glass.

(For details as to Shading, Watering, etc., *see* The Greenhouse, p. 231.)

VENTILATION AND ASPECT OF THE FRAME

Ventilation plays a great part in the use of the cold frame, and careful provision must, therefore, be made for it. Iron stays, fixed to the walls of the frame and made so that they may be fitted into slots in the lights, so graduated that more or less ventilation may be given, are often employed. A cruder method is to have blocks of wood, cut in steps, which are used to wedge the lights open to a larger or smaller degree as required.

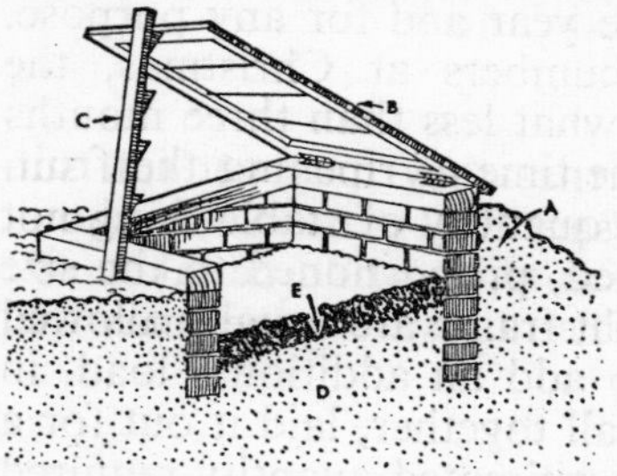

THE COLD PIT

A very good cold pit may be formed by building containing walls of turf or earth well beaten together, so that the back wall is higher than the front and in such a way that the sides slope from back to front, like the sides of a frame. Lights may be placed over the pit thus formed on frames covered with any protecting material. A cold pit of this kind, well and firmly built, will last a long time and is most useful in the winter for

FIG. 38. THE COLD PIT

In the accompanying diagram *A* shows a bank of earth thrown up against the back wall to increase the warmth of the pit; *B* indicates the light supported by the notched stick *C* when raised to admit air; *D* is the soil in which plants are set; *E* the top-dressing of leaf-mould or fibre.

247

sheltering vegetables liable to injury from frost and half-hardy plants, which will do well with this minimum of protection. If the bottom of the pit is sunk below the ground level, it will be all the warmer, and the containing walls above the surface of the ground need not be made so high. A cold pit of greater strength and permanence may be made in the same manner, by making an excavation in the earth about two feet deep and then surrounding it with brick containing walls about one foot above the ground level in front and two feet behind. These walls must be finished at the top with a wooden kerb and with bars from back to front to support the lights, if the latter are long enough to require them.

The Hot Pit

A single row of three- or four-inch hot-water piping may be run along the front and back of the brick pit mentioned above. These will convert it into a hot pit, which will be found of the greatest use.

THE HEATED FRAME

The heated frame is to all intents and purposes the same as the cold frame, save that it is furnished with heat in addition to that received from the sun through the lights. This heat is either supplied by means of 3 or 4-inch hot-water pipes along the front and back of the frame, or through the medium of a hot-bed upon which the frame is placed.

Management is in all respects identical with that of the cold frame, except that even more care must be given to ensure correct ventilation and a steady, even temperature.

THE HOT-BED

Hot-beds may be made at any time of the year and for any purpose. For example, if it is desired to have cucumbers at Christmas, the bed must be made early in October. Somewhat less than three months being required from the time of planting to the time of ripening the fruit.

If it is desired to commence in October, a quantity of stable dung not more than three weeks old should be collected, proportioned to the size of the frame; two double loads for a three-light frame are usually allowed for the body of the bed, but it is as well to add an additional load, in which to start the plants. Having shaken it all together, laid it out for a week, and then turned it over again, take the estimated quantity required for the size of the bed and stack the remainder in a compact heap. This heap should be covered to protect it from drying winds or excessive rain, or in very dry weather may be moistened lightly. The material to be used for the bed should then be thoroughly mixed with an equal quantity of compost or half-rotted leaves in order to reduce the first fierce heat and to make a steady heat last longer. Excessive heat may cause damage to the roots of the plants or lead to unbalanced growth.

248

When the material is ready, measure the frame, length and breadth, and mark out the bed, allowing 18 inches more each way for the bed than the length and breadth of the frame. At each corner of the bed, drive a stake firmly into the ground and perfectly upright, to serve as a guide by which to build the bed. Then proceed to build the bed, shaking up the dung well and beating it down with a fork. The whole should be equally firm and compact, so that it is not likely to settle more in one part than in another. The bed should be about 4 feet high at the back and 3 feet high in the front. The frame and lights may now be placed in the centre, but the lights should be left off, so that the rank steam may escape.

When the rank steam has passed off, which generally takes five or six days, place a 9- to 10-inch layer of good loam under each light. By the next day this will be warmed to the temperature of the hot-bed, and the plants may be planted in it.

Maintaining the Temperature

The heat of the hot-bed, if properly made, will last about two months, but the bed will require watching. It is advisable to have a thermometer in the frame, and as soon as the heat gets below 70 deg. F., to apply a lining of fresh dung, which has been prepared as before, to the front and one side of the bed. When the temperature again drops, add another lining to the back and to the other side. The bed can be kept at a growing heat for any length of time by this means, removing, at first, the old linings and replacing them by fresh.

Cloches

Cloches have developed from the old type of bell-jar and are now available in many forms, from the simple tent or barn consisting of two or four sheets of glass held in position by galvanized wire, to the larger and taller kinds which resemble frames or miniature greenhouses and are made up on a framework of wire or rigid metal. All serve the same purposes: they protect young plants, warm the soil and encourage early growth, and help late-maturing crops to finish off in good time. They check excessive evaporation yet allow sufficient ventilation and regulate moisture. Being light and easy to move, and so made that they can be placed end to end to cover continuous rows, they are specially useful for putting over crops sown for successional harvesting. In winter and early spring they may be used to cover winter lettuce, flower seedlings or early salads, and later on from March to May, put over such crops as young marrows, sweet corn, strawberries, outdoor tomatoes and melons. They are also valuable for protecting cuttings and for ripening onions and tomatoes especially in a wet or cold, sunless autumn. When not in use, cloches should be stacked on end, nested together, on a level piece of ground.

249

CHAPTER 33

FORCING

The process of making a plant flower or fruit out of its natural season is known as forcing. To effect this, cloches or frames and greenhouses with or without heat are used. For early forcing the heat of the sun's rays alone is not usually sufficient, and additional heat has to be applied either by means of a hot-bed or by the aid of hot-water pipes.

EARLY VEGETABLES

Vegetables may be forced in a heated frame, or in borders and boxes in the warm greenhouse.

The following paragraphs will show not only what may be done to produce early crops, but how it is possible to have supplies of many choice vegetables all through the winter.

Asparagus.—An early spring supply may be obtained by means of forcing. Place glass cloches or small frames over the crowns in the permanent beds early in February. Three-year-old plants are the best for forcing. Bottom heat is useful though not essential. If it is available, lift and replant the plants in January in a mild hot-bed in a frame with 3 inches of soil over the crowns. Keep the frame dark and the soil moist.

Beans, Broad.—Very early crops may be grown by means of forcing. Sow in pots or boxes in a compost consisting of two-thirds fibrous loam, one-third well-rotted and finely-sifted manure and leaf-mould. Place in a frame in January or February (Temperature 50° F. or below) and grow under glass in as natural a manner as possible. In the case of the later batches, they may be hardened off and set out in the open.

Beans, French.—To obtain the earliest possible supplies, sow at intervals in December, January, and February in a compost of loam, well-rotted manure, and coarse sand in 6-inch pots (3 seeds in each), and stand the pots 15 inches apart in an ordinary hot-bed made in the same way as for cucumbers. Water sparingly until the seeds are up, and grow close to the glass. The temperature should not fall below 60° F. Grow in as natural a manner as possible under glass.

Beans, Runner.—An early supply may be obtained by means of sowing in boxes in April (equal parts of loam and leaf-mould, with a little sand), and planting out at the end of May. They should be grown in as near to natural conditions as possible under glass.

250

Beetroot, Globe.—To obtain successional crops of early beetroots, sow batches of seed in a mild hot-bed in a frame from the beginning of January to the end of March and grow under glass.

Brussels Sprouts.—In order to obtain an early supply, sow seeds in boxes in a frame at the end of February and in March, and grow under glass in as near to natural conditions as possible.

Carrots, Stump-rooted.—For a successional supply of early carrots, sow seed in shallow drills 10 inches apart in 2-3 inches of finely-sifted soil over a mild hot-bed in frame early in January and at intervals until the first sowing outdoors is made.

Cauliflower.—To obtain an early supply, sow seed of an early kind on a mild hot-bed in February or early March and cover with hand glasses. Thin the seedlings when fit to handle, and plant singly in 3-inch pots, harden off, and plant out in a warm, sheltered situation or under glass in April. Seed may be sown in frames in August and September, the seedlings being pricked out as soon as they are up. Autumn-sown plants in the open may be pricked out under frames and forced under glass to obtain an early supply.

Celery.—To force celery, sow over a heat of about 70° F. in light, sandy soil in shallow boxes or pans under glass in February or March. Prick out singly in 3-inch pots when fit to handle, and discontinue the bottom heat. Shift to a cold frame or cool greenhouse, and into bigger pots, preparatory to planting out in May.

Chicory.—Treat this in the same way as advised for seakale.

Cucumber.—Cucumbers may be had at any time by sowing seed in a hot-bed or under glass about 3 months before the fruit is required.

Endive.—To obtain an early supply, sow in the open early in August. Prick out in sheltered position, and transfer the plants to a pit or cold frame in October for the winter.

Leeks.—For an early supply, sow seed thinly in a finely-sieved compost of two-thirds loam and one-third leaf-mould and sand in 3 inch deep boxes towards the end of January or early in February, and keep in moderate heat (55°-60° F.). When 3 inches in height, prick off the seedlings into boxes (2-3 inches apart). Give ample light and air, and transfer to a cold frame about the middle of April. Harden off and plant out in May.

Lettuce.—To obtain early plants, sow batches of seed in a frame from January to March, and raise indoors, or plant out in the open in a warm, sheltered position when fit to handle. Autumn-sown plants outdoors should be pricked-off in October and transferred to a frame for the winter. Ventilate as freely as possible.

Mint.—An early supply of mint may be had by propagating by means of division of roots and planting in boxes in March. Stand the boxes in a heated frame.

Mustard and Cress.—To obtain a continuous supply, make sowings in boxes in the greenhouse from October to March.

Onions.—To obtain an early crop, sow in a compost of two-thirds loam and one-third leaf-mould and sand in boxes in January (Temp. 60° F.). Reduce the heat and thin out to 3 inches apart when the seedlings are fit to handle. Give

251

ample light and air, and transfer to a cold frame in April. Harden off and plant out early in May.

Parsley.—Early supplies of this may be had by transferring plants from outdoors to the cold frame in August, September, or October.

Peas.—In order to have an early supply, sow in December, January, or February, placing 9 or 10 seeds in each 5-inch pot, or say 5 seeds in a 3½-inch pot, and standing them in cold frames. A compost of loam, leaf-mould, and sand suits peas well. Thin out the seedlings to 6 plants in each pot. Give as much light as possible and ample air, harden off, and plunge the boxes nearly to their rims in rows in the soil in the open in a warm, sheltered position about the second week in March, or, if space permits, grow entirely under glass.

Potatoes.—To obtain early potatoes, plant sprouted "seed" potatoes of an early variety in boxes, small tubs, or large pots, towards the end of January or early in February (Temp. 50° F.). The pots should be only half filled with soil so that top-dressings may be added as the haulm grows. A suitable compost is two-thirds well-decayed leaf-mould and one-third fibrous loam. If more convenient, plant them 4 inches deep and 9 inches apart in the above compost on a gentle hot-bed or in an old melon pit in February and grow under glass.

Radishes.—A continuous supply may be obtained by sowing seed in a frame or on a gentle hot-bed between rows of potatoes or other crops, from October to February, and growing under glass.

Rhubarb.—To force early rhubarb, cover young shoots in early spring with seakale pots or drain pipes, and surround them with rotted manure, etc., or lift the roots of plants two or more years old, and pack in boxes in a warm, dark place in October or November.

Seakale.—Lift the corms about the end of November or early in December, and pack them closely in light soil, and place in a dark, warm position. Water liberally.

Fresh roots should be lifted and treated weekly to provide a succession.

Tarragon.—Propagate by means of division of roots in March, and plant in boxes in a heated frame.

Tomatoes.—To obtain a continuous supply, seed may be sown from September to March in pots, pans, boxes, etc. (*See* page 443).

Turnips.—An early supply may be obtained by means of seed sown early in February in drills, 8 inches apart, on a hot-bed in a frame. Thin the seedlings to 3 inches apart when fit to handle, harden off and plant out in drills in May.

Vegetable Marrow.—These may be treated in exactly the same manner as cucumbers.

See also the chapter on Vegetables.

FRUIT

For forcing fruit a greenhouse is necessary; cucumbers, figs, grapes, nectarines, peaches and tomatoes require a warm greenhouse, most other fruit can be forced in a cool greenhouse and is generally grown in pots. For cultural details and for the temperature required at the various seasons, the reader is referred to the articles on the cultivation of the different fruits in the chapter on *Fruit in the Greenhouse*.

FLOWERING PLANTS

Flowers

Of the flowers most suitable for forcing are those of a woody and shrubby nature and those with bulbous or large, fleshy roots. All plants to be forced must be vigorous and fully matured, or no blooms will result.

Bulbs

Bulbs for forcing must be firm and plump, and are best of medium size. For cultural details *see* Bulbs in Pots, page 174. After forcing, the bulbs should be placed in a cold frame for a fortnight or three weeks to harden-off and for the foliage to die down. Bulbs are useless for forcing a second year, but if naturalized in the wild garden or in grass, they will soon regain their vigour and will bloom for many years.

The following are the bulbs most usually forced:—*Alliums, crocuses, freesias, hyacinths, lilies, narcissus, scillas, snowdrops, tuberoses,* and *tulips*.

Flowering Shrubs

Shrubs for forcing must, above all things, be vigorous and the shoots should be firm, well ripened, and must show plenty of flower buds. Heat should be applied gradually, and too little rather than over much should be given. The shrubs are usually potted up in September and early in October, and are plunged outdoors until required. Early potting is essential. About the middle of November, some of the earlier-flowering subjects may be transferred to the greenhouse and placed in a temperature of about 45 deg. F. for the first fortnight; during this period, syringing overhead twice a day will be necessary in fine weather. After the first couple of weeks, the temperature may be raised to 60 deg. F., and as soon as the plants break into active growth, the temperature can be increased by another ten degrees. When the colour of the buds begins to show, lower the temperature by five or ten degrees and maintain this level while the plants are flowering. After forcing, some of the old wood that has borne flowers should be cut away and any weak shoots should be cut right back; the aim being to let air and light into the centre of the plant, so that the shoots shall become thoroughly ripened and be able to produce buds for the following season. After trimming, let the plants remain in the warm for three weeks or so, and syringe overhead in fine weather with tepid water, and feed once a week with weak liquid manure. Following this treatment they should be stood in the cold house or cold frame for a fortnight or three weeks to be gradually hardened-off, preparatory to being set out in the open for the summer early in June. Nearly all shrubs are the better if forced every alternate year only, and with lilacs this is essential. Roses, however, can quite successfully be forced for several years in succession.

253

FORCING

For details as to the pruning and special cultural requirements of individual shrubs, *see* Chapter 34.

The following is a selection of hardy shrubs for forcing:

Acer japonica and vars.
A. Negundo var. variegatum
Amelanchier canadensis
Azalea mollis
Ceanothus species
Chimonanthus præcox
Choisya ternata
Clematis Jackmanii types
Cytisus Dallimorei hybrids
Diervillea florida
Daphne Mezereum
Deutzia gracilis and Lemoinei
Forsythia spectabilis
Hydrangea paniculata, grandiflora and Mme Mouillère

Jasminum nudiflorum
Kalmia latifolia
Kerria japonica plena
Laburnum anagyroides
Lilac. *See* Syringa
Lonicera Standishii
Magnolia stellata
Malus floribunda var. atrosanguinea, M. purpurea and M. spectabilis
Philadelphus coronarius and hybrids
Pieris floribunda
Prunus Persica
P. subhirtella and triloba fl. pl.

Pyrus. *See* Malus
Rhododendron many vareities
Ribes sanguineum
Roses most varieties
Spiræa arguta, media and Thunbergii
Staphylea colchica
Syringa "Charles the Tenth", or "Marie Legraye"
Viburnum Carlesii, tomentosum var. plicatum, and Opulus sterile
Wisteria sinensis

Roses

The treatment of roses differs slightly from that of other shrubs in that they must be established in their pots for at least twelve months before forcing is to take place; that is to say, they must not be lifted straight from the open ground to be forced. They can, however, be repotted in October, if need be. Early in November, they must be placed in a cold frame, pruned about the middle of December, and transferred to the greenhouse. About a fortnight later the forcing heat should gradually be applied.

Other Plants

Other plants valuable for forcing are: *Astilbe japonica* and *Astilbe hybrids*, such as *Astilbe Fanal* (Dark Red), *Peach Blossom* (Pale Pink) and *Queen Alexandra* (Deep Pink), *Convallaria majalis*, *Dicentra spectabilis*, and *Polygonatum officinalis*.

These roots should be potted-up at the end of October or early in November, being kept in a cold, but frost-proof, frame to be transferred to the greenhouse, in batches as required, at any time from December to March or April. Gradually remove the pots farther from the glass as the days grow longer and the sun stronger, and to increase the time that they remain in flower, shade the plants while in bloom.

254

CHAPTER 34

ABC OF PLANTS

DESCRIPTION—CULTURE—SPECIES AND VARIETIES

NOTE.—*The words in the brackets following the species and varieties indicate first the colour of the flowers, then the time of blooming, and lastly the average height in inches or feet to which the plants may be expected to grow.*

Aaron's Beard. *See* Hypericum.

Aaron's Rod (Verbascum Thapsus).—*See* Verbascum.

Abelia.—Hardy and half-hardy evergreen and deciduous shrubs which in mild, sunny, sheltered positions may be grown out-of-doors. *Culture.*—Take cuttings with a "heel" in late summer and strike in a frame or layer in August. Plant out in March or October in a sunny position against a south wall and in well-drained peat, loam and leaf-mould, or pot-up for the cool greenhouse. Trim to keep in shape only, cut off dead blooms and thin old wood after flowering. *Species.*— *A. floribunda* (Purple-rose, June–July, 48 in.); *A. triflora* (Pink-white, Aug.– Sept., 36–39 in.); and the hybrid *A. grandiflora* (Pink-white, Aug.–Sept., 36–48 in.).

Abies (Fir).—Handsome evergreen coniferous trees, which thrive in open positions in good loam. *Culture.*—Plant in April or October. No pruning is required. To propagate, sow in the open in March or April. *Species.—A. alba* (Silver Fir); *A. balsamea* (Balsam Fir); *A. homolepis* (Nikko Fir); *A. cephalonica* (Grecian Silver Fir); *A. grandis* (Giant Fir) and *A. nobilis* (Noble Fir).

Abronia.—A small half-hardy annual trailing plant, thriving in sunny borders, or rock gardens, in light sandy soil. *Culture.*—Sow in pots under glass in spring and plant-out the following April or May. *A. umbellata* (Pink, Summer, 9 in.) is one of the best species.

Abutilon (Indian Mallow).—A handsome half-hardy shrub excellent for decoration in the greenhouse, or for sheltered beds and borders. There are many beautiful hybrids, but they are not so commonly grown at the present day. In the greenhouse it forms a good pillar subject if planted out. The flowers are pendant from the stalk, and the petals being generally incurved at the top, the flowers assume a somewhat globular form. Some varieties have beautifully variegated foliage. *Culture.*—For bedding-out increase by means of cuttings of young wood struck in moderate heat (60° F.) during the previous autumn, or early in February, grow on, and, if for summer bedding, plant out about the end of May. Two parts fibrous loam to one part of peat and sand makes a suitable compost. Trim and cut out old wood in February. *Varieties.—A. Boule de Neige* (White); *A. Golden Fleece* (Yellow); *A. Red Gauntlet* (Dark Red); *A. Thompsonii* (Mottled Green and Yellow Foliage). The beautiful half-hardy

255

species *A. vitifolium* has flowers varying from Pale Blue to Lavender. It requires a well sheltered position under a South wall. Another beautiful species to grow is *A. megapotamicum* which requires similar treatment. Flowers Red and Yellow. All flower from August to November, and grow 18 to 72 inches high.

Acacia (Mimosa).—Most of these evergreen trees and shrubs are greenhouse shrubs not sufficiently hardy to plant in the open except in warm, sheltered borders during the summer months. *Culture.*—Sow seed when ripe, or take cuttings of half-matured wood with a "heel" and strike in a close frame in July or August.

In the warm greenhouse, *A. armata* may be had in flower in early spring. Pot-up in summer after blooming, in 6– to 10–inch pots, and give liquid manure while growing. Stand in a sheltered position out-of-doors in summer and take in again in September. Cut back straggling shoots after flowering. For Hardy or Rose Acacias, *see* Robinia. *Species.*—*A. armata* (Yellow, Jan.–March, 3–10 ft.); *A. Baileyana* (Yellow, Jan.–May, 3–20 ft.); *A. dealbata* [Mimosa] (Yellow, Jan.–May, 3–50 ft.); *A. hastata* (Pale Yellow, Feb.–April, 3–4 ft.); *A. longifolia* (Yellow, April–May, 12–50 in.); and *A. l. var. mucronata* (Yellow, Jan.–March, 18–50 in.).

Acæna (New Zealand Burr).—A genus of trailing plants, the dwarf-growing kinds of which are useful for carpeting in the rock garden. They do well in sun or shade in ordinary light, sandy soil. *Culture.*—Sow under glass in March, place cuttings in a cold frame in sand during August, or propagate by means of division in April. Plant-out in spring or early autumn. *A. Sanguisorbæ*, with its pretty grey-green foliage in summer, is a useful little trailer for the wall garden. *Species.*—*A. adscendens* (Purple, June–Aug., 6 in.); *A. Buchananii* (Yellowish-red, Summer 2–3 in.); and *A. microphylla* (Bright Red, June–Aug., 3 in.).

Acantholimon (Prickly Thrift).—Useful little rock plants, which like a warm, dry sunny position and a gritty, well-drained loam, and which are best propagated by means of cuttings with a "heel" in July and placed in a cold frame, or by layering, and in the case of *A. glumaceum*, by division of roots. *Species.*—*A. Echinus* (White); *A. glumaceum* (Pale Pink); and *A. venustum* (Pale Pink), probably the best but not easy to propagate. All flower from July–August, and grow from 5 to 6 inches high.

Acanthus (Bear's Breech).—A hardy perennial useful for beds, borders, and the cold greenhouse. It likes a sunny, sheltered site with light soil. For culture, *see* Perennials, p. 156. *Species.*—*A. mollis var. latifolius* (Rose, Summer, 24 in.); *A. mollis* (Lilac, Pink, or White, Aug. 40 in.); *A. spinosus* (Purple-pink or White, July and Aug., 40 in.).

Acer (Maple).—Hardy deciduous trees for the pleasure grounds and park in positions with well-drained ordinary soil. The leaves of the various species vary greatly in size, colour, and shape. *Culture.*—Plant in November. No pruning is required. Propagate by means of seed, layering and budding in the open in August. *Species.*—*A. Negundo variegatum, A. palmatum vars.* (Japanese Maples), *A. platanoides* (Norway Maple), *A. Pseudo-Platanus vars.* (Sycamores), *A. rubrum* (Red Maple), and *A. saccharinum* (Silver Maple).

Anemone, Giant French

Narcissus, Cheerfulness

PLATE 25

Anemone, St. Brigid

Daffodil, King Alfred

Alexander & Brown and Sutton & Sons

PLATE 26

DIANTHUS

Dobbie & Co.

Above and below,
various hybrid forms
of dianthus.

Allwood Bros.

R. & G. Cuthb

Border carnation,
Sussex Beauty

Dianthus Heddewegii
superb mixed

Sutton & Sons

Dianthus, Delight

Allwood Bros.

Achillea (Milfoil, Yarrow, and Double Sneezewort).—This genus includes a number of hardy perennials. The dwarf-growing kinds are invaluable for crevices and ledges in the rock garden. *A. tomentosa* and *A. rupestris* are delightful subjects for the paved and wall gardens. They like a sunny situation and light, dry, ordinary soil. For culture, *see* Perennials, p. 156. *Species.—A. argentia* (White, May and June 3–4 in.); *A. clypeolata* (Yellow, Silver foliage, July–Aug., 18–24 in.); *A. filipendulina* (Yellow, July–Sept., 36–40 in.); *A. Mille-folium* [Cerise Queen] (June–Aug., 24 in.); *A. tomentosa* (Yellow, 6–9 in.).

Achimenes.—A genus of beautiful scaley-stoloniferus-rooted plants, suitable for the living-room or greenhouse, and adapted for culture in hanging baskets. They combine great individual beauty with a variety of rich and brilliant colours. *Culture.*—Use a compost of equal parts of leaf-mould, loam and silver sand. Plant 5 to 6 tubers an inch deep in a 5- or 6-inch pot in February, cover them with about an inch of compost, and place in a house with a temperature of 55° F. to 60° F. Shade from the hot sun and feed with liquid manure. To keep up a succession, commence starting them in heat in January and continue until May. The stems should be tied up or they will fall down and get injured. Dry-off after flowering, lift the rhizomes and store. Propagate by offsets in February, or by cuttings in May under glass. *Species and varieties.—A. Admiration* (Red-purple); *A. Celestial* (Pale Mauve); *A. coccinea* (Scarlet); *A. grandiflora* (Large Violet); *A. longiflora* (Blue); *A. longiflora alba* (White); *A. Pink Perfection* (Rose-magenta). All flower from July–September, and grow from 12–18 inches high.

Aconite.—*See* Eranthis.

Aconitum (Monkshood or Wolfsbane).—Hardy perennial, *poisonous* plants. For culture, *see* Perennials, p. 156. *Species.—A. Carmichælii* (Pale Lilac-blue, Sept.-Oct., 36 in.); *A. Lycoctonum* (Yellow, July–Aug., 36 in.); *A. Napellus* (Blue and White, June–Oct., 48 in.).

Acorus (Sweet Flag, Sweet Sedge, or Myrtle Grass).—A genus of hardy perennials 6 to 30 inches high, flowering in July and August. Excellent subjects for the marsh or water garden. *Culture.*—Propagate by means of division in March, and plant-out in sunny, marshy situation, or in shallow water. *Species.—A. Calamus* (Yellow, 30 in.); *A. C. var. variegatus* (Leaves Striped with Red and White, 30 in.).

Adenophora (Gland Bellflower).—Hardy perennials which thrive in sunny borders, in well-drained ordinary soil. For culture, *see* Perennials, p. 156. *Species.—A. cælestis* (Large Blue, June–Aug., 12 in.), one of the best; *A. ornata* (Blue, June–Aug., 24 in.); *A. lilifolia* (Blue, June–Aug. 12–40 in.).

Adiantum (Maidenhair Fern).—*See* Ferns.

Adonis (Pheasant's Eye).—A genus of useful rock plants, annuals and peren-nials, thriving in shade in a mixture of loam, peat, and leaf-mould. For culture, *see* Annuals, p. 139, and Rock Plants, p. 196. *Species.—A. æstivalis* (Crimson, May–June, 12 in.); *A. annuus* (Blood Red, June–Aug., 12 in.); * *A. amurensis* (Yellow, Feb.–April, 12 in.); * *A. vernalis* (Yellow, March–April, 10 in.). Perennials marked *.

Ægle sepiaria. *See* Poncirus.

Æsculus (Horse Chestnut and Buckeye).—One of the most handsome of flowering trees. *Culture.*—Plant in November in a sunny position with ordinary soil. Thin out branches when overcrowded only. To propagate, sow in March, layer in autumn, or graft in the spring. *Some good Species.*—*A. californica* (Californian Horse Chestnut); *A. carnea* (Red Horse Chestnut); *A. Hippocastanum* (Horse Chestnut); *A. Hippocastanum fl. pl.* (Double Horse Chestnut); A. *indica* (Indian Horse Chestnut); *A. Pavia* (Red Buckeye).

Æthionema (Burnt Candytuft).—A genus of dwarf-growing, shrubby perennials that are excellent subjects for the rock garden or dry walls. They thrive in the sun in gritty or sandy loam. *Culture.*—Sow under glass in March or take cuttings in July and insert in cold frame. Trim in all straggly shoots after flowering. *Species and Varieties.*—*A. cordifolium* (Rose, June–July, 6 in.); *A. grandiflorum* (Rose, May–July, 12 in.); *A. pulchellum* (Pink, May–June, 9 in.); *A. Warley Rose*, hybrid (Carmine-rose, May, 9 in.).

Agapanthus.—Beautiful African lilies blooming in August and September, and combining graceful foliage with large handsome heads of blossom. In flower beds or grown in masses, the blue species *A. orientalis* is very lovely. Planted in strong, rich soil, it produces a splendid show, and when mixed with gladioli, the effect is unique. *A. o. albus*, a white variety, forms a good companion and makes an excellent contrast. These plants will thrive in the open in warm, sunny borders in rich sandy loam and leaf-mould, but are more suitable for the cool greenhouse. *Culture.*—Pot-up in March, using a 9-inch pot and compost of 2 parts loam to 1 part of leaf-mould, rotten manure, and sand. A large pot or tub is required for several plants. During summer, give abundance of water and liquid manure twice a week. In winter, protect from frost, and give water sparingly. Large plants may be stood out during the summer. Sow seed under glass or propagate by means of division in March. *Species.*—*A. orientalis* (Blue); *A. orientalis maximus* (Light Blue); *A. orientalis minor* (Blue); *A. orientalis albus* (White). All flower in August and September and grow to a height of from 18 to 40 inches.

Agastache mexicana (syn. Brittonastrum mexicana).—A beautiful herbaceous plant, which in the south has proved quite hardy. It may require winter protection in the less favourable parts of the country. It requires a well-drained sunny position. Propagate by seed in spring or division of rootstock in spring. It grows from 2 to 2½ feet in height and from June to August bears Cerise flowers.

Agave.—The best known kind is the *Agave americana* or American Aloe, which in the cool greenhouse usually grows from 20 to 40 inches high, though much larger plants are obtainable. It is a slow-growing plant, consisting of a number of broad, fleshy leaves with sharp points, and throwing up from the centre a long flower spike, from which proceed branchlets sustaining flowers white and tinted with a yellowish-green colour. The popular belief that the plant dies after flowering is a fallacy. The main stem does, certainly, but off-shoots from the base carry on the growth. It is chiefly used for the ornamentation of terraces when placed in tubs or large pots, and is equally effective for this purpose in the greenhouse. *Culture.*—Pot-up firmly every 4 or 5 years in a well-drained compost of 2 parts of rich fibrous loam to 1 part of leaf-mould, sand, and brick-rubble. The plants may be stood out-of-doors in summer. Propagate by means of seed in heat in February, or by offsets in the summer.

258

Species.—*A. americana* (Aug., 30 in.); *A. americana variegata* (Variegated); *A. densiflora* (Sept., 40 in.); *A. filifera* (Aug., 2–3 ft.).

Ageratum (Floss Flower).—A useful half-hardy annual for the rock garden, and for edgings to beds or borders. For culture, *see* Annuals Half-hardy, p. 140. *Species.*—*A. Houstonianum* (Blue and White, May–Sept., 6–18 in.). *Named Varieties.*—Blue Perfection (Amethyst Blue); Imperial Dwarf (Deep Blue); Lavender Band (Lavender); Little Dorrit (Pale Blue); and Snowflake (White).

Ailanthus (Tree of Heaven).—A fine hardy deciduous tree, growing from 60 to 70 feet in height, and flowering in August. *Culture.*—Plant in November in a sunny, open position and in ordinary soil. Thin out the wood when overcrowded. To propagate, place root cuttings in a frame in August. *Species.*—*A. altissima* (*glandulosa*).

Ajuga (Bugle).—Although *Ajuga reptans*, the Common Bugle, is hardly worthy of notice, this genus includes several pretty little rock plants with attractive foliage. The best of these is, probably, *A. reptans var. metallica crispa*, which has crinkled, dark green leaves with a metallic lustre, and blue flowers. These little plants thrive in almost any situation and in ordinary, gritty soil, and are usually propagated by means of division in March or April. Other attractive varieties are *A. r. atropurpurea* with purple leaves, and *A. r. variegata*.

Alchemilla (Lady's Mantle).—*Alchemilla alpina* is a low-growing little rock plant of tufted habit with silvery green, strawberry-like foliage, and carries tiny, greenish flowers in summer. It is useful for carpeting in the paved or rock garden, and likes a sunny, open position, and a well-drained, gritty, ordinary soil with a little lime in it. Propagate by means of division in spring or autumn. *A. pentaphyllea*, with tiny white flowers, is also deserving of a place in the rock garden. There are several other species all with similar flowers.

Alisma Plantago-aquatica (Water Plantain).—Hardy perennial of tufted habit, useful for bog or water margin in ordinary soil. It grows about 30 inches high, and the rosy-white flowers are borne from June to August. *Culture.*—Sow in March in peat, or propagate by means of division in April, and plant in a sunny position with from 1 to 12 inches of slow-moving water above the crowns.

Allium.—Attractive hardy bulbous plants which grow from 6 to 18 inches high, and bloom from May to July. They like a sunny position and light loam to which a little sand and leaf-mould have been added. *Culture.*—Plant in September or October, 3 inches deep and 4 inches apart. Lift from the ground when overcrowded and replant immediately. Propagation is by means of seed in frame in slight heat in March, or by offsets in October. Many species. *A. Beesianum* (Blue, 12–18 in.); *A. cyaneum* (Pale Blue, 6 in.); *A. Ostrowskianum* (Deep Pink, 6 in.), and *A. Moly* [The Lily Leek] (Yellow, 12 in.), are best suited for the rock garden. *A. albopilosum* (Lilac, 18 in. Large heads) is the most imposing species; *A. cæruleum* (Blue, 18 in.) is suitable for the border. *A. neapolitanum* [Daffodil Garlic] (White, 12–18 in.), and *A. roseum* (Lilac-rose. 12–15 in.) thrive in both border and rock garden, and the former may also be grown in pots and forced in the early spring. *Pot Culture.*—Pot-up in October, half a dozen bulbs in a 6-inch pot, in a compost of two-thirds loam and one-third leaf-mould and sand. Stand the pots, covered with fibre or ashes, in a cold frame. When about one inch of growth has been made, transfer to the green-

259

house, expose gradually to the light, and let the heat rise gently to 60° F. Water liberally while growing and after flowering, withhold water.

Almond.—*See* Prunus communis.

Alnus (Alder).—A deciduous tree which grows well in sunny, open positions and in moist, swampy soil. *Culture.*—Plant in November. No pruning is necessary. May be propagated by means of seed, layering, or grafting. *Species.*—A. *cordata* (Italian Alder), *A. glutinosa* (Common Alder), *var. imperialis, A. incana* (Grey Alder), and *A. japonica* (Japanese Alder).

Aloe.—A greenhouse evergreen plant, generally in the form of a rosette. Plant firmly in summer, in pots or tubs, in a compost of sandy loam, peat, and well-rotted manure. Stand in a sunny position, and water freely in summer, but sparingly in winter (Temp. 45° to 60° F.). Propagate by means of suckers in spring or sow seed in heat. *A. variegata* succeeds in a cool greenhouse.

Alonsoa (Mask Flower).—A pretty half-hardy, dwarf annual suitable for sunny beds, or for pot culture in the cool greenhouse. *Culture, see* Annuals, p. 140. If "stopped-back" periodically through the summer, some plants can be lifted and potted-up in September for flowering indoors, during autumn and winter. *Pot Culture.*—Pot-up in 5 to 6-inch pots, keep close for three weeks, then give ample light and air. Pinch out young shoots occasionally. Water carefully and give weak liquid manure until the buds show colour. *Species.*—A. *caulialata, A. linifolia,* and *A. Warscewiczii.* All scarlet, July to Aug., 18 in.

Aloysia. *See* Lippia.

Alstroemeria (Herb Lily or Peruvian Lily).—Tuberous-rooted perennials, some of which are hardy and suitable for sunny borders, in which the soil is well drained, rich, and light, with a little old mortar, leaf-mould, and sand mixed with it. They are also useful for pot culture. *Culture.*—Propagate by means of division in spring or autumn. Plant 4 inches deep and 10 inches apart. Water freely and mulch in summer when growing and protect from severe frost in winter. Do not lift the rhizomes. Seed may also be sown in gentle heat in January, the seedlings being planted out in May or June. *Species.*—A. *aurantiaca* (Orange-red, May–Aug., 30–36 in.); *A. chilensis* (Red, Pink, or Yellow, July, 30 in.); *A. hæmantha* (Bright Red, tipped Green, July, 18–24 in.); *A. Ligtu* (Whitish Lilac or Pale Red, streaked Purple, 1½–2 ft.); many beautiful forms; *A. Pelegrina* (Pinkish with Purple Spots, July, 12–18 in.). Greenhouse species marked *.

Alyssum (Madwort).—Useful dwarf annuals and perennials, for sunny beds, edgings, or the rock garden. The annual species, which are quite hardy, bloom nearly the whole summer; the perennials are amongst the earliest and most attractive spring flowers. They like a sunny position in sandy soil. *A. saxatile* (Rock Madwort or Gold Dust, as it is sometimes called) is a favourite rock plant. For culture *see* Annuals, p. 139, *and* Perennials, p. 156. *Species.*—A. *maritimum* [Sweet Alyssum] (White, May–July, 4–6 in.); * *A. montanum* (Yellow, May–June, 3 in.); * *A. saxatile var. citrinum* (Yellow, May, 6–10 in.). Perennials marked *.

Amaracus (Origanum).—A small genus of more or less hardy herbaceous, or sub-shrubs, which were at one time called Origanums. They require a well-drained soil in hot, sunny position. All are suitable for the rock garden. They may require covering with a sheet of glass in winter to guard against excessive wet. Propagate by means of seed sown in spring in pots, division of roots in March, or by cuttings inserted in sandy soil in cold propagating frame from August to September. *Species.*—*A. Dictamnus* (Pink to Purplish, leaves and stems woolly), should be given a warm sheltered position, well drained. *A. hybridus* (Pink), very similar to above species. Propagate by division in spring and soft cuttings in early summer.

Amarantus (Love-lies-bleeding, and The Prince's Feather).—Half-hardy annuals growing from 12 to 36 inches high, and flowering from July to October. They thrive in sunny beds or borders with shallow, light soil, or in the cool greenhouse. For culture, *see* Annuals, p. 139. *Species.*—*A. caudatus* (Crimson, July–Oct., 10–40 in.); *A. c var. ruber* (Crimson, with Carmine Foliage, July, 30 in.); *A. c var. tricolor* (Crimson, with Red, Yellow and Green Foliage, July, 36 in.); *A. hypochondriacus* (Crimson, July–Oct., 36–40 in.).

Amaryllis Belladonna (Belladonna Lily).—This beautiful species is very variable in the size and colour of its flowers, frequently producing flowers variously-shaded from white to a reddish or purplish hue. There is only one species. Some of the varieties are *A. Belladonna var. rubra major*, *A.B. var. kewensis*, *A.B. var. pallida*, and *A. B. Parkeri*, a cross between *A. Belladonna* and *Brunsvigia Josephinæ*. They succeed out-doors in well-drained soil at the foot of warm plant-house walls. The bulbs should be planted during the summer, when dormant, being covered with about 6 inches of rich loamy soil mixed with leaf-mould and silver sand. If planted too deep they do not flower freely. The blooms are produced during August and September, and the leaves, in common with those of many South African bulbs, during the winter and spring. Leave the bulbs in the ground but protect with fibre in winter. *Greenhouse Culture.*—If grown in the greenhouse, they require very large pots or pans. Even so, they do not flower freely; thus in the colder parts of the country, they should be planted out in raised beds in a cool greenhouse, or in a cold frame.

Amelanchier (June Berry or Service Berry).—Hardy deciduous trees and shrubs that thrive in sunny, sheltered positions and in moderately light and moist soil. *Culture.*—Plant in October or November. Do not prune, but cut out dead wood and thin when necessary after flowering. Propagate by means of seed in March, by grafting on the thorn in March, by cuttings struck in the open in October, or by layering. *Species.*—*A. alnifolia*, *A. canadensis*, and *A. rotundifolia*. All bear white flowers from April to May. The first two grow from 20 to 30 feet in height, the latter from 6 to 15 feet.

Ammobium alatum (Everlasting Sunflower).—A beautiful half-hardy biennial, growing about 18 inches high and blooming from June to August. Excellent for warm, sunny borders. For culture, *see* Biennials, p. 141.

Anagallis (Pimpernel).—Half-hardy annuals, suitable for a warm, sunny rock garden or for the greenhouse. *A. tenella* (Bog Pimpernel) said to be perennial, thrives on a moist bank in the bog or marsh garden. It grows about 3 inches high, carries pink flowers in July, and is best treated as an annual. For culture, *see* Annuals, p. 140. *Other Species.*—*A. arvensis var. carnea* (Pink, Summer, 6 in.); *A. a. var. cærulea* (Blue, Summer, 6 in.); *A. linifolia* (Blue, Summer, 10 in.); *A. l. var. collina* (Scarlet, Summer, 6 in.).

261

Anchusa (Alkanet).—The annuals are unimportant. The half-hardy biennials and perennials like a sunny position, but do not require very rich soil. For culture, *see* Biennials, p. 141, *and* Perennials, p. 156. *Species.*—*A. capensis* (Blue, July, 20 in.); * *A. italica var. Dropmore* (Rich Blue, June–Oct., 40–60 in.); * *A. sempervirens* (Deep Blue, June, 24 in.). Perennials marked *.

Andromeda (Marsh or Wild Rosemary).—Hardy, evergreen, heathlike shrubs, which thrive in the sun in boggy or moist peaty soil, and also make good pot plants for the cold greenhouse. Their roots should never be quite dry, but they will grow in well-drained, fibrous loam if ample moisture is provided and no lime is present. The flowers, borne in sprays at the end of the branches, are exactly like those of the Lily of the Valley. *Culture.*—Plant in October. Propagate by means of ripe seed in pans or boxes under glass in October, or divide the roots or layer in September. *Species.*—*A. polifolia* (Rose-white, May and June, 20 in.). Vars. *angustifolia* and *major*.

ANDROSACES (EASILY GROWN)

Name	Colour of Flowers	Height in Inches	Soil and Site	Remarks
A. carnea	Bright Rose and White	3	Cool, Sandy, Stony Loam. Moraine or Rocky Ledge	Small, bright, glossy green tufts. Needs no glass protection in winter.
A. Chumbyi	Brilliant Car-mine	4	Well-drained Gritty Loam. Rocky Ledge or Moraine	Silvery rosettes of woolly foliage. Needs glass cover in winter.
A. foliosa	Rose-lilac	6	Well-drained Sandy Loam and Leaf-mould. Rocky Limestone Ledge	Long, grey-green tufts. Coloured foliage in autumn. Spreads rapidly. Needs glass protection in winter.
A. lanuginosa	Rose-pink	4	Well-drained Loam. Rocky Ledge or Moraine	Trailing stems form silvery-grey carpet. Needs glass protection in winter.
A. obtusifolia	Pink	2–4	Good Gritty Soil	Keep fairly dry and do not water overhead. Position Sunny.
A. primuloides	Rose, White Eye on Red Stems	4	Well-drained Gritty Loam, Rocky Ledge	Forms large silvery-green rosettes of woolly foliage, and spreads rapidly. Needs glass covering in winter.
A. villosa	Rosy-white, Yellow Eye	3	Well-drained Sandy and Stony Loam, Rocky Ledge	Foliage forms tufts of small, woolly ro-settes. Needs glass protection in winter.
A. v. arachnoidea	Pinkish-white Yellow Eye	3	Well-drained Sandy Loam. Limestone Ledge.	Forms silvery, hairy rosettes. One of the best.

Androsace (Rock Jasmine).—These most beautiful, low-growing, and typically alpine plants are divided into two main groups: those of rather rampant growth that require a sunny site, ample drainage, and a gritty, sandy loam; and the high alpine or rock-loving class, which need a dry, hot, rocky crevice with a deep root-run, or a sunny position in shingle. In many cases, they are rather like very woolly, thin-leaved houseleeks. They must have ample moisture in the growing season, but it must not come in contact with the minute, furry cushions of foliage. To the second section belong such plants as: *A. alpina, A. ciliata, A. cylindrica, A. helvetica, A. imbricata, A. pubescens,* and *A. pyrenaica.* These are extremely difficult to grow outdoors in this country, but are charming for the Alpine house. Most androsaces have silky or woolly leaves and these need a covering of glass in winter to keep out excessive wet. The masses of starry, primula-like flowers are pink or white and are borne in early summer, with the exception of those of *A. lanuginosa,* which flowers from July to September, on short, erect stems some 3 to 6 inches high. *Culture.*—Sow seed under glass in March, take cuttings in September and strike in sandy soil under glass, or propagate by means of division in April. Plant out in the open in spring or early autumn. Androsaces may also be increased by layering in July.

Anemone (Windflower).—Anemones of both kinds, hardy fibrous-rooted herbaceous perennials and the tuberous-rooted, thrive best in semi-shade in a moist, light, rich medium loam, but generally succeed in any which is well drained, well dug, and manured. The dwarf-growing kinds are excellent for the rock garden, while *St. Brigid* anemones are favourites for beds and borders. *Culture.*—(TUBEROUS.) Plant from October to the end of March. Set the tubers about 3 inches deep and 5 inches apart. The roots are best left undisturbed, but may be taken up for removal or for drying-off as soon as the leaves have died down, being replanted in the autumn. A change of position is recommended at intervals of two or three years, for the maintenance of size, beauty and richness of the flowers. This may be effected by taking up the roots, digging the bed over, and adding some decayed manure to enrich the soil and nourish the plants in the following spring. Sea sand, or a little salt, mixed with the soil is a good preventive of mildew. These anemones may be propagated by means of division of dry rhizomes from September to March. FIBROUS-ROOTED HERBACEOUS PERENNIALS.—Sow thinly in the reserve garden in April, in drills a foot apart and $\frac{3}{4}$ inch deep. Shade from the sun until the seed is up. Thin-out the seedlings to 3 inches apart, and leave them in the reserve garden until the leaves have died down after flowering the following spring, replant in their flowering positions, 12 inches apart, early in September. *Greenhouse Culture.*—Plant in the autumn, using 6-inch pans and a compost of deep, rich, sandy loam, and place in the cool greenhouse. Dress annually with fertilizer and lift the tubers when the foliage has died down. *Species.*—*A. alpina* (Cream, May–July, 18 in.); *A. Hepatica* and *vars.* (Blue, Red, Pink and White, March–May, 6 in.); *A. hybrida* (*japonica*) (White-Rose, Aug.–Oct., 30 in.); * *A. apennina* and *vars.* (Blue or White, March–May, 9 in.); * *A. blanda* and *vars.* (Blue, Pink, White, March–April, 6 in.); * *A. coronaria* (Various, May–June, 12 in.); * *A. fulgens* (Scarlet, May–June, 12 in.); * *A. hortensis* (Purple-rose and Whitish, April, 10 in.); * *A. nemorosa* and *vars.* (Blue or White, April, 6 in.). Tuberous marked *.

263

Antennaria.—Useful little dwarf-growing rock plants of creeping habit that form silvery tufts of foliage, and bear in summer masses of tiny pink or white flowers. They spread rapidly in the sun, in sandy, gritty loam, and are extremely useful for carpeting, etc., in the paved and rock gardens. These little flowers are best propagated by means of division of roots in spring or autumn, and require no protection in winter. *Species.—A. dioica* (Rose) and *A. d. var. tomentosa* (White).

Anthemis (Chamomile).—Hardy perennials that like a sunny border or rock garden with sandy loam. For culture, *see* Perennials, p. 156. *Species and Varieties.—A. Cupaniana* (White, Silver foliage, June–Aug., 12 in.); *A. montana* (White, June–Aug., 12 in.); *A. Sancti-Johannis* (Orange, June–Aug., 12–18 in.); *A. tinctoria* (Yellow, June–Oct., 18–24 in.); *A. tinctoria, var. Kelwayi* (Pale Yellow, June–Oct., 18 in.).

Anthericum Liliago (St. Bernard's Lily).—Hardy tuberous-rooted perennials, which thrive in a warm, sunny border with moist, light, rich soil, or in a 6-inch pot in the cold greenhouse. They grow to a height of 30 inches and carry white flowers in June and July. For culture, *see* Perennials, p. 156.

Antholyza paniculata (African Corn Flag).—Hardy bulbous-rooted perennial, which thrives in a sunny position in well-drained borders with sandy loam, and grows to about 30 inches high, carrying scarlet and yellow blooms from June to August. *Culture.*—Propagate by means of offsets in March or October, and plant 5 inches deep and 6 inches apart.

Anthyllis (Kidney Vetch and Ladies' Fingers).—Pretty little shrubby rock plants which like a sunny position and warm, gritty loam. They flower in June and July, and reach a height of 10 inches. For culture, *see* Rock Plants, p. 196. *Species.—A. montana* (Purple-pink); *A. Vulneraria* (Yellow, sometimes White or Pink). *A. Hermanniæ* (Yellow) is a taller growing species, up to 2 to 3 feet in height.

Antirrhinum (Snapdragon).—These are among the most graceful and lovely of all summer bedding plants. There is a large number of varieties, and these include every conceivable colour. There are three types, namely—tall, intermediate, and dwarf. The tall make excellent border plants, the intermediate and dwarfs are those most employed for bedding, for the rock garden, and as edging plants. Antirrhinums are grown both as biennials and perennials. They like a dry, well-drained, well-manured loam, and a sunny position, and are extremely useful for dry beds, borders, wall, rock, and wild gardens. *A. Asarina* is a useful alpine with creamy-yellow flowers. It is best to raise this from cuttings each year, as it is not over hardy. These may be inserted in sandy soil in a cold frame during August or September. For culture, *see* Biennials, p. 141, *and* Perennials, p. 156. *Varieties.*—TALL.—*Cottage Maid* (Pink and White); *Crimson King*; *Moonlight* (Apricot); *Primrose King*; *Scarlet Prince*; *Snowflake* (White, tinged Yellow); *Torch Light* (Orange scarlet); and *Yellow King.* All flower from April to October, and grow from 30 to 48 inches in height. INTERMEDIATE.—*Amber Queen* (Yellow and Pink); *Black Prince* (Deep Crimson); *Bonfire* (Orange-red); *Bronze Queen*; *Buff Beauty*; *Coccinea* (Orange-scarlet); *Cottage Maid* (Pale Pink and White); *Mauve Beauty*; *Pink Perfection*; *Prima Donna* (Apricot and White); *Rosy Queen*; *The Fawn* (Apricot); and *Yellow Queen.* All

264

flower from April to October, and grow from 15 to 30 inches in height. DWARF. —*White Prince, Yellow Queen*. Both these flower from April to October, and grow from 6 to 15 inches in height.

Aponogeton distachyum (Cape Water Hawthorn or Pond Weed).—A hardy aquatic plant which spreads over the surface of the water and carries masses of small white flowers from May to October. It does equally well in sun or shade in water with an ordinary soil bottom, and is excellent for ponds, fountains, or basins, but must be kept in check or it will soon smother other aquatics growing with it. *Culture.*—Propagate by means of offsets or by division in March. Plant in a weighted basket in slowly-moving water with from 6 to 30 inches of water above the crowns. There is also a variety *A. d. roseum* with pink and white flowers.

Aquilegia (Columbine).—Hardy herbaceous perennials and biennials, that thrive in rather shady borders in moist, cool, well-drained, deep loam and leaf-mould. They are also useful for greenhouse culture, and the dwarf kinds for the rock garden. For culture, *see* Perennials, p. 156, *and* Rock Plants, p. 196. The columbines cross-fertilize with one another so profusely that they are very difficult to raise true from seed. If seed is used, it should be sown under glass in March or August, or, if preferred, the plants may be propagated by means of division in April or September. *Species and Varieties.*—*A. alpina* (Violet-blue, May and June, 10 in.); *A. canadensis* (Red, May, June, 12 in.); *A. cœrulea* (Pale Blue and White, May–July, 12–18 in.); *A. chrysantha* (Golden Yellow, May–July, 30 in.); *A. longissima* (Yellow, long spurs, May–June, 30 in.); *A. Skinneri* (Dark Scarlet and Greenish Yellow, May–July, 24 in.).

Arabis (Rock Cress).—Hardy perennial rock plant which likes a sunny position in ordinary, well-drained soil or sandy loam. It rapidly increases and thus should not be planted in close proximity to more choice plants, as it is likely soon to smother them. For culture, *see* Rock Plants, p. 196. *Species.*— *A. alpina* (White, May–July, 6 in.); *A. androsacea* (Rose, May, Trailer); *A. caucasica fl. pl.* (White [Double], May-June, Trailer); *A. muralis* (Rose, May–July, 6 in.); *A. verna*, a pretty annual (Violet, April–May, 6 in.).

Aralia.—Hardy shrubs which like a sunny position and sandy soil. *Culture.*— Plant in November. No pruning is required. Propagation is by means of root cuttings in autumn or suckers in spring. *Species.*—*A. chinensis* and *vars*. (Angelica Tree); *A. spinosa* (Hercules' Club).

Araucaria (Chili Pine or Monkey Puzzle).—Coniferous trees which like a sunny position and well-drained, deep loam. *Culture.*—Plant in April or September. No pruning is necessary. Propagate by seeds under glass. These trees are unsuitable for town gardens. *Species.*—*A. araucana. Pot Culture.*—*A. excelsa* (Norfolk Island Pine) is only suitable for the cool greenhouse. Pot-up in March, using two parts of sandy loam to one part of leaf-mould. Propagate by means of cuttings in heat in summer, or by "ringing".

Arbutus (Strawberry Tree).—Evergreen trees or shrubs which thrive in a warm, sunny, sheltered position in moist well-drained peat and loam. Trim back the long, straggling shoots in April and cut out dead wood. To propagate, sow seed in a frame when ripe. Grow in pots till ready to plant-out, and do not transplant more than necessary. Cuttings of young shoots may also be taken in July and struck in a frame. *Species.—A. Andrachne* (White, tinted Green, March and April, 10–30 ft.); *A. andrachnoides* (White, Winter, 15–30 ft.); *A. Menziesii* (Madrona), (White, May, 20–100 ft.); *A. Unedo* (Cream-pink, Sept.–Oct., 10–20 ft.).

Arctostaphylos Uva-ursi (Bearberry).—This is a pretty little trailing evergreen shrub, with small, roundish, leathery leaves, and in April and May flowers shading from white to rose. It is indigenous to certain moorland and mountainous districts, and if similar conditions are provided, can be grown quite easily from seed. It dislikes lime in the soil. *Arctous alpina* (The Black Bearberry), with white to red flowers in September, is a delightful little shrub, which rarely grows more than 10 inches high. It requires the same treatment as *Arctostaphylos*.

Arctotis stœchadifolia.—Half-hardy annual for sunny, sheltered beds and borders. It grows about 24 inches high, and carries pearl-grey, daisy-like flowers in summer. For culture, *see* Annuals, p. 140.

Ardisia.—These are evergreen shrubs, several species of which will flourish and fruit in a moderately warm greenhouse (Temp. 55–65° F.). *A. crenata* is a favourite species. *Culture.*—Pot up in March into 5 or 6-inch pots, using a mixture of loam and peat for the soil. Propagate by means of cuttings struck in sand under glass in March. Seed may also be sown in January in a propagating case.

Areca Catechu (Betel-nut Palm).—These are greenhouse palms with long, bright green, feathery leaves, and which grow from 10 to 25 feet high. They thrive in the shade in a compost of two parts of loam to one part of leaf-mould and sand. *Culture.*—Pot up annually in March or April, using 6 to 10-inch pots. Sponge the leaves frequently with warm soft water, and give water in moderation, but regularly. Temperature of the house, 50° F. in winter to 60° F. in summer. To propagate, sow seed one inch deep in heat in March.

Arenaria (Sandwort).—Dwarf hardy perennial creeping plants, useful for carpeting, for the paved garden and for the rock garden. They like a moist, sandy, gritty loam. For culture, *see* Rock Plants, p. 196. *A. balearica* likes a shady spot and ample leaf-mould in the compost, but *A. montana* loves to tumble over the sides of a rock in the full sun. *Species.—A. balearica* (White, May and June, 3 in.); *A. montana* (White, May–July, 3 in.); *A. purpurascens* (Reddish-purple, June and July, 3 in.); *A. tetraquetra* (White, June, 3 in.). One of the best and suitable for the moraine or scree.

Aristolochia.—*A. Clematitis* (Yellow, July, 3 ft.) is a hardy herbaceous perennial. Cut down each year. This and *A. macrophylla* (*Sipho*) [Dutchman's Pipe] a deciduous perennial climber (Brown and Yellow, June–July, 20 ft.), are hardy in sheltered situations, but others are only suitable for the warm greenhouse.

The following are the best for growing as climbers in the stove or tropical houses; *A. elegans* (Dark Brown, Summer, 20 ft.); *A. grandiflora* (Purple, Summer, 10 ft.). *Culture.*—Sow under glass in March, or take cuttings under glass in April. Plant-out in the following March (hardy species) or in the greenhouse in a mixture of light, sandy loam and leaf-mould. Thin-out the wood during the spring.

266

Armeria (Thrift, Sea Pink, Cushion Pink, etc.).—Dwarf hardy perennials mainly seen in the rock garden. They like a sunny, open position in dry, deep loam. For culture, *see* Perennials, p. 156. *Species.*—*A. cæspitosa* (Pinky-lilac, June, 4 in.); *A. maritima* and *vars.* (Rose, Red, Lilac, White, June–July, 6–12 in.); *A. plantaginea* (Rose, May–July, 18 in.).

Arnebia (Prophet Flower).—Hardy annuals which thrive in the sun in sandy loam and are excellent for border or rock garden. For culture, *see* Annuals, p. 140. *Species.*—*A. cornuta* (Yellow, Black Dot, June–Aug., 15 in.).

Aronia arbutifolia (Chokeberry).—White flowers followed by small red berries. Requires the same conditions as *Malus*, which see.

Artemisia (Old Man, Lad's Love, etc.).—Hardy herbaceous perennials and evergreen and deciduous shrubs thriving in ordinary soil. Several of the dwarf-growing kinds make excellent rock plants. *Culture.*—Propagate by means of division in October, or by cuttings in July. *Species.*—*A. Abrotanum* (Yellow, Aug.–Oct., 36 in.). Well known for its fragrance (Southernwood); *A. argentea* (Yellow or White, June–Sept., 20 in.); *A. caucasica* (Yellow, Silvery Foliage, July, 10 in.); *A. Dracunculus* [Tarragon] (Whitish Green, 24 in.). Leaves used for flavouring; *A. lanata* (Yellow [Silver Foliage], July-Aug., 6 in.).

Arum Lily. *See* Zantedeschia.

Arundinaria.—A genus of bamboo, the species of which thrive in a moist climate, a deep, rich loam holding ample leaf-mould, and plenty of protection from north and east winds. All species, save *A. japonica*, quickly suffer from drought, and it is essential that they shall receive attention in dry weather, if planted where the soil is apt to dry quickly. Of the hardy kinds *A. japonica* [Syn. Bambusa Metake], 10 to 15 feet, is the most generally grown. There are also many half-hardy species for the warm greenhouse. *Culture.*—Propagate by means of division in May and plant in sheltered positions. Cut out dead wood in April. *See also* Bambusa and Phyllostachys. Other *Hardy Species* are: *A. Falconeri* (25 ft.); *A. fastuosa* (20 ft.); *A. nitida* (10 ft.); *A. Simonii* (15 ft.); *A. Veitchii* (15 in.). *Variegated Species.*—*A. auricoma* (4 ft.); and the dwarf-growing *A. Fortunei* (24 in.). The genus is now divided up but for convenience sake all are included here under Arundinaria.

Arundo (Great Reed).—A perennial which thrives in semi-shade on slightly swampy banks in light, rich loam, and grows to a height of 10 feet. It is very attractive, but only suitable to large marsh or water gardens. *Culture.*—Propagate by means of division in May. *Species.*—*A. Donax* (Glaucous Foliage, 10 ft.); *A. Donax var. variegata* (Leaves Striped White, 10 ft.).

Asarum europæum.—A curious and useful little rock plant, growing about 2 inches high, and during the spring bearing purplish bell-shaped flowers amidst a mass of dark, heart-shaped, leathery leaves, which almost smother them. *Culture.*—Propagate by means of division from September to March, and plant out in permanent position in a shady spot under shrubs, and in moist and rich soil. No protection is necessary in winter. *A. canadense* (Brown, May–June, 8–12 in.); *A. caudatum* (Reddish Brown, July, 4–6 in.).

Asparagus (Asparagus Fern, Sparrow Grass).—Hardy and greenhouse evergreen and deciduous climbing and trailing plants, which thrive in a compost of two parts loam to one part of leaf-mould, peat, and sand. *Culture.*—Pot-up in

March, using 6 to 10-inch pots. Syringe and water well in summer. The vigorous climbers, such species as *A. plumosus* and *A. asparagoides*, should have their stems trained up strings or wires stretched from the ground to the roof of the house and running up within three or four inches of the back wall. *A. scandens* and *A. Sprengeri* make excellent basket plants, but care must be taken to see that the roots never become too dry. Propagate by means of seed in March in heat, by cuttings in a propagating case at the same period, or by division in March. If raised from seed, pot-off singly as soon as the seedlings can be handled. Give plenty of light, and keep the temperature steadily at about 60° F. The hardy species do well in a warm, sunny position in rich, sandy soil. *See also* Smilax. *Species.*—*A. plumosus* and *var. nanus*; *A. plumosus var. tenuissimus*; *A. retrofractus*; *A. Sprengeri*; *A. verticillatus*.

Asperula (Woodruff).—Hardy annuals and dwarf-growing perennials useful for beds, borders, edgings, rock garden, etc. The annuals like semi-shade; the perennials a sunny site, and soil with ample grit in it. *A. suberosa* dislikes lime in its soil. For culture, *see* Annuals, p. 139, *and* Perennials, p. 156. *Species and Varieties.*—*A. orientalis*, annual (Blue, June–Sept., 4 in.); *A. Gussonei* (Rose, May–Aug., 4 in., requires a well-drained site); *A. odorata* (White, May–June, 9 in.); *A. arcadiensis* (Pink [Silver Foliage], June and July, 3 in., best planted in moraine, in well-drained gritty soil cover with glass in winter).

Asphodeline.—Hardy herbaceous perennials that thrive in a sunny situation, in rich, well-drained soil. Closely allied to *Asphodelus*. *Species.*—*A. luteus* (Golden-yellow, May–July, 24–36 in.).

Asphodelus (Asphodel).—Mostly hardy perennials that thrive in the sun in any soil, though rich, sandy loam is most suitable. For culture, *see* Perennials, p. 156. *Species.*—*A. acaulis* (Pink, May–July, 12–24 in.); *A. albus* (White, May–July, 24–36 in.); and *A. ramosus* [King's Spear] (White, May–July, 24–36 in.).

Aspidistra (Parlour Palm).—These are plants bearing dark green, broad, lanceolate and leathery leaves on long stalks. They usually accommodate themselves to indoor conditions and are, therefore, favourite room plants. The flowers are very small and insignificant, and grow close to the ground. *Culture.*—Pot-up moderately firmly triennially in April, using a compost of 2 parts of peat and loam to 1 part of leaf-mould and sand. The pots should not be too large. Stand in the shade (Temp. 50° F. in winter to 60° F. in summer). Sponge the leaves with warm soft water when dusty, and water well and regularly during the summer. Propagate by means of division in April. *A. lurida*, the best known, is very popular as an indoor plant. There is also a variegated form, *A. l. variegata*.

Aspidium (Shield Fern).—*See Polystichum* under Ferns.

Asplenium (Spleenwort).—*See* Ferns.

Aster (Michaelmas Daisy, Starwort).—Hardy perennial asters, which thrive in the sun in ordinary well-drained soil and are excellent for borders and wild gardens; while the dwarf kinds make excellent subjects for the rock garden. They flower from July to November, and grow from 6 inches to 6 feet in height according to species. *Culture.*—Sow seed in the open in April, or propagate by means of division in March or October. Lift and divide the roots triennially. NAMED VARIETIES OF A. AMELLUS.—*Beauté Parfait* (Dark Blue); *Beauty of Ronsdorf* (Mauve); *General Pershing* (Pale Pink); *King George* (Purple-blue); *Perry's Favourite* (Pale Pink); and *ultramarine* (Deep Blue). NAMED VARIETIES OF A. CORDIFOLIUS.—*Diana* (Lilac); *Edwin Beckett* (Lilac-blue); and *Silver Spray* (Pale Lilac). NAMED VARIETIES OF A. ERICOIDES.—*Enchantress* (Pink); *Grey Dawn* (Light Blue); *King Edward VII* (Pale Lilac); *Ophir* (Mauve); *Perfection* (White); and *Simplicity* (Blue). NAMED VARIETIES OF A. NOVÆ ANGLIÆ.— *Barr's Pink* (Pink); *Mrs. F. J. Rayner* (Crimson); and *Purple Prince* (Purple). NAMED VARIETIES OF A. NOVI BELGII.—*Aldenham Pink* (Pink); *Beauty of Colwall* (Blue); *Beechwood Challenger* and *Beechwood Rival* (Red shade); *Brightest and Best* (Purple-rose); *Climax* (Heliotrope-blue); *Empress of Colwall* (Heliotrope); *Grey Lady* (Opal Grey): *King of the Belgians* (Pale Mauve); *Little Boy Blue* (Bright Blue); *Little Pink Lady* (Pink); *Peace* (Lavender); *Plenty* (Light Blue); *Sam Banham* (White); *The Bishop* (Purple); *The Sexton* (Rich Blue). There are also many other good species and varieties well worth growing, such as *Aster Frikartii* a hybrid (Single Blue, Aug.–Oct., 3 ft.); *A. subcæruleus* (Lavender, May–June, 1 ft.); good for rockery; *A. yunnanensis-Napsbury variety* (Large single Blue, May, 2 ft.) good for cutting.

For China Aster *see* Callistephus.

Astilbe (Goat's Beard).—The astilbe is closely allied to the spiræa, having the same loose foliage. It needs a cool, deep, and moist loam, either in sun or shade, and is thus a suitable subject for the marsh or bog garden. When grown in the sun, ample water must be afforded in dry weather and a mulch of leaf-mould should be given every November. These plants grow from 2 to 6 feet in height and flower from May to September. *See also* Spiræa. *Culture.*—Propagate by means of division in autumn or spring, and plant out in permanent position, which should be enriched with ample well-decayed cow-manure or hop-manure. Do not lift or divide the roots for three or four years after planting. *Species.*—A. *Arendsii* and hybrids; *Gloria purpurea* (Dark Pink); *Granat* (Dark Crimson); *Gruno* (Salmon-rose); *Pink Pearl* (Pink); *Prof. V. D. Wielen* (White); *Tamarix* (Bright Red). There are also other good kinds. *Astilbe astiboides* (White, 2–3 ft.); *A. chinensis* (White and Pink, 1–2 ft.); *A. Davidii* (Rose Purple, 3 in.); *A. japonica* (White, 2 ft.). This latter plant is erroneously called *Spiræa japonica* by Florists.

Astragalus (Milk Vetch).—Hardy, dwarf-growing plants of the broom genus, some of which make excellent subjects for the rock garden. They thrive in the sun, in deep loam, sand and mortar. *Culture.*—Sow in the spring or summer, or propagate by division in autumn. *Species.*—A. *alpinus* (Purple, June–Aug., Trailing); *A. danicus var. albus* (White, May–July, 5 in.); *A. massiliensis* (Violet-purple, May–July, 24 in.).

Astrantia (Masterwort).—Hardy perennials, which like a shady position with cool, moist loam and leaf-mould. The dwarf-growing kind are excellent for the rock garden. Propagate by means of root division in spring or autumn. *Species.* —A. *Biebersteinii* (Rose, May–July, 30 in.); *A. major* (White, tinged Pink, May–July, 18 in.); *A. minor* (Pale Rose, May–July, 6 in.).

Athyrium (Lady Fern) *see* Ferns.

Aubrieta (Rock Cress).—Pretty evergreen perennial trailing plants, which are useful for edgings, spring bedding, or the rock garden. They thrive in the sun in dry, rich, sandy loam and leaf-mould. For culture, *see* Perennials, p. 156. *Varieties.*—*Barker's Double* (Rosy Lilac); *Bridesmaid* (Blush-pink); *Carnival* (Reddish-purple); *Crimson King* (Ruby-red); *Dr. Mules* (Violet-blue); *Gloriosa* (Pink); *Godstone* (Violet Purple); *Gurgedyke* (Violet); *J. S. Baker* (Violet-blue, White Eye); *Lavender*; *Lilac Queen*; *Magician* (Purple); *Pritchard's A*1 (Purple). There are many other good varieties worth growing. All flower from April to June and grow about 4 inches in height.

Aucuba japonica (Spotted or Variegated Laurel).—A hardy evergreen shrub, growing some 8 feet high, and well suited for shady places and town gardens, in which the air is often close and smoky. They may also be grown in large pots for decorative purposes, but do best out-of-doors in the shade in well-drained ordinary soil. There are many useful varieties with spotted and deep green foliage. The male and female flowers are borne on separate bushes, and when the two sexes are grown near together, the female bush produces large bright red berries in autumn. *Culture.*—Plant in March or October. Cut back long weak shoots in May. To propagate, take cuttings and strike in frames or in the open in autumn, or sow seeds in frame when ripe.

Auricula (Primula Auricula).—Auriculas are divided into two classes, namely, Show Auriculas and Alpine Auriculas, the latter being more hardy and easier to grow. Show Auriculas are classed according to the colour of the edge, there being *White-edged*, *Green-edged*, and *Grey-edged* varieties. If there is no edge beyond the ground colour, it is called a *Self*. Thus, there are four classes of Show Auriculas. In the Alpine Auriculas, which may be single or double, the eye is yellow, cream, or white; there is no edge, but the ground beyond the eye is generally shaded to a darker colour round the edge. The best compost is a good fibrous, rather heavy loam, adding a little decayed manure and leaf-mould, with a liberal addition of silver sand and a sprinkling of charcoal or wood ashes.

Culture.—(*Show Auriculas.*)—Sow in pans in a warm house on the surface of a compost of half loam and half leaf-mould and gritty sand, when ripe or from January to March. Moist moss should be kept over the surface of the soil until the seedlings are up. When these have three or four leaves, transplant into 3-inch pots. Four to 5-inch pots are large enough for full-sized plants. Where it is essential that the flowers shall come true to type and in the case of choice specimens, it is better to propagate by means of offsets or root divisions in February or March, or in August after re-potting. Offsets may be placed singly in 3-inch pots, or three in a larger pot. Keep the pots in the open in a cool, sheltered site, and remove to the cool greenhouse at the end of September. The auricula blossoms, and is in full growth from February to June, when the plants should be removed from the glazed shelter under which they have been flowering, being placed in the open air on a shelf or stage having a north or north-east aspect, and if possible with some glass lights rigged up overhead. In August, when the fresh growth commences, the plants should be re-potted, the tap roots being shortened with a sharp knife. In November, place the plants under glass. Keep the plants within 18 inches of the glass, but shade from direct rays of the

270

sun. When the biting east winds are prevalent in March, close the ventilators on that side of the house and let in the air from the opposite quarter. Never allow water to fall on the foliage or to settle on the leaves at the base. Very little artificial heat is required and a close atmosphere is fatal. (*Alpine Auriculas.*) Sow seed in a light, sandy soil in a little heat in March and just cover with sand. Prick-off into boxes as soon as four leaves have formed. Harden-off in a shady cold frame at the end of May. Plant-out 6 inches apart in September or October in a partially shaded position facing north, in well-drained, rather heavy loam and cow-manure. Lift, divide, and re-plant triennially after flowering. A few good *Varieties* (*Show*).—White Edged: *Acme* and *Heather Bell*. Green Edged: *Dr. Horner* and *Prince Charming*. Grey Edged: *George Rudd* and *George Lightbody*. Self: *Gordon Douglas* and *Harrison Weir*. (*Alpines*).—*Admiration, Day Dream, Firefly, Majestic, Roxborough, Silver Wood*.

Azalea.—The azaleas common to our gardens, which are now frequently grouped with rhododendrons, are deciduous shrubs, varying from 2 to 6 feet or more in height. With azaleas, as with rhododendrons, the best garden varieties are hybrids. Azaleas are distinguished as Ghent (deciduous), Mollis (deciduous), and Indian (evergreen). The former two are more suitable for open-air culture and the latter for greenhouse decoration. A compost of sandy peat and loam, or two-thirds fibrous loam and one-third leaf-mould, is suitable for all varieties, but they will grow quite well in almost any soil that does not contain lime or chalk. *Culture.*—(Outdoors.) Plant from October to March, 3 feet apart in a semi-shaded and sheltered position, where they will form bushes of considerable size. When, however, they are to be used as bedding plants, it is better to plant them in full sun. They will then remain smaller. Azaleas in the open require ample moisture during dry summers. Do not prune, but merely keep in shape by means of "stopping" and removing straggly shoots and dead flowers in June.

Pot Culture (*A. indica and hybrids*).—Pot these plants up firmly from October to November, using 6 to 10-inch pots and the compost mentioned above. Keep in a cold frame until late November, then move in succession into the house, and gradually acclimatize to moist, warm conditions. After flowering, prune straggling shoots and remove all dead blooms. Re-pot if necessary (usually every second or third year), place the pots in the warmest corner and syringe overhead. Stand in the open in a cool, sheltered position on a bed of ashes or shingle from June to September, and water liberally and syringe overhead morning and evening in dry, warm weather. In September, return to the house. *A. mollis*, although hardy, is also useful for the warm greenhouse. *Forcing.*—See p. 253. To propagate, take cuttings of half-matured wood early in summer and strike in a frame (50°–60° F.); sow in moist heat and fine, sandy peat in spring; or layer. *Species.* —(*Hardy*)—*A. calendulacea* (Orange-red); *A. mollis* (Red, Yellow, etc.); *A. nudiflora* (Pink or White); *A. occidentalis* (Pink and White); *A. pontica* (Yellow). All flower from May–July, and grow from 3 to 6 feet in height. (*Greenhouse*)— *A. indica* (Many Shades of Colour). They flower from Christmas to May according to the temperature of the greenhouse, and grow from 1 to 3 feet high, or more with age. Named varieties are numerous, and growers' catalogues should be consulted.

271

Azara.—Evergreen shrubs and climbers that are almost hardy, and which like a warm, sheltered position and well-drained sandy loam. *Culture.*—Plant in March or October. Thin out the branches when necessary, but otherwise do not prune. Propagate by means of cuttings under glass in summer or by layering in spring. *A. microphylla* is a beautiful shrub with pale yellow flowers in early spring.

Babiana (Baboon-root).—Dwarf half-hardy bulbs with brilliantly-coloured flowers of great beauty, and pale green "hairy" leaves. The plants grow from 6 to 10 inches high, and bloom from May to June. They are natives of the Cape of Good Hope and can be grown in a warm, sheltered position in the open, but are better suited to a cold greenhouse. There are many varieties and all shades of colours; reds, blues, and purples predominating. *Culture.*—Plant in October, 4 inches deep and 4 inches apart, in a warm, sheltered bed, or put four bulbs in a $4\frac{1}{2}$-inch pot in a compost of sandy loam mixed with leaf-mould and cow-dung. When the bulbs are sending up leaves and flowers they should be kept thoroughly moist. Feed after blooming with weak liquid manure water until the leaves turn yellow, then stop the water, and dry off in the pot, or lift from the bed. *B. stricta var. rubro-cyanea* has blue flowers with carmine centres, and is most attractive.

Balsam (Impatiens).—A pretty half-hardy annual for sunny beds or borders with rich soil or for the greenhouse. *Culture.*—*See* Annuals, page 139. Support with neat stakes. *Pot Culture.*—Pot-up as required, using 5 to 6-inch pots and a compost of half loam and half rotten cow-dung and leaf-mould with a little sand, and stand near the glass in a cool greenhouse. Syringe overhead, ventilate, and water liberally. As soon as the buds begin to form, water twice a week with a weak liquid manure. Do not "stop" back. When large specimens are desired, shift into 8 to 10-inch pots, using the richest compost available, and plunge the pots into spent hops or tan and feed with manure water. *Species and Varieties.*—*Impatiens Balsamina* (many vars.); *I. Holstii* (Vermilion); *I. Oliveri* (Mauve); *I. Sultanii* (Rose).

Bambusa (Bamboo).—There are three great classes of bamboos, namely *Arundinaria*, *Bambusa* and *Phyllotachys*. Most species do well in the open, especially if the soil is of a moist, deep, light, loamy nature, and has some peat or leaf-mould in it, but in exposed situations they require some protection. *Culture.*—Propagate by means of division in May. Cut out dead canes in April. *Pot Culture.*—Pot-up in March in a well-drained compost of two-thirds loam and one-third leaf-mould and sharp sand. Water liberally, syringe well overhead in summer, and give weak liquid manure twice a week during the growing period. A moist and moderately warm atmosphere is essential.

It is the dwarfer kinds, such as *Arundinaria Fortunei variegata* (Striped with Silver, 2 ft.), *A. pumila* (1–2 ft.), *A. vagans* (1–$1\frac{1}{2}$ ft.), and *Phyllostachys ruscifolia* (1–2 ft.), that are most suitable as pot plants in the greenhouse. Propagate by offsets (division) in March. *Species.*—(*Hardy*)—*B. disticha* (2 ft.) and *B. angulata* (4–8 ft.).

Bartonia.—*See* Mentzelia.

Basil [Sweet] (*Ocimum Basilicum*).—The kind known as Bush Basil (*Ocimum minimum*) is the most hardy, and is raised from seed sown in gentle heat in

PLATE 27   *Above*, a selection of seven begonias in flower and *below*, a selection of nine coleus showing the ornamental variegations in the leaves.

Ferocactus longihamatus　　　　　*Mammillaria longiflora*　　　　　*Leuchtenbergia principis*

PLATE 28 CACTI

Astrophytum myriostigma　　　　　　　　*Echinopsis multiplex*

March or April. It should be carefully thinned and given plenty of air to harden it. A rich, warm soil suits it best.

Begonia.—These plants, which grow from 6 to 20 inches high and flower nearly all the year round, thrive in sunny beds and borders with rich loam. They are also extremely useful in the greenhouse.

Culture.—(Tuberous-rooted Kinds.)—For bedding out or for greenhouse decoration from June to October. Sow in February, under glass, (Temp. 65° F.) in a finely sifted and just moist compost of two-thirds loam and one-third leaf-mould and sand. Water before sowing and keep the seed-pans moist by covering them with a piece of glass until germination takes place. Prick-off the seedlings into shallow boxes. Pot-off singly into pots, or transplant into boxes or frames. Plant-out in May or June, or pot-up into 5-inch pots for the green-house, keep near the glass, and shade when the sun is hot. Occasional spraying overhead when the weather is warm will help them. These young plants should flower in the late summer. Particular varieties may be propagated in spring by means of leaf cuttings, which consist of well-matured leaves scored with the point of a sharp knife across the larger nerves of the lower side. These should be laid on sand or coconut fibre in a propagating case and held in place by small pieces of broken pot. Bulblets will form at the end of the nerves, and these, when large enough, must be removed and potted up singly. Ordinary stem cuttings may also be taken in summer. When starting tubers, they should be planted flat or hollow side uppermost in February or March, being just covered in shallow trays, in heat (60° F.), with moist, sandy loam and well-rotted manure for soil. Water in moderation until growth commences. If for summer bedding, harden-off in May in a cold frame and plant-out in June, or, if for the greenhouse, pot-up in 4-inch pots in a compost of two-thirds loam and one-third leaf-mould, well-rotted manure and sand, re-potting when pot-bound into 7 to 8-inch pots. Water well in summer, shade from hot sun, and once the roots have filled the pots, feed with weak manure-water twice a week. Stake any shoots that need support and pick off all dead blooms. Greenhouse temperature 55° F. in winter to 70° F. in summer. The tubers should be lifted in October when the frost has turned the foliage black. If they must be removed from the beds before this, lift them with a good "ball" of soil, pack in boxes, and place in a sheltered spot to finish ripening. Then shake the soil and foliage away from the roots, allow them to dry for a day or so and store in dry soil in boxes in a cool, but frost-proof place. Start them again the following February or March in a tray of damp fibre in heat, and pot up with the crown of the tuber level with the surface of earth when sufficient growth has been made. Tuberous begonias grown in pots must be gradually dried-off and stood in a frost-proof shed or frame for the winter.

Culture.—(Fibrous-rooted Kinds.)—This is a very large and varied class, including as it does a large number of species and varieties of a sub-shrubby habit, which require an intermediate or greenhouse temperature. Some of them flower more or less all the year round, and a few of them may be used for summer-bedding. The most important for this purpose are the many beautiful varieties of *B. semperflorens*, which may be raised from seed sown during January in a temperature of 60° F., or by means of basal cuttings from plants lifted and potted up and kept in a warm house over the winter. The sub-shrubby and perennial species, generally, are propagated by means of ordinary cuttings, or by means of leaf-cuttings, in a temperature of from 60° to 70° F. In the case of leaf-cuttings, they are usually pegged down on boxes of sandy fibre, the principal veins being scored in places with a sharp knife. The winter-flowering section, which is represented by *Gloire de Lorraine* and its varieties, may be increased by means of leaf-cuttings, or by young basal shoots. They are usually secured from plants that have flowered and that have been rested for a few weeks. These are then partly cut back and started in a temperature of from 65° to 70° F., cuttings being secured during March. The other winter-flowering section, which is represented by varieties raised from crossing the species *B. socotrana* with the tuberous-rooted varieties, are by no means easy to grow successfully, and require very careful management during their resting period. After flowering, they should be stood in a house with a temperature of from 55° to 60° F. They should have very little water at the root; on the other hand, they must not suffer, for it is important that their foliage should, so far as possible, be retained in a fresh condition until they start to throw up young shoots from the base during May. They should then be given more water at the root. When the young shoots are about three inches in length, they should be secured as cuttings, and inserted singly in small pots of sandy compost. They root readily in a close case with a bottom heat of 70° F. During the summer months they should be grown in an average temperature of from 55° to 65° F. During the summer, they enjoy ample atmospheric moisture, and must be shaded during the hottest part of the day.

All begonias are very subject to attacks of begonia mite "rust". This must be guarded against, by spraying with a nicotine compound, or by the use of a sulphur vaporizer.

Culture of Ornamental and Variegated-leaved Species.—Pot-up in March or April in a compost as recommended above, keep in a moist atmosphere, never letting the temperature fall below 50° F., and shading from the strong sun. At that time, water liberally and give a little weak liquid manure. Decrease the water supply in winter, but do not dry off entirely. Propagate by means of seed, leaf-cuttings, or by cuttings of unflowered shoots (Heat 60° to 65° F.).

Species, Hybrids and Vars.—(FIBROUS) *B. acutifolia* (White, tinted Red); *B. albo-coccinea* (White and Red); *B. coccinea* (Red); *B. Dregei* (White); *B. echino-sepala* (Pink and White); *B. fuchsioides* (Scarlet); *B. Luzerna* (Deep Pink); *B. man-icata* (Shell-pink); *B. semperflorens* (Many Varieties); *B. socotrana* (Bright Rose). This species and *B. Dregei* are the parents of the winter-flowering *Gloire de Lorraine.* (WINTER-FLOWERING.) *B. Gloire de Lorraine* (Reddish Pink); *Turn-ford Hall* (Blush White); *Mrs. L. de Rothschild* (Soft Pink); *Glory of Cincinnati* (Pink); *Mrs. Petersen* (Dark Foliage, Flowers Rosy-red); *Eges Favourite* (Red). All these are varieties of *Gloire de Lorraine.*

The following are some of the hybrids between *B. socotrana* and tuberous-rooted varieties, viz.: *Mrs. Heal* (Carmine); *Fascination* (Orange-salmon); *Exquisite* (Pink and White); *Emita* (Orange-scarlet); *Optima* (Salmon); *Her Majesty* (Coppery-orange); *Altrincham Pink*; *Clibran's Crimson*; *Clibran's Red*; *Duchess of Westminster* (Soft Pink); *Scarlet Beauty*; *The Gem* (Rosy-scarlet).

274

Other winter-flowering begonias are: *Gloire de Sceaux* (Pink with Dark Foliage); *B. manicata* (Pink); *B. Digswelliana* (Red); *B. Froebelii* (Scarlet); *B. nitida* (Flesh); *B. nitida alba* (White); and *B. Corbei le de Feu* (Red).

(FIBROUS-ROOTED FOR BEDDING AND GREENHOUSE.) *B. semperflorens* in many varieties, some of the best being: *Bonfire* (Scarlet); *Pink Perfection* (Pink); *Prima Donna* (Pink); *Glory of Erfurt* (Pink); *Erfordia grandiflora* (Silvery-pink); and *Triumph* (White).

(TUBEROUS-ROOTED.) *Albatross* (White); *Canary Bird* (Yellow); *F. C. Calthorpe* (Scarlet); *General Allenby* (Red); *Hilda Langdon* (Rose-pink); *James Baird* (Red); *Lady Carew* (Cerise); *Millicent* (Flesh-pink); *Mrs. F. C. Calthorpe* (Salmon); *Sir J. Reid* (Orange).

(*For Hanging Baskets*). *Alice Manning* (Yellow); *Betha* (Salmon-pink); *Golden Shower* (Yellow); *Lena* (Rosy-crimson); *Meteor* (Scarlet); and *Rose Cactus* (Rose-pink).

(*Ornamental-leaved*). *Begonia Rex* in many varieties; *B. imperalis* (Olive and Greyish Green); *B. maculata* (Silver and Green).

Bellis (Daisy).—Dwarf-growing hardy perennials, which thrive in the sun in moderately rich soil. Among the most beautiful are the *Large Double*, the *Large Quilled*, and the *Hen and Chickens*. All grow from 6 to 12 inches high, and produce masses of flowers in the spring and early summer. *Culture.*—Sow seed in the open in June, or propagate by means of division of roots after flowering. Plant out in permanent position in October. All daisies flower better if the roots are periodically divided. *Species.*—*B. perennis. Named Varieties.*—*Alice* (Shell-pink, double); *Eliza* (Red); **Dresden China* (Pink); **Rob Roy* (Crimson, double); *The Bride* (White); *Victoria* (Pink and White). **Suitable for the rock garden.

Bellium minutum [syn. *B. rotundifolium*].—An attractive little dwarf-growing daisy-like perennial with flowers from May to September that are whitish inside and darkish purple on the outside. They are very suitable for the paved or rock garden. These little plants will grow almost anywhere, but thrive in the sun in a mixture of sandy loam and leaf-mould, growing to about 3 inches high. *Culture.*—Sow seed under glass as soon as ripe or in March, or propagate by means of division in April.

Benthamia. *See* Cornus.

Berberidopsis corallina (Coral Barberry).—A half-hardy evergreen climbing shrub, which thrives in a cool greenhouse, or in a border in the south, in well-drained, light loam against walls facing south or west and partially shaded. It carries coral-red flowers in June, and grows to a height of 20 feet. *Culture.*—Take cuttings early in summer, or propagate by means of layering in October. Plant-out in April and October, and thin-out branches when overcrowded.

Berberis (Barberry).—Beautiful hardy flowering shrubs, there being both evergreen and deciduous species, among which are some of the most useful and attractive shrubs in cultivation. The stems are very thorny, and many species bear lovely orange or yellow flowers in spring or early summer, and in autumn carry handsome black, purple, or red fruit. Others have gorgeously tinted foliage in autumn. *Culture.*—Plant evergreens from March to April or from October to November, and deciduous kinds from November to March when the weather and soil permit, in ordinary soil or sandy loam. Thin-out shoots when overcrowded after flowering, or in winter after fruiting, and trim to shape. Trimming should be delayed until the leaves fall in the case of shrubs grown for autumn foliage. Most species are propagated by means of seeds in the open in October, by half-matured cuttings in a frame in July or August, or by layering in August. *B. stenophylla*, being a hybrid, must be propagated by cuttings or by layering. *B. Wilsonæ*, with its golden-yellow flowers in May, is a small-leaved and dwarf-growing plant. The coral-red berries appear in the late autumn and last a long way through the winter. *B. Darwinii* is useful for pot culture in the cold greenhouse. Pot-up in November, using 8 to 10-inch pots and a compost of two parts of sandy loam to one part of leaf-mould and rotten manure. *Species and Varieties.—(Evergreens)—B. candidula* (Yellow, April–May, 2 ft.). Useful in rock garden; *B. Darwinii* (Orange, April–May, 8–10 ft.); *B. stenophylla* (Yellow, April–June, 8–10 ft.). *(Deciduous)—B. polyantha* (Yellow, May, 6–8 ft.); *B. Thunbergii* (Yellow, April–May, 3 ft.); *B. vulgaris* (Yellow, April–May, 4–15 ft.); *B. Wilsonæ* (Yellow, May, 2–4 ft.); and *B. yunnanensis* (Yellow, May, 4–6 ft.). *Hybrid Barberries.* The barberries most useful as ornamental fruiting bushes are a race of hybrids which have originated in gardens chiefly as the result of the cross pollination of several Chinese species (*B. polyantha, B. Wilsonæ, B. sub-caulialata*, etc.) by insects. Some of the most distinct and attractive of those raised at Wisley have been given distinctive names; *Comet, Firefly*, and *rubro-stilla*. Being hybrids, these can only be propagated true by layering or cuttings. The raising of seedlings, however, is so easy and offers so much of interest and so many possibilities that many shrub lovers are raising seedlings.

Betula (Birch Tree).—Plant in November in sunny, open, moist positions. All species will thrive in a poor, gravelly soil. No pruning is necessary. Propagate by means of seeds, layering, or grafting. *Species.—B. verrucosa* (Silver Birch); *B. v. var. dalecarlica* (Cut-leaved); *B. v. var. pendula Youngii* (Weeping); and *B. v. var. purpurea* (Purple Birch); *B. papyrifera* (Paper Birch).

Bignonia (Trumpet Flower). Some of these are fine half-hardy perennial climbers, closely allied to the Tecoma, they thrive best planted out in borders of the stove or greenhouse and may be either trained to cover walls, pillars and up wires, as the case may be. *B. capreolata* (Orange, Summer, 6 ft.); *B. Tweediana* (Yellow, Summer, 6–8 ft.) are two species worthy of note. *See also* Campsis and Clytostoma.

Blechnum (Hard Fern).—*See* Ferns.

Bloomeria.—Half-hardy, bulbous-rooted plants that may be grown in the open in a warm, sheltered rock garden. In more exposed places, however, they should be kept indoors. They do well in a sandy soil, growing from 10 to 15 inches high, and flowering in May and June. *Culture.*—Plant in September or October, 2 to 3 inches deep and 3 inches apart. Propagate by means of offsets in September. *B. aurea* (Golden-yellow) and *B. Clevelandii* (Yellow) are among the best species.

Bocconia—*See* Macleaya.

Boltonia (False Starwort.)—A hardy perennial for border or wild garden, thriving in any moist and moderately good loam. For culture, *see* Perennials, p. 156. *Species.—B. asteroides* (White, July–Sept., 48–60 in.); *B. a. decurrens* (Whitish-pink, Aug.–Sept., 48 in.).

276

Boronia.—Evergreen shrubs which do best in the cool greenhouse in equal parts of sandy loam, peat, and leaf-mould. *Culture.*—Pot-up from April to May in 5 to 7-inch pots. Stop-back young plants, give ample air and liquid manure while growing. Prune after flowering, and stand outdoors from June to September. To propagate, take cuttings of young shoots in May and strike in sand, peat, and charcoal under glass (60° F.). *Species.*—*B. elatior* (Carmine); *B. heterophylla* (Cerise); *B. megastigma* (Brownish-purple and Yellow); *B. serrulata* (Scarlet). All flower from February to April and reach a height of 12 to 24 in.

Borago (Borage).—*B. laxiflora* is a pretty little hardy perennial. It is of trailing habit and is sometimes grown in the rock garden. In summer it carries quaint rosettes of foliage and bell-shaped, violet-blue flowers. Seed should be sown in the open in March, and fresh plants should be raised every year as it is not long lived.

Bougainvillea.—These are excellent shrubby climbers for the cool greenhouse, and grow well in pots of sandy loam in a sunny position. Cut laterals hard back in February. *B. glabra var. Sanderiana* is a good variety and carries rose-purple bracts in summer. *B. spectabilis* has brick-red bracts in June and July.

Bouteloua (Grama Grass).—A genus of hardy perennial flowering grasses, growing about 12 inches high, and thriving almost anywhere in ordinary soil. *Culture.*—Sow in the spring, or propagate by means of division in spring or autumn. *B. curtipendula*, flowers in long spikelets in summer.

Bouvardia (Jasmine Plant).—A winter-flowering evergreen shrub, which likes a mixture of fibrous loam, leaf-mould, peat, sand, and a little well-rotted cow manure. *Culture.*—Pot-up in March in 5 to 8-inch pots. Keep in a frame from June to September, water liberally and syringe. In September, return to the greenhouse, and give liquid manure once the buds begin to form. Cut hard back after flowering, and stop-back young shoots until August. (Temp. 50° to 60° F. in winter to 60° to 65 F. in summer.) Propagate by cuttings of young shoots or root-cuttings in February and March in heat (70° F.). *Species.*—*B. Humboldtii* (White, fragrant, 2 ft.); *B. leiantha* (Red, 3 ft.); *B. triphylla* (Red, 3–4 ft.). *Varieties.*—*Bridal Wreath* (White); *King of Scarlets* (Scarlet); *Mrs. R. Green* (Single Salmon); *President Cleveland* (Scarlet); *President Garfield* (Double Pink); *Priory Beauty* (Pink).

Brachycome (Swan River Daisy).—A beautiful summer-flowering, dwarf-growing, hardy annual, covered during the greater portion of the summer with a profusion of pretty cineraria-like flowers. It grows about 9 inches high, and makes a very effective subject in the rock garden. *Culture.*—Sow seed thinly in light, rich soil in April in the open, or in March or April in gentle heat. Thin out, or plant out 9 inches apart in a sunny position about the end of May. This plant does best when sown where it is to flower. *Species.*—*B. iberidifolia* (Blue or White, Summer, 1 ft.). There are also named varieties such as, *Azure Fairy*, (Pale Blue); *Blue Star*; and *Red Star*.

Bravoa geminiflora (Twinflower).—A half-hardy bulbous plant, which likes a sunny, sheltered position in rich light soil mixed with old leaf-mould. It grows about 15 inches high and flowers in July and August. *Culture.*—Plant in a warm

277

border or in the greenhouse in September, 4 inches deep and 6 inches apart, and protect with fibre during winter.

Brevoortia (Crimson Satin Flower).—Half-hardy bulbous summer-flowering plants growing up to 30 inches high. *Species.*—*B. Ida-Maia* (Dark Crimson and Green, Summer, 20 in.). For culture, *see* Brodiæa.

Brodiæa (Californian or Missouri Hyacinth).—Hardy and half-hardy bulbous plants with hyacinth-like foliage. They thrive in well-drained deep sandy soil mixed with leaf-mould, in sunny borders, cool greenhouse or rock garden. *Culture.*—Plant in October, 3 inches deep and 5 inches apart. Protect with ashes during winter, and lift the bulbs from the soil every fourth year only. Propagate by means of offsets in October. *Species.*—*B. grandiflora* (Violet-blue, June and July, 15 in.); *B. ixioides* (Yellow, Summer, 6 in.); *B. (Ipheion) uniflora* (White or Blue, April–May, 6 in.).

Bruckenthalia spiculifolia.—These little dwarf-growing evergreen shrubs, which are closely allied to the heath family, rarely exceed 7 or 8 inches in height, and make excellent subjects for the rock garden. They prefer a light, peaty soil, and the pretty pale-rose, bell-shaped flowers are borne in June and July.

Brunnera macrophylla (Pale Blue, Forget-me-not-like flowers, May–July, 12 in.). Perennial *see* p. 156.

Bryanthus.—*See* Phyllodoce.

Buddleia.—Flowering shrubs. Most species are not quite hardy enough to endure severe weather out of doors, but flourish in well-drained, deep, ordinary soil or good loam in warm, sunny, sheltered positions, on a wall, or in the greenhouse. *Culture.*—Plant *B. globosa* in March or October, the others from November to March. Do not prune *B. alternifolia* or *B. globosa*, merely cut out a little old wood after flowering, but in the case of *B. Davidii*, cut the last year's shoots back to within a few inches of the old wood in February. Propagation is by means of cuttings in a frame in late summer or autumn, or by means of seeds when ripe. *Hardy Species.*—*B. alternifolia* (Pale Purple, June, 20 ft.); *B. Colvillei* (Rose, July, 20 ft.); *B. Davidii and vars.* (Lilac, Aug. 15 ft.); *B. globosa* (Orange, June, 10 ft.).

Bulbocodium (Spring Meadow Saffron).—A pretty little hardy bulb, with crocus-like blooms, which likes a well-drained, sandy soil and a sunny position. *Culture.*—Plant in August 3 inches deep and 4 inches apart, or pot-up if for indoors. Lift from the soil every fourth year and propagate by means of offsets in August. *B. vernum* (Purple-red, Jan.–March, 5 in.) is the best species.

Buphthalmum (Ox-eye).—A tall hardy perennial, which thrives in the sun in well-drained loam. For culture, *see* Perennials, p. 156. *Species.*—*B. salicifolium* (Yellow, July–Sept., 24 in.); *B. speciosum* (Golden Orange, July, 60–70 in.).

Butomus umbellatus (Flowering Rush).—A hardy aquatic perennial of tufted habit, which likes a warm, sunny position in a bog or on a muddy bank, or in sheltered, still water, with from 1 to 12 inches of water above the crowns. It grows some 30 inches high, and carries pink flowers from June to August. Propagate by division in March.

Buxus (Box).—Plant in April or September, in light, well-drained soil. Clip in May and August. Propagate by means of cuttings in August or September under bell-glasses, division in September, or by layering in October. *Species.*—

278

B. sempervirens (Common Box); and varieties *argentea* (Silver); *aurea* (Golden); *myrtifolia*; and *suffruticosa*, a dwarf variety of the common box, which is the sort that is used for the edging of borders. March is a good time for breaking up old plants and replanting.

Cacalia coccinea [syn. Emilia flammea] *which see.*

Cacti.—Nearly all species may be grown in a moderately-heated greenhouse. They like a compost of one-half fibrous loam and one-half a mixture of sand, broken bricks, and lime rubble, and a sunny position, except *Epiphyllums*, *Rhipsalis* and *Zygocactus*, which prefer shade and a compost of two-thirds fibrous loam and one-third sand, peat, and brick rubble. Pot-up firmly in February or March, and re-pot every three or four years, keeping the pots as small as possible. A few pieces of charcoal in the compost are beneficial. Give ample ventilation, and syringe with tepid water twice a week from April to September. Decrease the water supply from October to April. Propagate by means of cuttings (partially dried) in summer, by grafting in March, or by offsets.

Hardy Cacti should be planted in spring in a well-drained, sunny, sheltered site in the rock garden or on a wall or bank in light loam with a mixture of brick rubble, sand, and gravel. *Aporocactus*, *Notocactus* and *Mammallaria*, and those with stems likely to hold moisture, should be covered with glass in winter. None of them can be regarded as hardy, except in warm and favoured situations. They are, however, excellent for cool greenhouses, while many of them are well suited for growing in windows, especially *Aporocactus flagelliformis* (Rat-tail Cactus). *Species.*—(Hardy)—*Cereus Engelmanni* (Purple, June, 18 in.); *Ferocactus acanthodes* (Greenish-yellow, Summer, 12–30 in.); *Mammallaria setispina* (Pink, Summer, 9 in.); *Opuntia pulchella* (Purple, Summer, 10 in.); *O. Rafinesquei* (Sulphur-yellow, June–Sept., 10 in.). (*Greenhouse*)—*Aporocactus flagelliformis*, Whip or Rat-Tail Cactus (Pink, June, 12–30 in.); *A. peruvianus* (White, May–July, 20–100 in.); *Cephalocereus senilis* (Old Man cactus) (Purple-Red, Summer, 15–100 in.); *Echinopsis cristata purpurea* (Rose, July, 10 in.); *E. multiplex* (Pale-Pink, fragrant); *Epiphyllum Ackermannii* (Rich Rose, Summer, 18 in.); *E. Aurora boreale* (Orange, June, 18–24 in.); *E. Edwardsii* (Red, Summer, 24 in.); *E. oxypetalum* (Creamy-white, June–Sept., 20–30 in.); *Ferocactus Lecontei* (Lemon-yellow, Summer, 10–30 in.); *Mammalaria applanta* (White tinged Red, July–Aug., 4–6 in.); *M. fuscata* (Purple, Summer, 6 in.); *M. Sulphurea* (Yellow, Summer, 3 in.); *Melocactus communis*, Turk's Cap Cactus (Red, June, 12–30 in.); *Notocactus Haselbergii* (Red and Yellow, April–May, 12 in.); *Opuntia aurantiaca* (Orange, June, 30 in.); *O. Ficus-indica*, Prickly Pear (Yellow, June, 30 in.); *Pediocactus Simpsonii*, Hedgehog Cactus (Red, June, 5 in.); *Rhipsalis cassutha*, Mistletoe Cactus (White, April, 15 in.); *Schlumbergera Russelliana*, Leaf-flowering Cactus (Pink, Nov., 10–24 in.).

Calamintha alpina (Calamint).—A hardy aromatic plant, forming a thick carpet of foliage, and carrying sprays of violet flowers all through the summer. Grow in a sunny site in gritty loam. Propagate by means of seeds in March, or by division in March or September. *C. grandiflora* is a taller species (12 in.), with purple-red flowers in July and August.

Calandrinia (Rock Purslane).—Attractive little dwarf-growing, annual and perennial plants, that thrive in the sun in sandy loam. For culture, *see* Annuals,

p. 139, *and* Perennials, p. 156. *Species.*—*(Annual)*—*C. discolor* (Lilac, 12–18 in.); *C. grandiflora* (Rose, 18 in.); *C. Menziesii* (Purple, 9 in.). *(Perennial)*—*C. umbellata* (Crimson, 9 in.). All flower from July to September.

Calceolaria (Slipper Flower).—There are three distinct kinds of calceolaria, the *herbaceous* (*C. herbeohybrida*), raised and reared under glass; the *shrubby* (*C. fruticohybrida*), grown for bedding-out; these thrive in fibrous loam mixed with leaf-mould and sand. The third type, being hardy herbaceous perennials and annuals, make excellent subjects for the rock garden.

Culture.—*(Herbaceous* or *Greenhouse Calceolarias)*—Sow lightly and thinly in a propagating case in June. Pot-up singly in July, and keep in a frost-proof frame. Re-pot into 3 or 4-inch pots in September, and take into the greenhouse. Keep warm and moist at night, and give a steady even temperature. Pot-up finally in February or March (before the flower buds begin to move), using 7 to 8-inch pots and a compost of two parts loam to one part leaf-mould and sand, and keep near the glass in a cool greenhouse. Stake securely, shade from the strong sun, and do not over-water. Weak liquid manure should be given at fortnightly intervals, as soon as the buds appear. Seeds should be sown afresh each year to attain the best results.

Culture.—*(Hardy Herbaceous Calceolarias)*—Sow seed when ripe or during March in pots in a frame. As soon as germinated and when large enough to transplant, prick off into pans or boxes, and keep in a closed frame until established; then give more air until sufficiently hardened off to transplant into permanent positions in a sunny position in the rock garden. Most of the varieties may be split up during April and May, or cuttings can be inserted in sand in a propagating frame during the autumn.

Culture.—*(Shrubby Calceolarias)*—Take cuttings of vigorous young basal shoots in September and strike under glass, or in a warm north border, and cover with a hand-glass. If the weather turns frosty, throw some covering over the hand-glass. About the middle of February, the cuttings must have their growing points pinched back. A fortnight later, they may either be potted or kept as cool as possible 3 to 4 inches apart in the pit, being finally transferred to the flower garden and set about 9 inches apart towards the end of May or early in June. Seed may also be sown under glass in March (temp. 50°–60° F.). Transplant the seedlings into boxes as soon as they can be handled, and next pot-up singly into 3 to 4-inch pots. Transfer to a cold frame in May, and before the plants become pot-bound, re-pot into 5 or 6-inch pots, if for greenhouse use, or if for summer bedding, harden-off, and plant-out early in June.

Shrubby Species and Varieties for Bedding.—*C. amplexicaulis* (Pale Yellow); *C. Bronze Prince*; *C. Burbidgei* (Yellow); *C. Sultan* (Maroon); *C. Veitchii* (Creamy-white); and *C. Clibranii* (Deep Yellow). All flower from May to September and grow from 9 to 48 inches in height. *Species.*—*(Perennial)*—*C. acutifolia* [known in gardens as *C. polyrrhiza*] (Yellow, 6–12 in.), *C. biflora* (Yellow, 9–12 in.); *C. tenella* (Yellow, Summer, 1–2 in.); *C. uniflora* (Bronze-yellow, 2–4 in.). *(Annual)*—*C. mexicana* (Yellow, 12 in.). All flowering during late summer and autumn.

Calendula (Pot Marigold).—Hardy annuals which thrive in beds or borders and in almost any soil. For culture, *see* Annuals, p. 139. *Named Varieties.*—

Favourite (Sulphur-yellow); *Lemon Queen* (Lemon-yellow); *Orange King* (Bright Orange); *Prince of Orange* (Orange, striped Pale Yellow); and *Yellow Queen* (Golden Yellow). All double, flowering from June to October and growing about 18 inches in height.

Calla palustris (Bog Arum).—This is a hardy aquatic plant, which spreads over the surface of shallow, still water. It likes a sunny position in firm soil at the margin of ponds. The white flowers are borne from June to August. *Culture.* —Plant in March with not more than 12 inches of water above the crowns. Propagate by means of division in March.

Callirhoë (Poppy Mallow).—*C. involucrata*, a trailing perennial species with beautiful purple-red flowers in July and August, is worthy of a place in any rock garden. It likes a sunny site and well-drained ordinary soil, and is best propagated after flowering by cuttings in September. Seed may also be sown in spring or autumn under glass.

Callistemon (Bottle Brush Plant).—Greenhouse evergreen shrubs which thrive in full sun, in a cool house, in equal parts of sandy peat and loam. They carry crimson and golden flowers in May and June on stems from 3 to 6 feet in height. *Culture.*—Pot-up in 6 to 10-inch pots, stand out-of-doors from June to September, and trim after flowering. To propagate, take cuttings of matured wood in the late spring and strike in a frame. *Species.*—*C. citrinus var. splendens* (Scarlet) and *C. speciosus* (Scarlet).

Callistephus chinensis (The China Aster).—A half-hardy, autumn-flowering annual particularly adapted for small beds, edgings, the rock garden, or for pot culture. All varieties thrive best in a deep, rich, light soil, and in hot dry weather, should be mulched with well-rotted manure, and frequently supplied with manure-water. For culture, *see* Annuals, p. 140. *Pot Culture.*—Sow in the open in May. Pot-up three plants in a 6-inch pot in a compost of two-thirds fibrous loam and one-third well-decayed manure. Stand in the open on a hard bed of ashes or on slates, and cover to the rims of the pots with a layer of fibre. Transfer under glass as soon as the buds begin to colour. *Species and Varieties.*—*C. chinensis* [single] (18 in.); *Chrysanthemum-flowered* (12 in.); *Comet* [Broad Florets] (24 in.); *Dwarf Bouquet* (6–9 in.); *Giant Ray* [Stiff and Prominent Florets] (18 in.); *Mignon* (10 in.); *Ostrich Plume* [Branching with Double Flowers] (18 in.); *Quilled* [Tubular Florets]; *Pæony-flowered* [Incurving Florets] (18 in.); *Victoria* [Double] (15 in.). (*See also* Aster).

Calluna vulgaris (Ling-Heather).—A hardy evergreen shrub, thriving in full sun and in peaty, non-calcareous soil. *Culture.*—Plant in October or April, trim-off dead flower-heads in April. To propagate, take cuttings in summer and strike in peaty soil in a frame, or layer. *See also* Erica. *Varieties.*—*C. v. var. alba* (White Scotch Heather); *C. v. Alportii* (Crimson-pink, July–Sept., 15 in.) *C. v. var. aurea* (Golden Foliage, July–Sept., 12 in.); *C. v. var. flore pleno* (Double Ling, July–Sept., 1 ft.); *C. v. var. alba Serlei* (White, July–Sept., 18 in.).

Calochortus (Butterfly Tulip, Star Tulip, and Mariposa Lily).—Half-hardy bulbous plants, that thrive in full sun and in sandy leaf-mould. *Culture.*—Plant in late October, 3 inches deep and 3 inches apart. Cover with straw or fibre in winter, and lift the bulbs when the leaves die down. *Pot Culture.*—Pot-up ten bulbs in a 4 to 5-inch pot in November in a compost of two-thirds sandy loam and one-sixth part each of peat and leaf-mould. Keep covered with fibre in a cold frame until late December, when transfer to the greenhouse; dry-off after flowering. Propagate by offsets in November. *Species.*—*C. Howellii* (White, July–Aug., 18 in.); *C. pulchellus* (Yellow-orange, July–Aug., 12 in.); *C. venustus and vars.* (Yellow and Red, July and Aug., 15 in.).

Calonyction aculeatum (Ipomœa Bona-nox, *I. grandiflora*).—Tropical and sub-tropical climbing herb, known as the common Moonflower, allied to Ipomœa and sometimes included in that genus. It bears large fragrant White flowers often with a green bud.

Caltha (Marsh Marigold).—A useful hardy perennial for the waterside or moist border. *Culture.*—Propagate by means of division of roots in March or July, and plant-out in moist, rich soil and in full sun or partial shade. *Species.*—*C. palustris var. fl. pl.* (Rich Yellow [double], May–July, 12 in.); *C. leptosepala* (Deep Yellow, Flushed Maroon, May–July, 15 in.); *C. polypetala* (Golden, May–July, 20 in.).

Calycanthus floridus (Carolina All-spice).—A hardy deciduous shrub, which likes a partially shaded, moist position, and which carries purple-red flowers in May and June, and grows to a height of 5 feet or more. *Culture.*—Plant in November, and cut-out dead wood after flowering. Propagate by means of cuttings or layering in summer.

Camassia (Quamash).—Hardy bulbous plants, which thrive in moist, but sunny, borders in a mixture of loam, leaf-mould, and rotten manure. *Culture.*—Plant in October 4 to 5 inches deep and 10 inches apart; and lift from the soil every fourth year. Propagate by means of offsets in October, or by seed under glass in March. *Species.*—*C. esculenta vars.* (Purple-blue and Silver-white, May and June, 20–30 in.); *C. Leichtlinii* (Cream-white, May and June, 40–60 in.).

Camellia.—Hardy evergreen shrubs which thrive in sheltered and semi-shaded positions and in practically any soil, provided it is lime-free. They are also useful for greenhouse culture. *Culture.*—Pot-up firmly in May, using 8 to 12-inch pots. They do best when under-potted. Use a compost of one-half part turfy loam and a quarter part each of sand and peat or leaf-mould. As soon as re-established, gradually harden-off, stand out-of-doors in partial shade on a firm base of ashes or bricks, and keep the roots moist, but not too wet. Move the plants into cold frames or the cold house in September. Trim-back all straggling shoots after flowering, syringe daily, sponge the leaves occasionally, and disturb the roots as little as possible. Propagate by grafting in a close propagating frame in early spring, using seedling *C. japonica* as a stock, or by cuttings of half-matured shoots in a frame in July or August. Seeds may be raised in a moist heat. *Named Varieties.*—*C. alba plena* (White, Dbl.); *C. Chandleri elegans* (Dbl. Pink); *C. cuspidata* (White, Single); *C. Donckelaarii* (Rose); *C. Henri Favre* (Rose-salmon); *C. Lady Clare* (Pink); *C. Jupiter* (Rosy-red, Single); *C. Mathiotiana* (Rose-red, Dbl.); *C. reticulata* (Semi-dbl., Rose-crimson); and *C. Waltham Glory* (Scarlet), etc. All bloom between February and May.

Campanula (Bellflower).—A genus, including annuals, biennials, and perennials, and providing plants for the greenhouse, border, and rock garden. The species themselves are numerous, but as they intermarry freely, the hybrids are bewildering in their names and almost overpowering in number. The alpine

282

species are most delightful little plants, and quite indispensable in the rock garden. A few of these, however, are lime-haters and need special treatment. Of the tall-growing perennials, *C. pyramidalis* (The Chimney Bellflower) grown in pots, produces a most striking effect. Of the dwarf species, also perennials, *C. carpatica* is a most valuable bedding plant. Some species are grown in pots or baskets in the greenhouse. *C. fragilis*, *C. isophylla* (Blue or White), and *C. Mayi* (China Blue) are trailing plants, excellent for hanging baskets. They are best grown in 4 to 5-inch pots, and will bloom from midsummer until the autumn. These plants love plenty of sun and should be watered liberally while growing in summer, but in winter must be kept nearly dry. After flowering, cut the trailing shoots hard back. Of the biennials, most important are the popular Canterbury Bells (*C. Medium*). The annual campanulas are few in number and the least important of the genus. Almost all species thrive in an open position in sun or semi-shade in well-drained, light, sandy loam with ample grit and leaf-mould. For culture, *see* Annuals, p. 139, Biennials, p. 141, and Perennials, p.156.

Pot Culture.—(*C. pyramidalis*). Sow in small pots, and place in a well-ventilated frame. Move into 5 to 6-inch pots in October, and keep in a frost-proof frame for the winter. Pot-up again in March, using 7 to 8-inch pots and a compost of two-thirds sandy loam and one-third leaf-mould, rotted cow manure, and a little old mortar rubble, harden-off, and stand in the open. Stake as the flower spikes form, move into the house about July, and give liquid manure when the buds form. *C. pyramidalis* and other tall species for the greenhouse may also be increased by means of cuttings in a frame in March or August. *Greenhouse Trailing Species.*—Propagate by means of seed in heat in March, by cuttings in a frame in August, or by division in March.

Species.—*C. dahurica* (Pale Purple, June–Sept., 18 in.); *C. lactiflora* (Pale Blue or White, June–Aug., 36–48 in.); *C. latifolia* (Pale Blue, June–Sept., 24–48 in.); *C. latifolia var. macrantha* (Large Purple flowers); *C. Medium* (Canterbury Bells) (Colours vary from White, Pink, Lavender to Purple, June–Aug., 10–50 in.); *C. persicifolia* (Blue and White, June–Aug., 24–30 in.); *C. pyramidalis* (Chimney Bellflower) (Blue or White, July–Sept., 40–70 in.); *C. sarmentosa* (Pale Blue, Summer, 12–18 in.).

NAMED BORDER VARIETIES OF C. PERSICIFOLIA—*Faerie Queen* (Pale Blue); *Fleur-de-Neige* (White, Double); *Newry Giant* (White, Semi-double); *Shirley* (Blue, Semi-double); *Telham Beauty* (Pale Blue).

ALPINES.—*C. Allionii* (Blue, June, 2–3 in.); *C. alpina* (Violet, June–Sept., 4 in.); *C. cæspitosa* (Blue, June–July, 5 in.); *C. carpatica, vars.* (Purple, Blue, or White, May–Sept., 6–12 in.); *C. garganica* (Mauve, White, or Pale Blue, June–Sept., 4 in.); *C. kewensis* (Violet-purple, June–July, 4 in.); *C. muralis* (Purple-blue, June–Aug., 4 in.); *C. cochlearifolia* (Deep Blue or White, June–Aug., 3 in.); *C. Portenschlagiana* (Purple, Summer, 9 in.); *C. Poscharskyana* (Powder Blue, June, 12 in.); *C. Raddeana* (Violet, late Summer, 12 in.); *C. Raineri* (China Blue, June–July, 3 in.). Requires sun and lime; and *C. Waldsteiniana* (Blue-mauve, June and July, 3–6 in.).

Campsis (Trumpet Flower).—Shrubs climbing by means of aerial roots. They thrive in well-drained, light soil if grown against a warm sunny wall. *Culture.*—Strike cuttings of ripe wood in a frame with bottom heat in autumn.

283

Species.—*C. grandiflora* [*Tecoma and Bignonia chinensis*] (Orange); *C. radicans* [*Tecoma and Bignonia radicans*] (Orange). Both flower from July to August and grow to a height of 20 feet.

Canary Creeper.—*See* Tropæolum.

Canna (Indian Shot).—Half-hardy perennials for the cool greenhouse, or for summer-bedding in warm, sunny beds and borders with well manured rich loam. *Culture.*—Sow seed ½ inch deep in sandy loam and leaf-mould in a propagating case (Temp. 75° F.), in February or March (the seed having previously been soaked for a day in warm water). Pot-up singly as soon as possible, or propagate by means of division of roots in spring, dividing them so that each section of root contains an eye. Pot-up early in March or April in single pots and, if for outdoor culture, plant-out in June about 24 inches apart. If for greenhouse culture, pot-up into 6 to 12-inch pots, using a rich and porous compost of one-half-loam and one-quarter part each rotten cow manure and sandy leaf-mould. At the end of September pot-up those grown out-of-doors, and winter under glass. Keep moderately dry and allow the leaves and stems to die off gradually. *Named Varieties.*—*Assaut* (Scarlet); *Beethoven* (Orange); *Italia* (Orange and Yellow); *Oiseau de Feu* [Fire Bird] (Scarlet-red); *President* (Scarlet); *J. B. Van der Schoot* (Yellow Spotted); and *R. Wallace* (Canary Yellow). All flower from August to October and grow to a height of from 3 to 6 feet.

Caragana (Altagana or Pea Tree).—Hardy deciduous trees and shrubs of the cytisus family, which thrive in sunny positions on dry banks and in light, sandy or ordinary soil. *Culture.*—Plant in October; cut out dead wood after flowering. Propagate by means of seeds in the open in May, or by layering in July. *Species.* —*C. arborescens* (Yellow, 10–15 ft.); *C. aurantiaca* (Orange-yellow, 4 ft.); and *C. frutescens* (Yellow, 5 to 8 ft.).

Cardamine pratensis (Lady's Smock, Bitter Cress, or Cuckoo Flower).—A hardy perennial growing from 6 inches to 2 feet in height and flowering from May to July. It grows well in sun or shade and in marshy land in the bog garden. *C. pratensis var. fl. pl.*, which grows about 12 inches high and carries pretty double lilac-coloured flowers, is the form most suitable for cultivation. *Cardamine trifoliata* which grows about 4 inches high has glossy leaves and bears pretty white flowers in summer. It does well in a cool spot, and is suitable for rock garden. There are some annual species also, but these are of no practical interest. *Culture.*—Propagate by means of division in March, and plant out in permanent position.

Carlina acaulis.—A pretty little dwarf-growing rosette-shaped plant for the rock garden. The flowers, which appear in summer, are like miniature thistles, nestling closely to the rosette. This plant will thrive almost anywhere, and is easily raised by means of seed sown in spring or autumn.

Carnation (Dianthus Caryophyllus).—Carnations are classified as Selfs, Flakes, Bizarres, and Fancies. *Selfs* are carnations of one colour only. *Flakes* are those which have the ground colour striped with one other shade. *Bizarres* are those which have the ground colour marked and flaked with two or three other tints. *Fancies* are varieties that do not come within the other classes. Carnations, picotees and pinks, which are closely allied, are all propagated by seeds, layers and cuttings.

Carnations in the Border.—Three weeks before planting time, the bed (well-drained medium loam) should be double-dug, and a little well-rotted stable manure should be dug in to at least 6 inches below the surface, but manuring must not be overdone. Plant in September or early in October, but in heavy and cold soils, it is often wise to keep the young plants in a frame until May, and then plant-out. In April, the flowering stems should be supported, and, as soon as it is apparent that the principal bud is a healthy one, the less important of them should be pulled off. A small dose of weak liquid manure or soot-water twice a week after watering should be given from the time the buds begin to form until the colour shows. Carnations are perennials, and the beds may, if so desired, be replanted only every third year. It is, however, usual to layer every year in order to maintain a stock of healthy young plants.

Carnations under Glass.—In September or early in October, pot-up the young layers singly into 3-inch pots in a compost of two-thirds turfy loam and one-third well-rotted leaf-mould and coarse sand, well sifted and sterilized by baking (*see* p. 54). Then stand the pots in a cold frame for the winter. Keep slightly moist, but no water must settle on the leaves. In March, repot into 6-inch pots, adding a little well-decayed manure and old mortar rubble to the compost. Keep close after potting until established, then give more air, and finally, remove the lights. In May, repot into 8-inch pots and return to the frame for a fortnight. Then stand in the open in a sheltered position, on a firm bed of ashes or on slates. Water liberally, syringe in dry weather, and stake, manure and disbud as advised for those in the open border. When the young plants are some 6 inches high, the heads should be pinched off, and as soon as the side shoots are from 6 to 8 inches in length, they will, in turn, require pinching-back; not later than mid-June, however, for ordinary July-flowering carnations, or mid-August for perpetual-flowering species. Transfer to a light position in the cool greenhouse as soon as the flowers show colour (about July).

Propagation.—Choice varieties should be raised from cuttings or layers. *Seed.*—Sow 1 inch apart in April or May in seed pans, in a compost of two-thirds loam from decayed turf, one-third well decomposed cow dung, and a little old mortar rubble and bonemeal, and place in a sheltered part of the garden. When the plants show five or six leaves, plant-out from 10 to 15 inches apart in sunny, well-drained beds. Protect during winter with a cold frame. In cold and heavy soil, some gardeners prefer to sow in August, winter in a cold frame, and plant-out in spring. *Layering.*—The season for this is in July or August, and the process is fully dealt with on p. 113. *Cuttings.*—Cuttings may be struck in a frame with a bottom heat of 60° F. at any time from November to February (the best time is January). Early in March, these cuttings, if struck in January, will need potting on into larger pots.

Perpetual or Tree Carnations are invaluable for winter blooms. The cultivation and requirements as to soil are much the same as for the ordinary carnation. The cuttings, which will be furnished by the side shoots, may be struck in silver sand in February, August or September in gentle heat (55° F.), or the non-flowering shoots of the old plant may be laid down in a cold shaded frame in the last-mentioned month. When rooted (in about a month), pot-up in 2½-inch pots, and winter in a cool greenhouse near the glass, and give ample air. The following summer, pot-on into 6-inch pots, and then into 8-inch pots, potting being more firm at each move. Pinch back, stand outdoors, and stake as advised. About the beginning of September, the plants may again be taken into the house and watered occasionally with weak liquid manure or soot water as soon as the roots have filled the pots. They must be securely staked at an early period. Syringing overhead on bright days is helpful, but water should only be applied to the roots when dry. Give ample air, and keep the temperature at about 50° F. Under this management, they will bloom freely during the winter months, and if planted out in the border early in May and watered well, will continue to flower all through the summer. Seed may be sown in gentle heat (55° F.) in February.

Malmaison Carnations require treatment as detailed for border carnations but only require one "stopping", and a cooler atmosphere; the winter temperature should rarely rise above 45° F. These carnations should not be placed in the open in summer. Propagate by layers in a frame in July and August, or by cuttings in a propagating frame with bottom heat in May or June.

Clove Carnations are a hardy border type, best planted-out in March or April. The following are a few of the many varieties which are in cultivation.

BORDER, SELFS.—*Bookham Apricot*; *Blush Clove* (Blush-white); *Bookham Clove* (Crimson); *Bookham Rose*; *Bookham Scarlet*; *Border Yellow*; *Coral Clove* (Coral-pink); *Crystal Clove* (White); *Fiery Cross* (Scarlet); *Glamour* (Yellow); *Janet* (Pink); *Margaret Keep* (Blush-pink); *Orangeman* (Orange-apricot); *Purple Clove*; *Royal Scot* (Scarlet); *Salmon Clove*; *The Grey Douglas* (Heliotrope); *Trumpeter* (Rose-madder); *White Clove*.

FANCIES.—*Centurion* (Yellow and Scarlet); *Endymion* (Canary-yellow, streaked Blood-red); *Highland Mary* (Primrose-yellow and Rose-pink); *Kelso* (Golden-apricot and Blue-grey); *Linkman* (Yellow and Scarlet); *Mona* (Buff and Rose); *Mrs. Hawksbee* (White and Rose-Crimson); *Ravenswood* (White and Maroon-crimson); *Saracen* (Slate-grey, striped Crimson and Rose); *Steerforth Clove* (White and Crimson-maroon); *The Cadi* (Rose-madder, striped Blue and Scarlet); *Viceroy* (Yellow and Carmine-crimson).

PERPETUAL BORDER.—*Sussex Avondale* (Salmon-pink); *Sussex Beauty* (Heliotrope); *Sussex Bizarre* (Peach, flaked Heliotrope); *Sussex Crimson*; *Sussex Maid* (White flaked Rose-pink); *Sussex Pink*.

PICOTEES.—(*Yellow ground*). *Exquisite* (Scarlet Edge); *Her Majesty* (Purple Edge); *Margaret Glitters* (Rosy-scarlet Edge); *Mrs. J. J. Kean* (Rose-pink Edge); *Niel Kenyon* (Rose Edge); *Togo* (Crimson Edge).

TREE OR PERPETUALS.—*Baroness de Brienen* (Salmon-pink); *Edward Allwood* (Scarlet); *Eileen Low* (Salmon-pink); *Laddie* (Salmon-pink); *Lady Northcliffe* (Salmon-pink); *Mikado* (Heliotrope); *Mary Allwood* (Reddish-salmon); *Mrs. A. J. Cobb* (Crimson); *Saffron* (Yellow); *Tarzan* (Scarlet); *Topsy* (Scarlet); *White Enchantress*.

MALMAISONS.—*Baldwin* (Pink); *Calypso* (Soft-flesh); *Duchess of Westminster* (Rose-pink); *Maggie Hodgson* (Crimson); *Nell Gwynne* (White); *Princess of Wales* (Pink).

Carnations, Marguerite.—Half-hardy annuals, which thrive in open beds and in rich, gritty loam. They grow about 18 inches high, and flower from August to October. If lifted before damaged by the frost, they will furnish flowers in the greenhouse throughout the winter and spring. For culture, *see* Annuals, Half-hardy, p. 139.

Carpanthea pomeridiana.—*See* Mesembryanthemum.

Carpenteria californica (Californian Mock Orange).—Half-hardy climbing shrubs, which like a warm, sheltered position, and well-drained loam. They grow from 5 to 10 feet high, and flower about mid-summer. *Culture.*—Propagate by means of cuttings of young wood in April in a frame, by layering in September, or by suckers in autumn. Plant in autumn, and prune-out weak wood and dead flowers after flowering.

Carpinus Betulus (Hornbeam).—A hardy deciduous tree, which thrives in sunny, open positions in almost any soil, and makes a good hedge plant. *Culture.*—Plant from November to February; no pruning is necessary. Propagate by seeds, graft in March on the common hornbeam, or layer. *Species.*— *C. Betulus* (Common Hornbeam) *vars. columnaris, incisa,* and *pyramidalis*; and *C. japonica* (Japanese Hornbeam).

Carya (Hickories).—These are fast-growing, stately, large trees allied to the Walnuts. The large compound leaves turn a clear yellow in autumn. *Species.*— *C. alba* (Shell-bark Hickory); *C. amara* (Bitter Nut); and *C. glabra* (Pig Nut).

Cassia.—Half-hardy evergreen greenhouse plants. (Temp. 45° F. in winter to 65° F. in summer.) *Culture.*—Pot-up in March, using 6 to 10-inch pots and a compost of peaty loam or sandy leaf-mould. Prune back, and start into growth in early spring. Keep quite dry in winter. Propagate by means of seed or cuttings in a close propagating case during the spring. *Species.*—*C. corymbosa* (Yellow); and *C. marylandica* (Yellow). The latter is quite hardy.

Cassinia.—Beautiful evergreen flowering shrubs, very branching by nature, which like a sunny position and ordinary soil. They grow from 3 to 6 feet high, and flower from July to September. *C. fulvida*, 4 feet, with creamy-white flowers, is a good species. *Culture.*—Plant from October to November, and thin-out the branches when they are overcrowded. To propagate, strike cuttings in a frame in August.

Cassiope tetragona.—Beautiful dwarf evergreen shrubs with white flowers hanging like small bells from erect, heath-like stems, in April and May. They rarely exceed 6 inches in height, and make excellent additions to the rock garden. *Culture.*—Propagate by means of layering in July, or by cuttings in August placed under a bell-jar in a compost of sand and peat. Plant out in April. A cool, moist, semi-shaded site is desirable, also sandy loam and leaf-mould. *C. fastigiata* and *C. Mertensiana* are useful subjects for the miniature rock garden. They are lime-haters.

Castanea (Sweet or Spanish Chestnut).—Hardy deciduous trees, which thrive in full sun and in light, gravelly loam. *Culture.*—Plant in November, and thin-out the branches when overcrowded. To propagate sow in the open. *Species.*— *C. sativa* (Sweet Chestnut, 60–100 ft.).

Catalpa (Indian Bean Tree).—Hardy deciduous trees, which thrive in full sun and in moist, but well-drained, rather light loam. They are good town trees, and grow to a height of from 25 to 50 feet, and flower in July and August. The blooms are white with yellow and purple markings, and somewhat resemble

287

those of the Horse Chestnut. *Culture.*—Plant from November to February. When seeds are not available, take cuttings of the leafy shoots in July, and insert them in gentle bottom heat, or layer in July. *Species.*—*C. bignonioides* (Indian Bean Tree) and *C. speciosa* (Western Catalpa).

Catananche (Cupidone).—Hardy perennial or annual plants, which like a sunny spot in a warm, dry border and ordinary soil. For culture, *see* Annuals, p. 139, *and* Perennials, p. 156. *Species.*—*C. lutea* (Yellow, July, 9 in.); *C. cœrulea* (Blue, July–Aug., 30 in.); *C. c. var. alba* (White, July–Aug., 20–30 in.).

Ceanothus (Californian Lilac).—Half-hardy shrubs, which like a warm, sunny position and well-drained ordinary soil and leaf-mould. There are two distinct classes, one flowering in spring, the other from July to September. The latter are hardy deciduous shrubs and the others evergreens, suitable for sheltered walls and the mild climate of the south and west. *Culture.*—Plant in March or October. Cut spring-flowering species back in May; late-flowering plants must be pruned in early spring. Plants of evergreen species grown as bushes will not need severe pruning. To propagate, take cuttings in July and August and strike in a frame, or layer during the same months. *Species and hybrids.*—EVERGREEN, SPRING-FLOWERING: *C. Burkwoodii* (hybrid) (Rich Blue) one of the best; *C. dentatus* (Blue); *C. rigidus* (Purplish-blue); *C. thyrsiflorus* (Pale Blue); and *C. Veitchianus* (Bright Blue). HYBRID (DECIDUOUS), LATE SUMMER AND AUTUMN-FLOWERING. *Ceres* (Rose-pink); *Gloire de Versailles* (Lavender); *Henri Defosse* (Dark Blue); *Indigo* (Indigo Blue); *Marie Simon* (Rose); and *Perle Rose* (Rose Carmine).

Cedar.—*See* Cedrus.

Cedronella cana.—This plant bears crimson-purple flowers in June on stems 3 feet high. It is not altogether hardy in some parts of the country, and is best grown in a sheltered spot in well-drained soil. For culture, *see* Perennials, p. 156.

Cedrus (Cedar).—Hardy evergreen trees, suitable only for large gardens. *Culture.*—Plant in September or October, when about between 1 and 4 ft. high, in a sunny position and in well-drained, gravelly, chalky, or sandy soil. No pruning is necessary. To propagate, sow in March or April. *Species and Varieties.*—*C. atlantica* (Mt. Atlas Cedar, 80 to 100 ft.), *var. glauca* (Blue Cedar); *C. Deodara* (Deodar, 150 ft.); and *C. Libani* (The Cedar of Lebanon, 100 ft.).

Celastrus (Bitter Sweet, Staff Tree, etc.).—Hardy perennial climbing plants, which thrive in most soils and positions. They are particularly attractive when growing through and over the branches of trees and vigorous shrubs. They are freely furnished with hundreds of brilliant golden-yellow fruits in autumn, which, when ripe, open to show the scarlet-coated seeds. *Culture.*—Cut out weak wood, and tip stray shoots in February. Propagate by means of seeds and layering young shoots in October. *Species.*—*C. obiculatus* and *C. scandens.*

Celmisia.—A genus of tufted, dwarf-growing plants with long, hairy leaves and pretty, white, daisy-like flowers in summer. The hardy species make delightful subjects for the rock garden. They like a dry warm position in full sun or semi-shade and a gritty, sandy soil. *Culture.*—Sow seed under glass as soon as ripe or in March. Protect with glass in winter. *Species.*—*C. coriacea; C. grandiflora; C. holosericea* (easiest grown); *C. Lindsayi;* and *C. spectabilis.* These all grow from 12 to 18 inches high.

PLATE 9 *TWO POPULAR VARIETIES OF SAXIFRAGE Above, WENLOCK PEACH, Below, GLASNEVIN BEAUTY*

Celosia (Prince of Wales' Feathers, or Cockscomb).—Half-hardy annuals, which thrive if planted out in June in a warm, sheltered situation in southern districts. Grown in pots in the greenhouse, they may, with a little management, be had in flower the whole winter. *Culture.*—Sow thinly in pans in March, in rich, sandy loam and leaf-mould, with bottom heat (70° F.), and just cover with very fine soil. Transplant into boxes as soon as possible, and when big enough, pot singly into 2-inch pots, which should be placed on a shelf close to the glass. Syringe the seedlings constantly, give free ventilation, and do not keep the roots too moist. Re-pot frequently, harden-off, and plant-out 4-12 inches apart in June, or pot-up for the greenhouse as required, using 5 to 7-inch pots and a well-sieved compost of one-half part rich loam and one-half leaf-mould and sand. Keep the seedlings in a warm, moist, and fairly close atmosphere, not too wet at the roots, until the flowers appear in the late summer. As soon as the buds form water twice a week with weak liquid manure until the colour shows. (Temp. 45° to 55° F. in winter to 60° to 65° F. during summer). *Species and Varieties.*—*C. argentea* (Silvery); *C. cristata* (*Cockscomb*) (Crimson, July–Aug., 18 in.); *C. cristata var. coccinea* (Scarlet); *C. cristata var. pyramidalis* (Scarlet, Crimson or Gold, July–Sept., 30 in.).

Celsia (Cretan Mullein).—Half-hardy biennials and perennials, which thrive in the cool greenhouse, in a compost of sandy loam and a little leaf-mould. For culture, *see* Biennials, p. 141, *and* Perennials, p. 156. *Species.*—*C. Arcturus* (Deep Yellow, spotted Purple, June–Nov., 20 in.); *C. cretica* (Golden-yellow, spotted Brown, June–July, 60 in.).

Centaurea.—A large genus comprising hardy annuals, biennials, and perennials, all of which thrive in a sunny position and in any good garden soil. The perennials (Knapweed) make good border plants; *C. Cyanus* (Cornflower) and *C. suaveolens* (Sweet Sultan) are annuals. *Culture.*—(*Annuals*). Sow cornflower seeds thinly, ½ inch deep, in March or September in beds or borders. Do not transplant, but thin-out to 12 inches apart when fit to handle. Sow Sweet Sultans thinly, ½ inch deep, in March in a frame, and transplant singly into pots as soon as possible, planting-out in May in light, chalky soil. (*Biennials*). Sow in the open in May or in pots in a cold frame, and plant-out when fit to handle, or take cuttings and strike in a cold frame in August. (*Perennials*). Sow in the open in April, or propagate by means of division in April or October. Plant-out in an open, sunny position and in ordinary loam in April or October. *Pot Culture.*—*C. gymnocarpa* (Dusty Miller) and *C. ragusina* are useful in the cold greenhouse. They should be potted up in March in loamy soil, in 6 to 8-inch pots. Water well while growing. To propagate sow in heat in January and August, or take cuttings in September. *Species and Varieties.*—HARDY ANNUALS —*C. Cyanus* (Cornflower) (White, Pink, Blue, July–Oct.: 6–36 in.); *C. depressa* (Blue, Crimson Centre, July–Oct., 12 in.); *C. moschata* (Sweet Sultan) (White to Yellow, Rose and Purple, July–Oct., 20 in.). HARDY PERENNIALS—Some good species.—*C. babylonica* (Yellow, 6–8 ft., July–Sept.); *C. dealbata* (Rose, Silver Foliage, July–Sept., 24 in.); *C. glastifolia* (Yellow, Summer, 40–50 in.); *C. hypoleuca* (Large Mauve, July–Aug., 12–18 in.); *C. macrocephala* (Deep Yellow, July and Aug., 50–60 in.); *C. montana* (Blue, White, Pink, and Yellow, July and Aug., 24–30 in.); *C. ruthenica* (Sulphur Yellow, Aug., 50–60 in.).

Centranthus.—*See* Kentranthus.

Cephalotaxus.—A small family of evergreen trees and shrubs, allied to the Yews, and found only in Eastern Asia. They thrive in most soils, are quite hardy, and particularly useful evergreens to plant in semi-shade. Increase is by cuttings, layering, and seeds. There are male and female flowers, as in the case of the Yew, and these are nearly always borne on different bushes. The female produces an egg-shaped or oval drupe-like fruit, 1–1¼ inches long, and green or brown in colour. *Species.*—Three species are usually listed: *C. drupacea, C. Fortunei,* and *C. Wilsoniana. C. drupacea var. fastigiata* is an upright growing form comparable in habit to the Irish Yew.

Cerastium (Mouse-ear, Chick-weed, Jerusalem Star).—A genus of dwarf-growing hardy perennials that are useful for carpeting or for the rock and paved gardens. For culture, *see* Rock Plants, p. 196. After flowering, all straggling growths should be cut back, or less vigorous neighbours will be suffocated. No protection in winter is necessary. *Species.*—*C. Biebersteinii* (White, Silver Foliage, May–June, 6 in.); *C. tomentosum* (White, Silver Foliage, June–Aug., 6 in.).

Ceratostigma (Leadwort).—Low-growing rock plants, which thrive in the sun and in gritty loam. For culture, *see* Rock Plants, p. 196. *C. plumbaginoides* (Cobalt-blue, July–Sept., 9 in.) sometimes named *Plumbago Larpentæ,* and *C. Willmottianum* (Rich Blue, July–Oct., 2–4 ft.) are the best known.

Cercis (Judas Tree).—Tall deciduous shrubs or small trees which thrive in full sun in moist, sandy, and well-drained loam. They carry pea-shaped flowers in May. *Culture.*—Plant in October or November. To propagate, sow in a frame, or layer in September. *Species.*—*C. chinensis* (Bright Pink); and *C. Siliquastrum* (Rosy-lilac), *var. album* (White).

Cestrum (Habrothamnus).—Handsome evergreen climbing shrubs, suitable for the cool greenhouse. They may be grown out-of-doors on a wall in a very sheltered position. *Culture.*—Pot-up annually in March in a compost of two-thirds fibrous loam and one-third leaf-mould, well-rotted manure, sand, and a little old mortar rubble. Water well while growing, and give liquid manure when the buds form, but keep the roots dry in winter. Prune fully-grown plants back to within two buds of the old wood in February; younger plants should be allowed to retain about a third of the new wood each year. Propagation is by means of cuttings struck in a temperature of from 60° to 65° F. in late summer.

Species.—*C. auranticum* (Golden Yellow); *C. elegans* (Red); *C. Newellii* (Crimson); and *C. Smithii* (Soft Pink).

Chænomeles.—Hardy deciduous flowering trees and shrubs, which thrive in sunny positions and in ordinary soil, either in the open border, or against a wall. *Culture.*—Plant in October or November. Cut-out old wood and shorten side shoots in June. Propagation may be carried out by means of seeds, budding, layering, suckers, or cuttings in October. *Pot Culture.*—Pot-up in November, in 8 to 10-inch pots and take into the cold greenhouse. Sink the pots in ashes outdoors from May to November. *Species and Varieties.*—*C. lagenaria* (Orange-red) *varieties: aurora* (Rose, shaded Yellow), *cardinalis* (Rich Deep Red), *nivalis* (White) and *rubra grandiflora* (Crimson); *C. japonica* [*C. Maulei*] (Orange-flame) hybrids: *Knap Hill Scarlet, Simonii* (Deep Crimson), and *C.*

superba (Orange-scarlet). They flower from January to June and grow from 3 to 9 feet high.

Chamæcyparis (False Cypress).—Quick growing Conifers at one time included under Cupressus. They succeed under the same conditions as that genus. *C. Lawsoniana* and its many varieties, i.e. *Allumii, luteus, erectaviridis, Hillieri* (Golden Yellow) and *Triomphe de Boskoop* (Glaucous-blue) are the best. For small gardens *C. obtusa* and varieties *ericoides, nana* and *pygmæa* are best. *C. tetragona minima* is suitable for the rock garden. *C. Lawsoniana* and *C. nootkatensis* make good hedge plants.

Charieis heterophylla (Cape Aster).—A pretty little free-flowering hardy annual, which is very effective in the rock garden. It grows some 6 inches high, and flowers from June to September, thriving in any good garden soil. For *Culture, see* Annuals, p. 139. *C. heterophylla* (Blue or White) is the most common species.

Cheiranthus.—*See* Wallflower.

Chelone (Shellflower).—Hardy perennials, many species of which are now classed with penstemons, which like a sunny or semi-shaded site and moist, sandy loam with humus in it. For culture, *see* Perennials, p. 156. *Species and Varieties.*—*C. coccinea* (Red); *C. Lyonii* (Rosy Purple); *C. obliqua* (Pink, 24–30 in.); *C. o. var. alba* (White). All flower from June to September, and grow from 24 to 36 inches in height.

Chimonanthus præcox (Winter Sweet).—A winter-blooming, hardy deciduous shrub, which likes a sunny, sheltered position and deep, moist, sandy loam. It bears pale yellow flowers stained purple in the centres, and reaches a height of 7 feet or more on walls. *Culture.*—Plant in October or March, and when grown as a climber, cut back side shoots to within five to six "eyes" of the main stems after flowering. Propagate by means of layering in August, or by suckers or seeds in March.

C. præcox var. grandiflorus has larger leaves and flowers. *C. præcox var. luteus* has more showy yellow flowers.

Chionanthus (Fringe Tree).—Hardy deciduous shrubs or small trees, which like a sheltered position and a well-drained, moist loam, and bear white flowers in June and July. *Culture.*—Plant from October to November, and trim to shape after flowering if required. Propagate by means of layering in September, or strike cuttings of half-ripe shoots in a close frame during July and August. *Species.*—*C. retusa* and *C. virginica.*

Chionodoxa (Glory of the Snow).—This bulbous plant requires similar treatment to that accorded to bulbs generally, and thrives in sun or shade and sandy loam in the border, rock garden, or greenhouse. *Culture.*—Plant in October 2½ inches deep and from 3 to 4 inches apart. Lift from the soil, only when over-crowded, when the leaves die down. *Pot Culture.*—Pot-up in the autumn, in a compost of sandy loam and leaf-mould, putting about 10 bulbs into a 6-inch pot, stand in a cold frame, and cover with fibre until growth starts. Then, move into the cold greenhouse. After blooming, place in a frame and continue to water until the foliage dies down; keep quite dry in summer. Propagate by offsets in October or raise from seed. *See also* Bulbs, p. 170. *Species.*—*C. Luciliæ gigantea* (Soft Mauve, Blue, and White, March, 9 in.); *C. Luciliæ* *grandiflora* (Lavender-blue, White Centre, March–April, 9 in.); *C. L. var. sardensis* (Deep Blue, March–April, 7 in.).

Chlidanthus fragrans.—A half-hardy bulbous plant, that thrives in warm, well-drained sunny borders or in pots in a mixture of peaty loam, leaf-mould, and sand. It grows about 9 inches high, and flowers in May and June. *Culture.*—Plant in April 3½ inches deep and 2 inches apart. Lift in October. Propagate by means of offsets in April.

Choisya ternata (Mexican Orange Blossom).—A half-hardy evergreen shrub, which likes a wall or a sunny, sheltered position and sandy loam. It grows from 6 to 10 feet high, and from May to September bears small white flowers. *Culture.*—Plant in April or September, and in April cut out old wood or trim if required. Propagate by means of layering in August, or by cuttings in a frame in August. *Pot Culture.*—Pot-up in spring in a 6 to 8-inch pot and a compost of peaty loam, leaf-mould, and sand. Prune straggly shoots after flowering, and put out, with pots sunk in ashes, from July to October.

Chorizemas.—Greenhouse evergreen shrubs, growing from 24–40 inches high and carrying red or yellow blossoms almost the whole year round. They thrive best in the cool greenhouse (Temp. 45° F. in winter to 55° F. in summer), in a compost of 2 parts of sandy peat to 1 part of fibrous loam. *Culture.*—Pot-up in the spring (biennially), using 6 to 8-inch pots. Keep dry until growth starts, and then water moderately, giving occasional doses of liquid manure. Stop-back during the first and second years. Prune out weak wood and dead flowers after flowering, and stand out-of-doors from June to September. Propagation is by means of cuttings of half-ripened wood, 3 inches long, with a "heel", under glass in June. *Species.*—*C. cordata* and *C. ilicifolia* are good species, of which there are several varieties.

Christmas Rose.—*See* Helleborus niger.

Chrysalidocarpus lutescens.—This is a greenhouse palm, requiring the same treatment as Areca.

Chrysanthemum.—The chrysanthemum is one of the hardiest plants, but owing to the fact that it flowers somewhat late, its beautiful blooms are subject to injury from the weather when grown out-of-doors, unless the protection of glass is provided.

Chrysanthemums of all varieties may be classified, according to the time of their blooming, as: early-flowering, blooming from July to October; semi-early, blooming in September and October in the open; and ordinary or late-flowering, flowering in November and December.

CULTURE OF INDOOR CHRYSANTHEMUMS.—If seed is used, it should be sown as soon as ripe (February) in a pan of sandy soil in a temperature of 60° F.: transplant, and pot-on as necessary. *Propagation by Cuttings.*—After the plants have finished blooming, the stems and all weak shoots from the base should be cut down to within a few inches of the ground, the pots being given a position in the cold greenhouse or in a frost-proof frame. A half-inch mulch of fine loam and leaf-mould, and a little water, will help the old roots to throw up sturdy young shoots for cuttings. *See* Cuttings, p. 108. Grow in pots in a mixture of well-rotted leaf-mould, grit or silver sand and fibrous loam, in about equal parts, and a dusting of wood ashes, all well sieved. Once the cuttings are rooted (in

Campanula pyramidalis

Campanula Medium

Celmisia insignis

Calceolaria herbeohybrida

PLATE 29

G. Preston

Alexander & Brown and Sutton & Sons

Baroness de Brienen

White Clove, Orangeman and Bookham Scar

PLATE 30 CARNATIONS

Endymion, Border carnations

Kelso, Border carnations

from three to five weeks), stand the pots near the glass in a frost-proof frame, and give ample ventilation in fine weather. Cuttings of Japanese types must be taken in December or January. Nearly all growers differ as to the best time for striking cuttings of the "Decorative" types. Some recommend November; some succeed admirably by inserting them in May; the latter date only when propagating plants to flower in small pots in December. Perhaps it is better to make a compromise by striking in February or March. *Potting-on.*—December-struck cuttings should be well rooted by the middle of February, and should then be potted-up into 3 or 3½-inch pots, adding to the compost one-third part well-rotted manure. They should receive their next shift into 5 or 6-inch pots about the first week in April. Disturb the roots as little as possible, and add a little more manure and a dusting of bonemeal and powdered charcoal to the compost, which do not sieve. The cultivation should be continued in a frame or on a shelf near the glass. Shade from the sun, then in about a fortnight's time harden-off, stand out-of-doors by the middle of May, and give a final shift a month or six weeks later. *Summer Treatment.*—The pots should be stood in the open on slates or a bed of ashes in a sheltered position, facing south or west. As soon as the pots are full of roots, the plants should be placed in 8 to 9-inch pots; about the middle of June is a good time to complete the final potting-up. No soil is better for them than a compost of two-thirds lumpy fibrous loam, one-sixth well-rotted cow-dung, and one-sixth leaf-mould and a little old mortar rubble and sharp sand liberally coloured with bonemeal and soot. There need not be much drainage. *Staking and Tying.*—The plants must be properly supported. *See* Staking and Tying, p. 39. *"Stopping" and Disbudding.*—If bushy plants are to be grown, pinch out the tip of the central shoot, when the plants are some 5 or 6 inches high. A second "stopping" will be necessary in early summer. If you grow blooms for exhibition only, no stopping will be needed until the "break-bud" appears in early summer. Pinch-out this bud and all the young shoots just below it, save the three strongest and best placed, and concentrate the whole strength of the plant into these stems and the strength of these stems into a single bud at the top. *Feeding and Autumn Treatment.*—From early in August, the plants should be fed two or three times a week alternately with sulphate of potash and with weak manure water. Feeding must cease as soon as the blooms are three-parts open, and early in October the plants should be moved under glass. This is a critical change for them, and the leaves should be kept well syringed, *except in dull, damp weather,* two or three times a day for a few weeks. In fine weather, the plants must be kept as cool as possible and ample ventilation given, a little at night even. Late-flowering varieties, that normally flower in December, should be kept in the open as long as possible. They must, however, be protected from frost. Never should the temperature of the house be allowed to rise above 55° F.

OUTDOOR CULTURE OF BORDER CHRYSANTHEMUMS.—Plant-out in March, or in the case of less hardy sorts, towards the end of May. They should receive the same general treatment in training and watering as those grown indoors, except that the majority should not be "stopped". The soil should be well-drained and well-dug in winter, but it must not be too rich. A mulch of well-rotted short stable manure in June is beneficial. In planting, 24 to 36 inches should be allowed between each plant, and an open, sunny, sheltered position is essential. Most varieties form bushy plants naturally, but with others it is necessary, from time to time, to pinch-back the tips of the shoots. This pinching-back must not be continued after the end of July. If large blooms are desired, the plants should be disbudded. Towards the end of June the taller border chrysanthemums will need staking with good strong sticks. *See* page 39. In hot dry weather, a good watering once a week should be given and a little weak liquid manure may be provided occasionally, once the buds have formed. As soon as the flowers are over, cut the plants down to the ground, lift them, shake the soil from the roots and place them, close together, in shallow boxes of light, sandy soil, and store in a frost-proof place. In March, divide the crowns, retaining the younger and more vigorous portions only, and plant-out again in the border, or take cuttings as advised for the indoor kinds. In light and warm soil, it is not always necessary to lift the crowns in autumn.

Varieties.—GREENHOUSE. JAPANESE EXHIBITION.—*Alice Burgess* (Salmon); *Birmingham* (Crimson); *Duchess of Kent* (Pink); *Duke of Kent* (White); *Edna Green* (Golden Yellow); *F. E. Luxford* (Apricot); *James Bryant* (Chestnut); *John Pockett* (Rosy Crimson); *Majestic* (Golden Amber); *Mrs. John Woolman* (Rose); *Mrs. R. C. Pulling* (Lemon Yellow); *Red Majestic* (Terra Cotta); *Thos. W. Pockett* (Pink); *W. Meadows* (Chestnut Brown).

JAPANESE DECORATIVE—(Mid-season Flowering).—*Ada Stevens* (Yellow); *Adonis* (Salmon Pink); *Crensa* (Gold); *In Memoriam* (Crimson); *Primrose Beauty*; *Oldland Bronze* (Bronze); *Sussex White*. (Late Flowering).—*Baldock's Crimson*; *Bronze Favourite*; *Friendly Rival* (Yellow); *Imperial Pink*; *May Wallace* (Shell Pink); *Molly Nicholson* (Salmon Bronze); *Sovereign* (Amber); *Sussex Gold* (Golden Yellow); *The Favourite* (White).

INCURVED VARIETIES.—*Golden Pride* (Yellow); *Monument* (White); *Ondine* (White, Green Tipped); *Progress* (Silver Mauve).

SINGLE VARIETIES.—*Artist* (Red); *Chesswood Beauty* (Crimson); *Mason's Bronze*; *Molly Godfrey* (Pink); *Phyllis Cooper* (Orange and Yellow); *Rowena* (Yellow); *Susan* (Rose, and Bronze).

ANEMONE-CENTRED SINGLES.—*Aphrodite* (Mauve-pink); *Elspeth* (Mauve); *Golden Nymph* (Straw-yellow and Gold); *Mary Godfrey* (Pink); *Thora* (Rose-pink); *Winsome* (Crimson).

POMPONS.—*Bubbles* (Chestnut Bronze); *Jante Wells* (Golden Yellow); *Mosquito* (Yellow); *Salmon Bouquet*; *Shell Bouquet* (Pink); *White Bouquet*.

HARDY BORDER VARIETIES.—*Arnheim* (Bronze); *August Pink*; *Carefree* (Chestnut); *Corona* (Orange); *Florence Horwood* (Bright Rose); *Golden Harvest* (Golden Yellow); *Hurricane* (Crimson); *Imperial Yellow* (Yellow); *Mary Mona* (Salmon); *New Countess* (Rose Pink); *Royal Pink*; *Serenus* (White); *Sweetheart* (Salmon Pink); *Zenith* (Maroon).

HARDY SINGLES.—*Carrie Luxford* (Crimson); *Doreen Woolman* (Golden Flame); *Maidenhood* (Primrose); *Mrs. H. Woolman* (White); *Shirley Crimson*; *The Dome* (Salmon and Gold).

Chrysanthemum, Annual (Corn Marigold, Crown Daisy).—These showy plants thrive in sunny beds or borders. For culture, *see* Annuals, p. 139. *Named Varieties.*—*Eastern Star* (Yellow, Brown Eye); *Evening Star* (Golden

Yellow); *Morning Star* (Primrose); *The Sultan* (Maroon); and *White Pearl* (White Double). All flower from June to September and grow to a height of about 20 inches.

Chrysanthemum frutescens (Marguerite).—These popular half-hardy plants like a soil that is not too rich. *Culture.*—Sow under glass in April, or strike cuttings of young shoots in a cold frame in September; protect in severe weather. Pot-up into 4-inch pots in March, harden-off, and plant-out towards the end of May; if for greenhouse decoration the following spring they should, late in May, be re-potted into 6-inch pots, hardened-off, and stood on ashes in the open until September, then moved into 7-inch pots and transferred to a cool, but frost-proof, house for the winter. Young plants grown on for pot culture should be "stopped" during the spring and summer. *Varieties.*—*Broussonetii* (White, Single), *Etoile d'Or* (Yellow) and *Queen Alexandra* (White, Double).

Chrysanthemum, Perennial (Ox-Eye Daisy).—These, like the annual species, make a good show in sunny borders and ordinary soil. For culture, *see* Perennials, p. 156. *Species.*—*C. alpinum* (White, June–Sept., 5 in.); *C. arcticum* (White, tinged Pink, Oct., 18 in.); *C. coccineum* (Scarlet, June–Sept., 36 in.); *C. maximum* (White, July–Sept., 36 in.); and *C. uliginosum* (White, Sept.–Oct., 3–5 ft.). *Named Varieties of C. maximum* (Moon Daisy); *Beauté Nivelloise* (White fimbriated); *Esther Read* (Double White); *Ian Murray* (White, incurved petals in centre); *Mayfield Giant* (Large Creamy White); *Wirral Pride* (Large White Anemone centred).

Chrysogonum virginianum (Golden Knee).—A showy herbaceous perennial, somewhat like a sunflower. The star-shaped, golden-yellow flowers are borne all through the summer. It grows to a height of about 10 inches, and will be quite happy in a shady spot in the rock garden. This plant likes a rich, loamy soil and needs ample water in dry weather. *Culture.*—Seed may be sown in April, but it is better to propagate by division of roots in March or September.

Cimicifuga (Bugwort, Bugbane or Snake-root).—A hardy perennial, which thrives in a deep, moist loam and a fairly sunny position. For culture, *see* Perennials, p. 156. *Species.*—*C. cordifolia* (Creamy-white, July–Aug., 36 in.); *C. racemosa* (Cream-white, July–Aug., 36–48 in.); and *C. simplex* (White, Aug.–Oct., 36 in.).

Cineraria.—Beautiful greenhouse perennials which, by careful management, may be had in flower from November to May, though February and March are the months in which they flower most easily. Available colours are: maroon, purple, red, rose, blue, white, and in some varieties the flowers are self-coloured; in others they are edged with white or with a second colour. Few plants are so effective for decorative purposes. They thrive in a compost of 2 parts fibrous loam to 1 part of leaf-mould, well-decayed cow manure and a little sand and old mortar rubble, and are best grown from seed. *Culture.*—The first sowing should be made in April in pans filled with equal parts of loam and leaf-mould and one-sixth part of sand. They should be well-drained, made firm, the seed should be lightly covered, and the pans placed in slight bottom heat. Cover with glass and paper, and keep slightly moist. Stand the seedlings in partial shade, move into 3-inch pots as soon as possible, gradually harden-off, and remove the lights of the frame entirely by day from July to the end of September.

295

Shift the young plants into 4½ to 5-inch pots as required, and give them their final shift in September into 6 to 8-inch pots. After each potting, keep the frame closed until the plants are re-established, then again gradually admit full air. Keep moist, and syringe every afternoon in hot weather, then towards the end of September, the plants should be placed in a cool greenhouse, and weak liquid manure or soot water given alternately with water. Another sowing may be made in a cold frame in May, and a third in June. Pot-on as above, but at proportionately later dates. *Cineraria maritima* (*Senecio Cineraria*) is a beautiful foliage plant for summer bedding, or decoration in the cold greenhouse. Sow under glass in March. *Species and Varieties.*—*C. maritima* (*Senecio Cineraria*) (Silver Foliage, Summer, 18 in.); and *Senecio cruenta* (*Cineraria*), of which there are many varieties, usually divided into the following classes, viz.; the large-flowered florist's varieties, the intermediate, and the stellata varieties [star Cineraria] (Various, Winter and Spring, 18–30 in.).

Cistus (Rock Rose).—Evergreen perennial shrubs mostly hardy in warm sheltered sites. They grow from 2 to 5 feet in height, and bear very pretty flowers. These are usually white, rose, or purple, in colour, spotted with a different shade, generally purple or yellow, at the base of each petal. Each flower, unfortunately, lasts little more than a day, but a succession of blooms keeps the bushes gay from June to August. They are commonly known as Rock Roses from the fact that the flowers resemble a large single rose. These plants make admirable subjects for the rock garden. They love the sun and do well in dry, well-drained, sandy loam, or in ordinary soil to which ample lime-rubble has been added. *Culture.*—Do not prune, merely keep the shrubs in shape by means of "stopping" in March and by removing dead blooms. Propagate by means of layering in August, sow seed in April, or take cuttings of half-matured wood in August and strike in a shaded frame. Grow in pots till ready for planting-out. *Species and Hybrids.*—*C. algarvensis* (see *Halimium ocymoides*), *C. cyprius* (White, Spotted Red, 48–60 in.); *C. ladaniferus* (White [Spotted Red], 48–60 in.); *C. laurifolius* (White, 48–60 in.); *C. lusitanicus* (White [Blotched Carmine], 36 in.); *C. purpureus* (Purple-red [Blotched Crimson], 36–48 in.). All flower from June to July.

Citrus sinensis (Dwarf Orange).—The dwarf fruiting species which are usually grown in the cool greenhouse are grafted plants. They thrive in a compost of three-quarters turfy loam and one-quarter leaf-mould, rotten manure and sand. In winter they need full sun, but in summer should be shaded from direct sun. Trim to shape only. The trees may be propagated by seed in gentle heat (65° F.), by budding in July, or by grafting in March; but cuttings struck in spring produce bushes which fruit earlier. The culture of the lemon (*Citrus Limonia*) and the lime (*Citrus aurantifolia*) is identical.

Clarkia.—Hardy annuals, which thrive in fairly moist rich soil in the border or cold greenhouse. For culture, *see* Annuals, p. 139. For the greenhouse, sow in a frame in August, and pot-up as required, using 6 to 7-inch pots for three plants. *Varieties.*—*Brilliant Rose* (Rose); *Firefly* (Crimson); *Marginata* (Pink, margined White); *Orange King* (Orange); *Scarlet Beauty* (Scarlet); *Purple Queen* (Purple); *Salmon Queen* (Salmon); and *Snowball* (White). All flower from July to October and grow about 24 inches high.

Claytonia (Spring Beauty).—Dwarf-growing hardy perennials, which thrive in sun or shade and in any soil. *Culture.*—Sow in March where the plants are to flower. *Species.*—*C. sibirica* (Rose) and *C. virginica* (White). Both flower in the spring and grow about 6 inches high.

Clematis.—Beautiful hardy climbers, which do well against walls and on trellises, facing north, east, or west, or in the greenhouse. If planted in a sunny position, the lower part of the stems require shade. Although not particular as to soil, they prefer light to heavy land if it has been well manured; a mixture of well-drained loam, well-rotted manure, and old mortar rubble is the most satisfactory compost. *Culture.*—Propagate by means of layering in summer. Plant in March. Cut away dead and weak wood, giving ample light and air to the growths retained, and fasten the shoots up securely. Propagation may also be carried out by means of grafting, by cuttings, or by seed. Most varieties require pruning after flowering, but *C. vitalba* is best pruned in March, while *C. Jackmanii* and *C. viticella vars.* should be cut down to 6 inches in November or to a foot in spring. *Pot culture.*—Use 5 to 10-inch pots and a compost of 2 parts fibrous loam to 1 part of leaf-mould, well-rotted manure, mortar rubble, and sand. Place in a cool or cold greenhouse early in the year. Water liberally while growing and keep well thinned. *Varieties.*—EARLY-FLOWERING—(Florida Group) *Belle of Woking* (Silvery Mauve); *Countess of Lovelace* (Lavender-blue); *Duchess of Edinburgh* (Double, White). LATE-FLOWERING—(Jackmanii Group) *Gipsy Queen* (Purple); *Jackmanii* (Purple); and *Snow White Jackmanii* (White). (Lanuginosa Group) *Crimson King* (Crimson); *Henryi* (White); *Beauty of Worcester* (Blue-violet); *Fairy Queen* (Flesh Pink); *Lady Northcliffe* (Deep Lavender); *Mrs. Pope* (Lavender); and *Nellie Moser* (Mauve, with Pink Bars). (Patens Group) *Duke of Edinburgh* (Purple-violet); *Miss Bateman* (White); and *The Queen* (Lavender); *C. montana* (White) *and var. rubens* (Rosy Red); *C. tangutica* (Golden Yellow); and *C. Flammula* (White). (Viticella Group) *C. Ascotiensis* (Azure Blue); *Ville de Lyon* (Carmine); and *C. viticella alba* (White, Semi-double).

Clerodendron.—Beautiful deciduous shrubs or small trees, which thrive in a sunny, sheltered position in well-drained, rich loam. *Culture.*—Plant in October or November. Propagate by means of seed, cuttings of half-ripened shoots in a frame, or by root cuttings. *C. fœtidum* is a good plant for the cold greenhouse, or, in favourable localities, it may be grown in a sheltered spot under a wall. *C. fallax* (Orange-scarlet) is a warm greenhouse shrub. *Hardy Species.*—*C. Fargesii* (White, Red Calyx, 10–12 ft.); *C. fœtidum* (Purple, 3–6 ft.); *C. trichotomum* (White, Red Calyx, 10–12 ft.). All flower from July to September.

Clethra (Sweet Pepper Bush).—Choice flowering shrubs that will thrive in a warm, sunny, sheltered position in the south and west of England. They grow to a height of 5–6 feet, and carry white blossoms from July to September. A compost of rich, moist loam and leaf-mould or peat suits them. Propagate by cuttings of semi-matured shoots in a frame in June, or by division. *Species.*—*C. alnifolia*; *C. canescens*; and *C. tomentosa* are among the most hardy.

Clianthus.—Evergreen climbing shrubs, which succeed best in the warm, sunny border of a cool greenhouse and in sandy peat and fibrous loam. *C. puniceus* (Crimson), *vars. magnificus* (Red) and *carneus* (Flesh), Parrot's Bill and

297

Lobster's Claw, blossom freely out-of-doors against a trellis or south wall. *Culture.*—Sow seeds in February singly in pots, and when 3 to 4 inches high, move into 4½-inch pots and keep in these until ready for planting-out in April, or, in the case of *C. Dampieri* (Glory Pea), into a border in the house, or into a good large pot or large basket. In summer, the plants must be kept well-watered, but never must the soil become stagnant or sour. The great thing is to grow these plants on without a check. Once the roots become over-dry, they will not recover; they are also impatient of disturbance. Protect from frost, and water sparingly in winter. Syringe house plants daily in hot dry weather, and train the shoots up trellis work or wires placed some 10 inches from the glass, and trim back straggling shoots after flowering. They may also be raised by means of cuttings in a frame (Temp. 70° F.) in May or June. *C. Dampieri* is a difficult plant to grow successfully on its own roots, and does best when the young seedlings are grafted on seedling stocks of the "Bladder Senna," *Colutea arborescens.*

Clintonia [syn. Downingia]. *Which see.*

Clivia (Imantophyllum).—Beautiful evergreen plants, with lily-like blooms, suitable to the greenhouse. *Culture.*—Plant in February, in 9-inch pots, in a mixture of rich, sandy loam, leaf-mould, and old manure. Keep in a cool place, and let the roots fill the pots, as the plants flourish best when root-bound. Water well in summer, keep cool and on the dry side during winter, and sponge the leaves occasionally with tepid water. Weak manure water should be given twice a week while the buds are forming. Propagate by means of division of suckers in February, or by seed sown when ripe. *Species.*—*C. citrina* (Yellow); *C. miniata and vars.* (Orange-scarlet); *C. nobilis* (Red and Yellow). All flower from March to April and grow about 20 inches in height. Clivias make very useful room plants.

Clytostoma.—An evergreen climber for cultivation in a warm greenhouse. It requires the same treatment as Bignonia, (*which see*). *Species.*—*C. callistegioides* (Purple, Spring and early Summer); *C. purpureum* (Mauve and White, Summer).

Cobæa (Cup and Saucer Plant).—Beautiful evergreen climbers, that thrive in the cool greenhouse. They grow to a height of 20 feet and flower from July to September. *C. scandens* (Purple and Greenish-white) will also thrive in the open in warm, sheltered positions in the south and west of England; in more exposed situations it must be treated as an annual and be raised afresh each year. *C. scandens var. variegata* is a beautiful greenhouse climber, and must be propagated by means of cuttings. *Culture.*—Sow thinly under glass (Temp. 45° F.) in light rich soil in February, or propagate by cuttings of young shoots in January or February, and raise in a propagating case. Pot-up into 3 to 4-inch pots, harden-off, and if for growing in the open, plant out 24 inches apart in June in equal parts of loam, leaf-mould, and sand, or grow on in pots and keep in the cool greenhouse. In February prune laterals back to two buds, and cut out all weak growth.

Codonopsis.—These are beautiful little perennials with twining stems and a strong odour. They may with advantage be grown in some wild place in the rock garden. Their pretty creamy-white to pale blue flowers appear in summer, and hang like bells from a twining mass of greyish stems and leaves, which when disturbed give off a pungent smell. They thrive in the sun and in ordinary garden loam. *Species.*—*C. clematidea* (White and Blue, 2–3 ft.); *C. ovata* (Pale Blue funnel-shaped flowers, 12 in.); *C. Meleagris* (Purple-mauve mottling, 8–12 in.). For Culture, *see* Perennials, page 156.

Colchicum (Meadow Saffron or Autumn Crocus).—Hardy bulbous *poisonous* plants usually grown in the rock garden. *Culture.*—Plant in July or August in full sun, 5 inches deep and 6 inches apart in moist, cool loam. Lift from the ground (triennially) in August to increase. *Species.*—*C. autumnale* (Lilac-rose, Sept.–Oct., 6 in.); *C. montanum* (Lilac or White, Sept.–Oct., 4 in.); *C. speciosum* (Crimson, Purple or White Eye, Sept.–Oct., 10 in.).

Coleus Blumei.—Half-hardy annual and perennial foliage plants, useful for bedding-out or the cool greenhouse. *Culture.*—Sow thinly in heat (70° F.) in March. Named varieties must be propagated by means of cuttings at any time from spring to autumn, struck singly in pots sunk to their rims in fibre in a frame with good bottom heat (70° F.), and in a moist atmosphere; the best time is March. These plants like a light, rich soil; 2 parts of loam to 1 part of leaf-mould and sand being recommended. Place near the glass, but shade from strong sun. When rooted, re-pot into 3-inch pots, pinch-back, and pot-on till they are finally in 5 to 6-inch pots, or 10-inch ones if large specimens are required. Ventilate freely, being careful that the temperature does not fall below 50° F. Syringe and water well in warm weather, and dress with fortnightly applications of weak liquid manure water. When grown from seed, discard all purely green-leaved seedlings. Pot up firmly into thumb pots as early as possible. *Varieties.*—*Beckwith's Gem*; *Countess of Dudley*; *Decorator*; *Pride of the Market*; *Sunset*; and *Verschaffeltii*, which is largely used in summer bedding schemes. All flower in the summer, and grow from 6 to 24 inches high. *Coleus thyrsoideus* are winter-flowering greenhouse species, with beautiful blue flowers.

Collinsia (Collin's Flower).—Hardy annuals for sunny beds, borders, or for the greenhouse. For culture, *see* Annuals, p. 139. *Species.*—*C. bicolor* (Reddish-purple and White, July–Oct., 12 in.); *C. grandiflora* (Purple-blue and White, July–Oct., 12 in.).

Collomia coccinea.—This is the best of a series of annuals with bright red flowers. They grow to 18 inches in height. Sow in April outdoors in a sunny position.

Colutea (Bladder Senna).—A deciduous broom-like shrub, thriving in almost any position or soil. *Culture.*—Plant in October or November and in March cut the previous year's growth well back. To propagate, take cuttings in September, or sow in the open in spring. *Species.*—*C. arborescens* (Yellow, June–Aug., 10 ft.); *C. cruenta* (Red and Yellow, June–Aug., 6–8 ft.); *C. media* (Reddish Brown, June–Aug., 10 ft.).

Commelina (Day Flower).—Annual and perennial plants, which thrive in a sunny position in warm, well-drained borders and rich light soil. For culture, *see* Annuals, p. 139, *and* Perennials, p. 156. *Species.*—*C. cælestis* (Rich Blue, Aug. and Sept., 18 in.).

Conandron ramondioides.—Beautiful little dwarf-growing semi-hardy plants of tufted habit, that will make a pretty show in a sheltered site in the rock garden. The violet-blue or white flowers, in shape like those of the potato plant, are borne in summer on short stems rising from the glossy, bright green begonia-like foliage. The plants will thrive best in semi-shade and in a well-drained, sandy, and peaty loam.

Culture.—Seed may be sown under glass as soon as ripe, or in March. Protect with glass in winter.

Convallaria majalis (Lily of the Valley).—To grow Lilies of the Valley well, the roots should be set in bunches a foot apart, in a mixture of sandy loam, leaf-mould, and old manure in a partially-shaded position; they can hardly be treated too liberally. Plant in October, only just covering with soil, and mulch with a 2-inch layer of leaf-mould, which should be removed in the spring. Dress annually in summer with leaf-mould and rotten manure, lift from the soil every fourth year, and propagate by means of division in October. *Pot Culture.*—Plump crowns should be potted-up, 1 inch apart, in November, using 5 to 6-inch pots and a compost of sandy loam and leaf-mould, so that only the tops obtrude. Water well and keep in a cool frame for a few days, then take into the house in batches as bloom is required. The pots must be kept in the dark until the shoots are 5 or 6 inches in height; after this, gradually admit light, raise the temperature to between 60° and 70° F., and give warm water in increasing amounts as growth goes on. After flowering, plant the crowns in the border.

Convolvulus (Bindweed).—A large family of hardy annual and perennial climbing and trailing plants, most of which like a sunny position. Any rather poor soil is suitable for the annuals and many of the perennials, but some of the less hardy kinds require a compost of fine loam, peat, and leaf-mould, especially for cuttings. *Culture.*—ANNUALS—Sow seed thinly in the open from May to June against a trellis or suitable support, and thin out to 10 inches apart when fit to handle. DWARF-GROWING KINDS.—Sow from March to June and thin out to from 5 to 10 inches apart. PERENNIALS.—Propagate by means of seed, cuttings, or by division. *Species.*—ANNUALS—*C. tricolor* (White to Purple and Blue, June–Oct., 8–9 ft.); *C. tricolor alba* (White, July–Oct., 12 in.). PERENNIALS—*C. Cneorum* (Soft Pink with Silver Foliage, June–Sept., 18 in.); *C. mauritanicus* (Blue, June–Sept., 12 in.).

Cordyline (Dracæna, Dragon Plant, and Club Palm).—These are handsome foliage plants. Some species are suitable for living rooms, but others require a greenhouse. *Culture.*—Pot-up in March, using 6 to 10-inch pots and a mixture of one-half peat and one-quarter part each of sand and loam, or two-thirds fibrous loam and one-third leaf-mould. (Temp. 50° F. in winter to 60° F. in summer). Water well and syringe daily in fine weather during the summer. Sponge the foliage with soft warm water and shade from the hot sun. *Species.*—Among the best species are *C. australis*; *C. indivisa* (Green and Yellow Mid-rib); *C. australis var. lentiginosa* (Purple-leaved); and *C. australis var. Doucettii* (Variegated-leaved). In warm, sheltered positions, *C. australis* may be grown outdoors. Plant out from September to March in a moderately dry, sunny position and in good loam. Propagate by seed sown, 1 inch deep, in heat (60° to 70° F.) in March, by root-cuttings in fibre in a hot-bed, by cuttings, or by "ringing" in spring.

300

Chrysanthemum, annual

Calendula, double Yellow Queen

PLATE 31

Chrysanthemum, Japanese Exhibition Variety

Crocus

Alexander & Brown and Dobbie & Co.

PLATE 32 Chrysanthemum, " Hurricane ", a medium-flowered early (reflexed).

Coreopsis (Tickseed).—Hardy annuals, biennials, and perennials, most of which are best treated as biennials. The tall species are effective in mixed borders, and the dwarf kinds make fine bedding plants. A moist, sandy loam and a sunny position are most suitable, and ample water is needed in summer. *Culture.*—ANNUALS—Sow seed thinly, ¼ inch deep, from March to June or in September, and transplant or thin out to from 9–12 inches apart when 3 or 4 inches high. Seed may also be sown, in heat in a frame, in February or March. BIENNIALS—Sow seed in the open in June. Transplant 12 inches apart into a warm reserve garden when 4 leaves have formed, and plant out some 15 inches apart in position for flowering in October. PERENNIALS—Sow seed in the open in April, or propagate by means of division in March or October. *Species.*— ANNUALS—*C. tinctoria* (Yellow and Bronze, July–Oct., 12 in.); *C. coronata* (Orange and Brown, July–Oct., 18 in.); *C. Drummondii* (Golden-yellow, July– Oct., 24 in.). PERENNIALS—*C. grandiflora* (Golden-yellow, July–Oct., 24–30 in.); *C. lanceolata* (Yellow, July–Oct., 24–30 in.); *C. pubescens* (Golden-yellow, spotted Crimson, June–July, 24–48 in.); *C. rosea* (Reddish-pink, July–Sept., 18 in.); *C. verticillata* (Golden-yellow, July–Sept., 24 in.).

Cornus (Cornel, Dogwood, Cornelian Cherry).—Deciduous shrubs and trees and hardy herbaceous perennials. *Culture.*—Sow under glass, or propagate by means of layering in October, or by suckers in November. Plant-out in spring or early autumn in the shade, in a mixture of moist leaf-mould and peat or in ordinary soil. *C. mas*, the Cornelian Cherry, (10 to 25 ft.) thrives quite well in a dry soil. Thin-out after flowering when the branches are overcrowded. *Species and Varieties.*—*C. alba sibirica variegata* (Silvery-white, Variegated Leaves); *C. alba var. Spæthii* (Golden Foliage); *C. capitata* (Syn. *Benthamia fragifera*), a half hardy evergreen shrub which may be grown in the open in a warm sheltered situation in the south (Cream and Pink flowers, Spring, Scarlet Fruits, 12 ft.); *C. florida rubra* (Rosy-pink Floral Bracts); *C. Kousa* (White Floral Bracts) *var. chinensis* (Large White Floral Bracts); and *C. Nuttallii* (Tree Cornel with Large Cream Bracts). All flower in May, and grow from 7 to 12 feet in height.

Corokea.—Half-hardy evergreen flowering shrubs, which thrive in a warm sunny position and in ordinary soil. *Culture.*—Plant in April or October, and prune only to keep in shape. To propagate, strike half-matured cuttings in a frame in August. *Species.*—*C. buddleoides* (White, April–May, 3–4 ft.); *C. Cotoneaster* (Yellow, May, 6 ft.); *C. macrocarpa* (Orange, May–June, 6 ft.).

Coronilla (Crown Vetch or Scorpion Senna).—Half-hardy evergreen or deciduous shrubs and herbaceous perennials, which succeed well against a south wall with a little winter protection, also in the rock garden, or cold green-house. *Culture.*—Plant in March or October in well drained ordinary soil, or in sandy loam (rock garden species). *Pot Culture.*—Pot-up in March, using 6 to 8-inch pots and a compost of 2 parts sandy loam to 1 part of peat. Prune into shape and cut-out old and dead wood in February, and stand in the open after flowering until September. To propagate, sow in a frame in March, or take cuttings of young wood in April or August (greenhouse plants) and strike in a frame (Temp. 60° F.). The rock garden species are propagated by seed as above, or by division of roots in October. *Species.*—*C. cappadocica* [syn. *C.*

301

iberica] (Creamy-yellow, July–Aug., 4 in.); *C. minima* (Yellow, June–July, 3 in.); *C. varia* (Lilac-pink, Aug.–Sept., 12–18 in.). SHRUBS—*C. Emerus* (Yellow, June to August) and *C. glauca* (Yellow, April–May).

Cortaderia (Pampas Grass).—Cortaderia is a new name for *Gynerium*, a very beautiful perennial grass, which throws up long, silky plumes in the late summer. A sunny, sheltered position is desirable, also well-drained soil. It grows some 6–8 feet high, and flowers in autumn. *Culture.*—Sow seed in April, or propagate by means of division of roots in April or May. *C. Selloana* has creamy-white plumes, and in *C. conspicua* the plumes are silvery-white.

Cortusa Matthiolii (Bear's Ear).—Dwarf-growing rock plants, closely allied to the Primula and very similar to it in appearance. Throughout July they carry heads of rosy-purple flowers, and thrive in partial shade and in rich, sandy loam and leaf-mould. Seed should be sown in March under glass, or the roots may be divided in March or October.

Corydalis (Fumitory).—Hardy annual and perennial rock garden or border plants, which require semi-shade and comparatively poor soil. For culture, *see* Annuals, p. 139, *and* Perennials, p. 156. *Species.*—PERENNIALS—*C. cava* (Purple and Rose, May, 12 in.); *C. Capnoides* (Cream, May–Sept., 12 in.); *C. lutea* (Yellow, June–Sept., 6–12 in.); *C. thalictrifolia* (Yellow, July–Sept., 6–12 in.) which is excellent for the cool greenhouse; *C. Wilsonii* (Canary Yellow, 10–15 in.).

Corylopsis.—Hardy deciduous shrubs, which like a sunny, sheltered position, and well-drained, ordinary soil. *Culture.*—Plant in October or November. Little pruning is required. Propagate by means of layering in the summer. *Pot Culture.* —Pot-up from October to February, using 6 to 8-inch pots and turfy loam. Sink the pots in ashes in the open from May to December, then take into the cold greenhouse. After flowering, prune-out weak wood and dead flower shoots. *Species.*—*C. glabrescens; C. pauciflora; C. spicata;* and *C. Willmottiæ.* All have primrose-yellow flowers from March to April and grow from 4 to 8 feet high.

Corylus (Filbert, Hazel Nut).—Best known as bearing edible nuts, but several trees and shrubs are valuable subjects for ornamental gardening. *C. Colurna*, the Constantinople Nut, growing up to 70 to 80 feet, is a beautiful ornamental tree. *C. maxima atropurpurea* (Purple-leaved Nut) and *C. Avellana aurea* (Yellow-leaved Nut) are useful shrubs to provide colour in the borders and pleasure grounds. For culture, *see* Filbert.

Cosmos (Mexican Aster.)—Half-hardy annuals and perennials, which thrive in warm, dry borders and in ordinary soil. The early-flowering annuals should be chosen. For culture, *see* Annuals, p. 139, *and* Perennials, p. 156. *Species.*— ANNUALS—*C. bipinnatus* (Pink, White and Crimson, June–Oct., 30–70 in.); *C. sulphureus* (Yellow, June–Oct., 20 in.); *C. tenuifolius* (Purple, June–Oct. 24 in.). *Named Varieties.*—*Early Dawn* (Pink and White); *Klondyke* (Yellow); *Rose Queen* (Rosy-Red); and *White Queen* (White).

Cotinus.—A genus of shrubs or small trees, allied and sometimes included under Rhus. They require a well-drained and not too rich soil. Propagated by seed, root cuttings and layers. *Species.*—*C. americanus* (*Rhus Cotinoides*) growing up to 30 ft. Leaf colouring attractive in the autumn; *C. Coggygria* (*Rhus cotinus*, Smoke or Wig Tree), Leaves Red and Yellow in the autumn.

Cotoneaster (Rockspray).—Hardy shrubs or small trees, most of which grow best in poor or chalky soil. The species vary greatly in habit. Some grow as small trees; many kinds make erect bushes, others grow in long, arching shoots; while others, again, are prostrate and creeping by nature. The last-named class is valuable for the rock garden. *C. adpressa* is tight and neat in habit and its leaves assume a deep red in autumn. It is excellent for a small rock garden. *C. congesta* is also of a neat habit, its leaves being slightly larger than those of *C. adpressa*. *C. Dammeri* has larger leaves again, and is good for a fairly large garden. *C. microphylla* is a useful species; it grows well near the sea, in the shade, and under the drip of trees. *C. microphylla var. thymifolia* is of straggling habit, grows to a height of 12 inches, and bears pinkish flowers in April. The cotoneasters are attractive in habit and several are beautiful shrubs, bearing white or pink-tinted flowers in spring. The best of these are *C. multiflora* and *C. frigida*, but their greatest beauty is in their brilliant red fruits, occasionally black, purple, etc., in autumn and winter. *Culture.*—Plant from October to March. No pruning is necessary, though certain species require thinning-out after flowering or fruiting. To propagate, take cuttings of hard wood in a frame in July or August, or layer in September or October. Cotoneasters also grow freely from seed sown in the open in March or September. *Species.*—*C. buxifolia* (E) (8–12 ft.); *C. Dammeri* (E) (prostrate); *C. Franchetii* (E) (7–10 ft.); *C. frigida* (15–20 ft.); *C. Henryana* (10–12 ft.); *C. horizontalis* (E) (2–4 ft.); *C. microphylla* (E) (2–3 ft.); *C. microphylla var. thymifolia* (E) (9–12 in.); C. *multiflora* (10–12 ft.); *C. rotundifolia* (4–8 ft.); *C. salicifolia* (E) (6 ft.). (E) denotes evergreen.

Cotula.—Hardy little trailing perennials with attractive, fern-like foliage and tiny yellow composite flowers in summer. They thrive in sun or shade and in gritty loam in the chinks of a paved garden. *Culture.*—Propagate by means of division of roots in March or October. *C. dioica* and *C. squalida* are the best known.

Cotyledon (Pennywort).—Dwarf-growing rock plants which thrive in sun or shade in dry, gritty loam, and sand, and which flower in June. They may be propagated by means of seed sown under glass as soon as ripe or in March, by division of roots in spring, or by cuttings that have been dried in the sun for a few days before they are set in the soil. This is to dry up some of the sap in the succulent stems. *See also* Echeveria.

Crassula.—This plant grows to a height of from 6 to 20 inches, and carries red, rose, or white flowers in summer or winter, according to species. The crassula grows well in a compost of two-thirds sandy loam and one-third crushed brick and old mortar-rubble. *Culture.*—Pot up in August or September. Keep fairly dry in winter (Temp. 45° F. Winter, to 65° F. Summer). Water carefully, and keep the foliage dry while growing. These plants bloom well for several years. Propagate by means of cuttings in sand on a sunny shelf in the house in the summer, or by division in the spring. The cuttings should be dried in the sun for 2 or 3 days before insertion. *C. sarcocaulis* (Red, July–Sept., 12 in.) is a good species. *C. sarcocaulis* is hardy in most parts of the British Isles; no other species is hardy. *C. lactea*, with white starry flowers, in loose terminal racemes, is a decorative plant for the greenhouse.

Cratægus (Thorn).—Hardy deciduous trees or shrubs, useful for hedges, etc. *Culture.*—Plant in October or November in a sunny position and in ordinary soil. Thin-out the branches when overcrowded. To propagate, sow seed when ripe, bud or graft. *See also* Pyracantha. *Species.*—*C. Crus-galli* (White); *C. Oxyacantha fl. albo pl.* (White, Double); *C. o. fl. roseo pl.* (Pink, Double); *C. o. punicea* (Scarlet, Single). All flower in May and grow about 15–25 feet high.

Crinum (Cape Lily).—A half-hardy bulbous plant for the cool greenhouse. *C. Powellii* and its *var. album* will grow outdoors in a sunny, sheltered moist border, in well-drained, deep, and rich sandy loam and peat. *Culture.*—Plant 6 inches deep in March, surrounded with coarse sand and protect with fibre in winter. Do not disturb unless overcrowded. *Pot Culture.*—Pot-up in the spring (triennially), one bulb in each 9 to 10-inch pot in a compost of two parts fibrous loam to one part sandy peat. Propagate by means of offsets in March. *Species and Varieties.*—*C. longifolium* (Pink or White); *C. Moorei* (Pink and White); *C. Powellii* (Rose-red or White). All flower from June to August and grow from 24 to 36 inches in height.

Crocus.—Besides those which bloom in the early spring (usually in February), there are species and hybrids that flower in the autumn and winter. *Culture.*— They like a good light soil to which a little bonemeal has been added, and thrive in sun or shade in a warm rock garden, border, or in pots, and are also useful for naturalizing in grass or for the wild garden. Crocuses are increased by off- sets or by seed, the former being the usual method. Offsets are treated in the same way as old bulbs and will bloom the second year. Seed should be sown in pans of light sandy loam as soon as ripe, being placed in a sheltered situation out-of-doors until late autumn. During heavy rain and cold weather, protect with a cold frame. They may remain in the same pans during summer, but should be lifted in autumn and planted in beds of mellow loam in the re- serve garden, 2 inches apart and 3 inches deep. Here they will form strong bulbs during the third summer, and a few of them may flower, most of them, however, deferring to do so until the fourth spring. Crocuses are very accom- modating in reference to the depth at which they are planted. Plant mature bulbs from 2 to 3 inches deep and 4 inches apart; autumn-flowering species from July to August; spring-flowering species in September or October. Divide and replant every third year. *Pot Culture.*—Plant about seven corms half an inch deep in a 5 to 6-inch pot or pan in autumn, using a compost of good, fairly light, sandy loam and leaf-mould, and keep covered with ashes or fibre in a frame until growth commences, then water and transfer to the cool house. Stand out in the open and keep dry in summer, and re-pot in September. *Species.*—EARLY SPRING FLOWERING—*C. biflorus* (White, veined Violet); *C. chrysanthus* (Orange-yellow and Red); *C. Imperati* (Lilac or Buff and Black); *C. mæsiacus* (Golden Yellow); *C. Sieberi* (Lilac-blue and Gold); *C. Tommasini- anus* (Lavender and Orange), one of the best for naturalizing in grass, as it spreads rapidly; *C. versicolor* (White, feathered Purple); *C. vernus and vars.* (Various). AUTUMN FLOWERING—*C. asturicus* (Purple); *C. byzantinus* (Lavender); *C. ochroleucus* (Yellow); *C. pulchellus* (Lavender-blue and Orange Throat); *C. sativus* (Violet, Mauve and Orange); *C. speciosus* (Violet-blue and Orange); *C. zonatus* (Lilac-pink with Orange Throat). NAMED VARIETIES—*Grandeur*

PLATE 10

POETAZ
VARIETIES OF
NARCISSUS

m a painting by Emily Sartain)

E.SARTAIN

Triomphante (White and Blue); *King of the Whites* (White); *Large Yellow* (Yellow); *L'Unique* (Lilac-pink); *Van Speyk* (Purple, veined White); and *Yellow Hammer* (Yellow). All 3 to 4 inches.

Crucianella stylosa.—A dwarf-growing rock plant, which is sometimes used for filling a gap in the paved garden. It spreads rapidly, grows about 5 inches high, and from May to September carries clusters of small, rose-coloured flowers. A sunny position is desirable, also a gritty loam. *Culture.*—Sow seed under glass as soon as ripe or in March, or propagate by means of division in March or October. This plant must be kept in check, or it will spread overmuch.

Cryophytum crystallinum.—See Mesembryanthemum.

Cryptogramme crispa (Mountain Parsley Fern).—A hardy evergreen fern, growing some 5 inches high and thriving in partial shade or sun and in dry, sandy loam, peat, and leaf-mould. This fern is a very effective plant for more or less shaded positions in the rock garden, though difficult to establish in many gardens. *Culture.*—Plant in April. Propagate by division in April. *See also* Ferns.

Cryptomeria japonica (Japanese Cedar).—Handsome evergreen trees, which thrive in deep sandy loam in a sheltered, sunny situation. *Culture.*—Plant from September to November. No pruning is required. To propagate, sow in March or April or strike cuttings under hand lights in August. The variety *elegans* is an attractive small tree.

Cucurbita (Ornamental Gourds).—Half-hardy climbing plants, including the ordinary Pumpkin, Gourd, and Vegetable Marrow, many of which are very ornamental. Treated in a similar way to ordinary marrows, most will thrive in the open and are very effective if trained up poles. Any catalogue will give a dozen and more good varieties.

Cuphea (Cigar Flower).—Hardy and half-hardy annuals, perennials, and shrubs, all better treated as half-hardy. *Cuphea ignea* (12 inches, with Scarlet, Black, and White flowers) is a half-hardy shrub much grown in the greenhouse. *C. lanceolata* (Red-violet) and *C. ocymoides* or *C. æquipetala* (Purple-violet), both annuals, grow to a height of about 24 inches. The perennial species, if sown early, can be used for bedding plants during the first year. For culture, *see* Annuals, p. 139, *and* Perennials, p. 156. (*Shrubby Species*).—Propagate by cuttings of young wood in bottom heat (70° F.) in spring. Trim the following January, and re-pot, if necessary, in February.

Cupressus (Cypress).—Quick-growing conifers of pyramidal habit. Good specimen trees on lawns and for planting in general. They thrive in sunny, sheltered positions and in almost any soil. *Culture.*—Plant in April or September. No pruning is required, except in the case of hedge plants. They may be propagated by means of cuttings (3 inches long with a "heel"), struck in a frame in August or September; some of the species, however, are best raised from seed in March. *C. macrocarpa* (the Monterey Cypress) thrives near the sea. This makes a good hedge plant. *C. sempervirens* has dark green foliage and grows 50 to 60 feet. There are a number of distinct varieties.

Cyananthus lobatus.—This is a useful little perennial trailing plant of rather tufted habit, which thrives in a shady position in the higher and drier parts of the rock garden and in moist, sandy loam, and peat. Masses of lovely purple-blue, bell-like flowers are borne on 5 to 6-inch stems in June, July, and August. Other species are—*C. Delavayi* (3–4 in.); *C. incanus* (2–3 in.) and *C. microphyllus* (2–3 in.), all being worthy of a place in the rock garden. *Culture.*—Sow seed under glass as soon as ripe or in March, or propagate by means of division in spring or autumn.

Cyathea.—This is a genus comprising stove and greenhouse evergreen tree ferns. The most useful species to associate with palms and flowering plants for conservatory decoration are: *C. dealbata* (New Zealand), *C. excelsa* (Mauritius), *C. insignis* (Jamaica), and *C. medullaris* (New Zealand). A compost of light fibrous loam and peat in equal proportions, with about one-quarter part coarse grit, is a suitable soil.

Cyclamen (Sowbread).—Tuberous-rooted plants, useful alike for rock garden, border, naturalizing in grass, and for greenhouse culture. Of the hardy cyclamen, there are two types, the spring-blooming and autumn-blooming.

Culture.—*Hardy Species.*—Plant in August, 2 inches deep and 2½ inches apart, in a shady position, in light sandy loam mixed with peat or leaf-mould and mortar. Keep moist during the spring and summer and dry in winter. Do not lift from the ground, but protect with fibre in winter and top-dress annually with leaf-mould and rotten manure. Propagate by means of seed in gentle heat in spring, and do not plant the young corms in their permanent positions until of moderate size.

Pot Culture.—(*C. persicum*).—Soak the pot and corm that have been dried-off in water and stand on a shelf in the greenhouse. Pot-up in August, placing one corm in a 5-inch pot in a fresh compost of rich sandy loam and leaf-mould, and keep close for a few days, then give ample air and not too much heat (60° F.). Moist, steady heat, and shade from strong sun are essential. Water moderately when growth begins and increase the supply until the plants bloom, about November with some plants and lasting until March. After flowering, decrease the water supply, dry-off, and keep the roots cool and almost dry until next potting-up. Keep the plants indoors from September to May, and in a cold frame with the pots on their sides from June to August. Only use the same corms for pot-culture for two years in succession.

One-year-old plants give the finest flowers, cyclamen are, therefore, best raised annually from seed.

Propagation.—To propagate, sow thinly in pans in a finely-sieved compost of two-thirds loam and one-third leaf-mould and sand, at any time between early August and late November, and place in a cold frame or on a shelf near the light in the cool greenhouse. Prick-off into pans, then pot-up singly into thumb pots and subsequently into larger pots until, in July, they are in 5 to 6-inch pots, in which they may be flowered. *Species.*—*C. coum* (Purple, Red, and White, Jan.–March, 3 in.); *C. europæum* (Red and White, July–Nov., 3 in.); *C. neapolitanum* (Rose, White and Purple Throat, Aug.–Sept., 6 in.); *C. persicum* (White to Crimson, Nov.–March, 6–10 in.).

Cydonia (Quince).—A hardy deciduous tree which thrives in a sunny position in ordinary soil. Plant in October or November. Propagated by seed, layering, suckers or cuttings in October. *C. oblonga* (Common Quince) has White flowers and is grown for its edible fruits.

Cynoglossum (Hound's Tongue).—Annuals, biennials, and perennials, many of which are now to be found under other generic names. They thrive in rather poor, ordinary soil, and bear deep blue, forget-me-not-like flowers from June to August. *C. nervosum* is one of the few still included under this genus and is worthy of a position in the rock garden. It needs good soil and a fairly sunny position.

Cyperus rotundus (Nut Grass, Galingale).—This is a large genus of grasses or sedges, that thrive in the marsh or water garden. They like a sunny site in marshy bog or soil at the edge of still water, and grow some 2 feet high, flowering in July and August. *Culture.*—Propagate by means of seeds, or by division of roots in March, and plant with up to 6 inches of water above the crowns.

Cypripedium (Lady's Slipper).—A genus of beautiful hardy orchids, which thrive in semi-shade and in a compost of moist, sandy peat, or moist loam and leaf-mould. They make very choice subjects for a sheltered spot in the rock garden, and are easily propagated by means of division of roots in April or September. *C. Reginæ* (20 in.), with pink and white flowers in June and July, is a useful plant for the bog or marsh garden. It is best planted in masses on a moist bank. *Other species.*—*C. humile* (Rose and Purple, May–June, 6 in.); *C. Calceolus* (Brown and Yellow, May and June, 15 in.); *C. japonicum* (Pink, White, Green, June, 6–12 in.); *C. macranthum* (Rosy-purple, May–July, 9–12 in.); *C. montanum* (Brown, Red, White, May–July, 10 in.).

Cystopteris (Bladder Fern).—This is a genus of hardy deciduous ferns, growing from 5 to 20 inches high and thriving in the shade in a compost of dry, sandy loam, leaf-mould, and old mortar-rubble. They make very decorative subjects for the rock garden. *Culture.*—Plant in March or April. Propagate by means of division of roots in March or April, or sow spores under glass in July. *Species.*—*C. alpina*, *C. fragilis* and *C. montana*. *See also* Ferns.

Cytisus (Broom).—A genus of shrubs, mostly hardy and deciduous, which thrive in light ordinary soil, in a dry, sunny position. The species and hybrids *C. Ardoinii* (Deep Yellow), *C. Beanii* (Golden-yellow), *C. kewensis* (Cream), and *C. purpureus* (Rose-purple), flowering in May and June, are all prostrate or trailing in habit, and suitable for the rock garden, or as carpet shrubs in shrub borders. *C. albus* (White) is the Spanish Broom, *C. nigricans* (Yellow, July, 4–5 ft.) and *C. scoparius* (Yellow) is the common broom; the latter has a better variety, however, in *C. s. Andreanus*, which carries ruddy bronze and yellow flowers from May to June, and forms a spreading bush about 6 feet high. *C. præcox* (Sulphur-yellow, April–May, 6 ft.), the purple-flowered hybrid brooms *Dallimorei*, *Donard Seedling* and *Dorothy Walpole* and many other coloured hybrids (May, 5–6 ft.) are the best border subjects, while for pot culture *C. canariensis*, and *C. racemosus* (Yellow, 3–6 ft.) will flower in the house from January to March. There are many other good species and varieties.

Culture.—Cut back all branches by at least a third, and plant in October. Small plants give little trouble. Except when quite young, only trim to keep in shape; pruning must be systematic and regular so that it is not necessary to cut into old wood. Spring-blooming species and varieties should be trimmed and pruned directly after flowering; late-flowering kinds must not be pruned until the following February or March. To propagate, sow in the open in September, take cuttings in March or August and strike in a frame, and grow in pots near the glass until ready for planting-out. Young plants need occasional "stopping-back". The Genista is closely allied to the Cytisus.

Pot Culture.—Pot-up in May, after flowering, using a compost of two parts turfy loam to one part lumpy leaf-mould and coarse sand. Prune hard back after flowering, then keep in the warm and syringe in fine weather. Harden-off and sink the pots in ashes outdoors from May to October, then move into the cool greenhouse. Keep fairly dry until growth starts and then water moderately, and give weekly doses of weak liquid manure as soon as the buds commence to form.

Dabœcia (Irish Heath).—Hardy evergreen shrubs, which thrive in sandy peat and loam with no lime in it. *Culture.*—Plant-out in March or October, and cut-off dead blooms in October. To propagate, strike cuttings in a frame in July or August, layer in September or sow seeds. *Species and Varieties.*—*D. cantabrica* [*syn. D. polifolia*] (Rosy-purple); *D. c. alba* (White); *D. c. atro-purpurea* (Reddish-purple, Dark Foliage); *D. c. bicolor* (Purple and White). They flower from June to September and grow about 1 foot or more in height.

Daffodils (Narcissus Family).—No spring flower is fairer or more graceful than the daffodil or narcissus. Technically speaking, the terms daffodil and narcissus are synonymous, for daffodil is merely the English for narcissus. The word *daffodil* is, however, popularly applied to those types of narcissi with long, trumpet-like coronas, the term *narcissi*, which really includes the whole genus, being reserved for those kinds with short cup-shaped corollas. For cultural details, *see* Narcissus.

Dahlia.—The dahlia is easily grown in ordinary garden soil, and in warm districts can be left in the ground all winter if a heap of ashes or sand is placed over the tubers. It is somewhat tender, however, and it is better to lift it as soon as the plants have died down, and to store the tubers for the winter. The ideal soil is a rich, sandy loam containing sufficient humus to make it retentive of moisture.

Culture.—Dahlias may be multiplied by seeds or by dividing the base of the old stem in April, taking care that an "eye" and a tuber or two are attached to each portion. Another way is to cut off the young shoots at their base and strike them in small pots. *Seed.*—Sow the seeds about 1 inch apart in shallow pans or boxes in March. The soil should be light and sandy with a mixture of leaf-mould. Place the pans on a warm shelf, and in April pot-off either singly or round the edge of 6-inch pots. Place in a cold frame, gradually harden-off, and plant out 2 to 3 feet apart, early in June. When flowering is over, the young tubers are taken up and treated as old tubers. *Cuttings.*—In February, March, or even the first week in April, tubers which have been wintered in a dry place are placed in shallow boxes containing a slightly moist compost of two-thirds finely-sieved loam and one-third leaf-mould and sand, which does not quite cover them, and are set over a hotbed close up to the glass. (Temperature 65° F.). A number of strong shoots soon appear; when these are 3 to 4 inches long, they are taken off and struck round the edges of 4-inch pots, filled with equal parts of sandy loam and leaf-mould. They should be watered, and again placed in the same hotbed, and shaded from the sun. Pot-up singly as soon as

308

Joan Baxter (incurved)   Carefree (reflexed)

PLATE 33   CHRYSANTHEMUMS

Florence Horwood (incurving early)   Ondine (incurving late)   *F. Kyle*

PLATE 34 *Above,* Darwin tulips interplanted with wallflowers to give a most pleasing effect. *Below,* daffodils planted in irregular groups in grass to give a natural appearance.

H. & V.

the cuttings have struck (about three weeks) and transfer to a cold frame. Pot-on as required, harden-off, and plant-out early in June. Others prefer to cut up the tubers and replace either in the soil of the hotbed or singly in pots. To obtain short-jointed, stout, and healthy plants, however, it is desirable that they shall be rooted from cuttings taken off in February and March.

Preparing the Ground and Planting.—In autumn, the beds should be prepared. They should be in an open, but sheltered, position and should catch the morning sun, but must have a little shade in the afternoon. Damp, low-lying situations should be avoided. Dahlias will be best displayed in beds 3 feet wide with alleys between. The beds should be marked by stakes placed at each corner, 4 inches of the surface soil being removed and 4 inches of thoroughly rotted manure and bonemeal at the rate of 3 oz. to the square yard being put in its place. The whole is then dug to a depth of 18 inches or 2 feet, and the manure thoroughly mixed with the soil. Towards the end of May, the soil should be top-dressed with wood ashes, which should then be thoroughly raked in. The three foot beds will receive each a row of plants, and the four to five-foot stakes are firmly fixed at planting time 3, 4 and 5 feet apart, according to the size of the plants, which are planted 4 inches deep, so that the crown is just above the surface. After planting, a good watering should be given, soot being sprinkled around. Syringe every evening in dry weather, and search for slugs, earwigs, and other pests.

After Care.—During June and July, water as often as twice a week in hot, dry weather, and assist the roots by stirring the soil with a fork every two or three weeks. Remove all dead or straggling shoots and keep the plant trim and well staked. A surface mulch of rotted manure, 3 inches deep, will help to keep the roots cool and moist; if this is not applied, weak liquid manure should be given every third or fourth day throughout August and September.

Disbudding.—When dahlias are intended either for exhibition or for highly developed flowers, early in July, when the plants are 18 inches high, pinch-out the top, and thin-out the stems that form after this, to six at the most, and leave only one bud on a shoot. Where a show of colour, or flowers for picking, is required, eight or nine main stems may be left; constant thinning-out of stems is necessary. Flowers for exhibition should be protected both from the sun and rain. As the autumn approaches, examine the shoots tied-up and slacken the raffia or bass where necessary. When the frost turns their foliage brown or black, take up the plants, leaving 6 inches or so of stem attached. Hang the tubers up to dry with the stem downwards for a few days, then plunge them with a little old soil still left on them into a box of ashes, fibre, chaff, or sand, in order to preserve them from damp, frost, and heat.

Varieties.—LARGE AND MEDIUM DECORATIVE TYPES.—*Ballago's Glory* (Red, tipped Gold); *Blaze* (Orange, Scarlet); *Chas. L. Mastick* (Orange-salmon); *Clara Carder* (Rich Pink); *Daily Mail* (Yellow and Orange); *D'Arcy Sainsbury* (White); *Earl Baldwin* (Lilac-rose); *Jersey Beauty* (Salmon-pink); *Liberator* (Velvet-crimson); *Pink Daily Mail*; *Pius XI* (Yellow and White); *Queen Elizabeth* (Yellow); *Thos. A. Edison* (Purple). SMALL DECORATIVE TYPES.—*Baby Fonteneux* (Rose); *Bloodstone* (Crimson); *Catalina* (White and Lavender); *Craig Park Gem* (Scarlet); *G. K. Moltke* (Salmon); *Verity Wadsworth* (Yellow);

Willy Den Ouden (Red and Orange). LARGE AND MEDIUM CACTUS TYPES.—
Boldness (Crimson-scarlet); *Brother Justinus* (Apricot and Yellow); *Miss
Belgium* (Orange); *New Vision* (Pink); *Nagel's Bijou* (Salmon-orange); *Pink
Spiral* (Pink and Yellow); *Royal Velvet* (Crimson); *Skua* (Rose-pink); *Trent*
(Scarlet); *Yellow Miss Belgium* (Yellow). SMALL CACTUS TYPES.—*Andries
Orange*; *Baby Royal* (Salmon-pink); *Barrie* (Red); *Kennet* (*Crimson*); *Little
Fawn* (Fawn and Pink); *Market Glory* (Lilac and Rose); *Mia* (Mulberry Red);
Peaceful (Pink); *Snow Queen* (White); *Tip* (Yellow); *Spencer's Darling* (Pink
and Yellow). CHARM AND PÆONY-FLOWERED TYPES.—*Bishop of Llandaff*
(Scarlet, dark foliage); *Dorothy Russell* (Scarlet); *Lemon Beauty* (Yellow);
Morning Glow (Orange, Scarlet); *Mabel Smith* (Fawn); *Norah Bell* (Pink and
Yellow). BEDDING TYPES, NOT HIGHER THAN 2 FEET.—(S) *Coltness Gem* (Scar-
let); *Maureen Creighton* (Red); *Park Beauty* (Orange); *Mrs. M. Hoyle* (Crim-
son); (S) *Mrs. W. Clarke* (Rose and Gold); (S) *Princess Marie-Jose* (Pale Pink);
(S) *Shirley Yellow*; *Windermere* (Rose and Yellow). SMALL POMPON TYPE.—
Little Beeswing (Scarlet and Gold); *Raider* (Yellow); *Apiary* (Crimson); *Doria*
(Ruby); *Johnnie* (Maroon); *Jill* (Orange); *Mrs. J. Telfer* (White); *Tunis* (Scarlet);
Muriel Ann (Pink). LARGE POMPON TYPE.—*Pride of Berlin* (Violet); *Jean Lister*
(White); *J. Van Citters* (Crimson and Gold); *Yellow Prince* (Yellow); *Nerissa*
(Rosy Pink). DOUBLE SHOW AND FANCY TYPE.—*Bonney Blue* (Violet); *W. H.
Williams* (Scarlet); *David Johnson* (Salmon); *Duke of Fife* (Cardinal Red);
Gloire de Lyon (White); *Marjorie* (Fawn and Yellow.) SINGLE COLLARETTE
TYPE.—*Admiral* (Crimson with White collar); *Bonfire* (Scarlet with White
collar); *Canopus* (Yellow self); *Glenmore* (Carmine tipped Straw); *Meg. Nichol*
(Lavender self); *Ooty* (Scarlet tipped Gold); *Radiance* (Scarlet self); *Swallow*
(White self). All bloom from July to October, and grow from 18 to 72 inches
in height.

(S)=single.

Daphne.—Dwarf-growing deciduous and evergreen shrubs, remarkable for
their fragrant, waxy flowers, and for their bright red *poisonous* berries. They
thrive in a sunny sheltered position and in well-drained deep, sandy loam and
peat. *Culture.*—Plant in March or October. No pruning is necessary. Propagate by layering in August, grafting in May, or seeds. *D. Mezereum* (Purple,
Rose and White, 2–4 ft.), which is usually propagated by means of seed, is the
best known of the hardy deciduous species. It thrives in ordinary garden loam,
but needs shade from the hot sun. If trimming is necessary, it should be done
in April. For the rock garden none are better than *D. alpina* (White, May, 1½ ft.),
D. Blagayana (Ivory, May, ½ ft.), and *D. Cneorum* (Purple-pink, May–Aug., 1 ft.).
They thrive in partial shade in sandy loam and peat or leaf-mould. *D. pontica*,
with greenish-yellow flowers in April and May, will grow quite well under the
drip of trees. *D. petræa*, syn. *rupestris* and one or two others are lime-lovers.

Greenhouse Culture.—*D. odora* (Pink, 2 ft.); and *D. odora alba* (White), often
but wrongly named *D. indica* in gardens, are too tender for the open air, except
in the south-west. In the cool house (Temp. 45° F. in winter to 65° F. in summer) they may be had in flower in December. Pot-up in April, using 5 to 7-inch
pots and a compost of peaty loam and sand. Plunge the pots in a cool, shady
position out of doors from May to September, syringe daily in fine weather,

310

and keep just moist. Move into the house in September and gradually give more heat. Treatment as advised for *Forcing*, p. 253, will bring the blooms out by December. Propagate by means of cuttings under glass from April to July.

Datura (Thorn Apple).—Half-hardy annuals and shrubs, succeeding in the sun in any light rich soil, preferably fibrous loam, sand, and a little good manure. *Culture.*—Sow seed thinly in March in the cool house, pot-up singly in 4-inch pots when fit to handle, harden-off, and plant out 24 inches apart in June. If preferred sow in the open in April or May, and thin out when fit to handle. The shrubs are propagated by cuttings in spring, and are only suitable for large greenhouses. Brugmansia (the shrubby species, known as the Trumpet Flower), an evergreen half-hardy shrub bearing white or scarlet flowers in May and June or August and September, thrives in a compost of turfy loam, peat or leaf-mould, coarse sand and well-rotted manure. After blooming stand in the open until the end of September. Water sparingly in winter. Prune in closely into the main stem in March, syringe and re-pot if necessary as soon as the young shoots appear. Summer temperature 60° F., winter 50° F. *Shrubby Species.*—*D. sanguinea* (Red); *D. suaveolens* (White); *D. s. var. Knightii* (Double White). *Annual Species.*—*D. ceratocaula* (White and Purple); *D. chlorantha fl. pl.* (Golden-yellow [Double], May and June, 36 in.); *D. fastuosa* (Purple Outside, White Within, July–Sept., 30 in.).

Davidia (Chinese Dove Tree).—Hardy deciduous trees, which thrive in a sunny position and in moist, deep loam. *Culture.*—Plant in October or November. No pruning is necessary. Propagate by means of seeds and by layering. *Species.*—*D. involucrata* and *D. Vilmoriniana*, both have large white floral bracts and reach a height of from 40 to 60 feet.

Delphinium (Larkspur).—A large genus of hardy annuals, biennials and perennials, which like a sunny site and a deep, highly enriched and well-drained friable loam, and need ample water in hot, dry weather. If flower stalks are cut down as soon as they have bloomed, a second crop of bloom will be obtained in early autumn. *Culture.*—All kinds may be raised from seeds sown under glass from March to May, or in July or August, though the annuals and many of the perennials do well if sown in the open and transplanted when large enough. The perennials may also be increased by means of division of the roots in March, April, or October, or by means of cuttings of young shoots 3 to 4 inches long struck in spring in a frame. *Pot Culture.*—Pot-up in October or November, in 5 to 6-inch pots, and winter well up near the glass in a cool house. *D. Gayanum* and *D. consolida*, the annual larkspurs (which see), belong to this genus. *Species.*—PERENNIALS—*D. cardinale* (Scarlet); *D. cashmerianum* (Purple-blue); *D. nudicaule* (Orange-scarlet); *D. tanguticum* (Blue and White); *D. sulphureum* (Sulphur-yellow). All flower from June to August, and grow from 24 to 60 inches in height. For named varieties, *see* growers' catalogues.

Desfontainea spinosa.—These evergreen shrubs are almost hardy in England, and thrive in warm, sheltered borders, or in pots in the greenhouse, in a well-drained compost of equal parts of loam and peat with a little sand added. They grow to a height of 10 feet and flower from July to September. *Culture.*—Plant in spring or autumn. Propagate by means of cuttings in slight heat in spring.

311

Desmodium (Tick Trefoil and Telegraph Plant).—Hardy perennials and shrubs, also greenhouse deciduous shrubs. The former thrive in sunny sheltered borders and in ordinary soil, the latter in the cool greenhouse. For culture, *see* Perennials, p. 156. *Greenhouse Shrubs.*—Pot-up in March in a compost of sandy loam and peat and keep in the cool greenhouse (Temp. 45° F. in winter to 65° F. in summer). Water well in summer and keep moist only in winter. Propagate by means of cuttings in a frame or from seed. *Species.—D. gyrans* [Telegraph Plant] (Greenhouse) and *D. tiliæfolium* (Lilac [hardy] July–Oct., 3–4 ft.).

Deutzia.—Hardy deciduous flowering shrubs, which thrive in a sheltered, partially shaded position and in rich, well-drained ordinary soil in the shrubbery, or in the greenhouse. *Culture.*—Plant in October or November, mulch annually after flowering, also thin-out well and cut away weak and old wood. To propagate, strike cuttings of soft wood in June in a frame with bottom heat. *Pot Culture.*—Pot up from September to November, in rich, sandy loam, using as small a pot as convenient. Keep cool, but frost-proof, then in December or January move into the greenhouse and gradually raise the temperature to 65° F. As soon as the buds form, water with weak manure water, or dress with artificial manure once a week until the colour of the flowers is visible. Deutzias are well adapted for forcing, but should be exempted from this process every alternate year. *Species and Varieties.—D. discolor grandiflora* (Pink); *D. d. major* (White); *D. gracilis* (White); *D. longifolia Veitchii* (Rose-purple); *D. magnifica* (Double White); *D. scabra* (syn. *crenata*) *fl. pl.* (Double Pink); *D. Vilmorinæ* (White); and *D. Wilsonii* (Tall White). All flower from May to June, and grow from 3 to 6 feet in height.

Dianthus.—A beautiful and extensive genus, which embraces the Carnation, Picotee, Pink, and Sweet-william. These are all dealt with separately under their common names.

Dicentra (Dielytra or Bleeding Heart).—Hardy perennials, which thrive in a sheltered, sunny site and in a light, dry soil with ample leaf-mould in it. They produce masses of fern-like foliage, above which rise long, tapering stems, from which hang the most charming little heart-shaped flowers of exquisite colour. Although hardy, it is safer to winter them in a cold frame. These plants are often forced in the greenhouse in late winter. *Pot Culture.*—Pot-up in September in well-manured sandy loam, stand in the cold frame, plunged in ashes and keep just moist, until November, then move into the greenhouse (55° F.). After flowering, continue to water until the leaves die down, and stand in the open from May to September. Dicentras require ample moisture and, when making full growth, the pots may be stood in saucers of water. Propagate by division in April or September, and plant-out during those months. In the open, the flowers are borne from May to July. *Species.—D. Cucullaria* (White, 5 in.); *D. eximia* (Purple, 15 in.); *D. formosa* (Red, 9 in.); *D. spectabilis* (Red or White, 24 in.).

Dicksonia.—A genus of stove and greenhouse ferns of easy culture in a moist, heated greenhouse. The best-known and most useful species for conservatory decoration are two tree ferns: *D. antarctica* (Australia) and *D. squarrosa* (New Zealand). As a potting compost use equal proportions of light, fibrous loam and peat, adding to this about one-fourth part coarse grit. *See also* Ferns.

Dictamnus (Burning Bush, Dittany, or Fraxinella).—Hardy perennials, suitable for sunny or semi-shaded borders and dry, light soil. For culture, *see* Perennials, p. 156. *Species.—D. albus* (White) and *D. albus var. purpureus* (Purple-red). Both flower from June to August, and grow about 30 inches in height.

Diervilla (Bush Honeysuckle or Weigela).—Hardy deciduous shrubs, which thrive in sun or semi-shade and in almost any soil, though moist, fibrous loam and leaf-mould suits them best. *Culture.*—Plant in October or November, and after flowering cut out old and straggly wood. To propagate, strike cuttings of soft wood in June in a frame, or matured cuttings in the open in October. *D. rosea* will flower in March in the cool greenhouse. Pot-up annually in October, using 8 to 12-inch pots, and a compost of two parts sandy loam to one part of leaf-mould and rotten manure. Plant-out in June after flowering, and don't re-pot for at least two seasons. Prune as above. *Species and Varieties.—D. amabilis* (Pale Rose, April–May, 6 ft.); *D. Abel Carrière* (Carmine-red, April–May, 5 ft.); *Conquete* (Deep Rose, 5 ft.); *D. Eva Rathke* (Crimson-purple, May–Sept., 3–4 ft.); *D. florida* (Deep Rose, 5–6 ft.); *D. f. candida* (White); and *D. f. foliis purpureis* (Purple Foliage).

Digitalis (Foxglove).—Handsome biennials and hardy perennials, that thrive in the shade and in almost any fairly rich soil. For culture, *see* Biennials, p. 141, *and* Perennials, p. 156. *Species.—D. ambigua* (Yellow spotted, 2 ft.); *D. ferruginea* (Wine coloured, 3–4 ft.); *D. lanata* (White, 2 ft.); *D. lutea* (Pale Yellow, 2 ft.); *D. purpurea* (White, Purple, 3–4 ft.). All flower from June to September, and grow from 10 to 50 inches high.

Dimorphotheca aurantiaca (Cape Daisy or Star of the Veldt).—A beautiful half-hardy annual, that grows to a height of about 12 inches and bears a profusion of orange-yellow marigold-like flowers with a black disc in the centre, from July to September. There are also several hybrid varieties arising from *D. aurantiaca* and *D. pluvialis*, the latter bearing white flowers on foot-high stalks, the petals being dark maroon below. These hybrids are salmon, pale yellow, and rosy-cream in colour. They like a sunny position and a light soil, and are extremely useful subjects for inclusion in the rock garden. *Culture.*—Sow seed thinly in May in a sunny position and in light soil, or sow in March under glass, ¼-inch deep in boxes in a compost of sandy loam, and plant out about 6 inches apart early in June.

Dodecatheon.—The American Cowslip, which thrives well in cool, shady borders, or the rock or marsh garden and in rich, deep loam. It carries umbels of small, cyclamen-like flowers on long pedicels at the apex of rigid stems. For culture, *see* Rock Plants, p. 196. *Varieties.—D. Hendersonii* (Rose, May, 9 in.); *D. Jeffreyi* (Purple-rose, June–July, 18 in.); *D. Meadia* (Lilac, Rose, and White, May–June, 12–18 in.).

Doronicum (Leopard's Bane).—Hardy perennials, which thrive in sunny borders and ordinary soil, or under almost any conditions. Cut down the shoots that have flowered, and dress with well-rotted manure to encourage a second crop of bloom. For culture, *see* Perennials, p. 156. *Species.—D. austriacum* (Golden-yellow, April–May, 18 in.); *D. plantagineum excelsum* (Yellow, March–June, 24–36 in.).

313

Dorotheanthus gramineus.—*See* Mesembryanthemum tricolor.

Douglasia (syn. Androsace).—These are very effective dwarf-growing rock plants, which thrive in moist, gritty loam. They grow about 3 inches high and flower in June. They are of rather trailing habit and the foliage feels soft and silky to the touch. *D. laevigata* (Pink) and *D. Vitaliana* (Yellow) are the best species. *Culture.*—Sow seed under glass as soon as ripe or in March, or propagate by means of division of roots in March or September, and plant out in semi-shade.

Downingia elegans and pulchella (Clintonia).—Half-hardy annuals, growing to about 6 inches high and carrying from June to September bright blue flowers with yellow or white eyes. *Culture.*—Sow seed thinly in March in a cool house in sandy loam. Prick off 4 inches apart into boxes, harden off, and in May plant out 6 inches apart in sunny beds and borders.

Draba.—Dwarf-growing rock plants, which thrive in a moderately sunny spot and in well-drained gritty loam. They grow in little bright green rosettes, which form a compact mat that is studded from March to May with tiny flowers. The species *D. Aizoon* is also worthy of cultivation in the Alpine House. *Culture.*—Sow seed under glass as soon as ripe, or in March or April, or propagate by means of division of roots in April. No protection is necessary in winter. *Species.*—*D. Aizoon* (Bright Yellow); *D. Dedeana* (White); *D. pyrenaica* (Pale Mauve-pink). All flower from March to May, and grow to about 3 inches in height.

Dracocephalum (Dragon's Head).—Hardy perennials useful for cool shady borders, or rock gardens with light soil. For culture, *see* Perennials, p. 156. *Species.*—*D. grandiflorum* (Blue, 15 in.); *D. Isabellæ* (Blue, 8 in.); *D. Ruyschianum* (Purple, 15 in.). All flower from July to August.

Drosera (Sundew or Youthwort).—Curious dwarf-growing plants, which thrive in a warm, sheltered position in the bog or wild garden. They grow some 3 inches high and flower about midsummer. Propagate by means of seed or by means of root cuttings in March. *Species.*—*D. intermedia* (White); *D. longifolia* (Red and White); and *D. rotundifolia* (Pink and White).

Dryas (Mountain Avens).—Evergreen trailing hardy perennials, which like sun or partial shade and a cool, gritty loam with lime and leaf-mould in it. They grow about 3 inches high, flower in the summer, and are excellent subjects for carpeting and for planting on ledges in the rock garden, for they are lovely in winter as well as in summer. *Culture.*—Sow seed under glass as soon as ripe, or in April, or take cuttings 2 inches long and strike in sandy soil in March or September. Plant out in permanent position in spring or early autumn. They require no protection in winter. *D. octopetala*, which in June and July has large, white, strawberry-like flowers on stems 3 inches high, is the best known.

Other good species are *D. Drummondii* with golden-yellow flowers in June and July, and *D. Suendermannii*, with creamy-white flowers in July and August.

Dryopteris (*Nephrodium*) (Male fern, Buckler fern).—*See* Ferns, p. 216.

Eccremocarpus scaber.—A half-hardy climber, which thrives in any well-drained light loam against south walls, trellises, and pillars, and is also useful as a greenhouse climber. *Culture.*—Propagate by means of cuttings in a frame in autumn, or sow in heat in January; plant-out in April. After flowering cut

314

away dead wood, and protect the roots in winter. *Species.*—*E. scaber* (Orange-red); *E. scaber, var. roseus* (Rosy-red). Both flower from July to September, and grow to a height of about 10 to 20 feet.

Echeveria.—Half-hardy dwarf-growing, rosette-shaped plants, which thrive in warm, sunny sheltered positions, but which must be brought indoors in October. The red and yellow flowers are borne on short stems. *Culture.*—Pot-up in March in 4 to 5-inch pots in a compost of loam and mortar-rubble. Propagate by means of offsets or leaf-cuttings in summer. *See* also Cotyledon.

Echinacea.—Hardy perennials, which thrive in sunny borders and well-drained, light loam. They reach a height of about 3 feet, and flower in August and September. *E. purpurea* (Reddish-purple) is the best species. For culture, *see* Perennials, p. 156.

Echinops (Globe Thistle).—Hardy perennials, that thrive in the sun and in light loam, but do not like being disturbed. For culture, *see* Perennials, p. 156. *Species.*—*E. bannaticus* (Blue, July–Sept., 36–60 in.); *E. exaltatus* (White, July–Aug., 60–70 in.); and *E. Ritro* (Blue, 50–60 in.).

Edelweiss.—*See* Leontopodium.

Edraianthus.—*See* Wahlenbergia.

Elæagnus (Oleaster or Wild Olive).—Hardy evergreen and deciduous shrubs, which grow freely in full sun and in almost any soil. *Culture.*—Plant in March, or from September to November, and cut-out old wood when required. To propagate, strike cuttings of matured wood in October in a frame, or layer. *Species and Varieties.*—*E. argentea* (6–12 ft.); **E. glabra* (15–20 ft.); *E. multiflora* (6–10 ft.); *E. orientalis* (10–18 ft.); **E. pungens* (10–15 ft.); **E. p. aureo-variegata* and *E. umbellata* (12–18 ft.). **Evergreen.

Emilia flammea [syn. **Cacalia coccinea**] (Tassel Flower).—A hardy annual, which likes a light soil, with plenty of leaf-mould in it. In summer and autumn, it bears orange-red, daisy-like flowers on stems 18 inches high. For culture, *see* Annuals, p. 139.

Enkianthus.—Beautiful flowering shrubs, which thrive in a sunny, sheltered position and moist peat or non-calcareous, sandy loam and leaf-mould. *Culture.*—Plant in October or November; no pruning is necessary. To propagate, sow seeds or strike cuttings of mature shoots in a frame in October. *Species.*—*E. campanulatus* (Cream, Yellow, and Red, May, 4–8 ft.); *E. japonicus* (White, April, 3–6 ft.).

Epacris (Australian Heath).—Heath-like winter-flowering evergreen shrubs, that thrive in the cool greenhouse. *Culture.*—Pot-up when growth recommences (about May), using 5-inch pots and a compost of sandy peat. Keep close until established and then stand in a cool greenhouse during the summer months. Water moderately, and give liquid manure while growing, but do not syringe. Cut long shoots well back and thin-out after flowering. Propagate by means of cuttings of young wood with a little bottom heat in spring, or sow seed in pots of sandy peat during March.

Epilobium (The Willow Herb).—Hardy perennials, the dwarf-growing species of which are useful for the rock garden, and the marsh or water-garden. They do well in sun or shade and in moist ordinary soil, but prefer a gritty loam with some peat in it. For culture, *see* Perennials, p. 156. *Species.*—*E. angustifolium*

315

(Crimson, July–Aug. 36–40 in.); *E. latifolium* (Pink, July–Aug., 9–12 in.); *E. obcordatum* (Rosy-purple, Aug.–Oct., 3–6 in.); and *E. Dodonæi* (Rose-pink), June–Aug., 24–36 in.).

Epimedium (Barrenwort).—Dwarf-growing perennials, which thrive in sun or shade in the rock garden in sandy loam with a little peat. *Culture.*—Propagate by means of division of roots in August. Plant out in permanent position in spring or early autumn. No protection is necessary in winter. *Species.*—*E. alpinum* (Yellow and Crimson, April–June, 9 in.); *E. grandiflorum var. violaceum* (Large Violet, April–May, 8–12 in.); *E. Perralderianum* (Bright Yellow, May, 12–14 in.); *E. rubrum* (Red, April–May, 10–12 in.); *E. Youngianum var. niveum* (White, April–May, 6–8 in.).

Eranthis (Winter Aconite).—Dwarf early-flowering perennials with buttercup-like flowers of deep yellow, which open from January to March. They make quite a pretty show if planted in a shady corner, on the rock garden or along the fringe of a shrubbery in well-drained, moist sandy loam and leaf-mould. *Culture.*—Plant in October, 2 inches apart and 2 inches deep. Do not lift from the ground. Propagate by means of division in October. *Species.*—*E. cilicica* (Yellow with a Brownish Tinge); *E. hyemalis* (Yellow with a Greenish Tinge); and *E. Tubergeniana*, a hybrid.

Eremurus (Fox-tail Lily, Giant Asphodel, or King's Spear).—Tall hardy perennials, which thrive in sunny, sheltered borders in rich loam. For culture, *see* Perennials, p. 156. *Species.*—*E. Bungei* (Golden-yellow, June–July, 20–40 in.); *E. Elwesianus* (Soft Rose, June, 50–60 in.); and *E. robustus* (Pink, June, 60–120 in.).

Erica.—An important genus of hardy and greenhouse evergreen flowering shrubs, often known as Heath or Heather, and comprising several hundred species and varieties, many of them flowering when other blooms are scarce.

Culture.—(*Hardy Species*)—Plant in October in a sunny position and in well-drained sand and peat, or in any light garden loam without lime in it (except *E. carnea*, which do not mind lime). Do not prune, but keep in shape by removing dead blooms from the spring-flowering species in June, from the summer and autumn-bloomers in March, and from winter-flowerers in April. To propagate, strike cuttings of half-matured wood in July or August in a frame, sow seed in a frame in March, divide the roots, or layer in autumn.

Culture.—(*Greenhouse Species*)—Propagate by means of cuttings of tender tops of young shoots in March or April, or in September (Temp. 50° F.), in well-drained pots or pans, filled with sandy peat moistened and firmly pressed down. Pot-up into 2-inch pots as soon as rooted. Keep in a close frame for ten days, then gradually give more air, and when they have made a few inches of growth "stop-back" to make "bushy" plants. Re-pot in September into 5-inch pots and transfer to a light, airy position. Repot into 6-inch pots, if need be, in March, and summer on a hard bed of ashes in a cold frame in full sun. Mature plants should be potted-up in September, in 6 to 7-inch pots, in a compost of sandy loam and peat in equal proportions, and should be stood in the cold greenhouse. Trim after flowering. The winter-flowering kinds should be turned out into the frames after hardening-off in April; the summer-flowering species in July, when they have finished blooming. In the cool house *E. gracilis*

316

Pompons   Coltness, Mrs. Wm. Clarke

PLATE 35   DAHLIAS

Cactus, Altmark   Cactus, Paul Pfitzer

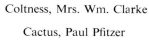

R. & G. Cuthbert

Daily Mail   Cactus, Snow Queen

PLATE 36   DAHLIAS

Ballegos' Glory   Collarette   *R. & G. Cuthbe*

(Red-purple) flowers in November and December, and *E. hyemalis* (Purple-pink) from December to February. In selecting plants it is of the utmost importance to choose healthy, dwarf-growing robust specimens. *See also* Calluna. *Hardy Species.*—*E. alpina* (White, Apl.–June, 6–9 ft.); *E. arborea* (White, Feb.–May, 15 ft. or more); *E. australis* (Rose-red, March–May, 3–6 ft.); *E. a. Mr. Robert* (White); *E. carnea* (Carmine-crimson and White, Nov.–April, ½–1 ft.); *E. cinerea* (Purple, Sept., ¾ ft.); *E. c. alba* (White, Sept., ¾ ft.); *E. c. pallida* (Very Pale Pink, Sept., ¾ ft.); *E. darleyensis* (Rosy-red, Nov.–Apl., 1–1½ ft.); *E. lusitanica* (White, Jan.–April, 6–10 ft.); *E. mediterranea* (Lilac-rose, March–May, 3–4 ft.); *E. m. alba* (White, March–May, 2 ft.); *E. tetralix* (Pink, May and June, 1 ft.); *E. t. alba* (White); *E. vagans* (Rosy-purple, July–Oct., 1–1½ ft.); and *E. Veitchii* (White, Feb.–Apl., 6–10 ft.).

Erigeron (Fleabane).—These are aster-like plants. The species grown are hardy perennials, which thrive in sunny borders or in the rock garden and in ordinary soil. For culture, *see* Perennials, p. 156. *Species and Varieties.*—*E. B. Ladhams* (Orange-rose, May–Sept., 30 in.); *E. Pink Pearl* (Pink, June–Aug., 18–30 in.); *E. Quakeress* (Pale Lilac, July–Sept., 30 in.); *E. alpinus* (Purple, July, 10 in.); *E. aurantiacus* (Orange, July–Aug., 6–12 in.).

Erinacea pungens [syn. Anthyllis Erinacea] (Hedgehog Broom).—This beautiful little shrub, which in April carries pale purple-blue, pea-shaped flowers on spiny, almost leafless bushes, is of the Broom family and native of Spain. It loves a hot, dry situation.

Erinus (Summer Starwort).—A hardy evergreen rock garden or wall plant, thriving in sun or shade and in sandy loam and old mortar rubble.

For culture, *see* Rock Plants, p. 196. *Species.*—*E. alpinus* (Lilac-rose and white); *E. a. carmineus* (Carmine). All flower from May to July, and grow about 4 inches high.

Eritrichium.—Beautiful hardy alpines, that grow best in sheltered, semi-shaded positions, in a cool compost of gritty loam, leaf-mould, peat, and sand mixed with broken limestone and sandstone. Propagation is by means of division in April, or by seed. They need protection from frost and moisture in winter. *E. nanum* is a dazzling sky-blue flower with a yellow centre and woolly, silvery-grey leaves arranged in a tuft—like a pincushion. It should be grown in the alpine house, and great care must be taken not to water overhead in winter. The flowers are borne on 2-inch stems in May.

Erodium (Heron's Bill).—Partly hardy and partly half-hardy perennials, which do well in sandy loam in dry, warm, sheltered situations in the rock garden. In many species, the fern-like leaves are silvery and fragrant and add greatly to the interest of the plant. *E. amanum* (White, May–July, 6 in.); *E. chrysan-thum* (Yellow, June–Aug., 5 in.); and *E. petræum* (White, June–Aug., 3 in.) are valuable as subjects for culture in the Alpine House, *see* p. 197. *Culture.*— Sow seed under glass as soon as ripe or in March, take cuttings in July and strike in sandy soil in a frame, or propagate by means of division of roots in April, and plant out in permanent position. *Other Species.*—*E. chamædryoides* (White, veined Pink, May–Sept., 3 in.); *E. hybridum* (Pale Crimson-purple, May–Sept., 10–20 in.); *E. macradenum* (White, tinged Rose, blotched Violet, June–July, 6 in.).

Eryngium (Sea Holly).—Tall hardy perennials, which like a dry, sandy soil and a sunny position in a warm border. For culture, *see* Perennials, p. 156. *Species.*—*E. amethystinum* (Metallic Blue, June–Aug., 24 in.); *E. Bourgatii* (Bluish, June–Aug., 18–24 in.); *E. giganteum* (Bluish, July–Sept., 30–40 in.); and *E. planum* (Blue, July–Aug., 24 in.).

Erysimum (Fairy Wallflower, Hedge Mustard).—Hardy annuals, biennials and perennials, excellent for sunny borders and rock gardens. They should be grown in gritty and sandy loam. For culture, *see* Annuals, p. 139, Biennials, p. 141, *and* Perennials, p. 156. *Species.*—*E. Perofskianum* (Yellow and Orange, July–Oct., 12–18 in.); *E. linifolium* (Lavender, May–Sept., 6 in.); *E. pumilum* (Yellow, June–July, 3–6 in.); and *E. rupestre* (Sulphur, June, 9 in.).

Erythræa scilloides.—This is perhaps the best of the dwarf-growing centaurys and is worthy of inclusion in the paved garden. It likes a sunny site and a gritty loam, and grows about 3 inches high. The rose-coloured flowers are borne in summer over dense little clumps of glistening green leaves. Seed should be sown under glass as soon as ripe or in March.

Erythronium.—A genus of extremely lovely little bulbous plants which does well in any light soil, and is useful as an edging to borders or in the rock garden. *Culture.*—Plant 4 to 6 inches deep and 4 inches apart in partial shade in September in moist well-drained sandy loam and ample leaf-mould. Surround the tubers with about an inch of silver sand and do not lift more often than necessary, but mulch annually with well-rotted manure and leaf-mould. Propagate by means of seed in a frame in August. Thin-out, but do not plant the seedlings out until the third September after sowing. The plants are also increased by offsets. *Pot Culture.*—Plant in August in 5 to 6-inch pots, using a compost of loam, peat and leaf-mould, and keep in a cold frame during the winter, giving but little water until February. Then increase the supply and take into the cold greenhouse. *Species and Varieties.*—*E. citrinum* (Yellow); *E. dens-canis* [Dog's Tooth Violet] Rose); *E. revolutum* (Pink); *E. Hartwegii* (Creamy-white). All flower from April to May, and grow about 10 inches in height.

Escallonia (Chilian Gum Box).—Half-hardy evergreen (except *E. Philippiana*, which is deciduous and hardy) shrubs, which succeed in sheltered situations and in well-drained soil. They flower during June and the succeeding months. The height varies from 6 to 10 or 12 feet. *Culture.*—Plant in October and November or in March and April. Cut-out old wood, shorten lateral shoots after flowering (August), and trim to shape. The autumn-flowering species should not be pruned until the following March. To propagate, strike cuttings of half-matured shoots in July or August in a frame. *Species and hybrids.*—*E. floribunda* (White); *E. Donard Brilliant* (Dark Red); *E. Donard Seedling* (Flesh-pink); *E. edinensis* (Rosy-pink); *E. langleyensis* (Rosy-carmine); *E. macrantha* (Rosy-crimson); *E. Philippiana* (White); and *E. rubra* (Deep Red).

Eschscholzia (Californian Poppy).—Hardy annuals, which thrive in hot, sunny beds or in the rock garden (dwarfs) in poor, light soil. *Culture.*—Sow seed thinly in the open from March to June or in the autumn, and thin-out to 9–12 inches apart when fit to handle. The autumn-sown plants bloom in the early summer. *Species.*—*E. cæspitosa* (Yellow, May–Oct., 9 in.); *E. californica* (Orange and Yellow, Red, etc., May–Oct., 18 in.).

318

Eucalyptus (Gum Tree).—Half-hardy evergreen trees, which with one or two exceptions, namely, *E. Gunnii*, *E. Gunnii*, var. *Whittinghamensis* and *E. urnigera*, can be grown outside only in mild localities. They thrive in the cool greenhouse in a compost of two parts of fibrous loam to one part of leaf-mould and charcoal. *Culture.*—Pot-up in March, using 6 to 8-inch pots; plant outdoors in a sunny position from June to September. To propagate, sow in gentle heat (60° F.) in early spring, or strike cuttings of mature shoots under glass in June.

Eucomis punctata (Pineapple Flower and King's Flower).—An ornamental half-hardy bulb from South Africa, with curious spikes of flowers. It grows about 24 inches high, and flowers in the open during the summer. *Culture.*—Plant in September in sunny, sheltered beds, 2½ inches deep and 10 inches apart, in well-drained, sandy loam. Protect with fibre in winter. Pot-up in March for greenhouse culture.

Eucryphia glutinosa.—An evergreen shrub from Chili. It produces beautiful white flowers in late summer. Plant out of doors in sunny, sheltered positions and in well-drained, light loamy or peaty soils. *Culture.*—Plant out about mid-April. If grown as a pot plant, in the greenhouse, it should be given a compost of two-thirds fibrous loam, and one-third leaf-mould, together with a sprinkling of sand and, if possible, a little peat. To propagate, sow seeds when ripe, or increase by means of layering.

Eulalia (Zebra-striped Grass).—Hardy perennial grass, suitable for borders and cool greenhouses. It thrives in ordinary soil, and is propagated by means of division in March or April.

Euonymus (Spindle Tree).—Deciduous and evergreen shrubs and small trees, which like a sunny position and good loam. *Culture.*—Plant the evergreen kinds in April or September and October; and the deciduous kinds from November to March. No pruning is necessary, except to shape the bushes. Propagate in autumn by means of cuttings from previous summer's growth or by seeds. *Species and Varieties.*—*E. alatus* [syn. *amurensis*] (D.), (Scarlet Leaves, Autumn, 6–9 ft.); *E. europæus* (Pink Fruit, Autumn, 10–25 ft.); *E. e. atropurpureus* (Purple Foliage, 6 ft.); *E. japonicus* (E.), (Deep Glossy-green Foliage, 6–10 ft.); *E. j. argenteo-marginatus* (Silver-edged Leaves); *E. j. aureo-pictus* (Golden Foliage); and *E. j. ovatus aureus* (Golden Foliage). *E. radicans* is a useful low-growing evergreen to plant in poor soil and beneath trees. *Note.*—D: deciduous. E: evergreen.

Eupatorium (Hemp Agrimony).—Evergreen greenhouse shrubs and hardy perennials. *Culture.*—(*Shrubs*)—Propagate by means of cuttings in heat in spring. Keep the cuttings warm and near the glass, harden-off, and plant out-doors in the sun in June. Stop-back occasionally until July, and cut old plants well back after flowering. Pot-up in September, using 6 to 8-inch pots and a compost of rich loam with some peat in it, and place in a cool house. (*Perennials*)—Propagate by division of roots in March. *Species.*—*E. cannabinum* (Pink, June–Sept., 48 in.); *E. perfoliatum* (White, June–Sept., 40 in.); *E. purpureum* (Purple, June–Sept., 48–60 in.); *E. ianthinum* (Lilac, Jan.–Feb., 15 in.); *E. petiolare* (White, April–May, 30–40 in.).

Euphorbia (Spurge).—A large genus, including annuals, biennials, and perennials. Many of them are stove and greenhouse plants. The hardy peren-

319

nials are the only ones that interest us here. *E. epithymoides*, 15 inches high with yellow blooms; *E. Myrsinites*, 6 inches, with glaucous foliage and yellow flowers; and *E. portlandica*, 9 inches, are subjects for ledges in the rock garden and like a well-drained, gritty loam and full sun. *E. palustris* (Marsh Spurge), 3 feet, may be grown in the drier parts of the bog or marsh garden. *Culture.*—Sow seed under glass as soon as ripe or in March, take cuttings in July and strike in sandy soil under glass, or propagate by means of division of roots in April or September.

Eurya japonica.—A half-hardy evergreen plant with handsome foliage, which thrives in the cool greenhouse or in warm, sunny sheltered situations out of doors. It requires a soil of sandy peat and loam. Pot-up in March, and water well until after flowering, then decrease the quantity. Propagation is carried out by means of cuttings of half-matured wood struck in heat in summer.

Eustoma Russellianum (Lisianthus Russellianus).—A handsome biennial with purple flowers in July and August. *Culture.*—Sow in a cool greenhouse in the middle of May. Prick out when fit to handle, pot-up singly into 3 to 4-inch pots in September, and winter under glass (50° F. to 55° F.). The following March, re-pot into 6-inch pots, using a compost of loam and leaf-mould, sufficient sand to keep the whole porous, and a little charcoal. Water in moderation, and grow on for greenhouse use, or plant out in a sunny position in the open when coming into flower.

Evening Primrose.—*See* Œnothera.

Everlasting Pea.—*See* Lathyrus latifolius.

Exochorda (Pearl Bush).—Hardy deciduous shrubs, closely allied to the spiræas. They thrive in sunny, sheltered positions and in rich loam. *E. grandiflora* (White, May–June, 5–10 ft.) is the best species. *Culture.*—Plant in October or November, and cut-back straggling shoots after flowering. To propagate, in late summer strike cuttings of half ripe shoots in a close frame.

Fabiana (False Heath).—These are half-hardy evergreen, summer-flowering shrubs, suitable for outdoor culture in sandy loam with some peat in it in warm, sheltered situations. In northern counties, it should be grown only in the cool greenhouse. *Pot Culture.*—After flowering, cut-back weak and straggling stems, pot-up, and summer in the open on a bed of hard ashes. Return to the house in September. Water liberally in spring and summer. Propagate in April or May by means of cuttings of young shoots in a warm frame, or sow in heat in March. *F. imbricata* (3–6 ft.) has white flowers.

Fagus (Beech).—This well-known tree thrives in chalk soils and is a good tree for woodland planting. *Culture.*—Plant in October or November. No pruning is necessary. Propagation of the varieties is usually carried out in March by means of grafting on the common beech. *Species and Varieties.*—*F. sylvatica var. aureo variegatus* (Golden Beech); *F. sylvatica* (Common Beech); *F. s. cuprea* (Copper Beech); *F. s. heterophylla* (Fern-leaved Beech); *F. s. pendula* (Weeping Beech); *F. s. purpurea* (Purple Beech).

Fatsia japonica (Japanese Aralia).—An evergreen shrub on the borderland of hardiness, which thrives well in sheltered town gardens and in the cool house. Only in good loam in warm, sheltered positions will it grow out of doors. This plant will grow 12 feet high and carries cream-white flowers in October and

320

November. *Culture.*—Plant in March or April, or pot-up in March, using a compost of two parts of loam to one part of leaf-mould and sand. Water well, syringing in spring and summer, and shade from the sun. To propagate, sow seed when ripe in heat (70° F.), insert 2-inch pieces of stem in sandy soil in a propagator in spring or September, or increase by "ringing". *F. Sieboldii* is synonymous.

Ferns.—*See* Chapter 25.

Ficus elastica (India-rubber Plant).—Greenhouse or room plants, that thrive in the shade in a compost of 2 parts of sandy loam to 1 part of peat (Temp. 50° F. in winter to 65° F. in summer). Pot-up in March, using 6 to 8-inch pots; these should be as small as possible in proportion to the size of the plant. Sponge the leaves when dusty, and water well and syringe overhead, daily, in fine weather in spring and summer, but not too freely in autumn and winter. Propagation is carried out by means of cuttings in a propagating case in March, or by "ringing" in the case of leggy plants. The variety *variegata* has attractive foliage.

Filipendula (Meadowsweet).—Perennial herbs once included under Spiræa, useful for planting in the hardy border, also for moist places. *Species.*—*F. camtschatica* (*Spiræa camtschatica*) (White, 8 ft.); *F. hexapetala* (*Spiræa Filipendula*) [Dropwort] (White, 3 ft.); *var. flore-pleno* has double flowers; *F. palmata* (*Spiræa palmata*) (Pink, 3 ft.); *F. rubra* (*Spiræa lobata*) (Peach blossom Pink, 4 ft.); *F. Ulmaria* (*Spiræa Ulmaria*) [Meadowsweet] (White, 3 ft.).

Forget-me-Not.—*See* Myosotis.

Forsythia (Golden Bell Tree).—Hardy deciduous shrubs, thriving in ordinary soil and in sunny positions. *Culture.*—Plant from October to November, and cut well back after flowering. To propagate, strike cuttings of soft wood in a frame in June or July and layer. *F. suspensa Sieboldii* looks well when grown against a wall or over pergolas and arbours, and *F. spectabilis* is useful for the cold greenhouse. Pot-up from October to December, using an 8 to 10-inch pot and a compost of two parts of loam to one part of leaf-mould and sand; sink the pot in ashes outdoors from May to December, then take into the cold greenhouse. *Species and Varieties.*—*F. x. intermedia vars. densiflora* and *spectabilis* and *F. suspensa* and *viridissima* (Golden-yellow, March and April, 6–10 ft.).

Fothergilla.—Hardy deciduous shrubs, which like a moist, sandy loam and peat. They grow some 3 to 6 feet high and flower from April to June. *Culture.*—Plant from October to March. Propagate by means of cuttings in late summer, by layering in autumn, or sow in heat in spring. *Species.*—*F. major* and *F. monticola*, both white.

Francoa ramosa (Bridal Wreath).—A graceful cool greenhouse plant with small white or rosy-red flowers in late summer. *Culture.*—Sow in March with slight bottom heat (55° F.), or propagate by means of cuttings under glass in June. Pot-up from February to March, using 6 to 8-inch pots and a compost of sandy loam and leaf-mould. Keep the seedlings in a cool, airy frame during the summer, and then transfer them to the warm greenhouse in autumn. Temperature in summer, 60° F.; winter 45° F. Discard the old plants, and raise a fresh batch annually. *Other Species.*—*F. appendiculata* and *F. sonchifolia*, with pink flowers spotted with red. They succeed under the same conditions.

Frankenia lævis and **F. pulverulenta** (Sea Heath).—Hardy evergreen plants of dwarf habit, that are useful for the paved or rock garden. They grow from 3 to 6 inches high, and flower from June to August. *Culture.*—Sow seed under glass as soon as ripe or in March, or propagate by means of division of roots in the spring. They like plenty of sun and a gritty loam to which a little peat has been added.

Fraxinus (Ash).—These well-known trees like a sunny position and ordinary soil. *Culture.*—Plant in November. Thin out the branches when overcrowded. To propagate, sow in a frame in autumn. *Species.*—*F. americana* (White Ash) 100 feet; *F. excelsior* (Common Ash) 100 feet; *F. oregona* (Oregon Ash) 80 feet; *F. Ornus* (Manna Ash) 50 feet.

Freesia.—A species of almost hardy bulbous plants suitable for the warm, sunny border or cold greenhouse. *Culture.*—Plant in August, 2 inches apart in light, well-drained soil, protect with fibre in winter, and lift after flowering. *Indoors.*—Pot-up in succession from July to December, 1 inch deep and 2 inches apart, in equal parts of sandy loam, leaf-mould, and rotten manure. Place the pots under a south wall, or in a frame in the case of coloured varieties, until the bulbs begin to grow (about six weeks). Then, if standing in the open, transfer to a cold frame, and in a fortnight place on a shelf near the glass. Thin stakes are necessary for support, and freesias require bi-weekly doses of liquid manure as soon as the buds form. The bulbs will bloom from January to April. After flowering, decrease the water supply and keep dry in a sunny frame from May to July. Shake clear of soil and pot-up each year. They can be increased easily from seed. Sow the seed when ripe, in August or September, in 5-inch pots in well-sieved sandy loam and leaf-mould, and place in a cool frame exposed to the sun's rays. Thin-out to leave five or six plants in each pot. Soak the seed for twenty-four hours before sowing. Freesias do not like transplanting. They may also be propagated by means of offsets in July or August. *Named Varieties.*—*Purity* (White); *Excelsior* (Cream); *La France* (Cream and Mauve); *Lemon King* (Yellow); *Orange King* (Orange-yellow); *Sunset* (Brownish-yellow); *La Charmante* (Rose-apricot); *Rose Beauty* (Rose); *Wisteria* (Mauve).

Fremontia californica.—A handsome semi-evergreen Californian tree. It grows from 15 to 30 feet high, and carries cup-shaped, golden-yellow flowers in summer. Plant in full sun and in a sheltered position. It should be given the protection of a wall in northern gardens.

Fritillaria.—Hardy bulbous plants, which succeed in any garden soil, although a dry, deep, rich (*F. Meleagris* moist), sandy loam gives the most satisfactory results. They are excellent for shady borders, the rock garden, for naturalizing in grass, and (some species) for pots. *Culture.*—Plant in October, 4 inches deep and 7 inches apart (except *F. imperialis*, which should be 10 inches apart), and do not lift from the ground, unless overcrowded; when necessary lift and re-plant immediately. *Pot Culture.*—Plant in the autumn, in 4 to 5-inch pots, in a mixture of loam, peat, leaf-mould, rotten manure, and sand, and give occasional doses of liquid manure when the buds form. Propagate by means of bulbous offsets in October. *Species.*—*F. aurea* (Golden-yellow, 8 in.); *F. citrina* (Yellow-green, 8–12 in.); *F. imperialis* (Red or Orange and Yellow, 30 in.); *F. libanotica*

(Lilac and Yellow, 15 in.); *F. Meleagris* (Purple or White, 10 in.); *F. persica* (Persian Lily) (Violet, 24 in.). All April to May-flowering.

Fuchsia.—Few flowers are more pleasing either in form or colour than the fuchsias. The plants have a grace and beauty peculiar to themselves. They grow in almost any soil, and are excellent for the cold greenhouse or the open border in summer. Turfy loam and leaf-mould in equal proportions, with some broken charcoal, old mortar rubble, and sand, suits them very well. Feeding them with weak manure water of any kind is preferable to mixing manure with the soil, and after they are well rooted, they should never be watered with clear water, but should always have a stimulant. A carefully-shaded house, guarded against the ingress of bees, is the best place for them when in blossom. In such a situation, they will continue to bloom for three months if the seeds are constantly picked off.

Culture.—Sow in heat (70° F.) in the spring, but the more satisfactory way is to take cuttings in spring or autumn. Plants that have been at rest during the winter should be started in February or March and large early-flowering specimens will be produced by cutting down the old plants and re-potting them in good, rich compost. When re-potted keep them in a temperature of 55° F., and syringe overhead daily in fine weather. Insert cuttings taken from these plants in pots filled with two-thirds fibrous loam and one-third leaf-mould, well-rotted manure, and old mortar rubble, and plunge the pots in a bottom heat of 60° F. In three weeks, they may be potted into 3-inch pots, and re-plunged in the same bed, keeping the temperature from 50° to 60° F. As soon as necessary, shift into fresh pots, until they receive their final shift into 6, 9, or 12-inch pots towards the end of June; or into the open about the end of May, if for summer-bedding. The size of the pot must be regulated by the period at which they are wanted to bloom. If in July, a 6 to 9-inch pot will suffice; if in September or October, a 12-inch pot will not be too large. Cuttings can also be taken of semi-matured wood in August. The plants should be kept close up to the glass and will require "stopping" at least six times, and careful training. Never "stop" a plant within two months of the time it is required to bloom. A regular, moist temperature must be maintained, and the foliage should be sprayed in warm weather. During bright sunshine the glass should be slightly shaded, *see* Chapter 31, The Greenhouse.

In July or August, the plants should be stood in a sunny position in the open.

Hardy Fuchsias.—In addition to the many named varieties so often met with in the greenhouse, there are hardy kinds that will thrive out-doors, even through severe winters. A great many that are looked upon as tender can stand a winter in the open if they are covered with 3 or 4 inches of dry cinder ashes at the first approach of frost. The best plan, in exposed positions, is to cut them right down in November and to cover the whole bed with a good coating of ashes or fibre. The ashes should not be removed until the fuchsias begin to shoot in the spring. If the bushes have not been cut down to the ground in winter, the dead ends should be trimmed off in March. Hardy fuchsias make a good show in late summer in mild districts, when several kinds are planted together, the colours being judiciously blended. They are also useful if used to form a hedge, and make effective plants for large rock gardens.

323

Except in the south and west of England, a sheltered position is necessary. They are best planted out in March or April in light, well-drained soil with some leaf-mould in it.

    Species.—(HARDY)—*F. corallina* (Purple and Red); *F. magellanica* (Scarlet); *F. m. globosa* (Violet and Purple); *F. magellanica var. Riccartonii* (Bright Red). (HALF-HARDY)—*F. cordifolia* (Red and Green); *F. corymbiflora* (Scarlet); *F. excorticata* (Purple). All flower from July to September and grow from 5 to 6 feet in height. There are numerous named varieties.

    Funkia.—*See* Hosta.

    Gaillardia (Blanket Flower).—Annuals and perennials both kinds being usually treated as half-hardy annuals and biennials. They thrive in any light, rich soil in sunny beds. *Culture.*—ANNUALS—Sow seed thinly, ½ inch deep, from March to June, and thin-out to about 12 inches apart when fit to handle. They may also be treated as half-hardy annuals, i.e. sown in moderate heat in March, in which case they should be pricked out early, hardened-off, and planted out early in June. BIENNIALS—Sow seed in the open in May. *Named Annual Varieties*—*The Bride* (White); *Crimson Glow* (Crimson); *Lorenziana* and *Picta* (Red and Yellow). *Named Perennial* (treated as Biennials, *see above.*) *Varieties.* —*Grandiflora*; *Masterpiece* (Red); *The King*; and *Sunset* (Red and Yellow). All flower from June to October and grow from 12 to 30 inches in height.

    Galanthus (Snowdrop).—Snowdrops thrive in the shade, in well-drained moist, gritty loam, and are excellent for beds, for the rock garden, for growing in pots, or for naturalizing in grass. *Culture.*—Plant in August or September, 3 inches deep and 3 inches apart; lift every fourth year only, and propagate by means of offsets. *Pot Culture.*—Plant 1 inch deep in September or October, using 4 to 5-inch pots and a compost of two parts of ordinary soil to one part of leaf-mould and sand, and keep in a cold frame covered with ashes or fibre until growth commences. Dry-off after flowering. *Species and Varieties.* —(EARLY)—*G. Elwesii* (White, marked Green, Jan., 8 in.); *G. nivalis* (White, Jan., 6 in.); *G. plicatus* (White, Jan., 12 in.). (LATE)—*G. Ikariæ* (White, March– April, 8 in.). (WINTER)—*G. Fosteri* (White, 8 in.).

    Galax aphylla (Fairies' Wand or Carpenter's Leaf).—This is a beautiful little creeping evergreen with white flowers borne in summer on 6-inch-long spikes. It has richly tinted foliage in autumn, and thrives in partial shade in the rock garden and in a mixture of moist sandy loam and leaf-mould, or preferably in peat. It is best propagated by means of division of roots in spring or early autumn.

    Galega (Goat's Rue).—A hardy border perennial, which thrives almost any-where and in any soil. *Culture.*—Sow seed in the open in April, or propagate by means of division in March or October. *Species.*—*G. officinalis* (Lilac-blue, White and Pink, June–Oct., 48 in.); *G. officinalis var. Hartlandii* (Pale Lilac-blue and White), June–Oct., 50 in.).

    Galtonia candicans (Cape Hyacinth).—Tall hardy bulbous plants, flowering in August and September, and loving a sunny border and well-manured, deeply-dug, sandy loam and leaf-mould. *Culture.*—Plant in March or October from 4 to 6 inches deep and 15 inches apart, letting the bulbs rest on sand. If the soil is cold and heavy, the bulbs must be lifted annually. *Pot Culture.*—Place

Hibiscus Trionum

PLATE 37

Helichrysum bracteatum, vars.

Fuchsia

Gloxinia, Modern Strain

Sutton & Sons and Dobbie & Co.

Gaillardia, grandiflora

Godetia, double flowered

PLATE 38

Helenium autumnale

Hollyhock, double

Alexander & Brown and Dobbie & Co.

one bulb ½ inch deep in a 6-inch pot and set in a cold greenhouse. Only grow in a pot for one year, after which plant-out. Propagate by means of seed in the open as soon as ripe, or by offsets in autumn.

Gardenia.—Evergreen flowering shrubs suitable for hothouse or warm greenhouse, and remarkable for their beautiful sweet-scented single or double flowers. The various species bloom at different seasons and so provide bloom over a long period. They require much heat and plenty of water when growing, and thrive in equal parts of peat, loam, and rotten manure with a little charcoal added. *Culture.*—Prune into shape and pot-up in February or March, putting year-old plants into 5 to 6-inch pots; 8-inch pots should be large enough for old specimens. Syringe daily, and give liquid manure when the buds form. Propagate in February or March by means of shoots with a "heel," struck in sandy peat in pots, in a propagating frame with a bottom heat of 70° to 80° F. *Species.*—*G. jasminoides* (Cape Jasmine); *G. j. var. Fortuniana* and *G. Thunbergia.*

Garrya (Californian Garrya).—Hardy evergreen shrubs with yellow or greenish-white flowers from November to March. *Culture.*—Plant in May in ordinary soil and a sunny, sheltered position. In May trim back long shoots a little and cut out dead wood. To propagate, strike cuttings in August in a frame or layer. *Species.*—*G. elliptica* (6–12 ft. or more). Male and female catkins are borne on different bushes.

Gaultheria (Winter Green, Shallon, etc.).—A genus of evergreen shrubs, some of which are hardy and suitable for the woodland or rock garden in lime-free soil. The best of the creeping or dwarf species are *G. nummularioides* with white bell-shaped flowers in August and September; *G. procumbens*; and *G. Veitchiana*, which is somewhat larger. The tiny bell-shaped flowers, white or pink and borne in summer, are quite insignificant. *Culture.*—Plant in April or October in cool, moist ordinary soil, and leaf-mould, in a partially-shaded position. Thin-out old shoots when overcrowded. Propagate by means of seed in heat in March or by division or layering in Oct. *Other Species.*—*G. procumbens* (White and Pink, July-Aug., Creeping); *G. Shallon* (White and Red, May–July, 3–6 ft.).

Gaura.—Hardy perennials, which are best treated as annuals, and which thrive in light, warm, rich soil in sunny borders. They reach a height of 36 inches, and flower from June to Oct. *Culture.*—Sow seed in a frame in February, and plant out in April. *Species.*—*G. Lindheimeri* (White and Red).

Gazania (Treasure Flower).—A showy summer bedding-plant with yellow and bronze flowers from June to October; also useful for cool greenhouse decoration. *Culture.*—Propagate by means of basal cuttings in summer in a cold frame; plant-out in June in a sunny position. Protect from frost in winter. For indoors, pot-up in March in sandy loam and peat. Water moderately while growing, but decrease the quantity of water after flowering until March, the following year. *Species.*—*G. nivea* (White, 6–8 in.); *G. Pavonia* (Orange, 12 in.); *G. rigens* (Golden-yellow, 12 in.) etc.

Genista (Broom).—The genistas, which are closely related to the Cytisus, are hardy flowering shrubs, valuable for the border, shrubbery or rock garden. No plant makes a finer show when in bloom or does better on a dry, sunny bank than *G. hispanica*, the Spanish Broom, with its golden flowers in May and June.

It is a prickly and compact shrub, forming a bush rarely more than 3 feet in height. All the species here recommended have yellow, pea-shaped flowers, which come in clusters at the end of the branches and are borne over a long period, usually in May and June, and in July and August. *Culture.*—Plant in October, in dry, light soil in a sunny position. The early-flowering types should have the old wood thinned-out and should be trimmed into shape directly after flowering; the later bloomers should be cut hard back in February or March. Do not prune *G. ætnensis*, *G. cinerea*, or *G. virgata*, merely keep in shape by means of "stopping" and removing dead blooms. To propagate, sow in a frame when ripe, or strike cuttings of half-matured wood in a frame during August, and grow on in pots until planted-out, as they do not transplant readily from nursery beds. *Species.*—*G. ætnensis* (July–Aug., 10–20 ft.); *G. cinerea* (June–July, 8–10 ft.); *G. dalmatica* (June–July, 4–6 in.); *G. hispanica* (May–June, 1–3 ft.); *G. pilosa* (May–June, 1 ft.); *G. tinctoria fl. pl.* [Double] (July–Aug., 1–2 ft.); *G. virgata* (June–July, 6–12 ft.).

Gentiana.—Many of the gentians are beautiful and desirable little rock plants, that seem to hold a special lure for the rock garden lover. They vary from the most minute foliaged of plants to large dock-like specimens, and in every case carry erect and charmingly coloured cup-shaped flowers in all shades of blue and white. Most of them, save, say, *G. acaulis*, *G. asclepiadea*, *G. Kurroo* and *G. septemfida*, are none too easy to grow. At least, most of them will grow, but so many are shy flowerers, as, for instance, *G. bavarica*, *G. ciliata*, and *G. imbricata*. The gentians need great care and as much approximation to alpine conditions as possible. In town gardens their cultivation is almost impossible. A moist, but well-drained, gritty, peaty loam and leaf-mould, to which has been added a fair amount of old mortar rubble, suits them well. Ample moisture is essential through the summer and most species do best in partial shade. For culture, *see* Rock Plants, p. 196. The gentians are impatient of root division, and indeed of transplanting. *Species and Varieties.*—*G. acaulis* (Deep Blue, May–June, 2–3 in.); *G. asclepiadea* (Violet, Sept., 12–14 in.); *G. Farreri* (Pale Blue, Sept.–Oct., 4 in.); *G. Freyniana* (Rich Blue, Aug.–Sept., 3–4 in.); *G. lutea* (Yellow, May–June, 24–36 in.); *G. Pneumonanthe* (Violet, Aug., 6–9 in.); *G. septemfida* (Clusters of Soft Blue, July–Aug., 6 in.); *G. sino-ornata* (Dark Blue, Oct.–Nov., 4 in.); *G. verna* (Deep Blue, April–May, 2 in.).

Geranium (Crane's Bill).—Ordinary garden soil, provided it is fairly light and well-drained, suits the hardy geraniums; a sunny, open site is preferable. The dwarf kinds are suitable for the rock garden, and thrive in ordinary gritty soil. An autumnal dressing of granite chips will help them to survive the winter. *Culture.*—Sow in March or August (under glass) or in April in the open, or the plants may be increased by division from October to March. Cuttings of matured side-shoots can also be struck in August in a frame. For half-hardy greenhouse bedding-plants and show varieties, *see* Pelargonium. *Species.*—(HARDY)—*G. armenum* (Red-purple, 18–24 in.); *G. Endressii* (Rose-pink, 15 in.); *G. grandiflorum* (Blue, 18 in.); *G. pratense* (Mauve, Blue or White, 20–30 in.). (DWARFS)—*G. Farreri* (Pink, 6 in.); *G. sanguineum* (Crimson-purple, 9 in.); *G. s. album* (White, 9 in.); *G. s. lancastriense* (Rose and Crimson, 6 in.). All flower from June to September.

326

Geum (Avens).—Hardy perennials, which thrive in sunny borders and in almost any well-drained, light, rich soil; the rock garden species love a deep, gritty loam, and *G. reptans* and *G. rivale* require plenty of moisture. *Culture.*— Sow seed in the open in April, or propagate by means of division in March or October, and plant out in permanent position. *Species and Varieties.*—*G. Borisii* (Orange-scarlet); *G. Lady Stratheden* (Double, Golden-yellow); *G. montanum* (Yellow); *G. Mrs. Bradshaw* (Bright Red); *G. Orangeman* (Orange); *G. reptans* (Golden-yellow); *G. rivale* [Leonard's] (Crimson-pink). All flower from April to October and grow from 6 to 24 inches in height.

Gilia (Ipomopsis).—Hardy annuals and half-hardy biennials, which thrive in ordinary soil in warm, sunny borders. *Culture.*—(ANNUALS)—Sow seed thinly, ¼ inch deep, from March to May, and thin out to 3 inches apart when fit to handle. In light, warm soils, a September sowing may be made. (BIENNIALS) (also known as Ipomopsis)—Sow seed under glass in June, grow on in pots, and plant-out the following May. They require the protection of a slightly heated frame in winter. *Species.*—(ANNUALS)—*G. densiflora* (Lilac-pink, 12 in.); *G. micrantha, var. aurea* (Yellow, 5 in.); *G. tricolor* (Pale Purple, White and Yellow, 10–20 in.). (BIENNIALS)—*G. aggregata* and *G. coronopifolia* (Crimson-scarlet, 24–48 in.). June to October flowering.

Ginkgo biloba (Maidenhair Tree).—A hardy deciduous tree, thriving in deep loam in a sheltered position. *Culture.*—Plant in October or November. No pruning is required. Propagate in March by means of seed in a frame. A good town tree, upright in growth, ultimately 60 feet or more high. Native of China.

Gladiolus (Sword Lily and Corn Flag).—Gladioli are divided into two sections, namely, the early-flowering (blooming from June to July) and the late-flowering (blooming in August and September). They like a deep, well-dug, firm loam, and a warm spot well exposed to the sun and sheltered from cutting winds.

Culture.—Line the hole or pocket in which the bulbs are to rest with a little coarse sand. Plant in March or April, 4 inches deep and 4 to 6 inches apart, in rows 15 to 20 inches apart. Each flower spike will need staking securely. If seed is not an object, the first flower stems should be cut down, when many of the bulbs will throw up a second flower-stem. The bulbs are taken up in October or November and stored. Prepare for planting in the following March or April by rubbing off the old roots and soil adhering at the bottom of the bulbs, and save the debris.

Propagation.—Examine this debris, and thousands of little scaly-looking rubbish will be found, which are young gladioli bulblets. Draw a drill 2 to 3 inches deep on a bit of rich soil in the reserve garden, and sow the bulblets thinly in March. Keep moist, and some of these will flower late in autumn if allowed to do so, many the second year, and all the third year. These young bulblets require exactly the same treatment as the old ones. Gladioli may also be raised from seed in May in a cold frame. If, however, it is desired that all the young plants shall come "true to type", propagation must be effected by offsets.

Pot Culture.—Place one corm, 3 inches deep, in a 6-inch pot, in a compost of 2 parts sandy loam to 1 part of leaf-mould and rotten manure and ample sharp sand, in October or November; cover with fibre till growth starts, and keep in a

327

frame until March. Then put in a light, airy position in a cold greenhouse to bloom. Water well while growing, and give weak liquid manure as soon as the buds begin to form, but discontinue this as soon as the colour shows. Dry-off after flowering, store, and keep dry ïrom May to October. *G. Colvillei* is good for pot culture, and makes a good room plant.

Species.—(EARLY)—*G. bizantinus* (Purple-red, 20 in.); *G. cardinalis* (Scarlet, White Spots, 30 in.); *G. Colvillei* (Purple, White Spots, 18 in.); *G. C. alba* (White, 18 in.). All flower from June to July. (LATE)—*G. brenchleyensis* (Scarlet); *G. gandavensis* (Various); *G. primulinus* [hybrids] (Various); *G. ramosus* (Purple, Rose, and White). All flower from August to September and grow to a height of about 24 inches. Named varieties are innumerable and catalogues should be consulted.

Glaucidium.—These are beautiful herbaceous perennial flowering plants introduced from Japan. They grow to about 24 inches high, and flower at midsummer. They are quite hardy, and thrive best in half shade, woodland conditions, in soil containing plenty of peat and leaf mould. *Species.*—*G. palmatum* (Violet).

Gleditschia triacanthos (Honey Locust).—A North American tree growing up to 60 feet or more high. It thrives in open, sunny positions and in well-drained soils. This tree deserves to be more commonly planted, for it has beautiful fern-like foliage, which turns bright yellow in autumn. Raise from seeds sown in a cold frame.

Globularia (Globe Daisy).—Dwarf-growing perennials, which thrive in the sun and in moist, light loam. They are useful for the paved or rock garden. For culture, *see* Rock Plants, p. 196. *Species.*—*G. cordifolia*; *G. trichosantha*. Both carry blue flowers from May to July, and grow to a height of about 8 inches.

Gloxinia.—Tender tuberous-rooted perennials, which thrive in a fibrous peaty loam mixed with leaf-mould, cow-dung, sharp sand, and charcoal. *Culture.*— Start the tubers in succession from January to April by placing them in a box in a 2-inch layer of the above compost (Temperature 60° F.). Keep just moist, and as soon as from 2 to 3 inches of growth has been made, plant one tuber in each 4-inch pot in the above-mentioned compost, so that the tops of the tubers are just above the soil level. Maintain the same heat and moisture, shade from the sun, and water liberally when well rooted. Pot-up into 5-inch pots as soon as potbound, and again into 6-inch pots when the buds are forming. As soon as the buds open, lower the temperature and give less moisture. After flowering, dry-off gradually, and store the tubers in peat or coconut fibre. Propagate at the end of January by means of seed in a compost of peat, sand, and fine rich loam, thinly covered with coarse sand only, and exposed to a bottom heat of about 70° F. Prick-off 1 inch apart as soon as possible, and gradually reduce the temperature to 60° F. As soon as large enough, pot-up singly into 4-inch pots, and place near the glass. Maintain the temperature, and keep moist, but do not let moisture touch the leaves. Pot-up by stages, until the flowering pots (5 to 7 inches) are reached. As soon as the buds mature, give a weekly dressing of weak liquid manure. Seed may also be sown in a cold house in June. Old tubers, when started in heat in February in boxes of damp fibre, supply shoots from which cuttings may be made; these should be placed in a close propagating frame and subjected to moist and gentle heat. Another method of propagation is by means of leaf-cuttings taken at any time. These should be inserted in the same kind of soil as that prescribed for seed. (*See* Leaf-cuttings, p. 114.) *Varieties.*—*Mauve Queen* (Mauve); *Beacon* (Crimson); *Cyclops* (Rose-scarlet and White); *Pink Beauty* (Pink). All flower from June to October, and grow about 12 inches in height.

Godetia.—Hardy annuals, useful for summer-bedding. (*See* Œnothera.) For culture, *see* Annuals, p. 139. *Named Varieties.*—*Duchess of Albany* (White); *Apple Blossom* (Pink); *Lady Albemarle* (Crimson); *Duke of York* (Red and White); *New Lavender* (Mauve); and *Azalea-flowered* (Various). All flower from June to October, and grow from 6 to 24 inches in height.

Golden Rod.—*See* Solidago.

Gomphrena globosa (Globe Amaranth).—Half-hardy annuals, which thrive in the cool house (Temp. 45° F. winter to 65° F. summer) in a compost of sandy loam, leaf-mould, and rotten cow-manure. *Culture.*—Sow seed in pots in March (Temp. 70° F.), and transplant 1 inch apart as soon as they can be handled. Move on singly into 5-inch pots by June, and place near the glass to flower.

Grammanthes.—Dwarf-growing, succulent, half-hardy annuals, growing from 4 to 6 inches high, and flowering from July to September. They do best in the sun and in light, sandy soil, and are valuable for growing in warm, sheltered portions of the rock garden. *Culture.*—Sow seed thinly as soon as ripe or in spring under glass in a cool house, prick-off into boxes when fit to handle, harden-off gradually, and plant out 4 inches apart in June. *G. dichotoma* (*gentianoides*) (Yellow) is the best-known species.

Grevillea robusta (Silk-bark Oak).—A graceful shrubby evergreen plant. It is generally grown in the greenhouse or living-room. To propagate, sow seed in a frame with gentle bottom heat in March, or take cuttings of half-ripened shoots in summer and strike under hand-lights. *Pot Culture.*—Pot-up every 2 to 3 years in March, using 5 to 8-inch pots and a compost of fibrous loam and coarse sand. Temp. 50° F. in winter to 65° F. in summer. Ventilate freely, but avoid draught.

Gunnera.—Hardy perennial foliage plants, which thrive in rich soil and sheltered, shady positions. They are valuable for margins of lakes, and for shrubberies. The crowns require slight protection in winter. See Perennials, p. 156. *G. chilensis* (Crimson fruit, Aug., 5 ft.) is the best. *G. manicata* has leaf stalks with red hairs.

Gypsophila (Chalk Plant, or Gauze Flower).—Hardy annuals and perennials, which thrive in dry, well-limed loam, in sunny borders or the rock garden. The rock garden species like the addition of coarse grit to the soil. *Culture.*— (ANNUALS)—Sow seed thinly from March to June, or in September, in a well-drained border, and thin out to from 3 to 6 inches apart when 1 inch high. (PERENNIALS)—Sow seed in heat in March, or in the open in April; propagate by division in March or October; or by means of cuttings (double varieties) in the spring. Plant out in permanent position in October and November or in March and April. *Species*—(ANNUALS)—*G. elegans* (White [large], 18 in.); *G. muralis* (Pink, 6 in.); (PERENNIALS)—*G. cerastioides* (White, Veined Red, 3 in.);

G. paniculata (White [Single and Double], 30 in.); *G. repens* (White and Pink, 4–6 in.). All May to September-flowering.

Haberlea.—Hardy perennials suitable for a shady spot in the rock garden. For a compost they need moist peat, leaf-mould, and sand. For culture, *see* Rock Plants, p. 196. *H. rhodopensis* (Lilac, May–July, 6 in.) is a favourite.

Habranthus pratensis. *See* Hippeastrum pratense.

Habranthus texanus [syn. *Zephyranthus texana*].—(Yellow flowers from May–Sept., 6–12 in.). Culture *see* Zephyranthus.

Halesia (Silver Bell or Snowdrop Tree).—Hardy deciduous summer-flowering trees or shrubs (8–30 ft.) which thrive in well-drained, moist, sandy loam in a sunny, sheltered position. *Culture.*—Plant in October and November; thin-out branches when overcrowded. To propagate, sow in a frame in March, or take cuttings in October. *H. corymbosa*, *H. hispida* and *H. carolina* are the best-known species. (The proper names of the first two species are *Pterostyrax corymbosa* and *P. hispida*.) All carry white flowers in May.

Halimium.—Small shrubs at one time united with *Helianthemum*, from which they differ by their short straight style. *Species.*—*H. halimifolium* (Yellow with dark spots, 3–4 ft.); *H. lasianthum* (Yellow with Purple spots—3 ft.); *H. Libanotis* (White, 18 in.); *H. ocymoides* (Yellow, Purple base, 2 ft.). For culture see *Helianthemum.*

Hamamelis (Witch Hazel).—Small deciduous flowering trees or shrubs, which thrive in sunny positions and in moist, but well-drained loam with peat and leaf-mould in it. They are suitable subjects for planting in a sheltered shrub border. *Culture.*—Plant October to November. Just thin-out and trim the branches in April when overcrowded. To propagate, sow seed when ripe in a frame, layer in late summer, or graft. *Species.*—*H. japonica* (Yellow, Jan.–Feb., 8–15 ft.); *H. j. arborea* (Yellow, Jan.–Feb., 15–20 ft.); *H. j. Zuccariniana* (Pale Yellow, Dec.–Feb., 3–6 ft.); *H. mollis* (Golden-yellow, Dec.–Feb., 8–10 ft.).

Hebe (Veronica).—Shrubs, chiefly native to New Zealand, formerly united with *Veronica*. They can be grown outside in mild climate. The dwarf species are suitable for the rock garden. *H. Andersonii* (Purple or Blue, July, 2 ft.); *H. Autumn Glory* (Deep Violet, Sept., 1½ ft.); *H. buxifolia* (White, June–Aug., 2 ft.); *H. cupressoides* (Pale Purple, July, 2 ft.); *H. Hectori* (Pale Lilac, July, 1 ft.); *H. speciosa* and *vars.* (Rose, Purple, Blue, July–Sept., 3–4 ft.); *H. Traversii* (White, 5–6 ft.).

Hebenstretia comosa.—A half-hardy perennial, growing about 18 inches high, with fragrant, semi-double, orange-red and white flowers from July to September. *Culture.*—Sow seed thinly in March under glass in a cool house, or in April in the open. Plant out 12 inches apart in June.

Hedera (Ivy).—There are many kinds of this well-known climber. The common sorts thrive against walls and in ordinary rich soil; the variegated kinds prefer walls facing south or west, and like ample lime in the soil. *Culture.*—Strike cuttings in autumn in sandy soil in a shady border, or layer. Plant-out in showery weather between the following October and April. When established, old leaves and untidy shoots need clipping hard back in April. *Species and Varieties.*—*H. Cænwoodiana* (Small Green Leaf); *H. colichica var. dentata* (Large Green Leaves); *H. Helix* (Common Ivy); *H. H. var. angularis aurea*

(Yellow); *H. H. argentea variegata* (Large Leaves, Margined White); *H. H. hibernica* (Irish Ivy. Very useful under trees); *H. H. Lee's Silver* (Small Silver Variegated Leaves); *H. H. minima* (Small Triangular Leaves); *H. H. purpurea* (Bronze Leaves in Winter). The tree or shrubby ivy *H. H. var. arborescens* is the adult or flowering stage of the Common Ivy, a useful evergreen shrub to plant under trees; in open positions it produces clusters of black fruits.

Hedysarum.—A genus of hardy biennials, perennials, and shrubs, useful for borders and the rock garden. They thrive in the sun and in ordinary soil. *Culture.*—(BIENNIALS)—Sow seed in the open in May. Shelter or place in a frame during winter, and plant out in flowering position in April or October. (PERENNIALS)—Sow seed in the open in April, or propagate by means of division (some species) in March; other species, by means of cuttings or layering in the autumn. Plant out in permanent position in March. *Species.*—(BIENNIALS)—*H. coronarium* (Scarlet, June–Sept., 36 in.). (PERENNIALS)—*H. capitatum* (Rose, Summer, 24 in.); *H. microcalyx* (Purple, June–July, 20 in.); *H. obscurum* (Purple-red, June–Aug., 6 in.); *H. utahense* (Rosy-purple [Grey Foliage], April–May, 6 in.). (SHRUB)—*H. multijugum* (Purple-red, June–Sept., 36–72 in.).

Helenium (Sneezeweed).—Hardy perennials, which thrive in sunny borders and in rich, ordinary, well-drained soil. For culture, *see* Perennials, p. 156. *Species and Varieties.*—*H. autumnael* (Yellow, July–Oct. 48 in.); *H. autumnale var. pumilum* (Yellow, June–Oct., 12–24 in.); *H.a. var. Riverton Beauty* (Yellow, [Chocolate Centre], Aug.–Oct., 36–60 in.); *H. a. var. Riverton Gem* (Red [Shot Gold] Aug.–Oct., 36–60 in.); *H. Hoopesii* (Orange, July–Oct., 30 in.).

Helianthemum (Sun Rose).—These beautiful, brilliant, shrubby evergreens are of trailing habit, and flower in the spring and summer. They make lovely clumps of bluish-green foliage, thickly splashed for two or three months in the year with brightly-coloured flowers very like those of the strawberry. These, unfortunately, fall the day they open, but this defect is made up for by the fact that the buds on the same bush open over a period of two or three months. The flowers of the varieties of *H. nummularium* (*vulgare*) (4–12 in., flowering in June and July), which are single or double, may be had in almost any shade of crimson, scarlet, rose, orange, yellow, or white. Yellow is the prevailing colour of the flowers of the other species. The dwarf-growing kinds, 2 to 12 inches high, love the sun, and do best on dry banks, or on walls or rocky ledges in the rock garden and in sandy soil. *Culture.*—Plant in March or October. "Stop" back long, weak shoots in August. They need no protection in winter. To propagate, sow seed under glass as soon as ripe or in March, or take cuttings in July or August and strike under glass in sandy soil. *See also* Cistus. *Species and Varieties.*—*H. glaucum, var. croceum* (Yellow, May–Sept., 6 in.); *H. nummularium varieties*: *Fireball* (Brick-red); *Rose Queen*; *Rubens* (Orange); *Sudbury Gem* (Crimson); *The Bride* (White); *tigrinum* (Salmon-pink) and *venustum plenum* (Double, Scarlet). There are many other good varieties.

Helianthus (Sunflower).—Hardy annuals and perennials, which grow freely in a sunny site and in any rich, well-dug soil. For culture, *see* Annuals, p. 139, *and* Perennials, p. 156. *Varieties.*—ANNUALS. *Named Varieties of H. annuus*—*Golden Nigger* (Deep Yellow); *Langley Gem* (Primrose, flushed Pink, Double); *Primrose Dame* (Pale Yellow). All flower from July to October.

Named Varieties of H. annuus.—*Apollo* (Gold and Maroon); *Mars* (Golden-red); and *Venus* (Cream, tinged Yellow). PERENNIALS—*H. mollis* (Orange-yellow, Sept.–Oct., 50 in.); *H. decapetalus* (Yellow [single or double], Aug.–Oct., 60–100 in.); *H. orgyalis* (Yellow [Black Centre], Sept.–Oct., 100 in.); *H. rigidus var. Miss Mellish* (Yellow, Sept.–Oct., 100 in.).

Helichrysum ("Everlasting Flowers").—These are mostly half-hardy or hardy perennials or annuals, which thrive in sunny positions and in gritty loam. They are mostly suitable for borders, or as pot plants indoors, while the dwarf species make excellent rock plants. *Culture.*—(ANNUALS)—Sow seed thinly, in February or March, under glass in moderate heat, using a compost of one-half loam, one-quarter leaf-mould, and one-quarter well-decayed stable manure. Prick-out 3 inches apart and harden-off. Transplant in mid-May 9–12 inches apart. Hardy species may be sown in the open in April, being thinned later to 12 inches apart. (PERENNIALS)—Propagate by means of division in the spring, or take cuttings in April and strike in gentle heat. *Species.*—(HALF-HARDY ANNUALS)—*H. bracteatum* and *vars.* (White, Brown, Red, Pink, and Yellow, July–Oct., 36 in.); *H. orientale* (Yellow, July–Oct., 24 in.). (HARDY PERENNIALS) —*H. bellidioides* (White, July–Oct., 5 in.); *H. frigidum* (White [Grey Foliage], July–Oct., 2–3 in.). These are suitable for the Alpine House.

Heliotropium peruvianum (Cherry Pie).—Soft-wooded shrubs, for summer bedding and pot-culture, and succeeding best in light, rich loam and leaf-mould. *Culture.*—Seed sown thinly in spring in moderate heat makes good plants for summer and autumn decoration. Pot-off in April into 4-inch pots, pinch-back when 3–4 inches high, harden-off, and plant-out, about 12 inches apart, in June. The finest plants are obtained from cuttings taken in the same way as advised for verbenas and bedding calceolarias. Take the cuttings in spring or autumn (preferably late August) and strike in boxes in a frame with moderate heat. Syringe in hot weather, and in five or six weeks pot-up into 3 or 4-inch pots and move into the cool house. They are very sensitive to frost, and like an average temperature of 60° F. from October to early June. *Pot Culture.*—Pot-up annually in March, using 6 to 8-inch pots and a compost of two parts loam to one part of leaf-mould and sand. "Stop" back to make bushy, and prune well back in February. As soon as the flower buds form, give bi-weekly dressings of weak liquid manure. Water well while growing, but keep dry during winter. Temperature 45° F. in winter to 60° F. in summer. *Named Varieties.*—*Lord Roberts; Mrs. J. W. Lowther; President Garfield; Swanley Giant; The Speaker;* and *White Lady.* All flower from May to September and grow from 12 to 36 inches in height.

Helipterum.—These half-hardy annuals, which now include the acroclinums and the rhodanthes, are everlastings, valuable alike for greenhouse (rhodanthes) and flower garden. They succeed best in a light, rich soil, and in warm sheltered positions. For culture, *see* Annuals, p. 139. *Pot Culture.*—(*Rhodanthes*). Sow ¾ inch apart in August (50° F.). Place the seedlings near the glass and keep fairly dry at first. Pot as soon as possible into the flowering pots. *Species.*—*H. Manglesii* (Rose and Silver); *H. Manglesii var. maculatum* (Pink, Yellow, or White); *H. roseum* (Rose). All flower from June to October and grow from 12 to 18 inches in height.

Lilium auratum

L. chalcedonicum

PLATE 39 LILIES

L. speciosum magnificum

L. Henryi

Alexander & Brown and Sutton & Sons,

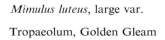
Mimulus luteus, large var.

Linum grandiflora

PLATE 40

Tropaeolum, Golden Gleam

Myosotis syrenaica

Sutton & Sons, Dobbie & Co. and Alexander & Br.

Helleborus.—The various species of this charming genus form one of the garden's greatest assets, for they flower at a time when there is little else. They are hardy perennials which thrive in well-dug, light and moist soil in a border facing preferably east or west or in a cool house. *Culture.*—Propagate by division in February or March, but do not split into clumps of less than 5 to 6 crowns. Plant out 18 inches apart. Top-dress annually after flowering, and in summer and autumn give doses of weak liquid manure. *Pot Culture.*—Sow seed in a frame in March or October, or propagate by root division in July. Pot-up in October, using 6 to 8-inch pots and a compost of 2 parts fibrous loam to 1 part of rotten manure. Water liberally while growing. Select fresh plants annually, planting the old ones out in April or May. Perhaps the finest species are *H. niger* [Christmas Rose] (White, Oct.–April, 6–12 in.) and *H. orientalis* [Lenten Rose] (Jan.–April, 18–24 in.). There are many colour forms of this species. *Named Varieties.*—*Admiration* (White, spotted Red); *Bluebird* (Slaty-blue); *Bronze Beauty*; *Darkness* (Red); *Eastern Queen* (Yellow); *Gertrude Jekyll* (White).

Helonias (Stud Flower).—Hardy herbaceous plants, which thrive in moist, sandy, and peaty loam in semi-shade, and which grow about 15 inches high, and flower in April and May. *Culture.*—Sow in a frame in April, or propagate by means of division in April or October. *Species.*—*H. bullata* [syn. *H. latifolia*] (Pink or Purplish).

Helxine Soleirolii.—This is a creeping plant with pretty green foliage and inconspicuous flowers. It makes an excellent subject for cultivation in the paved or rock garden, and will do in sun or shade in gritty loam, though not quite hardy in the north. Propagation is best effected by means of division of roots in the spring.

Hemerocallis (Day Lily).—Hardy perennials, which do well in moist, light, and deep soil in a shady border or marsh garden. As the name implies, the flowers, once open, last only a day or so, but a succession of bloom extends over two or three months. The flowers are useful for cutting. Propagate by division in April or November. *Species and Varieties.*—*H. aurantiaca* (Apricot-orange); *H. Dumortieri* (Yellow and Red-brown); *H. Gold Dust* (Golden-yellow); *H. Sovereign* (Orange-yellow); *H. fulva var. Kwanso fl. pl.* (Bronze-yellow). There are many new varieties in varying colours from Pale Yellow, Orange Red, Brown and Pinks. (*See* Catalogues.) All flower from May to August and grow from 12 to 36 inches in height.

Hepatica.—*See* Anemone.

Heracleum (Cow Parsnip).—Tall hardy biennials and perennials most suited to the wild or woodland garden or to the shrub border. The biennials are hardly worth growing. *Culture.*—(*Perennials*)—Sow seed in April in the open, or propagate by means of divison of roots in April or October. *Species.*—(BIENNIAL)—*H. asperum* (3 ft.). (PERENNIAL)—*H. Leichtlinii* (6 ft.); *H. persicum* (10 ft.); *H. villosum* [syn. *H. giganteum*] (10 ft.). All carry white flowers; the biennials blooming from May to July, the perennials from June to October.

Herniaria glabra and others are useful little creeping plants for the paved or rock garden. They like a sunny position and gritty loam, and are propagated by means of division in the spring.

333

Heuchera (Alum Root).—Hardy perennials, which do well in warm, rich, and light soil, in a sunny border, where they send up spikes of red and pink flowers like those of the London Pride. The dwarf-growing species are useful for the rock garden. For culture, *see* Perennials, p. 156. *Species and Varieties.—H. brizoides* (Rosy-red); *H. hybrida* (Red to White); *H. sanguinea var. gracillima* (Coral-scarlet). All flower from May to Sept.and grow 20 to 30 inches in height.

Hibiscus (Rose, Shrubby, or Syrian Mallow).—Beautiful hardy and half-hardy plants, suitable for borders and indoor decoration. *Culture.*—Plant the hardy sorts in sandy loam in March in a sheltered position in sun or shade. Do not prune, merely keep in shape by "stopping" and by removing dead blooms after flowering. Propagate by sowing seeds about April, or by cuttings in a frame in September, or by grafting. Those intended for indoor culture require a compost of fibrous peat and rich fine loam with a large proportion of sand; a little charcoal in the soil is often beneficial. Propagate these from seeds sown over gentle heat, or by cuttings struck early in spring in a close frame. *Species.*—(HARDY ANNUALS)—*H. Trionum* (Purple, July–September, 2–4 ft.). (PERENNIAL HERB)—*H. coccineur* (Bright Scarlet, August–October, 4–5 ft.). (HARDY SHRUBS)—*H. syriacus* and *varieties*. [SINGLE] *cæleste* (Light Blue); *Hamabo* (White, Crimson Blotch); *rubis* (Ruby-red); *totus albus* (White). [DOUBLE]—*amplissimus* (Vinous Rose); *Duc de Brabant* (Red); *Jeanne d'Arc* (White and Rose). These all flower from August to October and grow to a height of from 7 to 10 feet. (GREENHOUSE SHRUBS)—*H. Rosa-sinensis* (Rose-red, 10 ft.) many varieties; *H. schizopetalus* (Red, 10 ft.).

Hieracium (Hawkweed).—Hardy perennials, some of the dwarf-growing species of which thrive in ordinary soil in a sunny rock garden or border. For culture, *see* Perennials, p. 156. *Species.—H. alpinum* (Yellow, July, 6 in.); *H. aurantiacum* (Orange, June–Aug., 20 in.).

Hippeastrum (Equestrian Star).—A large genus of bulbous plants, including Amaryllis, Habranthus, etc. (*which see*). Jacobea Lily, now *Sprekelia formosissima*, is usually grown in pots in the warm greenhouse in well-drained, rich and heavy loam, to which bone dust and charcoal have been freely added, but succeeds at the foot of a south wall. *H. pratense* (*Habranthus pratensis*), is suitable for a sunny border, rock garden or pot culture. Plant in October and protect with fibre in winter. *Culture.*—Other Hippeastrums should be planted in February; water well, and give liquid manure when the buds appear; and keep dry after flowering. Re-pot every three or four years, and propagate by offsets treated as old bulbs.

Hippophæ rhamnoides (Sea Buckthorn).—Hardy deciduous shrubs or trees (10–40 ft.), which thrive in moist ordinary soil in open positions (preferably near the sea). *Culture.*—Plant in October or February, and cut back weak shoots in February. Propagate by means of seed in the open, by suckers or layers in autumn, and by root-cuttings in spring. Male and female flowers are borne on separate shrubs.

Holly.—*See* Ilex.

Hollyhock (Althæa rosea).—Though really perennials, these are best treated as biennials. They like a sunny position and a well-drained and deeply worked rich loam. In summer, give a liberal supply of water, and a good mulch of well-rotted manure. A dose of weak liquid manure every ten days should be given as soon as the plants reach a height of $3\frac{1}{2}$ to 4 feet. *Propagation.*—Sow seed thinly in drills 1 in. deep early in May in the open. When about 4 inches high, transplant 8 inches apart in a nursery bed, and plant-out 3 feet apart in October. On cold, heavy soils, it is better to sow in boxes in May or June, pot-up in winter, place in a frame, and plant-out in April. For Staking and Tying, *see* p. 39. *Cuttings.*—As soon as the first flowers of an old plant open sufficiently to judge of the flowering, the superfluous side branches that have no flower buds may be taken off with two or three joints and leaves. Cut the shoot through with a clean cut just under the lower joint, leaving the leaf entire. Cut it also at about 2 inches above the joint—either joint will do, provided it has growing eyes with a leaf and piece of ripened wood to support the bud until roots are formed. These cuttings, planted in a light sandy soil, placed under a hand-glass, and watered occasionally and shaded from the sun, will require little further care. When rooted, pot them off in 60-sized pots, and put them in a cold frame, where they can remain during the winter. In spring, plant them out in the open. The plants can also be increased by division just as the new growth is starting. *Species and Varieties.*—*A. alba superba* (White); *A. delicata* (Cream); *A. Queen of the Yellows* (Yellow); *A. Constance* (Pink); *A. James Vert* (Salmon); *A. Britannia* (Scarlet); *A. Palling Belle* (Silvery-pink); *A. King Albert* (Purple); *A. Black Knight* (Black); *American Fringed* (Various, Semi-double); *A. ficifolia*, the *Fig-leaved hollyhock* (Red, Orange or Yellow, Single or Double). All flower from July to September, and grow from 6 to 10 feet in height.

Holodiscus discolor.—[syn. *Spiræa discolor*]. Shrub, 8–12 ft. For culture, *see* Shrub *Spiræa.*

Honesty.—*See* Lunaria.

Honeysuckle.—*See* Lonicera.

Horminum pyrenaicum (Pyrenean Clary).—A hardy perennial which grows about 10 inches high and bears purple-blue flowers from June to August. It does well in dry ordinary soil in sunny borders or in the rock garden. For culture, *see Perennials*, p. 156.

Hosta (Plantain Lily).—Hardy herbaceous plants, suitable for the border, rock garden, shrubbery, or cold greenhouse. They require rich, well-dug soil, and thrive in sun or shade. *Culture.*—Propagate by means of division in spring or autumn, or pot-up in March. *Species.*—*H. ovata* (Lilac-blue, July–Aug., 12–18 in.); *H. plantaginea* (White, July–Sept., 18 in.); *H. Sieboldiana* (Pale Lilac, July–Aug., 18 in.).

Hottonia palustris (Water Violet).—These beautiful hardy aquatic perennials should be grown in a sunny position and in still water. The showy lilac and yellow flowers, which are borne at water-level, appear in May and June. *Culture.*—Sow seeds in ordinary soil in shallow water in March, or propagate by means of division of roots in April, and plant at the water's edge with from 1 to 3 feet of water above the crowns. *See also* instruction for planting in the chapter on the Water Garden.

Houstonia cærulea.—This is a pretty little evergreen rock plant of creeping habit and is smothered with pale blue, star-shaped flowers in May and June. It only grows about 3 inches high, and thrives on shady ledges in well-drained, moist, sandy loam and peat. Seed may be sown under glass in March, or propagation may be carried out by means of division of roots in September.

Humea (Incense Plant).—A handsome foliage plant, which thrives in rich, sandy loam and leaf-mould in sunny beds or borders, and which may be grown in the cold greenhouse in an 8-inch pot. The best known species is *H. elegans*, a half-hardy biennial. For culture, *see* Biennials, p. 141.

Humulus (Hop).—Hardy annual and perennial climbers, delighting in rich, deep, sandy loam. *H. Lupulus aureus* (Golden Hop), perennial and *H. japonicus variegatus* (Silver Variegated Hop), annual, must have poor soil. For culture, *see* Annuals, p. 139, *and* Perennials, p. 156. Cut the latter down to the ground in late autumn.

Hutchinsia.—Dwarf-growing hardy annuals and herbaceous perennials, which thrive in semi-shade and in cool, sandy, and gritty loam. The best-known species is *H. alpina*, a pretty little plant with evergreen fern-like foliage, that looks well in the paved or rock garden. It grows about 6 inches high, and from June to August bears small white flowers. *Culture.*—Seed may be sown as soon as ripe in March under glass, or propagation may be carried out by means of division of roots in spring or autumn.

Hyacinth (Hyacinthus).—Hyacinths can be divided into two classes; the *early-flowering Roman Hyacinths*, so useful for pot work and for forcing, and the *Dutch Hyacinths*, also good for pot work, and specially suitable for spring-bedding. The best soil for hyacinths is a well-manured, deeply-dug, sandy loam with leaf-mould in it, but they will grow in almost any soil or in coconut fibre, water, or sand. Several of the dwarf species of hyacinth should be employed to obtain early colour in the rock garden. *Hyacinthus azureus*, which grows about 4 inches high and carries beautiful blue flowers in February, is well worth growing. *Culture.*—Plant in a sunny position from September to November, about 4 inches deep, and from 5 to 10 inches apart, according to variety. *Pot Culture.*—To obtain bloom from December to April, plant in succession from August to November. A free, porous soil composed of two parts of turfy loam to one part of well-rotted manure, leaf-mould, and sand, thoroughly incorporated and sieved, is necessary. For three bulbs a 5½-inch pot will be sufficient. *See also* general cultural details in the chapter on Bulbs, p. 170. *Named Varieties.*—(White) *L'Innocence*; (Yellow) *City of Haarlem*; (Pink) *Pink Pearl*; (Red) *La Victoire*; (Blue) *King of the Blues* (dark); (Deep-blue) *Ostara*; (Light Blue) *Myosotis. See also* catalogues.

Hyacinthus candicans.—*See* Galtonia.

Hydrangea.—The common hydrangea—*H. macrophylla*—is a half-hardy summer-flowering deciduous shrub, which thrives in a sheltered position and in well-drained and richly-manured, sandy loam. *H. paniculata* and *var. grandiflora* (Creamy-white) are quite hardy. *Culture.*—The same treatment, both indoors and out, will suit these species, bearing in mind that although *H. paniculata* is quite hardy, *H. macrophylla* is not. The two species also require different treatment as to pruning. *H. macrophylla* should be pruned in summer and should have all weak wood cut out. The stems should be thinned and all dead flower-heads must be cut off. The strong shoots that are left should then be cut back to within 6 or 7 buds of the old wood. *H. paniculata* should be

336

PLATE 11

DUTCH IRIS
WEDGEWOOD

(n a painting by Emily Sartain)

pruned in March; the stems being thinned out to from 6 to 12 to each plant, according to the size of the bush; all remaining shoots should then be cut hard back to within a couple of eyes of the hard wood. Plant in March. *Pot Culture.* —Pot-up from February to March, using from 5 to 12-inch pots and a compost of two parts rich loam and one part of rotten manure and sand. For the cultivation of the blue-flowered Hydrangeas, use peat or leaf-mould instead of loam, as the latter usually contains lime. When grown in small pots, one stem only is encouraged. After flowering, stand in the open until September. *H. macrophylla* is also suitable for forcing in the warm greenhouse, and if transferred from frame or cold house to the warm house as required, a succession of bloom can be had from March to September. Blue flowers may be procured by planting in a lime-free soil and by watering freely with a weak solution of alum; one teaspoonful in one gallon of rain-water, or with 3 oz. of aluminium sulphate in one gallon of water. Both these solutions should stand for at least twelve hours before use. To propagate, strike cuttings of young wood in May, or of strong matured shoots that have not flowered in August; both in a frame. Autumn struck cuttings should be wintered in a frame with an even temperature of 40° F. *H. petiolaris,* also grown in nurseries as *H. scandens,* is a climber which ascends trees, walls or whatever support it has in much the same way as ivy does. The white flowers are borne from May to July. *Named Varieties of H. macrophylla.—Etincelant* (Carmine); *Helge* (Dark Rose); *Krimhild* (Salmon-rose); *Le Cygne* (White); *La Marne* (Mauve); *Mme. Moullière* (White); *Mme. de Vries* (Apple-blossom Pink); *Marie Matthes* (Rose); *Parsival* (Deep Red); *Peer Gynt* (Rose-red); *Rubis* (Red); *Triumph* (Rose-pink). Good varieties for bluing are: *Blue Prince; Goliath; Mme. A. Riverain; Niedersachsen;* and *Vicomte de Vibraye.*

Hymenocallis.—Hardy and half-hardy bulbous plants from 12 to 24 inches high and which carry white or yellow flowers from February to October. They require a light, rich loam. *Culture.*—Plant about 4 inches deep in September, and protect with ashes or fibre in winter. Lift about every fourth year. Propagate by means of bulbils, or seed.

Hypericum (St. John's Wort, Aaron's Beard, or Rose of Sharon).—This genus includes a number of hardy shrubs, evergreen and deciduous, as well as hardy annuals and perennials. The annuals are hardly worth growing, but some of the dwarf-growing perennials and evergreen shrubs make excellent rock or edging plants. Sandy loam and a sunny site suit them best, though the shrubs will thrive in partial shade, and *H. calycinum* is the best dwarf flowering shrub to plant beneath shade of trees. It is also useful for growing in town gardens. For culture, *see* Perennials, p. 156. (*Shrubs*)—Plant in November; cut well back in March. Propagate by means of cuttings in July, and by sowing seeds when ripe. *Species.—*(PERENNIAL)*—H. fragile* (8 in.); *H. gracile* (5 in.); *H. tomentosum* (6–9 in.). (SHRUB)*—H. calycinum* (12–18 in.); *H. Coris* (3 in.); *H. elatum* (48–60 in.); *H. Hookerianum* [syn. *oblongifolium*] (3–5 ft.); *H. Moserianum* (12–18 in.); *H. patulum Henryi* (18–36 in.). All carry yellow flowers from July to August, except *H. tomentosum,* which blooms from August to October.

Iberis (Candytuft).—Hardy annuals and perennials, both of which succeed in any soil with lime in it, but prefer dry, sandy loam and a sunny position. For culture, *see* Annuals, p. 139, *and* Perennials, p. 156. *Species.*—(ANNUAL)—*I. umbellata* (Purple, Crimson, and Pink, July–Oct., 12 in.). (PERENNIALS)—*I. gibraltarica* (Lilac-pink, May–July, 12 in.) [needs warm, sheltered position]; *I. semperflorens* (White, Nov.–April, 8–12 in.); *I. sempervirens* (White, May–June, 6–12 in.).

Ice Plant.—*See Cryophytum* (Mesembryanthemum crystallinum).

Idesia polycarpa.—A hardy, deciduous, flowering tree, which grows from 6 to 10 feet high, and flowers in June or July. It likes a sheltered sunny position and a well-drained, deep ordinary soil. All dead wood should be cut out annually. To propagate, sow seeds in the spring, or take cuttings of half-ripened shoots in late summer.

Ilex (Holly).—Hardy trees and shrubs, which thrive in sun or shade in almost any well-drained soil. Plant in May or September; prune with secateurs in April (hedges in May or August). To propagate, sow in March in shallow drills in the open. The seeds usually take two years to germinate, and many people prefer to strike cuttings of half-matured wood in August, in a cold frame, or to layer in summer.

Impatiens.—Handsome border and greenhouse plants, called also *Noli me tangere.* The common balsam, or *Impatiens Balsamina*, is included in this genus, and under this name the general culture of plants of this class is described. The perennials of this genus are warm greenhouse plants, and require much care in their culture and management. Propagate from seeds sown in gentle heat in spring, or by cuttings struck at that time. *Hardy Annual Species.*—*I. amphorata* (Rosy-pink, July–Sept., 4–5 ft.); *I. Roylei* (Pink and White, July–Sept., 4–5 ft.). *See also* Balsam.

Incarvillea.—Hardy annuals and tuberous-rooted perennials growing from 12 to 36 inches high and flowering from May to August. They thrive in well-drained, rich loam in sunny borders. *Culture.*—Sow in pans in a frame in April, thin, and plant-out in spring or autumn. Seed can be sown in the open early in May. Increase also by division in March or October. *I. Delavayi* (Crimson-pink or Purple, 15 in.) and *I. grandiflora* (Bright Pink, 6 in.) are popular perennial species.

Inula (Fleabane).—Hardy perennials useful for sunny borders or for the wild garden. For culture, *see* Perennials, p. 156. *Species.*—*I. ensifolia* (Yellow, 6–12 in.); *I. grandiflora* (Orange-yellow); *I. Hookeri* (Yellow); *I. Oculis-Christi* (Golden-yellow). All flower from June to August, and grow from 24 to 36 inches in height.

Ionopsidium (Violet Cress).—A plant so called from its violet-like appearance. Only two kinds are grown—*I. acaule*, with white flowers tinged with purple or with lilac flowers, and *I. a. album*, with white flowers. Both are small, not exceeding 3 inches in height, and flowering profusely all summer. These dwarf hardy annuals are reproduced by self-sowing in their growing positions. They should be grown in the shade and in any rich, damp soil. They make pretty little plants for crevices in the rock garden, and are ideal for pans in the Alpine House for early spring.

Ipomœa (Moon Flower, Morning Glory, etc.).—A large genus of half-hardy climbing plants, closely allied to the convolvulus, all requiring a rich, light soil.

Culture.—(ANNUALS)—Sow seed singly in April, in small pots under glass, and plant-out 24 inches apart in May or June against a trellis or sunny wall. It likes a warm, sunny, sheltered position and a rich, well-drained soil. (PERENNIALS)—These are best propagated by means of cuttings of side shoots struck in a frame between March and August. *Species and Varieties.*—*I. Learii* (Blue Dawn Flower). A sub-tropical perennial, herbaceous climber. Flowers Blue turning Purple. (ANNUALS).—*I. purpurea* (Various [Single and Double]); *I. tricolor* (*rubro-cærulea*) (Sky-blue). All flower from June to September and grow 8 to 10 feet high.

Iresine.—Half-hardy ornamental foliage plants, suitable for warm, sunny, and sheltered beds or for pot culture indoors. They grow about 18 inches high and thrive in ordinary soil. *Culture.*—Strike cuttings of young shoots in a frame in late summer or in spring. Plant out in June, 8 inches apart, or pot-up in March, using 5 to 8-inch pots and a mixture of peat, loam, leaf-mould, and sand.

Iris.—A genus of hardy plants, usually divided into two sections—namely the bulbous and the non-bulbous or rhizomatous-rooted. To the latter class belong the Flags or Bearded Irises, the Kæmpferi or Japanese group, and the Sibirica Irises; to the bulbous class belong the English, Dutch, and Spanish Irises. The Dutch Iris comes into flower about the middle of May. It is followed in June by the Spanish, and later in June comes the English Iris. The Tall Bearded Iris (4 feet) flowers in June, the Medium Bearded (2 feet)) bloom in May, while earlier still we have the Dwarf Bearded Iris. The Bearded Irises love a moist, cool soil, but will grow in any ordinary border, if it is mulched and well manured. They resent disturbance. The cultivation of irises is simple, the plants succeeding in a sunny position in any light, rich garden soil, though sandy loam with 50 per cent. peat or leaf-mould is most suitable for the bulbous species. The English Iris needs a heavier and cooler soil than the Dutch and Spanish species, and it is necessary to lift bulbs of the last two triennially, rest them for a few months, and then re-plant. For the Tall Bearded Iris the soil should be deeply dug, well manured, and should have some old mortar-rubble incorporated; it will, however, as said above, grow in almost any well-drained soil. The Japanese Irises love marshy land, require a position in full sun, and should occasionally be transplanted and divided in August after blooming. The three following types also belong to the rhizomatous group:—the *Evansia* section, in which are included *I. cristata* (Lavender, May, 6 in.); *I. lacustris* (Blue, June, 4 in.); and *I. tectorum* (Purple-blue, June, 9 in.). They are easily grown in a light, well-drained soil, and in a sunny and open position. The other types are the *Oncocyclus*, or Cushion Irises, and the *Regelia Irises*. Plant in November in a sunny site in a raised and well-drained bed of light gritty loam. As soon as the flowers have faded, a frame should be set over the bed to ripen off the bulbs.

Culture.—(BULBOUS-ROOTED)—Plant 3 to 4 inches deep in September or October, with a little sand round the bulbs (Spanish, 4 inches; Dutch, 5 inches; and English, 6 inches apart). Most spring and autumn-flowering species require to be lifted from the ground in August; summer-flowering kinds should be lifted every third year, in October, after the plants have died down. English irises should be left undisturbed: the Dutch irises need just the same treatment as the

Spanish. *Pot Culture.*—Many of the bulbous irises make good pot plants; among these are *I. alata, I. persica, I. reticulata,* and the English and Spanish kinds. They need a compost of two-thirds fibrous loam, one-third leaf-mould and sand. Plant five bulbs in a 6-inch pot in September or October. They may be propagated by offsets in October.

NON-BULBOUS OR RHIZOMATOUS SPECIES.—Sow seed in April in a cold frame, or propagate by division in August. Plant-out in August or September; Bearded Irises (tall) 20 inches apart; (medium) 15 inches apart; (dwarf) 5 inches apart. The upper part of the rhizomes should lie on the surface of the soil, so as to be exposed to the air and sun. The Dwarf Bearded Rock Species may be propagated by seed sown in September under glass, by off-shoots in October, or division in the spring after flowering. Lift and re-plant the rhizomes triennially.

Species and Varieties.—BULBOUS-ROOTED. SPRING-FLOWERING—*I. Histrio* (Lilac-blue and Yellow, Jan.–Feb., 6 in.); *I. orchioides* (Yellow, Lilac Spots, March–May, 20 in.); *I. persica Heldreichii* (Purple, Yellow, and Green, March, 4 in.); *I. reticulata Krelagei* (Purple, Red, and Orange, Jan.–Feb., 8 in.). SUMMER-FLOWERING—*I. xiphioides* (*English Iris*) (Purple, Mauve, Pink, and Blue, July, 10–25 in.); *I. Xiphium* (*Spanish Iris*) (Blue, Yellow, and White, June, 20 in.). AUTUMN-FLOWERING—*I. alata* (Sky-blue and Yellow, Nov.–Jan., 4 in.).

NON-BULBOUS OR RHIZOMATOUS—*I. fulva* [syn. *cuprea*] (Red-bronze, June–July, 20 in.); *I. fœtidissima* (Bluish-lilac or Yellow, June, 30 in.); *I. Kœmpferi* (Various, July–Sept., 18–30 in.); *I. Monnieri* (Yellow and White, June–July, 36–48 in.); *I. Monspur* (Light Blue, Lavender or Violet, July–Aug., 50 in.); *I. ochroleuca* (White and Yellow, June–July, 48 in.); *I. sibirica* (Blue, White, and Yellow, May–June, 36 in.); *I. spuria* (Deep Blue, June, 40 in.); *I. unguicularis* [syn. *stylosa*] (Various, Nov.–March, 6–12 in.). Named varieties are innumerable and catalogues should be consulted.

Ismene.—A genus of handsome summer-blooming plants suitable for warm sheltered borders or for in-door decoration. They like a light loam and rich vegetable soil. The culture is the same as that recommended for the hardy and half-hardy Amaryllis. Lift the bulbs and store during the cold months. The best-known species is *I. calathinum,* the Peruvian Daffodil.

Itea virginica.—Hardy deciduous summer-flowering shrubs (3 to 5 feet), which like a moist, peaty soil, and partial shade. Plant in October, and thin-out the branches when overcrowded. Propagate by means of seed in the open in April, or by suckers in October. *I. ilicifolia,* from China, grows tall, but it is rather tender and only suitable for a wall, except in the south and west.

Ivy.—*See* Hedera.

Ixia (African Corn Lily).—Half-hardy bulbs, which thrive in warm, dry, sunny borders or in the rock garden in rich, sandy loam and leaf-mould or peat, or in pots in the cold greenhouse. *Culture.*—Plant in September, 4 inches deep and 3 inches apart. Do not lift, but in winter, cover the bulbs with ashes or fibre. *Pot Culture.*—Pot-up from August to September, placing six bulbs in a 6-inch pot, in a compost of two parts turfy loam to one part each of leaf-mould, rotten cow-dung, and sand. Keep cool but frost-proof during the winter. In early spring, give light and air. Water well after blooming until the foliage dies, then dry off. Propagate by means of seed in a frame in September or by offsets in October. Seedlings take three years to flower. *Named Varieties.*—*Bridesmaid* (White); *King of the Yellows* (Yellow); *Queen of the Roses* (Rose); *Excelsior* (Red); *Alice* (Pale Yellow and Lavender); *Azurea* (Blue, Purple Centre). All flower in May and June and grow about 15 inches in height.

Ixiolirion montanum (Ixia Lily).—Half-hardy bulbous plants, which grow about 15 inches high, flower in June, and do well in well-drained sandy loam in a warm, sunny border or rock garden. *Culture.*—Plant in September, 5 inches deep and 3 inches apart. Do not lift the bulbs, but protect them with fibre during the winter. If grown in pots, treat as advised for the Ixia.

Jacobæa Lily.—*See Sprekelia formosissima.*

Jamesia americana.—A hardy deciduous flowering shrub, 4 to 7 feet high and with white flowers in May. It is allied to the Deutzias, and likes a damp, rich soil and a sunny position. *Culture.*—Plant from October to November; thin-out branches when overcrowded. To propagate, sow seed when ripe, or in autumn strike cuttings.

Jankæa Heldreichii.—Allied to *Ramonda* which it closely resembles. A choice rock garden plant which thrives in shady position and well-drained soil in a mixture of loam, peaty and leafy mould. Best suited for a pan in the Alpine House. If grown outside, plant in vertical crevices in full shade. Needs the protection of a sheet of glass in winter to keep the woolly grey leaves dry. Flowers Pale Blue, May–June, 4–6 in. Propagate by leaves and seed.

Jasione (Sheep's Scabious).—These are pretty dwarf-growing plants, forming tufts of narrow leaves, and carrying rounded heads of blue flowers on slender stems in summer. They like a semi-sheltered, but sunny, position, and do best in a sandy and gritty loam. Seed may be sown under glass as soon as ripe or in March, or the plants may be propagated by division of roots in spring or early autumn. *Species.*—*J. humilis*, 5 in.; *J. Jankæ*, 6 in.; and *J. perennis*, 9 in., are all good species.

Jasminum (Jasmine).—*J. officinale*, the common white jasmine, which blooms in June and July, is the best known; *J. revolutum*, with yellow flowers in May, is better grown in bush form; *J. nudiflorum* has yellow flowers in winter, is valuable for north walls and fences, and will thrive in town and suburban gardens. It is also useful in the cold greenhouse. There are also several beautiful hot-house species, viz., *J. nitidum*, flowers White, part climber; *J. Sambac* (Arabian Jasmine), flowers White, very fragrant, 5 ft. COOL HOUSE KINDS.—*J. azoricum*, White, evergreen climber; *J. polyanthum*, flowers White, Reddish outside, very fragrant; *J. primulinum*, flowers Yellow, like *J. nudiflorum*, only larger, evergreen climber. Hardy kinds like rich loam, and most do well against walls, trellises, and pergolas facing north or west. *Culture.*—Strike cuttings of ripe wood in summer in a frame, or layer. Plant-out from October to March, and after flowering, prune shoots that have bloomed. *Pot Culture.*—(COLD HOUSE)—Pot up in February or March, using 6 to 8-inch pots and a compost of two-thirds loam and one-third leaf-mould and well-rotted manure with a little sand. Give weak liquid manure twice a week as soon as the buds form. (WARM GREENHOUSE)—Pot-up in March. Keep moist and syringe frequently until the plants have bloomed; then keep moderately dry.

341

Juglans (Walnut).—Hardy deciduous nut-bearing trees, which thrive in well-drained loam in a sunny, open position. *Culture.*—Plant in October when three to four years old. Thin-out branches when overcrowded. To propagate, plant nuts 4 inches deep in the open. *Species.*—*J. nigra* (Black Walnut). A good timber tree; *J. regia* (Common Walnut), many varieties.

Juniperus (Juniper).—Evergreen shrubs and trees which thrive in the sun in moist, well-drained, and deep loam with mortar rubble. *Culture.*—Plant in May or September; no pruning is required. To propagate, strike cuttings in a frame in September, or raise from seed. *Species and Varieties.*—*J. chinensis* (40–60 ft.); *J. communis* (6–12, rarely 20 ft.) *vars. compressa* (a rock garden gem), and *var. hibernica* (Irish Juniper); *J. pachyphlæa* (young plants, silver-blue for the rock garden); *J. Sabina* (4–15 ft.) *vars. Knap Hill* and *tamariscifolia* (for rock garden); and *J. virginiana* (40–100 ft., Red Cedar of N. America), of which there are many varieties.

Kalmia (American Laurel).—Hardy evergreen shrubs, which should be treated as the rhododendron (*which see*). They are suitable for gentle forcing, and in this case should be treated as Azaleas. To propagate, sow in a frame in spring, strike cuttings in a frame in October, or layer in October. *Species.*—The best known are: *K. polifolia* (The Swamp Laurel), with its purple flowers in April and May, which grows about 2 feet high; *K. latifolia* (The Calico Bush or Mountain Laurel), with its rose and white flowers in June and which grows to a height of 8 to 15 feet; *K. angustifolia* (The Sheep Laurel), which makes a bush some 3 feet in height and bears clusters of rosy-red flowers in June. *Vars. rubra* (Deep Red) and *nana* are excellent for the rock garden.

Kentia see **Howea** (Curly Palm). *See* Palms, p. 365.

Kentranthus (Valerian).—A hardy perennial, which likes a sunny position and dry, limy soil, and is useful for border, rock garden, or walls. For culture, *see* Perennials, p. 156. *Species.*—*K. angustifolius* (Crimson, May–July, 24 in.); *K. ruber* (Crimson, Rose, June–Aug., 24–36 in.); *K. r. var. albus* (White, June–Aug., 24 in.), *K. macrosiphon* is a good annual (Red, June–July, 24 in.).

Kerria (Jew's Mallow).—Hardy deciduous shrubs, bearing orange flowers in March and April. *K. japonica* (4 ft., Single), *K. japonica flore pleno* (8–9 ft., Double), and *K. japonica aurea variegata* (Yellow Margined Leaves) are the only species and varieties. As climbers they run up to double the heights mentioned. They do well in sandy soil in sunny positions against walls facing south or west and in shrub borders. *Culture.*—Strike cuttings of young shoots in a frame in late summer, or propagate by division of roots in late autumn. Plant-out from October to March. About June or early July cut out the oldest wood. *Pot Culture.*—In the cool greenhouse, *K. japonica flore pleno* may be had in flower in February. Pot-up annually in October, using 8 to 10-inch pots and a compost of two parts of sandy loam to one part of leaf-mould and rotten manure. Prune after flowering, and plant outdoors.

Kniphofia (Tritoma, Red Hot Poker, Flame Flower, Torch Lily).—Tall hardy perennials, which thrive in well-drained, deep, sandy soil in sunny or partially-shaded borders. *Culture.*—Sow seed indoors during March or April, or propagate by means of division in March, and plant out from 18 to 30 inches apart. Protect the plants from frost in winter, and mulch with well-rotted manure in

342

the spring. They may also be potted-up in April or November, in 8 to 10-inch pots, and grown in the cold greenhouse. *Species and Varieties.*—K. *caulescens* (Red and Yellow, May, 40 in.); K. *modesta* (White, May–Sept., 30 in.); K. *Nelsonii* (Orange-scarlet, July, 24 in.); K. *uvaria grandiflora* (Orange-red, July–Sept., 70 in.). *Named Varieties.*—Golden Spur; Harkness Hybrid; Mount Etna; W. G. Mills; Royal Standard.

Kochia (Summer Cypress).—Half-hardy annuals, useful for summer-bedding, for borders, and the cold greenhouse. *Culture.*—Sow seed in the open in April, or in March under glass in moderate heat. Pot up singly in 4-inch pots, harden off, and plant out 12 inches apart in borders at the end of May, or use in the greenhouse. These plants grow from 2 to 3 feet in height, and flower from July to October. *Species.*—K. *scoparia* (2–4 ft.) and K. *s. var. trichophylla* (2–4 ft.).

Kœlreuteria.—Small trees with attractive pinnate leaves and large terminal panicles of yellow flowers followed by bladder-like fruits. They thrive in light soils and sunny positions. They are good town and suburban trees, which are readily propagated by root cuttings and seeds. *Species.*—K. *apiculata* and K. *paniculata.*

Laburnum (Golden Rain or Golden Chain).—Hardy deciduous trees with yellow flowers in May. Almost any soil and a sunny position suit them well. *Culture.*—Plant in November; trim back weak shoots after flowering, and cut-out dead wood in winter. In the cool greenhouse, L. *anagyroides* will flower from February to April. *Pot Culture.*—Pot-up in October, using 8 to 10-inch pots and a compost of two parts sandy loam to one part of leaf-mould and rotten manure. Prune as above after flowering and plant-out in the open. Do not re-pot for forcing for two seasons. To propagate, sow in a frame in spring; budding and grafting are sometimes resorted to. *Species and Hybrids.*—L. *alpinum* (Scotch Laburnum); L. *anagyroides* (Common Laburnum); L. *Vossii*; L. *Watereri.* L. *Adamii*, the Purple Laburnum, is a graft hybrid between Common Laburnum and *Cytisus purpureus.*

Lachenalia (Cape Cowslip or Leopard Lily).—Bulbous-rooted flowering plants suitable for greenhouse culture. *Culture.*—Pot-up in August, ½ inch deep in a compost of peaty loam with decayed cow manure and sand. Put one bulb in a 4-inch pot, or five bulbs in a 6 to 7-inch pot. Keep in a cold but frost-proof frame until early December, watering only when dry, then transfer to a shelf near the glass in the greenhouse (50° F.), and water as growth commences. Keep quite dry in pots from May to August. Propagate by means of offsets in August. *Species and Named Varieties.*—L. *pendula* (Red and Yellow); L. *tricolor var. Nelsonii* (Golden Yellow); L. *tricolor var. luteola* (Yellow-green, tipped Red).

Lampranthus.—*See* Mesembryanthemum.

Lantana (Surinum Tea Plant).—Bushy evergreen half-hardy shrubs, 6 to 8 inches high, and flowering from June to September. They are useful for the greenhouse and flower garden. *Culture.*—Pot-up as soon as the young shoots break after pruning, using 6 to 7-inch pots and a compost of two parts of loam to one part of leaf-mould, well-rotted manure, and sand. Syringe in spring and summer. If planted out during the summer, they must be wintered indoors. Seeds sown in heat (75° F.) in March make the summer and autumn blooming plants. They are also propagated in spring or autumn by cuttings of half-matured wood in heat. Stop back young shoots, and pot-up into larger pots as the plants become pot-bound. *Varieties.*—*Drap d'Or* (Yellow); *Favorita* (Yellow and Red); *La Neige* (White); and *Magenta King* (Purple-red).

Lapageria.—Beautiful evergreen climbers for the cool greenhouse, which require a well-drained, turfy loam, plentifully mixed with sand, an equal portion of peat, and a little charcoal. They grow to a height of 10 feet, and flower in October and November. *Culture.*—Propagate by seed sown as soon as ripe in gentle heat, or by layers after flowering, the latter being the best way. Pot firmly, or plant in the border in March, shade, and water well. Cut out weak shoots only after flowering. *Species and Varieties.*—*L. rosea* (Rose); *L. r. var. albiflora* (White), and *L. r. var. Nash Park* (Rosy-red).

Lapeyrousia (Flowering Grass).—Bulbous plants growing about 15 inches high, and flowering from June to September. They do well in warm, sunny borders, or in the greenhouse, and in light, sandy loam and leaf-mould. *Culture.*—Plant in October, 5 inches deep and 3 inches apart. Propagation is by means of offsets in October.—*Species.*—*L. cruenta* (*Anomatheca cruenta*) (Red) and *L. c. alba* (White).

Larix (Larch).—One of the few deciduous conifers. It grows from 30 to 100 feet in height, and thrives in a sunny position and in ordinary soil. *Culture.*—Plant in October. Remove dead wood when necessary. Propagate by means of seed in the open in November. *Species.*—*L. decidua* (*L. europæa*) (Common Larch); *L. leptolepis* (Japanese Larch); *L. occidentalis* (Western Larch); and *L. pendula* (Weeping Larch).

Larkspur (Annual Delphinium).—A showy hardy annual; the dwarf kinds (12 in.) are excellent for edging; and the taller sorts being grown in mixed borders. *Culture.*—Sow seed in March, in the open. Thin moderately when 3 inches high. Seed may also be sown in a frame in August; in this case, winter the seedlings in the frame, and plant out in April or May.

Species.—*D. cardiopetalum* (Blue); *D. Consolida* (Purple-blue); *D. Gayanum* [syn. *Ajacis*] (Blue).

Lathyrus (Everlasting Pea, Sweet Pea).—Annual and perennial climbing plants, the most popular of which are the *Sweet Pea*, *which see* under that heading; *L. grandiflorus* and *L. latifolius* (The Everlasting Pea). The latter two are beautiful hardy climbers. Moist, good soil and a sunny position suits it best. For culture, *see* Perennials, p. 156. *Named Varieties.*—*White Pearl* (White), and *Pink Beauty* (Carmine-rose). Both flower from June to September and grow about 6 feet in height. *L. pubescens* (Lavender-blue, 50–60 in.) is a beautiful sweet-scented, half-hardy, climbing species, which succeeds out-doors on a warm wall in the south or in a cool greenhouse, flowering for several months during the summer. Raise from seed during spring in a cool greenhouse.

Laurel.—*See* Prunus Laurocerasus.

Laurus.—This genus includes two species only, viz. *Laurus* or *Lindera Benzoin* (deciduous) and *L. nobilis* (evergreen), the true Bay Laurel or Sweet Bay. The latter thrives in well-drained, fibrous loam, leaf-mould, and peat, and in a sheltered position in sun or shade. To propagate, strike cuttings in a frame in August.

344

Lavandula (Lavender).—The best known species, *L. spica* (Mauve to White), the common lavender, thrives in light and well-drained soil and in sunny, open positions, grows about 3 feet high, and flowers in July and August. *Culture.*— Plant in March or September, and clip after flowering. To propagate, strike cuttings in October.

Lavatera (Mallow).—Hardy annuals, biennials, and perennials, which thrive in the sun and in any soil. *Culture.*—ANNUALS—Sow seed thinly, ½ inch deep, in April, or in autumn. Do not transplant, but thin out to about 20 inches apart. BIENNIALS—Sow seed in April in a frame (60° F.). Thin to 12 inches apart as soon as fit to handle, and plant out in May. PERENNIALS—*See* p. 156. *Species.* —ANNUAL—*L. trimestris* (Rose or White). BIENNIAL—*L. arborea* (Violet). PERENNIAL—*L. thuringiaca* (Blue). All July to September flowering, and growing to a height of from 30 to 60 inches.

Layia (Tidy Tips).—Hardy annuals suitable for sunny beds, borders, or rock gardens. *Culture.*—Sow seed thinly, ¼ inch deep, in April, and thin out when fit to handle to about 6 or 9 inches apart. *Species.*—*L. densiflora* (Mauve and White); *L. elegans* (Yellow, margined White); *L. glandulosa* (White). All flowering from July to September and growing about 10 inches in height.

Ledum (Labrador Tea).—Hardy evergreen shrubs, which thrive in cool, moist peat or loam deficient in lime, and in sun or semi-shade. *Culture.*—Plant in May or September. No pruning is necessary. Propagate in September by means of layering or cuttings, or by seed in spring. *Species.*—*L. grænlandicum* (*latifolium*) (White, tinged Pink); *L. palustre* (Pink). Both April to May-flowering and 10 to 40 inches high.

Legousia (Specularia, Corn Violet, Venus' Looking Glass).—Hardy little annuals, which thrive in sandy loam and peat in the rock garden. Sow in autumn, and thin-out to at least 6 inches apart. *Species.*—*L. falcata* (Blue); *L. hybrida fl. pl.* (Lilac or Blue); *L. perfoliata* (Purple and Blue); *L. Speculum Veneris* (Purple or White). All June to September flowering.

Leiophyllum buxifolium (Sand Myrtle).—Hardy dwarf evergreen shrubs for the rock garden, that thrive in fibrous loam in the sun, and produce white flowers freely in May and June. *Culture.*—Plant in April or September. Propagation is by means of seed in a frame in spring, by cuttings in August, or by layering in September.

Leontopodium alpinum (Edelweiss).—A hardy plant, which requires a sunny position, and sandy loam and old mortar rubble. The cream-white, star-shaped flowers are borne from June to September on stems 6 inches high. *Culture.*—Sow under glass as soon as ripe or in March, or propagate by means of division of roots in April, and plant out in permanent position. As it cannot stand too much damp, in winter the plant should be covered by a sheet of glass.

Leptospermum.—Evergreen shrubs, which thrive in the cool greenhouse in a compost of two parts peat to one of loam and a little sand. *L. scoparium* (White) may be grown outdoors in a sunny, sheltered situation. Propagate by means of cuttings (with bottom heat) in May, or by seed in slight heat in March. *Species and Varieties.*—*L. Donard Beauty* (Red, margined Rose, 50 in.); *L. grandiflorum* (White, 80 in.); *L. scoparium Chapmanii* (Rose-scarlet, 50 in.); *L. s. var. Nichollsii* (Carmine, 50 in.). All June to August flowering.

345

Leptosyne.—Annuals and perennials, which thrive in ordinary soil in sunny positions. For culture, *see* Annuals, p. 139, *and* Perennials, p. 156. *Species and Varieties.*—ANNUAL—*L. Douglasii* (12 in.); *L. Stillmanii* (20 in.). PERENNIAL—*L. maritima* (30 in.). All Yellow, flowering in Summer.

Leucojum (Snowflake).—Hardy bulbs, with bell-like blossoms, which thrive in any garden soil in semi-shade, and are useful for borders or the rock garden. *Culture.*—Plant in September, 3 to 4 inches deep and 5 inches apart; lift every seven years. Propagate by offsets or by seed. *Species.*—*L. æstivum* (White, spotted Green, May, 15 in.); *L. autumnale* (White, Oct., 10 in.); *L. vernum* (White, March, 9 in.).

Lewisia (Bitter-root).—Useful little rock plants for a dry, sunny crevice and in gritty loam. Protect from wet in winter. *Culture.*—Sow seed under glass in March, and plant out in permanent position in April. *Species.*—*L. Cotyledon* (Pink, striped Buff or White, May–June, 4 in.); *L. Howellii* (Pink, May–June, 6–12 in.); *L. rediviva* (Pink and White, May–Aug.); *L. Tweedyi* (Salmon-pink, May, 8 in.).

Leycesteria (Flowering Nutmeg).—This is a hardy (in south and west of England) deciduous shrub, only one species of which is at all extensively grown, that is, *L. formosa*. It grows from 6 to 8 feet high, and in July and August carries drooping racemes of purple and white, funnel-shaped flowers at the end of the current year's growth; these are followed by purple-black fruit in autumn. The plant thrives in maritime districts and by the water-side and in light, well-drained soil, and will even flourish under the shade of trees. *Culture.*—Plant in October or March. Cut out wood that has flowered. To propagate, sow seed in the spring, or take cuttings in October and strike in a frame.

Liatris (Blazing Star, or Kansas Feather).—Hardy perennials, better grown as biennials. They thrive in almost any soil in a warm, sunny border. For culture, *see* Biennials, p. 141. *Species.*—*L. graminifolia* (Pink, 36 in.); *L. scariosa* (Mauve, 36 in.); *L. spicata* (Mauve-purple, 40 in.). All flower from Aug. to Oct.

Libertia.—Herbaceous perennials for the border or rock garden. They need a light soil. For culture, *see* Perennials, p. 156. *Species.*—*L. formosa* (White, 20 in.); *L. grandiflora* (White, 20 in.); *L. ixioides* (White, 40 in.). All March to May flowering.

Libocedrus (Incense Cedar).—Hardy and half-hardy evergreen coniferous trees, the most popular species of which is *L. decurrens*. It likes a well-drained loam and a warm, sheltered position. *Culture.*—Sow seed from October to April, or strike cuttings in a frame in September.

Ligularia.—Showy herbaceous perennials sometimes included in *Senecio*. *Species.*—*L. clivorum* (*Senecio clivorum*) (flowers Orange-yellow, large leaves, Aug.–Sept., 4 ft.); *L. Veitchiana* (*Senecio Veitchianus*) (flowers Yellow, numerous, long toothed leaves, Aug.–Sept. 6 ft.); *L. Wilsoniana* (*Senecio Wilsonianus*) (flowers Yellow, leaves heartshaped, 5 ft.); Of easy culture, propagated by seed and division. Good plants for moist positions.

Ligustrum (Privet).—Hardy evergreen and deciduous shrubs, usually grown as hedge-plants, but poisonous to cattle. They thrive in ordinary soil. *Culture.*—Plant from November to March; clip hedges several times in summer and cut out dead wood. To propagate, strike cuttings in the open in autumn. *Species.*→

346

L. ovalifolium (Oval-leaved Privet); *L. o. foliis aureis* (Golden Privet) are those most used; and *L. lucidum* is a tall evergreen privet.

Lilac.—*See* Syringa.

Lilium (Lily).—There are many different species and varieties of lilies, but they are for the most part hardy bulbous perennials requiring practically the same management. Lilies thrive in deep, well-dug garden soil, or in a moist, well-drained fibrous loam with well-decayed leaf-mould and gritty sand in it. A few, such as *L. auratum*, *L. giganteum* and *L. pardalinum*, love a peaty soil, but with the majority, the presence of peat in their soil will cause failure. *L. candidum*, *L. Martagon*, *L. pyrenaicum*, and *L. testaceum*, will succeed in calcareous soil.

Culture.—Plant in October in groups of five or seven, 4 to 5 inches deep (about three times their own depth), and from 6 to 12 inches apart, according to species. The bulbs should, as a rule, when planted, rest on sand, and for the first winter a few dried leaves should be placed on the surface above them. They must not be disturbed oftener than every three years. It is wise to plant medium-sized bulbs, as they will do better in successive years, although not so well in their first summer. A yearly top-dressing of well-decayed manure each spring will be beneficial. Lilies which form roots from the base of the stem as well as from the bulb should be planted among low-growing shrubs, which will afford shade to the base of their stems. These particular lilies may be planted at any time, and somewhat deeper than the non-stem-rooting kinds. Though loving shade at the root, the bulbs should not be planted directly underneath trees. When in bloom, all lilies must be carefully staked, and all dead flowers should at once be removed, but the stems must not be cut down until they have died off. *The Madonna Lily* (*L. candidum*) requires different treatment. Transplant this lily in August. It likes deep, well-dug loam and cow manure for soil. This lily resents disturbances, and should only be lifted when necessary. Top-dress with well-rotted manure each spring. *Pot Culture.*—Plant in late autumn. A 12-inch pot will take six bulbs; a large bulb of *L. auratum* would require a 10-inch pot to itself. The bulbs should be covered by 1 inch of soil, which should be made firm, and care must be taken that the bulbs do not touch the sides of the pots. They should be treated in their first stage of growth exactly as hyacinths grown in pots, except that the pots must be only partly filled with soil. The pots should remain buried in ashes or fibre, in a frame till the plants begin to grow, when, as the stems grow, the pots are gradually filled up to within about an inch of the rim. Those intended to flower early should be placed under glass, while late bloomers should remain out-of-doors in a sheltered situation. Propagation is carried out by means of offsets in October, by planting scales from bulbs in sandy soil in a cold frame, or by seed in pans in a cold frame in August. Seedlings will flower when they are from two to five years old, according to species.

Species and Varieties.—*L. auratum* [Golden-rayed or Japanese Lily] (White, Yellow, and Crimson, Aug.–Sept., 40 in.); *L. candidum* [White Madonna Lily] (White, June–July, 50 in.); *L. carniolicum* [Carniolan Lily] (Scarlet with Black Spots, July, 30 in); *L. chalcedonicum* [Turk's Cap] (Bright Scarlet, July–Aug., 40 in.); *L. croceum* (Orange, July–Aug., 36–60 in.); *L. Davidii* (Orange-red,

347

36–40 in.); *L. elegans* [syn. *Thunbergianum*]; (Red, Shades of Yellow, with Black Spots, May–June, 20 in.); *L. formosanum* [Trumpet Lily] (White, July–Aug., 30 in.); *L. Hansonii* (Orange-yellow spotted Brown, 48–60 in.); *L. Martagon* (Rosy-violet, Wine-red, and White, July, 40 in.); *L. monadelphum* (Deep Yellow, 48 in.); *L. pardalinum* [Panther Lily] (Scarlet, Orange, and Yellow, July, 60 in.); *L. pyrenaicum* [Pyrenean Lily] (Yellow and Black, May and June, 30 in.); *L. regale* (White and Yellow, July, 24–40 in.); *L. speciosum magnificum* and *vars.* [Japanese Lily] (Carmine, Margined White, Aug.–Sept., 50 in.); *L. superbum* [Swamp Lily] (Scarlet and Yellow, Dotted Purple, July–Aug., 24–84 in.); *L. testaceum* [syn. *excelsum*] [Nankeen Lily] (Nankeen Yellow, Anthers Scarlet, June–July, 60 in.); *L. tigrinum splendens* [Tiger Lily] (Scarlet-orange, Dark Purple Spots, Aug.–Sept., 50 in.); *L. umbellatum erectum* (Red-orange, June and July, 20 in.).

Lily of the Valley.—*See* Convallaria.

Limnanthemum.—*See* Nymphoides.

Limnanthes Douglasii.—A dwarf hardy annual, which flowers in summer, and is useful for edging or rock garden. *Culture.*—Sow seed thinly in a sunny bed in April or September, cover lightly with soil, and thin out to 9 inches apart when fit to handle. *Species.*—*L. alba* (White, 4–5 in.); *L. Douglasii* (White and Orange, 4–5 in.).

Limonium [Statice] (Sea Lavender).—These extremely beautiful "Everlasting" flowers thrive in sunny borders or in the rock garden, in well-drained, sandy loam and leaf-mould. For culture, *see* Annuals, p. 139. Nearly all the annuals are better treated as half-hardy. For Perennials, *see* p. 156. *Pot Culture.*—Pot-up half-hardy species in a compost of two-thirds fibrous loam and one-third peat to which has been added a little leaf-mould and sand and some well-decayed cow manure. Pot-on as the roots fill the pots, until 8 to 9-inch pots are reached. *Species.*—(HALF-HARDY ANNUAL)—*L. Bonduellii* (Yellow); *L. sinuatum hybridum* (Mauve, White, and Rose, June–Oct., 15–30 in.); *L. Suworowii* (Rosy-purple or White, June–Oct., 12–18 in.). (HARDY PERENNIAL)—*L. Gmelinii* (Purple-blue, July–Sept., 18–24 in.); *L. incanum* (Red or Pinky, July–Aug., 15 in.); *L. latifolium* (Lavender-blue, July-Sept., 2–3 ft.); *L. tataricum* (Red, July–Sept., 20 in.).

Linaria (Toad Flax).—These are mostly hardy annuals and perennials. All species like a light, sandy soil, and a sunny, dry position; the rock garden species need a gritty soil. For culture, *see* Annuals, p. 139 *and* Perennials, p. 156. *Species.*—(ANNUAL)—*L. bipartita* (Red, White, or Purple, 12 in.); *L. Broussonnetii* (Yellow, Black spots, 10 in.); *L. maroccana* (Violet-purple and Yellow, 15 in.); *L. reticulata* (Yellow and Purple, 12–18 in.). (PERENNIAL)—*L. alpina* (Violet, blotched Orange, 3 in.); *L. Cymbalaria* (Mauve and Orange, Trailer); *L. dalmatica* (Orange and Yellow, 40 in.); *L. purpurea* (Blue, 30–50 in.); *L. triornithophora* (Violet-purple and Orange, 30 in.). All June to September flowering.

Linnæa borealis (Twin-flower).—A hardy evergreen trailing shrub, which thrives in a mixture of sand and peat in the shade on moist banks, and in June and July, carries in pairs small, but dainty, white flowers flushed with pink. *Culture.*—Propagate by means of division in March or October, or increase by layering.

348

Linum (Flax or Linseed-oil Plant).—Hardy annuals and perennials which thrive in dry, light soil, in a sunny position. The rock garden species need the addition of ample grit. They are also useful as pot plants. *Culture.*—(ANNUALS) —Sow seed thinly, ¼-inch deep, in loamy soil from March to June, and thin out to from 4 to 9 inches apart when fit to handle. (PERENNIALS)—Sow seed in the open in April, or under glass in March, or take cuttings and strike in sandy soil in July. Plant out in April or October. *Pot Culture.*—Pot-up in March or April, using 5 to 6-inch pots and a compost of loam and peat with a little sand mixed. In February or March, prune back the previous year's growth to within an inch of the base. *Species.*—(ANNUAL)—*L. grandiflorum* (Crimson-scarlet, Black Centre. Oct., 12 in.); *L. usitatissimum* (Common Flax), (Blue, July–Oct., 24 in.). (PERENNIAL)—*L. alpinum* (Blue, May–June, 6–9 in.); *L. campanulatum* (Yellow, Summer, 12–18 in.); *L. flavum* (Golden-yellow, June–Sept., 10 in.); *L. hirsutum* (Blue and White, May–Sept., 9 in.); *L. narbonnense* (Deep Blue, May–Sept., 12–24 in.); *L. perenne* (Pale Blue, May–Sept., 12–24 in.); *L. salsoloides* (Creamy White, July–Aug., 4–8 in.).

Lippia (Sweet Verbena).—Only one kind of this sweet-smelling deciduous shrub is grown to any extent. *L. citriodora*, with purple blooms in August. It can be grown in the open or against a wall in the south and west of England and in other parts it is suitable for the cold greenhouse, but requires protection from the frost in winter, even under shelter. *Culture.*—Re-pot into a smaller pot in the spring, in rich mould, loam, and sandy peat or leaf-mould for preference; when well rooted transfer to a larger pot. It succeeds also in the warm greenhouse. Cut young shoots hard back to the old wood in February, and pinch back the young shoots from time to time, but not later than June. Propagate by means of cuttings of young wood in gentle heat in spring. *L. nodiflora* is a dwarf-growing prostrate perennial, about 6 inches high, carrying white, pink, or purple flowers from June to August. It does best in the sun and in gritty loam, and is a useful subject for cultivation in the wall or paved garden. Propagate by means of division in March, or by cuttings of young wood in a cold frame in autumn. *L. citriodora* [syn. *Aloysia citriodora*] has lemon-scented foliage.

Liquidambar styraciflua (Sweet Gum).—Hardy deciduous trees growing 40 to 80 feet high, and which like a cool, moist ordinary soil, and a sunny position. Propagate by seeds. In autumn its leaves turn to brilliant shades of orange and crimson.

Liriodendron (Tulip Tree).—Tall deciduous trees, flowering in July and August, and which thrive in well-drained soil in a sunny position. *Culture.*—Plant in November; in autumn cut-out dead wood. To propagate, sow seed in a frame in March. *Species.*—*L. chinense* and *L. Tulipifera*.

Liriope graminifolia (L. Muscari).—A cool greenhouse or half-hardy plant, a native of China and Japan. The average height is from 9 inches to 1 foot. The spikes of violet-blue flowers push up freely among the arching green leaves in autumn. As an ornamental pot plant, *var. variegata*, with yellow and green leaves, is more useful than the green-leaved type. The plants thrive in a loamy potting compost, and are readily increased by division of the clumps in spring.

Lisianthus.—*See* Eustoma.

349

Lithospermum (Gromwell).—Hardy trailing evergreen shrubs and perennials, which do well in a mixture of gritty loam and peat in moderately sunny positions, and are excellent for dry walls, rock gardens, and for edging. For culture, *see* Rock Plants, p. 196. *Species.*—*L. diffusum* (Blue); *L. graminifolium* (Sky-blue); *L. intermedium* (Deep Blue); *L. oleifolium* (Sky-blue); *L. rosmarinifolium* (Bright Blue). All June to September flowering.

Lobelia.—A genus of half-hardy annuals and perennials, of which the low-growing kinds are suitable for edging, thriving in deep, well-manured and moist soil in sunny positions. *L. gracilis* is equally beautiful in pots or beds. All varieties of the greenhouse perennial, *L. Erinus*, are valuable for edging and for hanging baskets or vases. Treat all these as half-hardy annuals. The tall perennial species are valuable in the mixed border.

Culture.—(ANNUALS)—Sow seed thinly under glass (Temperature 60° F.), in March, on the surface of pans of very fine, moist, sandy soil. Prick off 1 inch apart in boxes, harden off in a cold frame in April, and plant out from 6 to 9 inches apart early in May. If required for greenhouse use, pot-up singly into 3 to 4-inch pots in the compost mentioned below. (PERENNIALS)—Sow seed in a frame in April, take cuttings of young growths in March, or propagate by means of division in late April, and plant out 8 inches apart in permanent position in rich, moist soil. Water liberally while the plants are making growth. As soon as the foliage is dead in autumn, the stems are cut down and the roots lifted and stored in boxes of dry soil in a frost-proof frame. Water is given in March to re-start growth, and late in April the roots are divided and planted-out.

Pot Culture.—(*L. cardinalis* and *vars.*)—Pot-up in March, using 6 to 8-inch pots and a compost of fibrous loam, leaf-mould, rotten manure, and sand. Keep in a frame on ashes until about to bloom, then transfer to the cool greenhouse. After blooming, cut down the flower stems, return to the frame in October, and cover with ashes for the winter. Give a good watering in February, and a month later, divide and re-pot if necessary.

Species and Varieties.—(ANNUAL)—*L. Erinus*—*Kathleen Mallard* (Double, Dark Blue); *Celestial* (Cobalt Blue); and *Imperial Blue* (Dark). All flowering from July to October and growing about 6 inches in height. *L. gracilis* (Celestial Blue, 12 in.); *L. tenuior* (Blue, White Eye, 12 in.). (PERENNIAL)—*L. cardinalis* (Crimson-scarlet, 24–36 in.); *L. fulgens* (Scarlet, 30 in.); *L. linnæoides* (Pinky), a prostrate creeping plant suitable for the rock garden; *L. syphilitica* (Blue and White, 24–30 in.). All June to September flowering. *Named Perennial Varieties.*—*Kimbridge* (Magenta); *B. Ladhams* (Scarlet); *Queen Victoria* (Red); *Purple Emperor; Salmon Queen.*

Loiseleuria procumbens (syn. *Azalea procumbens*).—(Trailing Azalea).—This is an attractive and valuable little shrubby plant of trailing habit. It has purple-pink flowers in summer, and is a valuable subject for moist situations in the rock garden, thriving in sandy peat and leaf-mould. Propagate by means of cuttings in a frame in September.

Lomaria (*see* Blechnum). Ferns, Chapter 25.

Lonicera (Honeysuckle).—A genus comprising all the trailing and climbing hardy and half-hardy deciduous or evergreen plants known as Honeysuckles. These thrive in any good, moderately dry garden soil and frequently in shaded

350

positions. *Culture.*—Strike cuttings of ripe shoots in the open in late summer; let the cuttings stand in the bed for a year, then plant-out from October to April. If preferred, propagate by layering or from seed. After flowering, cut away old wood and trim back shoots. For garden use *L. Periclymenum var. belgica* and *L. P. var. serotina*, the early and late Dutch honeysuckles, are excellent deciduous flowering climbers. Two valuable evergreen flowering climbers are *L. japonica flexuosa* and *L. j. Halliana*. *L. sempervirens* forms a beautiful greenhouse climber, and *L. Standishii* and *L. fragrantissima* (Bush Honeysuckles) flower outside early in February. *Pot Culture.*—Pot-up in the late autumn, in a compost of sandy loam, leaf-mould, and rotten manure, and keep in a cold greenhouse until February, then move to a sunny position in the cool house. The plants may be stood outdoors from June to October. Two other useful Bush Honeysuckles are *L. Maackii* and *L. tatarica rubra*.

Lophospermum.—*See* Maurandias.

Lotus (Bird's Foot Trefoil).—The hardy perennial species of this plant, which grow well in ordinary soil, are well suited for sunny borders or for the rock garden. For culture, *see* Perennials, p. 156. *Species.*—*L. corniculatus* (Yellow, July–Aug., 6 in.); *L. Bertholetii* [syn. *peliorhynchus*] (Scarlet, June, 10 in.); *L. Tetragonolobus purpureus* (Purple, July–Sept., 6–12 in.).

Lunaria annua (Honesty).—Hardy biennials growing from 24 to 30 inches high, and carrying purple, mauve, or white flowers from May to July. They thrive in partially-shaded borders or in the wild garden in moderately rich soil. *See* Biennials, p. 141.

Lupinus (Lupins).—Hardy annuals and perennials valuable for borders and the wild garden. The dwarf species are excellent for bedding. They thrive in light, rich, and well-drained soil deficient in lime, and in sunny positions. Stake the plants early. *Culture.*—(ANNUALS)—Sow seed, 1 inch deep and 5 inches apart, from March to May. Do not transplant, but thin out to about 18 inches apart, when fit to handle. (PERENNIALS)—Sow seed under glass in March or in the open from April to August, and thin to six inches apart. As an alternative, take cuttings in April and strike in sandy soil. Plant out in permanent position in March or October. Cut the stems to the ground after blooming, and mulch with well-decayed manure or with a phosphatic artificial. *Species and Varieties.*—(ANNUALS)—*L. Hartwegii* (Pale Blue); *L. nanus* (Lilac-blue and White). (PERENNIALS)—*L. arboreus* (Yellow, White and Blue); *L. leucophyllus* (Rose-pink); *L. polyphyllus* (Blue, White, and Rose). All flower from May to October and grow from 12 to 60 inches in height. *Named Varieties.*—(White) *Snowbird*; (Cream) *Mrs. Morris*; (Yellow) *Canary Bird*; (Coral Pink) *George Russell*; (Cerise Pink) *Joan of York*; (Salmon) *Nellie Allen*; (Bright Orange) *Flaming June*; (Crimson) *Downer's Delight*; (Bright Red) *City of York*; (Sky Blue) *Lady Diana Abdy*; (Slate Blue) *Gladys Cooper*; (Blue and White) *Admiration*; (Violet Purple) *Ruth Phillips*; (Purple and Yellow) *Jealousy*; (Violet and White) *Jane Ayr*.

Luzula (Wood Rush or Cuckoo Grass).—This is a genus of rush-like plants sometimes useful for growing in the water garden at the moist edges of ponds and streams. They are, as a rule, propagated by means of division of roots in April.

351

Lychnis (Catchfly, Campion, Ragged-Robin, Rose of Heaven).—Hardy annuals, biennials, and perennials, which thrive in any good soil, especially in rich, light loam, and which like a sunny position. The rock garden species need a gritty loam. *Culture.*—(ANNUALS)—These are easily raised from seed in the usual manner. (BIENNIALS)—Sow outdoors in April. Transplant 7 inches apart when fit to handle, and plant out in October or April. (PERENNIALS)—Sow seed under glass in March or in April in the open, or propagate by means of division in April or October. *Species and Varieties.*—*L. alpina* (Rose, April–June, 6 in.); *L. chalcedonica* (Scarlet and White, June–Sept., 30 in.); *L. fulgens* (Salmon, June–Sept., 12 in.); *L. Haageana* (Crimson, July–Aug., 12 in.); *L. Viscaria splendens var. fl. pl.* (Rose, June–July, 12–18 in.).

Lycium chinense (Box Thorn).—Hardy deciduous climbing shrubs, which thrive in shrub borders and against sunny walls. *Culture.*—Strike cuttings of ripe shoots, or layer in the open in October. Let the cuttings stand in the beds for a year, then plant-out from October to March. In winter, cut-out weak wood and top strong shoots.

Lysimachia (Creeping Jenny, Moneywort, or Loosestrife).—These herbaceous perennials do best in moist, rich, ordinary soil and in semi-shade. The low-growing species make excellent subjects for carpeting in the rock garden; the taller kinds for border or wild garden. *Culture.*—Propagate by means of division in April or October; no protection is required during winter. *Species.*—*L. clethroides* (White, 30 in.); *L. punctata* (Yellow, 30 in.); *L. vulgaris* (Common Loosestrife) (Deep Yellow, 24–36 in.) (DWARFS)—*L. Nummularia aurea* [Creeping Jenny] (Yellow, Trailer). All June to September flowering.

Lythrum (Purple Loosestrife).—Hardy perennials, thriving in rich, sandy soil in shady, moist borders, or in the wild garden. *Culture.*—Sow seed in the open in April or propagate by means of division in March, and plant out. *Species.*—*L. Salicaria* (Purple and Rose, 50 in.); *L. virgatum* [Rose Queen] (Rose, 40 in.). All June to September flowering.

Macleaya [*Bocconia*] (Plume Poppy).—A hardy perennial which thrives in sunny borders and in light, rich soil. For culture, *see* Perennials, p. 156. *Species.*—*M. cordata* (Whitish-cream, June–Oct., 70 in.); *M. microcarpa* (Creamy-bronze, June–Oct., 90 in.).

Macrotomia [syn. *Arnebia*] (Prophet Flower).—Hardy dwarf-growing perennials, requiring the same conditions as Arnebia. *Species.*—*M. echioides* (Pale Yellow with black dots, May–Aug., 9–12 in.).

Magnolia.—Hardy and half-hardy deciduous and evergreen shrubs, to which a good, deep, well-drained loam with ample leaf-mould and a sunny position are essential. Transplant as little as possible, and prune when required (which is but rarely) in summer. They grow from 15 to 60 feet high and flower spring and summer. *Culture.*—(HARDY SPECIES)—*M. denudata* (White); *M. salicifolia* (White); *M. Sieboldii* (White, Claret Centre); *M. Soulangeana* (White, stained Purple); *M. Soulangeana var. Lennei* (Rose-Purple); and *M. stellata* (White). Plant in April or October. Propagate by means of grafting under glass in spring, layering, cuttings, and seeds. *M. grandiflora*: Plant in April or September. To propagate, sow seed in a frame, strike cuttings of matured wood of the current year in heat in autumn, or layer during that period. *Pot Culture* (generally

M. stellata).—Pot-up in October or November, using 8 to 12-inch pots and a compost of sandy loam, leaf-mould, and rotten manure. Keep fairly dry in a cold greenhouse until growth commences, then water moderately. After flowering, prune-out weak wood and dead flower shoots, and sink the pots to their rims in ashes outdoors from May to December, when the pots should be moved into the house.

Maianthemum (Twin-leaved Lily of the Valley).—Beautiful little hardy perennials, useful for carpeting in the rock garden, and which like a mixture of loam and leaf-mould, also a shady position. *Culture.*—Propagate by means of division in April or September. No protection is necessary in winter. *M. bifolium* (5 in.), with white flowers like those of a small spiræa in June, is a good species.

Malcomia maritima (Virginian Stock).—Hardy annual, which thrives in sunny beds and in fairly light soil, and which is useful for edgings. For culture *see* Annuals, p. 140. *Varieties.*—(Crimson) *Fairy Queen*; (Purple and Crimson) *Crimson King*. Both flower from June to October, and grow about 6 inches in height.

Malope (Mallow-wort).—Tall hardy annuals, useful for sunny beds or borders. *Culture.*—Sow seed thinly, ½ inch deep in the open, in April or May, and thin out to about 18 inches apart when fit to handle. *Species.*—*M. trifida* (Crimson, Red, or White).

Malus (Crabs).—A genus of hardy deciduous trees at one time included under Pyrus. Most species bear delicate blossom and ornamental fruit. *Culture.*—Plant in November in a sunny position, sheltered from cold winds, in deeply dug and well-manured soil. *Pot Culture.*—Many of them when small are useful for culture in the cool greenhouse. Pot up annually in October, using 8 to 12-inch pots and a compost of two parts of sandy loam to one part of leaf-mould, and rotted manure. Sink the pots in ashes outdoors, from May to December. Propagate by means of seed, grafting, or budding in the open. *Species and hybrids.*—A few of the best flowering Crabs are *M. aldenhamensis*; *M. Arnoldiana*; *M. Eleyi*; *M. floribunda*; *M. f. atrosanguinea*; *M. Niedzwetzkyana*; *M. purpurea*; *M. Scheideckeri*; *M. spectabilis*.

Malva (Marsh Mallow).—Hardy and half-hardy annuals and perennials, which like a well-drained border of ordinary soil and a sunny position. *Culture.*—(ANNUALS)—These are easily raised from seed sown in the usual manner. (PERENNIALS)—Sow seed in the open in April, take cuttings in August and strike in sandy soil, or propagate by means of division in March or October, and plant out. *Species.*—(HARDY ANNUALS)—*M. crispa* (White, 60 in.). (HARDY PEREN-NIALS)—*M. Alcea* (Purplish-red, 50 in.); *M. moschata* (Rose and White, 30 in.). All June to September flowering.

Marguerite.—*See* Chrysanthemum frutescens.

Martynia (Elephant's Trunk or Unicorn Plant).—A half-hardy annual thriving in sunny borders or in the greenhouse. For culture, *see* Annuals, p. 139. They like a compost of leaf-mould, loam, rotten manure, and sand. *Species.*—*M. fragrans* (Violet and Orange, August, 10–18 in.); *M. lutea* (Orange-yellow, August, 15–20 in.).

Marvel of Peru.—*See* Mirabilis.

Maurandia.—Beautiful, but somewhat tender, deciduous climbers, which will grow in the open in rich, ordinary soil in a warm, sheltered position. *Culture.*—Sow in heat in March, or strike cuttings of young shoots under glass in summer. Plant-out in June. *Pot Culture.*—Pot-up in March, using 6 to 7-inch pots and a compost of two parts of loam to one part of leaf-mould and sand. Trim straggly shoots in autumn. *Species.*—*M. Barclaiana* (Violet-purple); *M. erubescens* (Rose); and *M. scandens* (Purple). All July to September flowering and growing to a height of about 10 feet.

Mazus.—Hardy creeping perennials that are excellent for the paved or rock garden, and which thrive in a mixture of well-drained loam and leaf-mould, and in sunny positions. For culture, *see* Rock Plants, p. 196. *Species.*—*M. Pumilio* (Purple-mauve); *M. reptans* (Mauve).

Meconopsis.—The best of this genus are hardy herbaceous perennials or biennials. They thrive in gritty loam and peat, and in partial shade in borders or rock garden. For culture, *see* Biennials, p. 141, *and* Perennials, p. 156. *Species.*—(BIENNIALS)—*M. integrifolia* (Yellow, 18–20 in.); *M. paniculata* (Yellow, 4–6 ft.); *M. Prattii* (Blue-purple, 20–36 in.); *M. regia* (Yellow, Silvery foliage, 4–5 ft.); *M. superba* (White, Silvery foliage, 4–5 ft.); *M. Wallichii* (Pale Blue), 4–6 ft. (PERENNIALS)—*M. betonicifolia* [syn. *Baileyi*] (Blue, 3–4 ft.); *M. cambrica fl. pl.* (Yellow, Orange, Double, 12–18 in.); *M. quintuplinervia* (Lilac-blue, 12–18 in.). All flower from May to August.

Mentha (Mint).—A large genus of hardy herbaceous perenn als, which includes several useful little plants of very dwarf nature. Thesei will thrive in crevices in the paved or rock garden. One of the best is *M. Requienii*, with its pretty little lilac flowers in the summer and minute foliage like that of the *Arenaria balearica*. Once disturbed, it will fill the air with its delightful fragrance. The mints require a shady site and a moist, gritty loam. Propagation is best carried out by means of division of roots in March.

Mentzelia Lindleyi (Bartonia).—A pretty little hardy annual for the border or rock garden. It grows to a height of 15 inches and bears bright yellow flowers from June to October. *Culture.*—Sow seed thinly ¼ inch deep in a warm, sunny position, or in gentle heat, from March to May, or in September. Thin out to 18 inches apart.

Menyanthes trifoliata (Bog Bean).—A hardy perennial, which thrives in ordinary soil and a sunny position in bog or in still, shallow water. It flowers from March to June and bears rosy-lilac flowers. *Culture.*—Strike cuttings in mud in summer; plant-out in March, with from 6 to 12 inches of water above the crowns.

Mertensia (Lungwort and Oyster Plant).—Hardy perennials, which thrive in almost any moist, cool soil with a little peat in it, and in shady borders, or in the rock garden. *Culture.*—Sow seed under glass in March or September, propagate by means of division in April or September, or take cuttings of young shoots in a frame in July or August, and plant out in a permanent position. Lift and divide triennially. *Species.*—*M. echioides* (Blue); *M. maritima* (Pink, later Blue); *M. primuloides* (Deep Blue, Yellow Centre); *M. sibirica* (Purple-blue); *M. virginica* (Purple and Blue, 24 in.). All flower from May to August and grow from 4 to 24 inches in height.

354

Mesembryanthemum (Ice Plant).—This is a very large genus of succulent plants, largely natives of South Africa and other parts of that continent. A few are found in New Zealand, Australia, the Canary Islands, and in the Mediterranean region. Generally, they may be regarded as greenhouse plants, although some of them are hardy at the seaside, along the south and west coasts, and in a few favoured situations on the east coast. Some of them are excellent for window gardening, while many of the strong-growing and sub-shrubby species are excellent flowering plants for the cool greenhouse, or for hot, sunny positions out-doors during the summer months. The genus is now divided up but for convenience they are all included under *Mesembryanthemum*.

Propagation.—Most of them are readily propagated by means of seed, cuttings, or division.

Culture.—They thrive in a compost of good medium loam with a little leaf-soil, and enough sand, old mortar rubble or broken bricks to keep the whole open and porous. Perfect drainage is essential, and water must be carefully afforded during the winter months.

Species.—While most of them are perennials, there are a few ANNUAL SPECIES which have for many years been fairly common in gardens; the best-known being: *M. crystallinum* (*Cryophytum crystallinum*) (Ice Plant); *M. pomeridianum* (*Carpanthea pomeridiana*) with yellow flowers; and *M. tricolor* (*Dorotheanthus gramineus*) with rose, red, and white flowers. The following are a few of the most showy SUB-SHRUBBY SPECIES: *M. aurantiacum* (*Lampranthus aurantiacus*) (Deep Orange); *M. aureum* (*Lampranthus aureus*) (Orange); *M. blandum* (*Lampranthus blandus*) (White, changing to Rose and Red); *M. Brownii* (*Lampranthus Brownii*) (Purple, changing to Reddish-yellow); *M. coccineum* (*Lampranthus coccineus*) (Scarlet); *M. falciforme* (*Lampranthus falciformis*) (Purplish-pink); *M. spectabile* (*Lampranthus spectabilis*) (Red); *M. roseum* (*Lampranthus roseus*) (Rose); and *M. violaceum* (*Lampranthus emarginatus*) (Violet). All reach from 12 to 18 inches in height.

The other section, with compressed stems and very thick, fleshy leaves, are very interesting on account of their many strange forms and coloration, which, in many cases, has a striking resemblance to the ground and stones or pebbles among which they grow. On account of their small size, a large collection may be accommodated in quite a small greenhouse, while many of them may be successfully grown in sunny windows. Generally, they are only a few inches high, and flowering is very uncertain. In this section, the growing period is, in most cases, during our winter. This entails the need for great care in affording them water, especially during spells of dull weather. The following are some of the fairly common and distinct species: *M. Bolusii* (*Pleiospilos Bolusii*), *M. calcarium* (*Titanopsis calcarea*), *M. ficiforme* (*Conophytum ficiforme*), *M. fissum* (*Rimaria dubia*), *M. fulviceps*, *M. Lesliei* (*Lithops Lesliei*), *M. pseudotruncatellum* (*Lithops pseudotruncatillo*), *M. simulans* (*Pleiospilos simulans*), *M. testiculare* (*Argyroderma testiculare*), *M. thecalhum* (*Conophytum minutum*), *M. tigrinum* (*Faucaria tigrina*), *M. truncatellum* (*Conophytum truncatellum*), etc.

Metasequioa glyptostroboides.—A recently introduced conifer of which little at present is known regarding its hardiness. Closely allied to Taxodium distichum and requiring the same cultural treatment.

355

Michaelmas Daisy (Starwort).—*See* Aster.

Michauxia.—Tall hardy biennials, which thrive in moist, sandy loam in sunny borders. *Culture.*—Sow seed in a warm position in the open, or in a cold frame, in April. Pot-up in September, and winter in a frame. Plant out in flowering position in April. *Species.*—*M. campanuloides* (Pink, White, July–Aug., 50 in.).

Mignonette.—*See* Reseda.

Mimulus (Musk or Monkey Flower).—Hardy and half-hardy annuals and hardy perennials. Seed of the annuals sown in spring makes good bedding plants, and seed sown in autumn produces early-flowering plants for the greenhouse. They like a shady site with moist, rich soil. The smaller species are useful for edging and for the rock garden. For culture, *see* Annuals, p. 139, Perennials, p. 156. In cold localities it is wiser to lift the roots and store them in a frame. Cuttings may be taken in summer. *Pot Culture.*—Pot-up in May, using 5 to 6-inch pots and a compost of two parts of loam and one part of leaf-mould, peat, and sand. Pinch back young shoots to make bushy plants, and keep cool in winter. *Species and Varieties.*—(HALF-HARDY ANNUAL)—*M. tigrinus* (Yellow, Spotted, June, 9 in.). (HARDY PERENNIALS)—*M. Burnetii* (Pale Brown, 10 in.); *M. cardinalis* (Scarlet, 20 in.); *M. cupreus* (Orange, 12 in.); *M. luteus* (Yellow Spotted, 9 in.); *M. moschatus* (Yellow, 6 in.); *M. ringens* (Pale Blue, 10 in.). All June to August.

Mina lobata.—*See* Quamoclit lobata.

Mirabilis (Marvel of Peru).—A genus of greenhouse and hardy perennials, which grow best in sunny positions and in a light, rich loam, but do well in any good garden soil. They should be treated in the same manner as dahlias, and can be grown from seeds sown in gentle heat from March to April, being hardened-off, and planted-out in May. *Species.*—*M. Jalapa* (Red, Pink, or White, July–Sept., 36 in.).

Miscanthus sinensis var. zebrinus (Striped Zebra Rush).—This is a hardy plant, that can be used with great effect in the bog or water garden. It thrives in the sun, and should be planted on banks in any ordinary soil. It grows to about 40 inches high, and flowers from June to September. Another good species is: *M. sacchariflorus*, which attains a height of from 7 to 8 feet and is very similar to the Bamboos. *Culture.*—Propagate by means of division of roots in April, and plant out in permanent position at that time.

Mistletoe.—*See* Viscum album.

Mitraria coccinea (Mitre Flower).—A half-hardy evergreen shrub that will grow outdoors during the summer, in warm, semi-shaded, and sheltered situations. Plant in April in a moist, peaty soil. *Pot Culture.*—Pot-up in March in a compost of two-thirds turfy peat and one-third part of sand. To propagate, strike cuttings of young shoots in a frame in summer.

Moltkia petræa [syn. *Lithospermum petræum*].—A small woody shrub, somewhat resembling the lavender in foliage, but carrying during May and June light and dark purple flowers, like those of the lithospermum. *Culture.*—Sow seed under glass during March or April, and pot off as soon as ready, or take cuttings during late summer and autumn, and strike in sand in a frame. Plant out in the rock garden in a position in full sun and in well-drained loam.

356

Monarda (Bee's Balm, Horse Mint, Oswego Tea, Red Sage, or Bergamot).—Useful perennials, thriving in deep, moist loam in sunny borders. They will, however, grow anywhere. *Culture.*—Propagate by means of division in March or October, by cuttings in September, or from seed in spring. *Species.—M. didyma* (Red, July–Sept., 24 in.); *M. fistulosa* (Pink, July–Sept., 24 in.). *Varieties.* —*M. Rose Queen* (Rose-pink); *M. violacea superba* (Deep Violet-purple) and *M. Sunset* (Deep Purple).

Montbretia.—*See* Tritonia.

Moræa (Butterfly Iris).—Pretty bulbous plants which may be grown outdoors in warm sunny sheltered situations, and thrive well in light rich sandy loam; but the best results will be obtained in pots in the cool greenhouse. *Culture.*—Plant in March, 4 inches deep and 2 to 3 inches apart. Lift after the foliage has died down and replant annually. *Pot Culture.*—Plant 4 or 5 bulbs in a 4½-inch pot in November, and protect from frost in a dark corner of the cool greenhouse; gradually introduce to the light early in March. Water well during growth, but keep dry after the foliage fades. Propagate by means of offsets. *M. Spathacea* (Yellow, striped Purple, Summer, 12–18 in.), is a good species.

Morina (Whorl-flower).—Half-hardy and hardy perennials, excellent for the border or rock garden. They like a warm, sunny position and a rich, gritty loam. In exposed districts, winter in a frame. Sow in March, or propagate by offsets. *Species.—M. longifolia* (Rose and White); *M. persica* (Pink).—Both July to August flowering and growing about 30 inches in height.

Morisia monantha [syn. **hypogæa**] (Mediterranean Cress).—Hardy little summer-flowering rock plants, which thrive in well-drained, deep, gritty loam in an open and fairly sunny spot. *Culture.*—Plant out in a sunny crevice in the rock garden. Propagate by seed sown in spring in a cold frame, or by root cuttings placed in sand in a frame. *See* Rock Plants, p. 196.

Morus.—*See* Mulberry, in the chapter on Fruit Culture.

Muscari (Grape Hyacinth).—Hardy bulbous plants, which thrive in good loam in warm, sunny borders or in the rock garden, or in pots. *Culture.*—Plant in October, from 2 to 3 inches deep and 3 inches apart; lift from the ground only when overcrowded. Propagate by means of offsets in October. *Pot Culture.*—Pot-up annually in October, 1½ inches deep in 5-inch pots, using a compost of two parts of loam to one part of leaf-mould and sand. Dry-off in a cold frame after flowering. *Species*—(EARLY)—*M. botryoides* (Blue and White varieties, Feb.–Mar., 6 in.). (LATE)—*M. conicum var. Heavenly Blue* (Sky-blue, April–May, 8 in.); *M. racemosum* (Deep Blue, April–May, 6 in.).

Mutisia.—A hardy climbing plant, usually grown in the cold greenhouse. *Culture.*—Pot-up in a large pot in a compost of two-thirds loam and one-third leaf-mould and ample sand, or plant out in a well-drained border. Water liberally and syringe from May to July, but keep only just moist during the autumn and winter. *Species.—M. Clematis* (Red, July–Aug., 20 ft.); *M. decurrens* (Orange-yellow, July, 12 ft.); *M. ilicifolia* (Rose, July–Aug., 15 ft.).

Myosotidium.—A half-hardy perennial, which needs a warm, sunny position and a fairly rich and moist soil. Propagation is by seed sown in May and June, or by root-cuttings in October. *Species.—M. nobile* (Blue and Cream, May, 20 in.).

357

Myosotis (Forget-Me-Not).—There are annual and perennial species, some of the latter being grown as biennials. All thrive in the sun and in ordinary soil. Many are useful for bedding, for the rock garden, and for the cool greenhouse. *Culture.*—(ANNUALS)—Sow seed thinly from June to July in the open, cover very lightly with mould, and thin-out to 5 inches apart when fit to handle. (PERENNIALS)—Sow seed in the open from April to July, or propagate by means of division in October, and plant out 5 inches apart. *Pot Culture.*—Pot-up in October, using 4 to 5-inch pots and sandy soil, and keep in a cold frame through the winter. Move into the cool house in early spring. *Species.*—*M. cæspitosa* [*M. Rehsteineri*] (Blue, April–May, 2 in.); *M. dissitiflora* (Light Blue, April–June, 6–9 in.); *M. pyrenaica* (Blue, Pink, and White, June–Aug., 6 in.). *M. scorpioides var. semperflorens* (Sky-blue and Yellow, May–Sept., 6–9 in.).

Myrtus (Myrtle).—Beautiful evergreen greenhouse shrubs, which will grow out-of-doors in warm, sunny, and sheltered situations. *Culture.*—Plant in May in loam and leaf-mould; the addition of a little peat is beneficial. Trim in April, not in autumn. *Pot Culture.*—Pot-up in March (triennially), using 5 to 12-inch pots and a compost of two parts of sandy loam to one part of leaf-mould. Stand outdoors from July to October, and prune in February. To propagate, strike cuttings in a frame in July, or layer in September. *Species.*—*M. communis* (Common Myrtle) and *M. Ugni* (*Eugenia Ugni*).

Narcissus.—Beautiful hardy bulbs, which are excellent for beds, borders, the rock garden (most species), for naturalizing in grass, and for pots. This genus is a large one, embracing the *Short-cup* or *Incomparabilis*; the *Barri*; the *Eucharis-flowered*; the "*Angel's Tears*"; the *Cyclamen-flowered*; *Jonquils*; the *Polyanthus Narcissus*; the *Hooped Petticoat*; the *Poet's Narcissus*, and many others. Most species thrive in well-dug and well-drained ordinary soil, though some few, notably the *Hooped Petticoat*, the *Cyclamen-flowered* and the *Angel's Tears*, prefer warm, deep, and moist sandy loam; the *Polyanthus narcissi* like a rather stiff soil. Partial shade is desirable, but they will grow well in full sun.

Culture.—Plant from August to October, the sooner the better, 4 inches deep in heavy soil and 7 inches deep in light soil, and about 4 inches apart; making exception of small species, which should be 2 to 3 inches deep, and the May-flowering double white narcissus, which must be not less than 9 inches deep in well-worked moist loam. If used for naturalizing, the bulbs should be left in the ground, but in beds or borders they should be raised triennially in July. Top-dress in August with bonemeal and well-rotted manure.

Greenhouse Culture.—Pot-up from August to November, using a compost of half fibrous loam to a quarter part each of sand and leaf-mould or rotten manure, and place from three large to twelve small bulbs in a 4 to 5-inch pot, and keep in the open in a cool, shady site under a 3-inch layer of coconut fibre until growth commences, then move into the cool house in batches. Dry-off when the foliage dies, and plant-out in the open the following year. The bulbs of the Polyanthus Narcissus being large, a 5-inch pot will be needed for a single specimen. Daffodils will not stand forcing, and only gentle heat should be used. Propagate by means of offsets at lifting time, re-planting the offsets immediately in a reserve garden; seed may also be sown in pans or boxes in August, but they take four to six years to flower. *See also chapter on* Bulb-Growing.

Named Varieties.—TRUMPET (Trumpet as long as or longer than the perianth segments)—(Yellow) *Dawson City;* (Golden-yellow) *King Alfred;* (White) *Peter Barr;* (Yellow) *Golden Spur;* (White) *Beersheba;* (Bi-colour; White or cream perianth with yellow trumpet) *Queen of the bi-colors.* SHORT CUP OR INCOMPARABILIS (Cup not less than one-third, but less than equal to the length of the perianth segments, outer petals yellow or white, cup yellow or red)—*Bernardine; Crœsus, Criterion, Damson, Fortune,* and *Sir Watkin.* BARRI (Cup less than one-third the length of the perianth segments, bright coloured cups, perianths yellow or white)—*Firetail, Lady Diana Manners, Conspicuus, Red Beacon, La Riante,* and *Chinese White.* LEEDSII OR EUCHARIS-FLOWERED (Outer petals white, with white or pale yellow or cream cups, sometimes tinged pink)—*Bridesmaid, Duchess of Westminster,* and *White Lady.* N. TRIANDRUS OR "ANGEL's TEARS" (Short cup and reflexed outer petals)—*Agnes Harvey, Queen of Spain* and *Venetia.* CYCLAMEN-FLOWERED (Pale yellow with darker and very narrow trumpet)—*N. cyclamineus.* JONQUIL-FLOWERED—*Buttercup, Jonquilla* and *N. odorus rugulosus.* TAZETTA OR POLYANTHUS (These are all bunch-flowered and white with yellow cups)—*Cheerfulness, St. Agnes,* and *Paper White.* POETICUS OR POET's (Petals white or yellow with red eye)—*Actœa, Sarchedon, White Standard,* and *Pheasant's Eye.* DOUBLE—*Inglescombe, Butter and Eggs,* and *Telamonius plenus.*

New varieties are so numerous, that catalogues should be consulted.

Nasturtium.—*See Tropæolum majus* and *nanus.*

Nemesia.—Half-hardy annuals, which make excellent bedding, rock garden, or pot plants. *Culture.*—In March sow thinly in deep boxes of moderately rich soil under glass (50° F.). Thin as soon as possible, harden-off in a cold frame, and plant out 7 inches apart in May, or pot-up and place in a cool greenhouse, standing the pots out in the open during the summer. Seed may also be sown in a frame in August. *Species.*—*N. floribunda* (White and Yellow); *N. strumosa* (Red, Pink, Orange, Yellow, Blue and White); *N. versicolor* (White and Mauve). *Named Varieties.*—*Aurora* (Red and White); *Blue Gem; Cherry Red; Orange Prince;* and *Twilight* (Mauve and White). All June to September flowering and growing about 12 inches high.

Nemophila (Californian Bluebell).—Dwarf-growing hardy annuals for edgings to sunny beds, or for the rock garden. For culture, *see* Annuals, p. 139. *Species.*—*N. insignis* (Sky-blue, White Centre); *N. Menziesii* (Purple, Blue, White, blotched Black); *N. M. discoidalis* (Maroon and White). All July to September flowering and growing to a height of from 3 to 9 inches.

Nepenthes (Pitcher Plant).—These curious stove evergreens thrive in a compost of 2 parts good loam to 1 part sphagnum moss. *Culture.*—Pot or plant in a basket in March, and grow near the glass. Good moist bottom heat is necessary. Temperature 65° F. in winter to 85° F. in summer. Water well while growing, but shade from the sun's rays. Syringe daily and keep the air moist. Propagation is by means of sucker-growths or cuttings in a bottom heat of 80° F.

Nepeta (Catmint).—Hardy perennials, which thrive in sunny positions and in ordinary soil, and which are useful for edgings to large borders, or for the rock garden. For culture, *see* Perennials, p. 156. *Species.*—*N. curviflora; N. marifolia;* and *N. Faassenii (Mussinii).* All Blue, May to September, 18 inches.

359

Nephrodium.—*See* Dryopteris.

Nerine.—Beautiful bulbous plants, which thrive in the cool greenhouse in rich loam, mixed with leaf-mould, cow-manure, and sand. *Culture.*—Plant singly in August in 4 to 5-inch pots, water well when the flower buds appear, and feed with liquid manure. Keep dry from June to August, with the pots exposed to the sun, and when the flower shoots again rise, soak the pots and top-dress with fresh soil. Re-pot every fourth year, and propagate by offsets in August, or sow seed when ripe. *Species and Varieties.*—*N. Bowdenii* (Pink); *N. curvifolia var. Fothergillii major* (Scarlet); *N. pudica* (White); *N. sarniensis* (Pale Salmon); *N. sarniensis var. corusca* (Orange-scarlet); *N. undulata* (Whitish to Soft Flesh); and *N. undulata var. alba* (White). There are many named hybrids. All September to December flowering and growing about 20 inches in height.

Nerium.—The best known of this genus of evergreen shrubs is *N. Oleander*, the Common Oleander. The blossoms and wood are *poisonous*.

Culture.—Pot when required in February, using 6 to 12-inch pots and a compost of two parts loam to one of leaf-mould, peat, and a little sand. Keep in a sunny position in the cool greenhouse, and sponge the leaves frequently. Remove shoots at the base of flower buds, and prune to within three buds of the old wood. Keep fairly dry during winter.

To propagate, place cuttings of well-ripened shoots in bottles of water, in a sunny frame in summer, or in a warm propagating case. When well-rooted, pot-up in light soil, and "stop" from time to time.

Nertera depressa (Coral-berried Duckweed).—This is a dwarf-growing plant, rarely exceeding 3 inches in height, that creeps along the surface of the ground and roots as it runs. It carries a quantity of small, green, ovate leaves, and tiny, greenish flowers followed by orange-scarlet berries, and is well worthy of a place in the rock garden in the South of England. It thrives in the shade and in warm, moist, sandy loam and leaf-mould, but must be protected from frost. *Culture.*—Sow seed in heat in March or April, or propagate by means of division in a warm greenhouse in the spring.

Nicotiana (Tobacco Plant).—Although treated as annuals, tobacco plants are perennials, and if the roots are protected from frost, they will come up again year after year. Among the sorts usually grown are: *N. alata* and *N. Sanderæ*. The first has white flowers, fragrant in the evening; the second bears rosy-red, bluish-red, or white flowers, but these are not so fragrant. They thrive in rich soil in sunny beds and borders. *Culture.*—In March sow seed thinly in fine soil under glass (Temp. 60° F.), and merely cover with fine sand. Prick off 6 inches apart into boxes of fairly rich soil, harden off, and plant out 12 inches apart early in June. For greenhouse use, seed sown in a frame in August will furnish bloom from January to March.

Nierembergia (Cup Flower).—Half-hardy perennials, which thrive in moist loam in a sunny position. *N. repens* [*syn. rivularis*] with creamy-white flowers streaked with purple, from June to August, is a useful little mat forming rock plant. *N. cærulea* (Lavender Blue), 12 in. and *N. frutescens* (Blue, shading to White at margin), 12 to 18 in., are pretty plants for the cold greenhouse, or mixed border outdoors. For culture, *see* Rock Plants, p. 196.

Nigella (Devil-in-a-Bush, Love-in-a-Mist, Jack-in-Prison). Hardy annuals, useful for sunny beds and borders. *Culture.*—Sow seed thinly, ¼ inch deep, in the open from March to April, or in autumn. Do not transplant, but thin out to about 4 inches apart when fit to handle. Seed may also be sown early in March under glass, being planted out in May. *Species and Varieties.*—*N. damascena* (Pale Blue or White); *N. damascena var. Miss Jekyll* (Deep Blue, double); *N. hispanica* (Deep Purple); *N. orientalis* (Yellow and Red). All June to September flowering and growing about 18 inches in height.

Nolana prostrata (Chilian Bell-flower).—The nolana is a pretty little hardy annual of trailing habit with velvety, bell-shaped flowers of blue or blue and white. They grow from 3 to 12 inches high, and are extremely valuable subjects for inclusion in the rock garden. Sow seed in March in light, gritty loam, and leaf-mould, and thin out the seedlings to 6 inches apart as soon as possible.

Nothofagus (Southern Beech). This tree comes from South America and Australasia. It is only suitable for cultivation outside in the milder parts of the country. The South American species are the hardiest, the best being *N. antarctica, N. obliqua,* and *N. procera.* These are thriving in gardens near London.

Nuphar.—A genus numbering but a few species, among which is *N. luteum,* the Yellow Water Lily. This is hardy and, like all of its kind, may be grown in a pond or a slow stream. The plants spread over the surface of water and flower from June to August. They like plenty of sun, and should be cultivated in the same manner as Nymphæa, *which see. Species.*—*N. advenum* and *N. luteum.* Both Yellow, June to August, 12 to 18 inches.

Nymphæa.—A genus of water-lilies including the common White Water Lily. The hardy species have white, rose, orange, or yellow, flowers. Most species like a sunny, sheltered position in slow-moving water. Those from hot countries require a hothouse. *Culture.*—Sow seed in spring in rich loam in a basket under water, or propagate by means of division from April to June, and plant in rich loam, leaf-mould, and cow-dung in weighted openwork baskets sunk with from 12 to 60 inches of water above the crowns, according to species.

Nymphoides peltatum (*Limnanthemum nymphæoides*). (Fringed Golden Buck Bean).—Hardy aquatic plants, flowering July and August, and enjoying a sunny position in slow-moving water. Sow seed, or propagate by division in March, and plant with not more than 12 inches of water above the crowns.

Nyssa sylvatica (Tupelo Tree).—A hardy deciduous tree, thriving in moist deep loam, or any good soil in sunny positions. *Culture.*—Plant in November (as young as possible). No pruning is necessary. Propagate by means of seed or layering. It does not transplant well.

Ocimum Basilicum (Sweet Basil); *O. minimum* (Bush Basil). For treatment *see* "Basil".

Œnothera (Evening Primrose, Godetia).—Annuals, biennials, and perennials, delightful for bedding, borders, or for the rock garden, and also grown in the greenhouse. All the species thrive in rich, sandy loam, or any good soil, and in sunny positions. For annuals, *see* Godetia, and for the Culture of Evening Primrose, *see* Biennials, p. 141, and Perennials, p. 156. *Pot Culture.*—Pot-up as required, using 6 to 7-inch pots and ordinary potting compost. Winter autumn-sown plants well up to the glass in a cold greenhouse. The genus is sometimes split up but for convenience are kept here under *Œnothera*. *Species.*—(BIENNIAL) —*O. (Lavauxia) acaulis* (White, tinted Rose, 10 in.); *O. biennis grandiflora* (Pale Yellow, 30 in.). (PERENNIAL)—*O. (Pachylophus) cæspitosa* (Pale Yellow or White, 4–6 in.); *O. (Kneiffia) glauca, Fraseri* (Golden-yellow, 20 in.); *O. (Megapterium) missouriensis* (Yellow, Trailer); *O. (Hartmannia) speciosa* (White to Rose, 30 in.). All June to October.

Olearia Hastii (New Zealand Daisy Bush).—Hardy evergreen shrubs, which grow from 4 to 9 feet high, and bear white flowers in late summer. They like a sheltered position and well-drained soil. *Culture.*—Plant in April or October. Trim to shape when necessary in March, and every four or five years, cut hard back. *Pot Culture of Greenhouse Species, O. stellulata (O. Gunniana).*—In the cool greenhouse these may be had in flower in March. Pot when required in October, using 5 to 7-inch pots and a compost of two parts of sandy loam to one part of leaf-mould and rotten manure. Sink the pots in ashes in a sunny spot outdoors from May to December, then take indoors, and keep fairly dry until growth starts. To propagate, sow in a frame in March, or strike cuttings in a frame in September.

Omphalodes (Creeping or Rock Forget-Me-Not, Navelwort).—Annual and perennial creeping plants, valuable for semi-shaded spots in the border or rock garden, and loving a moist, sandy, or gritty loam. For culture, *see* Annuals, p. 139, *and* Perennials, p. 156. *Species.*—(ANNUAL)—*O. linifolia* (White, July, 9 in.). (PERENNIAL)—*O. cornifolia (O. cappadocica)* (Porcelain Blue, May–June, 9 in.); *O. Luciliæ* (Lilac-blue, June–Sept., 6 in.); *O. verna* (Blue, April–May, 4 in.).

Onoclea sensibilis (Sensitive Fern).—*See* Ferns, p. 213.

Ononis (Rest Harrow).—Hardy perennials, which thrive in sunny rock gardens and in almost any soil. For culture, *see* Rock Plants, p. 196. *Species.*— *O. fruticosa* (Purple-pink, May–Aug., 24–36 in.); *O. spinosa* (Rose-purple, July–Sept., 10 in.).

Onosma (Alpine Comfrey).—Hardy perennial and biennial, rock plants, which thrive in well-drained, gritty loam, peat, and sand on hot, sunny ledges. Sow under glass in March, or strike cuttings in summer. *Species.*—*O. albo roseum* (White, tinged Rose); *O. cæspitosum* (Orange); *O. stellulatum* (Yellow); *O. s. var. tauricum* (Lemon). All June to July.

Ophiopogon (Snake's Beard or Japanese Hyacinth).—Beautiful half-hardy perennial foliage plants of dwarf growth, which thrive in a compost of two parts of loam to one part of leaf-mould and sand. Pot-up in March (only when pot-bound) using 6 to 7-inch pots. Water well and syringe the leaves daily from May to October, but keep fairly dry in winter. Propagate by means of division in March. Temperature, 40° F. in winter to 55° F. in summer.

Oplismenus hirtellus.—Variegated grass suitable for growing in baskets, etc., in warm greenhouses. It thrives in sandy loam with peat or leaf-mould and is readily increased by cuttings. The leaves are striped White and Pink, 3 ft.

Opuntia.—*See* Cacti, p. 279.

Orange.—*See* Citrus—Dwarf.

Orchids.—Besides the numerous beautiful orchids which may be grown in the greenhouse, there are many hardy species which thrive outdoors in sheltered borders, in the rock garden, or bog garden, notably, *Calopogon pulchellus* [Grass

Pink Orchis] (Purple or Yellow, June and July, 18 in.); *Calypso borealis* [Calypso Orchis] (Pink and Yellow, June and July, 5 in.); *Cephalanthera alba* [White Helleborine] (White, 9 in.); *Cypripedium humile*, etc. [Lady's Slipper] (Rose and Purple, Yellow and White, May–July, 6–30 in.); *Epipactus* [various] (Brown and Red, Summer and Autumn, 10–24 in.); *Goodyera pubescens* [Adder's Violet] (White, May–September, 6–10 in.); *Habenaria bifolia* [Butterfly Orchis] (White and Green, May–July, 12–15 in.); *Listera ovata* [Tway Blade] (Green, May–July, 12–18 in.); *Ophrys apifera* [Bee Orchis] (Purple, Brown, and Yellow, June and July, 10–18 in.); and *O. muscifera* [Fly Orchis] (Brown, Yellow, and Blue, May and June, 7 in.); *Orchis foliosa* [Various] (Green, Yellow, Mauve 5–24 in.); *Serapias Lingua* [Tongue-flowered Orchis] (Purple and Red, May and June, 12 in.); and *Spiranthes autumnalis* [Ladies' Tresses] (White, Late Summer, 6–8 in.). Most of these thrive in moist, sandy loam and leaf-mould or peat and in semi-shaded positions. The *Ophrys*, *Orchis*, and *Spiranthes* like a sunny position. Propagate most species by division in spring or autumn; in some cases by offsets. Greenhouse orchids vary considerably in their requirements, and need careful attention. Space does not permit of these being dealt with thoroughly, and the reader is referred to a work devoted to orchid-growing.

Origanum (Marjoram).—These are hardy herbaceous perennials for the rock or wall garden. They grow about 9 inches high and from June to September carry bracts of glistening rose-pink flowers. The leaves are small and rounded. The origanums thrive in moist, sandy loam and leaf-mould. *Culture.*—Sow seed under glass as soon as ripe or in March, take cuttings in the summer and strike in sandy soil under glass, or divide the roots in March or October.

Ornithogalum (Star of Bethlehem).—Hardy and half-hardy bulbous-rooted plants, suitable for warm borders, for the rock garden, and for naturalizing in grass, and (chiefly *O. arabicum*) for pots. They thrive in ordinary soil in sun or semi-shade. *Culture.*—Plant from September to October, 3½ inches deep and 3 inches apart, and protect from frost in winter. *Pot Culture.*—Pot-up from August to November, placing three bulbs in a 6-inch pot, or singly in a smaller pot, and using a compost of two parts of turfy loam to one part of leaf-mould and sand. Grow near the glass in a cold greenhouse. Propagate by means of offsets. *Species.*—*O. arabicum* (White with Black Centre, May and June, 30 in.); *O. nutans* [Wild Hyacinth] (Greenish-white, May 15 in.); *O. umbellatum* (White, Green Streaks, May, 10–15 in.).

Orontium aquaticum (Golden Club).—Hardy aquatic plants, which thrive in slow-moving water. Propagate by means of root division in March, and plant with from 6 to 12 inches of water above the crowns.

Osmanthus.—Hardy evergreen shrubs, some of which resemble hollies. *Culture.*—Plant in May or September in sandy loam and in sun or partial shade. No pruning is necessary, but long, straggling shoots should be cut back in June. To propagate, strike cuttings of ripened shoots in a frame in September, or layer in summer. *O. Delavayi* (White, March and April, 4–6 ft.) is the best species. *O. Aquifolium* is a good evergreen shrub with small, fragrant, white flowers in late autumn.

Osmaronia (Nuttallia) cerasiformis (Osoberry).—A hardy deciduous shrub, growing from 5 to 10 feet high, and bearing white flowers from February to

March. Male and female flowers are borne on separate bushes, so both should be grown if fruit is desired. The female has purple fruits in autumn. *Culture.*— Plant in October or November in sun or semi-shade and in ordinary soil. Increase by division in late autumn. Thin-out old wood in April after flowering when overcrowded.

Osmunda (Royal Fern).—*See* Ferns, p. 213.

Ourisia.—Hardy perennial creeping plants, which thrive in moist, sandy loam in the shade, and are excellent for moist ledges in the rock garden. *Culture.*— Sow seed under glass in March, or propagate by means of division in April, and plant out in permanent position. No protection is necessary in winter. *Species.* —*O. coccinea* (Scarlet, May–Sept., 7 in.); *O. macrophylla* (White, May–June, 8 in.).

Oxalis (Cape Shamrock, Wood Sorrel).—Hardy and half-hardy annuals, perennials, and bulbous plants, admirably adapted for pots, warm borders, and the rock garden. They succeed in any well-drained light, sandy soil and leaf-mould; the rock garden species need a gritty loam and a position in semi-shade. *Culture.*—(ANNUALS)—Sow seed thinly in March or April in a cool house. Prick off, 3 inches apart, into boxes, harden-off, and plant-out 6 inches apart in early June. (PERENNIALS)—Sow seed under glass in March, or propagate by means of division in March, and plant-out in permanent position. (BULBOUS SPECIES)—Plant from September to November, 3 inches deep and 10 inches apart. Hardy species should not be lifted from the ground, but half-hardy kinds must. In light warm soils, however, protection from frost by means of ashes or fibre will be sufficient. Propagation is by means of small bulbs removed from the parent and planted in September. *Pot Culture.*—Pot-up in March, ¾ inch deep, in 5 to 6-inch pots or pans, and in a compost of two parts of sandy loam to one of leaf-mould. Keep cool, and water sparingly until growth commences, then water liberally, and gradually give more light. *See also* Bulbs, p. 170. *Species and Varieties.*—(ANNUAL)—*O. corniculata* (Yellow, Aug.–Oct., 4 in.); *O. rosea* (Rosy with Deeper Veins, 15 in.). (PERENNIAL)—*O. adenophylla* (Lilac-pink, dark Eye, May–July, 5 in.); *O. enneaphylla* (White, May–Sept., 6 in.); *O. floribunda* (Red, Rose, Mauve, or White, March, 6 in.); *O. lobata* (Yellow, Sept.–Oct., 4 in.); *O. purpurata* (Carmine, Aug.–Sept., 8 in.); *O. tuberosa* (Rose, Oct.–Nov., 6 in.).

Oxydendrum arboreum (Sorrel Tree).—Hardy deciduous trees, which thrive in a loamy or peaty soil and in a sheltered position. They grow up to 30 feet high and have white flowers in July and August. Plant in May or October. To propagate, sow in a frame in March, or strike cuttings.

Ozothamnus rosmarinifolius (Snow in Summer).—A dark evergreen half-hardy shrub (8–10 ft.), bearing white flowers in May and June, and which needs the protection of a wall, except in the warm districts of the south and west. Plant in rich loam or peat in a sunny site, and propagate by cuttings of young wood in a frame.

Pæonia.—Pæonies are divided into two classes, the *herbaceous*, and the *tree or shrubby*. They are mostly hardy and thrive in sun or partial shade in sheltered beds, in well-dug loam enriched with rotted cow-dung, but they will grow in almost any soil.

364

Culture.—(HERBACEOUS)—Propagate by means of division in April or October, and plant-out 3 feet apart, with the crowns 3 inches deep. Transplant as little as possible, never oftener than every five years, and if root divisions are required, they should be cut out with the plant *in situ*. Mulch with well-decayed manure each spring. (P. MOUTAN, THE TREE OR SHRUBBY SPECIES)—Plant in September or early October, and protect from frost. If given gentle forcing in pots, they will furnish early blooms, but forcing should be permitted only in alternate years. Increase by means of layering, or by grafting on *P. officinalis* and *Moutan* stock.

Species (HERBACEOUS).—*P. Cambessedesii* (Pale Pink, 12–18 in.); *P. emodii* (Large White, 24 in.); *P. lactiflora* (White, 24 in.); *P. Mlokosewitchii* (Citron Yellow, 24–36 in.); *P. officinalis* (Dark Red, 24–36 in.); *P. peregrina* (Crimson, 24 in.); *P. tenuifolia* (Crimson, 18–24 in.); *P. Veitchii* (Small Pink, 18–24 in.); and *P. Wittmanniana* (Pale Yellow, 24 in.).

Varieties.—(HERBACEOUS). (SINGLE)—(White) *Bridesmaid;* (White and Pink) *Eastern Brocade;* (Rose-pink) *Avant Garde;* (Deep Pink) *Eva;* (Salmon) *Kelway's Gorgeous;* (Yellow) *Lemon Queen;* (Cherry Red) *Lord Kitchener;* and (Crimson) *Victor Hugo.* (DOUBLE)—(Large White) *Duchess de Nemours;* (Bluish-white) *Lady Alexander Duff;* (Coral-pink) *Kelway's David;* (Pale Pink) *Baron Schroder;* (Rose Pink) *Mme Jules Elie;* (Bright Pink) *Natalie;* (Crimson) *President Poincaré;* (Crimson) *Richard Carvell;* (Dark Red) *M. Martin Cahusæ;* and (Purple) *Louis Van Houtte.* All May to July flowering. P. MOUTAN (TREE PÆONY).—(SINGLE)—(White) *Queen Alexandra;* (Salmon-pink) *Countess of Crewe;* and (Crimson) *Eastern Queen.* (DOUBLE)—(White) *Aphrodite;* (Flesh-pink) *Duchess of Marlborough;* (Rose) *Reine Elizabeth;* and (Scarlet) *Eastern Prince.* All June.

Palms.—Some species require a considerable amount of heat, but such species as the *Areca* (Betel-nut Palm), *Chamærops* (Fan Palm), *Corypha* (Cabbage Palm), *Howea* (Curly Palm), and *Phœnix* (Date Palm), may be grown easily in a house merely protected from frost. Palms are usually bought by the amateur as small plants, and should be re-potted into pots of the same size, in a compost of fibrous loam and silver sand, or fibrous peat and grit. Spring or early summer is the best time for potting. The roots must not be injured, and they must be planted firmly the same depth as before. Water well both summer and winter, sponge the leaves with warm soft water, and syringe morning and evening in spring and summer. Partial shade is required in hot weather, and a little liquid manure made from cow-manure and soot is beneficial. Should the foliage turn yellowish, a small lump of sulphate of iron on the surface of the soil will remedy this. Propagation is usually by means of division in April, by suckers in September, or by seed.

Pancratium illyricum and P. maritimum (Mediterranean Lily, or Sea Daffodil). —Semi-hardy bulbous plants, which thrive in light, rich loam and peat, in warm and well-drained borders, and in sunny, sheltered positions. There are also many stove and greenhouse species. Both plants bear white flowers in May and June on stems 18 inches high. *Culture.*—Plant in October or March, 5 inches deep and 10 inches apart. Do not lift, but protect with fibre in winter. *Pot Culture.*—Repot every third or fourth year (in March) in two-thirds loam to one-third well-rotted manure and a little sand. Dry-off gradually after blooming, and stand hardy species in the open from May to September. Propagate by means of offsets in October or March.

Pandanus (Screw Pine).—This is a large genus of warm greenhouse and stove trees or shrubs. Botanists have described something like eighty species, but very few are grown outside botanic gardens. In fact, the only one generally cultivated is *P. Veitchii*. This is a native of Polynesia, and has green leaves broadly bordered with white. It is a very attractive and useful pot plant for table decoration. Increase is by offsets which develop round the base. Use a sandy, loamy compost, adding a little peat and leaf-mould.

Pandorea jasminoides [*Bignonia and Tecoma jasminoides*] (Bower Plant).—A charming climber for cool greenhouse, requiring rich soil and sunny exposure. (Flowers White sometimes suffused with Pink, Aug.–Oct.).

Panicum (Panick Grass).—A large genus of stove, greenhouse, or hardy, annual or perennial grasses of variable habit. *P. palmifolium* (*P. plicatum*) is a free-growing, green-leaved plant 1⅓ to 1½ feet high, useful as an under-growth in a heated greenhouse.

Pansy (Heartsease).—*See* Viola.

Papaver (Poppy).—Hardy annuals, biennials, and perennials, which thrive in the sun and in almost any soil, though a deep, rich soil is best. They are useful for beds, borders, and the wild garden. *P. alpinum* is a useful rock species; it needs a gritty loam, and is raised from seed sown in autumn. The dwarf-growing of *P. nudicaule* (The Iceland Poppy) is also an extraordinarily attractive little plant. All dead flowers must be picked off, or the season of blooming will be greatly reduced. *Culture.*—(ANNUALS)—Sow seed thinly, ¼ inch deep, in August, or from March to June, and just cover lightly with mould. Do not transplant, but thin out to about 5 inches apart when fit to handle. (BIENNIALS)— *See* p. 141. (PERENNIALS)—*See* p. 156. The latter hate disturbance and should not be lifted oftener than every three or four years. *Species.*—(ANNUAL)—*P. glaucum* (Deep Scarlet, June–Sept., 20 in.); *P. lævigatum* (Red, White, and Black, May–Sept., 25 in.); *P. somniferum* [Opium Poppy] (Crimson, Mauve, Rose, Violet, and White [Double and Fringed], July–Oct., 30 in.); *P. Rhæas vars.* [Shirley Poppy] (Orange, Pink, Red, Lavender, Blue and White [Single and Double], June–Sept., 24 in.). (BIENNIAL)—*P. alpinum* (Yellow, Salmon, White, and Orange, May–Sept., 6–9 in.). (PERENNIAL)—*P. bracteatum* (Scarlet and Black, May–Sept., 36–48 in.); *P. nudicaule* [Iceland Poppy] (Orange, Yellow, Buff, Salmon, and White, May–Sept., 6–24 in.); *P. orientale* (Various, May–June, 30–50 in.). *Named Varieties.*—(*P. orientale*)—(White) *Perry's White;* (Cerise) *Ethel Swete;* (Salmon Pink) *Mrs. Perry;* (Scarlet) *Lord Lamborne;* (Orange) *Orange King;* (Vermilion) *Goliath.*

Paradisea Liliastrum (St. Bruno's Lily).—These are beautiful bulbs, which grow about 20 inches high, bear white flowers in May and June, and grow in well-drained, light soil in sun or partial shade in the border or wild garden. *Culture.*—Plant from 9 to 12 inches apart in October or March, and mulch with old manure in March. Propagate by means of division in September or October.

Parnassia (Grass of Parnassus).—Hardy perennials suitable for the bog, marsh, or water garden, or for the moist shady border. *Culture.*—Sow in the open in autumn, or propagate by means of division in April. *Species.—P. fimbriata; P. nubicola; P. palustris.* All bear white flowers from June to August and grow 5 to 10 inches high.

Paronychia.—Little creeping plants for the paved or rock garden, which thrive in the sun and in gritty loam, and which are propagated by means of division in March, by cuttings under glass, or by seed. *Species.—P. capitata* and *P. serpyllifolia,* flowers insignificant.

Parrotia persica (Persian Witch Hazel).—Hardy deciduous trees, growing from 30 to 40 feet high, and which flower in March. They like a dry ordinary soil, and a sunny, sheltered position. *Culture.*—Plant in November. No pruning is necessary. Propagate by means of layering in summer.

Passiflora (Passion-flower).—A genus of beautiful climbing shrubs, which grow in almost any well-drained soil, though sandy loam is best, and which should be given a position against a sunny wall facing south or west; the root-run should be restricted to encourage flowering. *Culture.*—Strike cuttings of young shoots in a frame in summer. Plant-out in October or March. Cut back shoots to half their length in February or March, and cut-out weak wood. *Greenhouse Culture.*—Plant in March in a compost of two parts of fibrous loam to one part of peat and sand, and syringe and water well in summer. Prune back to within two buds of the old wood in winter, and cut away all weak shoots in spring. *P. cærulea* (Blue, June–Sept., 25 ft.) is the most hardy; for the cool greenhouse, or a warm outside wall, the white variety *Constance Elliott* (June–Sept., 25 ft.) is recommended.

Paulownia tomentosa (*P. imperialis*).—A round-topped deciduous tree, that grows from 30 to 50 feet in height, and which comes from China. The tree, itself, is fairly hardy, but the panicles of flower buds form in autumn and in severe winters are usually frozen, except in the south and west. In Paris, the panicles of blue-purple, foxglove-like flowers are a feature in gardens during May. This Paulownia is a useful subject for sub-tropical gardening. If the stems are cut down to the base each year in March, very vigorous stems, from 10 to 12 feet high, and with huge leaves, are produced in one season.

Pelargonium.—There is frequent confusion over the names *geranium* and *pelargonium.* The former term covers both sections of plants, but is correctly assigned to the hardy perennial sorts (*see* Geranium). The term "pelargonium" includes all half-hardy greenhouse and bedding plants and the show varieties. All pelargoniums need a light, airy position, but no draughts, and only sufficient artificial heat to keep out frost is needed.

Propagation.—About six months after cuttings are struck, the plants should come into bloom. March-struck cuttings should, therefore, flower in autumn and winter; plants raised in July or August, in early spring (those to be used for bedding in the open should, of course, have their early flowers nipped off); while April and May should see the first blooms of September-struck cuttings. June and July are, however, the best months for taking cuttings. The pots are prepared in the usual manner, and filled with a compost of five-eighths of loam to three-eighths parts of sand and leaf-mould. The cuttings should be taken in dry weather when the parent plant has had no water for some days, and they should be kept dry for twenty-four hours before potting. Place five cuttings

367

round the edge of each 4-inch pot and with their stems inserted to a depth of about an inch or an inch and a half. If the cuttings are struck in August or September, the protection of a frame is not essential and the pots may be sunk in a sheltered south border, where they will require no shading unless the sun is very hot. If a frame is used, the lights should only be put on as a protection against heavy rain. When struck in a frame, keep the atmosphere close, shade, and sprinkle the cuttings occasionally overhead till rooted. Gradually harden-off the cuttings for potting-off into 3-inch pots as soon as they are rooted. If they grow too freely before it is time to take them into the house or frames (September), the top shoots should be broken off. These tops may be used to provide another batch of cuttings. Through the winter months, little water and only just sufficient heat (50° F.) to exclude the frost should be given. Pick-off all flower-buds as they appear, and as the weather improves give more air. Late in March, or early in April, re-pot into 5 or 6-inch pots, so that they may be grown on to be hardened-off and planted-out late in May or in early June. From April onwards, plants grown for flowering in pots should receive weekly doses of liquid manure or soot water, and should be grown near the glass in a cool greenhouse, being pinched-back to make them bushy. Plants stopped-back not later than February will flower in May; when blooming is to be delayed until July, pinching back may be continued until towards the end of April. After flowering, ripen the growth in the sun in the open, then cut the stems back to from 3 to 4 inches from the base in July and rest the plants with the pots on their sides in a frame for two months. Then pot-up in fresh soil, keep in the frame, and remove all buds until the plants are moved into the house early in September.

Plants for Autumn and Winter Flowering.—A further batch of cuttings taken from old plants "started" in gentle heat in the greenhouse can, if desired, be struck in the spring (March). These two or three batches of cuttings will provide plants that will bloom, in the greenhouse, practically all the year round. March-struck cuttings should be potted-up singly into 3-inch pots about May. When these pots are full of roots, move the young plants into 4-inch pots; harden-off in a cold frame ready for setting out in the open on a hard bed of ashes in June, or into the open beds, if for summer-bedding. Plants for flowering indoors in autumn and winter should be stopped-back in July, and all flower buds picked off until September. Early in August, move them into 6-inch pots and transfer to a light and airy shelf in the greenhouse at the beginning of September. As the season advances, a little heat (55° F.) will make the plants blossom. Zonal, Ivy-leaved, and Scarlet-leaved pelargoniums, if treated in this way, will flower in autumn and winter; Regals so treated, however, will not come into bloom until March, and will continue to flower until the middle of June.

Plants may also be raised from seed, but this is rarely attempted by the amateur.

Varieties.—(REGAL AND DECORATIVE)—*Duchess of Kent, Bridesmaid, Carisbrooke, Elsie, Godfrey's Pride, Magpie, Mrs. W. J. Godfrey, Pictor, Pearl, Princess Mary, Purple Robe, Queen of the West.* (ZONAL). Single-Flowered for Pots—(Amaranth) *Amarantha*; (Scarlet) *Canopus*; (Magenta) *Mrs. Eddowes*; (Rose-pink) *Freyda*; (Salmon) *Harry Wood*; (Orange) *Janet Scott*; (Pink)

Carolina; (Salmon) *Gwendolen Lysley*; (Cherry-red) *Peach*; (Crimson-lake) *Ryecroft Gem*; (White) *Snowstorm*; (Rosy-pink) *W. A. Cull.* Double for Pots—(Crimson-maroon) *Dr. Despres*; (White, edged Purple) *Emperor Nicholas*; (Violet Red) *Hornsey Violet*; (Crimson) *Ryecroft Pride*; (White) *Ryecroft White*. Bedding—(Scarlet) *Paul Crampel*; (Salmon) *Salmon Crampel*; (White) *Dr. Nansen*; (Orange-scarlet) *Maxime Kovalesky*; (Salmon) *King of Denmark*; (Red) *Decorator*. (IVY-LEAVED)—(Rose) *Madame Crousse*; (Scarlet) *Scarlet Crousse*, and *Sir Percy Blakeney*; (Cream) *Alliance*; (White and Purple) *L'Elegant*; (Deep Pink) *Chas. Turner*; (Soft Pink) *Galilee*; (Crimson) *James T. Hamilton*. (SCENTED-LEAVED)—*P. crispum; P. odoratissimum;* and *P. querci-folium.*

Peltandra virginica (Water Arrow Arum).—A beautiful hardy aquatic plant which thrives in the sun and in ordinary soil at the water's edge. It grows from 24 to 36 inches high, and flowers in July. Propagate by means of division of roots in March, and plant out in permanent position in from 6 to 12 inches of slow-moving water.

Penstemon (Beard Tongue).—Useful and graceful perennials, both dwarf and tall. The dwarf species are excellent for the rock garden, while the taller species make beautiful bed or border plants if treated as half-hardy biennials. All kinds thrive in the sun and in a warm, sandy loam with a third part humus in it. *Culture.*—Sow in boxes of fine soil under glass (50° F.) early in March. Prick-off as soon as possible, harden-off gradually, and plant-out in April or May. Or sow seed in the open late in May, and winter the seedlings in a frame. If preferred, take cuttings of side shoots (three to four joints of young growth with a "heel") in August, and strike in a cold frame, 3 inches apart, in sandy soil. Plant-out 14 inches apart in April. In cold districts, they need a sheltered position and protection from frost. *See also* Chelone. *Species and Varieties* (ROCK GARDEN SPECIES).—*P. barbatus* (Scarlet); *P. Bridgesii* (Reddish); *P. Eatonii* (Red); *P. fruticosus var. crassifolius* (Lavender, 8–12 in.); *P. gentianoides* (Purplish-red); *P. Hartwegii* and *vars.* (Crimson); *P. Newberryi* (Cerise, 4 in.); *P. isophyllus* (Red, 12–18 in.); *P. ovatus* (Blue, 12–18 in.); *P. Roezlii* (Magenta, 6 in.); *P. Scouleri* and *var. alba* (Lavender and White). All June to October flowering. *Named Varieties.*—(BORDER)—(Scarlet and White) *Castle Forbes*; (Crimson) *Crimson Gem*; (Pink) *Daydream*; (Scarlet and White) *George Home*; (Mauve) *Mauve Bedder*; (Rose and White) *Mrs. Ed. Matthews*; (Crimson and Violet) *Mrs. John Forbes*; (Salmon Pink) *Montrose*; (Pink) *Pink Beauty*; (Crimson) *Southgate Gem*; (Scarlet and Cinnamon) *Thos. H. Cook*; (White) *White Bedder*. All grow from 20 to 30 inches in height.

Perilla nankinensis.—Half-hardy annuals with purple foliage, useful for summer bedding and greenhouse. *Culture.*—Sow seed thinly in March under glass. Harden off gradually, and plant out 12 inches apart in June.

Pernettya mucronata (Prickly Heath).—Hardy evergreen shrubs, which do well in moderate sun and in cool and moist, well-drained, peaty loam. *Culture.* —Plant in March or October. No pruning is necessary. *Pot Culture.*—Pot-up in October or November, using 6 to 8-inch pots and a compost of two parts of peat to one part of leaf-mould and sand, and place in the cold greenhouse. Plant outdoors when the berries fall. To propagate, sow in a frame in March, take cuttings in summer, or divide the roots in autumn. *Varieties and colour of Fruit.*—*P. mucronata alba* (White); *P. m. atrococcinea* (Deep Purple); *P. m. lilacina* (Pink); *P. m. speciosa* (Crimson). All bear small white flowers towards the end of May and grow to a height of from 2 to 5 feet.

Petasites.—Hardy herbaceous plants, the most popular, though weedy, species of which is *P. fragrans*, the Winter Heliotrope, which grows some 10 inches high, and carries whitish-lilac flowers in late winter. Almost any moist soil suits petasites well; it needs partial shade. Propagate by means of division in February or March, or seed can be sown in the open in May or June.

Petunia.—Half-hardy soft-wooded perennials, best treated as half-hardy annuals. They like a sunny position and a moderately rich, light soil, and may be used for borders, bedding, and (double varieties) pot culture. *Culture.*— See Annuals, p. 139. If pricked-off into pots for the house, they must be potted-on frequently until in their flowering pots. Double varieties should be propagated by means of cuttings of young wood in a temperature of 60° F. in the spring, or of mature shoots in a cold frame in August. *Pot Culture.*—Pot-up in May, using 6 to 10-inch pots and a compost of two parts loam to one part of leaf-mould and dry, well-rotted manure, and keep in cool greenhouse. Pinch-back to five joints from the old stem as soon as established in the flowering pots. Early training and staking is essential. Flowering may be retarded by standing the plants in a cold frame or on a bed of ashes in the open any time after the middle of May.

Species.—*P. violacea* [syn. *integrifolia*] and *P. axillaris* [syn. *nyctaginiflora*]. There are numerous varieties, both single and double, for which consult any good seed list. (Various, June–Oct., 12 in.).

Phacelia.—Dwarf-growing hardy annuals, suitable for edging, for the border, or the rock garden. They like a sunny or semi-shaded position and ordinary soil. *Culture.*—Sow seed in the open in April, and thin out to about 6 inches apart. Do not attempt to transplant. *Species.*—*P. campanularia* (Deep Blue, June–Aug., 8 in.); *P. tanacetifolia* (Pale Mauve, June–Aug., 20 in.); *P. Whitlavia* (Deep Blue, June–Aug., 8–10 in.).

Phædranassa Carmiolii (Queen Lily).—Half-hardy bulbous plants, with scarlet flowers, segments green margined yellow in spring, growing about 18 inches high. They like a well-drained, deep, sandy loam, and thrive in sunny, sheltered positions in warm borders, or in pots in the greenhouse. *Culture.*— Plant 6 to 9 inches apart and 5 inches deep in March or October, and protect with fibre in winter. Propagate by offsets in March or October.

Philadelphus (Mock Orange).—Hardy deciduous flowering shrubs known as "Syringa", a name which properly belongs to the Lilacs. They thrive in any good garden soil, and like a sunny position. *Culture.*—Plant in October or November. Thin-out the shoots well immediately after flowering and cut-back old and weak wood of the previous year to the young lateral growths at the base. If the shrubs are much overgrown, they should be cut hard back in March. *Pot Culture.*— In the cool greenhouse, *P. Lemoinei erectus* may be had in flower in March. Pot-up annually in October, using 8 to 10-inch pots and compost of two parts of sandy loam to one part of leaf-mould and well-rotted manure. Prune as described above, and sink the pots to their rims in ashes outdoors from May to

December, then take inside again and keep fairly dry until growth commences once more. To propagate, strike cuttings in a frame in July and August. *Species and Hybrids.—P. coronarius* (White); *P. microphyllus* (White); *P. Lemoinei erectus* (White); *P. Norma* [one of the best singles]; *P. Virginal* (White, Double); *P. purpureo maculatus* (White Petals, stained Purple); and *Voie Lactee* (Largest Single White Flowers, 2 inches across). All May to July flowering and growing to a height of from 3 to 15 feet.

Phillyræa (Mock Privet).—Hardy evergreen shrubs, which thrive almost any-where and in any soil. They are especially valuable under trees. *Culture.—*Plant in May or September. Propagate by means of cuttings in a frame, or by layering in September. *Species.—P. angustifolia* (White, May–June, 9 ft.); *P. decora* (White, April, 6–8 ft.); *P. media* (White, May, 6–8 ft.); *P. latifolia* (White, April, 6–15 ft.).

Phlomis fruticosa (Jerusalem Sage).—This is a hardy evergreen shrub that grows from 2–4 feet high and carries yellow flowers in July, August, and Sep-tember. It does well in sunny positions and in ordinary soil. *Culture.—*Plant in March or October. Cut out dead shoots and trim back to shape in March. To propagate, sow seed in a frame in March, or take cuttings in the summer and strike in a frame.

Other species are herbaceous perennials and die to the ground each winter. *Species.—P. cashmiriana* (Lilac, July, 2 ft.); *P. tuberosa* (Purplish Rose, June, 2 ft.); *P. Russellianus* (Yellow, July, 2–3 ft.).

Phlox.—A magnificent genus of annuals and perennials, which need a cer-tain amount of sun and enjoy an open position, but one sheltered from strong winds. The *Phlox Drummondii* varieties—half-hardy annuals—make good bed-ding and pot plants. *Phlox paniculata* [syn. *decussata*], and *P. maculata*, peren-nials, look fine in borders, while the dwarf perennials or *Mossy Phloxes* are excellent for the rock garden. The annual and herbaceous kinds succeed best in deep, rich and moist, but well-drained loam. Stake early and thin-out all weak growths.

Culture.—(HALF-HARDY ANNUALS)—Sow seed thinly in the open in April, or in February and March under glass in slight heat. Prick-out 4 inches apart as early as possible, harden-off, and plant out from 12–18 inches apart early in June. (PERENNIALS)—Sow seed in the open in April, take cuttings of young growths in the autumn, and strike in sandy soil over a little bottom heat under glass. Winter in the cool house near the glass, and in March harden-off in a cold frame ready for planting-out in May. It is also possible to propagate by means of division in February, March, or October.

Pot Culture.—(PERENNIALS)—Pot-up in October, using 5 to 6-inch pots and a rich, sandy soil. Stand in a cold greenhouse, and water freely from April to October, then decrease the water supply. Give liquid manure from May to September. (ANNUALS)—If seed is sown in a frame in August and the seedlings are potted-up and transplanted to the greenhouse, blooms may be had from January to March.

Species.—(ANNUAL)—*P. Drummondii* (Various, June–Oct., 6–12 in.). (PEREN-NIAL)—*P. paniculata* [syn. *decussata*]. (Various, July–Oct., 40 in.). *Named Varieties of P. paniculata—A. E. Amos* (Scarlet); *Antoine Mercier* (Pale Lavender); *Border Gem* (Violet Blue); *Daily Sketch* (Salmon Pink); *Flau. A. Buchner* (White); *Leo Schlageter* (Scarlet); *P. D. Williams* (Soft Pink); *San Antonio* (Purplish Red); *Spitfire* (Salmon Orange); *William Kesselring* (Violet); *William Ramsey* (Dark Purple). *Phlox Arendsii*—Hybrids between *P. canadensis* varieties and *P. paniculata*—(Lilac) *Amanda*; (White and Lilac) *Charlotte*; (Rose) *Hanna*. All flowering from July to September and reaching a height of from 12–18 inches. (ALPINE)—*P. adsurgens* (Pink), 6 in.; *P. amœna* (Carmine-pink, May–July, 6 in.); *P. argillacea* (Lilac-white, July–Aug., 8–15 in.); *P. divaricata* (Lavender-blue, May–July, 6–12 in.); *P. ovata* (Red, May–July, 10 in.); *P. subulata* and *vars.* (Pink, Mauve, Blue, and White, May–June, 4 in.); *P. stolonifera* (Rose-purple, June, 6 in.).

Phormium (New Zealand Flax).—Tall perennials, which require a fairly sheltered, sunny position and a well-drained loam, and flower from June to September. *Culture.*—Sow in a frame in March, or propagate by means of division of roots in April. *P. Cookianum* (Yellow, 60 in.) and *P. tenax* (Crimson, 70 in.) are the best species.

Phyllitis Scolopendrium.—This genus contains both hardy and greenhouse ferns, which grow from 5 inches to 2 feet in height. The hardy sorts thrive in sandy loam, peat, and leaf-mould, with a little mortar in it. They should be planted in the shade in a sheltered spot in the rock garden, or on a moist bank in the bog or marsh garden. *P. S.* (*vulgare*) is the common Hart's Tongue fern. *Culture.*—Plant in April. Propagate by means of division of roots in April or sow spores under glass in July. *See also* Ferns, p. 213.

Phyllodoce.—A race of dwarf heath-like evergreen plants, shrubby, rarely exceeding 7 or 8 inches in height, excellent subjects for the rock garden. They prefer a well-drained soil of equal parts of peat, leaf-mould, a little loam and sand and a moist position either in semi-shade or sun. *Culture.*—Plant in October or March. No pruning is required. Propagate by means of cuttings in a frame in October or layer at that time. All flower in early summer, having pretty bell-shaped flowers. *Species.*—*P. Breweri* (Yellowish, May, 8–12 in.); *P. empetriformis* (Pink pitcher-shaped flowers, June); *P. cærulea* (Reddish Purple, 6–8 in., June).

Physalis (Winter Cherry, Chinese Lantern, or Cape Gooseberry).—Half-hardy and hardy perennials, growing from 20 to 40 inches high, and flowering from June to October. They like warm, light, and rich soil, and a sunny position in a sheltered border. For culture, *see* Perennials, p. 156. *See also* Solanum capsicastrum. *Species and Hybrid.*—*P. Bunyardii* (*hybrid*) and *P. Franchetii* (both Orange Fruits).

Physocarpus.—A genus of hardy shrubs allied to the Spiræa. They are mostly planted in rough shrubberies where plants are left largely to take care of themselves. Increase by cuttings, removal of offsets from outsides of bushes, and by seeds. They thrive in ordinary cultivated garden soil. The best known Physocarpus is *P. opulifolia*, a native of Eastern North America. It grows from 6 to 10 feet high, and has clusters of small white, pink-tinted flowers in June. The variety *lutea* has yellow foliage, which is showy in early summer.

Physostegia (False Dragon's Head).—Hardy perennials, growing from 20 to 40 inches high, and bearing red flowers in late summer. They like partial shade and a rich, sandy soil. *Culture.*—Sow seed in the open in April, or propagate by means of division in March or October, and plant out in permanent position; cuttings may also be raised in a frame in summer. *Species.*—*P. virginiana var. speciosa* (Rich Pink) and *P. virginiana var. alba* (White).

Phyteuma (Horned Rampion).—Hardy perennials. The smaller species thrive in the rock garden in rich, gritty loam; the taller kinds in a deep, rich soil in the border, and love a sunny position. For culture, *see* Perennials, p. 156. *Species.*—*P. comosum* (Pale Blue, June–July, 3 in.); *P. Scheuchzeri* (Blue, May–June, 12 in.); *P. Halleri* (Violet, May and June, 6–20 in.); *P. spicatum* (Lilac, May–June, 2 ft.).

Phytolacca Americana (American Poke-root).—This plant is an excellent tuberous-rooted perennial for growing near the bog garden. The pinkish-white flowers are borne in summer, and are followed by spikes of dark-blue berries. To propagate, sow seed in March under glass or divide the roots and plant out in spring or autumn in any rich soil.

Picea (Spruce).—Hardy evergreen trees of the Conifer family, which thrive in well-drained loam and in sunny positions. *Culture.*—Plant from October to November or in March and April. No pruning is required. Propagate by means of seed. *Species.*—*P. glauca* (*P. alba*) (White Spruce, 60 ft.); *P. Abies* (*P. excelsa*) (Norway Spruce, 50–100 ft.); *P. Smithiana* (*P. Morinda*) (Himalayan Spruce, 60–100 ft.); *P. Omorika* (Serbian Spruce, 60–80 ft.); *P. orientalis* (Oriental Spruce, 60 ft.); *P. pungens glauca* (Blue Spruce, Grey-blue Foliage, 20 ft.). For the rock garden the best are varieties of *P. Abies*, namely, *Clanbrassiliana, Gregoryana, humilis, Ohlendorffi, pumila,* and *pygmæa.*

Picotees.—These are a kind of carnation, distinguished by a narrow, dark-coloured edging to the petals, or by the petals being covered with tiny dots; the ground colour is usually white or yellow. Only the yellow ground picotees are grown in the open; cultivation is in every respect the same as for the carnation, *which see.*

Pieris (Lily of the Valley Bush).—Hardy evergreen shrubs, which like a moist, peaty loam and sand, and a sheltered position in sun or partial shade. *Culture.*—Plant from September to October. Do not prune, but keep in shape by means of "stopping" and removing dead flowers in May. Propagate by means of layering in autumn.

Good kinds are *P. floribunda* [syn. *Andromeda floribunda*] (White, Upright panicles, April–May, 3–6 ft.) and *P. japonica* (White, pendulous racemes, March–April, 4–10 ft.). *See also* Andromeda.

Pinguicula (Butter-wort, or Bog Violet).—Hardy perennial bog plants, which thrive in moist, peaty loam, and in a shady position. *Culture.*—Propagate by means of division in April. *Species.*—*P. alpina* (White); *P. grandiflora* (Blue); *P. vulgaris* [Bog Violet] (Purple-violet). All carry tiny gloxinia-like flowers in April and May, and grow to a height of from 3 to 4 inches.

Pinks (Dianthus).—Beautiful hardy perennials, closely allied to picotees and carnations, and requiring very similar cultivation. They are excellent border and edging plants. New varieties may be obtained from seed sown in April, May, and June, and old plants may be increased by cuttings of basal shoots that have not flowered. These should be some 3 inches long, and should be struck 3 inches apart under a handglass or in a frame in sandy soil in July. Cuttings should be taken with a "heel" or cut square below a joint, and should have the bottom 3 to 4 leaves taken off before being inserted in the soil. When well-rooted, they should be planted in a bed in rows 6 inches apart and with 3 inches between the plants. If preferred, the cuttings can be struck in a sheltered north border. Here they should remain till September, when they may be planted in a bed or in pots, in a compost of two-thirds loam from decayed turf and one-third well decomposed cow-dung. The roots must not be sunk too deep. After being gently watered, the pots may be placed in a cold frame, the lights being closed for the following four-and-twenty hours. In March, re-pot into 24's in which they are to bloom. The best soil for this potting is a mixture of good loam and well-rotted manure from an old hot-bed, with a little white sea-sand and old mortar-rubble added if the soil is at all heavy. March is also the best time to plant border pinks out in the open. These resent disturbance and should remain in position for several years; the ground, however, should be limed periodically and an annual dressing with a phosphate manure must be given. Pinks are also easily increased by division if lifted in September, or they may be layered in July and the young plants can be moved to their new flowering positions in autumn; seed may also be sown under glass in July.

The biennial *Dianthus chinensis*, the Chinese or Indian Pink, is best raised from seed in the autumn, wintered in a frame, and set out in the following May; a sunny position is essential, and a well-limed or chalky soil is a great advantage. Its variety *D. c. Heddewigii* and its named sorts are best treated as annuals. Another delightful class includes the Alpine or rock garden pinks; these are easily grown in a sunny position and in sandy soil. Perpetual-flowering pinks (*D. Allwoodii*), if lifted in autumn and potted-up, will continue to bloom in the greenhouse throughout the winter. They are not particular as to soil, will stand the winter in the open border well, and are easily raised from cuttings or by layering in summer. *See also* Carnation.

Varieties.—(PERENNIAL). (*Border*)—(Pink) *Apple Blossom*; (Carmine, Red Centre) *Bookham Pride*; (Rose-pink) *Dainty Lass*; (Salmon, Laced Red) *Fair Rosamund*; (Salmon, Crimson Centre) *Jean Douglas*; (Shell-pink, Crimson Centre) *May Blossom*; (White) *Mrs. Sinkins*; (White, Margined Deep Maroon) *Peter Pan*; (Salmon-rose and Carmine) *Rosemary*; (Reddish-pink and Crimson) *Sunset*; (Salmon, Laced Crimson) *Vera*; (White) *White Ladies*. Consult the catalogues for numerous varieties. All May to July flowering, and growing to a height of about 12 inches. (ALPINE)—*D. alpinus* (Pink or White); *D. cæsius* (Rose); *D. neglectus* (Reddish-pink). All June flowering, and growing to a height of about 5 inches. (BIENNIAL).—*Named Varieties of D. c. Heddewigii and vars.*—*Aurora* (Salmon-red, Double); *The Bride* (White, Ringed with Purple, Single); *Crimson Bell* (Blood-red, Single); *Empress* (Crimson and Rose, Single); *Salmon Queen* (Single, Fringed); *Scarlet Queen* (Single, Fringed); *Snowdrift* (White, Double, Fringed); *Vesuvius* (Orange, Single, Fringed). All July to October flowering, and growing to a height of from 6 to 12 inches.

Pinus (Pine).—A large family of hardy evergreen trees growing, according to species, from 4½ to 200 feet high. They like a sunny position, and prefer light loam, but will grow well in most soils. *Culture.*—Plant in May or September when from 2 to 3 ft. high. No pruning is required. Never plant pines near a smoky city. *Species and Varieties.*—*P. Griffithii* [syn. *P. Wallichiana*] (Bhutan Pine), *P. nigra* [*P. Laricio*] (Corsican Pine), *P. nigra var. austriaca* (Austrian Pine). The best pine for chalk soils and windswept positions, *P. radiata*, [syn. *P. insignis*], a fast-growing pine for the seaside and mild districts, and *P. sylvestris* (Scot's Pine).

Piptanthus nepalensis (Himalayan Laburnum).—Hardy semi-evergreen summer-flowering shrubs, growing from 6 to 10 ft. high, and which like a sunny, sheltered position and well-drained ordinary soil. To propagate, sow in a frame in March, strike cuttings of semi-matured wood in a frame in summer, or increase by layering.

Plagianthus.—A genus of New Zealand trees and shrubs, also known as *Hoheria* and *Gaya*. They thrive in warm, sunny positions. *P. Lyallii* (*Hoheria Lyallii*) is a large shrub up to 15 feet high, or a small tree in mild districts. A second species, *P. glabrata* (*Hoheria glabrata*) is the hardier of the two shrubs. In July the branches are wreathed with tissue-paper-like white blossoms. Both are useful wall shrubs in cold districts. *P. betulinus* is an elegant birch-like tree some 30 to 40 feet high, and of moderate hardiness.

Platanus (Plane).—These are hardy deciduous trees, which thrive in sunny positions in any well-drained soil. *Culture.*—Plant in November. Prune in winter when the wood becomes overcrowded. To propagate, sow in March, take cuttings in autumn, or layer. *Species.*—*P. orientalis* (Oriental Plane) and the hybrid *P. acerifolia* (London Plane). The latter is a good subject for large town gardens and squares.

Platycodon (Chinese Bell-flower).—These are hardy perennials, which thrive in well-drained, deep, sandy loam, in open, shady positions, and are excellent for the border or rock garden. They grow from 10 to 25 inches high, and flower in July and August. *P. grandiflorum* with glaucous foliage and deep blue flowers, and *P. g. Mariesii*, 10 inches, with white and blue flowers, are good kinds. *Culture.*—Sow seed under glass as soon as ripe or in March, or divide the roots in March or October. No protection is necessary in winter.

Platystemon californicus (Californian Poppy, or Cream-Cups).—A hardy annual which likes a sunny position and light ordinary soil, and is useful for beds, borders, or rock garden. The yellow flowers are borne in summer on 10-inch stalks. For culture, *see* Annuals, p. 140.

Plumbago (Leadwort).—A genus comprising about ten species of plants, mostly perennials, some suitable only for the greenhouse and others hardy. The most noteworthy for greenhouse culture is *P. capensis*, an admirable pillar plant, with pale lavender-blue flowers in September; so also is *P. capensis var. alba* (White). *Culture.*—Pot-up annually in March in 6 to 8-inch pots, or plant in the cool house border. A compost of two parts of loam and one part of leaf-mould and coarse sand is best. Water well and syringe in warm weather, but keep dry from October to March. Young pot plants (not climbers) should be pinched back once or twice. In the case of bushes, cut back the shoots to within 10 inches of the previous year's growth in October. Climbers should be trained in a single stem in much the same manner as a vine. Cut back all laterals of climbers to within 5 inches of their base after flowering, and prune-back again to within 2 to 3 inches from their base early in February, and if grown in the greenhouse border, mulch annually in spring with well-rotted manure. Propagate by cuttings of semi-matured side shoots in gentle bottom heat in spring or early summer. *See also* Ceratostigma.

Podophyllum (Duckfoot or May Apple).—Hardy perennials, which thrive in partial shade and in moist, peaty loam, and which are useful for the bog, or rock garden. They grow from 10 to 30 inches high and in May carry purple or white flowers. Propagate by means of division of roots in April. *P. emodii* and *P. peltatum*, both white and growing to a height of 12–18 inches, are to be recommended.

Polemonium (Jacob's Ladder, or Greek Valerian).—Hardy perennials for sunny borders, or the wild garden, and requiring well-drained loam. Rock garden species need partial shade and a compost of gritty loam and leaf-mould. For culture, *see* Perennials, p. 156.

Species.—P. cæruleum and vars. (Blue or White, June–September, 18 in.); *P. carneum* (Blue, Flesh coloured or Yellow, May–June, 8–12 in.); *P. confertum* (Blue, June–July, 6 in.); *P. mellitum* (Bluish White, June–July, 6–8 in.); *P. reptans* (Slate-blue, March–June, 12 in.).

Polianthes tuberosa (Tuberose).—Half-hardy bulbous plants, growing 24 to 36 inches high, and flowering in September. They thrive in sunny positions in sheltered warm borders, and in a mixture of sandy loam, leaf-mould, and well-rotted manure, or they may be flowered in pots in the greenhouse. *Culture.*—Plant in March, 6 inches deep and 6 inches apart, and do not water until they begin to grow. *Pot Culture.*—Plant bulbs singly in 4 to 5-inch pots, (African kinds) late autumn, (American kinds) early spring, and plunge the pots in fibre in a warm frame (bottom heat 65° F.). When their roots fill the pots, re-pot, and repeat the treatment until the buds appear. The bulbs only flower for one season. Propagation is by means of offsets.

Polyanthus (Primula polyantha).—These are generally classified as: *Gold-laced*, *Fancies*, and *Selfs*, and make an excellent show, especially during April and May, in partially shaded beds and borders, mostly as edging plants. They need a moist, deep, good loam. There are innumerable named varieties. The *Munsted* strain is excellent; the colours are numerous and the flowers are borne from March to June on 8-inch stems. *Culture.*—Sow under glass in April or May, prick-off into boxes, and place in a cold frame. Harden-off, and plant out 9 inches apart in a shady and sheltered reserve border in June, and transfer to their flowering positions in October. Seed may also be sown in the open in July, or the polyanthus can be propagated by division immediately after flowering. *Pot Culture.*—Pot-up singly in 8-inch pots in October, and keep in a cold frame until just before bloom is required, when transfer to the cool house. *See also* Auricula.

Polygala (Milk-wort).—Useful little plants, mostly shrubby evergreens or hardy perennials, which thrive in a mixture of cool, moist, gritty loam and peat, or leaf-mould, and in partial shade in sheltered positions. They are excellent for the rock garden, border, or wild garden, and require no protection in winter. Propagate (HARDY PERENNIALS) by seed sown in the open in May or June, or increase by division of roots in March or October. SHRUBBY SPECIES are in-

376

creased by cuttings of young shoots struck in coarse sand in a propagating case in spring. *Pot Culture.*—(SHRUBBY SPECIES)—Pot-up in March, in a compost of one-half peat, one-quarter fibrous loam, and one-quarter sand. Shade from direct sun, and syringe. Remove all dead flower heads, and, after flowering, cut the shoots of the current year back to within 6 inches of the old wood; then syringe and stand in the sun to ripen the wood. Remove to the house in September. *Species.*—*P. calcarea* (Purple, Blue, Mauve, or Rose, May–Sept., 5 in.); *P. Chamæbuxus* (Purple and Yellow, June–July, 3 in.).

Polygonatum.—Hardy perennials, of which the best known is *P. multiflorum* (Solomon's Seal or David's Harp). It is a highly ornamental border or wild garden plant. The polygonatum will do well in almost any soil and situation. It thrives best, however, in moist good loam and in partial shade. For culture, *see* Perennials, p. 156.

Polygonum (Knot-wort).—A large genus, including hardy annuals, hardy and half-hardy perennials, shrubs, climbers, and trailers. The tall hardy perennials are useful for the wild garden or border, and grow in any ordinary loam, and in partial shade. *P. affine* (Pink, July–Oct., 8 in.); *P. capitatum* (Pink, Summer, Creeper); *P. vaccinifolium* (Pink, Aug.–Sept., Creeper) are rock species, the second being little more than an annual which comes up in the same place each year. *P. baldschuanicum* is a luxuriant perennial deciduous climber, with cream-pink flowers in May and June and again in September. For culture, *see* Annuals, p. 139, and Perennials, p. 156. In the case of shrubby species, do not prune, but cut out old wood from the centre, and trim away thin straggly shoots. *Other Species.*—(ANNUAL)—*P. orientale* (Purple-rose, June–Sept., 4–5 ft.). (PERENNIAL)—*P. campanulatum* (Pink, July–Sept., 3 ft.) and *P. polystachyum* (White, July–Sept., 5–6 ft.).

Polypodium (Polypody).—*See* Ferns, p. 213.

Poncirus trifoliata (Hardy Orange or Bengal Quince).—A hardy deciduous shrub, which likes a sunny position in well-drained fibrous loam and leaf-mould. *Culture.*—Sow in March in a frame, or take cuttings of half-ripened shoots. Plant-out in March or October. After flowering (April or May) cut out dead wood and trim to shape only.

Pontederia cordata (Water Plantain or Pickerel Weed).—These hardy perennial aquatic plants spread over the surface of water, and from June to October bear blue flowers in fine tufts. After flowering, they sink their heads in the water till the seed is ripe. They like a sheltered position and a good loam in still, shallow water. *Culture.*—Propagate by means of division of roots in April, and plant out with from 2 to 12 inches of water above the crowns.

Poppy.—*See* Papaver.

Populus (Poplar).—A large genus of hardy, fast growing, deciduous trees, suitable only for large gardens, and which thrive in moist loam in sunny positions. *Culture.*—Plant in November. No pruning is required. To propagate, strike cuttings of matured wood in the open in October. The Aspen or *Populus tremula*, commonly known as Trembling Poplar because its foliage is always in motion, thrives well almost anywhere, especially in damp places. There is also a very handsome variety, *P. tremula pendula*, a weeping form. *Species and Varieties.*—*P. alba pyramidalis* (White Bolleana Poplar), *P. canescens* (Grey

377

Poplar), *P. lasiocarpa* (A very Large-leaved Chinese Poplar), *P. nigra betuli-folia* (Manchester Poplar, a useful town and street tree), *P. tremuloides* (American Aspen), and *P. trichocarpa* (Western Balsam Poplar). Hybrid Poplars of very fast growth: *P. Eugenei*, *P. generosa*, and *P. robusta*. *P. nigra var. italica* is the Lombardy Poplar and is very useful to form a tall screen quickly.

Portulaca (Purslane).—These half-hardy plants, which grow about 6 inches high, and flower from June to September, are nice little plants for the rock and wall gardens. *P. grandiflora*, with purple, red, yellow or white flowers, is the best known. *Culture.*—Sow seed thinly in April in the open, or under glass as soon as ripe, or in March, and thin out the seedlings or transplant to 6 inches apart in May and June. They require a sunny site and a sandy soil. Their fleshy leaves will take on a pinkish tinge in autumn, forming a background to a mass of brilliant flowers. *See also* Calandrinia.

Potentilla (Cinquefoil).—A genus of plants, some species of which bear a resemblance to the strawberry in flower, and in some cases, to its manner of propagation. Many species, however, are of a low-growing or shrubby nature, others are hardy perennials. All do well in sun or semi-shade, in the border or rock garden (dwarfs), in deep, sandy soil. Sow seed in light loam in spring, increase by division in March or October, or strike cuttings of well-ripened shoots in a frame in autumn. The old and dead wood should be thinned-out in September. *Species and Varieties.*—(BORDER)—*P. argyrophylla var. atrosanguinea* (Crimson); *P. Gibson's Scarlet*; *P. grandiflora* (Yellow); *P. Hopwoodiana* (Apricot). All May to September flowering, and growing to a height of from 12 to 18 inches. (ALPINES)—*P. alba* (White); *P. nepalensis var. minor* (Crimson); *P. n. var. Miss Willmott* (Rose); *P. nitida* (Pale Pink); *P. Tonguei* (Orange, Spotted Crimson). All May to September flowering, and growing to a height of from 6 to 12 inches. (SHRUBBY)—*P. fruticosa* (Yellow); *P. f. var. Veitchii* (White); *P. f. var. Vilmoriniana* (Sulphur). All July to September, and 3 to 4 feet.

Poterium (Burnet).—Hardy perennials, which thrive in ordinary soil in sunny borders. For culture, *see* Perennials, p. 156. These plants grow from 10 to 30 inches high, and flower from July to September. *Species.*—*P. canadense* (Rosy-purple) and *P. obtusum* (Rose).

Pratia.—Hardy dwarf-growing rock plants, which thrive in sandy peat and leaf-mould in sunny positions on well-drained banks, and from May to August carry white or blue flowers on 3-inch stems. *Culture.*—Sow seed in heat, in sandy loam and leaf-mould as soon as ripe or in March; take cuttings in August and strike in sandy soil in a frame; or propagate by means of division of roots in spring. *Species.*—*P. angulata* (White); *P. begonifolia* (Blue); and *P. (Lobelia) linnæoides* (Pinky).

Primrose (Primula vulgaris).—*See* Primula.

Primula.—A large genus, including some of the most popular flowers, the auricula, the cowslip, the polyanthus, and the primrose. In the greenhouse, in the rock garden or bog garden, in beds, and growing wild in the woods, the primula is one of the most useful genus that exists. The majority thrive in rich, deep loam, and appreciate the admixture of leaf-mould and grit with the soil, with the exception of the higher alpine species, which appreciate a compost containing a quantity of old mortar rubble, and like a position in the sun. *P. marginata* (Blue) is an example of this class. They are all moisture-lovers, but must have a well-drained soil. The majority like partial shade, unless unlimited moisture is available in hot weather.

Culture.—Sow seed in pots or pans, under glass, in May, in a compost of equal parts of loam, leaf-mould, and sand, all sieved through a ½-inch mesh, and well mixed. Cover thinly with fine, sandy soil, and keep in a temperature of 60° F. Prick-off 1 inch apart into pans as soon as possible and, in about three weeks, pot-up singly into 3-inch pots, harden off, and keep on a bed of hard ashes in a shaded frame. Transfer to 5 to 6-inch pots in September. Propagate also by means of division in September, or in spring.

Pot Culture.—Pot-up firmly in September or October, using 5 to 6-inch pots and a compost of half loam and half leaf-mould, rotted manure, and coarse sand, and keep in a frame until November, pinching-off any flower buds that form; then transfer to the cool greenhouse for flowering. A little soot water may be given from time to time while the buds are forming. Discard the plants after flowering, except in the case of rare and choice varieties. *See also* Auricula, Polyanthus, etc.

Alpine primulas are of great value in the rock garden and the bog garden. The first group thrives among the rocks in rich loam; the second class loves a cool, moist, but well-drained soil. Space does not permit us to deal more fully with these, but below, the first group are marked with an * and the second †. *Species and Varieties.*—*P. vulgaris* [*Primrose*] (Various, April, 6 in.); *P. Auricula* (Golden yellow, March–May, 6 in.); †*P. Beesiana* (Magenta, May–June, 20–30 in.); †*P. Bulleyana* (Orange-scarlet, April–May, 12–18 in.); †*P. capitata* (Blue, April–June, 6–12 in.); *P. denticulata* (Lilac and White, Feb.–April, 12–18 in.); †*P. farinosa* (Rose-purple, May, 6 in.); †*P. Florindæ* (Yellow, July–Aug., 1–3 ft.); †*P. helodoxa* (Yellow, June–July, 10–18 in.); †*P. japonica vars.* (Various, May–Aug., 12–24 in.); †*P. Juliæ* (Magenta, April and May, 4 in.); *P. kewensis* (Pale Yellow, April, 15 in. [Half-hardy]); †*P. Littoniana* (Reddish-purple, July–Aug., 12–24 in.); *P. malacoides* (Pale Mauve, Pink or White, Sept.–May, 12–24 in. [Half-hardy]); *P. marginata* (Lavender-blue, margined White, May, 6 in.); †*P. minima* (Rose-pink, May–June, 2 in.); *P. nivalis* (White, Feb.–May, 6 in.); *P. obconica vars.* [Tender] (Various, Spring, 9–12 in.); †*P. pulverulenta* (Crimson-maroon, April–May, 20 in.); †*P. rosea* (Rosy-pink, March–May, 4–7 in.); *P. Sieboldii vars.* (Red, Purple, Lilac, May–June, 12 in.); †*P. sikkimensis* (Sulphur-yellow, May–June, 20 in.); *P. sinensis* (Various, Sept.–April, 12 in. [Tender]); *P. stellata* (Various, Sept.–May, 12–24 in. [Tender]); †*P. Veitchii* (Magenta, May–June, 6–12 in.); *P. viscosa var. Mrs. G. H. Wilson* (Dark Blue, April–May, 4–7 in.). Those without distinguishing marks are for the greenhouse.

Prunella (Self-heal).—Dwarf-growing hardy perennials, thriving in moist, light, and rich soil, in the sunny border or rock garden. *Culture.*—Sow seed in the open in April, or propagate by means of division in April or October, and plant out in permanent position. *Species.*—*P. grandiflora* (Purple, Red, Blue, or White vars., 8 in.); *P. vulgaris laciniata alba* (White, 6 in.). All July to September flowering.

379

Prunus.—A large genus of hardy deciduous flowering and fruit-bearing trees, including *P. Amygdalus* [*communis*] (Almond), *P. Armeniaca* (Apricot), *P. Avium* (Gean), *P. cerasifera* (Cherry Plum), etc. No genus of trees adds more to the beauty of the garden in spring. They do best in a deeply dug and well-manured soil rich in lime, or in localities with a chalk subsoil. *Culture.*— Plant in October, in sunny positions sheltered from north and east winds. To propagate, sow seed, or bud in the open in summer on plum stocks. *Pot Culture.* —*P. sinensis* is a useful species for cultivation in the cold greenhouse. Pot-up in November, using 6 to 8-inch pots and well-manured ordinary soil. After flowering, sink the pots to their rims in ashes outdoors in a sunny spot from May to December, then take indoors. In the main, pruning should be as for ordinary fruiting plum trees (*which see*), but prune-out weak wood and dead flower shoots after flowering. The Japanese Cherries, varieties of *P. serrulata* var. *Lannesiana*; and *P. triloba fl. pl.*, may be grown in the cool house. Pot-up in October, using 8 to 12-inch pots and a compost of two parts of sandy loam to one part of leaf-mould and rotten manure. Subsequent treatment as described above.

The common Almond (*Prunus Amygdalus*) is well known from its being one of the earliest flowering trees in England, when it is literally covered with delicate pink blossoms, which appear before the leaves. The trees, which grow from 12 to 20 feet high or more, and flower during March and April, are hardy and very ornamental.

P. triloba fl. pl. is excellent on a south wall. The large, double, delicate pink flowers appearing in April. Plant in November, in a sunny position, in well-dug and well-manured ordinary soil containing lime. Prune hard back immediately after flowering.

P. (Amygdalus) tenella, a dwarf-growing species, is useful for pot culture in the cold greenhouse. Pot up in November, using a 6 to 8-inch pot and a compost of 2 parts of sandy loam to 1 part of leaf-mould and rotten manure. These dwarf specimens grow to from 12 to 18 inches high, and flower in April. Prune in December to shape only. *Varieties.*—*alba*, *georgica* and *Gessleriana*.

Prunus Laurocerasus (Laurel).—Evergreen shrubs, which thrive in almost any soil and are useful for hedges. Prune carefully in May and September with a knife—shears must not be used—and when some years old, cut-out old wood. Plant young bushes 2 feet apart in March or September, and cut the vigorous young shoots back below the level of the others. Propagate by means of cuttings and layering.

Pseudolarix amabilis (P. Fortunei) (Golden Larch).—Hardy deciduous coniferous trees, which thrive in well-drained loam in sunny, sheltered positions. *Culture.*—Plant in October or November. No pruning is required.

Pseudotsuga taxifolia (Douglas Fir).—Hardy evergreen coniferous trees, which thrive in full sun in a cool moist soil, and reach a height of between 100 and 200 feet. *Culture.*—Plant from September to November. No pruning is required. Propagate by means of seeds.

Pteridophyllum racemosum.—This is a minute plant in the poppy family, though seeming very far removed from it. It forms dense little tufts, and looks for all the world like a small Asplenium or Lomaria. Stems from 3 to 8 inches in height rise from the foliage and from these hang tiny ivory-white flowers. This is a useful plant for the Alpine House, and must be grown in a shady place and in a damp, well-drained, peaty, and sandy loam.

Pterocephalus Parnassii (*Scabiosa Pterocephalus*).—(Mauve, June–Oct., 4–6 in.). Closely allied to Scabiosa and succeeds with the same cultural conditions.

Pulmonaria (Lungwort).—These are hardy herbaceous perennials, growing from 6 to 12 inches high and flowering in April and May. They like a semi-shaded position and light, rich loam, and are useful subjects for planting in crevices in the rock garden. *Culture.*—Propagate by means of division of roots or cuttings in the spring or autumn, and plant out in flowering positions at those times. They require no protection in winter. *Species.*—*P. angustifolia azurea* (Rich Blue); *P. rubra* (Red); *P. saccharata* (Rosy-blue).

Punica Granatum (Pomegranate).—A deciduous shrub, which loves a light, rich loam and in the open requires the protection of a south wall. Cut out dead and weak wood in the autumn. Propagate by cuttings of semi-mature shoots in summer in slight heat, or graft in March. The fruit rarely develops in Great Britain.

Puschkinia scilloides (Striped Squill).—A hardy bulbous plant, which grows about 6 inches high and flowers in April and May. It thrives in deep, rich, sandy soil, mixed with leaf-mould, in warm, sunny borders or in the rock garden. *Culture.*—Plant in October, 3 inches deep and 3 inches apart. Protect with fibre in winter, and lift triennially.

Pyracantha (Fire Thorn, Evergreen Thorn, or Cratægus Pyracantha).—Very beautiful hardy evergreen bushes or climbing shrubs, which thrive in any good, light loam in sunny positions and against walls and fences. All bear white flowers from May to June. *Culture.*—Sow seeds when ripe, or strike cuttings in summer. Plant in October or April. Trim to shape only in early spring, but clip as little as possible. *Species and Varieties.*—*P. angustifolia; P. coccinea; P. coccinea Lalandii; P. Gibbsii; P. Gibbsii yunnanensis; P. Rogersiana.* See also Cratægus.

Pyrethrum [syn. Chrysanthemum coccineum].—Hardy perennials, now included under the genus Chrysanthemum, and which thrive in cool, light, deep, and moderately rich soil in sunny, open borders. For culture, *see* Perennials, p. 156. *P. aureum* (Golden Feather) is a popular foliage plant for summer-bedding, and grows about 5 inches high. *Varieties.*—(SINGLE)—(White) *Princess Marie*; (Soft Pink) *Eileen M. Robinson*; (Salmon Pink) *Salmon Beauty*; (Bright Red) *Brenda*, and *Firefly*. (DOUBLE)—(White) *White Madeline*; (Pink) *Queen Mary*; (Crimson) *J. N. Twerdy*. All flower in May and June and again in August, reaching a height of from 18 to 30 inches.

Pyrola (Winter Green).—This genus contains several pretty little dwarf-growing perennials of the Heath family, with spikes of flowers very like those of the Lily of the Valley. *P. chlorantha* (Greenish-white), *P. elliptica* (White), and *P. minor* (Pinky-white), all flowering in summer and growing about 3 inches high, are popular species for the rock garden. *P. rotundifolia* (White) grows from 6 to 8 inches high. *Culture.*—Propagate by means of division of roots in spring or sow seed. A semi-shaded site is desirable, also gritty, peaty loam.

381

Pyrus.—A genus of hardy deciduous trees, including *P. nivalis* (Snowtree) and *P. sinensis* (Sand Pear). *Culture.*—Plant in November in a sunny position sheltered from cold winds, in deeply-dug and well-manured ordinary soil. Thin-out the branches when overcrowded, and cut-out dead wood and weak shoots after flowering. Propagate by means of seed, grafting, or budding in the open. For Pyrus (Crab), *see* Malus. For Pyrus (Mountain Ash), *see* Sorbus.

Quamoclit (Star Glory).—Half-hardy climbers, closely allied to *Ipomœa*, and sometimes included in that genus. Most of them succeed under the same cultural conditions. *Species.*—*Q. coccinea* (*Ipomœa coccinea*), annual (Flowers Scarlet with Yellow throat, climber, 10 ft.); *Q. lobata* (*Mina lobata*); (Crimson and Pale Yellow, Climber, 20 ft.); *Q. pennate* (*Ipomœa Quamoclit*) (Scarlet, leaves pinnate, Climber) known as Cypress Vine.

Quercus (Oak).—A large genus of hardy deciduous and evergreen trees, the majority of which are too large for the average garden. Below will be found a small selection of the best species and varieties for pleasure-ground and hedge-row planting. *Culture.*—Plant young trees in October or November in a sunny position and in deep, good loam. Thin-out the branches in summer when required. To propagate, sow acorns in the open in September, or October, as soon as ripe, or graft in spring.

Species and Varieties.—(DECIDUOUS)—*Q. Cerris* (Turkey Oak); *Q. coccinea* (Scarlet Oak); *Q. c. splendens* (Knap Hill Scarlet Oak); *Q. palustris*; *Q. Robur* (Common Oak); *Q. rubra* (Red Oak); *Q. sessiliflora* (Durmast Oak). (EVERGREEN).—*Q. Ilex* (Holm Oak); *Q. Suber* (Cork Oak).

Ramonda (Pyrenean Primrose, Rosette Mullein).—A small hardy perennial rock plant, which thrives in the shade, in a mixture of loam, peat and leaf-mould. For culture, *see* Rock Plants, p. 196.

Species and Varieties.—*R. pyrenaica* (Pale Purple-blue, Orange Centre); *R. pyrenaica var. alba and rosea*; *Ramonda Nataliæ* (Deep Purple-blue). All flower from May to August and grow about 6 inches in height.

Ranunculus.—A large genus of herbaceous perennials and tuberous-rooted plants, including the common buttercup. Most species thrive in partial shade, in moist, deep, well-dug, rich, sandy soil with ample leaf-mould in it. They are also useful for pot culture. The dwarf-growing kinds are splendid plants for the moraine, if grown in good loam to which has been added ample coarse sand and a little well-decayed cow-dung and leaf-mould. The alpine species cannot stand a position in which the soil dries up very quickly, and they need ample water in summer. *R. aquatilis* and *R. Lingua* are valuable for the water garden. They are best planted in boggy soil in November. *R. aconitifolius* is a taller species that may be grown with advantage in the bog or marsh garden. *R. alpestris* is the best of the high alpine species. It is vigorous, and all through the summer carries masses of white flowers almost an inch in width. *Culture.*—(PERENNIALS)—Propagate by means of division in November or April. The plants should remain in position for several years. (TUBEROUS)—Plant the tubers, claws downwards, 2 to 3 inches deep and 4 to 6 inches apart, early in February or March, surrounding them with sand and charcoal. Lift the tubers after flowering. *Species.*—(FIBROUS-ROOTED)—*R. aconitifolius fl. pl.* (White [Double], May–July, 24–30 in.); *R. acris fl. pl.* (Yellow [Double], May–June, 24 in.); *R. aquatilis*

382

(White, May and June, 2–12 in.); *R. Lingua major* (Yellow, June–Aug., 30–50 in.). (TUBEROUS-ROOTED)—*R. asiaticus vars.* [Persian, French, and Turban] (Various, May–July, 6 in.). (ALPINE)—*R. alpestris* (White, May–Aug., 4 in.); *R. amplexicaulis* (White, May–Aug., 10 in.).

Raoulia australis.—This is a compact little creeper with silvery-grey foliage and inconspicuous flowers, which makes a very pretty carpet plant for some hot, dry, stony place. It likes a sunny position, and gritty loam and leaf-mould. Seed may be sown in March under glass, or propagation can be carried out by means of division of roots in April or May.

Raphiolepis.—A vigorous evergreen flowering shrub, which grows well in well-drained, ordinary soil. In cold districts, it should be given the protection of a south wall. Pruning is rarely necessary, but may be done in March. Propagation is by cuttings under glass. The best species are: *R. indica* (Rosy-red, 4 ft.); *R. umbellata* [*japonica*] (White, 3 ft.); and the hybrid *R. Delacouri* (Rosy-red, 4 ft.). All species may be forced in the greenhouse in spring.

Reseda odorata (Mignonette).—This sweet-scented perennial is commonly grown as an annual. It likes a fairly rich soil with lime in it, and a sunny position. *Culture.*—Sow seed thinly, ¼ inch deep, in a firm seed bed in the sun from March to June. Thin out to 12 inches apart when fit to handle. Seedlings grown in the open should not be transplanted. *Pot Culture.*—Sow in pots under glass in March, June, August, and September, using a compost of two parts of loam to one part of rotted cow-manure and a little crushed lime-rubble and sand, and placing several seeds in each 6-inch pot. Thin to four plants in each pot, and stand near the glass or grow in a frame. Cut-off all dead flowers, and prune back straggly shoots. *Named Varieties.*—*Crimson Giant*; *Golden Gem*; *Pearl* (Cream); *Machet* (Buff); *Salmon Queen* (Salmon-pink); *Giant Red* (Red). All flower from July to September and grow from 9 to 18 inches in height.

Retinospora.—*See* Chamæcyparis.

Rhamnus (Buckthorn).—These are small trees that will do well almost anywhere, provided they have shelter from wind. *Culture.*—Plant in the late autumn or early spring. Prune in February. Propagate by means of cuttings in the open in September, by layering in October or March, or sow seed outdoors in September. *R. cathartica* (Common Buckthorn); *R. Alaternus* (Evergreen, growing to a height of 12 ft.) is a good kind.

Rheum (Rhubarb).—The ornamental rhubarbs, which thrive on moist, sunny banks or in the water garden in deep, rich loam, are grown chiefly for their foliage. For culture, *see* Perennials, p. 156.

Rhododendron.—Among the most handsome and finest of all our flowering shrubs are the hardy rhododendrons. Most hardy species thrive best in a position sheltered from north and east winds and in positions sheltered from the midday sun. They prefer well-trenched and well-drained, moist, peaty loam, but will grow in almost any soil deficient in lime or chalk, providing it contains ample decaying vegetable humus, and is sufficiently porous. Most flower from April to June, but a few early kinds bloom from Christmas onwards. Rhododendrons bear frequent transplanting so long as the ball of earth round their roots is not broken. They are surface-rooters and will not grow on steep banks, where the roots will parch up in summer. Except in the case of such hybrids as

383

Bagshot Ruby, The Bride, or *Pink Pearl*, which will grow in full sun, rhododendrons require some sun, which should, however, be intermittent. These shade conditions are best supplied by trees and large bushes planted among the rhododendrons, and deciduous kinds will be found better than evergreens and conifers, in view of the leaf-mould with which they will annually mulch the soil. Rhododendrons will not, however, flower entirely under the shade of trees. For the majority of these bushy species, the atmosphere should be as damp as possible. Several of the early-flowering species are useful greenhouse plants, as they furnish bloom from January to early March. Chief among these are *R. dauricum, R. mucronulatum, R. moupinense* and *R. præcox*, all hardy plants. In addition to the hardy and half-hardy species, there are choice greenhouse kinds, which require moist warmth all the year; these are best grown in a cool house during the winter and kept under glass in summer (Temp. 50° F.).

When purchasing rhododendrons, care must be taken that species chosen are suitable for the climate.

Culture.—Plant and "heel-in" very firmly in October or November, or at any time in winter and spring, up to May, providing the soil is not water-logged and that there is no frost. When planting, add some well-rotted leaf-mould. Fresh stable manure must not be used. If the weather is dry, soak the hole well before planting, and in any case, a little leaf-mould should be placed at the bottom for the roots to rest upon. Bushy species should be set 6 feet apart, and smaller lime-hating subjects, such as azaleas, kalmias, daphnes, and heaths, can be used to fill the gaps until the rhododendrons have grown a bit. Do not prune young bushes, merely keep them in shape by means of "stopping" and removing dead blooms immediately after flowering. When it is necessary to cut back old and straggling plants, do so in April. Top-dress annually in March with good leaf-mould, and every second or third year give a top-dressing of old hot-bed manure or old mushroom bed manure in May.

Propagation.—To propagate hybrids, graft (on stock *R. ponticum*) under glass from January to May, layer well-matured shoots in late summer, or take cuttings. Species may be increased by means of seed sown thinly in March or April in pans, in a compost of equal parts of well-sieved leaf-mould, or peat, and coarse sand in a cold frame. Most species may be raised from cuttings of semi-matured shoots, struck in a frame with slight bottom heat, and practically all species can be layered in summer. For Pot Culture, *see* Azalea.

Species.—*R. Augustinii* (Lilac-blue); *R. discolor* (Late Flowering, Large White); *R. Fortunei* (Pale Pink); *R. hippophæoides* (Blue); *R. micranthum* (Small Clusters of White Flowers); *R. orbiculare* (Rose); *R. racemosum* (Pink to White); *R. rubiginosum* (Rose-lilac); *R. yunnanense* (Flesh-pink, Dark Markings).

Rock Garden Species.—*R. calostrotum* (Rose); *R. chryseum* (Yellow); *R. ferrugineum* (Rose); *R. hirsutum* (Rosy-pink); *R. impeditum* (Lavender-blue); *R. intricatum* (Pale Blue); *R. keleticum* (Rosy-purple); *R. ledoides* (Rosy-white); *R. muliense* (Primrose-yellow); *R. racemosum* (Rosy-pink to White); *R. repens* (Crimson); *R. rupicola* (Plum-purple); *R. salvense* (Rosy-crimson); *R. scintillans* (Lavender-blue); *R. telmateium* (Blue-purple); and *R. Williamsianum* (Rose).

Hybrids.—Alice (Deep Rose-pink); *Ascot Brilliant* (Deep Blood-red); *Bagshot Ruby* (Ruby-red); *Britannia* (Rich Red); *Charles Dickens* (Scarlet); *Countess of*

384

From paintings by Emily Sartain

PLATE 12 *Above, V A R I E T I E S   O F   R A N U N C U L U S ;   Below, Z I N N I A S*

Athlone (Mauve); *Countess of Derby* (Rose); *Cunningham's White* (White, tinged Pink); *Doncaster* (Bright Scarlet, spotted Dark Brown); *Duchess of Connaught* (White, flecked Lemon); *fastuosum fl. pl.* (Pale Lavender [Semi-double]; *Hugo de Vries* (Rich Pink); *Loder's White* (White); *Lord Palmerston* (Deep Rose); *Mrs. E. C. Stirling* (Pale Mauve); *Mother of Pearl* (Blush-white, Red stamens); *Pink Pearl* (Flesh-pink); *Sappho* (White, heavily spotted Maroon); *Snowflake* (White); *The Bride* (White, marked Green); and *Unknown Warrior* (Rose-crimson).

Rhodothamnus Chamæcistus.—This is a dwarf-growing, ericaceous, evergreen shrub, that carries pretty, pale pink flowers from March to May. The leaves are edged with spines, and the plants, which grow from 6 to 12 inches in height, do best in a well-drained, peaty soil, and are most pleasing subjects for semi-shaded sites in the rock garden.

Rhopalostylis Baueri.—This is a greenhouse palm and requires the same treatment as Areca.

Rhus (Lacquer Tree or Stag's Horn).—Hardy deciduous trees and shrubs, which like a sunny position and good loam. *Culture.*—Plant in October. Cut-out all old and dead wood. To propagate, strike cuttings of matured shoots under bell-glasses in September, or layer in September. *Species.*—*R. Toxico-dendron* [Poison Ivy] (Shrub 10 ft.); *R. typhina* [Stag's horn] (Greenish Flowers in June, Orange Foliage in Autumn, 10–25 ft.); and *R. verniciflua* [Varnish Tree] (Tree, 30–40 ft., attractive foliage).

Rhus Cotinus.—*See* Cotinus Coggygria.

Rhus cotinoides.—*See* Cotinus americanus.

Ribes.—Mostly hardy deciduous shrubs, akin to the currant and gooseberry, which thrive in sun or part shade in ordinary garden soil, and which should be treated in exactly the same way as gooseberries and currants, *see* Chapter devoted to Fruit Culture.

Species.—*R. alpinum* (Yellow); *R. sanguineum* (Flowering Currant) with rosy-red flowers in April; *R. sanguineum var. Brocklebankii* (Golden Foliage); *R. s. King Edward VII* (Crimson); and *R. speciosum* (Fuchsia flowered Gooseberry) (Red, 10 ft.) are the best known.

Richardia.—*See* Zantedeschia.

Ricinus communis (Castor-oil Plant).—Half hardy plants, which thrive in rich loam in warm beds, or in the cold greenhouse. One of the best varieties is *R. communis var. Gibsonii. Culture.*—Sow singly in pots, in March, under glass (Temp. 50° F.). Pot-on into 5-inch pots, harden-off, and plant-out in June, or pot-on into 6 to 8-inch pots and keep indoors.

Robinia (Hardy or Rose Acacia and False Acacia).—Hardy deciduous summer-flowering trees, which like a well-drained, light soil, and a sunny, sheltered position. *R. Pseudo-Acacia*, the Locust Tree or False Acacia (White, 50 ft.), is the most common and is a good town tree. The most attractive species for the garden, however, is *R. hispida*, the Rose Acacia (Pink, 9 ft.). *Culture.*—Plant in November. Do not prune, but merely trim to keep in shape. Propagate by means of seed or by grafting.

Rocket (Hesperis, Dame's Violet).—Early spring-flowering hardy annuals, biennials, and perennials, which grow freely in any light soil in a sunny position, and are excellent for the mixed border. *Culture.*—(ANNUALS)—These may be easily raised from seed in the usual way. (BIENNIALS)—Sow in the open in May, and thin-out as soon as fit to handle. (PERENNIALS)—Sow seed in the open in spring or summer, or divide the crowns in July or August, replant in reserve garden, and plant-out in March or October.

Species.—(BIENNIAL)—*H. tristis* (Cream, Brownish-red, Purple, May–Sept., 12–24 in.). (PERENNIAL)—*H. matronalis* (White, Red, Rose, Purple [Single and Double], June–July, 20 in.); *H. violacea* (Violet, May–July, 18 in.).

Rodgersia.—Hardy perennials, growing 4 ft. high and bearing pink or white flowers in June or July, and which thrive in partial shade in a moist border or by water's edge in peaty soil. *See* Perennials, p. 156. *R. æsculifolia* (Pink) and *R. pinnata* (Red) are good species.

Romneya (Californian or Bush Poppy).—Deciduous flowering shrubs or shrubby perennials. They are almost hardy, and thrive in the sun, and in well-drained, sandy, enriched loam, in a sheltered position or under a south wall. *Culture.*—Plant in March. Cut-out all dead wood in the spring and cut-back any weak growth. In severe winters, protect with straw, bracken, or sacking; in the north, these plants must be grown under glass. *Pot Culture.*—Pot-up annually in April, in a compost of sandy peat and leaf-mould in 6 to 7-inch pots. To propagate, divide the roots in March, or strike root-cuttings in a frame in the autumn.

Species.—*R. Coulteri* [*Matilija Poppy*] (White, June–Sept., 5 ft.) and *R. trichocalyx* (White, June–Sept., 5 ft.) are the best known.

Rosa (Wild Rose, Briar).—This name includes all the wild roses and the briars. Most species are strong growers. *Culture.*—Plant from November to March, in a sunny position, and in ordinary soil. In March, cut away old wood and cut back long shoots. To propagate, strike matured cuttings in the open in October or November. A few, like *R. spinosissima* (Scotch Rose), are readily increased by division.

Species.—*R. Hugonis* (Yellow, 6–8 ft.); *R. moschata* (Musk Rose, climbing up to 40–50 ft. on trees); *R. Moyesii* (Lurid Dark Red), 6–12 ft.; *R. omeiensis* (White, 6–10 ft.); *R. o. pteracantha* (Large Red Spines); *R. rubiginosa* (Pale Pink, 6–8 ft.) (Sweet Briar); *R. rugosa* (Purplish-rose, 4–6 ft.); *R. setipoda* (Rosy-pink, 6–10 ft.); *Attractive fruits in autumn.

Roses.—Roses are divisible roughly into several groups or classes. The two largest classes, containing most of the garden and exhibition roses of to-day, are the Hybrid Perpetuals and the Teas. These two groups include sub-divisions; thus, the Hybrid Perpetuals are often held to include Hybrid Teas and Perpetual Bourbons, while the Noisettes are classed with the Teas. Then we have the climbers and ramblers, including the Briar family and the Wichuraiana Roses. Many of the dwarf-growing species of roses are excellent for inclusion in the rock garden, and among them we have *Rosa pendulina* (*alpina*) *pyrenaica*, a crimson-flowered rose, only attaining to about 2 feet. With this may be grown *Rosa Seraphinii*, a Corsican native, which is trailing in habit, and only reaches a total height of about 10 or 11 inches. It bears very attractive bright pink single flowers in June. *Rosa nitida* is yet another of these delightful dwarf roses with very lovely foliage.

386

Soil.—The very best of all soil for roses is a deep stiff loam. The worst soil for roses, after pure sand, or nearly so, is the black soil of the town garden, very porous, and over-full of organic matter. Peaty soils, if rich in character, are quite good for roses, a general rule being that the more gravelly or sandy a soil the less favourable for the rose. An essential for good rose soil is that it should be well drained, and this means a substratum of porous material, chalk or gravel, not many feet below the surface. Gravel has had a bad reputation for roses, but it is not altogether deserved. It is usually considered too dry and hot for roses to thrive in, but really, if a little care is taken to improve it, it will grow very good roses. Tea roses, for example, bloom in perfection on a gravel soil, and many of the briars and the newer hybrids enjoy just such a light, dryish medium. Chalk, providing that it is deep enough below the surface, and that there is a good depth of soil on top, is not a bad sub-soil. It is well-drained, and not too dry in hot weather. Where it is very close to the surface, it is bad, and needs a lot of work and preparation if it is going to grow good roses. Eighteen inches of decent loam is the minimum for roses on chalk, and where the loam is shallower than this, special places must be prepared for the plants and extra soil supplied.

Situation.—Roses like shelter, and they like an open situation. They dislike wind, although they like fresh air, and hate to be shut in by big trees. The spot to look for, then, is one sheltered from frosts and violent winds, and not close to high hedges or trees. Shelter is desirable from north and east winds, and if there is room for choice, the rose garden should be on the highest part of the available land, other conditions of soil and shelter being equal. "Frost falls," as the country people say, and where the roses are planted on a slope, let the more delicate kinds be at the top.

Planting.—Early November is the best time of all for this operation, though it may be done right through the winter—should conditions be favourable—until the end of March. First, the soil must be thoroughly broken up to a depth of at least 2 or 3 feet. Next, the soil must be perfectly drained. Before the roses arrive, the soil should be re-turned to a depth of about 18 inches, and a good allowance of manure incorporated with it. The lowest layer of soil in the bed should consist of rich, fairly retentive soil, which will hold a certain amount of water, while the upper layers should be lighter and more friable, to encourage the plants to produce plenty of good fibrous roots. The holes to receive the roots should be dug, from a foot to 18 inches, square and deep enough where bush roses or dwarfs are to be planted, for the point of junction of the scion and the stock to be covered when planted to a depth of about an inch. Where standard roses are being planted, the holes should be about 6 inches deep. (*See also* Planting Fruit Trees, p. 458.)

Pruning Roses after Planting.—When roses are planted during the autumn and winter months, their first pruning should be left until the spring, but when spring-planted, it should be done at the time of putting in. The trees should be gone over carefully and all dead wood cut clean out, together with weak and sappy, unripened wood, also any shoots which have received injury. Standards should then be cut back to within about 4 inches of their union with the stock, bush trees being dealt with a little less severely, having about 6 inches of every shoot left above the ground. This pruning is only meant to be carried out the first time after planting. The subsequent treatment varies with the variety.

Pruning Established Roses.—The time of pruning roses differs with the variety. Hybrid Perpetuals, both dwarf and bush, as well as standards and Hybrid Teas, are pruned during March, bush and standard Teas and Noisettes during April, while the climbing roses, Hybrid Perpetuals, Hybrid Teas, Teas and Noisettes should be looked over twice in the year, being well thinned as soon as they have flowered in the summer and pruned properly in March. If required for exhibition, the plants must be pruned much harder than plants for bedding or garden decoration. As a general rule weak-growing varieties should be pruned hard, and strong-growing sorts lightly. (*See also* Pruning, p. 461.) Roses may be roughly divided into classes for purposes of pruning. The first with which we are concerned is that of the Hybrid Perpetuals, Hybrid Teas, Teas, and Noisettes, which require hard pruning. All dead, unripe, and weak shoots should be cut clean out, and the centre of the plant thinned well to allow good room either with a sharp knife or the secateurs. The shoots retained should be cut back to from four to six buds. Examples of this type are: *Admiration, Dickson's Perfection, Earl Beatty, Glory of Rome, Mme Constant Soupert, McGredy's Pride, Mrs. Henry Morse, Rev. F. Page Roberts, Richmond, Sam McGredy, The Doctor, William Moore,* and *Victory.*

The Hybrid Perpetuals, Hybrid Teas, Teas, and Noisettes, which require moderate pruning, are the next class. These should have the dead unripe and weak shoots cut clean away. The shoots which cross, or may cross when full grown, should be cut out, the plant never being allowed to get crowded in the middle. The strong, well-ripened last year shoots which are left should be cut back to from six to eight eyes. Examples of roses needing this treatment are: *Anna Neagle, Apricot Queen, Autumn, Betty Uprichard, Captain Hayward, Christopher Stone, Clarice Goodacre, Covent Garden, Dainty Bess, Earl Haig, Elizabeth Arden, Emma Wright, General Jacquemont, General McArthur, George Dickson, Ena Harkness, Etoile de Hollande, Innocence, Lady Hillingdon, Los Angeles, Margaret McGredy, McGredy's Orange, Pink* and *Triumph, Madame Butterfly, Mrs. Barraclough, Mrs. Edward Laxton, Mrs. Herbert Stevens, Mrs. Henry Bowles, Mrs. Sam McGredy, Mrs. van Rossem, Ophelia, Phyllis Gold, Poinsettia, Red Letter Day, Shot Silk,* etc.

There are also varieties of Hybrid Perpetuals, Hybrid Teas, Teas, and Noisettes which require light pruning. They should be treated as the previous classes, but still less wood should be cut away. The centre of the plant should be kept open, but beyond this the strong shoots from the base should be left about 8 inches long, while the other shoots should be cut back till on their laterals or side shoots there are from one to three buds left. The base shoots should be left 12 inches long, while the laterals on the older wood may be reduced to four or five eyes.

Roses needing pruning of this kind are such plants as *Caroline Testout, Frau Karl Druschki, Hugh Dickson, Irish Elegance, K. of K., Lady Waterlow, La France, Miss Willmott, Mrs. Herbert Taylor, Souvenir de Claudius Denoyel,* and *Sunstar.* Very strong-growing varieties are best pegged down, the shoots being left from 3 to 6 feet in length.

388

PLATE 41   Rose, Apricot Queen.

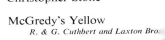

Poinsettia

Christopher Stone

PLATE 42 ROSES

Southport

McGredy's Yellow

R. & G. Cuthbert and Laxton Bros.

The next section includes the climbing kinds of Hybrid Perpetuals, Hybrid Teas, and Teas, as well as some of the other climbers. These roses need very little pruning, most of them doing best if left to grow naturally. The necessary thinning out of dead wood and of the shoots which are likely to overcrowd the plant, together with the worn-out wood of over two years' growth, will keep the plants in full vigour and blossom. The removal of the old worn-out wood is as well done in the summer, directly after the plants have done blooming, and the young shoots should at once be tied in to take the place of those removed. It is at this time that any necessary re-shaping of the rose should be done, crowded growths being thinned and the branches re-spaced over the wall or trellis so as to keep as much flowering wood as possible. Where the base of the plant becomes bare, as often happens with climbing roses, the space may be filled either by bending down one or more of the lower shoots to cover the bare space or by shortening one or two of the base shoots to induce them to throw out laterals. Among these climbing roses are: *Ards Rover, Climbing Caroline Testout, Cramoisie Superieure* (Climbing), *Gruss an Teplitz, Mme. Edouard Herriot* (*Daily Mail Rose*), *Irish Fireflame, Climbing Lady Hillingdon, Climbing Lady Waterlow, Climbing Ophelia, Climbing Mrs. Henry Stevens, Sunburst* and *Wm. Allen Richardson,* etc.

Propagating Roses.—The most usual method of propagating the rose is by budding. The operation of budding is fully described on page 115, but in the case of the rose, the selection of the bud is so important a part of the operation that it must be touched on separately. The bud must be taken from a shoot which is mature enough to have borne or to be able to bear a flower—what is called a "ripe" shoot. A ripe shoot may be selected by trying it with the finger, which should be gently rubbed over the prickles. If these latter fall off easily, the shoot is in a fit condition for budding. Budding should be done in the summer, between June and September, the earlier season being good if enough really ripe shoots can be found. This is an important point, however, and if there is any doubt, the budding should be put off. The stock is chosen with reference to the soil or situation in which it is to be grown. Certain kinds do best in light soils, others in heavy, some in dry, and some in moist ground. Some varieties of rose, again, do better on one stock than another. Very few of the choicer kinds are grown on their own roots. Roses are often propagated from cuttings, and, certainly, where the roses do as well on their own roots, they are easier to deal with than when budded. There is always a risk that the stock may shoot out vigorously and choke the more delicate scion. Climbers and ramblers, as a rule, do well grown in this way, as do a good number of the Hybrid Perpetuals. When making cuttings it is simplest and best to take cuttings from well-ripened wood, which carries a good number of strong healthy leaves, in the summer, after the roses have done flowering. These cuttings will root well in the open air. A shoot should be selected which has borne a flower, and should be cut off with about three or four leaves attached. The leaf nearest the flower should be removed, the shoot being cut off short above the second leaf and just below the lowest. If the cuttings are to be rooted absolutely in the open, a bed should be prepared in a shaded situation, the soil being worked up a little with decayed manure, sand, and leaf-mould. A frame is perhaps more satisfactory than the open ground, but is not essential. The cuttings should be set 3 to 4 inches apart, and should be well watered in, water being again given with a sprinkler morning and evening. The cuttings do as well or better planted in pots, as they seem to root more quickly. A hand light or a cold frame placed over them will help rooting. (*See also* Cuttings, p. 108.)

Where roses are grown from seed, a method only employed where new varieties are being raised, the essential point is that the seed shall be allowed to ripen thoroughly and shall never become dry. The pods should be left on the plant until they are almost dropping, and should then be picked, stalk and all, and the latter set in damp sand until the following November or December, when the seed is to be sown. The seeds often take a complete year to germinate, so that hope need not be given up if the seedlings show no sign of life for many months. Where seedlings are being raised for the sake of new varieties, the tiny plants are budded on to briars even during their first year; as soon, in fact, as it is possible to take a bud from them. The seedlings will usually flower in their first year, but a bud should in all cases be secured if possible, as the little plants often die after flowering, the effort seeming to exhaust them completely.

Varieties.—So innumerable are the varieties of the rose and so much depends on the taste and preferences of the individual, that it is impossible, in the space available, to give any adequate list of varieties. The reader is, therefore, referred to the growers' catalogues.

The National Rose Society gives a list of more than a hundred of the best roses for general garden cultivation. Here is a brief selection from a recent list.

Hybrid Teas.—*Anna Neagle, Apricot Queen, Betty Uprichard, Christopher Stone, Dainty Bess, Etoile de Hollande, Emma Wright, Elizabeth Arden, Elizabeth of York, Glory of Rome, Joyous Cavalier, K. of K., Lady Sylvia, Margaret McGredy, McGredy's Pink, Triumph, Yellow, Mme. Butterfly, Mrs. Edward Laxton, Mrs. Henry Bowles, Mrs. Henry Morse, Mrs. A. R. Barraclough, Ophelia, Picture, Phyllis Gold, Caroline Testout, General McArthur, Mme. Abel Chatenay, Clarice Goodacre, President Herbert Hoover, President Jac Smits, Richmond, Scarlet Queen, Sir Henry Seagrave, The Doctor* and *Violinista Costa.*

Pernetianas.—*Mrs. Wemyss Quin, Mme. Edouard Herriot* (The *Daily Mail* rose), *Golden Emblem, Angèle Pernet, Christine,* and *Isobel.* Of the remaining two, *Frau Karl Druschki* is a beautiful white, scentless Hybrid Perpetual, and *Mrs. Herbert Stevens,* a Tea.

Rosmarinus officinalis (Rosemary).—Hardy evergreen shrubby perennials, which like a sunny position and a light, dry soil, but which will grow almost anywhere, except in wind-swept areas. They are good shrubs for a dwarf evergreen hedge. The shrubs grow from 3 to 6 feet high and flower in April and May. *R. o. prostrata* is a trailing rock plant, not quite hardy. *Culture.*—Plant in March or September. Trim to shape after flowering. To propagate, sow in a frame in April, or strike cuttings under bell-glasses in July.

Rubus (Bramble, Raspberry, etc.).—A large genus of mostly hardy deciduous flowering shrubs and climbers, including the blackberry, loganberry, and raspberry. These like a shady position and rich loam. A few, such as *R. deliciosus,*

390

are grown in bush form; many, as in the case of *R. candicans fl. pl.* (White, Double) and *R. ulmifolius bellidiflorus* (Pink, Double), are selected for the beauty of their flowers; some, such as *R. flagelliflorus*, for the decorative value of their foliage; and others, notably *R. biflorus* and *R. Giraldianus*, for their white stems in winter. *Culture.*—Plant in October. Cut-out old and dead wood after flowering. Propagate by means of suckers in the autumn.

Rudbeckia (Cone-flower).—Hardy annuals and perennials, which like a well-drained ordinary soil and a sunny position. Stake early. For culture, *see* Annuals, p. 139; Perennials, p. 156. *Species.*—(Annuals)—*R. bicolor* (Yellow and Purple, 24 in.), *R. hirta* (Yellow and Purple-brown, 30 in.). (Perennials)—*R. grandiflora* (Yellow and Purple, July–Sept., 40 in.); *R. laciniata fl. pl.* (Golden-yellow [Double], Aug.–Sept., 60 in.); *R. purpurea* [*see* Echinacea purpurea] (Purple, July–Sept., 70 in.); *R. speciosa* [syn. *Newmanii*] (Orange, Purple-black Centre, July–Sept., 24 in.).

Sagina (Pearl-wort).—These are very charming little plants with tufts of moss-like foliage and white flowers in the summer. They are of creeping habit, and should be planted in the sun, in gritty loam. These plants should certainly be introduced into rock and paved gardens. Propagation is best carried out by means of division of roots in the spring. *S. glabra* and its varieties are the best known.

Sagittaria (Arrow Head).—Hardy aquatic plants, which thrive in a mixture of clay, sandy loam, and rotted manure, grow from 10 to 30 inches high and flower from June to October. *Culture.*—Sow seed ¼ inch deep in April, or pro-pagate by means of division in March. Plant in March in weighted baskets in shallow, still water. *Species.*—*S. sagittifolia* (White).

Salix (Willow).—A genus of hardy deciduous trees and shrubs excellent for growing near water. *S. babylonica* is the common Weeping Willow. There are a few species with brightly-coloured stems, the best being *R. vitellina* (Golden Willow) and *R. v. britzensis* (Cardinal Willow). These are usually cut hard back annually in spring. The most attractive in flower (Palm) are the staminate catkins of *S. Caprea, S. cinerea* and *S. Medemii. Culture.*—Plant in November in a sunny position and in moist soil at the water's margin or in deep, heavy loam. Pruning, except when the trees are cut hard back annually as mentioned above, is not necessary, but dead wood should be cut out. To propagate, strike cuttings of matured wood in the open in November or March.

Salpiglossis.—Half-hardy annuals suitable for a rich soil in sunny beds, or for pot culture. *Culture.*—Sow seed thinly in light, rich soil in the autumn or early in March under glass with moderate heat (Temp. 50° F.). Pot-up as soon as possible in 3-inch pots in light, rich, sandy soil, harden-off, and plant out 9 inches apart late in May. A few twigs a foot or so high should be used to stake the plants. Autumn-sown seed potted up and transferred to the green-house will produce blooms from January to March. *Species.*—*S. sinuata* (Purple, etc.). They flower from July to September and grow about 18 inches in height.

Salvia.—There are many species belonging to this genus; annuals, biennials, and perennials, which are grown in the greenhouse or in the garden as orna-mental bedding-plants. All thrive in the sun in rich, ordinary soil. *Culture.*—(Annuals)—Sow seed thinly, ¼ inch deep, in April in the open, or in February under glass. Prick out into boxes 2 inches apart, and plant out 9 inches apart in April. (BIENNIALS)—Sow seed in a frame from May to June, transplant into a nursery bed when fit to handle, and set-out permanently in September. (PERENNIALS)—Sow seed in the open in April, take cuttings in spring or in August and strike in sandy soil in a cold frame, or propagate by means of division in October, and plant out in permanent position in March or October. *Pot Culture.*—Sow in moderate heat in February, prick-off early, and pot-on as required, never allowing the plants to become pot-bound, and using eventually 6 to 8-inch pots and a compost of two-thirds turfy loam, and one-third coarse sand, leaf-mould and well-rotted manure. Grow-on in an average temperature of 60° F., harden-off in a cold frame, summer with the pots plunged in ashes in the open, and take into the cool house early in October. Pinch back occasionally till August, and syringe daily. After blooming, keep the roots fairly dry and cool till March, then give more moisture and slight heat. Rather than raise from seed, however, strike cuttings of young wood in April. *Species.*—(HALF-HARDY ANNUAL)—*S. carduacea* (Lilac-blue); *S. coccinea* (Scarlet); *S. Horminum* (Various). All June to September flowering and growing to a height of from 12 to 18 inches. (HARDY PERENNIAL)—*S. argentea* (Pale Rose); *S. glutinosa* (Yellow); *S. hæmatodes* (Lavender-blue); *S. superba* [syn. *virgata nemorosa*] (Purple-blue); *S. uliginosa* (Deep blue). All June to September flowering and growing to a height of from 24 to 60 inches. (HALF-HARDY PERENNIAL)—*S. azurea* (Azure-blue); *S. Grahami* (Purplish-scarlet); *S. involucrata var. Bethelii* (Rose); *S. leucantha* (Rosy-mauve); *S. patens* (Deep-blue); *S. rutilans* (Scarlet); *S. splendens var. Harbinger* (Scarlet); and *S. splendens var. Pride of Zurich* (Scarlet). June to December-flowering and growing to a height of 18 to 70 inches.

Sambucus (Elder).—Deciduous shrubs or small trees, bearing white flowers in summer. *S. nigra* is the Common Elder; its two varieties, *S. n. albo-variegata* (silver-leaved) and *S. n. foliis aureis* (golden-leaved) are very attractive. *S. racemosus*, the Berried Elder, flowers a month earlier. The flowers are followed by large clusters of red fruits, *Culture.*—Plant in October in partial shade, and in moist loam, or if need be, in almost any soil and situation. Cut well back in spring. To propagate, strike cuttings in the open in October.

Sanguinaria canadensis (Bloodroot).—A hardy perennial, which likes sandy loam, and a sunny position in the border or rock garden. It grows 6 inches high and flowers in spring. For culture, *see* Perennials, p. 156.

Santolina Chamæcyparissus (Lavender Cotton, Holly Flag).—These are hardy evergreen shrubby perennials with greyish-white leaves, growing from 10 to 24 inches high, and bearing yellow flowers from June to August. They like a dry ordinary soil, and a sunny position. For culture, *see* Perennials, p. 156.

Sanvitalia procumbens.—A pretty trailing hardy annual, carrying yellow flowers with purple centres from June to September, and useful for edgings and the rock garden. For culture, *see* Annuals, p. 139. Sow ¼ inch deep in April; thin-out to 8 inches apart when fit to handle.

Saponaria (Soapwort).—Hardy annuals of tufted habit and perennials, the creeping species of which are excellent for edgings or for the rock garden, and bear cutting back, if necessary, for a late autumn display. The taller kinds are useful in the woodland and the wild garden. All like a sunny position and dry,

392

light, gritty loam. For culture, *see* Annuals, p. 139, *and* Perennials, p. 156. *Species.*—(ANNUAL)—*S. calabrica* (Rosy-red, June–Oct., 6 in.); *S. Vaccaria* [*Vaccaria pyramidata*] (Rose and White, June–Aug. 20 in.). (PERENNIALS)— *S. cæspitosa* (Rosy-pink, June–Sept., 4 in.); *S. ocymoides and alba* (Rose and White, May–July, 6 in.); *S. officinalis* [Single and Double] (Rose or White, July and Aug., 20 in.).

Sarcococca.—Low-growing and hardy evergreen shrubs with fragrant flowers, and which may be planted in any soil in the shade and even under the drip of trees, but which prefer a mixture of sandy loam and peat. Propagate by division, or strike cuttings of semi-matured wood under glass. *Species.*—*S. humilis*; *S. ruscifolia; S. saligna.* All bear white flowers in early spring and grow from 1 to 3 feet high.

Sarracenia (Huntsman's Horn).—These are half-hardy insectivorous peren- nials, growing from 6 to 20 inches high and flowering in June. Their leaves are in shape like huntsman's horns standing erect and some 6 inches to a foot in height, down which inquisitive blow-flies are lured and then absorbed. The sarracenias like a sunny position and a fairly cool, but moist, compost of half- peat and half-sphagnum moss. *S. purpurea* (Purple, 10 in.) is a quaint species for a moist bank in the bog or marsh garden. It is best propagated by means of division of roots in April but can be raised from seed sown as soon as ripe on chopped sphagnum moss.

Saxifraga (Saxifrage, Rockfoil).—A large genus, including numerous species of which there are many varieties, and the group is swelled by a seemingly endless number of hybrids. In addition, this genus is the most useful among alpine plants, for with it alone one could almost furnish the whole rock garden, so varied are the species both in characteristics and habit. Of the species in cultivation, the majority are perennials, which are very hardy and easy to grow. They vary in height from 2 inches to 3 feet, according to species, and furnish bloom from January until October, though the majority flower in May and June. There are kinds that will suit any position in the rock garden. Some love the shade; others require a rocky crevice in the sun; a few thrive in the moraine, in the paved garden, or in the Alpine House; and yet others do best at the side of a pond or stream. The species are grouped into a number of sections; all the plants in one section are of more or less the same habit and have approximately similar wants. We will give the cultural requirements of each section and a list of a few of the chief species in each group. By far the most important sections are, firstly, the Encrusted or Silvery Saxifrages (*Euaizoonias*), and, secondly, the Mossy Saxifrages (*Dactyloides*).

Euaizoonias (Encrusted or Silvery Saxifrages) are happiest among limestone rocks or in the moraine, but will grow almost anywhere if given a rather gritty soil and a warm, sunny site. Seed can be sown when ripe in pans of light com- post in a frame, or the roots can be divided in summer. *Species and Varieties.*— *S. Aizoon* and *vars.* (Creamy-white, Yellow or Rose, 6–10 in.); *S. Cotyledon and vars.* (White, 18 in.); *S. Hostii* [syn. *elatior*] (White, Spotted Pink, 15 in.); *S. lingulata* (White, 15 in.); *S. mutata* (Orange, 18 in.). All May to July flowering.

Dactyloides (Mossy Saxifrages).—These plants will grow in almost any well- drained soil, but prefer a compost of gritty loam, leaf-mould, and sand, and should be given a cool position in semi-shade. Increase by division of roots in summer, or sow seed in spring in gentle heat. *Species and Varieties.*—*S. Clibranii* (Crimson, 5 in.); *S. decipiens* [syn. *cæspitosa*] (Red to White, 6 in.); *S. hypnoides* (White, 5 in.); *S. Miss Willmott* (Cream, blotched Chocolate, 6–9 in.); *S. moschata* and *vars.* (Creamy-white, Rose, and Red, 2–6 in.); and *S. muscoides* (White or Red, 4 in.). All flower from May to June.

Kabschias ("Cushion" or Tufted Saxifrages).—These plants need an open and cool, but fairly sunny site, facing preferably east or west, in the rock garden. The most suitable compost consists of one-third stone chippings and two-thirds calcareous loam, leaf-mould, and sand. Above all, the soil must be well-drained, and ample moisture should be available in summer. Plants in the open may, in winter, be given the protection of a frame-light, or a sheet of glass. Increase by division of roots after flowering, by cuttings in the spring, or autumn, or raise from seed in gentle heat in spring. *Species and Hybrids.*—*S. Bertolonii* (Pink and Yellow, April–May, 4 in.); *S. Boydii* (Yellow, March–May, 3 in.); *S. Burseriana* and *vars.* (White or Yellow, Feb.–April, 4 in.); *S. cæsia* (White, May–June, 3 in.); *S. corymbosa var. luteoviridis* (Yellow, April–May, 5 in.); *S. Elizabethæ* (Citron-yellow, March–May, 4 in.); *S. Grisebachii* (Crimson, April–May, 5 in.); *S. lilacina* (Lavender-rose, April–May, 2 in.); *S. marginata* and *vars.* (White or Yellow, March–May, 5 in.); *S. media* (Purple, April–May, 4 in.) and a host of others.

Porphyrions.—Give these plants a cool position in partial shade and a well-drained compost of moist, gritty loam and leaf-mould. Increase by division. *Species.*—*S. Hirculus major* (Golden, July–Sept., 5 in.); *S. oppositifolia* and *vars.* (Crimson-purple, March–May, 2 in.); *S. retusa* (Rose, May–July, 4 in.).

Megasea (Bergenia).—These thrive in sun or semi-shade and in ordinary garden loam, and may be propagated by seed (gentle heat) in the spring; or by division in the autumn. *Species.*—*Bergenia cordifolia* (Rose, 12–18 in.); *B. ligulata speciosa* (Purple-rose, 12–24 in.); *B. Stracheyi* (Pink and White, 10 in.). All April to May flowering. The section *Megasea* is by many placed in the genus Bergenia, but is sometimes included under *Saxifraga.*

Diptera.—This section likes a position in the Alpine house and light, gritty loam or a sheltered situation in the rock garden. Propagate by means of seed, by division, or layering. *Species.*—*S. cuscutaeformis* (White, June, Trailing); *S. Fortunei* (White, Sept.–Oct. 10 in.); *S. sarmentosa* (Mother of Thousands) (Yellow or White, June–Sept., 10 in. [tender]).

Robertsonia.—These like a shady position in light, gritty loam. Propagate by means of seed (gentle heat) in the spring, or by division in the summer. *Species.*—*S. cuneifolia* (White, 5 in.); *S. umbrosa* and *vars.* (*London Pride*) (Rose and White, 10 in.); *S. umbrosa var. primuloides* (Rose, 5 in.). All May to June flowering.

Trachyphyllum.—These thrive in semi-shade and in moist, gritty loam. Propagate by means of seed (gentle heat) in the spring, or by division in summer. *Species.*—*S. aspera; S. flagellaris.* Both Yellow flowering from May to June and growing 3 to 5 inches high.

Scabiosa (Scabious or Pincushion Flower).—Annuals, biennials, and perennials, which thrive in sunny, open borders, and in well-drained, rich, and light soil. They also make good pot plants for bearing winter blooms if lifted and taken into the greenhouse in September. For culture, *see* Annuals, p. 140, Biennials, p. 141, *and* Perennials, p. 156. *Species.*—(ANNUAL)—*S. atropurpurea. Named Varieties.*—*Black Prince* (Maroon); *Coral Pink* (Pink); *Fairy* (Pale Lavender); *Fire King* (Crimson); *Scarlet King* (Scarlet); and *Yellow Prince* (Yellow). All June to October, 24 to 36 inches. (PERENNIAL)—*S. arvensis* (Lilac, June–Oct., 18 in.); *S. caucasica* and *vars.*; NAMED VARIETIES OF S. CAUCASICA—*Annie* (Pale Lavender); *Collarette* (Violet); *Diamond* (Violet-blue); *Edith* (Silver-lavender); *Elsie* (Pale Blue); *Isaac House* (Deep Blue); *Mrs. House* (White); and *Princess* (Deep Lavender). All May to September flowering and growing to a height of from 24 to 36 inches.

Schizanthus (Butterfly Flower, Fringe Flower, Poor Man's Orchid).—A half-hardy annual, which thrives in a compost of two parts of fibrous loam to one part of leaf-mould and a little pounded mortar-rubble. The species chiefly grown in the open ground is *S. pinnatus. Culture.*—Sow thinly in the open in April, or under glass with moderate heat in late February for summer bloom; in August for spring flowers. Prick-off 3 inches apart, harden-off, and plant-out 9 to 12 inches apart in April. *Pot Culture.*—Sow several seeds in a 5-inch pot in September, keep in a temperature of 60° F., and moderately moist. Thin-out to five seedlings in each pot, and top the young plants occasionally. Winter on a sunny shelf near the glass in a cold greenhouse, and in February, pot-up with three plants in 6 to 7-inch pots and stake carefully. In three weeks' time nip-out the heads. Only slight heat is needed to bring the plants into bloom. *Species.*—*S. Grahamii* (Scarlet) *S. pinnatus* (Purple and White); *S. pinnatus var. grandiflora* (Orange Marking); *S. retusus* and *vars.* (Salmon-rose and Orange); *S. wisetoniensis* (Various). All March to October flowering and growing to a height of from 18 to 48 inches, except *S. pinnatus*, which flowers from June to September.

Schizocodon.—Pretty little evergreen plants of tufted habit, which thrive in shady, sheltered sites in the rock garden. They love a moist, but well-drained, compost of two-thirds sandy peat and one-third loam, together with some grit and charcoal. *S. soldanelloides*, with rose-coloured, fringed soldanella-like flowers in summer, is the best known; it grows about 4 inches high. Seed may be sown under glass as soon as ripe or in March, or propagation can be carried out by means of division of roots in the spring, or by rooted offsets in late summer.

Schizopetalon Walkeri.—A fragrant little half-hardy annual, bearing white flowers on stems a foot high in summer. A succession of sowings should be made in the open in a warm, rich soil from May onwards.

Schizostylis coccinea (Kaffir Lily, Crimson Flag, or Winter Gladiolus).—This is a half-hardy South African plant, which increases freely by means of underground stolons or rhizomes. There is a fine rose-coloured variety named *Mrs. Hegarty*. These plants grow from 20 to 30 inches high, and flower in October and November. They thrive in sunny, sheltered borders with a south aspect, and moist but well-drained, light, rich soil. They are also useful for pot culture in the cool greenhouse. *Culture.*—Plant in March or October; protect with fibre in winter. Lift and divide the roots every few years in March, and propagate by means of offsets during that month. *Pot Culture.*—Plant in

November in a compost of two-thirds loam and one-third leaf-mould, well-rotted manure, and coarse sand. Stand in a cold frame, giving no water until growth commences. Sink pots outdoors in a sunny position in summer, and late in September, when the buds show, transfer to the cold house.

Scilla (Squill).—Hardy spring-flowering bulbous plants, which do well in warm, sunny borders, in the rock garden, or in pots. *Culture.*—Plant in September or October, 2½ inches deep and 4 inches apart, in good garden or sandy soil. Propagate by means of offsets in September. *Pot Culture.*—Pot-up from August to November, placing about eight bulbs in a 5 to 6-inch pot, and using a compost of two parts of light, rich loam to one part of leaf-mould. Keep the pots in a frame and covered with fibre until growth starts, then transfer to the cold greenhouse. Plant-out in the open after flowering. *Species.—S. bifolia* and *vars.* (White, Pink, Blue, Feb. and March, 6 in.); *S. hispanica* and *vars.* [*Spanish Squill*] (White, Pink, Blue, April and May, 15–20 in.); *S. nonscripta* (*nutans*) [*Bluebell*] (Blue, Rose, or White, May, 15 in.); *S. peruviana* (Blue and White, May and June, 12 in.); *S. sibirica* (Blue, March, 6 in.).

Scirpus (Club Rush).—Hardy perennial marsh or aquatic plants, of which *S. lacustris*, the Common Bulrush, is the best known. *Culture.*—Propagate by means of division in March, and plant-out in shallow water at the edge of a pond or stream. *Pot Culture.—S. cernuus* (*Isolepis gracilis*, 1 ft.). Tufted with threadlike stems, and *S. nodosus* are greenhouse species, thriving in a compost of two parts of loam to one part of leaf-mould and sand. Pot-up, when necessary, in March, the first in 60s or 54s, the latter in 32s pots.

Scolopendrium.—*See* Phyllitis.

Scutellaria (Skull-caps).—These pretty little rock plants grow in poor, shallow, and dry soil, and carry pink or purple flowers on 6 to 10-inch stems from August to October. *Culture.*—Sow in the open in May or June, or increase by division in March or October. *Species.—S. alpina* (Purple, 6 in.) and *S. minor* (Pink, 6 in.).

Sedum (Stonecrop).—A large family of hardy plants, mostly perennials, the low-growing species being chiefly suitable for the rock, paved, or wall garden; the taller kinds are useful in the border. Sedums do well in a dry, light soil with lime in it; the summer-flowering kinds like a sunny position; autumn-flowering species do equally well in sun or shade. The smaller kinds require the protection of glass in winter. For culture, *see* Perennials, p. 156. *Species.*—(PERENNIAL)—*S. acre var. aureum* (Yellow, May and June, 3 in.); *S. album* (White, May and June, 6 in.); *S. anglicum* (Pink and White, June–Aug., 4 in.); *S. dasyphyllum* (Pink and White, June–Aug., 3 in.); *S. Ewersii* (Rose-purple, June–Aug., 6 in.); *S. pulchellum* (Rosy-flesh, June–July, 3–6 in.); *S. spathulifolium* (Yellow, June–Aug., 3 in.); *S. spectabile* (Rosy-flesh, July–Sept., 12–18 in.).

Selaginella.—An extensive genus of stove, greenhouse, or hardy evergreen plants resembling mosses and allied to ferns. But unlike ferns, the selaginellas are readily increased by cuttings. They thrive in an ordinary loamy potting compost with plenty of coarse grit and a little peat or leaf-mould added. The best-known hardy species for the rock garden is *S. helvetica*. Useful cool greenhouse kinds are: *S. apus, S. Braunii, S. Kraussiana, S. Mertensii,* and *S. Watsoniana.* For stove culture: *S. atroviridis, S. caulescens, S. Galeottei* (a beautiful

Crimson Excelsior

Hooded Grandiflora

PLATE 43 SWEET PEAS

Christina

Princess Elizabeth

R. Bolton & Son and Sutton & Sons

PLATE 44   Four stages in growth of sweet peas.   *Top left*, seedlings in April, *top right*, well-grown plants in May, *bottom left*, flowering in June and *bottom right*, layering in July.

Sutton & Sons

basket plant), *S. plumosa, S. serpens, S. uncinata*, a nice basket plant, and *S. Willdenovii*, a climbing plant growing with age to a height of from 15 to 20 feet.

Sempervivum (Houseleek).—A large genus of curious succulent plants, mostly hardy perennials, although some require the protection and warmth of a green-house. They are well suited to sunny chinks or bare ledges in the rock garden, and thrive in sandy loam. For culture, *see* Rock Plants, p. 196. Except for *S. arachnoideum*, the Cobweb Houseleek, with its cobweb-like white down, the hardy kinds need no protection in winter.—*Species.*—*S. arachnoideum* (Reddish-pink, June–Aug., 5 in.); *S. arenarium* (Yellow, June, 8 in.); *S. tectorum* [Common Houseleek] (Red, July, 10 in.); and *S. triste* (Red, June, 6 in.).

Senecio (Groundsel or Ragwort).—A large genus of annual and perennial plants, some hardy and others only suitable for the greenhouse. Those in culti-vation like a moist, deep, and moderately light loam, and a sunny position. For culture, *see* Annuals, p. 140, *and* Perennials, p. 156. *Greenhouse Culture.*—Pot-up in March, in a compost of two-thirds fibrous loam and one-third sand, leaf-mould, and a little well-rotted manure. Propagate by cuttings struck in spring in a frame with slight bottom heat.

Species.—(HARDY ANNUAL)—*S. elegans* and *vars.* (Purple, Rose, or White, June–Oct., 12–20. in.). (HARDY PERENNIAL)—*S. Doria* (Yellow, Aug., 4 ft.); *S. pulcher* (Purple, Aug.–Oct., 20 in.); *S. tanguticus* (Yellow, Aug.–Oct., 3–6 ft.).

Sequoia.—These are hardy ornamental evergreen coniferous trees, which, in California, grow to a height of 300 feet. They thrive in a sunny position, and in well-drained deep loam. *Culture.*—Plant in May or September; no pruning is required. *Species.*—*S. sempervirens* (Redwood).

Sequoiadendron giganteum (Sequoia gigantea).—At one time included under Sequoia, but now separated into a separate genus. A stately conifer of Cali-fornia 100 ft.

Shortia (Crimson Leaf).—Hardy dwarf-growing perennials, which thrive in a moist, but well-drained compost of two-thirds sandy peat and one-third loam, together with some rough grit and charcoal. A sheltered, shady position in the rock garden suits them. In spring, they carry white or rose flowers on stems 4 to 6 inches high, and throughout autumn and winter, their leaves are tinted with reddish-brown. *S. galacifolia* (Pink and White, 6 in.) and *S. uniflora grandiflora* (Pink, 5 in.) are two good species, and the latter may be grown to advantage in the Alpine house. *Culture.*—Propagate by means of division of roots in April, and plant out firmly in permanent position.

Sibthorpia.—This genus includes perennial creeping plants, some of which thrive outdoors on moist, shady banks, and in sandy loam and leaf-mould. They bloom in July, and are much used for carpeting in the bog and rock garden. *S. europæa*—(Yellow, 1 in.) is the best-known species. *Culture.*—Take cuttings in August and strike in sandy soil in a frame, or propagate by means of division of roots in April, and plant out in permanent position.

Sidalcea.—Hardy perennial plants, which do well in sunny borders and in a moist loam. For culture, *see* Perennials, p. 156. *Species and Varieties.*—*S. candida* (White); *S. malvæflora rosea* (Pink); *S. neo-mexicana* (Bluish-pink); *S. Rosy Gem* (Bright Pink). All July to September flowering and growing to about 36 inches in height.

Silene.—A genus containing a considerable number of species including the plants known as the Campion and Catchfly. They are for the most part hardy annuals, biennials, and perennials, excellent for borders or the rock garden, and like a sunny, open position, and a well-drained sandy loam. Most of the alpine species need a moist gritty loam. For culture, *see* Annuals, p. 140, Biennials, p. 141, *and* Perennials, p. 156. *Species.*—(ANNUAL)—*S. Armeria*—(Pink, June–Aug., 24 in.); *S. pendula compacta* (Blue, White, Rose, Spring–Summer, 4–6 in.). (PERENNIAL)—*S. acaulis* [Moss Campion or Cushion Pink] (Pink, May–June, 2 in.); *S. alpestris* [syn. *Heliosperma alpestre*] (White, May–June,, 5 in.); *S. Elizabethæ* (Rose, June–Aug., 6 in.); *S. laciniata* (Scarlet, July–Aug., 8–10 in.); *S. virginica* (Crimson, June–Aug., 6 in.).

Sisyrinchium (Satin Flower).—Hardy perennials useful in the border, the rock garden, or the Alpine house. A cool and fairly moist loam with one-third part leaf-mould and sand, or sandy peat, suits them best. *Pot Culture.*—Pot-up annually in September, and place in a sunny position in the cold house. After blooming, keep in a cold frame until re-potting. For culture, *see* Perennials, p. 156. *Species.*—*S. angustifolium* (Light Blue, May–July, 5–10 in.); *S. bermudianum* (Deep Blue, May–June, 10 in.); *S. californicum* (Yellow, May–July, 12–18 in.); *S. filifolium* (White, March–May, 6–8 in.); *S. grandiflorum* (Purple, March–May, 10 in.); *S. iridifolium* (Creamy-yellow, June–July, 12–24 in.).

Skimmia.—Hardy evergreen shrubs, which like a sunny, sheltered position, and a deep rich loam. They grow about 3 feet high, flower in April, and carry scarlet berries in autumn. *Culture.*—Plant in March or October, grouping one male plant with six females. No pruning is necessary. To propagate take cuttings, or layer in the summer. The common species is *S. japonica.*

Smilax (Greenbrier).—Beautiful evergreen climbing plants, which thrive in the cool greenhouse in a mixture of two parts of loam to one part of leaf-mould and sand. There are also a few hardy species which may be grown in the open. *Culture.*—Pot-up in March, using 5 to 6-inch pots, stand in semi-shade, syringe and water well in hot weather. Cut old plants right back each March. Propagate by means of seed sown during the spring in a temperature of 60° to 65° F., or by division in March. *S. herbacea* is an herbaceous species.

There are a number of hardy climbing Smilax, the best-known being *S. laurifolia* and *S. rotundifolia.*

Snowdrop.—*See* Galanthus.

Solanum Capsicastrum (Berried Solanum or Winter Cherry).—Beautiful evergreen greenhouse shrubs, which do well in a compost of rich loam, peat, and sand, and which in winter bear red cherry-like berries. *Culture.*—Sow in March (Temp. 60° F.), or strike cuttings of young growths after blooming (February) in moderate heat. Pinch-back when 4 inches high, pot-up in June in 5-inch pots, and stand outdoors in a sunny, sheltered position for the summer. Pinch-back again two or three times before July, and early in October move into the house, and place near the glass. Cut back shoots of old plants in February.

Solanum jasminoides (Jasmine Nightshade).—A half-hardy climbing perennial, which should be grown in leaf-mould, sand, and loam mixed in equal proportions and in warm and sheltered positions, or in a greenhouse in cold districts. It carries white flowers from June to October. *Culture.*—Propagate by means

398

of cuttings of young wood in a frame with bottom heat during March. Cut back any weak shoots in February. *S. crispum*, grown under similar conditions, is an attractive climber up to 20 feet or more and carries bluish-purple flowers from June to September. *Other species.—S. Seaforthianum* (Climber, 10 ft., star-shaped Blue flowers); *S. Wendlandii* (Shrubby prickly climber, large Lilac-Blue flowers).

Soldanella (Moon-wort).—A pretty hardy perennial rock plant thriving in the shade, and in moist, gritty loam and peat, and which in winter must be protected with a pane of glass. For culture, *see* Rock Plants, p. 196. *Species.—S. alpina* (Violet-blue, May–June, 4 in.); *S. alpina var. pyrolæfolia* (Lilac, March, 6 in.); *S. pusilla* (Violet, June–July, 3 in.).

Solidago (Golden Rod).—A genus of hardy border perennials, yellow in colour, and growing from 2 to 4 feet in height. They flower throughout autumn, and thrive in sun or shade in almost any soil. There are numerous varieties, and the following are a few of the best species: *S. canadensis; S. elliptica; S. graminifolia; S. rigida; S. Virgaurea.*

Sophora.—Hardy deciduous shrubs and trees, which thrive in sunny positions and in well-drained soil. *Culture.*—Plant in October or November. Thin-out the branches when overcrowded. Propagate by means of seed; the bushy species can also be layered, and cuttings may be rooted. *Species.—S. japonica* (White, 50–80 ft.); *S. tetraptera* (Half-hardy, plant against a wall, Yellow); *S. vicifolia* (Bluish-white, 6–8 ft.).

Sorbaria Lindleyana [syn. *Spiræa Lindleyana*].—Shrub with white flowers up to 20 ft. *Culture.*—See shrubby *Spiræa.*

Sorbus.—A distinct genus of tree and on account of its pretty white flowers in April and May and their handsome foliage and bright berries, which appear in the Autumn, a great attraction in any garden where they make good specimen trees. *S. Aria* (White Beam), *S. Aucuparia* (Mountain Ash), *S. A. fructu-luteo,* bright Yellow fruit, *S. A. asplenifolia, S. discolor,* fruits White or Yellowish, *S. domestica* (Service-tree). *Culture.*—Plant in November in a sunny position and in deeply dug and well manured ordinary soil. Cut out dead wood and weak shoots in winter.

Sparaxis.—Half-hardy bulbous plants, which may be grown in the open in sunny positions in warm sheltered borders and in well-drained, sandy soil, or in pots in the greenhouse. *Culture.*—Plant in September or October, 2½ inches deep and 3 inches apart, and cover with fibre in winter. *Pot Culture.*—Pot-up in September, placing six bulbs in a 5-inch pot, and stand in a cold frame covered with fibre until growth commences. The culture of these plants is very similar to that required for Ixias (*which see*). *Species.—S. grandiflora* and *vars.* (Violet, White, or Crimson, April–May, 18 in.); *S. tricolor* (Orange-red and Purple, May, 20 in.).

Sparmannia africana (South African Hemp).—Greenhouse evergreen shrubs, which thrive in the cool house in a compost of two parts of sandy loam and peat to one part of rotten manure. Prune hard back in February. Pot-up from March to April, using 6 to 12-inch pots, and from June to September stand in the open. Propagate by means of cuttings of semi-matured shoots in heat (55° to 60° F.), in March or April.

399

Spartium junceum (Yellow Spanish Broom).—Evergreen shrubs, which thrive in a sunny position and in poor, dry, or sandy soil. They grow some 8 to 12 feet high, and carry yellow flowers from July to September. *Culture.*—Plant in October. Cut back long shoots in March. To propagate, strike cuttings of young wood in a frame in July, or sow seeds; grow the young plants in pots until ready to be planted out. The Spanish Broom is a splendid town shrub.

Specularia.—*See* Legousia.

Sphenogyne (Ursinia).—A small genus of half-hardy annuals which can be grown in the open during summer in well-drained soil and sunny position. Propagated by means of seed sown thinly in situ. Thin in seedling stage. May be sown also in pots or boxes. Prick out 4 to 5 in 3-inch pots and grow in a cool frame or greenhouse. Useful for flowering in the conservatory. *Species.*—*S. anthemoides* (Yellow, 6–12 in.); *S. crithmifolia* (Yellow, 12–14 in.); and *S. pulchera* (Orange, 12 in.). All flower best during a hot Summer.

Sprekelia formosissima (Jacobea Lily). For culture *see Hippeastrum.*

Spiræa.—A genus of plants, both herbaceous and woody and mostly hardy perennials, which thrive in moist, rich loam, and in a semi-shaded position. They are excellent in the border, for forcing indoors, and as room plants. *Culture.*—Propagate by means of division in March or October; cuttings of young wood may also be struck in a frame in autumn. Thin-out the older wood of spring-flowering shrubs after flowering, if the bushes have become unshapely. Shrubs that flower between July and September should have all weak wood cut right away in February, and all other shoots that have flowered must be cut back by at least one half. *Pot Culture.*—Pot-up in October, using 8 to 10-inch pots and a compost of two-thirds sandy loam and one-third leaf-mould and a little well-rotted manure. Keep almost dry in a frost-proof frame till growth starts, then take into the cool house in succession as bloom is required. In a fortnight's time, raise the temperature by five degrees or so, and give bi-weekly doses of weak liquid manure. Stand in a saucer of water in hot weather. Prune as advised above, harden-off in a frame, and sink the pots in ashes out-doors from May to October, then re-pot, if necessary, and place in a cold frame. *Species* (SHRUBS)—WHITE FLOWERS.—*S. arguta* (6–8 ft.); *S. bracteata* (4–8 ft.); *S. canescens* (6–10 ft.); *S. prunifolia fl. pl.* (6–8 ft.); *S. Thunbergii* (3–5 ft.). PINK.—*S. Douglasii* (4–6 ft.); *S. japonica Anthony Waterer* (1–2 ft.); *S. Margaritæ* (4–5 ft.); *S. Menziesii triumphans* (4–6 ft.).

Stachys (Betony).—A genus of attractive plants, annuals, biennials, and mainly perennials, a few of which are suitable for the cool greenhouse.

All thrive in almost any well-drained good warm soil. The tall species are suitable for sunny borders. Dwarf species can be grown on the rock garden. *Culture.*—Propagate perennials by division in April or November or sow seed in spring or autumn and give cold frame treatment. Cuttings may be struck in September. *Species.*—*S. Betonica* (Violet, 12–24 in.); *S. b. var. alba* and *var. rosea* (12–24 in.); *S. grandiflora* (Purple, 24–28 in.); *S. citrina* (Yellow, 6–12 in.); *S. alpina* (Purple, 24 in.); and *S. lanata* (Lavender, 6–12 in. grey woolly foliage).

Staphylea (Bladder Nut).—Hardy deciduous shrubs, which like a semi-shaded position, and a well-drained deep loam. *Culture.*—Plant in October or November. Do not prune, but merely trim to shape. Propagate by means of

MDE. F. T. CHAUVIN   NORMA

PLATE 13   *RHODODENDRONS*

CHINTZ   BLUE PETER

seed, by cuttings, or by layering in autumn. *Species.*—*S. colchica* and *S. pinnata* (both White); *S. holocarpa* (Pink). May to June flowering.

Statice (Sea Lavender).—*See* Limonium.

Steironema ciliatum (Lysimachia ciliata).—A herbaceous perennial growing up to 48 in. high with Yellow flowers in July, allied to *Lysimachia* and requiring the same treatment.

Sternbergia (Yellow Star Flower, Winter Daffodil).—Half-hardy bulbous plants, which thrive in sunny positions in warm borders, in the rock garden or greenhouse. They need sandy soil mixed with a little leaf-mould and mortar rubble. *Culture.*—Plant in April, 4 inches deep and 5 inches apart; *S. Fischeriana*, which flowers in February, should be planted in July or August. Protect from frost with fibre, and lift from the ground triennially. If to be grown in the greenhouse, pot-up in July. Propagate by means of offsets in April. *Species.*—*S. colchiciflora* (Yellow, Aug.); *S. lutea* (Yellow, Aug.–Sept.); *S. Fischeriana* (Yellow, Feb.–March). All grow to a height of about 10 inches.

Stewartia (Stuartia).—Hardy deciduous shrubs requiring a sunny, sheltered site, and rich, sandy loam and leaf-mould. Cut away all dead and weak wood every two or three years. Propagate by means of cuttings of ripened wood struck under glass in late summer, or by layering. *Species.*—*S. Malachodendron* (Virginica), *S. pentagyna*, and *S. Pseudo-Camellia*. All carry creamy-white flowers from June to July and grow to a height of from 6 to 10 feet.

Stock.—These are beautiful half-hardy annuals and biennials, which thrive in the sun and in a rich and not too dry soil with lime in it.

Before being set out in their flowering positions, seedlings should be examined to see that they are double, the single-flowered being discarded. Seedlings that will produce double-flowered plants generally have long, pale green, concave leaves; the foliage of the single-flowered is, as a rule, deeper in colour, somewhat convex and more rigid.

The Ten-weeks' Stock (*Matthiola annua*) is a favourite for bedding. This half-hardy annual grows 6 to 24 inches high, and usually blooms ten or twelve weeks after being sown. *Culture.*—Sow seed thinly, $\frac{1}{8}$ inch deep, in March, in a compost of loam, leaf-mould, and sand in boxes under glass (Temp. 60° F.), or in April in the open, in sandy soil. The seedlings must not be over-watered or given too much heat. Prick-off as soon as possible, 3 inches apart, into boxes, harden off early in April, and plant out firmly late in May, 12 inches apart, keeping the "ball" intact as much as possible. The over-vigorous seedlings should be thrown away, as they are usually single-flowered. Choose a sunny position, and do not plant deep in the soil. After planting, water liberally and mulch with a layer of old manure.

Intermediate Stocks.—These furnish flowers in the borders from June to October, and are excellent in a cold greenhouse for flowering in late winter and early spring. For spring-flowering, sow thinly in light soil in boxes or pots in a cold frame in August. Thin or transplant singly into small pots when fit to handle, using a compost of two parts of turfy loam to one part of well-rotted manure. Stand the pots in the open until frost is imminent, then transfer to a frost-proof frame. Pot-up from October to February, using 6 to 7–inch pots, transfer to the cold greenhouse in January, and keep near the glass, or if for summer-flowering in the open, keep them in a frame until April, when harden-off and plant-out in May. If preferred, treat as Ten Weeks' Stocks.

East Lothian Stocks.—These are half-hardy biennials, which bloom from June to September, and are popular for bedding. For early-flowering, sow during July in a compost of two-thirds loam to one-third leaf-mould and sand, in a cold frame. Winter in cold frames, or pits, and plant out the following spring. *See* Biennials, p. 141. If preferred, these stocks may be treated as half-hardy annuals.

Brompton or Giant Stocks.—These are half-hardy biennials, flowering in May, June, and July. The seed should be sown in July thinly in drills about 6 inches apart in a light, sandy bed with an east aspect. When about 3 inches high, thin-out the seedlings to 6 inches apart, winter in a cold frame and plant-out in March.

Nice or Winter-flowering Stocks.—These are useful in the cool greenhouse. For winter-flowering, sow in a cold frame in June, pot-up three seedlings in a 5-inch pot, grow on in a frame, and transfer to the cool house early in December. For spring-flowering, sow in a frame in August, grow in a frame as above, and take into the house when the winter-flowering plants are over.

Varieties.—BROMPTON—(White) *Cottager's White;* (Rose) *Sunrise;* (Scarlet) *Old English Scarlet;* (Purple) *Cottager's Purple;* (Green) *Improved Green.* EAST LOTHIAN—(White) *White Wallflower-leaved;* (Crimson) *Crimson Wallflower-leaved.* INTERMEDIATE—(White) *Crystal White;* (Lilac) *Queen Alexandra;* (Scarlet) *Covent Garden.* NICE OR WINTER FLOWERING—(White) *Mont Blanc;* (White and Rose) *Riviera Market;* (White, Rose, Salmon, Mauve, or Crimson) *Beauty of Nice;* (Pale Yellow) *Yellow Prince;* (Pink) *Empress Elizabeth;* (Lilac) *Queen of the Belgians.* TEN-WEEK—(White) *Snowdrift;* (Primrose) *Princess Mary;* (Salmon) *Salmon Beauty;* (Pale Red) *Almond Blossom;* (Crimson) *Crimson King;* (Scarlet) *Fireball;* (Mauve) *Mauve Beauty;* (Violet) *Violet Queen;* (Blue) *Celestial;* (Various) *Giant Perfection, Perfection Ten-week,* and *Superb Bedding.*

Stock, Night-scented (Matthiola bicornis).—This most fragrant of hardy annuals likes a fairly rich soil, with lime or old mortar rubble in it. For culture, *see* Annuals, p. 140.

Stokesia (Stoke's Aster).—Hardy perennials, which thrive in sunny borders and in light, well-drained soil. They grow some 1 to 2 feet in height, and bear blue or white flowers in early autumn. *See* Perennials, p. 156. *Species.*—*S. lævis* (Blue); *S. l. var. alba* (White).

Stratiotes aloides (Crab's Claw or Water Soldier).—Hardy perennial aquatic plants with long sword-like leaves, that grow below the surface of the water. They grow about 20 inches high, bear white flowers in June, and like a position in shallow, still water. Unfortunately, they increase so rapidly that they are apt to become a nuisance in ornamental waters, so must be kept in check. *Culture.*—Propagate by means of division of roots in March, and plant in ordinary soil with from 3 to 12 inches of water above the crowns.

Streptocarpus (Cape Primrose).—A lovely perennial, suitable for culture in the heated greenhouse. *Culture.*—Pot-up annually in February or March, using 6-inch pots and a compost of equal parts of sandy loam and leaf-mould. Propagate by means of seed in gentle heat (60° F.) in February, by leaf-cuttings, or by division in March. If seed is sown, the small plants should be pricked-off singly into small pots and gradually re-potted until in 6-inch pots. They must be kept moist and shaded from strong sun. *Species.*—*S. caulescens* (Pale Blue); *S. Dunnii* (Rose); *S. Galpinii* (Mauve and White); *S. Rexii* (Blue); *S. Wendlandii* (Rose or Blue). There are many garden varieties in varying shades of purple, blue, white, and rose. All May to October flowering and growing to a height of from 10 to 20 inches.

Styrax (Storax).—Hardy deciduous shrubs or small trees, that like a sunny, sheltered position, and a moist, rich sandy loam. *Culture.*—Plant in October. In autumn thin-out any weak shoots. Propagate by means of layering in autumn. *Species.*—*S. Hemsleyana* (10–20 ft.); *S. japonica* (8 ft.); *S. Obassia* (8 ft.). All carry white flowers from June to July.

Sweet Pea (Lathyrus).—Sweet Peas enjoy a rich soil properly prepared prior to sowing. A trench 2 feet wide should be dug out to a depth of from 2 to 3 feet, while a plentiful supply of well-rotted horse manure should be worked into the lower strata some 10 inches below the surface. With the top-spit may be incorporated a little leaf-mould, bonemeal, soot, and lime, but no stable manure. Sweet Peas can be sown in the open on a dry day, generally early in March, but rather earlier in a warm, sheltered situation. It is often beneficial to soak the seeds in warm water overnight, especially if the weather is very dry. The seed should be sown 1½ inches deep and 3 inches apart, the surface being dusted with soot. When about 4 inches high, thin-out to 6 inches apart, and support by means of twigs. As the plants grow taller, stakes 7 to 8 feet in height should be placed in position. Wire peaguards or strands of black cotton should be used to keep the birds from the seeds. To secure the finest blooms, however, the seeds should be sown in late autumn or early in February in 5-inch pots, placing six seeds in each, or a single seed in a small pot. The seeds may also be sown some 2 inches apart in boxes about 4 inches deep, but the seedlings must be potted-off singly as soon as possible. A compost of two-thirds fibrous loam and one-third leaf-mould, to which a sprinkling of bonemeal, wood ashes and coarse sand have been added, will be found most suitable. Raise the young plants on a shelf near the glass in a cool greenhouse or in a frost-proof frame. Before being planted out into the open, early in March, when the plants are about 4 inches high, the plants should be hardened-off in a cold frame. Not more than three growths should be allowed to spring from each root, if exhibition blooms are desired. They should be planted out one foot apart in rows, and confined to a single stem, all tendrils being kept cut off. The stems should be tied singly to tall canes, and when the plants have grown to 3 or 4 feet high, they should be given, after rain or a soaking with clear water, a little soot-water or weak liquid manure (the colour of weak tea), once a week. The application of the latter must not be overdone. Water applied to sweet peas must have been exposed to the air for at least twenty-four hours; cold water may cause the buds to drop. The tips should be pinched-out when they reach 6 to 8 inches above the top of the stakes, and the soil between the plants should be kept continually stirred. Plants so raised should flower from early June to late September; if desired, early May blooms may be had by growing the peas throughout in the greenhouse. The after-attention is very simple, but it is of prime importance to

403

keep the plants free from seeds. If seeds are required, a portion of the row or one clump may be set apart for the purpose. Named varieties are innumerable and catalogues should be consulted.

Sweet-William (Dianthus barbatus).—A beautiful hardy perennial, best treated as a biennial. For culture, *see* Biennials, p. 141. Sweet-williams can also be propagated by means of cuttings and by division of roots. *Varieties.*— *Auricula-eyed* (Rich Colours and White Eyes); *Giant White* (Self); *Harlequin* (Multi-coloured); *Nigricans* (Deep Purple); *Pink Beauty* (Self); *Pheasant's Eye* (Double Strain, Crimson and White Eye); and *Scarlet Beauty* (Self). All June to September flowering and growing to a height of from 9 to 18 inches.

Symphoricarpus (Snowberry).—Hardy deciduous shrubs, which thrive in sun or shade and in ordinary soil. They grow some 5 feet high and flower in July and August. In autumn the flowers are followed by white fruits. *Culture.* —Plant in October or November. Cut-out dead wood and weak shoots annually in March, and every few years, lift the shrubs in autumn, divide the roots, and replant the younger and more vigorous parts.

Those bearing the largest and most attractive fruit are *S. albus* and *S. a. var. lævigatus.*

Symphyandra.—These are charming plants for crevices and ledges in the rock garden. They grow from 6 to 24 inches high, and in July and August carry white, blue, or pale yellow flowers. The symphyandras thrive in well-drained, gritty loam. Seed may be sown under glass in March, or propagation can be carried out by means of division of roots in spring or autumn. *Species.*—*S. Hofmannii* (White, 18 in.); *S. pendula* (Creamy-white, 8–10 in.); *S. Wanneri* (Violet, 6–10 in.).

Syringa (Lilac).—Hardy deciduous shrubs, which thrive in the sun in moist, well-manured, well-drained, and rather heavy loam. They grow from 5 to 15 feet high, and flower in April and May. *Culture.*—Plant in October or November. Periodically cut away all suckers from the roots of grafted plants, disbud surplus buds in spring, and cut-out old and weak wood after flowering, but never trim away the young or half-matured shoots. Propagate by means of layering in June, by matured cuttings in the open in October, or by suckers in October. *Forcing.*—For decoration in the greenhouse, pot-up in October or November, using 6 to 10-inch pots and a compost of two parts sandy loam to one part of leaf-mould and a little sand and bonemeal, stand in a sheltered, frost-proof position, and move into the house in succession as bloom is desired. After flowering, remove all dead blooms, syringe and keep up the heat for three weeks or so, then harden-off and sink the pots in ashes outdoors from May until the October of the following year. Never force two years running. Prune as above. Named varieties are frequently increased by crown or cleft-grafting in March. For Mock Orange or *Philadelphus coronarius*, commonly called Syringa, *see* Philadelphus. *Named Varieties.*—(Single) (White) *F. C. Van Tol* and *Marie Legraye*; (Rich Red) *Congo*; (Crimson Purple) *Massena*; (Purple) *Souvenir de Louis Spath*; (Rich Mauve) *Charles X*; and (Slate-blue) *Hugo Koster*. (Double) (White) *Madame Lemoine*; (Rosy-pink) *Belle de Nancy*; (Violet) *Alphonse Lavallée*; (Soft-mauve) *Kathleen Hovermeyer*; (Red-purple) *Charles Joly*; (Lilac-blue) *President Grevy*.

PLATE 45   RHODODENDRONS

Left

R. Falconeri
R. Cunningham White
R. Doncaster

Right

R. Pink Pearl
R. Orbiculare
R. Mrs. Stirling

Sparaxis, Fire King

Polianthes tuberosa

PLATE 46

Scabiosa atropurpurea

Viburnum Opulus var. sterile
Alexander & Brown and Sutton & Sons

Tagetes (AFRICAN AND FRENCH MARIGOLDS).—Half-hardy annuals, that will make a delightful show in warm, sunny beds and borders. *T. erecta* requires rich soil; *T. patula* thrives in poor soil. For culture, *see* Annuals, p. 139. *See also* Calendula. *Species.—T. erecta* (AFRICAN MARIGOLD). *Named Varieties.* —*Giant Orange* (Double); *Lemon Queen* (Single). Both flower from June to September and grow to a height of from 20 to 40 inches. *T. patula* (FRENCH MARIGOLD). *Named Varieties.—Cloth of Gold; Yellow Bedder; Star of India* (Crimson-red, Striped Yellow); and *Silver King.* All June to September flowering and growing to a height of from 9 to 18 inches. *T. tenuifolia* (*T. signata*). Yellow flowers and finely-cut foliage, 12–18 inches.

Tamarix (or Tamarisk).—Hardy deciduous or evergreen shrubs, which do well anywhere in light ordinary soil. They grow from 5 to 10 feet high and carry pink flowers from May to September. *Culture.*—Plant in October or November. Prune summer-flowering species in March, spring-flowering kinds after flowering. Strike cuttings in the open in October. *Species.—T. pentandra* (*æstivalis*) and *T. tetrandra.*

Taxodium distichum (Deciduous Cypress).—Hardy deciduous trees, which thrive in full sun and in moist or swampy soil. *Culture.*—Plant from October to November. No pruning is required. Propagate by means of seed in a frame.

Taxus (Yew).—Hardy evergreen trees or shrubs, which thrive in sun or shade, and in ordinary soil. *T. baccata* is the Common Yew, usually used for hedges. *Culture.*—Plant in May or September. When necessary, trim in May or August. Propagate by means of seed in the open in March, or by cuttings of young wood in a frame in September. A selection of the best varieties of the Common Yew should include: *T. baccata vars. adpressa, aurea* (Golden Yew), *Dovastonii, fastigiata* (Irish Yew), *fastigiata aurea* (Golden Irish Yew), *fructu-luteo* (Yellow Fruits) and *pendula.*

Tecoma (Trumpet Flower).—Beautiful climbing shrubs, which thrive in well-drained, light soil, if grown on warm sunny walls or in the greenhouse. *Culture.* —Strike cuttings of ripe wood in a frame with bottom heat in autumn. Plant in dry, open weather between October and April. *Species.—T. Garrocha,* shrub for the cool house (Yellow, Salmon and Scarlet, leaves pinnate, 5–6 ft.); *T. Smithii,* shrub, (Yellow and Orange, Winter).

Tecomaria capensis (Tecoma capensis).—Cape Honeysuckle. Partially climbing (Orange-red). At one time included under Tecoma and needing similar treatment. Suitable for cool house.

Teucrium (Germander).—This genus includes some useful little herbaceous plants and a few evergreen shrubs. The herbaceous perennials thrive in the sun and in gritty loam in the border or rock garden. For culture, *see* Perennials, p. 156. The shrubs need a warm sunny, and sheltered position; a sandy loam suits them best. They are increased by cuttings of young shoots. *Species.*— (PERENNIAL)—*T. Chamædrys* (Bluish-red, July–Aug., 10 in.); *T. Marum* (Deep Pink, Aug.–Sept., 10 in.). (SHRUBBY)—*T. flavum* (Yellow, Aug.–Sept., 30 in.); *T. fruticans* (Pale Lavender-blue, March–Sept., 4–6 ft.).

Thalictrum (Meadow Rue).—Hardy perennials, which thrive in well-drained, rich, sandy loam, in sunny or shady borders, or by the side of a stream. The dwarf kinds are useful rock plants. *T. minus var. adiantifolium* and *T. diptero-*

carpum are excellent for the cold greenhouse. For culture, *see* Perennials, p. 156. *Pot Culture.*—Lift from the open and pot-up in November, using 5 to 6-inch pots and a compost of equal parts of rich loam and leaf-mould. *Species.*—T. *minus var. adiantifolium* (Yellow, June–Sept., 20 in.); *T. alpinum* (Greenish-yellow, May–June, 4–6 in.); *T. aquilegifolium* (Purple, July–Aug., 3–4 ft.); *T. Delavayi* (Rosy-purple, July–Aug., 18–30 in.); *T. dipterocarpum* (Rose, Purple, or White, June–Sept., 36–50 in.); *T. glaucum* (Yellow, July–Aug., 48–72 in.).

Thermopsis (False Lupin).—Hardy perennials, which grow from 12 to 30 inches high, and flower in summer. They do well in sheltered, sunny borders and in rich, sandy soil. *Species.*—T. *barbata* (Purple); *T. fabacea* (Yellow); *T. montana* (Yellow). *See* Perennials, p. 156.

Thlaspi rotundifolium.—These pretty little rock plants are easily raised by means of seed sown under glass in March, or by division of roots in spring or autumn. The fragrant flowers, which appear in July and August, are rosy-lilac in colour.

Thunbergia alata.—Evergreen climbers, carrying pretty flowers from June to September. and much used for hanging baskets, and for greenhouse staging. They like a rich, fibrous loam mixed with leaf-mould and sand, and are raised from seed in March in sandy soil, in a temperature of 60° F., or from cuttings subjected to gentle bottom heat. Pot-on for flowering into 4 to 5-inch pots, or harden-off and set out in the open in June in a warm, sheltered bed. *T. Gibsonii*, a trailing plant, has brilliant orange-coloured flowers, and is very beautiful when planted for the summer on a hot, sunny bank.

Thuja (Arbor-vitæ).—Hardy evergreen trees, often used instead of yew as hedge plants. They succeed in sunny positions and in any moist garden soil. *Culture.*—Plant in May or September. No pruning is necessary. Trim hedge plants in April and September. Propagate by means of seeds in a frame, or by cuttings in a frame in September. *Species.*—T. *occidentalis*, *T. orientalis*, *T. plicata* (*gigantea* or *Lobbii*).

Thymus (Thyme).—Hardy trailing plants, that are useful for the rock or paved garden, and which thrive in the sun and in well-drained sandy loam. For culture, *see* Rock Plants, p. 196. *Species.*—T. *nitidus* (Pink Flowers, 12 in.); *T. Serpyllum* (Purple Flowers, Green Foliage, 3 in.); *T. S. album* (White, 3 in.); *T. S. citriodorus* (Purple Flowers Trailing); *T. S. lanuginosus* (Purple Flowers. Grey Leaves, 3 in.); *T. vulgaris argentea* (Silver Leaves, 8 in.). All flower from June to August.

Tiarella cordifolia (Foam Flower).—Hardy perennials, which like a shady position in the border or rock garden, and a moist, ordinary soil. They grow some 9 inches high, and carry creamy-white flowers from April to June. For culture, *see* Perennials, p. 156.

Tigridia (Tiger Iris).—Half-hardy bulbous plants, which do best in a light, rich sandy loam and leaf-mould, in a warm, sunny position in a dry border or rock garden, or in the greenhouse. *Culture.*—Plant about the middle of April, 4 inches deep and 6 inches apart, letting the bulbs rest on sand. Lift from the ground in November. For Pot Culture, six bulbs may be placed in a 6-inch pot, the latter being kept in a frame or cool house until growth has started. Propagate by means of offsets in April. *Species.*—T. *Pavonia* (Scarlet, marked

Yellow and Purple); *T. P. var. conchiflora* (Yellow, Purple spots); *T. P. var. grandiflora rubra* (Crimson Scarlet). All May to July flowering, and growing to a height of from 12 to 18 inches.

Tilia (Lime).—Hardy deciduous trees, which thrive in sunny, sheltered positions, and in moist, rich soil. They bear fragrant, yellowish-green flowers from June to August. *Culture.*—Plant in October or November. Thin-out the branches when overcrowded. To propagate, sow seed, or layer basal shoots, which will be produced after the tree has been cut down close to the ground. *Species.*—*T. dasystyla* (40–60 ft.), *T. petiolaris* (60–80 ft.), *T. platyphyllos* (70–100 ft.), *T. tomentosa* (60–100 ft.), *T. vulgaris* (80–100 ft.).

Torenia.—Half-hardy annuals of trailing nature, which flower in August, and are suitable for hanging baskets. They need a compost of sandy loam and leaf-mould. *T. flava* (*T. Baillonii*) (Yellow and Purple, 1 ft.); *T. Fournieri* (Violet, Blue and Yellow, 1 ft.). For culture, *see* Annuals, p. 139.

Trachelium cœruleum (Throat-wort).—A half-hardy biennial which thrives in leaf-mould and sandy loam in sunny beds or borders. It grows about 18 inches high, and flowers in July and August. For culture, *see* Biennials, p. 141. It is a good pot plant for the cool house.

Trachelospermum.—This is a small genus of evergreen twining shrubs with leathery leaves and fragrant flowers. Being on the borderland of hardiness, the trachelospermums should be planted on a sheltered wall outside, or grown in cool greenhouses. *T. divaricatum*, with creamy-yellow flowers and *T. japonicum*, with white flowers, are Japanese species. *T. jasminoides* (white flowers) and its var. *variegata*, come from China. Cuttings and layering provide ready means of increase. Trachelospermum are sometimes named Rhyncospermum.

Tradescantia (Spider-wort).—Hardy and half-hardy perennial plants, suitable for beds and the cool greenhouse. They thrive in sun or shade in any good well-drained soil. For culture, *see* Perennials, p. 156. *T. canaliculata* (*reflexa*) (Blue, June–Sept., 20 in.); *T. virginiana* (Purple, Red, Blue, or White, June–Sept., 20 in.), the Common Spider Wort, and its varieties, are good representatives of the hardy species.

Trichomanes.—A genus of filmy ferns, requiring a very humid atmosphere. For this reason, they are usually grown under bell-glasses or hand-lights on the north or shady side of a greenhouse. The most ornamental and generally cultivated species are: *T. radicans* (Killarney Fern), *T. reniforme* (New Zealand), *T. alatum* (W. Indies), *T. javanicum* (India, Java, etc.), *T. parvulum* (Japan and China), and *T. venosum* (Australia and New Zealand). The trichomanes are best cultivated in square pans or dwarf pots. Plenty of drainage is necessary. Most suitable is a compost of fibrous peat and soft sandstone. This should be raised towards the centres of the pots or pans, so as to form mounds with small pieces of sandstone protruding.

Trientalis (Starflower and Chickweed Wintergreen).—Small hardy perennials, suitable for a light, rich, peaty soil, in a shady and moist position in the rock garden. They may also be used as a border edging. *T. americana* (Starflower) bears white flowers on 6-inch stems in June or July, and *T. europæa* in April or May. Propagation may be carried out by means of seed in summer, or by division in spring.

Trifolium (Clover, Shamrock, Trefoil).—Hardy annuals and perennials, which thrive in any light soil, and which are easily raised from seed or propagated by means of division of roots. They may be introduced into the rock garden, if so desired. *T. alpinum*, 4 inches high, once established throws up large pink flowers that make the plant well worth growing. *Other species.—T. incarnatum* (Crimson Clover) (Crimson, 2–3 ft.); *T. pannonicum* (Hungarian Clover) (Pale Yellow, 2 ft.); *T. uniflorum* prostrate (Rosy Pink) ideal for pan in alpine house or rock garden.

Trillium (Wood Lily or Trinity Flower).—Hardy tuberous-rooted perennials, which thrive in well-drained, moist, peaty soil, in partial shade in the border or rock garden, or in pots in the cold greenhouse. *Culture.*—Plant in October. Lift from the soil when overcrowded. Propagate by means of seed sown in a frame in March, or in the open in June, or increase by division of roots in October. *Species.—T. grandiflorum* (Rose or White, June–July, 6–12 in.); *T. erectum* (Deep Purple, May–June, 5–10 in.); *T. ovatum* (Pale Purple, May–July, 8 in.); *T. sessile californicum* (White, May–June, 8 in.).

Triteleia.—*See* Brodiæa.

Tritonia (Montbretia).—Hardy bulbous plants, which thrive in rich, sandy loam and leaf-mould in warm, sunny beds or borders, or in pots. *Culture.*—Plant in April, 4 inches deep and 4 to 6 inches apart. Cover with fibre in winter, and lift every four years only; half-hardy varieties must be lifted each October. *Pot Culture.*—Pot-up in April, placing five bulbs in a 7 to 8-inch pot, and using a compost of two parts of peaty loam to one part of leaf-mould and sand. Sink the pots in ashes in a frost-proof frame, and transfer to the greenhouse early in June. Re-pot the plants every year; propagate by means of offsets. *Named Varieties.—Drap d'Or* (Yellow); *Etoile de Feu* (Orange); *Fire King* (Fiery Red); *His Majesty* (Orange-scarlet); *Kathleen* (Orange Scarlet); *Lady Hamilton* (Apricot); Lady Wilson (Golden-yellow); *Lord Nelson* (Scarlet); *Phare* (Crimson); *Prometheus* (Orange-red); *rosea* (Rosy-pink); *Salmon King* (Salmon); *Star of the East* (Golden-orange); *St. Botolph* (Yellow). All July to September flowering and growing to a height of 2 to 4 feet.

Trollius (Globe Flower).—Hardy herbaceous perennials, which thrive in rich, moist loam, in shady borders or in the marsh garden. For culture, *see* Perennials, p. 156. *Species.—T. asiaticus* (Yellow or Orange, May and June, 24 in.), *T. europæus var. napelliformis* (Orange, May–June, 30 in.), *T. Ledebouri* (Golden-yellow, April–May, 30–40 in.).

Tropæolum.—Beautiful climbers, mostly half-hardy annuals, invaluable for covering trellises out-of-doors and for training up pillars and rafters in the cool greenhouse. The best known are *T. aduncum* [*peregrinum*] (Canary Creeper), *T. majus*, and *T. nanus* (Nasturtium). *Culture.*—(*T. aduncum*).—This beautiful and well-known creeper flowers best in a rather poor, dry soil, and in a sunny position. *T. aduncum* (Yellow) is half-hardy. Sow late in April very thinly in the open, or under glass in March in a cool greenhouse. If planted indoors, pot-off singly, harden-off, and plant out 12 inches apart in May, otherwise thin out when fit to handle. (*T. majus* and *T. nanus*).—Many varieties are well known as climbers, the dwarf varieties are useful for bedding or edging, and for the rock garden. Sow thinly from March to June, ½ inch deep, in light, poor soil, and thin-out to from 12 to 18 inches apart when fit to handle. The double varieties do not seed, and cuttings must be struck in a cold frame in August or September. For outdoor use, *T. aduncum* and *T. majus* are especially good, also the perennial species *T. polyphyllum* (Yellow Trailer) and *T. speciosum* (Flame Nasturtium). *T. peltophorum* (*Lobbianum*) blooms beautifully through the winter months in the greenhouse, and likes a light, but not too rich a soil. Pot-up from March to April, in 6 to 10-inch pots and grow near the glass. Propagate by means of seed, or by cuttings in heat in March or April.

Tsuga (Hemlock Spruce).—Hardy coniferous trees, growing from 70 to 100 feet high and doing best in sunny positions and in moist, deep loam. They are suitable for pleasure ground and woodland planting. *Culture.*—Plant in May or September. No pruning is required. Propagate by means of seed sown in a frame. Three of the most ornamental species are *T. heterophylla* (*Albertiana*), *T. Mertensiana* (Mountain Hemlock), growing to 70 feet in height, and *T. canadensis*, which reaches 80 feet.

Tulips.—Tulips look best massed in beds or borders, carpeted with other spring flowers. The best tulip for all-round purposes is, probably, the *Keizer Kroon*. For planting permanently, the *Cottage* and *Darwin* tulips are best. Several of the dwarf species of tulip are useful for obtaining early colour in the rock garden. *T. silvestris* (Yellow, April–May, 10–15 in.); *T. Clusiana* (White with Crimson Eye, May–June, 6–9 in.); *T. montana* (Bright Red, May–June, 6 in.); and *T. patens* (*persica*) (Yellow, May–June, 6 in.) are all suitable.

Culture.—Tulips require a fair amount of sand in a well-drained, deeply-dug, rich loam with a cool, moist subsoil, and a sunny, sheltered position not subject to draughts and cold winds. Plant early in November, from 4 to 5 inches deep and from 8 to 10 inches apart. It is best to lift the bulbs and plant them in a different bed each year. If this cannot be done, the soil should be well dug and improved by the use of bonemeal or well-rotted cow-manure.

Pot Culture.—The early single and double dwarf *Duc Van Thol* tulips are excellent for this purpose. The former may be planted six or eight bulbs in a good sized pot; but of the latter, three bulbs are sufficient. All tulips require a good supply of water when in flower, and should be shaded from the sun; hard forcing will prevent flowering. The soil and treatment necessary for tulips grown in pots are the same as recommended for hyacinths. Propagation is carried out by means of offsets, separated from the bulbs when lifted in summer, and planted in September or October. *See also chapter on* Bulb Culture, page 170. Named varieties are almost innumerable and nurserymen's catalogues should be consulted.

Tunica.—Dwarf-growing hardy perennials, useful for inclusion in the rock garden and for edgings to borders. A sandy loam suits them best, in sun or shade. For culture, *see* Perennials, p. 156. *Species.*—*T. Saxifraga* (Pale Rose or White, June–Aug., Trailing).

Typha (Reed Mace, False Bulrush, or Cat-o'-nine-tails).—A genus of aquatic plants, which thrive on a swampy bank, in the marsh garden, or at the edge of a sheltered pond, with from 1 to 12 inches of water above the crowns. They grow some 6 feet high, and flower in late summer. *Species.*—*T. angustifolia* (Narrow-leaved Bulrush); *T. latifolia* (Reedmace).

Ulex (Furze, or Gorse).—Free-flowering evergreen shrubs, bearing yellow flowers, and which like a sunny position and a poor, dry soil. *U. europæus fl. pl.* (5 ft.), flowering from March to June, and *U. nana* (18 in.), flowering from September to December, are both useful for hedges. *Culture.*—Plant-out from pots at any time between March and October. Cut back when overgrown in April, and propagate by means of cuttings in a frame in August, or seed in a frame in March.

Ulmus (Elm).—Hardy deciduous trees, mostly growing up to 100 feet, which thrive in almost any soil and in practically any position. *Culture.*—Plant in October or November. Thin-out the branches in the summer when required. Propagate by means of seeds, grafting, or sucker growths. *Species.*—*U. procera* (English Elm); *U. p. Louis van Houttei* (Golden-leaved); *U. p. variegata* (Striped and Margined creamy-white); *U. hollandica var. major* (Dutch Elm); *U. glabra* (*montana*) (Wych Elm); *U. glabra pendula* (Weeping Wych Elm); *U. nitens*; *U. stricta* (Cornish Elm); and *U. s. Wheatleyi* (Guernsey Elm), the best elm for road and avenue planting.

Umbellularia californica (Californian Laurel).—An evergreen tree, or large bush, rather resembling the Bay Laurel in appearance and degree of hardiness. It is a very good evergreen for gardens in the south and west, and has a small, yellowish-green flower produced in April, followed by a roundish, pear-shaped purplish fruit one inch long. Increase is by cuttings, layering, and by sowing seeds.

Ursinia.—*See* Sphenogyne.

Vaccinium.—A large genus of shrubby plants, which includes the Whortleberry or Bilberry (*V. Myrtillus*). There are several species grown for the beauty of their flowers, fruit, and tinted foliage in autumn; these require a moist, sandy, and peaty loam. Propagate by means of cuttings struck under glass in spring and summer, by root-suckers, or by seed sown in autumn when ripe. Plant-out in March. *Species.*—*V. Arctostaphylos* [Bear Berry] (Greenish-white, 6 ft.); *V. corymbosum* [Blueberry] (Pale Pink or White, 5 ft.); *V. Myrtillus* [Whortleberry] (Pale Pink, 1½ ft.). All May flowering.

Valeriana.—Hardy perennials, of which the smaller species are useful for the rock garden. The best known are *V. officinalis* (All Heal) and *V. Phu.* They thrive in sunny borders and in any ordinary soil. For culture, *see* Perennials, p. 156. Both flower from June to October.

Vallota purpurea (Scarborough Lily).—Half-hardy bulbous plants, which thrive in a compost of two parts of sandy loam to one part of leaf-mould. They require the protection of the cool greenhouse or sunny window; and flower on stems 1 to 2 feet high in August and September. *Culture.*—Plant in July or August, singly in 5 to 8-inch pots, with the crowns 6 inches below the surface. Winter near the glass, and give liquid manure when the buds form. Water moderately till the leaves die in spring, and keep fairly dry and exposed to the sun from May to September. Leave in the same pot for three or four years. Propagate by means of seed in spring, or by offsets in August.

Venidium fastuosum.—Half-hardy annuals which thrive outdoors in sunny, dry, well-drained situations. Sow in flowering positions towards the end of April.

Veratrum (False Hellebore).—*Poisonous* hardy perennials, which thrive in deep, rich loam. For culture, *see* Perennials, p. 156. *Species.—V. album* (White); *V. nigrum* (Deep Purple); *V. viride* (Greenish-white). All July to September flowering and about 50 inches.

Verbascum (Mullein).—Hardy biennials and perennials, which may be grown in sunny borders or in the wild garden in light, ordinary soil. For culture, *see* Biennials, p. 141, *and* Perennials, p. 156. *Species.*—(BIENNIAL)—*V. olympicum* (Golden-yellow, Grey Foliage, June–Sept., 70 in.). (PERENNIAL)—*V. Chaixii* (Yellow, Mauve Centre, June–Sept., 50–90 in.); *V. Lagurus* (Yellow, June–July, 48–60 in.); *V. nigrum* (Yellow, Purple eye, July, 36–40 in.); *V. phœniceum* (Purple, White or Rose, June–Sept., 20–30 in.). Good hybrids are *Cotswold Beauty* (Amber, June–July); *Gainsborough* (Pale Lemon, June–July); and *Pink Domino* (Mauve Pink, June–July). All growing from 36–48 in. high, with bold spikes of flowers.

Verbena.—Half-hardy annuals, biennials, and perennials, which do well in rich, sandy loam, in sunny beds. For culture, *see* Annuals, p. 139, *and* Biennials, p. 141. *Culture.*—(PERENNIALS)—Sow in heat (Temp. 60° F.) in February and treat as biennials. With named varieties, at any rate, strike cuttings of sturdy shoots that have no flower buds in a frame in spring or early autumn. Autumn-struck verbenas are best left in the cutting pots until February; and, unlike calceolarias, if sufficient old plants are kept over the winter for stock, spring-struck cuttings are best. Plant-out 10 inches apart in June. *Pot Culture.*—Pot-up in March, using 5 to 6-inch pots and a compost of sandy loam and leaf-mould, and a little well-rotted manure. Stop-back the young shoots to make bushy plants. *Species.—V. chamædryfolia* (Scarlet); *V. venosa* (Rosy-purple). *Named Varieties.*—(HALF-HARDY PERENNIALS)—(White, Scented) *Boule de Neige*; (Pink) *Miss Willmott; Crimson King; King of the Scarlets;* and *Purple Emperor.*

Veronica (Speedwell).—SHRUBBY SPECIES—These, now included in the genus Hebe, are amongst the most valuable of summer and autumn blooming plants, both for greenhouse culture and for growing out-of-doors, where, with a dry sub-soil and somewhat sheltered, sunny situation, the plants will generally stand uninjured through the winter. *Culture.*—Plant in April or September. Trim annually to keep in shape only, but it is usually necessary to prune hard back every few years. To propagate, strike cuttings of matured wood in a frame in August. The young shoots should occasionally be pinched-back, but no "stopping" must be done after June. *Pot Culture.*—Pot-up in the early summer, using 6 to 8-inch pots and a compost of two parts of loam to one part of leaf-mould. Harden-off and stand in the open from May to September, then take into the cold house. After flowering, prune severely in March, and place the pots near the glass.

ANNUAL SPECIES.—The miniature species, such as *V. glauca, V. syriaca,* and *V. syriaca, var. alba,* make very pretty plants for small beds and edgings. *Culture.* —Sow in the open in September, and thin-out to 5 inches apart as soon as fit to handle.

HERBACEOUS PERENNIAL SPECIES.—These thrive in sunny positions and in any fairly good garden soil, especially if it is rather gritty. Every fourth year, the plants should be lifted and divided, the younger outer crowns only being re-planted. Propagate by means of division in March and (some species) in October. Some of the dwarf-growing species make excellent rock plants. For culture, *see* p. 156.

Species and Varieties.—(ANNUAL)—*V. alba* (White, Summer, 6 in.); *V. glauca* (Blue, Summer, 6 in.). (PERENNIAL)—*V. Allionii* (Deep Blue, May–July, 5 in.); *V. austriaca alba* (White, June–July, 12 in.); *V. caucasica* (Pale Red, June–Aug., 10 in.); *V. gentianoides*, (Blue, June–July, 6–8 in.); *V. incana* (Violet-blue, Silver Foliage, June–Sept., 6–9 in.); *V. longifolia var. subsessilis* (Deep Blue, July–Sept., 20–30 in.); *V. longifolia var. incarnata* (Pink, July–Sept., 30 in.); *V. prostrata* (Dark Blue, June–July, 2–3 in.); *V. (Leptandra) virginica* (White, July–Sept., 30–36 in.).

Viburnum.—Hardy deciduous trees and shrubs, which thrive in most soils, but prefer a moist, well-drained deep loam, and which are very useful for shrubberies. The best known shrubby species is *V. Opulus sterile*, the Guelder Rose or Snowball Tree. *V. tomentosum plicatum*, a splendid border shrub, is also a useful sort for the greenhouse. Pot-up in October, using 7 to 10-inch pots and ordinary loam. Prune after flowering, and plant-out for two years in the open. *V. Tinus* (Laurustinus) is an evergreen species making a bush 8 feet or more in height. It will thrive in sun or shade under trees and facing north. It flowers in autumn and all though the winter. It is also useful for pot-culture indoors. In the latter case, pot-up in the early autumn, using 6 to 10-inch pots and well-drained sandy loam. Cut well back after flowering, and put out in the open in semi-shade from May to October.

Other good species are *V. Carlesii* with pinkish-white flowers in April and May; *V. fragrans*, pink or white, January to March, and *V. tomentosum*, creamy-white, May and June. *General Culture in the Open.*—Plant in a sunny position, deciduous species in October, November, or March; evergreens in May or September. Trim into shape annually and, when necessary, cut-out old wood in July (deciduous) and May (evergreen species). Propagate by means of cuttings in a frame in June, or layer in October.

Vinca (Periwinkle).—The hardy periwinkles are evergreen shrubs, which grow in any well-drained, ordinary soil, and which look well in borders or on rock-work. *V. maior* (20 in.) and *V. minor* (9 in.) have purple-blue flowers from June to September. There are also mauve and white varieties. *Culture.*—Plant from March to October. Cut back straggling shoots in April. Propagate by means of division in March or October.

Viola.—The viola and pansy are so similar in their cultural requirements that we treat them under the one heading. Violas, sometimes called Tufted Pansies, are much used for bedding or as edging plants, where they will flower from May until well into November. Any ordinary, deeply-dug, moderately rich loam will suit them. A sprinkling of good compost and a dressing of soot or bonemeal should be scattered on the top. Heavy clay is not good for violas. A cool, but not damp position in partial shade is best.

Culture.—Violas may be propagated from seed, by cuttings, or by division of the roots. Seed intended for spring flowers should be sown in boxes in June, using a good light soil, and the box should be covered with a sheet of glass until

412

PLATE 47   A brick-built or frame porch can look very attractive with the right climbing plants *Above*, example with wisteria and *below*, with climbing rose, Lady Waterlow.

H. & V. Joel and Frank Cant & Co

PLATE 48

BLANCHING CELERY

Celery, like leeks, endives, etc., requires blanching to remove the green colouring matter and consequent bitterness of taste. The usual way of doing this is earthing up the soil round the stalks. This can, however, be considerably improved by adopting the drill illustrated on this page and described below.

Top, wrap wax paper round the stalks from the root to upper leaves and tie firmly with string or raffia. *Centre*, and *bottom*, firm earth round individual plants and fill in the trench. This method not only produces a cleaner plant but affords some protection from pests.

the seeds are up. When fit to handle, transplant 2 inches apart into other boxes; water liberally and shade from sun. As frosty weather approaches, the boxes should be placed in a cold frame for the winter. At the beginning of April, transplant about 9 to 12 inches apart into partially-shaded beds, keeping the "balls" as far as possible intact. Cuttings of new, but vigorous growths from the centre of the plant, may be struck in September in a shady frame and planted-out in March for blooming the following year. Propagation by cuttings may take place any time from April to the end of October, although August and September are the best months. For early flowering, it is best to propagate by division of old roots in September. The hardier kinds can be wintered success-fully in the open in any shady nook in the garden, but not under trees. The less hardy kinds should be wintered in cold frames. Pansies bear larger and brighter flowers if raised from seed. All dead blooms should be periodically picked-off.

Pot Culture.—Strike cuttings in July or August, and when rooted, plant in 4-inch pots, and plunge in ashes or coconut fibre in a cold frame, where they should remain until the end of March. Shift them into 8-inch pots, keep close for a few days, then admit air gradually.

Culture.—(*Alpine Species*)—There are also many delightful alpine species, which need similar treatment to that described for the bedding viola, but the soil should be somewhat more loose, gritty, and moist.

Species.—*V. biflora* (Golden-yellow); *V. calcarata* (Yellow, Blue, or Purple); *V. declinata* [syn. *V. bosniaca*] (Rosy-mauve, Rose); *V. gracilis* (Violet-purple); *V. hederacea* [syn. *Erpetion reniforme*] (Light Blue, White, a creeper, 2–3 in. high); *V. lutea* (Golden-yellow); *V. odorata* [Sweet Violet]; *V. pedata* [Birdsfoot Violet] (Rosy-purple); *V. p. var. bicolor* (Rosy-purple and Yellow, a most strik-ing plant).

Violet (Viola odorata).—Violets may be grown in pots, by placing two or three runners or offsets in a pot in April or May, and keeping them in a frame, slightly shaded from the hot sun in summer. Loam, leaf-mould, and sand suit them admirably, but the violet is not particular as to soil. Russian violets, and sometimes the Neapolitan, will flower from September to April, if given the protection of glass. True violets flower in March and April. There are many varieties, but their culture is so similar that they may all be considered together. The grower should start with good stock from a reliable source, and, although the violet is a perennial, it is best to renew the stock each year.

Cultivation.—The violet should be propagated annually in June. When the plants have flowered, remove them from the soil, divide them into single crowns, cutting off all runners and dead foliage and selecting the finest outside crowns only; then plant-out the single varieties 15 inches apart each way, and the double kinds 10 to 12 inches apart, and press the soil firmly round the roots, but do not bury the crowns. A rich, well-dug, and well-drained bed with an east aspect, where they can receive the morning sun, should be chosen. When the plants show signs of growth, stir the soil about their roots with a small hoe, water liberally, and syringe them in the evenings of dry, hot days. Pinch-off all runners as they appear, and give a little shade from the sun in hot weather. Nothing more, save fortnightly doses of weak liquid manure or dustings with an artificial fertilizer and soot, is required for their culture during the summer months. The double varieties should be wintered in pots under glass or in a frame. Violets may also be propagated by cuttings struck in a cold frame in September or October.

Pot Culture.—To obtain bloom during the winter months, the best compost consists of four parts of turfy loam to one part each of rotted manure, leaf-mould, and sand, and a sprinkling of soot, well mixed together. In September, raise the violets from the bed in which they have been growing with as much earth on their roots as possible, and remove all side-shoots and runners. One strong plant should be put in each 6 to 7-inch pot with the crowns just above the soil. The pots should be well drained with broken bones instead of potsherds, and after planting, the pots should be well watered to settle the soil about the roots. A sufficient number of frames should be arranged in a sunny, sheltered, southern aspect, placing them in such a manner that the lights will throw off rain quickly. Put in a layer of old tan, about 4 inches thick, and in this the pots should be plunged in rows up to their rims. The bed of tan should be 6 to 9 inches higher at the back than at the front, and should be raised so that the plants are from 6 to 9 inches from the lights. Keep the frame almost closed for three or four days after planting, and shade if the sun is strong. After the first fortnight, and when the temperature is above 50° F., the lights may be removed during the day, and at night they should be tilted up at the back for the admission of air. When the temperature is below 50° F., the lights should be left on, but even then air should be admitted from behind during the day-time. If the temperature is below 40° F., the admission of air should be very partial, if it is admitted at all. At no time after the plants begin to bloom should the lights be entirely removed, except for the purpose of watering or gathering the flowers. When the weather is cold, a covering of mats should be applied at nights. In hard frosts, two mats should be put on as well as litter round the sides of the frame. Care must be taken to wet the leaves as little as possible.

Varieties.—(DOUBLE)—(White) *Comte de Brazza;* (Lavender, Blue, and White) *Marie Louise;* (Violet pink) *Madame Millet;* (Pale Blue) *Duchess de Parme;* (Dark Blue, White Throat) *Mrs. Arthur.* (SINGLE)—(White) *White Czar;* (Rose-pink) *Cœur d'Alsace;* (Rose, Pink, and White) *Rosea Delicatissima;* (Rose and Lavender) *Mrs. Lloyd George* (Semi-double)—(Purple) *Admiral Avellan;* (Violet) *Princess of Wales.*

Virginian Stock.—*See* Malcomia.

Viscum album (Mistletoe).—This parasite is easy to cultivate. An incision should be made in the bark of the underside of a three-year-old branch of an apple tree—many other trees, such as the pear, plum, lime, black poplar, thorn, ash, birch, etc., answer equally well—and in February into this incision insert some ripe mistletoe berries, and carefully tie the bark over with a piece of bass, matting, or woollen yarn. Growth is exceedingly slow at first.

Vitis (Vine).—Hardy deciduous climbing plants, including the popular Virginian Creeper *Parthenocissus tricuspidata var. Veitchii* (*Ampelopsis Veitchii*). They grow well in deeply-dug, moist soil with a little lime in it, and should be planted only in sheltered positions. *Culture.*—Strike cuttings in a frame in September. Plant in dry and open weather from November to March. Trim in winter. *Species.*—*V. Coignetiæ* is known as the Japanese Crimson Glory Vine.

Other good species are *V. Henryana* (*Parthenocissus Henryana*), *V. Thunbergii* and *V. vinifera purpurea*, the Teinturier Grape.

Vittadenia australis (triloba).—A beautiful little dwarf-growing plant, also known as *Erigeron mucronatus* (which see), which may be set in semi-shady positions and in sandy loam. It grows about 4 inches high, and is excellent for ledges in the rock garden. The daisy-like flowers, which are white and pink, are borne from April to September. No protection in winter is required. For culture, *see* Rock Plants, p. 196.

Wahlenbergia (Edraianthus, Tufted Harebell).—Dwarf-growing, hardy perennial rock plants, which like a sunny position and gritty loam, with a little lime rubble. For culture, *see* Rock Plants, p. 196. *Species.*—*W. Pumilio* (*Edraianthus Pumilio*) (Violet-blue, 2 in.); *W. serpyllifolia major* (*Edraianthus serpyllifolius major* (Violet, 2–3 in.). All May to June flowering.

Waitzia (Everlasting Flowers).—Half-hardy annuals, which can be grown in warm, sunny borders or in the greenhouse. For culture, *see* Annuals, p. 139. *W. grandiflora* (Golden-yellow, July–Sept., 20 in.) is the best known species.

Waldsteinia.—Only a few species of this genus are cultivated, and these but seldom. They have sprays of yellow flowers, some in early summer and others in spring or autumn. These plants grow about 8 inches high, and their creeping stems form dense masses that spread over the rocks. They thrive in sun or shade and in ordinary soil, and are admirable plants for rocky ledges, banks, or dry walls. *Culture.*—Propagate by means of division of roots in March, and plant out in permanent position. They require no protection in winter. *W. geoides* and *W. sibirica* (Yellow, March–June, 6 in.) are perhaps the best known species.

Wallflower (Cheiranthus).—Hardy biennials and perennials, which may be grown in sunny, open beds or borders, in the rock garden, or in the cold greenhouse. They love dry, sandy loam with some lime in it. The double wallflowers do not seed and must be raised from cuttings. The Double German varieties are, however, raised from seed. Grown in pots, they are excellent for the cool greenhouse. The perennial species are usually grown as biennials. *Culture.*—(BIENNIALS)—Sow seed thinly in early June, in drills 12 inches apart, in an open position, or take cuttings (double varieties) in September and strike in a frame in sandy soil. Transplant the seedlings when 2 inches high to 10 inches apart, water well, and nip out the centres as soon as the plants are established. Plant out in position for flowering early in October. (PERENNIALS)—Sow seed in the open in April, in drills 10 inches apart, or take cuttings in September and strike in sandy soil. Plant out in permanent position in October. *Pot Culture.*—Pot-up in September, using 5 to 6-inch pots and ordinary soil, and keep in a cold frame until the buds appear. *Species and Varieties.*—*C. Allionii* (Bright Orange, 10 in.); *C. alpinus* (Pale Yellow, 6 in.); *C. kewensis* (Chestnut Brown, 12 in.); *C. Marshallii* (Orange-yellow, 6 in.). All April to June flowering. *Named Varieties.*—[*C. Cheiri*]—(Pale Yellow) *Primrose Dame*; (Bright Yellow) *Cloth of Gold*; (Golden-yellow) *Harpur Crewe* (Double); *Ivory White*; *Orange Bedder;* (Apricot) *Eastern Queen; Blood Red;* (Crimson) *Vulcan;* (Brown) *Harbinger; Purple Queen.*

Watsonia (Bugle Lily).—Half-hardy bulbous plants, which should be grown in sunny positions in warm, sheltered borders and in sandy loam, peat, and leaf-mould, or in the cold greenhouse. *Culture.*—Plant in October or March, 3 inches deep and 4 inches apart. Pot plants should be kept dry in winter. Propagate by means of offsets in October or seed sown when ripe. *Species.*—*W. coccinea* (Scarlet, 20 in.); *W. densiflora* (Pink, 15 in); *W. Meriana var. Ardernei* (White, 20 in.). All June to August flowering.

Weldenia candida.—This is one of the prettiest alpines, though as yet very rare. It is of tuberous nature, and dies down in winter, when it ought to be covered with a few branches or with glass. In spring it throws up shoots like those of *Iris alata.* In late spring these stems support exquisite white waxy flowers. Propagation may be carried out only by dividing the roots in early autumn and planting in a well-drained compost of peaty loam and sand and in a sheltered position.

Wistaria.—Hardy May-flowering deciduous climbers, that do well in any good garden soil, but which prefer moist, deep, and well-drained sandy loam. *W. sinensis* (*chinensis*) of which there are three or four varieties, is the best known; *W. floribunda var. multijuga* is a newer form with mauve, rose, or white flowers, and longer racemes. *W. floribunda var. multijuga alba* is the best white wisteria. *Culture.*—Propagate by means of layering young wood in the summer, and plant-out in permanent position in dry, open weather from October to April. Both winter and summer-pruning are essential to promote flower buds, and straggling shoots should be cut away, but sturdy laterals should be encouraged to grow out some 3 feet from the main stems. Once the climbers are trained in this way, the young shoots should, in winter, be cut hard back to within a couple of inches of the old wood. *Pot Culture.*—In the cool greenhouse, *W. sinensis* will flower from February to April. Pot-up in October, using 8 to 12-inch pots and a compost of rich, sandy loam. Prune in January or February, cutting back all weak growing and straggly shoots to within an inch of the base. Sink the pots to their rims in ashes outdoors in a sunny spot from May to December.

Wulfenia carinthiaca.—Hardy perennials, which like a shady position in the rock garden, and a compost of loam and peat. It carries purple-blue flowers in July and August on 9-inch stems. *See* Rock Plants, p. 196.

Xanthoceras.—Deciduous shrubs or small trees, which need a sheltered position and a light, rich loam. Propagate by means of seed sown under glass. *X. sorbifolia* is the species most usually grown. In April this carries a wealth of creamy-white blossom in erect racemes. In favourable conditions it reaches a height of 12 or more feet.

Xeranthemum (Immortelles).—A showy class of everlasting flowers, all of which are hardy and thrive in sunny beds or borders and in rich soil. The best-known are: *X. annuum* (Purple, Rose, or White) and *X. inapertum* (Purple or White Flowers). Both grow 12 inches high and flower from July to September. For culture, *see* Annuals, p. 140.

Xerophyllum asphodeloides (Turkey's Beard).—Hardy perennials, useful for the mixed border, marsh, or wild garden. They love partial shade, and a moist, gritty loam and leaf-mould. They carry tall graceful spikes of ivory-white flowers 2 feet high in May. Propagate by means of seed sown in the open in June, or by division of roots in March, and plant out in permanent positions.

416

PLATE 14   *Above, PHLOX SUBLATA IN A ROCK GARDEN and Below,*
BUSH OF AZURE BLUE FELICIA IN WHICH ARE INTERSPERSED
THE MARIGOLD "NAUGHTY MARRIETTA"

Yew.—*See* Taxus.

Yucca.—These are all practically hardy evergreen plants of quaint appearance, forming striking objects when planted on lawns, banks, or in the rock garden. They are also useful for winter bedding. Yuccas do best in sheltered, sunny positions and in well-drained ordinary soil. *Culture.*—Plant in March or April. Cut away dead leaves in March and dead flowers in October. *Pot Culture.*—Pot-up in a compost of two-thirds fibrous loam and one-sixth coarse sand, and one-sixth finely-crushed brick-rubble. Propagate by means of tops, with the leaves trimmed off, planted in pots of very sandy and porous soil, by rhizomes in spring, or by seed. *Species.*—*Y. recurvifolia*, one of the best species for the garden, carries greenish-white inflorescences in August and September; *Y. gloriosa* is known as Adam's Needle, and *Y. angustifolia* is a hardy and more or less dwarf species. *Y. filamentosa* and *Y. flaccida* should find a place in the rock garden.

Zantedeschia (Arum Lily).—The Arum Lily is easy to cultivate either in the greenhouse or in a room. Re-pot every October in rich, light mould, preferably loam with equal parts of sand and cow-dung, the offsets having been removed, and the old soil well shaken out. A 6-inch pot may be used for each plant, or three may be placed in a 9 to 10-inch pot. From this time till June, or earlier if the plants have flowered, they should have abundance of water and occasional doses of liquid manure; it is best to keep the pot always standing in a deep saucer full of water. After this, however, they must be planted-out in rich soil, or stood in the open in the semi-shade, kept moist, and be given occasional doses of manure water till October, when the same treatment should be repeated. Propagate by means of offsets. The yellow species are less hardy and thrive best in the warm greenhouse. Pot-up in February. Withhold water gradually after flowering and keep the pot in a frost-proof frame through the winter.

Species and Varieties.—*Zantedeschia æthiopica; Z. a. Childsiana* (White, 24 in.); *Z. a. Little Gem* (White, dwarf); *Z. Rehmannii* (Rose). *Z. melanoleuca* (Purple and Yellow); and *Z. Elliottiana* (Yellow, Aug. 24 in.); The arum (except the yellow varieties) usually flowers from February to May. In some catalogues the Arum Lily is still listed as Richardia.

Zauschneria (Californian Fuchsia).—Handsome perennials, which thrive in gritty loam in a sunny position in the rock garden. For culture, *see* Rock Plants, p. 196. *Species.*—*Z. californica* (Scarlet, July–Sept., 12–18 in.); *Z. cana* (Scarlet, small foliage, July–Sept., 18–24 in.).

Zea (Indian Corn or Maize).—Half-hardy annuals, which thrive in ordinary soil in warm, sunny situations. For culture, *see* Annuals, p. 139. *Z. Mays vars. variegata* and *quadricolor* (3 ft.) are generally grown, and are also useful for greenhouse purposes.

Zelkova.—A small genus of interesting and handsome hardy trees, nearly allied to the elms. They grow best in a deep, moist, loamy soil, where the position is moderately sheltered. They may be increased by seeds, but if these are not available, graft on the elm. *Z. carpinifolia* (*Z. crenata*), a tree up to 100 feet in height, and a native of the Caucasus, is the best-known species. *Z. serrata* (*Z. acuminata*), from Japan, is also listed in tree and shrub catalogues.

Zenobia speciosa.—This is a hardy, ericaceous shrub, that is semi-evergreen and which reaches a height of from 3 to 4 feet. From June to August it bears, on slender stems, drooping bell-like flowers of a waxy whiteness. It is a most interesting plant for growing in the bog or marsh garden. *Z. pulverulenta* is very similar to *Z. speciosa,* but has its leaves and stems covered with a steely-white, mealy dust, which makes it a very decorative plant, especially in winter. *Culture.* —Plant in a semi-shaded position in September or October and in well-drained, peaty soil or in a mixture of loam and leaf-mould (no lime). Cut off old flower shoots after blooming. Propagate by means of soft cuttings in a frame in June, or by means of division in September.

Zephyranthes (Zephyr Flower).—Bulbous-rooted plants, some species of which are sufficiently hardy to thrive in warm, sunny borders and in rich and well-drained peaty loam. The more tender kinds should be grown in pots in the greenhouse. *Culture.*—Plant in October, 4 inches deep and 3 inches apart, with the bulbs resting in sand, and protect with fibre in winter. Lift when overcrowded, and propagate by means of offsets in October. *Pot Culture.*—Pot-up from August to November, placing four to five bulbs in a 5-inch pot and using a compost of two parts of loam to one part each of leaf-mould and peat with a little silver sand. Dry-off gradually after flowering. *Species.*—*Z. candida* (White); *Z. grandiflora (carinata)* (Pale Pink); and *Z. rosea* (Rose). All May to September flowering and growing to a height of from 6 to 10 inches.

Zinnia.—Half-hardy annuals, which thrive in light, rich soil. The dwarfer hybrid varieties are valuable for warm, sunny beds; the taller kinds for borders and the cool greenhouse. For culture, *see* Annuals, p. 139. *Greenhouse Plants.* —Pot seedlings up singly in small pots, using a compost of two-thirds fibrous loam and one-third dry, well-rotted manure, and sand. Give ample light and ventilate freely, but do not let the temperature drop below 60° F.; avoid draughts. More water will be needed as growth increases. Re-pot before the plants get potbound, and as soon as the plants are re-established, reduce the temperature by about ten degrees and, as the buds appear, water weekly with weak manure-water and dress with bonemeal. *Species.*—*Z. elegans* (Various, 20–30 in.); *Z. Haageana* (Orange, 12 in.); *Z. pauciflora* (Red, 20 in.). There are many varieties, and catalogues should be consulted. All species and varieties flower from July to September.

418

CHAPTER 35

VEGETABLE CULTURE

In all but possibly the very smallest gardens, a part, at least, is usually set aside for the cultivation of vegetables, salads, and herbs. Nor does this necessarily involve any sacrifice of beauty or interest. For beautiful as are many of our hardy flowers, few of them surpass in form and colour many of those vegetables which are inevitably associated in our minds with the idea of English gardens. Peas, beans, scarlet runners, asparagus, globe artichokes, cabbages, rhubarb, parsley, and sage all possess a beauty and, for most of us associations which are of the very essence of gardening. Badly placed, indeed, must be the garden in which no vegetables can be grown. For the range is great, and nearly every soil and situation can be adapted and used for the cultivation of at any rate some of our English vegetables.

SOIL

As a general rule, we may take it that a deep, medium, heavy loam is best suited for the purposes of a kitchen garden, though much may be done to drain and lighten heavy soils and to enrich and moisten light soils so as to make them almost equally useful. Protection from strong winds is essential in the case of most vegetables, and walls, fences, or hedges, should, where necessary, be erected or planted for this purpose. Reasonable exposure to sunlight is also necessary.

Trenching

In any event, the ground must be carefully and thoroughly prepared if any success is to be gained. Deep digging or trenching and a liberal application of organic manure are the most important of these preparatory steps. *See* p. 45.

Manuring

The preparation and manuring of the soil should take place in the autumn, so as to be ready for sowing in the early spring. It is not usually possible to trench the whole of the vegetable garden thoroughly annually. About a third of the area should be trenched each year, and this will ensure that the whole is trenched at least once in three years. Where the ground is not trenched, it must be dug over every autumn to a depth of

419

12 to 15 inches. The surface of the soil should be left rough, to be acted upon by the sun, air and frost. For artificial and organic manures suitable to the various soils, *see* Table of Manures, p. 424. Trenching is, on the whole, the greatest secret of successful vegetable cultivation.

LAYING-OUT THE VEGETABLE GARDEN

The most suitable and economical form to adopt is a simple rectangle. All paths and borders and divisions should follow straight lines and should form right angles with each other. The paths should be strong and solid, and the garden should be well-drained and sheltered. The shadier parts should be the home of vegetables that do not primarily require warmth, such as rhubarb, seakale, Scotch kale, and the many varieties of salad. The pulses, potatoes, and cabbages require more sun, and it is a safe rule to follow that where the cabbage will grow to perfection almost any vegetable will do well. The sides of any available walls which face east and south and west should have borders at their base in which fruit trees may be placed, and here also, owing to their more genial situation, early crops of all kinds may be nursed. The width of such borders depends upon the amount of sunlight that visits them, and while they should in no case be so wide as to render cultivation difficult, those which get most sun may be wider than those whose aspect is less sunny. A bed should be given up to herbs, and since so many of these are beautiful and sweet-smelling, the strip they occupy may be placed as near the house as convenient.

BEST VARIETIES TO GROW

Naturally, it is impossible to say definitely what are the best varieties to grow as some kinds thrive on a moderately heavy soil, but do poorly on light soils, and vice versa. Certain varieties are best for the early crop, others for the main crop, others are preferable for late sowing. At the end of the paragraphs devoted to the individual vegetables, we have given varieties suitable for the various crops; some of the selections loving a light soil, others thriving in heavy soils.

CROP ROTATION

It will, with but few exceptions, always be found a good plan to vary the crops taken from any given plot, never growing the same kind of plant on it for two seasons running. Each crop takes out of the soil certain elements, and leaves it enriched by others. Thus, for example, leguminous crops, as peas, are able to extract nitrogen from the air, and besides using a part of it themselves, leave the soil richer in nitrogenous constituents than they found it. The nitrogen is stored in the roots, which for this reason should always be left in the soil. This is a good moment to sow in this soil plants such as the onion, which demands a good supply of nitrogen in

420

the soil ready for their use. It is a good rough rule that tuberous or bulbous-rooted plants should come after fibrous-rooted ones, and vice versa. Crops so similar in habit and nature as cabbages, broccoli, sprouts, and kale should not follow one another. Plants with shallow roots, as the pea, the lettuce, and the cabbage, should be grown alternately with deep-rooted plants like the beet, the carrot or the parsnip. The soil should not be freshly manured for root-crops, manuring for the previous crop being sufficient. If manure has not previously been given, it must be dug in very deeply to encourage good straight roots. Fresh manure should never come in contact with the roots. Related crops usually suffer from the same diseases; this is another reason for a rotation. (*See* Table, p. 422.)

Much time will be saved if the rotation is worked out and decided upon well before the planting time.

The following table, showing a strip of land divided into three plots, with a rotation on each covering three years, is a useful guide. It can, of course, be extended indefinitely, both with regard to the number of plots used or the successive number of years.

THREE YEAR PLAN

Plot	1st Year	2nd Year	3rd Year
A	Cabbages	Peas	Turnips
B	Leeks	Carrots	Seakale
C	Brussels Sprouts	Onions	Celery

Arranging a Succession of Crops

It is advisable to plant another crop as soon as the previous one has been cleared, for space is usually at a premium. The chief crops that are over early and permit of second cropping are early turnips, onions, cabbages, potatoes, and early peas. Quick-maturing crops useful to form the second crop to follow these are spinach, lettuce, onions, shorthorn carrots, turnips, cabbages, or broccoli for use the following spring. In selecting these crops, consideration must be given to the correct rotation of crops. (*See* Table, p. 422.)

Fast-Maturing Catch-Crops

Catch-crops are fast maturing crops, that may be planted between the rows of slower-growing vegetables, or even in the rows between the individual plants. Before the main crop has matured and claimed its full space, these "catch crops" will have matured and will have been cleared. Suitable catch-crops are shown in the last column of our table relating to Crop Rotation, page 422.

421

CROP ROTATION

The following table shows what crops a certain vegetable may follow and what it may *not* follow. It also indicates what crops a vegetable may be followed by and the crops that should not come after it.

Principal Crop	Crops it may follow	Crops it may not follow	Crops it may be followed by	Crops it may not be followed by	Catch-crops which may be planted between rows
Beans	Asparagus, borecole, cabbages, broccoli, turnips, parsnips, carrots, potatoes.	*Leguminous plants of its own family, i.e., peas, etc.	Beet, carrots, celery, leeks, lettuces, parsnip, salsify, turnip, and any of the Cabbage tribe.	*Leguminous plants of its own family, i.e., peas, etc.	Borecole, Brussels sprouts.
Beet	Cabbage tribe, and any crops but those specified in next column.	Spinach, turnips, parsnips, carrots, salsify, and scorzonera.	Peas, beans, cabbages, cauliflower, lettuces, onions and any spring-sown crop except those in next column.	Spinach, turnips, parsnips, and carrots.	Nothing.
Borecole and Brussels Sprouts	Peas, beans, lettuces, potatoes.	*Cruciferous plants of own order, i.e., any of Cabbage tribe, turnips, etc.	Peas, beans, beet, carrots, parsnips, onions, potatoes, kidney beans, celery, salsify, leeks, lettuce, endive, shallots, spinach.	*Cruciferous plants of own family, i.e., any of Cabbage tribe, turnips, etc.	Beans.
Broccoli	Peas, beans, kidney beans.	*Cruciferous plants of own family.	Any crop to be sown or planted when cleared off.	*Cruciferous plants of own family.	Nothing.
Cabbages	Peas, beans, kidney beans, potatoes, lettuces, onions, leeks, celery, etc.	*Cruciferous plants of own family.	Peas, beans, kidney beans, potatoes, lettuces, carrots, parsnips, beet, salsify, celery, seakale, onions, leeks, radishes, endive, shallots, spinach, etc.	*Cruciferous plants of own family.	Coleworts.
Carrots and Parsnips	Cabbage tribe and any crops except those in next column.	Any crops except root crops and *umbelliferous plants, as celery, parsley, etc.	Any crops except those in next column.	Any crops except root crops and *umbelliferous plants, as celery, parsley, etc.	Nothing.
Cauliflower	Peas, beans, potatoes, celery, kidney beans, onions, carrots, lettuces, beet.	*Cruciferous plants of own family.	Peas, beans, potatoes, celery, kidney beans, onions, carrots, leeks, salsify, endive, shallots, lettuces, beet, parsnip.	*Cruciferous plants of own family.	Spinach, lettuces, endive.

CROP ROTATION (continued)

Celery	Any crop except those in next column.	Parsnips, carrots, parsley.	Peas, beans, kidney beans, onions, potatoes, turnips, and any of the Cabbage tribe.	Parsnips, carrots, parsley.	Lettuces, endive, dwarf early peas, French beans.
Endive and Lettuce	Asparagus, potatoes, peas, beans and any of the Cabbage tribe.	Chicory, salsify, scorzonera, artichokes, cardoons, and any plants of the family *Compositæ.	Peas, beans, potatoes.	Chicory, salsify, scorzonera, artichokes, cardoons, and any plants of the family *Compositæ.	Nothing.
Kidney Beans and Peas	Potatoes, carrots, parsnips, turnips, broccoli, and any of the Cabbage tribe.	Beans and *leguminous plants of own family.	Broccoli, cabbages, of any kind, spinach, turnips, potatoes, late celery, parsnips, beet, salsify, onions, leeks, lettuce, endive, shallots.	Beans and *leguminous plants of own family.	Summer spinach, radishes, lettuce, broccoli, turnip, early carrots; borecole and Brussels sprouts between dwarf sorts.
Leeks, Onions, Shallots, etc.	Cabbage tribe, celery, potatoes, peas, beans, kidney beans, lettuces, endive, spinach.	Garlic, chives, and any crop of the onion tribe.	Cabbages, carrots, coleworts, celery, cauliflower, parsnips, potatoes, peas, beans, beet.	Garlic, chives, and any crop of onion tribe.	Nothing.
Potatoes	Any crop except those specified in the next column.	Carrots, parsnips, beet, salsify, scorzonera.	Any crop requiring a loose, clean, well-worked soil, and all *cruciferous plants, peas, beans, etc.	Root crops generally, as carrots, parsnips, beet, etc.	Brussels sprouts, cabbages, borecole, broccoli, and late celery if there is space enough for trench.
Seakale	Potatoes, peas, beans, carrots, parsnips, beet, celery, etc.	*Cruciferous plants of own family.	Potatoes, peas, beans, carrots, parsnips, beet, celery, etc.	*Cruciferous plants of own family.	Nothing.
Spinach	Peas, beans, kidney beans, cabbage, cauliflower, lettuces, etc.	Beet.	Peas, beans, kidney beans, cabbage, cauliflower, lettuces, etc.	Beet.	Nothing.
Turnips	Potatoes, spinach, peas, beans, lettuces, etc.	*Cruciferous plants of own family.	Potatoes, spinach, peas, beans, lettuces, beet, carrot, parsnip.	*Cruciferous plants of own family.	Nothing.

* NOTE.—To save space in the table, the above group names have been used and are here explained.
Cruciferæ.—Cabbage, cauliflower, broccoli, colewort, turnip, radish, cress, seakale, mustard, horse-radish.
Leguminosæ.—Peas, beans.
Umbelliferæ.—Carrot, parsnip, parsley, celery, fennel, carraway.
Compositæ.—Globe artichoke, Jerusalem artichoke, scorzonera, salsify, endive, lettuce, chicory.

423

Note.—A Dressing of 3 qrs. per ¼ Acre is equal to 2 lb. to the Square Rod, or 1 oz. to
to the farmyard manure, which is applied in the Autumn or Spring, according to the
ment, and for particular cultural details of

Name of Vegetable	Farmyard Manure	Artificial Fertilizers.*	
Beans. . .	Moderately heavy, 3–4 tons	Basic Slag	3 qrs.
		Vegetable or Wood Ashes	3 qrs.
Beetroot . . .	Organic manure for preceding crop only	Ammonium Sulphate	1½ qrs.
		Potash Salts	1½ qrs.
		Peruvian Guano	2 qrs.
Cabbage (including Broccoli, Brussels Sprouts, Cauliflower, Kale, etc.)	Moderately 3 tons	Salt	2½ qrs.
		Steamed Bone Flour	2½ qrs.
		Nitrate of Lime	1½ qrs.
		Sulphate of Potash	1 qr.
Carrots . . .	Organic manure for preceding crop only	Ammonium Sulphate	1½ qrs.
		Kainit	3 qrs.
		Salt	2½ qrs.
Celery . . .	Moderately, 3 tons	Ammonium Sulphate	1½ qrs.
		Potash Salts	1½ qrs.
		Salt	2½ qrs.
Leeks. . . .	Moderately, 3 tons	Ammonium Sulphate	1½ qrs.
		Potash Salts	1½ qrs.
		Steamed Bone Flour	3 qrs.
Lettuce . . .	Moderately, 3 tons	None necessary	
Onions . . .	Moderately, 3 tons	Ammonium Sulphate	1½ qrs.
		Kainit	3 qrs.
		Soot	1 cwt.
Parsnips . . .	Organic manure for preceding crop only	Ammonium Sulphate	1½ qrs.
		Kainit	3 qrs.
Peas	Moderately, 3 tons	Basic Slag	3 qrs.
		Potash Salts	1 qr.
		or Wood or Veg. Ashes	3 qrs.
		Nitrate of Soda	1½ qrs.
Potatoes . . .	Fairly heavily, 5 tons	Ammonium Sulphate	1½ qrs.
		Basic slag	3 qrs.
		Potash Salts	1½ qrs.
		or Wood or Veg. Ashes	3 qrs.
Radishes . . .	Moderately, 3 tons	None necessary	
Spinach . . .	Moderately, 3 tons	(a) Ammonium Sulphate (heavy soil) or	1½ qrs.
		(b) Nitrate of Soda (light soil)	1½ qrs.
Turnips . . .	Organic manure for preceding crop only	Ammonium sulphate	1½ qrs.
		Kainit	3 qrs.
		Steamed Bone Flour	3 qrs.

* In each case, *all* the fertilizers quoted should be used if the

time to apply.

¼ acre.)

the Square Yard. Unless otherwise stated, the artificial manures are given in addition soil; heavy in Autumn, light in early Spring. *See* also Chapter 4, on Soil Improve- the various vegetables, *see* Chapter 36.

When to Apply Artificial Fertilizer	Remarks
Autumn and Winter Spring	No farmyard manure is needed unless the soil is exhausted. On heavy soil substitute 2 qrs. of Superphosphate for the Basic Slag, and apply when the crop is maturing.
Spring. When sowing Spring. When sowing Before sowing When growing When growing When growing as top-dressing Early Spring Spring. When sowing	Soil should have been well manured with organic matter for previous crop, which crop should not have been a root one. Farmyard manure should be well dug in in Autumn in heavy soil, or in early Spring in light soil. On light soil Nitrate of Soda should be substituted for the Nitrate of Lime.
Spring or Autumn, according to soil When growing	Soil should have been well manured with organic matter for previous crop, which crop should not have been a root one. On heavy soil substitute 1 qr. of Sulphate of Potash for the Kainit and apply early in Spring.
When sowing When growth commences When growing	Farmyard manure should be well dug in in Autumn in heavy soil or in early Spring in light soil.
When sowing When growth commences When growing	Farmyard manure should be dug in in Autumn in heavy soil or in Spring in light.
When sowing Spring or Autumn according to soil When growing	The farmyard manure should be well dug in in Autumn in heavy soil or in Spring in light soil. On heavy soil 1 qr. Sulphate of Potash should be substituted for the Kainit, and applied in early Spring.
When sowing Spring or Autumn according to soil Autumn and Winter Spring, when sowing	Soil should have been well manured for previous crop, which should not be a root one. No farmyard manure is needed unless soil is exhausted. On heavy soils 2 qrs. Superphosphate should be substituted for the Basic Slag, and applied when the crop is maturing.
When growing When planting Autumn or Winter When preparing soil	Soil should be deeply worked and the farmyard manure incorporated in the Autumn. On heavy soil 2 qrs. Superphosphate should be substituted for the Basic Slag, and applied when the crop is maturing.
(a) When sowing (b) When growing	No artificial should be necessary if the farmyard manure has been dug in.
When sowing Autumn or Spring, according to soil When growth begins	Soil should have been well manured for previous crop, which should not have been a root one. On heavy soil substitute 2 qrs. Superphosphate for the Steamed Bone Flour and apply when the crop is maturing.

best results are desired. One fertilizer is, however, better than none.

SOWING SEED

Sowing in the open may begin about the end of February, on fairly dry soil, in warm situations—a few early peas, early beans, early horn carrots, and lettuce. (*See* table, p. 427). In March, some parsnips, onions, beets, turnips, and more peas, beans, and carrots may be sown. In order to obtain a succession of vegetables through the year, and not gluts at one time and none at another, it is desirable to sow the seeds of most vegetables in successive small quantities, so that crop may follow crop. Always sow in drills, not broadcast. It is then possible to keep the hoe busy between the rows. (*See also* Sowing in the open and under glass in Chapter 11.)

Thinning and Planting-out

If the crops have been sown thinly, little thinning will be necessary, but as soon as the plants can be handled, thin out to the distances advised for each vegetable. (*See* next chapter).

WATERING VEGETABLE CROPS

Seedlings

Towards the end of April and early in May, while many seedlings are still tender, we often experience hot, dry weather that would scorch up many of the seedlings unless they were watered. The hoe should be used unsparingly among the seedlings after watering. This will help to keep the earth moist, and will let the air into the ground. It is almost always essential to water transplanted seedlings thoroughly to make the soil firm about their roots.

Maturer Plants

Plants whose roots spread out near the surface of the soil and do not descend very deeply will need liberal watering every day should the summer be very dry; lettuce is a good example of this type of plant.

There are other crops which, in spite of the fact that their roots run down fairly deeply, need copious supplies of water in dry weather; beans, peas and celery may be instanced in this case.

On the other hand, root crops and many plants of the cabbage tribe, provided they are planted in deeply-dug, well-worked soil, will rarely need watering or mulching, even during the driest seasons. (*See also* Watering in Chapter 11.)

BLANCHING AND MULCHING VEGETABLES

These important operations are fully dealt with in Chapter 3, *which see.*

TIMES TO SOW THE VARIOUS VEGETABLE SEEDS OR TUBERS

The following table shows what seeds should be sown during the various months of the year. Full cultural details will be found in the paragraphs on the particular plants in the next chapter.

Seed or Tubers	Jan.	Feb.	Mar.	April	May	June	July	Aug.	Sept.	Oct.	Nov.	Dec.
Artichokes,												
Chinese	–	–	*	–	–	–	–	–	–	–	–	–
Globe	–	–	–	*	–	–	–	–	–	–	–	–
Jerusalem	–	–	*	–	–	–	–	–	–	–	–	–
Asparagus	–	–	*	–	–	–	–	–	–	–	–	–
Beans,												
Broad	–	*	*	*	*	–	–	–	–	–	–	–
Kidney or French	–	–	–	–	*	*	–	–	–	–	–	–
Runner	–	–	–	–	*	*	–	–	–	–	–	–
Beetroot	–	–	*	*	*	–	–	–	–	–	–	–
Borecole or Kale	–	–	*	*	*	–	–	–	*	–	–	–
Broccoli	–	–	–	*	*	–	–	–	–	–	–	–
Brussels Sprouts	–	*	*	–	–	–	–	–	–	–	–	–
Cabbages	–	–	*	*	–	–	–	*	–	–	–	–
Cardoons	–	–	–	–	–	*	–	–	–	–	–	–
Carrots	–	*	*	*	*	–	–	*	–	–	–	–
Cauliflower	–	*	–	*	–	–	–	*	–	–	–	–
Celery	–	*	*	–	–	–	–	–	–	–	–	–
Colewort	–	–	–	–	–	*	*	*	–	–	–	–
Kohl-rabi	–	–	*	–	–	–	*	–	–	–	–	–
Leeks	–	*	*	–	–	–	–	–	–	–	–	–
Onions	*	*	*	–	–	–	–	*	*	–	–	–
Parsnips	–	*	*	*	*	–	–	–	–	–	–	–
Peas	–	*	*	*	*	*	–	–	–	–	–	–
Potatoes	–	*	*	*	–	–	–	–	–	–	–	–
Salsify	–	–	–	*	–	–	–	–	–	–	–	–
Savoys	–	–	–	*	–	–	–	–	–	–	–	–
Seakale	–	–	*	*	–	–	–	–	–	–	–	–
Shallots	–	*	*	–	–	–	–	–	–	–	–	–
Spinach	–	–	*	*	*	*	*	*	*	–	–	–
Swedes	–	–	*	*	*	*	–	–	–	–	–	–
Turnips	–	–	*	*	*	*	*	*	–	–	–	–
Vegetable Marrows	–	–	–	–	*	–	–	–	–	–	–	–

* In the above table, the *'s denote when to sow or plant.

NOTE—Salads and Herbs are dealt with separately in Chapters 37 and 38.

CHAPTER 36

THE CULTURE OF PARTICULAR VEGETABLES

Artichokes. CHINESE ARTICHOKE.—This artichoke requires space and a well-drained, well-manured, deeply-dug soil. The tubers should be planted in March, in drills 6 inches deep, allowing 12 inches between the plants in the rows and 12 to 24 inches between the rows. The surface of the ground between the rows should be kept well hoed, and early in July a liberal top-dressing of manure should be given. During July and August, water should be freely afforded. In light soil the tubers may remain in the ground through the winter, being dug as required. Or they may be raised about the middle of November and stored under sand or fine soil covered with litter.

GLOBE ARTICHOKE.—Full exposure to the sun is desirable, and frost is less harmful than damp. The ground should be trenched and heavily manured in the autumn, and the planting should be done about the beginning of April. The best method of propagation is by root division or suckers, as seeds cannot be counted on to come true. No plants should be kept after three or four years old, and it is well to make a small fresh plantation each year. The flower-heads should be picked when about half-grown and closed. Liberal watering and mulching, and, if necessary, staking are the principal parts of its summer treatment.

At the approach of winter, some ashes or sand should be banked round the plant, and before frosts are expected, the plant should be covered with litter or leaves. About the middle of March, this should be removed, the earth between the rows being lightly forked and dressed with manure.

JERUSALEM ARTICHOKE.—The Jerusalem Artichoke does best in a somewhat light soil, deeply dug, and in an open situation. The tubers should be planted early in March, in drills 3 inches deep, 18 inches being allowed between the tubers, and 3 feet between the drills.

In very heavy soil, it is well to plant only just below the surface and to mix plenty of ashes with the soil.

Storing.—The stems should be cut down early in November, and the tubers may be left in the ground through the winter and dug as required.

Varieties.—Good varieties are *Old Red* and *White*.

Asparagus. On clay soils, the cultivation of asparagus presents somewhat of a problem, though even here, by throwing up the soil into ridges, placing broken bricks and other rubble for drainage, by the addition of burnt rubbish and leaf-mould, and by surface manuring, asparagus of no mean quality can be raised. Where, however, the soil is of a more sandy nature, and the natural drainage is efficient, every one, with a little care and attention, may easily grow this excellent vegetable.

428

Soil and Situation.—A warm situation should be selected, preferably with a southern aspect. Protection from the prevailing winds must be afforded. The soil, whether light or heavy, should be deeply dug, and while in the case of heavy soils, it is well only to enrich the top foot or so of soil so as to keep the roots near the surface, in the case of medium and light soils, the ground should be heavily enriched with decayed farmyard manure, preferably to a depth of 4 feet or more.

Planting.—The ground being dug and levelled, divide it into 5-foot beds, with alleys 2 feet wide between each bed. Strong one-year-old plants, without tops, should be selected and in April planted 1½ to 2 inches deep in three rows in each 5-foot bed, the rows a foot from each side of the bed, and the plants 2 feet apart in the rows. Water well after planting if the weather is dry. Throughout the summer, the principal work must consist in keeping the surface of the ground broken up by means of the hoe, and in destroying weeds as soon as they appear. Under no circumstances should any other crop be raised between the plants.

About the end of January a mulch of stable manure may be laid on the surface and a sprinkling of earth used to cover it; or alternately, a little nitrate of soda or guano may be applied in May. About the second week of February, each crown should be covered with a few inches of soil or preferably sand, or sand mixed with soil. Shoots may be cut, or better, broken, as low as possible, when about 8 inches in length, care being taken not to injure young shoots not yet fit for cutting. No cutting should be done for the first two years at least. In the case of older plantations, it is unwise to cut asparagus after the middle of June. Cut down all stems in autumn.

Forcing.—See p. 250.

Varieties.—*Perfection; Connover's Colossal;* and *Early Giant Argenteuil.*

Beans, Broad. *Soil.*—Broad beans like best a deep, somewhat heavy soil, which should be deeply dug and moderately heavily manured in the autumn before sowing.

Sowing.—The earliest sowing may be made in a warm and sheltered situation at the end of October or early in November. Seed should be sown in the open for main crop purposes in February and March, successional crops being obtained by sowing a few each month right up to May or June. About 9 inches should be allowed from seed to seed, and 2 feet between the rows. A little earth drawn up to the roots when the seedlings are 3 to 4 inches high induces them to put out fresh roots. When the stem is covered with about 18 inches of flowers, the top should be pinched off to encourage the growth of the pods. All laterals should be removed as they appear. Should the black fly attack the beans, immediately pinch-back all young shoots. This may arrest the pests. If this is not successful, the plants must be syringed with a solution of soft soap. *See also* Forcing, p. 250.

Varieties.—Earliest crop, *Mazagans* or *Early Green* and *Exhibition Longpods;* Main crop, *Giant Green* and *White Windsor.*

Dwarf Broad Beans grow some 12 to 18 inches high, are bushy in form, and occupy no more space than the tall varieties. *Little Marvel,* and *Dwarf Fan,* are popular varieties.

Beans, French or Kidney. *Soil.*—Dwarf Kidney Beans or French Beans like a deep, rich soil, which should be deeply dug and manured in the autumn. They should be grown in an open, unshaded situation.

Sowing.—By sowing partly in the open and partly under glass, French Beans may be obtained during practically every month of the year. In the open, the first sowing should be made under a south wall about the middle of April, the young plants being sheltered as soon as they come up with a little loose litter. The principal out-door sowing should be made early in May, but it is well to sow a few seeds at weekly intervals right on to the beginning of July. Seed should be sown 6 inches apart in drills 2 inches deep, 2 to 3 feet being allowed between the rows.

Thinning and Transplanting.—When the young plants appear, they should be thinned or transplanted so as to allow at least a foot from plant to plant in the rows. The pods must be gathered before the seeds are formed and the period of bearing will be prolonged if the pods are picked as soon as they are fit. *See also* Forcing, p. 250.

Varieties.—Early sowing, *Masterpiece, Ne Plus Ultra*; followed by *Negro Longpod*, followed again by *Canadian Wonder* and *Perfection*; latest sowing the *Newington*.

Beans, Runner. *Soil.*—The Runner Bean does best in a deep, moderately retentive soil, which has been well manured and deeply dug in the autumn. *See also* Table page 424.

Sowing.—The earliest seed should be sown in a sheltered situation about the middle of May. Successional crops may be obtained by sowing in the open until the middle of June. Sow in drills, 2 inches deep, 5 inches being allowed from seed to seed in the rows and 6 feet from row to row. Water and syringe liberally in hot weather. A weekly soaking with liquid manure as soon as some of the pods have set will increase the crop.

Training.—As soon as the plants have formed their first leaves, tall poles, 8 feet in height and firmly set in the ground, should be provided. Dust the young plants liberally with soot to keep away slugs.

The pods should be gathered as soon as ready, or they will become hard and stringy. *See also* Forcing, p. 250.

Varieties.—Earliest planting, *Earliest of All* and *Tender and True*; later, *Prizewinner, Scarlet Emperor, Streamline*, and *Mammoth White*.

Beetroot. The soil should be deep and of medium texture. No manure should be added just before sowing, but the beet should follow a crop, preferably leeks, for which the ground has been manured.

Sowing.—For early use, the turnip-rooted kind, of which *Sutton's Globe* and *Crimson Ball* are good varieties, may be sown on a mild hot-bed in a frame from the beginning of January to the end of March, or about the first week in April, in a warm border in the open, in drills 1 inch deep and 15 inches apart. A little salt dusted into the drills at the time of sowing, and sprinkled between the plants occasionally during June and July, will materially improve the roots. The soil should be made firm after sowing, and the young plants should be thinned to about 9 inches apart, the young shoots being dusted with soot or lime to protect them from the birds. The turnip-rooted kinds may also be used for later supplies, where the soil is too poor or shallow for the long-rooted kind. Where the soil is suitable, however, the long-rooted kind are to be preferred for all but the earliest crops. These should be sown in May under similar conditions to those suggested for the turnip-rooted kinds. *Cheltenham Green-top* or *Galloway Purple* are, perhaps, the best varieties of all this group. *Pineapple* and *Nutting's Old Dwarf Red* are excellent. *See also* p. 251.

Storing.—Any roots that remain in the ground should be lifted before the middle of October, the leaves should be twisted off, the roots dried and carefully packed away in dry sand in a cool but frost-proof place. If carefully and periodically looked over, the roots will remain in good condition until the following April.

Borecole. The Borecole or Kale is one of the most popular of our vegetables, for it is in season from October till April.

Soil.—A rather stiff, deeply-dug, and well-enriched soil is desirable. The manure should be added some time previously to planting.

Sowing.—The seeds should be sown from March to May in drills about 1 inch deep. The seedlings should be thinned out to 4 inches apart, where necessary, as soon as they appear.

Planting-out.—The plants may be planted out when about six to eight weeks old, about 2½ feet being allowed from plant to plant in all directions. Water liberally until the roots are firmly established.

Varieties.—Autumn supply, *A1* and *Dwarf Green Curled*; for Christmas, *Curled Scotch*, *Drumhead* and *Read's Improved Hearting*; for early spring, *Asparagus Kale*, *Welsh Kale*, and *Cottager's Kale*. Spring varieties may be sown in early autumn, often with advantage.

Broccoli. The broccoli, with care, will supply a succession of heads from November till June.

Soil.—A well-tilled, rich soil is necessary, as rapid growth is essential.

Sowing.—The seeds should be sown in an open position in drills ½ inch deep, 1 foot being allowed between the drills. The ground should previously be fined, dressed with soot, and rendered very firm.

Thinning and Transplanting.—Thin out to 6 inches apart as soon as possible, and finally to 2½ feet apart. Broccoli flourishes in ground that has been used for another crop and not retrenched. If the soil has been well manured, it should be beaten down hard round the roots. This will encourage hard stems and prevent too much leaf from forming. The plants should be kept well supplied with water until properly established, especially the autumn-flowering varieties, and these must also be liberally watered in all stages of their growth during dry, hot weather. Before severe weather sets in, the spring kinds should be laid over, with their heads facing the north. This operation checks the action of the roots and the plants consequently become less succulent and better able to resist frost. They are also put in the best possible position for covering with stable manure or any other litter when such protection becomes necessary.

Varieties.—Mid-winter supply, *Self-protecting*, *Snow's Winter White*, *Sandringham Winter White*, *King's Large* and *Superb Early White*; to succeed these: *Purple* and *White Sprouting Broccoli, Leamington, Late Queen, Nine Star* and *Model*.

431

Brussels Sprouts. Brussels Sprouts require a deeply-dug and previously heavily manured soil, well-trodden before planting.

Sowing.—The seed may be sown in a warm situation in drills about ¾ inch deep, and about 10 inches apart, at the end of February or the beginning of March. The surface should be covered with loose litter until the plants are well up. For Forcing, *see* p. 251.

Planting-out.—Late in April, the young plants should be moved either to their permanent quarters, or to fresh ground, about 8 inches apart, so that they can easily be again transplanted 3 feet apart. Water well after transplanting. For the earlier supplies, seed may also be sown very thinly early in August, the young plants being moved to their permanent quarters the following April, having been once transplanted in October. For a late supply, seed may be sown in rather rich soil about the end of April. If the plants are developing too quickly a few of the leaves should be cropped back to stumps in the autumn. This also greatly encourages the production of sprouts. The top growth should be left intact until all the sprouts are cleared, when the top may be cut and used as greens.

Should some of the lower leaves turn yellow in autumn, they must be removed or the sprouts may rot. Do not cut the tops or heads till late winter or the stems will stop growing and the production of sprouts will cease.

Varieties.—Early sowing, *Dwarf Gem* and *Matchless*; general crop, *Aigburth, Cambridge No. 1, Cambridge No. 5, Exhibition, Market Favourite.*

Cabbages. *Soil.*—The ground should be deeply dug and moderately enriched a few months previous to planting. Cabbages should be liberally supplied with water at all stages of their growth.

Sowing.—For an early spring supply, seeds should be sown about the end of July, and again about the middle of August. Sow a little seed at frequent intervals, so that the crop may mature successionally. The seeds should be sown thinly in rows 8 inches apart and about 1 inch deep. Keep the beds moist and give a liberal dusting of lime, salt, or soot now and then.

Planting-out.—About six weeks from the time of sowing, the plants may be placed in firm ground which has not been newly dug, but has been prepared some two or three months earlier. Fifteen inches should be allowed from plant to plant in the rows, and 20 inches between the rows. The ground should be thoroughly soaked after planting, and liberal supplies of water given, especially for the first few days.

Varieties.—*Ellam's Early, Flower of Spring, Greyhound, Harbinger, Primo,* and *Velocity.*

For a summer supply, such kinds as *Main Crop, Sutton's Favourite,* and *Miniature Marrow* may be sown at intervals during the second half of April and the whole of May. They should be treated much as advised in the case of spring cabbages, but they should be planted out into somewhat richer soil, as their growth is much more rapid. For autumn crops, we may rely largely on the Coleworts *Rosette* and *Hardy Green.* They may be sown in May and the first two weeks of June, being treated very much as recommended for spring cabbage. For late autumn, winter, and early spring use, savoys and hardy winter cabbages may be sown during the end of May and first half of June. The small-

432

headed kinds have the best quality, though the drumheads are large and hardy. Good winter cabbages are *Winnigstadt*, *St. Martin* and the *St. John's Day*. For later use, *New Year*, *January King*, and *Bijou* may be grown. Do not cut savoys before November.

Red Cabbages are grown almost entirely for pickling. The cultivation resembles that of other cabbages. Seed is best sown in March; good, compact heads may then be obtained ready for pickling in the autumn. The red cabbage should only be gathered when the head is thoroughly formed, the stem being thrown away as valueless. Useful sorts are *Dutch Blood-red* and *Dwarf Blood-red*.

Cardoons. The prickly Tours cardoon, the red-stemmed Marseilles, and the large-growing Puvis are all better than the Spanish variety.

Sowing.—Seed should be sown in a cold frame or under glass without heat early in April. It may also be sown early in June in the open.

Planting-out.—Early in May trenches, some 18 inches apart, should be dug to a depth of not less than 18 inches, about 6 inches of thoroughly decayed manure being placed at the bottom of the trench and dug in and thoroughly incorporated with the soil. Plant out the seedlings in the open about the end of May.

Blanching.—When the plant is 18 inches high, fasten it to a stake, and tie the leaves lightly to this, earthing up the stem at the same time like celery. Throughout the summer, water copiously and frequently with soft water (rain water if possible) and a little guano to prevent flowering. In September, the early crop will be fit for use.

Carrots. *Soil.*—A rather light, sandy soil, which has been recently enriched by the liberal incorporation of well-rotted manure, suits carrots best.

Where the soil is cold and heavy, it may be greatly improved by being well trenched and by the liberal addition of wood ashes, leaf-mould, or old potting soil. If these ingredients are not available, the soil may be broken up and then drawn with the rake into ridges about a foot high, and on these the seeds may be sown.

Sowing.—The first sowing may be made in a warm border at the end of February, *Early Shorthorns* or *Gem* being chosen. They are best sown about 1 inch deep in drills 15 inches apart, being thinned to about 8 inches apart. Further seed may be sown in April and May, *Scarlet Horn*, *Nantes Horn*, *Scarlet Perfection* and *James's Intermediate* being selected for this sowing. It is worth while to make a small sowing of *Early Nantes* about the end of June, with a view to obtaining some nice small roots in the early months of the year. In all cases, but especially in the case of these June sown carrots, it is wise to add a fairly liberal dressing of soot and lime to the soil in order to reduce the attacks of insect and other pests to a minimum.

Storing.—Carrots may be drawn for the table as soon as large enough; but the main crop for storing should not be taken up till the end of October, or even later, unless severe frosts set in. The carrots should be removed carefully so as not to damage the roots, being stored in a frost-proof and fairly dry place. A covering of straw or sacking should be given against severe frost. For Forcing, see p. 251.

Cauliflower. The cauliflower is in season from June to November.

Sowing.—In order to maintain a succession, three or four sowings should be made, the first being made on a slight hot-bed in February or early March. Good kinds for this early crop, which is ready about June, are *Early London*, *All the Year Round*, and *Snowball*. The seedlings should be thinned, hardened off, and planted out in the open in April. Early in April a second and larger sowing should be made in the open. For this crop, such varieties as *Dwarf Mammoth*, *Autumn Giant*, *Erfurt*, *Pearl*, *Purity*, and *Favourite* may be sown, young plants being planted out in May and June. A third sowing should be made about the middle of August to stand through the winter. For this sowing, such kinds as *Walcheren* will be best.

Planting-out.—When the plants are large enough to be handled, they should be transplanted 4 inches apart in rich and well-manured soil. In June, the April sowings will be fit to plant out where they are to grow; in September they will be heading, and will continue to improve until the frosts of early winter.

When the heads begin to appear, they should be shaded from sun and rain, some of the larger leaves being broken down so as to cover them. Water should be given liberally in dry weather.

Wintering.—On the approach of winter, the plants in flower may be taken up with as much earth at their roots as possible, being laid in by the roots on their sides in a light, sandy soil, in some frost-proof place.

Autumn-sown plants are generally pricked out under frames for protection during winter, plenty of air being given in fine weather.

Celeriac. Celeriac is hardy and of easy culture, growing well in almost any rich garden soil.

Sowing.—Seed should be sown in March, over moderate heat. The seedlings should be pricked out as soon as capable of being handled, and should be potted in 3-inch pots.

Planting-out.—About the end of May, the plants should be transferred to the open. The ground intended for their reception should have been deeply dug and well enriched, and should have been made firm previous to planting. Planting should be shallow, as at no stage should any earthing-up take place. Rather, indeed, should the soil be gradually drawn from the bulbs so that they may almost stand on the surface as do onions. Liberal supplies of water should be given throughout the summer, and it is well to keep the surface of the ground between the plants covered with a little leaf-mould or litter. From 12 to 15 inches should be allowed from plant to plant in the rows, and about 18 inches between the rows.

Storing.—At the approach of winter, the roots should be taken up and stored like beetroots (p. 431).

Celery. *Soil.*—Celery prefers a soil not too light. Deep cultivation is a necessity, and manure and water must be liberally afforded.

Sowing.—Seed should be sown under glass over a heat of about 70° F. March is the month for the principal sowing, but a pan of early seed may be sown in February. As soon as the seedlings are able to be handled, about 2 inches high, the young plants should be pricked out singly into 3-inch pots, containing soil rich with well-rotted manure. From this time onward, bottom heat is unneces-

434

sary, and the pots may be placed in a cold frame. Later, the plants may be transplanted into bigger pots preparatory to the final planting in beds or trenches.

Planting-out.—The ultimate planting-out, when about 6 inches high, takes place for the main crop about the end of June, the earliest plants from the February sowing being put out about the end of May and the late crop about the end of July.

The trench system of growing celery is that usually adopted. A common mistake is to make the trenches too deep. They should, it is true, be deeply dug, and even the sub-soil should be broken up to some extent, but it should be left in position, covered with a layer of manure, and manure should be liberally incorporated with the soil itself. When actually ready for planting, the trenches should be 4 feet apart, about 16 inches wide, and 4 inches deep. In the trenches, the young plants should be placed at intervals of about a foot, being firmly trodden in. In addition to the stable manure, celery will do all the better if a dressing of ½ oz. each of ammonium sulphate and potash salts to every square yard of soil is well dug into the ground before planting. Water should be liberally given at once, and some shade afforded. The soil between the plants should be kept mulched with old manure so as to afford additional nourishment and to check evaporation. As growth proceeds, earth should be gradually hoed up round the plants, about 4 inches at a time, being patted down firmly to keep out the rain, though the principal earthing-up, which must be done in dry weather, should take place about a month before the celery is required. The leaves should be held together while the earthing-up is in process, so that no soil may be allowed to enter between the stalks. The hearts must be kept well above the earthing-up, and any side growths should be removed. The last earthing-up in the case of the general crop should take place about the end of October, or later if the weather is mild and the plants growing.

Varieties.—For early use *White Gem.* For main crop, *Superb White*, and *Champion White. Reds.*—*Standard Bearer, Sulham Prize*, and *Mammoth Red.*

Chicory. Apart from its uses as a salad, Chicory affords two possibilities for culinary use. Its early growth may be forced and blanched after the manner of seakale (p. 441), and its unforced green leaves may be used in spring much as spinach is used.

Sowing.—Seed may be sown from the middle of April to the middle of June in fine soil which has been well manured for a previous crop, in rows 15 inches apart, the seedlings being thinned to about 9 inches apart in the rows.

Forcing.—About the end of October, the roots should be lifted, packed in deep boxes in moist, light soil, and blanched in perfect darkness. A little forcing should be applied if an early supply is wanted. The *Witloof* and *Christmas Salad* are good kinds.

Colewort. *See* Cabbages, p. 432.

Couve Tronchuda. The culture and treatment of this variety of cabbage are the same as for the ordinary cabbage. It is fit for use, like savoys, after frosty weather sets in.

Endive. *See* Salads.

Kale. *See* Borecole, p. 431.

Kohl-rabi. The Kohl-rabi is especially useful as an alternative to the turnip where the soil is light, as it will stand severe drought—frost has no effect upon it. The roots are most palatable when half grown.

Sowing.—For a summer supply, sow the seed in March in drills about ¾ inch deep, and 18 inches apart. The young plants should be thinned as soon as possible to about 10 inches apart. Transplanting is undesirable. For autumn and winter supplies seed should again be sown towards the end of July. (Store as for Turnips, p. 444.)

Varieties.—Short Top Green, Earliest White and *Early Purple.*

Leek. *Soil.*—Very deep, rich soil is essential.

Sowing.—For an early crop the seed may be sown in boxes early in February (with a layer of rotted manure at the bottom of the boxes), being kept in moderate heat. When some 2 inches high, the seedlings must be pricked-off 2 inches apart. They should be kept in a moderate heat till the middle of April, being then transferred to a cold frame, hardened-off, and planted out in May. Seeds may be sown thinly in the open successively in a warm border from the end of February till the end of March, ½ inch deep in drills about 6 or 8 inches apart. The seeds should be soaked in luke-warm water for about 12 hours previously to being sown.

Planting-out.—As soon as they are large enough to handle, the young plants should be thinned out, and may be transferred to their permanent sites when about 1 foot high, about June. They must be planted firmly with their lower leaves just resting on the ground. If the ground is rich and moderately heavy, the leeks may be planted on the flat in rows, 2 feet apart, about 12 inches being allowed from plant to plant. When the soil is not so rich and heavy, it is desirable to grow leeks in trenches. These should be about a spade's width in breadth, about 2 feet apart, and about 15 inches deep, and at the bottom of each should be placed a liberal dressing of well-rotted manure. On this should be placed a little soil, in which the plants should be planted. Liberal dressings of liquid manure must be given in late summer; and at all times the roots should be kept moist.

Blanching.—As they grow, earth is to be thrown into the trench, so as to keep an increasing portion of the stem blanched. When grown on the flat, they must be kept well earthed-up by means of the hoe.

Storing.—The leeks can remain in the ground through the winter to be dug as needed, or they may be stored in sand in a dry shed.

Varieties.—London Flag, The Lyon, Monarch, and *Musselburgh.*

Mushrooms. *Soil and Situation.*—Mushrooms merely require a supply of horse manure, and a certain degree of warmth and moisture. If the manure when crushed in the hand binds, but no excess liquid is pressed out, it contains the required proportion of moisture. During the months of summer and autumn, mushrooms may, perhaps, most conveniently be grown in the open air, but during late autumn, winter, and spring, some building or frame is necessary.

Making the Bed.—As a rule, about six to nine weeks must be allowed from the commencement of operations to the gathering of a crop. The longest litter should first be shaken out of the manure, all up to the length of about a foot being re-

436

Asparagus   *PLATE 49*   Broad beans, Longpod

Runner beans, Champion   Dwarf beans, Masterpiece
Beet, oval, long and round   Seakale beet   *C. W. Teager*

Winter broccoli   *PLATE 50*   Sprouting broccoli

Cabbage, Drumhead   Cabbage, Savoy
Cauliflower, Early   Forced chicory   *C. W. Teager*

tained. This should then be made up into a heap about 2 or 3 feet high and from 4 to 6 feet wide, and is best made on a gentle slope. In winter-time, this heap should be made up under cover, or the heat will too quickly evaporate. Every second day, the heap should be thoroughly turned, so as to bring the central portion to the surface and the surface to the centre, and during this process all lumps should be broken up. This turning should be continued for about a week in winter and for about two weeks in summer. The manure should then be placed in position, being well trodden down. The temperature of the heap should be taken by means of a thermometer plunged to a depth of about 8 inches.

Sowing the Spawn.—As soon as this temperature gets to about 75° or 80° F., the spawn, which must be fresh and which is bought in bricks composed of a mixture of manure and soil, containing dry mycelium of the mushroom, should be inserted in pieces about 2 inches square. These pieces should be firmly planted by means of a trowel, about 2 or 3 inches deep in the manure and about 8 inches apart. The heap of manure is then at once to be covered with about 2 inches of well-sieved, sandy loam. Old garden soil is totally unsuitable. The soil should be just, and only just, moist enough to hold together, and should be beaten firm with the flat of the spade. The whole must then be covered over with a layer of straw, 15 inches in thickness, or with other material to exclude all light. Additional protection should be afforded by mats or sacking, if the spawn is planted in winter.

Care of the Bed.—Little or no water should be given to the bed until the mushrooms begin to come up. As soon as the mushrooms appear, however, a moderate supply of tepid water may be given once a week, and it will be found that a little common salt, or, better still, saltpetre, will be beneficial. So far as possible, the temperature of the air of the building in which mushrooms are being grown should be kept at from 55° to 60° F. If the bed is to retain its health mushrooms should not be cut, but should be twisted off, separating the stalks as near the base as possible. Fresh soil must be added to fill the holes made by picking, and the bed must again be covered with straw.

Pests.—Woodlice play great havoc in mushroom beds. Traps baited with carrot or potato will do much to keep this pest down.

Onion. *Position and Soil.*—Onions require a sunny, open position, and prefer a rather strong, deep, and rich friable loam, though they grow quite well in any good light soil. Clay is not very suitable, while a newly-broken soil is impossible, as the foliage grows at the expense of the bulbs, which are also open to attack by insect pests, always present in freshly broken soil. The ground should be liberally dressed with lime and with plenty of well-rotted manure buried deeply, trenched thoroughly, and ridged in early autumn. The top-spit should be dressed liberally with soot or wood ashes (4 cwt. to the acre). On a light soil, kainit (3 cwt. to the acre) and ammonium sulphate (1½ cwt. to the acre) are the most suitable manures.

Sowing in the Open.—The main crop should be sown as soon as the ground is in working condition, between January and mid-March. The seed bed should be made (*see p.* 104) and the seed sown thinly in drills ¾ inch deep and 12 inches apart. Seed may also be sown early in January under glass in a temperature of

60° F. The seedlings should be hardened off in April, and planted out early in May.

As soon as possible after appearance of the plants, the surplus should be pulled out, without loosening those which remain. At least 3 inches should, at the first thinning, be left from plant to plant. Water should be given liberally during the summer if the weather is dry.

A sowing in the open should also be made about the middle of August to furnish young onions during the winter, and for use in summer before the main crop is ready. The seedlings are allowed to remain where sown until the end of February, when they should be planted out in a moderately but not too rich soil.

Storing.—Towards the end of September, the bulbs should be well formed and the tops should show indications of ripening. Where this is not the case, the crops should be bent or broken down with the back of a wooden rake, this operation being repeated as often as may be necessary to check the growth of the tops. As soon as the bulbs seem to be properly matured, which will be known by the decay of the leaves, they should be taken up, spread in a sunny situation in the open air until thoroughly dried and then stored in an airy shed or tied up in what are called ropes, hung on a shady outside wall, and protected from the wet. For Forcing, *see* p. 251.

Varieties.—Spring Sowing: *Bedfordshire Champion, Sutton's A1, James Long Keeping* and *Up-to-Date*; Autumn Sowing: *Autumn Queen* and *Giant Rocca*; Winter Sowing: *Ailsa Craig* and *Excelsior*.

Parsnip. *Soil.*—To grow the parsnip properly, deeply dug, rich, sandy soil, which has been previously well manured, is desirable. If manure is used, it should be well rotted, short farmyard manure, well buried to draw the long tap roots deep down and to discourage the production of side roots encouraged by the use of manure on the surface. The ground should be trenched 2 feet 6 inches deep, and ridged up as long as possible before sowing.

Sowing.—Seeds may be sown at intervals from February to May, the best-flavoured, though not the largest roots, being obtained by sowing at the later date. Drills should be made ¾ inch in depth and 18 inches apart. In these, seeds should be sown thinly, lightly covered, and well trodden in, and when the young plants appear, thinning should be begun, until ultimately not less than 6 inches remain between plant and plant. As soon as they are large enough, they may be pulled.

Storing.—During the winter, the roots are best left in the ground as when growing, but any that remain over should, after having had their tops trimmed off, be lifted and stored in sand in the dark early in March before growth re-starts. Should the winter frost prove very severe, the crowns must be protected by a layer of ashes, bracken, or straw.

Varieties.—*Student, Tender and True*, and *Hollow Crown*.

Peas. *Soil and Position.*—Peas require deep loam which has been well enriched and deeply dug, or trenched, in the autumn. It is a good plan to dig a shallow trench on each side of the rows, so that during the summer months manure and water can be easily supplied.

Sowing under Glass.—The very earliest peas are obtained by sowing early in

438

December at the rate of nine or ten seeds in a 5-inch pot in a cold frame. The plants should be thinned to six per pot. They must have little or no artificial heat, abundance of light, and free ventilation on every possible opportunity. These plants, after being hardened off, should be planted out in a warm, south border about the second week in March, in deep drills.

Sowing in the Open.—The first sowing in the open may be made towards the end of February, providing the land is not too wet. To secure a succession, sow once a fortnight from this time up till the end of May, or even the middle of June. The seeds should be sown 2 to 3 inches apart in flat-based drills, 3 inches deep and 4 inches wide. Before sowing the drills should be dusted with wood ashes. Dwarf peas should be planted in rows about 2 feet apart; medium, 4 feet; and tall, 12 feet. A handful of potash salts to every twelve plants, dug into the soil just before planting, will materially help the crops.

Sticking.—The peas should be sticked when 3 inches high, and between the main sticks small twiggy sticks should be inserted to give the peas a start. After sticking, they should be well mulched. (*See* p. 36.) In hot, dry weather, peas require a copious supply of water, and syringing overhead. The peas should be gathered directly they are fit, and if it is wished to prolong the fruiting period, no pods should be allowed to remain on the vine beyond this stage.

Varieties.—For earliest sowings: *Foremost* and *Little Marvel*; for early sowing in the open: *Gradus, Kelvedon Wonder, Marvellous, Peter Pan,* and *The Pilot.* To follow these *Duke of Albany, Giant Stride, Kelvedon Standby, Onward* and *Stratagem.* These may be followed by *Best of All, Lord Chancellor, Marrowfat, Matchless,* and *Veitch's Perfection.* These should carry us well into August. Following these we have the so-called late peas, such as *Autocrat, British Empire,* and *Ne Plus Ultra,* success with which can only be hoped for in favoured localities.

Potato. *Soil.*—Potatoes do best in a deep, sandy, well-drained loam. Before Christmas, farmyard manure should be applied at the rate of about 20 tons per acre. This manure may well be supplemented by a mixture of $1\frac{1}{2}$ cwt. ammonium sulphate applied in the drill at the time of planting, and 3 cwt. basic slag and $1\frac{1}{2}$ cwt. potash salts when preparing the soil.

Sprouting.—Tubers which are intended to be used for "seed" should be selected at the time of lifting. They should be evenly shaped and should weigh from 2 to 3 oz. each. They should be spread on the floor in an open shed until the skin is set and hard, and should then be packed in single layers in trays, being stored in a room inaccessible to frost, where, nevertheless, they are fully exposed to air and light. In the case of very early potatoes, these trays may be placed under the stage in the greenhouse or other warm place. A little fine soil may also be sprinkled over the potatoes, which should be slightly watered. By this means, a certain amount of growth results, and the potatoes, if carefully planted out without damage to the new rootlets, will be more forward than others not treated in this way. In all cases seed potatoes placed in boxes should be arranged with their crowns upwards. The eye in the centre of the crown is that from which growth should be encouraged, as it is much the more prolific, and makes the strongest plant. Only three or four shoots should be encouraged, the others should be rubbed off as soon as they appear.

439

For the earliest potatoes a south border, preferably sheltered by a wall, should be chosen. The potato is peculiarly susceptible to frost, and it is generally useless to plant before the middle of February, even in such a situation. In heavy soils, it is generally better to plant after the middle of March. For the main crop, March is the best month to plant, but some late kinds should also be planted in April.

Planting.—The soil having been prepared and levelled, drills should be drawn about 5 inches deep and 3 feet between the rows. The tubers should be laid at the bottom of the drills, at a distance of about 15 inches apart, and should then be covered by the hoe. When planting the early kinds, only 2 feet need be left between the rows. When the plants are 5 to 6 inches high, the first earthing-up should take place, and this should be continued every three or four weeks until the plants are nearly full grown.

Digging and Storing.—Except in the case of early potatoes for immediate use, which are dug up as required, the tubers should not be dug up until the tops are quite dead. One plant should be dug up as a trial; if the potatoes are ripe, the skin of the tubers will be set and the potatoes ready for eating. If they are to be stored, they should be left in the ground three weeks to a month longer. They are best lifted by means of a fork inserted deeply under the tubers, which will then not be likely to be damaged. They should be cleared of earth, dried by exposure to the sun for a day or two, then stored in a dry cellar or other dark frost-proof building.

Where no building for storage purposes is available, they may be piled up, interspersed with layers of straw, on some raised site, covered with straw, and a thick layer of earth.

Varieties.—Early: *Arran Pilot, Duke of York, Home Guard, Midlothian Early* and *Ulster Chieftain.* Mid-Season: *Arran Banner, Arran Comrade,* and *Great Scott.* Maincrop: *Arran Chief, Dunbar Standard, Kerr's Pink, King Edward, Majestic* and *Red King.*

Rhubarb. *Soil and Situation.*—To produce really good stems, a deeply-dug soil, somewhat heavily manured with farmyard manure, or if not obtainable, with bone manure, is essential. The situation should be sheltered from east winds.

Planting.—Carefully selected roots should be planted 5 feet apart in spring, with the top bud 2 inches below the surface. No stems should be cut during the first season. Nor should the plants be weakened by too many stems being pulled from any one plant in any one year. Any flower heads should, however, be immediately cut.

Forcing.—A mild degree of forcing can be effected by covering the young shoots (of plants at least two years old) in the early spring with seakale pots or drain-pipes, and by surrounding these with a heap of fermenting manure. A large dressing of well-rotted manure should be dug in about the roots as soon as one has finished pulling the leaves. The roots should be lifted and divided every three to four years. Or roots can be dug up in early autumn and allowed to remain exposed to the weather. The roots can then be placed under the greenhouse bench, or in the cellar and covered with soil or ashes to prevent evaporation. They should be well watered and kept supplied with an abundance of

440

moisture—water applied once a week—but guard against over-watering as this will result in light coloured stalks. To obtain the best rhubarb it should not be forced in full light, or total darkness. The temperature can range from 45° to 70° F. After forcing, the roots can be planted out in a nursery for a year or two before being forced again. Propagate by division of roots.

Varieties.—*Daw's Champion; Victoria* (for summer use); *Champagne* (for early use) and *Stott's Monarch.*

Salsify. *Soil.*—Salsify does best in a deep, sandy soil. The manure should be buried 9 or 10 inches deep, the surface only having been enriched either for a previous crop, such as celery or peas, or by the addition of some well-spent hot-bed soil or old manure.

Sowing.—Seed should be sown thinly about the end of April in drills 1 inch deep and 12 inches apart. As soon as the seedlings are about 2 inches high, they should be thinned to 5 or 6 inches apart. They will be ready for use in the early part of November.

Lifting and Storing.—The roots are best left in the ground throughout the winter, being pulled as required for use. If the frosts are severe, the roots should be protected with ashes, straw, or bracken. Any roots that remain in February must, however, be lifted before the growth recommences, being stored under sand, or earth and straw, as advised in the case of beetroot.

Varieties.—*Giant French, Improved Mammoth, Sandwich Island.*

Savoy. *See* Cabbages.

Scorzonera. Scorzonera requires similar treatment to that advised for salsify. Being a perennial plant, however, the surplus roots may, though undesirable, be left in the ground over the second year. But it is far better to raise a fresh crop each year.

Variety.—*Giant Russian.*

Seakale. Few vegetables yield a better return for the trouble they entail, than does seakale.

Soil.—The ground intended for a permanent plantation should be deeply dug, and a very liberal dressing of manure should be incorporated, the top of the sub-soil being broken up and left in situ.

Sowing.—Seed should be sown thinly in March or April in drills about 2 inches deep, 18 inches being allowed between the drills. As soon as the seedlings have made six leaves, they may be transplanted to rows 18 inches apart, allowing 9 inches from plant to plant. Water must be given liberally, and liquid manure applied frequently in hot weather. The following spring about 2½ feet should be allowed from plant to plant in every direction.

Propagation by Root Cuttings.—Far better than propagation by means of seed is propagation by root cuttings. Small roots, or rather pieces of root, about the size of the little finger, 5 to 6 inches long and ½ inch thick, should be planted vertically about the end of March, bud-side upwards; the bud or the top of the piece of root—where there is no bud—being cut straight, and planted just on a level with the surface of the ground. The bottom end of the cuttings should be cut slantwise. Eighteen inches should be allowed between the rows in which these are planted, about 15 inches being allowed from set to set. The surface between the rows should be kept broken up by the hoe, and 2 or 3 inches

441

of manure may be used as a top-dressing. On light soil, a dressing of salt, about ½ lb. to the square yard, may also be given with advantage. Early in May, all weak growths should be cut away and any flower stems must be removed, so that strong crowns may be formed for forcing in the winter. Water should be given liberally throughout the summer.

Forcing and Blanching.—If intended for early use, the roots should be lifted about the end of November, as soon as the leaves part readily from the crowns. These roots can be packed closely together in light soil, the crowns being on a level with, or just below, the surface. They should be placed in a dark cellar or darkened part of the greenhouse, a large case placed under the staging being excellent for this purpose. The roots must be exposed to a continuous temperature of about 60° F. or a few degrees less. The soil in which the roots are packed should be gently watered, being then covered with a layer of dry leaves or straw. The kale should be cut when about 7 inches long, and for a continuous supply, it is important to place a fresh lot of roots under the forcing conditions weekly. The roots which have been lifted for purposes of forcing and which are not wanted for the moment may be stored away in soil, crown uppermost so that they can be placed in the forcing house as required. Forcing takes about three weeks.

If it is intended to force seakale where it stands in the open, the plants should be covered with seakale pots (or large drain pipes covered with slates) about the second week in November, the space between the pots being piled up with leaves, or, if these are unobtainable, with fresh manure. Enough leaves should be used to cover the pots. They should be lightly trodden down. Every fortnight, a fresh supply of plants should be subjected to this process so as to yield a continuous supply. As soon as the crop has been cut, the bulk of the heating material should be cleared away, but a little should be left as protection against frost. Seakale should be cut when about 7 inches in length, and care should be taken to remove not less than ½ inch of the old wood at the same time. *Lily White* is a good variety.

Shallot. *Soil.*—Shallots are easily cultivated in almost any soil. They do best in an open situation, and in a medium well-drained soil that has been deeply dug and well manured for previous crops. The ground should have ¼ lb. of superphosphate to every square yard forked into it, and must be made fairly firm before planting.

Planting.—The bulbs, which should be of medium size, should be planted in February, or early in March, just deep enough to make them firm, but should not be quite covered with soil. Six to 9 inches should be allowed from bulb to bulb, and 12 inches between the rows. At the beginning of July, the soil should be drawn away from the bulbs, so that they may ripen, and about the end of July or early in August, when the stems begin to die down, the bulbs should be pulled up and dried, after which, they should be stored in a dry, moderately light room. If the bulbs are left in the ground, they are likely to sprout again. Though usually grown from offsets, shallots may be raised from seeds, and should be treated in the same way as spring-sown onions. The *Sutton Shallo* is one of the best to grow from seeds.

Varieties.—*Russian* is a good variety, and *True Shallot* for pickling.

Spinach. *Soil.*—A deeply-dug, rather moist soil is to be preferred, a sandy, gravelly soil, or a sloping situation being unsuitable. If the soil is not moderately rich, a light dressing of well-decayed manure should be applied, but this should be kept some distance under the surface.

Sowing.—It is a good plan to soak the seed in water for twenty-four hours before sowing. Seed should be sown thinly in the permanent quarters, in drills, 1 inch deep and 1 foot apart. When some 3 inches high, the seedlings should be thinned out to 6 to 8 inches apart. Sowing in the open may take place at three-weekly intervals from the end of February to early in May. The *Victoria Roundleaved*, and *New Zealand Spinach* are as good varieties as any for summer or autumn.

In gathering spinach, pick only the largest leaves; do not pick the whole of the leaves from any one plant.

If winter supplies of spinach are desired, the *Prickly Spinach* should be sown early in August, 3 inches apart in drills, with 18 inches between the rows, and liberally watered. Of this variety, the shoots and not the leaves are used. For a winter crop, a light, sandy soil is the most suitable. Early in February, use the hoe among the winter spinach, and dress with liquid manure.

Varieties.—Autumn supply: *New Zealand* and the *Carter*; winter supply: *Prickly* or *Long Standing*.

Tomato. In most parts of southern England, tomatoes of good quality can, in favourable seasons, be grown in the open air, preferably against a south wall or fence. In average seasons in almost all districts, some kind of glass structure is desirable if early ripe fruit is to be obtained.

Sowing.—Seed should be sown at weekly intervals through February and March, ¼ inch deep and 1 inch apart in pans covered with glass and paper and placed close to the glass in a warm greenhouse or moderately warm frame. (Night temperature, 60° F.; day temperature, 70° F.). The pans should be shaded from the strong sun till the seeds germinate. Seed sown in February should produce fruit in July. As soon as two leaves appear on the seedlings, they should be pricked-off singly into thumb pots, a good half of the stem being buried in the soil. In a small greenhouse, it is well that these young seedlings should be kept near the glass, to keep them short-jointed. As they grow, they should be moved on into larger pots, and in about 10 or 12 weeks, they should be ready for planting out into borders, 18 inches apart in the row, or into the final pots, some 10 inches in diameter, in which they are to be fruited. The first truss of bloom must be formed before the plants are planted out. Potting should be very firm.

Soil.—The soil required for the successful growing of tomatoes is fibrous loam, mixed with a little sharp sand, together with leaf-mould and some well-decayed manure. Too much soil must not be introduced at first. The plant should be started in a small mound of soil, well-up near the light, and more earth should be added as the roots grow and demand fresh compost. Over-manuring definitely tends to unfruitfulness, and no manure must be used which has not fully fermented.

It is desirable to add a pinch or two of kainit or nitrate of potash at intervals through the growing season.

443

Cultivation under Glass.—Generous watering is essential at every period of growth, though a permanently saturated condition of the soil is, of course, undesirable. Under glass, 3 feet should be allowed from plant to plant. Wires should be stretched 9 or 10 inches from the glass and the plants may be trained along these under the glass. All side shoots must be nipped off, only the flower trusses being allowed to break from the main stem. The plants should have their heads pinched out as soon as they reach the top of the wires. To "set" the fruit, pass a rabbit's tail over the flowers each day. Although warmth is necessary, over-heating is to be avoided. A night temperature of 55° to 60° F. and a day temperature of 60° to 70° or 75° F. should mark the extremes. Ample ventilation must be given. Seeds may be sown in June and July to furnish winter supplies.

Cultivation in the Open.—When it is proposed to grow tomatoes in the open-air, seeds should be sown in March under conditions similar to those already suggested. Suitable varieties, such as *Stonor's, M.P., Essex Wonder*, and *Market King*, should be selected for the purpose. The young plants, when some 15 inches high, should be cautiously hardened, and should be planted out about the end of May. A medium loam is the most suitable soil, and good drainage is essential.

The best situation in the open for tomato plants is against a south wall fully exposed to the sun. For the first week or so, the plants should be protected at night by means of seakale pots or drain-pipes. They should be well watered with liquid manure to keep up a rapid growth. As soon as the blossom-buds appear, watering should cease. The side-shoots must be stopped, the tops being nipped off, and all those sprays that show little signs of fruit must be thrown out, the plant not being allowed to grow much over 3 feet high. Water must be given only to prevent a check in case of drought. In dry weather, mulching with manure is beneficial.

If it is clearly apparent that the fruit will not ripen while growing outdoors, the branches on which full-grown fruit is found should be cut off and hung in a warm dry greenhouse.

Varieties.—Best of All, Harbinger, Golden Queen, Money Maker, Duke of York, and for early sowing *Early Market* and *Sunrise*.

Turnip. *Soil.*—The most suitable soil for this vegetable is a sandy loam which has been deeply dug and well manured for a previous crop.

Sowing.—Successional sowing may be made in the open in March, April, and May, the *Red* and *White Milan* varieties, *Early Paris Market*, and *Snowball* being chosen. The plants should be thinned to at least 6 inches apart as soon as possible.

Turnips intended for autumn and early winter use should be sown in an open situation in July, the *Redtop Mousetail* and *Veitch's Red Globe* are most suitable. Sown the first week in August for mid-winter crops, *Orange Jelly* and *Golden Ball* are good mid-winter kinds.

Storing.—When frost sets in, the turnips should be covered with a few inches of leaves or litter and be left in the ground. In the spring, any roots left will send up a crop of young green shoots—"turnip-tops"—which have considerable value as a green vegetable.

Ridge cucumber *PLATE 51* Endive, green curled

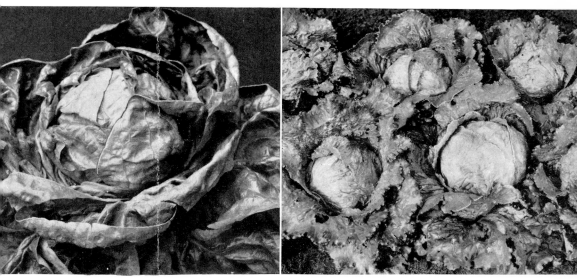

Lettuce, Arctic King Lettuce, Webb's Wonderful
Kale Kohl Rabi *C. W. Teager*

Leeks

Peas, Onward

Radish, Long variety

PLATE 52

Marrow, Table Dainty
Parsnips

Onions
Shallots

C. W. Teager

Vegetable Marrow. *Soil and Situation.*—This vegetable requires a deep, light, rich soil, and a fairly sheltered position, where ample water can be supplied in dry weather.

Early marrows can be grown in frames after the manner of cucumbers, *see* page 447, but as they require less heat, it is well to let the fermenting mass consist half of leaves and half of stable manure. Marrows require less water and more air than cucumbers, though the supply of water must be regular. The temperature at which these early frame marrows should be kept should vary from 55° F. to about 70° to 75° F. When the plants begin to bear fruit, 1 oz. each to the square yard of superphosphate and sulphate of ammonia should be applied and well watered in.

If slugs or snails are inclined to be tiresome, a dressing of soot over the soil will help to keep them away. But the majority of marrows, will, naturally, be grown in the open air.

Sowing.—Two seeds should be sown, 1 inch apart, early in April in each 3-inch pot or pan, filled with light, sandy soil, the seeds being covered by about 1½ inches of fine soil. The seeds are placed flat, on their sides, not vertically in the soil. The pans should be placed near the glass in gentle heat, and kept fairly moist, and as soon as the plants are sufficiently strong to handle, they should be potted-off into 7-inch pots, two plants being placed in each. The pots should then be replaced near the glass in the warmth. When well established, they should be removed to a cold frame, and gradually hardened off. Towards the end of May, or as soon as the weather is warm and appears to be settled, the seedlings should be planted out and protected for a time by handglasses or other means. Ample water should be given until the roots get hold of the soil. The shoots must be trained and regulated so that they shall not grow too closely together, being stopped, if necessary, to forward the growth of the fruit. After a few of the marrows have set, but not before, a weekly dressing of liquid manure should be given, or artificial manures may be applied as advised for frame marrows.

If it is impracticable to sow under glass, seeds may be sown in May on the bed itself. Three seeds are usually planted 1½ inches deep and 9 inches apart in the form of a triangle, each seed, or patch of seeds, being covered with an inverted flower-pot, the hole being covered with a piece of tile. When the young plants are up, they should be gradually hardened by the removal of the pots for increasing periods during the daytime.

Two of the three seedlings in each group should be removed as soon as the rough leaves appear.

Making the Bed.—The bed for marrows grown in the open should be made up in about the second week in May. A shallow trench about 4 feet wide should be dug, and about 18 inches depth of an equal mixture of leaves and half-rotten stable manure should be laid in this. This fermenting mass should then be covered with the soil taken out of the trench.

Cutting.—Marrows should be cut while the skin can still be broken by the thumb-nail, the earliest to be cut being some 9 inches long.

Varieties.—*The Melon, Moore's Cream, Tender and True, Long Green, Long White,* and *Table Dainty.*

445

VEGETABLE GROWING AT A GLANCE

Name	When to Sow or Plant	Amount of Seed or Number of Roots required for 50 Foot Row	Depth to Sow or Plant in Inches		Time of Germination in Days	Time to reach Maturity in Weeks
			Light Soil	Heavy Soil		
Artichoke— Jerusalem . .	March	7 lb. Tubers	3	1	—	30
Globe	Feb. (Heat) April (Open)	18 Plants	1	½	—	70
Asparagus . . .	March	½ oz. or 25 Plants	2	1½	14–25	170
Bean (Broad) . .	Feb.–May	1 Pint	3	2	7–14	15
Bean (Kidney or French) . . .	May	½ Pint	2	1½	7–14	12
Bean (Runner) . .	May	1 Pint	3	2	7–14	15
Beetroot . . .	April–May	1 oz.	2	1	9–18	17
Borecole or Kale .	March–May Sept. (for Spring Use)	½ oz.	1½	1	8	20
Broccoli . . .	April–May	1 oz. for 8 Square Yards	¼	¼	6–10	20
Brussels Sprouts .	Feb.–March	½ oz.	¾	½	5–12	25
Cabbage . . .	March–July	½ oz.	1	½	6–10	18
Capsicum . . .	Feb. (Heat, 65° F.)	½ oz.	½	½	12	30
Cardoon . . .	April (Cold Frame) June (Open)	½ oz.	1½	1	15–20	24
Carrot . . .	March–May	½ oz.	1	½	10–20	24
Cauliflower . . .	Feb. (Hot-bed) April and Aug. (Open)	½ oz.	½	¼	6–12	20
Celeriac . . .	March (Heat, 65° F.)	½ oz.	¼	¼	15	24
Celery	Feb. (Heat, 70° F.)	½ oz.	¼	¼	10–20	32
Colewort . . .	June–Aug.	½ oz.	½	½	5–10	24
Kohl-rabi . . .	March and July	½ oz.	½	¼	6–12	30
Leek	Feb. and March	½ oz.	½	½	6–12	28
Maize	April (Glass)	1½ oz.	2	1½	6–12	16
Onion	Jan.–March; July–Sept.	½ oz., or 1 Bulb per Foot of Row	Only cover	half-Bulb	10 (seed)	30 (seed)
Parsnip . . .	Feb.–May	½ oz.	¾	½	12–18	32
Pea	Feb.–June	1 Pint	3	1½	7–12	15
Potato	1st Early; Feb.–March 2nd Early: March Main Crop: April	1st Early 8½ lb. 2nd Early 4 lb. Main Crop 3½ lb.	6	4	14–21	16
Rhubarb . . .	Feb.	10 Crowns	2	1	—	108
Salsify or Scorzonera .	April	½ oz.	1	½	6–12	28
Savoy . . .	April	½ oz.	½	½	5–10	24
Seakale . . .	March–April	1 oz.	2	1	15–20	90
Shallot . . .	Feb.–March	1 oz.	¾	½	10	25
Spinach . . .	Late Feb.–Early May	½ oz.	1	½	10–20	12
Swede . . .	March–June	½ oz.	½	½	12	30
Tomato . . .	Feb.–March (Glass)	3 Seeds for every Plant required	½	½	7–14	15
Turnip . . .	March–Aug.	½ oz.	1	¾	6–12	12
Vegetable Marrow .	April (Glass) May (Open)	3 Seeds for every Plant required	1½	1	7–14	12

NOTE.—For Forcing Early Vegetables, *see* pp. 251–2. The times at which to plant out, the distances to which to thin-out the seedlings, and the most suitable soils for the various crops will be found in the paragraphs on the culture of the individual plants, pages 428 to 445.

CHAPTER 37

SALADS

Corn Salad. *Sowing.*—Sow in drills, about 3 to 6 inches apart, in light, rich soil in a warm situation. Successional sowings between February and September will give a supply almost all through the year. Water liberally. Protect from severe frost with a covering of hay or straw.

Cress. *Sowing.*—Sow four days earlier than the mustard, in order to have both ready at the same time. Sow thickly in the open in March or April in a sunny spot in a moist and sheltered position. Cover very lightly with soil. Sow every fortnight from April to September to ensure a succession. The seed leaves only are eaten. For winter use, sow from October to March in boxes placed in a greenhouse or window.

Cucumber. *Soil.*—Early in March a hot-bed should be prepared. (*See* p. 248.)

Sowing.—In a few days, when the steam generated by the hot-bed has been allowed to escape, seeds may be sown in the bed, rather more being sown than plants are required. The seedlings will be up in two or three days.

Cultivation and Training.—As soon as the plants appear, a day temperature of about 80° F. and a night temperature of 60° F. should be aimed at. (*See* Gardening under Glass.) Should the night temperature much exceed 60° F. it is well to wedge up the lights about ½-inch when shutting for the night and during hot weather this amount of night ventilation may be increased. When the plants are grown in a frame and have made two leaves in addition to the cotyle-don leaves, pinch out the point above the second; each plant will then send out two lateral shoots above the second leaf on each shoot; pick off the top. After that, stop them above every fruit, and as the plants grow, add fresh soil to keep the roots covered till the whole bed is level, taking care that the soil is of the same temperature as that in the bed. If the cucumbers are grown in the green-house, stakes should be placed to lead the stems up to the first wire and until this is reached, all side-shoots must be pinched out. The main-stems must be stopped when the top of the roof is reached. The laterals are run along the wires until they are some 2 feet in length when they must also be stopped. Liberal supplies of tepid water are essential, but the leaves should be watched, as should they turn yellow, it is an indication either that too much water is being given or that the temperature is too cold. Twice, or, in hot weather, three times a day, the plants and bed should be well wetted, either from the watering-pot by means of a fine rose, or by means of a garden syringe. In cold weather, the lights should be covered with matting at night. From two to four plants will be sufficient for a two-light frame. Liberal dressings of guano are very beneficial. (*See* p. 61.) The cucumbers should be gathered as soon as they have attained adequate size, and malformed ones should at once be removed.

Varieties.—*Challenger, Tender and True* and *Improved Telegraph.*

447

Dandelion. Seed should be sown from March till June in drills a foot apart, the seedlings being thinned to 9 inches apart in the rows. In November, the roots may be lifted and stored in sand until they are wanted, when by planting in boxes and the application of a little heat in a dark place, nice blanched growths are obtained (*see* Forcing, Seakale, p. 252). When used as a vegetable, the plants may be left out of doors, and the young leaves gathered from March till June. The improved thick-leaved and improved broad-leaved are both good varieties.

Endive. *Soil.*—Endive thrives in light, moderately rich soil. The ground should be trenched to a depth of 2 feet, and thoroughly manured.

Sowing.—The first sowing should be made about the middle of May. For the main crop, seed should be sown in the middle of June, and again about the middle of July. Plants to stand the winter should be sown early in August. Seed must be sown thinly, 1 inch deep, in drills 12 inches apart, and the plants, when ready, should be thinned out to 9 inches. Plenty of water should be given in dry weather, and liquid manure occasionally.

Blanching.—When nearly full-grown, the plants should be blanched. In the case of the earlier crops and the broad-leaved kinds, they must be tied up loosely when dry, after the same fashion as Cos lettuce, and the soil should be drawn up about each plant. But, as late crops intended for winter use are liable to be injured by frost, these and the curly-leaved kinds should be blanched by covering the plants with inverted pots, the hole in which should be closed with a cork. Blanching should be done at intervals, so as to have a continuous supply. The August sowing should be planted out in some sheltered situation. In many localities, these plants require the protection of glass in winter.

Varieties.—*Large Ruffec, Green Curled, Green Batavian* and *White Batavian.*

Lettuce. Lettuces are of two kinds—those coming under the heading of Cabbage lettuces, which are short and globular in shape, and the Cos kind, which have long leaves.

Soil.—Both kinds like a light, rich, and deep soil. For the main crop of summer lettuces, a piece of ground that has already been well cultivated should again be trenched, plenty of good fresh stable manure being incorporated in the process. The layer of manure should be placed a spade's depth below the surface. This process will prevent many of the lettuces from "bolting", as is so apt to occur in hot, dry weather. Abundance of moisture at the roots and ample room for leaf growth are essentials.

Sowing.—Lettuces may be sown under glass any time from January to March, but it is unsafe to sow them in the open until after this date, when successive sowings once a fortnight until August should be made in the bed in which the majority of them are to remain. Transplanting is necessary in the case of part of the crop, but the best plants are invariably obtained by sowing in the permanent position.

Sowing in the Open, Thinning, and Planting-out.—Early in March, the seed should be sown thinly in drills, a foot apart and ¾-inch deep, on the bed already prepared, and when the plants are big enough to handle, they should be thinned to about 6 inches apart, the thinnings being themselves planted out at the same interval elsewhere in the plot. Final thinning to 12 inches apart must be made

Forced rhubarb   Seakale   Garden Swedes

PLATE 53

Round or summer spinach   Turnips, White Milan

Selection of common herbs.   Reading from left to right they are mint, thyme and parsley.

Planting out sturdy seed-lings in a border near a south wall.

PLATE 54
CULTURE OF
TOMATOES

Plant at stage when blossom buds appear.

Firming in the soil ᵥ thumbs and forefing

Tying plants to st with raffia.

Plant with side sh removed, see page ⸝

if good lettuces are to be grown, and it is better to leave too few plants than too many. For two or three weeks after planting out, the young seedlings must be well dusted with soot to keep off the slugs and snails. Ample moisture will now be required.

Winter Lettuces.—Winter lettuces are obtained partly from special sowings and partly by the preservation of part of the late summer crop. Seed should be sown in successive lots from August to the latter part of October, the earlier sowings being made both in the open and in frames, but the later ones—those sown in October—in frames only. Fine soil, well mingled with old rotted manure, is necessary for the seedlings when pricked out. Of these seedlings some should be planted in frames on light soil, not too far from the glass, at 3-inch intervals, and when the young plants touch each other, they should be thinned out by pulling for use and for planting out. These thinnings may be planted out in a warm border at 6-inch intervals, a crop being still left in the seed bed. All the crop in frames needs careful handling, plenty of moisture being allowed, or warm, bright weather will cause the plants to bolt. Slight protection given to the outdoor crop will keep them safe through the hard weather, and it is probable that the plants will be crowded enough to need the removal and transplanting of every other one; a process which needs and is worth extreme care. If placed in March in a good warm sunny border, the lettuces will be useful in the very early summer.

Tying and Blanching.—Tie the leaves of Cos lettuces with raffia just above the centre when nearly ready for cutting, so as to blanch their hearts. Cabbage lettuces do not need tying.

Varieties.—*May King* (cabbage), *Improved Trocadero* (cabbage), *Paris White* (Cos), *Favourite* (Cabbage), *Giant White Cos, Imperial* and *Arctic King* (Cabbage), both good winter varieties, *Black Bath Cos* (Winter), *Webb's Wonderful* and *Tom Thumb* (Cabbage) (for frame).

Mustard. Mustard is grown in the same way as cress. (*See* p. 447.)

Onions. (*See* Vegetables, p. 437.)

Radish. The radish may be grown successfully all the year round by sowing the seed in a hot-bed (*see* p. 252) in frames from October to February, and in the open ground at fortnightly intervals during the remainder of the year.

Soil.—Radishes thrive best in a light and slightly limed loam, manured for a previous crop.

Sowing.—Seed should be sown thinly in drills, 1 inch deep, from 3 to 4 inches apart for long radishes, and from 4 to 6 inches apart for the larger sorts, as the *Spanish.* Any seedlings that press on their neighbours should be at once thinned out. Early sowings, about February, will require to be protected from frost by a covering of litter, but this must be removed every mild day, as soon as the plants appear above ground. Sheltered positions facing south are best for the early crops. When the weather is hot and the ground dry, the ground should be watered before the seed is sown; some days before the radishes are to be drawn, the beds should be watered well, and the soil should be kept moist until the crop is finished. (*See also* Forcing, p. 252.)

Varieties.—*Red Globe Short Top* (early use), *French Breakfast* (summer use), *Turnip Red, Turnip White*, and *Black Spanish* (winter use).

Rampion. Seed should be sown in drills about 10 inches apart, in March or April for use in autumn, and in May for a winter supply. Thin out to 4 to 8 inches apart in the rows. All remaining roots must be lifted in November and stored in sand in a dry, frost-proof shed. A rich soil and a shady position is necessary.

Watercress. This salad plant is best grown in a stream of pure running water with a good gritty bed. It is essential that this water supply should be uncontaminated. Vigorous shoots 15 inches long should be placed evenly over the surface of the bed in March. If the water is then gradually admitted, these shoots will form roots in a few days, when more water can be let in as the plants become established, but care must be taken not to admit the water too rapidly or the plants will be torn from their young roots. The watercress will be ready for cutting about August. Provided the soil is kept very moist, watercress can be grown in deep trenches, the seed being sown in May. By growing *Brown Winter Cress*, which is planted in August or September, watercress may be had almost all the year round.

SALAD GROWING AT A GLANCE

Name	When to Sow or Plant	Amount of Seed or Roots required for 50 ft. Row	Depth to Sow or Plant in Inches		Time of Germination in Days	Time of reach Maturity in Weeks
			Light Soil	Heavy Soil		
Chicory .	April–June	¼ oz.	1	¾	6–15	25
Corn Salad	Feb.–March and Aug.–Oct.	½ oz.	½	¼	9	10
Cress . .	April–Sept.	1 oz. for 2 Square Yards	⅛	⅛	5	1½
Cucumber.	Feb.–May	4 Seeds for every Plant required	1	1	7–14	15
Dandelion.	March–June	¼ oz.	½	¼	7–10	32
Endive .	May–Aug.	¼ oz.	1	¾	6–12	16
Lettuce .	March–Aug. (Open) Jan.–March (Glass) Aug.–Oct. (Glass)	¼ oz.	¾	½	6–12	10
Mustard .	April–Sept.	1 oz. for 1 Square Yard	⅛	⅛	5	1½
Radish .	Feb.–Sept. (Open) Oct.–Feb. (Frame)	½ oz.	1	¾	6	7

The times at which to plant out, the distances to which to thin-out the seedlings, and the most suitable soils will be found in the paragraphs on the culture of the individual plants, pages 447–450.

CHAPTER 38

THE HERB GARDEN

Every garden should contain a few herbs. They take up but little room, require but little care, and are useful in the kitchen.

Borage (*Borago officinalis*).—For culture, *see* Borago, p. 277.

Chervil. (*Anthriscus Cerefolium*).—Chervil well repays careful cultivation, deep digging, and moderate enrichment of the soil. In the warmer parts of the country, seeds may be sown early in September in a warm, dry situation, the seedlings being thinned to about 6 or 7 inches apart. When the nights are frosty this crop will need the protection of mats fastened on bent sticks. In other parts of the country, the seed may be mixed with fine soil or sand in the autumn, and the boxes containing the mixture may be placed in a frost-proof room for the winter. About the end of February, seed and soil may be sown together in drills in the situation that they are permanently to occupy.

Chives (*Allium Schænoprasum*).—The chive is of the onion tribe, and its shoots are used in soups and salads. It likes a good garden soil, and is propagated by division in March or October. Plant in rows a foot apart, with six inches between the plants. Replant each third year. Seed may be sown in the open in April.

Fennel (*Fœniculum vulgare*).—Fennel likes a rich soil, and is propagated by seed and root division. Seed should be sown in April in drills an inch deep, the drills being 18 inches apart, and when the plants are about 3 inches high, they should be transplanted and set 9 to 12 inches apart. Root division is done in March, the plants being replaced a foot apart in rows a foot apart. The flower stalks should be cut off as soon as they appear.

Garlic (*Allium sativum*).—Garlic requires to be treated as shallots. *See* p. 442.

Horseradish (*Cochlearia Armoracia*).—The ground should be trenched in late autumn to a depth of 2 to 3 feet, very little manure being applied, for a heavy dressing encourages a tendency to fork. Some old roots should be taken up, the crowns should be cut off about 1½ inches long, all fibrous roots being removed. Next, with a dibble, which is marked 2 feet from the lower end—that being the depth the crowns are to be planted—holes 10 to 12 inches apart in rows 18 inches apart are made. This done, a lath-stick, split at the end, is taken and the crown is inserted in the slit. The lath-stick is then thrust down to the bottom of the hole, and the crown is pushed out by another stick which is thrust down for the purpose. It is unnecessary to fill up the holes, as they gradually fill as the horseradish nears the surface. If a fresh row is planted every spring, and another taken up, the crop will be kept in good condition, and a fresh piece of improved ground offered every year for other crops. The roots will be ready for digging in November two years hence, when the roots should be dug up and stored in sand until required.

Lavender (*Lavandula vera*).—*See* Lavandula, p. 345.

Marjoram. Marjoram is cultivated for the use of its aromatic leaves for flavouring. *Origanum vulgare* (wild) is a hardy perennial. Two other species cultivated as well are the Sweet Marjoram (*Origanum Majorana*) and Pot Marjoram (*Origanum Onites*). *Sweet Marjoram* is usually treated as an annual. Sow seeds outside in April in a warm position or for early use under glass in March, and thin to 6–8 inches apart. Cut tops as they come into flower in July and dry off slowly. *Pot Marjoram* is a hardy perennial. It likes a light soil. Increase by division in spring or by cuttings during summer. Plant one foot apart.

Mint (*Mentha spicata*).—For culture *see* Mentha, p. 354.

Parsley (*Petroselinum crispum*).—Parsley requires light, rich, deeply-dug loam, with a good admixture of leaf-mould, sand, and a little old mortar. Two sowings should be made, one for the summer crop, sown in April, the other for winter and spring, sown in July. Seed should be sown thinly in drills 15 inches apart and an inch deep. Not until about seven or eight weeks after sowing will the seed begin to show, when it must be kept carefully weeded and well watered. The seedlings should be thinned out to 6 to 9 inches apart. Any flower-buds should be nipped off at once. The crop required for winter use should be picked close in September, when a fresh crop of leaves will shoot up. Parsley runs to seed in the second year, it is, therefore, necessary to make a sowing every year. Parsley needs semi-shade.

Rosemary (*Rosmarinus officinalis*).—Rosemary likes much the same conditions as lavender, and may be propagated by cuttings taken in April, and planted in semi-shade. They may be transplanted from the nursery bed in September or the following April.

Rue (*Ruta graveolens*).—Seed should be sown in gentle heat in April, or slips may be taken in June and September. The rows should be 18 inches and the plants 12 to 18 inches apart.

Sage (*Salvia officinalis*).—Seed should be sown in a sunny, sheltered spot in late March or early April, the seedlings, when large enough, being transplanted to a nursery bed about 4 inches apart, and later re-transferred to their final bed at about a year old. *Cuttings.*—Cuttings with a "heel" may also be taken in April. Fresh beds should be made every three or four years.

Savory [Summer, *Satureia hortensis*], [Winter, *Satureia montana*].—Savory likes a rich but not too heavy soil, and the summer kind should be sown in April in drills 12 inches apart, the seedlings being thinned to 9 inches apart. Winter savory may be raised in the same way, or old plants may be divided in March. Winter savory is the simplest to grow, as it does not need yearly renewal. Both kinds should be grown for a continuous supply.

Tarragon (*Artemisia Dracunculus*).—*Soil.*—A sheltered position and a light loam are needed. The plants are propagated by root division in March, the little plants being put in drills 3 inches deep and 18 inches apart, with 9 to 12 inches from plant to plant. The surface of the bed should receive a dressing of well-rotted manure, and another dressing each year in autumn, when the stems should be cut down.

Thyme (*Thymus vulgaris*).—For culture *see* Thyme, p. 406.

CHAPTER 39

FRUIT CULTURE

Although there are certain general conditions which are more or less applicable to all fruit trees, it must be borne in mind that different kinds do best in soils and under conditions to some extent peculiar to each kind; their individual requirements, are, therefore, noted in the paragraphs dealing with each sort of fruit. As a rule, it may be laid down that the most suitable soil is a medium loam, of moderate depth, resting on a well-drained subsoil. Soil that is water-logged is almost hopeless unless extensive drainage operations are undertaken, and very light, sandy soils are only satisfactory when kept frequently enriched by the addition of vegetable manure and by generous watering in dry weather. In any case, the soil should be prepared by digging or trenching, and in the case of poor soils, by the enriching of a foot of the soil nearest to the surface. Ordinary stable manure is the most generally satisfactory for this purpose, but must be used sparingly, and if some fibrous loam can also be added, so much the better. In any event, the subsoil should be broken up to a spade's depth, but it should not be brought to the surface, and no manure should be placed at the bottom of the trench.

Situation

The situation should be such as to afford shelter, particularly from winds from the east and north, cold biting winds from these quarters being common in the early spring, when the trees are in blossom and very susceptible to frost. Low-lying, damp situations should, where possible, be avoided. Exposure to sun is essential, as otherwise the wood becomes weak through incomplete ripening, and the fruit, if any forms, is likely to be of poor flavour and size.

Of course, most of us have our soil and situation determined for us, and we have to make the best of them. Much can in most cases be done to improve them, and by careful selection of the kind of fruit attempted to be grown, a moderate degree of success may be attained under the most unpromising conditions. Where natural protection is lacking, walls or hedges should be constructed, and, on the sunny side of the former, fruits may be grown which in our climate are almost impossible without wall protection. Many plants may be used for the making of effective hedges— the myrobalan plum, the privet, the elder, the hawthorn, and, if higher

453

shelter is required, the black Italian or the Lombardy poplar are but a few among the many possible selections. Then, again, much may be done to improve naturally unsuitable soils. (*See* p. 50.) Heavy soils may be lightened by deep digging, thorough drainage, the addition of stable manure, leaf-mould, sand, road sweepings (no tar or oil), or burnt earth. Light soils may be improved by the addition of stable manure and clay. The aim must be, in any case, to create a soil which shall be at least of moderate depth; which shall be capable of retaining moisture, yet be well drained from stagnant water; which shall be alive through the presence of a reasonable proportion of organic matter; which shall have a loose, open texture, and yet possess some cohesion and fibrosity. Basic slag, in the proportion of 1 lb. to every 5 square yards, may be mixed with the top-soil in the autumn.

On very chalky soil, little success can be expected, unless the chalk is taken out to a depth of 18 to 24 inches. Suitable soil must be substituted and renewed every few years.

SELECTION OF TREES

Needless to say, the selection of trees, as well as of the stocks on which they grow, should, to some extent, be regulated by the conditions one has to offer them. The grower with a walled kitchen garden can include in his selection of fruit-trees apricots, peaches, and nectarines, which the orchard-grower would have difficulty in protecting adequately. In the mixed garden, space is too valuable to allow of standard trees being planted. The bush and pyramid forms and the useful cordons and espaliers are here far preferable, as they can occupy spaces hardly larger than those required by, say, hardy perennials, while the quality of the fruit obtained from these forms especially the cordons and espaliers will be equal to any obtained from standard trees. Where standards are used in the mixed garden, they are best planted upon any small lawn or grass plot, where they will be seen to advantage.

FORMS OF FRUIT TREES
Round-shaped Trees

For a small garden, the bush form is generally considered the best of the round-shaped trees. Standards are most suitable for orchards.

Bush and Pyramid Trees.—The pyramid and the bush tree are formed in much the same way, except for the fact that the pyramid has a central stem, running as straight as possible up the middle of the tree, from which the side shoots spring, while the bush trees has no central stem but branches from the side shoots, the middle being kept clear. The bush and pyramid forms are suitable to apples, pears, plums, and cherries. They should be planted 8 feet apart.

The Standard.—The standard is a good form for apples, pears, plums, and cherries. It is not, in our climate, so suitable for those fruits—peach, apricot, nectarine, and so on—which require more heat properly to ripen them.

Half-Standards are similar in form to standards, except that the main stem up to the first branch, is only 4½ feet high instead of the 6 feet in the standard. Large heads are formed, which produce a highly profitable crop.

Flat-trained Trees

The Cordon.—This is an especially economical form in which the fruit is borne on either side of one or two main stems, all branches but the main ones being rigorously suppressed. The cordon assumes three directions— the horizontal, the vertical or up- right cordon, and the oblique cordon, which is mostly grown at an inclination of 45 degrees to the ground level. The cordon system of growing and training trees on supports is applicable to the apple in open ground; and to pears, peaches, nectarines, apri- cots, gooseberries, and currants, red or white, on walls or wires.

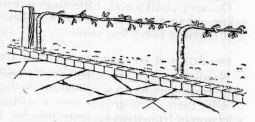

FIG. 39. APPLES TRAINED AS HORIZONTAL CORDONS

The trees should be planted 4 to 5 feet apart and at least a foot from the path edging. The posts carrying the supporting wire, which should be about 18 inches above ground level, should be set 12 feet apart.

The Espalier.—We have in this form a central stem, from which branches extend horizontally side- ways, giving the tree the form of a double ladder. Each of these branches is treated as a cordon and re- strained to its one main stem, all side shoots being removed. There should be a space of about a foot between the tiers of branches. Where the espalier stands by itself, a maximum height of five or six tiers is quite enough, but where the tree is grown against a wall, its size is practically only limited by the available space. Almost any fruit—especially apples and pears— that can successfully be trained as a cordon or bush may also be grown as an espalier. This system does not suit apricots, cherries, plums, nectar- ines, or peaches. Espaliers should be planted 15 feet apart.

The Fan.—As its name implies, the fan is shaped with radiating branches like a fan, and, like the espalier, may stand away from, or against a wall. Where it has wall support it may be much larger than where it has merely artificial trellises. The fan shape is excellently suited to plums, apricots, peaches, Morello cherries, and nectarines, the Morello cherry particularly enjoying a north wall. Fan-trained trees should be planted 15 feet apart.

455

FRUIT CULTURE

SUITABLE VARIETIES

Careful inquiries should be made as to varieties and the types of trees—espaliers, standards, or bushes, etc.—that thrive best in the locality, and note should also be taken of the stocks that have been found most reliable and successful. A great failing is to have too many mid-season varieties; early and late varieties should also be selected to extend the fruiting season as much as possible.

Self-sterile Varieties

Many of the best varieties of apples, cherries, pears, plums are self-sterile, that is to say, they cannot fertilize their flowers with their own pollen, but require the pollen from another variety of the same kind of tree to enable them to set their fruit. In selecting fruit trees for a garden or orchard, it is, therefore, necessary to have more than one variety of each particular kind of fruit. The different varieties must, however, be those that come into flower at approximately the same time. There are a few self-fertile varieties which can more or less effectively fertilize their own blooms and set a fair crop of fruit, but if good and regular crops are required, it is obvious that great care is needed in the selection of fruit trees. These self-fertile trees are marked with an asterisk in the tables showing the best varieties of fruit.

PLANTING

Time to Plant

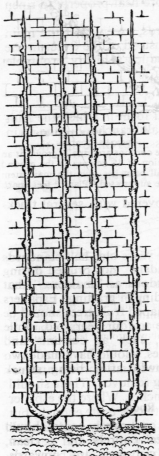

FIG. 40. PEARS TRAINED AS DOUBLE VERTICAL CORDONS Although the *oblique* is the most convenient of all cordon forms, the double vertical cordon may be employed to suit the requirements of space or situation.

For planting fruit trees, the time is between early November and March, but the best of all is November. Planting should, if possible, cease before mid-December, to be continued if necessary, late in February when the worst of the frosts are over. In very heavy soils, spring planting has certain advantages over autumn planting, but in the ordinary way,

456

November planting is preferable. When trees are planted in spring, especially on light soils, it is absolutely necessary to keep the ground continuously moist by frequent watering and surface mulching with manure.

Planting must never be done during frost, or when the ground is wet and sticky. If the latter condition prevails when the trees arrive from the nursery, they must be "laid in" by the roots in a sheltered position, that is to say, they must have their roots well covered up with soil until the weather is suitable for planting. In frosty weather, the trees cannot be "laid or heeled in"; they should be kept in a frost-proof shed with the roots covered with several thicknesses of sacking or paper.

FIG. 41. AN APPLE TRAINED AS OBLIQUE CORDON
Oblique cordons are usually grown at an inclination of 45 degrees to the ground level; all branches save the main stem must be suppressed. Plant 2 feet apart.

Age of Trees for Planting

Standards are best planted when three to four years old; half-standards as "two-year-old feathered trees," that is, "maidens" not pruned during the winter after their formation; bushes and cordons as "maidens," that is, trees that have made a year's growth after budding or grafting. Espaliers and fan-shaped fruit trees should be from three to four years old, while bush fruit, such as currants and gooseberries, should have made two years' growth after being struck as cuttings.

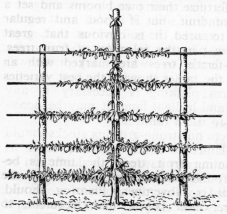

FIG. 42. AN ESPALIER-TRAINED PEAR
Each horizontal branch is treated as a cordon, all side shoots being removed. There should be a space of 12 to 18 inches between the tiers of branches. Plant 15 feet apart.

Pruning the Roots

Bruised or broken roots should be removed entirely by a clean, sharp cut outwards and upwards. Two or three spurs are sufficient, but if there are more good ones, they may remain after being pruned. Should the roots be dry, soak them well in water until the bark has become plump, then plant immediately. One great point in planting fruit trees is to keep the

457

roots of the plants as little exposed as possible. A dry wind or a cutting, frosty air is fatal to them.

Planting

A hole about 3 feet in diameter and 2 feet in depth is dug out in ground that has been well drained. In the bottom of this pit is laid 10 or 12 inches of brick or lime rubbish, the roughest material at the bottom; this is rammed pretty firmly so as to be impervious to the tap-root. The remainder of the pit should be filled in with earth suitable to the requirements of the tree.

The tree should be placed upright in the centre of the hole, and the lowest roots should be laid out horizontally. Fine earth should then be loosely thrown over them, and carefully pressed firmly over them.

The next layer of roots should be treated in a like manner and so on until the whole of the roots are covered. It is most important that the rootlets should, as far as possible, assume their natural position, thoroughly penetrating and permeating the surrounding soil. It is also most necessary to make the soil firm at each stage of the planting in order to minimize the depth to which the tree will sink.

Firm planting is necessary in any soil, and in light land, it may be necessary to use a rammer.

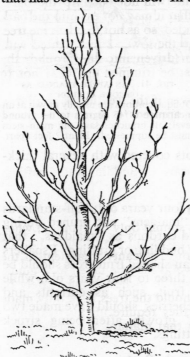

FIG. 43. THE PYRAMID APPLE
The pyramid has a central stem, running straight up the middle of the tree, and from which the side shoots spring. This form is used for apples, pears, plums and cherries.

Trees on strong-growing stocks should be planted to about the same depth as in the nursery garden; this depth can be seen from the marks of soil usually found on the stem. Fruit on dwarfing stocks, however, should be planted so that the union of stock and scion is just below the soil. It is rarely necessary to have more than 4 inches of soil over the upper roots; deep planting is the bane of fruit trees.

For best time to plant individual species of fruit and distance apart of forms of tree or bush, see Fruit Growing at a Glance table on pages 490 and 491.

458

STAKING AND TYING

It is necessary to support the newly-planted tree with a strong stake reaching to the lowest branch, but not higher, driven firmly into the ground before the earth is filled in round the roots. The stem is tied to it with soft cord, after the tree has been surrounded with hay or straw, or even a wrapping of old felt, so that the string will not cut into the bark. This cord should be renewed annually, so that it may not eat into the bark as the tree swells. The stake should be rounded, so as not to chafe the tree, should be pointed at the bottom, and have the lower 2 feet treated with creosote or tar. After the stake has been driven into the ground, the burred-over top, caused by the mallet, must be trimmed up so as not to damage the bark of the tree.

After planting, ample water should be given if the weather is at all dry, and a mulch of stable manure should be applied to protect the roots. (*See* p. 36.)

PROPAGATION

For the propagation of Fruit Trees by means of Budding and Grafting, *see* pp. 115 to 126.

MANURES: ARTIFICIAL AND ORGANIC

Whether they are young or old, the trees should only be manured when they are actually bearing a crop of fruit. It is no easy matter for the amateur to tell when the trees need generous or scanty treatment in the matter of manure, but the growth of the wood may be taken as a guide. If the wood has made an extension of 15 to 20 inches, it may safely be inferred that no manure should be given; should the trees have only made up to 5 inches of extension growth, then they require liberal treatment. Anything between these growths indicates that manure should be given only in moderation.

Artificial Manures

It must be remembered that all fruit trees will thrive the better for the occasional application of wood ashes, a small amount of lime, and a good dressing of soot to the surface soil. Of the artificial manures proper, nitrate of soda, sulphate of ammonia, superphosphates, basic slag, and kainit are those most used. It must be remembered that potash and phosphates check growth and encourage excessive fruit production, all the more so when pruning is not severe. On the other hand, nitrogenous manures, especially when accompanied with severe pruning, produce much woody growth and tend to decrease the yield of fruit.

(*See also* Chapter 5, devoted to Manures, Organic and Artificial, *and* Manuring Fruit Trees, p. 460.)

459

MANURES FOR FRUIT TREES

When and How to Apply

(Area ¼ acre)

NOTE.—3 qrs. per ¼ Acre is equal to 2 lb. to the Square Rod, or 1 oz. per Square Yard. The artificial manures are given in addition to the farmyard manure, which is applied in winter.

Fruit	Farmyard Manure	Artificial Manure	When to apply the Artificial Manures
Apple . .	Occasionally	Superphosphate, ¾ cwt. and Potash, ¼ cwt.	After pruning.
Apricot	Mulch annually in May	1 lb. Bone Meal	Winter.
Cherry. . .	5 tons	Sulphate of Potash, ⅓ cwt. and Superphosphate, 1¼ cwt.	Winter. When fruit is set.
Cucumber .	4 cart-loads for a two-light frame in March	2 oz. Dried Fish Guano per sq. yd. or 1 oz. Sulphate of Ammonia per sq. yd.	Summer. Spring.
Currant and Gooseberry .	5 tons	Sulphate of Ammonia, ¾ cwt., Sulphate of Potash, ½ cwt., Superphosphate, 1 cwt.	April. Autumn (triennially).
Damson (*see* Plum).			
Fig	Mulch annually in May	Not required	
Gooseberry (*see* Currant).			
Grape . . .	A slight top-dressing	Apply Liquid Manure weekly from time the fruit sets until ripe.	
Loganberry (*see* Raspberry).			
Medlar . .	5 tons	Superphosphate, ¾ cwt. and Superphosphate, 1 cwt.	April.
Melon . .	Six loads for a three-light frame when bed made up	Tepid liquid manure	At two-weekly intervals from the time the fruits begin to swell until ripe.
Nectarine (*see* Peach).			
Nut . . .	Not advised.		
Peach . . .	Mulch annually in May	1 lb. Bone Meal	Winter.
Pear . . .	5 tons	Superphosphate ¾ cwt., Sulphate of Potash ¼ cwt.	Autumn. Early Spring.
Plum and Damson .	5 tons	Bone Meal, 3 qrs.	Winter.
Quince (*see* Pear).			
Raspberry . .	5 tons (decayed)	½ cwt. Nitrate of Soda, 1 cwt. Superphosphate, Sulphate of Potash, ¼ cwt..	Half in March, half in June.
Strawberry . .	5 tons	Nitrate of Soda, ¾ cwt.	May.
Tomato . .	*In Pots:* ⅓ part (well decayed) *In Beds:* 5 tons	A pinch of Nitrate of Potash	At intervals through the growing season.

Liquid Manure

Liquid manure can with advantage be applied to all fruit trees about the end of May. It should never be given too strong. The liquid manure from the farmyard should be diluted until it is pale amber in colour, and is best applied after rain or after the soil has been moistened a couple of hours beforehand.

Liquid manure may be given more liberally on light, dry soils, than on cold, damp, heavy ground.

Farmyard manure contains nitrogen, phosphates, and potash—the three essential plant foods—but to secure a large crop of fruit, the trees should be given a little additional stimulant in the way of artificial manure. Farmyard manure is invariably spread during the winter; artificial manures are usually employed after pruning, when the fruit is set, or in the spring. according to the special characteristics of the fertilizer selected.

The table opposite gives the quantities of the various manures for different fruits. (*See also chapter on* Manures, p. 56.)

PRUNING

In pruning a tree, we aim at three main objects. The first is to promote healthy growth of wood, and this is the chief aim of the grower in pruning his young trees. The second, and one almost equally important in the early life of the tree, is to give the form desired, a point of great moment in the future of the tree as regards fruit or flower. These two ends are attained by the same means: first, the tree is shaped in such a way that when fully grown, it may be well balanced and well proportioned according to its natural habit; secondly, the branches are so thinned as to allow of perfectly free circulation of air and light throughout the tree, thus promoting the ripening of the wood and keeping it healthy; and thirdly, the tree is helped to produce good vigorous shoots and thus to come to maturity as soon as possible, by means of judicious cutting back of weak shoots and shortening of strong ones. The third main object is the increase of fruitfulness, which of course means increase of flowers in plants grown for their blossoms.

PRUNING KNIVES, SECATEURS, AND SAW

Two pruning knives will be required: one, very strong, for winter-pruning, where the wood to be removed is all hard and well-ripened; and another lighter and with a thinner blade, for the removal of young green shoots in summer-pruning, where the passage of a thick blade might bruise the young wood unnecessarily. Clean cutting is the first thing to aim at in pruning. The secateurs are used for certain operations, and for the amateur are useful, as they do away with the possibility of injury to other shoots by the slipping of the blade. Instead of a clean cut, the

461

secateurs are apt, however, to pinch and flatten the wood. This damaged end frequently withers, and if the cut has been made in the position which in pruning with the knife would be the correct one, the injury affects the bud, which is thus destroyed, and the pruning must recommence lower down.

The only other instrument needed is a small hand saw for the removal of branches too large for the knife. All these instruments must be kept very sharp, or they will bruise the wood and leave unhealthy wounds.

If it is necessary to cut away a branch altogether, no portion of it should be left on the main stem, as this stump would decay and encourage fungi and pests. The cut should be as nearly perpendicular as possible, smooth, and slightly bevelled, thus presenting the smallest possible extent of wounded surface. To avoid tearing the bark, should the branch fall before it is completely severed, it is wise to make a small cut on the underside of the branch before the main cut from above is commenced. Where the cut surface is very large, it should be covered as soon as possible with the composition known as "grafting" mastic, or failing this any other protective such as coal tar, creosote white paint, will do, as this prevents fungus spores entering the tissues and setting up disease.

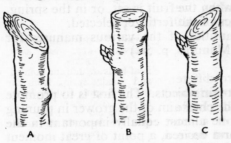

FIG. 44. PRUNING: HOW TO MAKE THE CUT. The perfect cut (A) begins on the side of the shoot opposite the selected bud, slants slightly upwards, and ends just above the tip of the bud. In B (incorrect), the cut is made too far above the bud; if cut as in C (incorrect), the bud will be weakened.

HOW AND WHEN TO PRUNE

How to Make the Cut

The way in which the cut is made is most vital. It should be as nearly as may be straight, and should not leave a surface slanting upwards from below the bud, with its lower edge below the spring of the bud and its upper on a level with it. This weakens the bud, which does not receive its full nourishment, and it results either in the shoot budding strongly from an undesirable bud lower down, or in the bursting of a new strong bud just below the one chosen, necessitating the re-pruning of the shoot down to that level. On the other hand, the cut should not be made too far above the chosen bud, or the wood left will wither up, and will have to be removed the following year. The perfect cut begins on the side of the shoot opposite to the selected bud, and slants ever so slightly upwards across the shoot till it ends immediately above the tip of the bud. It

462

should be clean and unbruised. Always prune back to a wood-bud, not a fruit bud, and see that the bud faces in the right direction, that is, usually outwards.

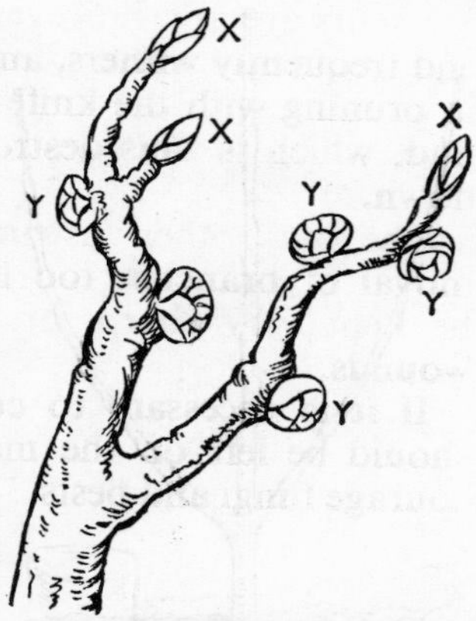

The first thing to be done before undertaking the operation of pruning is to study the trees to be dealt with, and to make up your mind clearly as to what effect you wish to produce. Where you are dealing with young trees, it is certainly not a good plan to prune for fruit. The trees are as yet weak and not firmly established, and their vigour should be devoted to the formation of good healthy, well-ripened wood, a well-shaped head, and healthy roots.

Leaf-bud or Fruit-bud

It is an essential but easy matter to differentiate, when pruning, between fruit-buds and leaf-buds. The latter are thin and pointed, and usually spring from the end of a spur, while the fruit buds are globular and have a plump appearance and generally sprout from the old wood and from near the base of the young shoot.

FIG. 45. DISTINGUISHING BETWEEN FRUIT- AND LEAF-BUDS
Leaf-buds are thin and pointed, and usually spring from the end of a spur; fruit-buds are globular and generally sprout from the old wood and from near the base of the young shoot.

In summer, the fruit buds are surrounded by a cluster of leaves. Several of these fruit-buds will be found in the fruit-spur, a short shoot springing naturally from the old wood and usually terminating in a leaf-bud. Fruit spurs may be formed artificially by summer-pruning. (*See* p. 464.)

Thinning Fruit Spurs

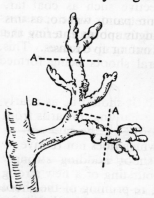

FIG. 46. THINNING FRUIT-SPURS
Thinning is accomplished in two stages; in the first year the spur is cut back to A, A. The next year the spur is cut back to B.

After a few years the fruit spurs are likely to have grown too big and may need thinning, otherwise the fruit will gradually decrease in size.

This thinning is best accomplished in two stages as shown in Fig. 46. In the first year, the spur is pruned back to A, A, which will encourage new growth nearer the base. The next year the spur is cut back to B, and will, in consequence, have greatly improved fruiting capacity.

463

FIG. 47. YOUNG TREE TO BE TRAINED AS AN ESPALIER
It is in this state that the young trees are usually received from the nursery.

Time for Pruning

All pruning of fruit trees should be done before the buds start swelling in spring. Any time after the leaves have fallen in autumn and not later than the end of February is a good time, although with such trees as Peaches, Plums and Pears which come into flower very early, it is advisable not to leave pruning any later than the end of January. With apples which usually come into flower much later, pruning can be extended for a few weeks. The pruner can select the best bud and can cut back to that without fear that the bud will dry up or become blind. Where young trees are concerned, any summer-pruning beyond that absolutely necessary to keep them in shape should be barred. Where the new growth shows some defect in shape, such as a bad side shoot or a very lop-sided branch, it may be removed in summer, but the less done in this way the better.

Only very hardy and well-established trees should be pruned actually during winter.

SUMMER-PRUNING

This operation consists in going over the trees on two or three occasions in summer, and pinching off, with the finger and thumb nail, a few at a time, the soft ends of the side shoots to about four or five leaves. This, if done too early, will result in fresh sub-lateral shoots being formed from the upper buds. Should these form, they must again be pinched back to one leaf.

Leading shoots should never be summer-pruned. The result of this pinching is the concentration of sap in the young leading shoot and the gradual change of the leaf-buds upon the remainder of the side shoots into fruit-buds. The best time to summer-prune varies with the variety of tree, the soil, and the climate. Fruit on light soil can usually be pruned

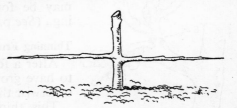

FIG. 48. PRUNING THE ESPALIER: FIRST YEAR
The side branches are trained horizontally, and pruned to two-thirds of their length, with a bud immediately below the cut. The stem is pruned to 12 to 18 inches above the side branches, leaving three buds immediately below the cut —one on each side, well placed, and a third in front to continue the stem.

464

PLATE 55 Before and after pruning. *Above*, standard rose and *below*, bush rose.

3

5

2

4

6

PLATE 56 1 and 2, before and after pruning an established bush fruit tree; 3 and 4, before and after pruning a pyramid form tree; 5 and 6, before and after pruning an open centre tree.

in July; trees on heavier land a month later. Pruning should be done early enough to prevent shoots from making excessive growth, but not so early that a mass of sub-laterals are formed. Black currants, raspberries, Morello cherries, nectarines, and peaches must not be summer-pruned, for the fruit forms along the length of the previous year's growth.

The above remarks refer to all forms of fruit trees, except the standard; this it is inadvisable to summer-prune.

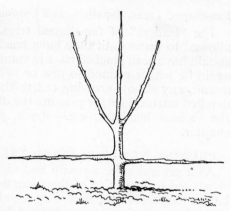

FIG. 49. THE ESPALIER IN ITS SECOND YEAR
By the autumn of the second year, the tree should have attained this form; a central stem and two extra untrained side shoots.

PRUNING ESTABLISHED TREES

Generally speaking, the rapid formation of leaves and wood is adverse to the production of fruit. Obviously, the tree has only a certain amount of energy and nourishment, and if this is all, or nearly all, expended on the formation of leaves, there will be little left over for the fruit. On the other hand, a certain amount of leaf growth is necessary for the proper nourishment of the fruit and the tree itself. On the whole, the slow growth of wood favours the production of fruit and blossom, and should be the end to be aimed at. Where trees have been summer-pruned, winter-pruning will consist in little more than cutting back laterals to within two or three buds of their base and in shortening the main shoots back to a good leaf-bud.

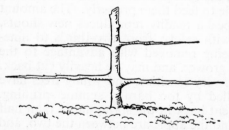

FIG. 50. PRUNING THE ESPALIER: SECOND YEAR
The new side shoots are trained horizontally and are pruned to two thirds of their length, and the main stem to from 12 to 18 inches above them as before, having three well placed buds to form the next tier. The first (lower) pair of laterals are pruned to two-thirds of the year's growth.

Pyramids, Bushes, and Standards

With pyramid, bush, and standard trees, it is merely necessary to keep the trees in shape, usually cutting back to an outward-facing bud, so that the resulting shoot may grow out from the centre of the tree, to admit of plenty of air space.

Crossing branches must, of course, be cut out.

Fan-shaped Trees, Espaliers, and Cordons

The "leaders" of fan-shaped trees, espaliers, and cordons should be allowed to grow until they have reached the desired length. All laterals should have been pinched back in summer (*see* Summer-pruning), and must again be winter-pruned to one or two buds. In trees trained up against a wall, any shoots growing out to the front must be cut right out. For detailed instructions for pruning the different kinds of fruit trees, *see* under the various headings, e.g.—*Apple, pear, cherry, etc.*, in the following chapter.

PRUNING NEWLY-PLANTED TREES

As a general rule, a young and vigorous tree should have its branches shortened to one-third of their length. Where the planting is done fairly late in the season, the necessary pruning may be done at once; where it is early the operation may well be deferred for a week or two, so that the buds may be past the danger of drying up, and in order that the best ones may be more easily selected. All the feeble shoots should be thinned out, being so selected that the head, when finished, may be balanced and evenly filled. The remaining one-year shoots should then be cut back to a good bud, care being taken to see that it is so placed on the stem, inwards or outwards, that the shoot produced from it may occupy a suitable position in the general "design" of the tree. The final shapeliness of the full-grown tree depends much on this first selection of shoots, and for the first year, at least, more thought must be given to the future shape of the tree than to the immediate production of fruit.

Much also depends on the judgment of the pruner in the matter of the amount to be cut from the young tree. The leaves and roots are inter-dependent. If the leaves are too few, the root growth will be feeble; if they are too many, the roots will be unable to feed them properly. The amount varies with the kind of tree. The peach readily reproduces new shoots, so that it may be cut back freely with safety, from two-thirds to nine-tenths of the last season's shoot being removed with advantage to the plant. The grape, too, is a vigorous grower, and may be heavily cut back, while the cherry, on the contrary, is very sensitive, and young trees have been severely injured and even killed by too hard a summer-pruning. Shoots of the cherry should not be cut back in the spring more than half their length at the most. The pear and the apple are between the two, and must be moderately pruned, without excess, but should usually be cut back by quite a half. The amount of cutting to be done varies also with the size of the fruit, and with other special conditions. For example, plum trees may be left fuller of wood than may apples, as the latter fruit is very much heavier, and the strain of a large crop much greater than in the case of the smaller plum. Again, the apple, to reach perfection, needs sunshine while on the tree; therefore the shoots must be so thinned that the sunshine may penetrate as freely as possible, while the pear, whose fruit is usually ripened after removal from the tree, may carry its shoots more closely packed.

Black currants, newly planted, should be cut hard back to two buds from the base; this applies to all the shoots. Red and white currants and gooseberries should have all the weak shoots cut back to within two buds of the base, but all strong growths should be shortened back by about one-half only.

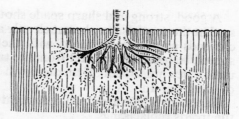

FIG. 51. ROOT-PRUNING

The lightly-shaded section shows the position of the trench to be dug round the tree, and where a sharp spade should be driven horizontally 1½ feet below the base of the tree to sever the downward-striking roots, shown by the dotted lines.

ROOT-PRUNING

Where the trees have been grown on proper stocks, and have been well looked after while young, root-pruning should not be necessary, but as a remedial measure where trees have, as it were, got out of hand, it has great uses and is best carried out in early autumn.

Root-pruning has much the same effect as top-pruning, but in addition, it may be used to direct the roots towards the surface of the ground so that they may lie in the upper layers of soil, these being the fullest of moisture and nourishment as well as the best aerated. Root-pruning of old and young trees differs in method.

Root-pruning Young Trees

These should be lifted completely out of the ground and transplanted. This process will in itself be sufficient root-pruning, and should be done to those trees whose summer growths are numerous and fruit buds few. Bush, espalier, and cordon trees that are pruned in hard, are the most likely

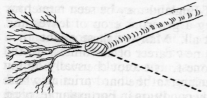

FIG. 52. ROOT-PRUNING

In root-pruning, always make the cuts upwards, as this keeps the rootlets in the top layer of soil.

to need root-pruning. Established standards but rarely need it. Young trees planted in deep, rich soil, may also require root-pruning. Trees with short, healthy growth and plenty of fruit spurs are best left alone; they do not need root-pruning.

Never attempt to root-prune unless it is quite obvious that the operation is a necessity.

467

A good, strong and sharp spade should be used in lifting the young tree, so that the rootlets may be cut cleanly and not broken and bruised, and all cut ends should be trimmed with the knife before replanting. The soil should be tried about 3 feet from the tree, and thence in towards the trunk until fibres are found. Then dig down below the tree and lift it bodily out of the ground.

Tap roots which are striking straight downwards may be removed before the tree is replaced.

Large and Established Trees

Large, established trees are difficult to root-prune. The operation is best carried out towards the end of the season, when the leaves are still on the trees. A trench, some 3 feet wide and 2 to 3 feet deep, is dug round the tree to be operated upon. The fibre roots should be preserved intact, tied together in bundles, and covered with sacking to keep them from being dried up by the sun or exposure to the air. All strong roots over an inch in diameter are cut off, care being taken to make the cuts upward, as this helps to keep the rootlets in the top layer of soil. A very sharp spade should then be driven horizontally under the tree, and 1½ feet below the base, to sever downward-striking roots. This completes the work, and the trench should then be filled up with good loam, mixed, if possible, with some spent manure—some that has been used in a hot-bed is best, as it will not be too strong.

If it is found that the fibrous roots are not very numerous, it will be advisable only to root-prune one side of the tree at a time, the other side being operated upon in the same manner the following autumn.

Should the tree be of considerable size, the branches must be reduced, and side shoots should be cut-in before root-pruning is attempted.

A pretty safe guide as to the position of the trench for root-pruning is the old saying that the roots of a tree spread out underground as far as its branches.

RENEWING OLD FRUIT-TREES

In every village and country district of England may be seen numerous old fruit-trees which, although producing a generous crop of leaves and fresh shoots, yield practically no fruit at all. Many of these might, by a little judicious treatment, be started on a new career of usefulness. In the case of plums, peaches, and all other stone fruit except cherries, nothing can be done in the way of renovation, seeing that the hard pruning which would be necessary is generally fatal to them. Pears in particular respond to vigorous treatment, as also in a lesser degree do apples. In the case of standard trees in orchards, directly the fruit is gathered the trees should be gone over, all the dead wood being removed, together with all boughs that have been bruised, barked, or split or injured in any way. The grass should then be mowed, thistles cut down, and the cuttings removed from the orchard. Salt should be sprinkled at the rate of two hundredweight to the acre over the ground, and as soon as new grass appears, some sheep should be turned in, being fed once daily with cake or corn. This treatment should be continued through the winter, and in the spring a dressing of kainit or soot should be given. In dealing with old pear-trees on walls, it is a good plan to cut out every other horizontal branch six inches from the main stem, and as soon as fresh shoots have replaced these, to cut out those previously left, and to allow them to be replaced by new shoots in the same way. Another plan is to remove the main stem with all its branches down to the level of the lowest pair of horizontal branches. By this operation, the formation of strong new shoots will be stimulated from the lowest tier; these can be encouraged to grow in an upright form at such regular distances as are required. In the case of overgrown pyramids and bushes of pears and apples, the centre of the tree should be opened up, crossing branches being removed. A trench also should be made round the tree at a distance of three or four feet, and any coarse roots burrowing downwards removed, great care being taken not to injure the horizontal roots and fine rootlets. (*See* Root-pruning, p. 467.) The following year, it will often be well to transplant such trees to a fresh situation.

Where the trees are very old and apparently quite useless, it is best to cut the main branches back in early winter, October to January, to within two feet of their base, and then to "Rind- or crown-graft" (*see* p. 125) suitable young grafts on to them. By this method, well-bearing trees may be had in three or four years.

THINNING-OUT THE FRUIT

The thinning of the fruit is a most important matter, firstly, because if too much fruit is left on a tree, all will be small, and secondly, because over-cropping weakens the trees. A heavy crop ripened one year almost certainly means but little fruit the following. Especially necessary is it for young trees to be heavily thinned.

Sturdy bushes or cordons may bear just a few fruit in their third year— say one fruit to each spur.

With older trees, only just as much fruit as the tree can mature satisfactorily should be left on the branches; the larger the probable eventual size of the fruit, the smaller the number that should be allowed to remain, and the more vigorous the tree, the more it may be permitted to bear. In thinning, all misshaped and badly placed fruit should be removed, and the operation of thinning should be performed, not all at once, but in two or three stages.

469

GATHERING AND STORING FRUIT

A gentle touch will always cause ripe fruit to leave the tree, that is to say, the fruit-stalk parts easily from the twig on which it grows if the fruit is gently raised to the horizontal position. Fallen or bruised fruit should never be mixed with that which is to be stored.

Time to Gather.—Fruit which ripens in summer and autumn should be gathered just a shade before it is ripe. A single day before they are perfectly ripe suffices for peaches and other delicate stone fruit; a week for apples and pears; but cherries are only gathered when completely ripe. Those apples and pears, which arrive at maturity in winter, are best gathered at the moment when the leaves begin to fall. It is better to lose a few apples through falling from the trees than to gather late-keeping varieties too soon. In the latter case, they will shrivel and lose their flavour when stored.

Of cooking apples, only a few should be picked before they are actually ripe, and this should be done in the process of thinning-out the fruit. Fruit that has been damaged by insects and fungus will drop a considerable time before the other fruit, and this must not be taken as an indication that the sound fruit is ripe.

Weather for Gathering.—All gathering should take place in dry weather, and the late morning and afternoon will usually be found to be the best time, as all the fruit should be quite dry when it is gathered.

Storing

Apples and Pears.—These fruits need to be stored in an even temperature of about 45° F., being looked over periodically once a fortnight, so that any decaying ones may be removed.

They should first be sweated, that is to say, laid in heaps and left to heat for ten days or a fortnight, and should then be stored away on trays, or in a dry, dark cellar in heaps, uncovered except during frost.

Pears, especially, need constant inspection. It is not always easy to tell when pears are beginning to ripen. With several varieties, however, the skin becomes a golden-yellow, or the tinge of red, if present, will become brighter.

Grapes.—Grapes should be cut when quite ripe so that the laterals removed with the bunches are about nine inches long.

These laterals should be inserted into wine bottles almost filled with water and containing a few lumps of charcoal. The bottles are then placed in racks or secured to the wall at an angle of 40 degrees, so that the grapes will hang naturally. The room in which they are stored must be kept cool and dark, but well aired. Bunches so kept will last well into the new year.

CHAPTER 40

THE CULTURE OF PARTICULAR FRUITS

Apple. The apple does well in any well-drained, moderate loam, providing the situation is not too low-lying, too exposed, or, on the other hand, too much shaded from the sun.

Forms of Trees.—In planting apples in an orchard on grass land, what is known as the standard form (*see* p. 455) is undoubtedly the one to be selected. For most purposes, however, the bush or the pyramid (*see* p. 454) form of apple-tree is well suited. Apples are also sometimes grown as cordons or espaliers, trained against a trellis or wire fence. Apples are propagated by budding in July, or by grafting in March or April, on suitable stocks. The types of stocks now in use for apples are considerable and vary according to the type of tree to be grown. For budding and grafting see pages 115–126.

Planting.—Standard trees should be allowed a space of 20 to 25 feet in all directions from tree to tree. Bush and pyramid trees should be planted 8 to 15 feet apart. For planting, see page 458.

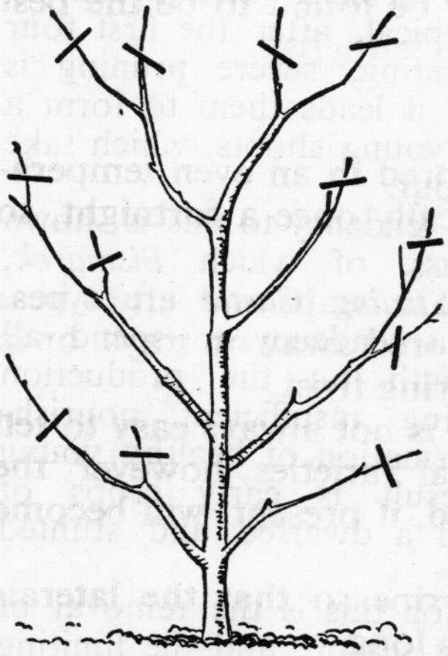

FIG. 53. PRUNING THE ESTABLISHED BUSH APPLE
The main branches should be cut back by one-third of the growth made in the previous year and all laterals to two buds. Prune, preferably, in December and January.

Summer Pruning is carried out in July and August, and again in September, the laterals or side-shoots being pinched back, a few at a time, to five or half-a-dozen leaves. Fresh shoots that develop after the "pinching back" are again stopped to two or three leaves. This encourages the formation of fruit buds and applies to all forms of tree, except the standard, which is not summer-pruned.

Winter Pruning. Newly Planted Trees.—For general instructions for pruning newly planted trees, the reader is referred to the section on *Pruning*. In the case of the apple, newly planted standards, bushes, or pyramids, should have their main shoots cut back to about one-third of their length. Trees trained fan-wise and as cordons must be shortened by about a quarter.

In espaliers, the "leader" must be shortened to 12 to 18 inches above the top pair of side-branches, which must be cut back by a half; any lower pairs of side-stems need only be slightly shortened, unless they have grown very rank. Laterals, on the main shoots, in all cases must be cut back to within two or three buds of their base. The pruning should be done in March.

471

Winter Pruning Established Trees.—This operation can be done any time between November and March, but is best done in December and January. Standards should be pruned as little as possible, only sufficient to keep them in shape and form; dead and diseased wood and all sucker growth must, of course be cut out. Bushes and pyramids will do best when their main branches are cut back by one-third, while trees trained on walls, or as espaliers and cordons, require only slight shortening until they have covered the desired space. In all forms, except the standard, laterals should be cut back annually to two or three buds. Short twigs 3 to 4 inches in length need not be pruned back as they will probably carry fruit; when they have borne fruit, they may be cut back to two buds like the more vigorous laterals.

Special Treatment.—So much do the varieties differ in habits of growth that what is excellent for one may be bad for another, within, however, the general rules of good pruning. Thus, some of the kinds usually make very strong young growth, and for these, of which *Blenheim Orange, Newton Wonder* and *Bramley's Seedlings* are typical, after the first four years after planting, severe pruning is not advised, as it leads them to form a mass of strong young shoots, which take all the tree's vigour.

The opposite tendency to this is shown by another class, of which *Bismarck, Grenadier* and *Stirling Castle* are types. This kind has a tendency to spend all its early strength on the production of fruit, leaving insufficient nourishment for the formation of healthy young wood. The result is early crops of small fruit, and a dwarfed and stunted tree.

The remedy for this is the removal of all fruit the first season, and the limiting of the crop to a small one in the second.

FIG. 54. SUMMER- AND WINTER-PRUNING THE APPLE

Between July and September, laterals should be stopped, a few at a time, to five or six leaves, as shown at *S*. Between November and March, main branches should be pruned by one-third, and all laterals to two or three buds as at *W*. Standards are never summer-pruned and are winter-pruned as little as possible.

A few apples—for example, *Lady Sudeley, Mr. Gladstone,* and *Irish Peach*—bear fruit on the ends of the young wood, and are known as tip bearers. In such cases, the tree should be pruned with a view to encouraging healthy side shoots, as by cutting these back in the autumn to six leaves and in the spring to two or three buds, good healthy young wood may be secured all over the tree.

472

With such varieties, therefore, summer-pruning will consist in topping crowded shoots in the centre of the fruit tree, also any lateral shoots that it is necessary to shorten to keep the tree in shape. All other shoots should be allowed to grow.

Thinning.—Each cluster should be thinned to two or three fruits, those at the centre usually being retained. Varieties bearing large fruit must be more severely thinned than this, one or two apples to each spur being sufficient. (*See also* Thinning, p. 463.)

Gathering the Fruit.—Different varieties of apples ripen in different months, and early varieties should, of course, be picked when they are ripe. Most of the later kinds, however, have to be gathered before they are strictly ripe, in order to be stored before the frosts. October is the great month of the apple harvest. (*See* Storing Fruit, p. 470.)

Varieties.—By careful selection, a supply of apples may be had almost the year through, at any rate from July to May. For those who are handicapped by a heavy soil, the following list may prove useful, all the varieties being comparatively able to withstand this unfavourable condition: *Bramley's Seedling, Lord Grosvenor, Wellington* and *Worcester Pearmain.*

(*See also* Manuring Fruit Trees, p. 460; Mulching, p. 36; and Root-pruning, p. 467.)

SOME OF THE BEST APPLES

Dessert

Name	Season	Name	Season
(S) Blenheim Orange. .	Nov.–Jan.	(I) Lady Sudeley . .	Aug.–Sept.
(I)* Charles Ross . .	Oct.–Nov.	(I) Laxton's Fortune .	Sept.–Nov.
(S) Cox's Orange Pippin .	Nov.–Jan.	(S) Laxton's Superb .	Dec.–March
(I) Ellison's Orange . .	Sept.–Oct.	(S)* Ribston Pippin . .	Nov.–Jan.
(I)* James Grieve . .	Sept.–Oct.	(S) Sturmer Pippin . .	March–May

Cooking

Name	Season	Name	Season
(S)† Anne Elizabeth . .	Mar.–April	(S) Lane's Prince Albert.	Dec.–Mar.
(S)† Beauty of Kent . .	Oct.–Feb.	(S) Lord Derby . .	Oct.–Nov.
(S)* Bismarck . . .	Oct.–Jan.	(S)* Newton Wonder .	Oct.–Mar.
(S) Bramley's Seedling .	Oct.–Mar.	(I) Rev. Wilks . . .	Oct.–Nov.
(I) Grenadier . . .	Aug.–Sept.	(I)* Stirling Castle . .	Sept.–Oct.

(S) = Storing. (I) = Immediate Use. * = Self-fertile Varieties. † Can be used for dessert or cooking.

Allington Pippin, Bramley's Seedling, Cox's Orange Pippin, Lady Sudeley, Lord Derby, Newton Wonder, Stirling Castle, and Sturmer Pippin make an excellent combination for cross-pollination.

Apricot. *Soil and Situation.*—This fruit is most suited to cultivation on a south wall or under glass, thrives in a good, well-drained, calcareous loam, and is best planted in October. Water should be given liberally in dry weather; a mulch of well-rotted manure early in June is very helpful. Netting of about ½-inch mesh which hangs in front of the trees, is the best means of protection from frost. Care must be taken that the wind cannot blow the netting against the flowers. Thin, partially, all fruit where it is thickly set, but reserve the final thinning, to 5 inches between fruits, until the fruit has stoned.

Pruning.—The apricot flourishes best trained as a fan with its main branches set some 9 inches apart. It will tend to produce spurs, which contain both wood and fruit buds, fruit buds proper borne on short growths not unlike spurs, and true wood buds, which should be thinned out to two or at the most three on each spur in April; good young shoots at the base of old wood being retained to train in where there is room between the main branches of the fan, as the ends of the main branches tend, as they grow, to diverge from each other. If the laying-in of good young wood is neglected, the tree will obviously become thinner and more sparse as it grows. All side shoots from this young wood should be cut back to four leaves in the summer.

FIG. 55. PRUNING THE APRICOT

Summer-prune all side shoots to four leaves, as at S. When the leaves fall, stop all leading shoots and prune all shoots not needed to fill spaces to two or three buds as at *W*.

In winter-pruning, which should be done when the leaves fall, all leading shoots should be stopped, all shoots not required to fill up vacant places on the wall being cut back to two or three buds. Useless wood should be cut away, young shoots being nailed in to replace them. All shoots which push out forwards from the wall should be removed. Propagate by budding in July or August on St. Julien plum stock.

Varieties.—*Large Early* (July-August); *Shipley's Blenheim* (August); *Moor Park*, *Powell's Late*, and *Royal* (very hardy) (August-Sept.).

Blackberry. *See* Rubus, p. 390, and Raspberries, p. 487. Best varieties, *Parsley-leaved*, *Wilson Junior*, *Himalayan Giant*, and *Merton Thornless*.

Cherry. *Soil and Situation.*—A well-drained, moderately deep loam is necessary for cherries; they do well on soil overlying chalk. They do not thrive on dry, gravelly soils, nor on heavy clay. They like an open situation, facing west or south, though Morellos and Kentish do well on a north or east wall. Protection from birds and from frost in the early spring is desirable. Cherries may either be grown as standards or against walls—trained horizontally—or as bushes or cordons. For planting and manuring, *see* pages 456 and 460.

474

Pruning.—Much cutting causes the tree to "gum", and for this reason, it is best, wherever possible, to form the young tree carefully and then confine all pruning to summer stopping of shoots to five or six leaves, with the finger and thumb. Any further pruning with the knife that is found needful should be done not later than October, when the sap is still in the wood; laterals being shortened to three or four buds. If pruning is done later than this, the tendency to gumming will be greater. Should the tree show an inclination to use up its energy on the formation of luxuriant wood and no fruit buds, it should be lifted and replanted, the check thus given to the root action being usually enough to remedy the bad habit. The cherry easily forms good fruiting spurs, and when the tree has a sufficient number of these to secure a good, but not exhaustive crop, it should be let alone as much as may be.

The cherry is propagated by budding in July or August on stocks selected from *Prunus Avium* (Gean) in the case of sweet cherries, or *Prunus Cerasus*, in the case of acid cherries. The Mahaleb Cherry stock is passing completely out of use.

It must be remembered that most cherries are self-sterile and require the pollen from another variety of cherry to set their fruit; more than one variety must, therefore, always be planted.

(*See also* Fruit in the Greenhouse, p. 493.)

FIG. 56. PRUNING THE CHERRY
The cherry should be summer-pruned to five or six leaves, as at *S*; further pruning should be as light as possible, because of the tendency to "gumming" and should not be done later than October, laterals being shortened to three or four buds, as at *W*.

SOME OF THE BEST CHERRIES

Name	Season		Name	Season
(D) Black Heart . .	July		(C) Kentish Red . .	July
(D) Early Rivers . .	June–July		(D) May Duke . . .	June
(D) Frogmore Early	Early July		(C)* Morello . . .	Aug.–Sept.
Bigarreau . .			(D or C) Royal Duke .	July
(D) Governor Wood . .	Early July			

(C) = Cooking.   (D) = Dessert.   * = Self-fertile.
NOTE.—At least four varieties should be planted together for cross-pollination purposes (*see* page 456).

Chestnut. (*See* Nuts.)
Cobnut. The Cobnut requires the same treatment as the *Filbert* (p. 478).

FIG. 57. PRUNING RED AND WHITE CURRANTS

Early in July young laterals should be pinched back to five or six leaves, in October being cut back to within three buds from the base. "Leaders" should not be summer-pruned and must not be winter-pruned by more than half. Old wood must be cut out periodically.

Currants. *Soil and situation.*—Red and white currants require the same treatment, which differs in several respects from that needed by the black variety. Ordinary deep loam, deeply dug and fairly well manured, and an open, sunny site, answer well for both red and white; but black currants require a cool, moist, rich soil, and a shady situation with plenty of water during the growing season.

Planting.—Currants should be planted 5 feet apart and so that the highest roots shall be but an inch or so below the surface. (*See* Planting, p. 458.)

White currants are not such vigorous growers as the red varieties, they should, therefore, not be planted in between the latter or they will be crowded-out. Each variety should be planted separately. Currant bushes need liberal water in hot dry weather, and a mulch of rotted manure applied in May will do much to keep the roots cool and moist, and will help the fruit. Every branch of newly-planted black currants should be cut hard back to two buds the following March to encourage the growth of vigorous shoots during the following summer and fruit the next year.

Suitable Forms.—For general purposes, the bush or standard form is most useful, but red and white currants also do well when trained as cordons against a wall. For late picking they are particularly useful when planted on a north wall. In forming these bushes, which are best if trained cup-shape, three main shoots are first grown, the second year these are each cut hard back so that two strong shoots will take the place of one, forming six in all. These main shoots must be cut back some 6 to 10 inches each winter, until the bushes are the required size. The subsequent pruning is described below.

Pruning.—Red and white currants fruit on spurs, and consequently, young "lateral" shoots should, early in July, be pinched back to five or six leaves, and then in October be cut back to about three buds from the base.

The "leaders" should not be cut back by more than one half, or the fruitfulness of the bush will be endangered, and care must be taken to cut back close to a good healthy bud. Old wood

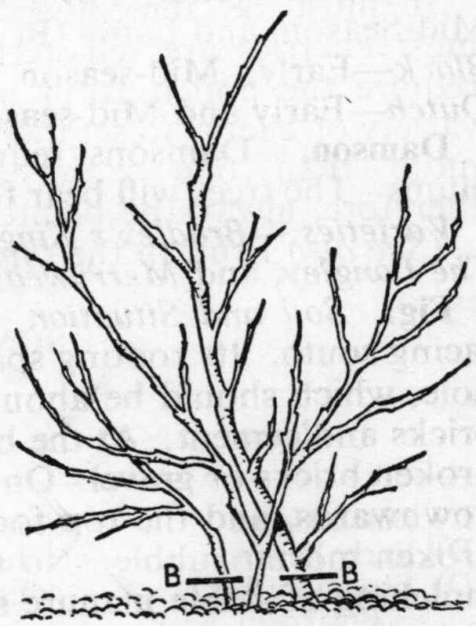

FIG. 58. PRUNING BLACK CURRANTS

Old wood should be cut well away to the base as at *B-B* each year. No summer-pruning should take place, as the young growths are the next year's fruit-bearers.

476

must periodically, though not too frequently, be cut away to permit young shoots to be trained in to take its place.

Summer-pruning must not be too rigorous at one time; a little should be done each day. The "leader" must not be summer-pruned, but must be left intact.

White currants are less vigorous in growth than the red kinds and, therefore, do not require to be pruned quite so severely as the red.

Black currants differ from red and white kinds in that their fruit is borne on one-year-old shoots only. Old wood should, therefore, as far as possible, be cut well back to the base every year, and the more thoroughly this can be done, the more vigorous will be the young growths on which the following year's crop depends. These young growths, which should be encouraged from the base of the bushes, must of course, not be summer-pruned, as advised for the red and white currants, as they are fruit-bearers for the next year. Black currants should not be grown on very light soil, and, like the raspberry, the soil must not be deeply worked between the bushes or the roots will be damaged.

The hoe must, of course, be used continually in order to keep the weeds down and the soil moist. Manure should be applied as described in the table on page 460.

Birds are usually very troublesome when the fruit is ripening, so before this time the bushes should be netted with muslin or other protective netting.

Propagation.—Currants are propagated by cuttings 9 to 12 inches long, taken in October and planted out in the open. Any buds below soil level being removed, except in the case of black currants when these buds must be allowed to remain. The bushes will bear fruit for some fifteen or twenty years.

Varieties.—(RED) *Fay's Prolific, Laxton's No.1,* and *Raby Castle*—Early, Mid-Season, and Late. (BLACK) *Boskoop Giant, Edina,* and *Daniel's September Black*—Early, Mid-season and Late. (WHITE) *White Versailles* and *White Dutch*—Early and Mid-season.

Damson. Damsons require exactly similar treatment to that advised for plums. The trees will bear for about twenty-five years.

Varieties.—*Bradley's King of the Damsons, Farleigh Prolific, Aylesbury Prune, The Langley,* and *Merryweather.*

Fig. *Soil and Situation.*—The fig should have a sheltered and sunny wall facing south. Its rooting space should be somewhat limited. Indeed, the actual hole, which should be about 3 feet deep and 4 feet square, is often walled in by bricks and cement. At the bottom of this hole should be placed about a foot of broken bricks or gravel. On this should be laid about a foot of turves, grass side downwards, and the top foot should consist of a mixture of fibrous loam and broken mortar rubble. No manure must be added at planting time, but a good mulching of stable manure should be given in May, and the borders should be liberally watered every ten days in summer. Fifteen to twenty feet should be allowed between trees.

Pruning.—The fig may be trained against a wall in a fan-shape, as advised for peaches. As many permanent leaders as are required should be fixed to the wall at from 10 to 15 inches apart; all unnecessary wood should be removed by disbudding, and the fruit-bearing shoots must be stopped back to five or six leaves at the end of August or beginning of September, according to the habit of the tree and the nature of the season. This stopping, the object of which is to induce the formation of fruit for the ensuing season, is a matter of much nicety. A too early stopping with most trees will cause a too early development of fruit, the consequence of which will be that it will not stand through the frost of winter. The fruit for next year must not be much larger than a pea when winter sets in. Other pruning is not much required, except so far as is necessary to maintain the shape of the tree, and to prevent overcrowding. The fruits mature principally on one- or two-year-old wood. Old wood should, therefore, be cut out in October where it is possible to train in well-ripened shoots of the previous year's growth. Each year a couple of vigorous young shoots from the base of the tree must be trained up to replace old and worn-out branches. When a tree is not bearing as well as it might be, it should be lifted in October and root-pruned (*see* Root-pruning, p. 467). Figs are propagated from suckers or cuttings of one-year-old wood in October. The trees will bear for thirty to forty years.

(*See also* Fruit in the Greenhouse, p. 493.)

Varieties.—(Early) *Castle Kennedy*. (Mid-season) *Black Ischia, Brown Turkey, Brunswick*, and *White Ischia*. (Late) *Bourjasotte Grise*.

Filbert. *Soil and Situation.*—Filberts are easily grown in well-drained, deeply-dug soil. The filbert, though smaller than the cobnut, has much the better flavour. The cultivation of both is the same. When planting a filbert plantation, a site should be chosen which is sheltered from east and north-east winds. A shrubbery or hedge of evergreens will do this quite satisfactorily. The nuts are best grown in the form of bushes, with a crown of five to six main shoots supported by a sturdy stem some 15 inches high. The main shoots should not be allowed to grow to more than 6 feet in height. The trees should be planted 15 feet apart in October.

Manuring.—A light dressing of organic manure, preferably shoddy or feathers, should be spread round the trees annually, and the soil should be well dug-over each year, preferably in December. To prevent the ground from becoming stale, a dressing of lime should be given triennially.

Pruning.—As soon as the pollen is shed, usually early in March, pruning may be begun. Vigorous side shoots should be cut back to a catkin a few inches above the base, some of the oldest wood being cut out each year. The small, twig-like wood of the previous year's growth must be left in, for this bears the fruit. Wood that has borne fruit the previous year should be cut hard back to two or three buds. All sucker growth must be twisted off from the roots, and the centre of the trees kept well open. Nuts should not be gathered until they are perfectly ripe and brown, late in September. If they are to be stored, they had better hang on the trees until they fall naturally.

Propagation.—This is usually accomplished by layering two-year-old wood in autumn, but grafting is sometimes effected in March.

Varieties.—The *Kentish White* and *Prolific* are among the best Filberts, whilst the *Kentish Cob*, the *Emperor Cob* and the *Cosford Cob* are among the best Cobnuts.

Gooseberry. *Soil and Situation.*—Though the gooseberry will grow on the poorest soil, it will not produce really fine fruit unless planted in a deep, rich, well-drained loam, and treated generously. Fresh air and sun are essential to the gooseberry.

478

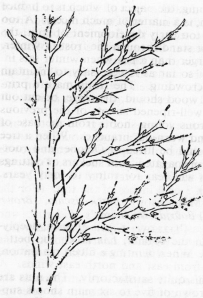

FIG. 59. PRUNING THE GOOSEBERRY
In July all unneeded shoots should be stopped to two or three leaves; in January main shoots should be shortened to seven or eight buds and side shoots to two or three. Old and weak wood must be cut out.

Planting.—Early and late varieties should be planted in separate groups, as they will want netting from the birds at different times. Weak growers must not be planted among varieties of more vigorous growth, or they may be overwhelmed by the latter plants. The bushes should be planted 5 feet apart, the bushes being cut back moderately hard after planting.

Pruning.—Gooseberries bear on the young as well as on the two-year-old wood, generally upon small spurs arising along the sides of the branches. Young growths required to form future laterals should, therefore, be allowed to make their full length. Young shoots not needed should, in July, be pinched back to two or three leaves to form fruit spurs. In winter-pruning gooseberries, for which January is a favourable season, the weaker of the young shoots should be cut out, and the old wood gradually removed so as to keep the tree thin of branches, but those left must be trained to some regular shape, and must never be permitted to grow across each other. They should radiate in a cup-like shape, if trained as bushes

or standards, so as to be 6 or 8 inches apart, leaving the centre of the bush open. The young shoots which are retained should merely have their soft ends cut off, just beyond a bud pointing upwards. Main shoots should be shortened down to seven or eight buds and the side shoots to two or three buds. In the case of many varieties, there is a distinct tendency to a weeping habit, and this should be fought against by pruning back to upward-pointing buds only, as the fruit is liable to become earth-stained.

Every year, liberal top-dressings of manure should be given in winter, and every third or fourth autumn, a dressing of basic slag in the proportion of 5 oz. to every square yard of soil should be applied. See also Manuring Table, page 460.

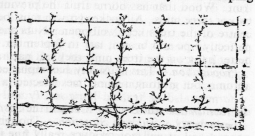

FIG. 60. A GOOSEBERRY TRAINED AS A CORDON
This method provides the branches with ample sun and air, and is very economical of space.

479

Protection from Birds.—If the bushes are dusted over with a mixture half of slaked lime and half soot early in March, the birds will be discouraged from picking off the buds. The best plan for protecting the fruit from birds is to encircle the bush with wire netting, and to cover the top with a piece of string netting, which can be removed when the fruit is to be gathered.

Gathering the Fruit.—A start can usually be made in June. First all the fruit from the centre of the bush should be gathered, then the large fruit on the lower branches; after this the fruit is picked in successive gatherings as it swells and ripens. No thinning is necessary.

Propagation.—Young bushes should be raised from cuttings so as to build up a stock to replace a few of the old trees each year. Cuttings should be struck in spring or autumn. Short-jointed, sturdy shoots of the previous year's growth must be selected, each some 8 to 10 inches long, and not root suckers. To secure a clean stem and prevent the formation of suckers, every bud should be removed with a knife from the base to within 3 or 4 inches of the top. (For the method of striking cuttings, *see* p. 108.)

Varieties.—(RED) *Crown Bob, Lancashire Lad, Whinham's Industry*, and *Lord Derby*—Early, Mid-season and Late. (YELLOW) *Gipsy Queen, Leveller*, and *Yellow Ball*—Early, Mid-season and Late. (GREEN) *Lancer* and *Keepsake*—Mid-season and Late. (WHITE) *Careless* and *White Lion*—Mid-season and Late.

Grape. CULTIVATION IN THE OPEN. *Soil and Situation.*—A situation at the base of a wall facing south, south-east, or south-west should be selected. Manure should not be added unless the soil is very poor, but it is advisable instead to incorporate with the soil a reasonable portion of gravel, wood ashes, old mortar, and rotten refuse.

Planting.—It is well to plant the young vines as single cordons 4 feet apart, about 6 inches distant from the wall and with the roots about 4 inches below the surface, late in October.

Pruning.—The rod should be cut down to within 12 inches of the ground in January, and during the first year only superfluous shoots should be removed, the young shoots intended to remain being allowed to grow to their full length. In the following November, these should be pruned back to two buds, with the exception of the leading shoot, which should be pruned back to about 30 inches from its base. Spurs will result, and the young shoots which grow thereon must, at an early stage, be reduced to one in each instance. Each of these shoots allowed to remain must subsequently be pinched back to two leaves beyond a bunch, if there is one, if not to five or six leaves, and the little shootlets that branch from it must be pinched back just beyond the first leaf, as soon as this appears. The following November, these laterals are cut back to one bud and the main shoot to 50 inches. In successive years the treatment is the same. The vine may also be trained horizontally and then vertically as also advised for culture under glass. The branches must at all times be kept carefully and closely attached to the wall or fence. Muslin bags should be used for protecting the ripened grapes from the attacks of flies and wasps. *See also* p. 494.

Varieties (Out-door).—(BLACK) *Black Cluster.* (WHITE) *Chasselas Dorée, Grove End Sweetwater*, and *Royal Muscadine.*

480

Loganberry. *Planting.*—The loganberry loves a moist, but well-drained, deep, rich loam, and is best planted 5 feet apart in October. It is usually trained fan-wise or as an espalier on a trellis or wire fence.

Pruning.—After the fruits are gathered, the old growths must be cut out right down to the base. Sufficient of the strongest new shoots of the year must be selected to cover the supports. These must be tied up to the supports, not being allowed to straggle over the ground. All weak, useless growths should be cut away. These new shoots must, however, be kept clear of the fruiting canes. As soon as the fruit is gathered, the old branches must be cut out and the new ones tied in to replace them.

Propagation.—The loganberry is best propagated by layering in August. The new plant may be severed from its parent and transplanted in November to its fruiting position. The loganberry may also be increased by division of roots in October. The plants will bear fruit for ten to fifteen years.

Medlar. *Soil and Situation.*—The medlar is easily grown in any good, well-drained, but retentive soil. It requires an open situation where it is protected from cold winds, and should be planted with 10 feet between the trees.

Cultivation.—The cultivation of the medlar, so far as pruning is concerned, is almost identical with that advised for the apple. The fruits should be gathered about the middle of November, and should be stored in a single layer, "eye" downwards, on some dry silver sand. It is usually

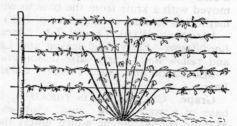

FIG. 61. TRAINING THE LOGANBERRY
The loganberry is usually trained fan-wise on a trellis or wire fence. It may also be trained up fir-poles in the same way as rambler roses and will reach a height of 10–12 feet.

necessary to store the medlars for at least a fortnight before they are ripe for eating.

Varieties.—*Nottingham* and *Royal.*

Mulberry. *Soil.*—The mulberry tree should be planted in October, 25 to 30 feet from tree to tree, in deep, well-drained, and moist loam. In the south it can be grown in the open as a bush or standard, but in northern districts it should be grown on a warm south wall.

The mulberry is easily propagated by cuttings or layers which root readily in October. It may also be increased by budding in August on a white mulberry stock.

Nectarine. (*See* Peaches and Nectarines, page 482.)

Nuts. The principal nuts cultivated in England for their fruit are: the Walnut, the Cob, the Filbert, and the Sweet Chestnut. The last, however, is grown primarily as an ornamental tree, *see* Castanea, p. 287. For Walnut, *see* Juglans, p. 342.

Little pruning is necessary, only sufficient to keep the trees in shape, and this is best done before the leaves fall. (*See also* the Filbert, p. 478.)

Peaches and Nectarines. *Soil and Situation.*—In the South of England, both peaches and nectarines may be grown in the open in sheltered situations against walls or fences facing south, south-east, or south-west, where ample protection from spring frosts can be given by means of blinds or a double thickness of fish netting.

The blinds or netting should be raised each morning, except when the weather is very severe, to allow the bees to approach and pollinate the blossom. They like best a calcareous, well-drained soil somewhat on the heavy side and previously well manured. When grown against a wall, they should be planted in autumn, about 4 inches from the wall at a sufficient depth for all the roots to be covered with at least 6 inches and not more than 9 inches of soil. Not less than 18 feet width of wall space should be allowed to each tree. The fan-shape is the most satisfactory for both these trees.

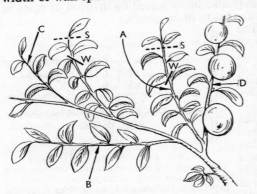

FIG. 62. PRUNING PEACHES AND NECTARINES
Laterals should be summer-pruned to nine or ten leaves as at *S*, and winter-pruned to seven or eight buds, as at *W*. Over-vigorous laterals, such as *B*, and extension shoots, as *C*, are neither summer- nor winter-pruned. *D* shows a previous year's shoot in fruit; shoot *A* has been allowed to grow from the base to replace it when cut away after fruiting.

Pruning and Disbudding.—The peach and nectarine are so closely related that the one description will cover the pruning of them both. Because they bear their fruit mainly on the young wood of the previous year, the beginner will often be confronted with the problem of how to remove a sufficient quantity of the old wood after the year's crop, while at the same time leaving enough of it to bear the young shoots for next year, as it does this mostly at the ends of the fruiting shoots.

The novice is apt to err on the side of leniency, and consequently his tree, after four or five years, will be found nearly barren, except at the extreme end of its branches. This may be prevented by the simple method of leaving, when the established shoot is disbudded as the spring growth starts, a good wood bud at the base of the shoot as well as one at the top, for this bud at the base will have to replace the fruit-bearing branch when the latter is cut away in the following winter. Should this shoot grow to more than 2 feet in length during the summer, its top must be pinched out. This shortening will probably cause the formation of sub-laterals, which must again be pinched back to one leaf. It is well to leave an "extension" bud at the upper end of the shoot, as it serves a useful purpose in helping to draw up the sap, and thus ensures a full supply of nourishment to the fruit buds on the intermediate part of the branch, but the top bud must be pinched back if it begins to extend too far—that is, shortened back to five or six leaves—and should be cut off with the old wood after fruiting and the lower one left to make the new wood. Buds must, of course, be left on where there

482

are gaps to be filled, and as far as possible, new shoots from the top of the old wood should be trained in to fill these spaces. The cutting out of the old wood may be done at any time after the fruit is removed.

This "disbudding" should be performed gradually, but vigorously; quite five out of every six young shoots will need to be removed. The work should be begun in April, before the buds are an inch long, and should extend over a month. All wood buds which push forward from the wall should be rubbed out, and with them all those which obviously will not easily be made to fill a convenient space in the tree. As soon as the young shoots are long enough to handle, they should be placed in position, some 4 inches apart, and secured. A tree which makes much wood and bears little fruit should not be disbudded too severely. If a good deal of strong young wood is laid in, the tree will soon cease to produce wood buds as freely as before, and a good crop will result. On the other hand, a weakly tree should be sternly dealt with. As soon as the fruit is set, the ground should be well watered, and liquid manure may, with advantage, be given.

Thinning.—The fruit should be exposed to as much air and sunshine as possible; this is done by tying back the foliage that shades it. It is best to thin out the fruit as soon as it is the size of a filbert, starting with the smallest and most crowded on the underside of the branch, and removing a few at intervals of a week or so. A final thinning should be given as soon as the fruit has stoned, so as to leave two peaches to every square foot of wall space, that is, about one fruit on every year-old shoot.

Propagation.—Peaches and nectarines are propagated by budding on an almond or plum stock in July.

(*See also* Fruit in the Greenhouse, p. 498.)

Varieties.—PEACHES.—(Early) *Amsden June*, *Waterloo*, *Royal George*, *Crimson Galande*, and * *Hales's Early*. (Late) *Barrington*, *Golden Eagle*, and *Sea Eagle*.

NECTARINES.—*Early Rivers*, *Elruge*, *Lord Napier*, *Pineapple*, and *Victoria*.

Pear. *Soil and Situation.*—The best soil for the pear is a sandy, slightly clayey loam with a clay sub-soil. The least suitable are light soils over gravel or chalk and cold, damp clays. (*See* Manuring Table, p. 460.) It is useless to plant in a north aspect, even as espaliers or fan-shaped trees against a wall. Shelter is, of course, required on the east and north. In the case of trees grown against walls, protection from frost may be afforded by hanging netting about 9 inches from the wall. Abundance of warmth and sunshine is essential.

Propagation.—The pear is propagated by budding in July and August, and by grafting in March and April on a suitable Quince stock.

Planting.—See p. 458.

Summer-pruning.—Pears should be kept to their regular number of well-spreading branches, each branch kept thin like a cordon, with the side-shoots, which must not be less than 8 inches apart, shortened in July to five or six leaves. This summer-pruning must start from the top of the tree and should be carried out gradually, at intervals of two or three days, until the shoots at the bottom of the tree are finally pinched back. Do not stop-back the leading shoots. The

---

* Denotes those kinds which will grow on a south wall in the open.

Jargonelle pear and one or two other varieties fruit on the tips of the young shoots and not on spurs. Such varieties should be carefully summer-pruned; only shoots in the crowded centre of the tree being "stopped". Well-placed young shoots should be encouraged to grow and thus form vigorous branchlets to bear fruit the following season.

Winter-pruning, which is carried out in the early spring, consists in cutting the side-shoots back to two or three buds, always cutting back to an outward-pointing bud to preserve a good shape in the tree. All dead wood and any branches growing across other wood must be cut away, and where the fruit spurs are too numerous for the tree to mature all the crop, or where the fruit is too crowded, some of the spurs should be cut right out. Where spurs have aged and become weak, they should also be cut clean away, as fresh ones will spring from their bases. Where the pear is grown as a pyramid or as a trained tree, it will require lifting every two or three years to check rampant growth, or the tree will run to wood. As with apples, standard-trained pears must not be so severely pruned as fruit grown in the cordon, espalier, or bush form. The fruit buds of the pear are smaller than those of the apple, while its wood buds are smaller still, and darker in colour.

Rootstocks for Pears.—Pears are propagated by budding or, in some cases, by grafting on to a suitable type of Quince stock. The Quince is a close relative to the pear and although it is a weaker growing stock it enables the Pear to crop much earlier than if it were on a Pear stock. It has been found after careful research that at present there are three types of rootstocks suitable for Pears.

FIG. 63. PRUNING THE PEAR

Side-shoots should be shortened in July to five or six leaves, as at *S*; leaders must not be stopped back. In spring side-shoots must be cut back to two or three buds, as at *W*. Standards must not be severely pruned.

(1) Quince "A". For general purposes this rootstock has been found to be very good for bush and smaller trees.

(2) Quince "B". This stock is very similar to No. 1 both in vigour and cropping.

(3) Quince "C". Pears which are on this stock crop very heavily, at a very early age and it is therefore to be recommended for heavy cropping varieties, cordons, espaliers and trees for the small garden.

PLATE 57 Watering and mulching a fruit tree. *Top left*, hollow out a shallow bowl at foot of tree ; *top right*, fill with water, *bottom left*, fill in hollow and *bottom right*, mulch with manure.

PLATE 58 *Above*, Cox's Orange Pippin pruned and trained as a fan tree and *below*, the same variety of tree pruned and trained as single oblique cordons.

H.

East Malling Research S

Thinning.—Each fruit should have ample room to develop. Varieties bearing large fruit naturally need thinning more drastically than the smaller fruiting kinds, which may be allowed to carry two or even three pears on each spur. *See also* Thinning, p. 469.

Gathering and Storing.—The fruit of the early kinds should be gathered before it easily separates from the tree, when gently raised on a level with the stalk, which means that it is ripe. Early fruit should then be laid out singly and allowed to ripen for a few days, being eaten at once, as few of the early varieties will keep. Choice fruit should be protected whilst still growing on the tree from the attacks of birds and wasps by means of thin muslin bags. (*See* Storing, p. 470). Late dessert pears, especially, need care, and should be allowed to hang on the trees until the middle of November and then must be stored as already directed. Most of the fruit, however, should be gathered before the beginning of November.

Many varieties of pear are self-sterile, and, therefore, require trees of other varieties in the same garden or orchard (*see* p. 456).

SOME OF THE BEST PEARS

Dessert

Name	Season	Name	Season
(I)* Beurré Diel . . .	Oct.	(S) Easter Beurré . .	Jan.–Feb.
(I) Beurré Superfin . .	Oct.	(S) Emile d'Heyst . .	Oct.–Nov.
(I) Bon Chrétien	Sept.	(S) Glou Morceau . .	Dec.–Jan.
(William's)		(I) Jargonelle . .	Aug.
(I) Clapp's Favourite . .	Aug.–Sept.	(S)* Josephine de Malines .	Dec.–Jan.
(I)* Conference . . .	Oct.–Nov.	(I) Laxton's Superb. .	Aug.
(I) Danas Hovey . .	Oct.–Nov.	(S) Louise Bonne of Jersey	Oct.
(I)* Doyenne d'Eté . .	July–Aug.	(S) Pitmaston Duchess .	Oct.–Nov.
(I)* Durondeau . . .	Oct.–Nov.	(I) Souvenir de Congres .	Aug.
(I) Doyenne du Comice .	Oct.–Nov.	(S) Winter Nelis. . .	Nov.–Jan.

Stewing

Name	Season	Name	Season
(S) Bellissimo d'Hiver. .	Nov.–March	(S) General Todleben .	Nov.–Jan.
(I) Beurré Clairgeau . .	Nov.–Dec.	(S) Uvedalis St. Germain .	Jan.–May
(S) Catillac	Dec.–May	(S) Verulam . . .	Jan.–March
		(I) Vicar of Winkfield .	Nov.–Jan.

(S) = Storing.   (I) = Immediate Use.   * = Self-fertile (*see* page 456).

NOTE.—There is no better way of growing any pear than as a cordon, except in the case of the Jargonelle. Pears also grow exceptionally as espaliers.

Plum. *Soil and Situation.*—The plum likes best a fairly deep, well-drained loam, providing it contains lime or chalk in some form or another. It does not thrive in sandy or gravelly soils, though by heavy manuring (*see* table, p. 460) and the addition of a quarter of a bushel of lime for each tree much may be done even with these. Undrained soil in which stagnant water remains and low-lying sites suit plums no better than pears or apples. At any rate, for the dessert varieties, a southern aspect is necessary, but for cooking kinds a north or north-east aspect will often serve.

Shelter should be afforded from the east and north, and the shade of buildings or trees must be avoided. Plums are grown, apart from on walls, as standards, pyramids and bushes.

Planting.—In any case, they should be planted in October or February, and not too deep. In the first nine or ten years, the plum is apt to make too much woody growth. This can be got over by growing the plums in the form of bushes or pyramids.

In this form, they may be lifted, root-pruned, and replanted every third or fourth year, during the first dozen years, to ensure adequate fruit-spurs.

Mulching, manuring, watering, and thinning are as necessary in the case of plums as in the case of other fruit trees. As many plums are self-sterile, more than one variety blooming at about the same time should always be planted in the garden or orchard.

Pruning.—The plum fruits on spurs and on the previous year's wood. It has the habit of producing an intermediate kind of shoot, neither quite a shoot nor quite a spur, which is generally called a "stub". The shoots proper, those which extend from the framework of the tree, usually bear no fruit buds, and are found in great quantity on young trees. The pruner should select from among them those which he needs to form his tree. Where this is already well shaped and filled, the shoots may be left untouched, as they will then merely lengthen, but where the tree is thin and "unfurnished", the tips of some few selected ones should be cut back, that they may break sideways and fill the vacant places. The useful growths in a plum tree are the "stubs" which do not make long wood. A tree which produces these in number is a good bearer, and they should be touched as little as possible. With standards, pyramids, and bushes, once the tree is properly formed, all buds not wanted for training in to replace old wood should be rubbed off in spring. In July all useless side-shoots should be stopped back, and in winter the "stubs" should be pruned back to two or three buds. All old, broken, and diseased wood must be cut out, the mere process of keeping the tree open usually secures a good supply of healthy ripened wood, and this will produce fruit-bearing spurs spontaneously. Wall-trained fruit has a tendency to make vigorous growth towards its top and for the base of the trees to become bare. During July and August, the side shoots of these wall-trained trees should be stopped to six to eight leaves to encourage the formation of fruit spurs, and should again be cut back to two or three buds in winter, at which time the main shoots should be shortened a little each year until the trees have covered the wall, the lower branches being trained well downwards. Plums require thinning, and a start is usually made in June or early July. (*See* Thinning, p. 469.)

486

Propagation.—Plums are propagated by grafting in March and by budding in July on the St. Julien, *Brompton, Damas C., Myrobalan B.*, the Mussel, or the Common Plum stock, according to variety.

The plum will bear well for twenty to twenty-five years.

Varieties.—(COOKING) *Belle de Louvain* and **Monarch*. (DESSERT) *Coe's Golden Drop*, **Early Transparent Gage*, *Greengage*, and *River's Early Prolific.* (COOKING AND DESSERT) **Czar*, **Pond's Seedling* and **Victoria.*

Quince. *Soil and Situation.*—The quince requires a somewhat moist, deep soil of moderate richness, and enjoys an open situation. Although it does well in our southern counties, in the more northern parts it seldom ripens its fruit. (*See* Manuring Fruit Table in the previous chapter, p. 460.)

Pruning.—The quince and the pear are very closely related, and they require much the same kind of pruning. The quince should be judiciously thinned as to the main branches, and should have unproductive or straggling wood cut out. This is best done in early autumn.

The quince may easily be propagated by means of layers, cuttings, or suckers in October.

Gathering and Storing.—The fruit of the quince should not be gathered until the end of October, unless the autumn is unusually frosty. When gathered, they should be stored by themselves (they will affect the flavour of other fruit) in a cool, frost-proof place on layers of straw on a shelf, until they have turned yellow. They are then fit for use. Here they will keep for from two to three months. (*See also* Gathering and Storing, p. 470.)

Varieties.—The three existing varieties of quince are known as the "*Apple-shaped*", the "*Pear-shaped*", and the "*Portugal*".

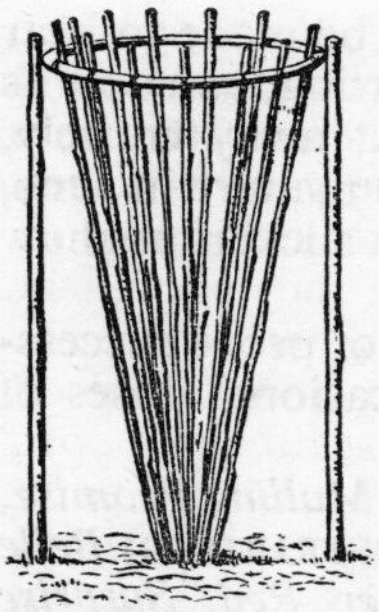

FIG. 64. SUPPORT-ING A RASPBERRY CLUMP

Alternatively to planting in rows, raspberries are often planted in clumps of three roots, each clump being set 3 to 4 feet apart.

Raspberries.—*Soil and Situation.*—Raspberries do best in partial shade and in rather damp, but well-drained, soil. Early in the autumn this soil should be dug to a depth of 2 to 2½ feet, and a liberal dressing of manure (preferably cow or pig dung) should be incorporated with it. (*See* Manuring Table for Fruit Trees, p. 460.)

Planting.—The canes, which should be young ones, are best planted in November, though when this has been impossible, they may be planted in February.

The canes should be planted singly, 2 feet apart, in rows 5 feet from one another. The top roots should be but an inch below the surface.

It is usually well to cut down the canes in March to about 10 inches from the soil. In the following year new rods will be produced from the base, and these will bear raspberries the year after.

Alternatively to planting in rows as described above, raspberries are often planted in clumps of three roots, each clump being set 3 to 4 feet apart, and the canes are supported as shown in our diagram (Fig. 64). This method is usually favoured in small gardens.

* Denotes self-fertile varieties.

487

Pruning.—In June, the bushes should be gone over, all suckers being removed, except about six of the strongest. It is only on the one-year-old shoots that fruit is borne, so that in autumn all old canes that have borne fruit should at once be cut down to the ground, and burned. All weak young shoots should be cut out at the same time, about four of the strongest being left to bear fruit the following season. The only other pruning that is required consists in cutting off the sappy curved tops of the young mature canes in March to encourage the formation of laterals on which the berries are borne. The ground in which raspberries are grown should not be broken up, as the roots remain near the surface, but a liberal dressing of manure should be given as a mulch early in the spring and again in June. If the weather is hot while the fruit is swelling, the canes should be watered liberally and the hoe used constantly. The autumn varieties should have their canes cut down to about 4 inches from the ground in February.

Supporting the Canes.—Raspberries need some form of support, the simplest and most useful consisting of three wires strained horizontally at heights of about 2 feet, 3½ feet, and 5 feet from the ground. To these wires the canes should be tied in autumn, some 9 inches apart from each other. The canes should not be tied up during the summer, as they ripen better if left untied.

Raspberries are propagated by division of roots in October. The canes will bear well for from seven to fourteen years. Care should be taken to plant only strong healthy stocks obtained through a reliable source. Some varieties of raspberries can become badly infected with diseases particularly one known as Virus which soon causes the plants to be stunted and weak and so produce a poor crop. Some varieties are more resistant to the disease than others, notably *Norfolk Giant*.

An Autumn Crop.—By a little management, raspberries may be made to bear a crop of fruit during September and October. For late bearing, as soon as suckers show themselves in June, the old canes should be cut away entirely, so as to prevent summer fruiting; and by a mulch of well-rotted manure in June, encouragement should be given during July and August to such suckers as show blossom-buds, for these will bear fruit in autumn.

Autumn-bearing raspberries must be kept thin or they will not prove successful. Water should be given liberally in dry weather and occasional doses of liquid manure applied.

Varieties.—(SUMMER-FRUITING) *Hornet, Laxton's Bountiful, Malling Promise, Norfolk Giant, St. Walfried, Newburgh, Pynes Royal.* (AUTUMN-FRUITING) *Belle of Fontenaye, Hailsham Berry, November Abundance, October Red, Surprise d'Automne,* and *Laxton's Autumn Giant.*

Strawberries. *Soil and Situation.*—Strawberries do best in a deeply-dug, well-drained loam which has been well dressed with manure some two or three months previously to planting. (*See* Manuring Fruit, p. 460.) In many gardens, the strawberry crop is all too soon over. By using early and late varieties and by planting in borders with different aspects, strawberries may be had in fruit for quite a long time. Those in the south border will be ready early in June; those in a bed facing north will form the late crop. An open, sunny position is essential.

Planting.—Planting should take place during the latter half of September; late planting will give the strawberry little chance of becoming established before the winter sets in, and results in small and scanty fruit. Just previously to planting, the soil should be well watered and made firm. Planting must be carried out so that the crown is left just above the surface of the soil. The plants should be watered in their pots before planting, and water should be liberally given for a few days if the weather is dry. (*See* Planting, p. 458.) Every October, a liberal top-dressing of manure should be given between the rows, being forked-in early in March. In May, before the flowers open, the ground between the plants should be well hoed, dusted with soot, or nitrate of soda at the rate of 1 oz. to the square yard, and should then be covered with fairly short straw to keep the fruit from being splashed with mud. If late frosts are severe, the straw may be pulled up over the bloom to protect it. About 18 inches should be allowed from plant to plant, and 2 feet to 2 feet 6 inches between the rows. After the fruit has been gathered, the straw should be removed, also the oldest of the leaves, and all the runners except those required for layering. The surface of the soil must also be loosened gently. For Forcing, *see* p. 252.

Propagation.—As a rule, strawberries crop best in their first season in the beds and deteriorate very much, in size, if not in quantity, after their second or third year. About a third of the bed should, therefore, be laid down, on a fresh site, with fresh runners each year, so that no plants shall become more than three years old. The usual and the best method of propagation is by layering early in July. Early and vigorous runners with good compact centres from one-year-old, heavy-fruiting plants should be selected. (*See* Layering, p. 113.) It is best to peg the layers down early in July into 3 to 3¾-inch pots rather than into the ground. These potted layers should be transplanted into their permanent positions in August or September, and they should then bear an abundance of fruit next year and furnish new layers as well. It is essential where possible to propagate from clean healthy plants free from disease.

Autumn-bearing Strawberries.—The *St. Fiacre* is large-fruited and of fine flavour, and is one of the best varieties of this kind of strawberry, which, if well-manured late in June, bears in summer in the ordinary way, and again in September.

Alpine Strawberries also produce fruit in the autumn. They are usually planted some 10 inches apart in March as edgings to borders. Cultivation is similar to that of ordinary strawberries. Three of the best varieties are the *Bergère* (red), *Baron Solemacher* and the *Improved White*.

See also Fruit in the Greenhouse, p. 499.

Varieties.—(EARLY) *The Duke, King George V*, and *Royal Sovereign*. (MID-SEASON) *British Queen, Huxley Giant (Brenda Gautrey), President*, and *Veitch's Perfection*. (LATE) *Dr. Hogg, Auchincrieve Climax, Latest of All*, *Sir Joseph Paxton*, and *Tardive de Leopold*.

Vines. (*See* Grape).

* Denotes varieties suitable for heavy soil.

FRUIT-GROWING AT A GLANCE

Fruit	Form of Tree	Distance between Rows	Distance between Trees	Most Suitable Aspect	Best Soil	When to Plant	When to Prune	Time and Method of Propagation	When Ripe
Apple	Cordon (Vertical) Bush Half-Standard Standard Pyramid or Espalier	— 8 ft. 20 ft. 25 ft. 10 ft.	2 ft. 15 ft. 20 ft. 25 ft. 10 ft.	Any; open best	Medium, Moist Loam on Stiff Sub-soil; Sandy Loam	Oct. and Nov. Feb. and March	Winter-pruning March, Newly-planted; Dec. and Jan. Established; Summer-pruning July and Aug.	Budding, July; Grafting, March and April	July–May
Apricot	Pyramid in Houses; Fan on Wall	15 ft.		East by South to West	Good Loam	Oct.–Feb.	Winter-pruning, October; Summer-pruning, May	Budding, July and Aug.	June–Sept.
Blackberry	Espalier	4 ft.	10 ft.	Any	Any Soil	Oct.–Feb.	After Fruit is Gathered	Cuttings or Layers, March	Sept.–Oct.
Cherry	Standard Pyramid or Bush Cordon (Vertical) Fan on Wall or Espalier	30–40 ft. 10–12 ft. — —	30–40 ft. 10–12 ft. 2 ft. 15 ft	East, South and West	Light, Sandy Loam Chalky Soil	Oct.–Feb.	Winter-pruning, Sept.–Oct.; Summer-pruning, May–July	Budding, July and Aug.; Grafting, March	June–Sept.
Currant	Standard Bush Cordon (Single) Cordon (Double) Cordon (Treble)	6 ft. 5 ft. — — —	8 ft. 6 ft. 2 ft. 3 ft. 4 ft.	Any	Red and White, Good Loam; Black, Cool, Moist and Rich	Oct. or Nov.	Winter-pruning, Sept.–Oct.; Summer-pruning, July	Cuttings, Oct. (Open)	July–Sept.
Damson	Espalier Standard or Half—Standard	20–25 ft.	9 ft. 20–25 ft.	Any	Strong Loam	Oct.–Feb.	Winter-pruning Early Spring; Summer-pruning, July–Aug.	Budding, July Grafting, March	Aug.–Oct.
Fig	Fan on Wall	—	15–20 ft.	South or South-West	Well-drained, Fibrous Loam and Broken Rubble	Oct. to Feb.	Winter-pruning, Oct.; Summer-pruning Aug.–Sept.	Suckers or Cuttings, Oct.	July–Sept.
Gooseberry	Standard Bush Cordon (Single) Cordon (Double) Cordon (Treble) Espalier In House	6 ft. 5 ft. — — — —	8 ft. 6 ft. 2 ft. 3 ft. 4 ft. 9 ft. if Grown as Single Stem	Any	Medium Loam	Oct. and Nov.	Winter-pruning, Jan.; Summer-pruning, July	Cuttings, Oct. or March (Open)	May–Sept.
Grape	In House	—	3–4 ft.		Fibrous Loam, Wood Ashes, Lime Rubble, Charcoal and a little Soot. Also Crushed Bone, see page 494	Oct. to Feb.	Winter-pruning, Dec.; Summer-pruning, June	Eyes, Jan. (see p. 497)	April–June (heat from Nov.); July–Dec. (heat from March)

FRUIT-GROWING AT A GLANCE—continued

Fruit	Form of Tree	Distance between Rows	Distance between Trees	Most Suitable Aspect	Best Soil	When to Plant	When to Prune	Time and Method of Propagation	When Ripe
Loganberry Medlar	Espalier Standard	4 ft. 10 ft.	10 ft. 10 ft.	Any Any	Any Soil Any Good Soil; Deep-dug and Well-drained	Oct.–Feb. Oct. to Feb.	After fruiting Winter-pruning, Early Spring; Summer-pruning, July	Cuttings or Layers Grafting, March-April	Sept. Oct.–Jan.
Nectarine.	Fan on Wall Cordon on Wall	— —	15 ft. 2 ft.	East to South-West	Open, Deep Calcareous, not too Moist	Oct.–Nov.	Winter-pruning, Autumn; Summer-pruning, April–May	Budding, July	May–Sept. (glass); July–Sept. (open), according to Variety
Peach	Fan on Wall Cordon on Wall	— —	15 ft. 2 ft.	East to South-West	Open, Deep Calcareous, not too Moist	Oct.–Nov.	Winter-pruning, Autumn; Summer-pruning, April–May	Budding, July	May–Sept. (glass); July–Sept. (open), according to Variety
Pear .	Cordon (Vertical) Bush Standard Pyramid Espalier or Fan	8–12 ft. 20–30 ft. 12–18 ft.	2 ft. 8–12 ft. 20–30 ft. 12–18 ft. 15 ft.	Any; East and West for Wall Trees	Deep Loam on Clay Sub-soil	Oct.–Feb.	Winter-pruning, Early Spring; Summer-pruning, July	Budding, July and Aug.; Grafting, March and April	July–March according to Variety
Plum .	Espalier Fan Bush Standard Pyramid (*see* Bush)	10–15 ft. 25–30 ft.	20 ft. 20 ft. 10–15 ft. 25–30 ft.	Any; South or West for Wall Trees	Strong, Well-drained Loam, not too Deep, containing Lime and Chalk	Oct.–Feb.	Winter-pruning, Early Spring; Summer-pruning, July–Aug.	Budding, July; Grafting, March	Aug.–Oct., according to Variety
Quince	Cordon Standard Pyramid	20–30 ft. 8–12 ft.	2 ft. 20–30 ft. 8–12 ft.	Any	Moist, Deep Medium Loam	Oct.–Feb.	Winter-pruning, Early Spring; Summer-pruning, July	Cuttings or Layers, Oct.	Sept.–Oct.
Raspberry	Canes Clumps of Three	5 ft. 6 ft.	2 ft. 4 ft. between Clumps	Any	Deep, Rich, Moist Loam	Oct.–Feb.	Winter-pruning, Oct.; Summer-pruning, June	Division, Oct.	June–Sept.
Strawberry	—	2½ ft.	1–2 ft.	South or South-West	Deep, Rich, Well-drained Loam	Aug.	Not needed	Runners, July	June–Sept.

491

CHAPTER 41

FRUIT IN THE GREENHOUSE

Fruit may be grown under glass, either planted in borders or in pots, in lean-to or span-roofed houses, the latter being the more suitable form of house for fruit-culture in pots.

The Border

The border may be entirely in the house, all outside, or half in and half out. For early forcing, however, the whole border should be entirely under glass.

Instructions for preparing the borders and composts to suit the various trees will be found in the following paragraphs on the cultivation of each species.

Training

Strong galvanized wire should be stretched along the roof, some 18 inches to 2 feet from the glass; it must not be closer or the foliage will be scorched by the sun. The wires must be about 9 inches apart; and on these the trees will be trained.

Fruit Growing in Pots

Under certain conditions, it may be advisable to grow the trees in pots, placing them in the open for a part of the year, and bringing them into the fruit house in succession as they require shelter and warmth. The trees selected for this purpose should preferably have been grown in pots from the time they were first budded or grafted, should be three or four years old, and must have a good show of fruit buds. The compost should be prepared in September, and have a clear month in the open, under cover, to amalgamate. It should be composed of a barrow-load of leaf-mould, one of coarse sand, one of old mortar rubbish, one of rotted dung, and five of yellow loam. This is further enriched by the addition of two gallons of bonemeal, and another gallon or so of some good fertilizer or vine manure. A bushel of quarter-inch bones is also mixed in the compost. Every year, in about the middle of October, when the leaves commence to drop, the trees should be repotted. They should be taken out of their pots while the soil is fairly dry, so that their roots may be easily freed from it. (*See* chapter on Potting.)

492

Scase

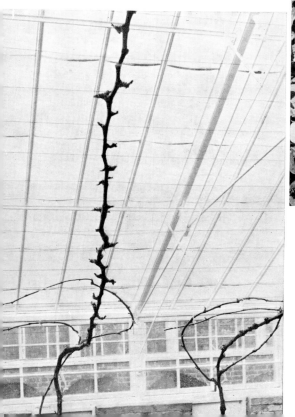

PLATE 59

GREENHOUSE FRUITS

Below, a good crop of peaches from a tree fan-trained on wire to a wall exposed to long periods of sunshine.

Above left, an unpruned vine in a steam-heated greenhouse. *Below left*, the same vine after pruning.

Mustograph

PLATE 60 Gooseberries growing as vertical or upright cordons.

Wintering in the Open

The trees, when potted, should be watered well and plunged to the rims of the pots in ashes in the open, the pots being covered with a layer of litter 6 to 10 inches in depth to exclude the frost. This should be done not later than the first week in November, and if possible earlier by a fortnight. They will then require little further care or attention until February, when they are moved into the house, except that in January they will need looking over, and the pruning of the pears and plums should be completed.

Before bringing in the trees, at the end of January, the orchard-house should be thoroughly cleaned, and the brickwork limewashed.

Instead of repeating our remarks on heating, ventilation, and the general management of the greenhouse, we refer the reader to the chapter dealing with the greenhouse, and to the details as to the temperature, ventilation, and cultural requirements of each fruit given in the following pages.

Apples—Pears—Plums. Apples, pears and plums need no artificial heat and may all be successfully grown in the cold greenhouse. Cultural details are here unnecessary and the reader is referred to the chapter on *Potting* and to the separate articles describing the culture of these fruits in the open, pp. 471, 483 and 486.

Cherries. *Soil.*—This fruit thrives best in a compost of two-thirds loam and one-third old mortar rubble, wood ashes, bone-meal, and charcoal. For Potting, *see* Chapter 12.

Temperatures.—Only slight heat should be applied and that very gradually. Until the flowers open, the thermometer should not be allowed to drop below 40° F. at night, but it must not rise above 50° to 55° F. by day. Once the fruit has set, the temperature may be allowed to rise to between 45° and 50° F. by night and 55° and 60° F. by day.

Pollination.—When the flowers are out, dust them over daily about noon, when the air is driest, with a rabbit's tail to ensure good pollination; this is an important point. While the fruit is setting, syringe the trees twice daily in fine weather, and keep a good look out for insect pests. As soon as the fruit has set, the trees may be assisted by the application of dilute liquid farmyard manure or soot water. This may be varied by guano or a compound fruit manure. When applying manure, it is important not to use it when the soil is dry. If dry, the plants should be first watered with clear water; this applies to all plants, especially to pot grown subjects.

Pruning.—*See* p. 461. *See also article on* the Cherry, p. 474.

Cucumbers. (*See* The Culture of Salads, p. 447.)

Figs. In the case of the fig, the first crop is borne on the shoots of the previous year, the second on the growth of the current year, and the third on the sub-laterals from the shoots made that season. The third crop, however, is rarely of any value and, to avoid weakening the tree, should be picked off as soon as it forms. Artificial heat will only be necessary when fruit is required before August.

Where no artificial heat is used, full advantage should be taken of the sun's heat, and the house should be closed early in the afternoon. When plants are started in January and plunged in a hot-bed with a temperature of about 75° F., and are given an air temperature of 60° to 65° F. by day and 50° to 55° F. by night, increasing gradually to some 10° above this, the fruit should be ready in June. The second crop in August.

Compost and Planting.—As the roots should be confined, small pots should be used (*see* Potting, p. 127.) For suitable compost and for border-planting details, *see* p. 477. February is the best time for planting. Until the plants break into active growth but little moisture is required, but once moving, ample moisture must never be lacking, even in winter, or the fruit will shrivel and drop. During the ripening period, the water must be somewhat withheld or the fruit may crack. If this happens, ventilation should be more freely given and the floor sprinkled instead of the foliage being syringed.

Where artificial heat is used, the leaves should be freely syringed twice a day to keep the atmosphere moist, and the house should be shut early in the afternoon to ensure a high night temperature.

Pruning.—To avoid overcrowding, all unnecessary growth must be removed as early as possible, and as soon as the fruit has set the shoots should be pinched back to five or six leaves. At the winter-pruning, it will only be necessary to cut out old and useless wood. This pinching back, in summer, is very necessary in the case of the fig, as if this is not done, the extension grows very fast and diverts the nourishment from the young fruit, which is then very liable to turn yellow and drop.

Thinning.—As soon as the fruits are the size of a pea, they should be thinned out so that, on an average, not more than three remain on each shoot. Once the fruit commences to ripen, syringing should be discontinued and more ventilation given.

See also Fig Culture in the Open, p. 477.

Grapes. *Soil.*—The grape vine should be planted in a border in the house, and this should be dug out to a depth of from 2½ to 3 feet, and should, where space is available, be about 10 feet wide. The bottom of the border should be concreted, with a slight fall to the front. On the top of this should be placed 6 to 9 inches of draining material, consisting of broken bricks, clinkers, etc. On this base should be laid a mixture of two-thirds fibrous loam with one-third wood ashes, lime rubble, charcoal, and a little soot. A hundredweight of crushed bones may be added for each load of loam. On the broken bricks and other drainage, turves a couple of inches thick should be laid, grassy side down, and on this the mixed soil should be placed.

Planting.—The vines are best planted 3 to 4 feet apart, if grown as single stems, 1½ to 2 feet from the front wall, and about 1 inch deeper in the soil than the old planting mark. The surface of the ground should be covered with about 3 inches of short manure as soon as planting has taken place. A good time to plant indoors is early in January, when the canes should be cut back to about 18 inches long. As vines for planting are usually purchased in pots, they should, before planting, be washed free of all soil. This allows the roots to be spread out evenly.

494

Training, Pruning and Disbudding.—During the first year, the main shoot only should be allowed to grow to its full length, other shoots must be removed. When the vines have shed their leaves, the leading shoot should be cut back to about 2 feet from the start of the current year's growth. Each year the same treatment should be carried out, except that after the first year of growth, side-shoots are allowed to form on the wood that has been cut back the previous winter; these laterals are pruned to one bud from the base to form spurs. When the main shoot is sufficiently strong and has reached the top of the house, no young growth is allowed to form at the top of the main stem, but is rubbed off to promote vigour in the fruiting spurs below; these are annually cut back to one bud shooting outwards. Only one shoot is desired from each of these spurs, therefore, when the young shoots push out in spring, the most vigorous one only is retained. The inexperienced gardener, however, should wait until the small bunches of fruit are visible on these shoots; then he should select the best bunch and discard all the other shoots. When a rod has not been fruiting well, it is a good plan to train in another shoot from the bottom to take its place, the old rod being cut out when the young growth has reached the top of the house. The young shoot should be cut back when some 3 feet long and should then be treated as advised above for the young vine.

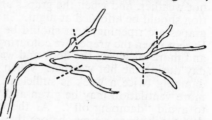

The above method of training is applicable when several vines are grown in one house. Where only one vine is planted, instead of training one shoot to run vertically up the glass, two shoots are grown horizontally, running in opposite directions to each other, and are pruned as for the single vertical stem.

FIG. 65. PRUNING THE GRAPE VINE
In winter, prune the side shoots made the previous summer to within one bud, (shooting outwards) of the base. Cut back the main shoot annually to about 2 feet from the start of the current year's growth.

Laterals are allowed to form from the upper side of these stems and are trained vertically upwards at intervals of 3 to 4 feet, these eventually being pruned and trained as for the single main-shoot. The vines should be tied to wires, fixed 9 inches apart, and kept 18 inches from the roof-glass. The rods frequently produce shoots from their tops before any young growth has formed near the base. To encourage this lower growth, the rods must be unfastened from the wires and should have their heads bent down towards the ground. This will arrest the flow of sap and young growth will soon form at the base. When the laterals all up the rods are in an even state of growth, the rods may again be tied to the wires in an upright position. Vines should not be allowed to bear grapes the first year. If the vine is a strong one, a few bunches of fruit may be taken off during the second year, but not until the third season should anything like a crop be allowed to mature.

Temperatures.—Newly-planted vines should be allowed to become well established before any unnecessary heat is employed, fires being only lit to exclude frost. When the fruit is required in July or August, the temperature

495

may be raised to a minimum of about 55° F. early in March, and from the middle of April onward, the temperature from sun heat alone may be allowed to rise to 85° F., a night temperature of about 55° F. being afforded. From the time the young leaves are fairly developed until the grapes are in flower, a night temperature of 55° F. to 60° F. should be given.

Fertilization.—When the flowers are open, they should be lightly dusted over each day, about noon when the air is warm and dry, with a soft camel-hair brush to distribute the pollen from one flower to another. As the atmosphere should be kept dry while the blooms are being fertilized, the borders should be well watered before the flowers open, so that, unless the weather is very hot, water will not again be required until the bloom has set.

Ventilation.—Ventilation should always be started just before the sun rises, or the vines will be scorched, and should be increased as the heat increases, until noon. After two o'clock, the ventilation should be diminished, and the house should be finally closed at about half-past five (summer-time). During very hot weather, and when the grapes are beginning to colour, a little top ventilation should be afforded at night. Should the weather be cold and dull while the grapes are ripening, heat should be given, but ventilation should be provided. Except when the grapes are colouring, when the heat must be somewhat reduced and more air given, the floor and walls should be freely damped several times a day during the hot weather. When the grapes are colouring, however, a good damping twice a week is sufficient. As soon as the grapes are well coloured, more ventilation may be given and the heat must be reduced to the minimum to avoid "damping off". As the laterals grow, they must be gradually bent down, a little at a time, before they touch the glass and should be first loosely tied to the wires with raffia, being later more securely fixed when they have become more used to the position. It is a job that must be done gradually, as the stems are brittle and will snap if treated drastically. The shoots must be evenly distributed over the wires so that each receives ample sun and air. Water when the vines are "starting", shortly before the flowers open, while the fruit is stoning, liberally while the grapes are swelling, and after the fruit has been harvested.

Application of liquid manure should be given weekly from the time the fruit sets until it is ripe.

Thinning.—As soon as the bunches have set their berries, it should be decided how many bunches are to be left, and how many grapes on each bunch. It has been estimated that each foot of rod of a well-matured vine should bear about 1 lb. weight of grapes. Thus a fully-established vine about 20 feet long, of such a variety as *Muscat of Alexandria* or *Black Hamburgh*, should not be allowed to bear more than about seven or eight bunches, averaging 3 lbs. a bunch, whilst of such varieties as *Trebbiano* or *Grosse Guillaume* not more than three or four bunches, each averaging from 6 to 7 lbs. in weight, are as much as it should be permitted to hold. No lateral should be allowed to carry more than one bunch, and the bunches retained should be compact and neat in form, not long, straggling ones. Surplus bunches should be removed as early as possible, and on the bunches that are allowed to remain the grapes should be thinned-out at an early stage, so as to make shapely bunches. The centre especially should be

PLATE 15 *Above left. APPLES, WORCESTER PEARMAIN and Above right, PLUMS, VICTORIA, Below, A BUNCH OF RIPE CHERRIES, KENTISH RED*   *Shell Photos*

thinned and ¾ of an inch should be allowed from berry to berry. Grape-thinning scissors and a forked stick some 10 inches long to separate the grapes should be used, as on no account must the grapes be touched by the hand. Care must be taken not to injure the grapes.

Propagation.—To propagate, several eyes or buds, that is, short pieces of the previous year's side growth some 2 inches in length, each with one good bud upon it, and having a slanting cut ½ inch long directly under the bud, are planted in January horizontally, with the bud just above the soil in small pots, in a compost consisting of loam with one third leaf-mould and a liberal addition of sand. The pots are placed in a mild hot-bed and the soil kept moist and shaded. The eyes start growth quickly under these conditions, and should then be moved to a cooler, but light position. As soon as the roots have well filled the pot, they should be repotted singly into 6-inch pots. As the vines grow, they must be carefully staked, and by midsummer the plants will be about 6 feet in height. They should be moved into 8-inch pots, then again into 10-inch pots, being kept in the open from September to November, and planted in the house in January.

Storing Grapes.—*See* Storing Fruit, p. 470.

See also Grape-growing in the Open, p. 480.

Varieties.—*Black Alicante, Black Hamburgh,* and *Gros Colman* (all black); *Muscat of Alexandria* (amber); and *Cannon Hall Muscat, Foster's Seedling,* and *Mrs. Pearson* (all white).

Melons. *Preparing the Bed.*—The hot-bed should be made as described on p. 248, and then covered with about 6 inches of good, stiff garden loam, with an admixture of a little old mortar rubble, sand, and a few handfuls of crushed charcoal. This should bring us to about the end of March.

Sowing.—Seed may be sown in the bed itself, or young plants may be raised two in a pot of sandy soil, in a temperature of about 70° F. early in March, being planted out, 2 feet apart, as soon as an even temperature of about 80° F. may be counted upon. Double as many seeds should be sown as plants ultimately required.

Pruning.—If grown in a frame, the main shoot should be pegged down on to the soil and stopped when about 2 feet in length. Three or four laterals should be permitted to form. These should be trained evenly over the bed, being pinched back when sufficient flowers are visible. In a house the plant should be allowed to grow up as a single cordon supported by a cane, being stopped back when 3 feet high. Laterals will be thrown out and should be trained along horizontal wires ten inches apart, being stopped when some 18 inches long. The female flowers have small globular growths at their base, and four or five of these on each plant require "setting". This is done by picking the male flower, which has no globular formation at its base, removing the yellow petals, and by pressing the pollen-covered remainder into the female flower. The best time to do this is early in the morning when the sun is shining and the plants are dry. While the fruit is ripening, it is essential to allow the shoots from beyond the fruits to thrive, in order that nourishment may be drawn out to the fruit; all unnecessary side growth, however, must be stopped to avoid crowding. Only one fruit must be allowed on each lateral.

Watering and Ventilation.—During the early periods of growth, the plants must never be allowed to be dry at the root, and twice a day in bright weather the leaves should be syringed with water; preferably in the morning and again when closing the house for the night. Tepid water should always be used. When the flowers open, very little water at the roots should be given, and the plant should not again be syringed overhead until the fruits begin to swell. During the whole period of growth, air should be liberally afforded, a careful eye being, of course, kept on the temperature, which should not fall below 60° F. at night, or below 70° F. by day. Should the thermometer rise above 85° F. while the sun is shining, a little more ventilation should be afforded until the temperature has dropped. It will be difficult to maintain these temperatures when frames are used, but much may be done by covering the lights closely with mats and sacking on cold nights. Throughout their whole lives melon plants require free ventilation and an abundance of light, and this is especially true during the period of fruit ripening. Once the roots of the plants are established, they cannot have too much sun.

Ripening the Fruit.—Fruit sown in March takes some four months from the time of sowing to ripen, later-sown fruit will only require three months. As soon as the fruits begin to swell, fertilizers should be applied or tepid liquid manure should be given at weekly intervals. As the fruits swell, more water, which must be tepid, is needed and more syringing in bright weather until they begin to ripen, when the syringing and water supply must be diminished and more air given, but the plants must never be allowed to flag. The fruit is heavy, and when the size of a tennis ball, arrangements should be made for supporting it by means of small wooden "rafts", or nets, suspended from the roof. Ripeness is indicated by the stalk appearing to separate from the fruit.

Second and Third Crops.—Where artificial heat is available, by planting a strong young plant as soon as the fruit has been gathered from the old one, three crops of melons may often be obtained in one season. Seed sown in January will bear fruit in June, the plants put in at this time will ripen their fruit in August, and the last crop should ripen off by October.

Varieties.—*Blenheim Orange* (Scarlet flesh); *Superlative* (Scarlet flesh); *Emerald Gem* (Green flesh); *Ringleader* (Pale Green flesh); *Hero of Lockinge* (White flesh). *King George* (Scarlet flesh) will grow under cooler conditions, even in a cold frame, as will *Munroe's Little Heath* and *The Earl's Favourite*.

Peaches and Nectarines. Under glass the cultivation of these fruits is essentially similar to their outdoor culture. The house must be kept very cool until the first or second week in February, when a temperature of 45° to 50° F. should be given. After ten days, the temperature should be raised by about 10°. Ample ventilation should be given when outside conditions are suitable. In order to ensure fertilization, the flowers must be dusted over about noon with a soft camel's hair brush or a rabbit's tail. No syringing should be done while the trees are in bloom, but should be continued twice daily with soft water as soon as the fruit has set, when the temperature should be raised to 65° F. The ground should also be sprinkled with water three or four times each day while the fruits are forming and swelling. Not more than one fruit for every 9 inches square of wall space should be allowed.

498

Ripening the Fruit.—As the fruit approaches the ripening period, it should be fully exposed to the sun and given as much ventilation as possible. The shoots should be kept laid in closely, obstructing leaves removed, and a mulch of manure given. Syringing should cease as soon as the fruit begins to colour, as a drier atmosphere is needed at this period. Once the fruit is gathered, the roots must be given ample water, and the border dressed liberally with lime. The foliage should be syringed and ventilation freely given.

For methods of planting, training, pruning, thinning, etc., *see* p. 482.

Strawberries. *Compost and Potting.*—For cultivation under glass, the young plants should be propagated as described on p. 489, and should be potted-up about the middle of August, with the crowns appearing just above the soil in 6-inch pots, in a compost consisting of a mixture of three parts coarse turfy loam, one part well-rotted manure, and one part brick rubble and broken pieces of lime; the whole should be well mixed together and then dusted over with a good sprinkling of bonemeal and soot. Drainage must be good. (*See* Potting, p. 127.) The pots should be stood on a floor of hard-rammed ashes or brick rubble, in a position in which they will be protected from the full sun. In fine weather the plants should be syringed three or four times daily, and the roots must never be allowed to become dry, but the soil must not become sodden. In ten days' time, when the roots are fully established, the pots must be transferred to a position where the plants will have full sun, soot water should be given every three or four days, the foliage being syringed morning and evening in fine, warm weather. Any runners that form should immediately be cut off, as they divert nourishment from the plants.

Wintering in Frame.—In November, or earlier should the frosts become severe, the pots should be placed in a cold frame for the winter. The pots should be sunk to their rims in ashes, but the foliage must come close up to the glass. Free ventilation must be given in fine weather and never must the pots become dry.

Forcing.—Early April is about the earliest that we can expect good fruit from forced strawberries, and to have fruit ripe by this time, some of the pots should be moved from the cold frame about the middle of January, to be placed on shelves near the glass in the vinery or peach house, if a special forcing house is not available, or in a heated frame. Every three weeks, until the middle of March, a few more pots should be brought into the heat; this will provide a succession of fruit from April until the open-air fruit is ready in June.

The Use of Bottom Heat.—A mild hot-bed will stimulate the root action and thus produce more vigorous plants and crops, so that where this is available, the pots should be plunged into the hot-bed when moved from the cold frame, and before removal to the house, the first batch about the middle of January. They should be left there for about a month, when the flower spikes will have formed. Each morning a little air should be admitted, and when fine and bright the foliage should be syringed daily early in the afternoon, at which time the frame should be closed to preserve the heat of the sun through the night. Once the flower spikes have formed, the plants should be transferred to shelves, about 15 inches from the glass of the house, or should be so placed in the heated frame that the plants are that distance from the lights.

499

Temperature and Ventilation.—The heat should, at first, be gradually applied, a temperature of 50° F. being quite sufficient at night, rising 5° to 10° F. by day in accordance with the heat of the sun. The atmosphere should be kept dry while the plants are in flower, and each day, about noon, when the air is driest, the flowers should be gently shaken, or better still the centre of each should be dusted with a rabbit's tail, to ensure cross-pollination and consequent fertilization. Once half a dozen to eight fruits have set on each plant, the atmosphere should be kept moist, the temperature being allowed to rise gradually to 60° F. by night and 65° to 70° F. by day. The plants should be syringed and the floors damped early each afternoon when fine and warm. The house should be closed early in the afternoon to preserve the heat through the night. As free ventilation as possible should be given during the morning, but the temperature must not be allowed to drop below the figures mentioned above. Greenfly are liable to appear at this period and careful watch must, therefore, be kept, the house being thoroughly fumigated on the first sign of them. If the undersides of the leaves are syringed daily, when fine, there should be little trouble from red spider. When the weather is very hot, water may be required twice or even three times a day.

Thinning and Ripening.—Should more than eight berries have formed on any plant they must be thinned out, only the largest and best shaped berries being retained. Once the fruits commence to swell, weak liquid manure should be applied once a week. As soon as the fruit begins to turn colour, the temperature must be gradually lessened, freer ventilation should be given, and syringing and the application of manure water must stop.

The berries may be prevented from becoming soiled by contact with the soil by being each supported on a short prong of wood pushed into the soil below the berry. When the fruit has been gathered, the plants must be taken out of their pots and planted out in the open where, if watered and well cared for, they will in all probability fruit again in the early autumn. *See also* Fruit Culture in the Open, p. 488.

CHAPTER 42

DISEASES AND PESTS

The harm done by diseases and pests varies from season to season, but even in the lightest year the damage over the whole country is very considerable. Plants of all kinds may be killed or damaged and crops severely reduced or lost. Even when crops of fruit, vegetables or flowers may be obtained in reasonable quantities, the quality and appearance often fall far below the standard desired and the gardener gets but a poor reward for all the time and money he has spent on good cultivation, seeds, plants and manures. To avoid such disappointment it is necessary to have some knowledge of the common pests and diseases, to know how to control them and above all to be ready to act at the best and earliest opportunity, remembering always that much damage can be done under the soil or within a plant before the symptoms of attack become clearly visible.

The words diseases and pests are here used in their broadest sense. Diseases may conveniently be divided into two main groups, those of a physical character due to poor growing conditions or lack of some essential plant-food, and those caused by parasitic agents such as fungi, bacteria or viruses. The second group is the more important and the organisms concerned are among the simplest forms of vegetable life, minute or microscopic, with the viruses beyond microscopic recognition. Fungi may live on or inside the plant and many of them go through well-defined phases of development, finishing in a fruiting stage which produces the spores that spread the disease further. Bacteria multiply by simple cell-division and with the viruses are usually spread through some intermediary such as a sucking insect, the gardener's hands, boots, or tools, by taking cuttings or dividing the roots of an infected plant, or less commonly by using infected seed.

Among pests, the gardener includes all those animals which attack plants; insects, mites, slugs, snails, birds, etc. But many are beneficial and these should be carefully preserved. Ladybirds, lacewings, hover flies, centipedes and some of the ground beetles live on other insects. Shrewmice and hedgehogs are also good friends and birds do much more good than harm, particularly if seedlings and fruiting crops are protected by netting or cotton or a suitable bird-scarer is used. The largest group of pests is formed by insects, most of which develop in four stages, egg, larva or grub, pupa or chrysalis and adult. The grub stage is generally the most damaging

501

for it is then that the insect needs the most food, and the adult stage is usually the most infective when the females seek new quarters for egg-laying. Many insects produce more than one generation a year and some, like aphides, produce living young as well as eggs.

From the gardener's point of view, insects are of two kinds, those that bite and eat the tissues of the plant and those that pierce the tissues with their tongues and suck the sap. The first are generally controlled by applying a poison on to their food, the second by applying a toxic substance on to the insects themselves or, in greenhouses, by using a fumigant. A sucking insect cannot be controlled be using a spray or dust designed to act only as a surface poison.

Up to fifty years ago there were very few sprays or dusts capable of controlling diseases and pests satisfactorily, but modern research has given an effective answer in all but a very few cases. A few of the most-recently discovered methods which are highly-successful on a commercial scale are, however, unsuitable for private gardens. Some require the operator to wear special protective clothing and a respirator and others may damage adjoining crops if the spray drifts in the wind. Such remedies are quite safe on farms and market gardens but may be extremely dangerous in a residential area with its children and domestic pets and where fruit, flowers and vegetables are grown together in a small area and there is always the risk of causing damage to plants in a neighbour's garden. For these reasons, only the safest of the effective treatments are here recommended, but even so, this involves the use of several poisonous or harmful substances and the most sensible plan is to regard them all as dangerous and store them under lock and key.

The mixtures recommended can be made up by the gardener or bought in convenient sizes under various proprietary names. In addition many other preparations are available. They are carefully manufactured and tested and can be used with every confidence. But since different active principles may be used and the strengths of the concentrate vary, it is most important that the manufacturer's instructions are properly carried out.

EQUIPMENT

Even the smallest garden will require some form of equipment for applying spray fluids or dusts, and manufacturers offer a wide choice.

Sprayers.—For large gardens or where there are fruit trees a knapsack-type of sprayer which is strapped to the shoulders and has its own "one-hand" pump and flexible hose and lance is perhaps the most suitable. Smaller machines of the stirrup-pump type are available in many forms and for the small garden there are various types of syringe and "atomisers" which blow the fluid out as a misty spray. All machines and syringes should have a fine as well as a coarse nozzle.

Dusting machines.—These are smaller and lighter. The larger kinds are generally carried on the shoulder and have a "one-hand" bellows and a flexible spout which can be directed up to a tree or down to a ground-level crop. For small-scale work there are many kinds of hand "puffers", some of them being incorporated in the container as bought from the shop.

But whatever method is used the principal aim must be to cover the whole plant thoroughly, including the undersides of the leaves. This can best be done by putting on the spray or the dust in the finest particles possible and for this reason it is important to buy good-quality dusts which use a very fine base powder as a carrier or to add a spreading agent to the fluids and use a fine nozzle on the sprayer. The work should be carried out on calm, dry days and dusting should preferably be done in the early morning or evening when the normal dampness on the leaves will help the dust to cling. Once the spray or dust has dried on, only heavy rain will wash it off. Dusts are of course washed off more easily and therefore have to be applied more frequently than sprays, but against this, the job is lighter and quicker.

GENERAL RULES

There is no short cut to the control of diseases and pests and since most of them appear at different times of the season on a wide variety of crops and develop in various ways with their most vulnerable stages occurring at different times there is, as yet, no cure-all or once-for-all magic available. With the inevitable but few exceptions, fungicides have no effect on insects, nor insecticides on fungi. Some of the soil fumigants will however control many soil insects as well as fungi and it is sometimes possible to incorporate an insecticide with a fungicide when spraying a particular crop, e.g. apples attacked by aphis and scab at the same time.

In the average garden where fruit, flowers, shrubs and vegetables are generally grown close to each other, the control of diseases and pests is not always easy and certain fundamental precautions are necessary.

1. Winter washes, e.g. tar oils, must be used only in the dormant period and should not be applied to fruit trees if leafy vegetables or herbaceous plants are growing underneath. Spring spraying, e.g. with nicotine, should be done instead.

2. Fruit and ornamental trees or shrubs should never be sprayed with an insecticide while the blossom is open owing to the danger to bees and other pollinating insects.

3. Non-volatile surface poisons such as arsenate of lead must never be applied to a food crop nearing its harvesting time.

4. Insecticides containing BHC (benzene hexachloride) should not be applied to black currants, potatoes or root vegetables nor to trees growing above them as they may taint the crops.

503

5. DDT and Derris should not be used where they may contaminate a stream or ornamental pool containing fish.

6. Boxes or sheds used for storing fruit or vegetables should be cleaned every year with hot water and soda and not with any disinfectant which may affect the flavour of the stored produce.

GREENHOUSE FUMIGATION

Fumigation is the most convenient way of controlling the more serious pests and diseases in greenhouses, particularly red spider and white fly. Various substances are used, the active principles being nicotine, hydrocyanic acid gas, azobenzene, tetrachlorethane, sulphur, BHC or DDT. They can all be bought as proprietary articles, many of them in the convenient form of "smokes". But as most of them are exceedingly poisonous the maker's instructions must be followed precisely and on no account should a greenhouse or conservatory leading into a dwelling house be fumigated in this way.

The best time to do the job is in the evening when the plants are dry. Tender plants and those in full flower should be removed and treated separately. The house must be made as airtight as possible and the work done quickly, starting from the far end, and moving towards the door. When finished, the door should be locked. In the morning when the house is opened up ample time must be allowed before going inside.

SOIL FUMIGATION

A different type of fumigation is sometimes used in the open. It is rarely necessary in well-managed gardens but may be the best way of dealing with the heavy infestations of leather-jackets and wireworms which often occur when old, rough turf or neglected land is broken up. Naphthalene is used in powdered form and raked in, and as it does not harm growing plants (except very young seedlings) it can be used at any time of the year. Formalin and cresylic acid are used as liquids, but as they are harmful to plants when freshly applied they should only be used when the land is uncropped. Both of them will control a number of soil fungi.

STERILIZATION

In greenhouses where plants are grown in beds or borders the soil may become infected with certain serious root diseases or pests like eelworms. It must then either be replaced with fresh clean soil or sterilized. The best sterilization is by steaming but in a private garden the second-best, formalin or cresylic acid, has to be used in the same way as for soil in the open. After sterilizing the house should be well-aired for 10–14 days.

Small quantities of soil for potting can be sterilized at home by baking or steaming. *See* Chapter 4.

504

GENERAL HYGIENE

Plants that are well-grown and well-managed are much less liable to be attacked by diseases or pests than those which are unhappy in their surroundings. But even the strongest are by no means immune and everything possible must be done to prevent trouble or to act as soon as it is seen. General tidiness does much to remove potential sources of infection. Weeds should be kept down, hedges trimmed and cleared of rubbish at their base, and boxes, pots, stakes, etc. kept clean and stacked tidily instead of being left lying about the garden.

Very often, the prompt removal and burning of an attacked shoot or plant will prevent any further spread, and sometimes it may pay to scrap an unhealthy crop entirely and buy in fresh, clean plants or follow with a different crop altogether. Broken branches on trees and shrubs or accidental wounds should be pared off smoothly and covered with white lead paint or grafting wax, and as soon as flowers or vegetables are finished the remnants should be taken up and composted. Anything showing signs of rotting, such as rotten fruit or slimy growth, should be collected and burned.

ANTS

Ants do not attack plants themselves but cause damage by helping to spread aphids which they often "nurse" for the honeydew, and they may tunnel among the roots of young seedlings.

Treatment. The nests must be destroyed with boiling water, liquid derris, paraffin, sodium cyanide or a proprietary "ant-killer". If the nest cannot be discovered, a little sugar should be sprinkled about; the ants will carry this away to their homes.

APHIDES

These are the well-known Greenfly or Blackfly, which attack a wide range of both outdoor and greenhouse plants. They may be black, green, reddish, almost white or bluish. There are several generations a year, with or without wings. They feed by sucking the sap and in so doing frequently spread virus diseases. They occur on the roots of some plants, e.g. lettuces and brassicas, as well as above ground. Most of them exude a sticky "honeydew" on which sooty moulds frequently grow, further spoiling the appearance of the plant. The Woolly Aphis (American Blight) commonly seen on apple trees, exudes a white fluffy covering.

Symptoms. Attacks generally start on the undersides of the leaves or tips of the shoots. Curling and malformation follow, making spraying difficult. Prompt attention is therefore essential.

Treatment. Spray or dust with nicotine, derris or pyrethrum. Several applications may be necessary. On fruit trees the routine winter-washing

505

must not be missed, and in greenhouses annual fumigation should be carried out.

APPLE BLOSSOM WEEVIL

A dark-coloured weevil about ¼ inch long, covered with greyish hairs with a yellowish V-shaped mark across the wing cases. The insect has a long snout which the female uses to bore a hole in the flower bud ready for laying an egg. Usually only one egg is laid in each bud. Pears, quinces and medlars are sometimes attacked but apples suffer the most.

Symptoms. When the grub hatches it feeds on the growing flower which wilts, turns brown and fails to develop a fruit. The brown petals form a "cap" under which a grub is usually found.

Treatment. Spray with DDT just before buds begin to burst, or dust with a 5% DDT dust when the flower buds are "breaking" and again just before bursting. An alternative method is to tie bands of sacking or corrugated paper around the trunks in June, to offer shelter for the adults. Remove and burn the bands in October.

APPLE SAWFLY

The adult is about ⅓ inch long, black, with legs and underside yellowish red. It appears at blossom time, laying its eggs, one to a flower. The grub is creamy white with a black head which later becomes brown.

Symptoms. The grub tunnels into the developing fruit which often shows the tunnelling as a ribbon-like scar. By June the attacked fruits show a hole from which dirty brown "frass" exudes. One grub may attack several fruits. When fully fed it drops to the ground and pupates in the soil.

Treatment. In small gardens, affected fruits should be picked or gathered up and burned. On a larger scale, a nicotine spray should be used at petal fall or within the next few days.

Note. The damage done by Apple Sawfly must be distinguished from that of Codling Moth (see p. 513) because the control measures are different.

APPLE AND PEAR SCAB

Two species of fungi are concerned, each confined to its own host. Infection can occur at any time during the growing season, the winter stage being passed under the bark or on fallen leaves. Many of the best varieties suffer the worst.

Symptoms. As the leaves develop, dark olive-green patches appear and later become brownish or black. Blister-like swellings and cracks occur on the shoots. Later the fruits are attacked, the skin becoming cracked or covered with scattered dark or black spots.

Treatment. Diseased material should be collected and burned, and the trees sprayed with lime-sulphur at the following stages of growth:

1. When the flower buds are fully developed but still green, lime-sulphur 1 gallon to 40 gallons of water.
2. When the flower buds are showing pink but have not opened, lime-sulphur 1 gallon to 50 gallons of water.
3. When most of the petals have fallen, lime-sulphur 1 gallon to 100 gallons of water.

As far as possible, the sprayings should be spaced at intervals of 14 days, and on no account must heavier concentrations be used otherwise damage will be done to some varieties. Doyenne du Comice pears must not be sprayed with lime-sulphur but with colloidal sulphur.

APPLE SUCKER

Small flattened yellowish insects are often seen around the young leaves and blossoms. They excrete a sticky fluid and white waxy threads. Later they become green and when adult have wings. Small, oval, creamy eggs are laid in the autumn on the fruit spurs.

Symptoms. Flower buds die or fail to set fruit. A badly-attacked tree looks as though it had been damaged by frost.

Treatment. The best control is obtained by routine spraying with a winter wash. If this has been missed spray in spring just before the blossoms burst, with nicotine.

ASPARAGUS BEETLE

The beetle is about $\frac{1}{8}$ inch long and has a greenish-black head and orange wings with black bars. The eggs are greenish black and laid in rows on the shoots of asparagus.

Symptoms. The beetles eat the buds and later the grubs feed on the foliage.

Treatment. Spray or dust with derris or pyrethrum. After cutting is finished nicotine can be used. As the beetles hibernate in old stems or surrounding rubbish, the beds and the garden around must be kept tidy.

BACTERIAL ROTS

Most of the more common bacterial diseases of plants cause varying forms of wet or slimy rot. The first visible sign may be a sudden wilting, and at this stage discoloured tissues are usually seen if the affected part is cut across. Many herbaceous plants and vegetables are attacked, especially potatoes (Blackleg), cucumbers under glass (Wilt), tomatoes, rhubarb (Crown Rot), French beans (Halo Blight), carrots, onions, iris and other bulbs. The "drier" forms of bacterial diseases produce typical cankers on

507

trees and shrubs (see **Dieback**) or galls on the roots of fruit and other trees, roses and certain root vegetables such as beetroot (Crown Gall).

Treatment. The only satisfactory method is to remove and burn infected plants. After completing the work, the hands and any tools used should be disinfected in formalin (2%).

BEAN WEEVIL

The beetles are small, about ¼ inch long, generally yellowish-brown with striped wing-cases, and the short snout characteristic of weevils. They attack peas as well as beans, but are only serious on seedling plants.

Symptoms. The beetles eat circular patches from the edges of the leaves which take on a scolloped appearance.

Treatment. Good cultivation and manuring to help the crop grow away quickly is generally sufficient. In cold, slow-growing weather, the plants should be sprayed or dusted with DDT.

BEET FLY

A greyish-black fly about ⅛ inch long lays its eggs on the underside of the leaves of beetroot in the seedling or young stages. There are two or three generations a year.

Symptoms. Pale blotches appear on the leaves caused by the grubs burrowing in between the upper and lower surfaces. The plants wither and may die.

Treatment. Hoe regularly and top-dress with nitrate of soda to help the plants grow away quickly.

BIG BUD

This is caused by the Black Currant Gall Mite which is widespread throughout the country. It is minute, just too small to be visible to the naked eye, and its main host is black currants. Red and white currants and gooseberries are occasionally attacked.

Symptoms. The mites live in the buds which swell to about twice the normal size and fail to open normally. In the following spring, the infested buds dry up and die and the mites move on to fresh healthy buds.

Treatment. On a small scale hand-picking of all infested buds if done in good time will reduce attacks, but the best control is by spraying with lime-sulphur (1% solution) when the leaves are about as big as a two-shilling piece and before the flowers open. The mites are then exposed as they begin to move to fresh buds. Some scorching may result and the crop be reduced, but in the following year spraying should be unnecessary and a full crop be obtained. In severe cases the bushes should be grubbed and burned and replaced by healthy stock.

See **Reversion**, a virus disease which can be spread by these mites.

BLACK SPOT

Roses may sometimes be seriously affected. Some varieties are more resistant than others.

Symptoms. Black spots or blotches appear on the leaves and sometimes on the shoots.

Treatment. Spray with Bordeaux mixture. Remove and burn affected shoots and all fallen leaves.

BLOSSOM WILT

The many separate strains of this disease affect cherries, plums, apricots, peaches, pears and apples including many of the ornamental varieties. They are closely related to the fungi causing Wither Tip in plums and Brown Rot, and their severity varies widely from year to year. The most important is the Blossom Wilt of apples.

Symptoms. The fungus enters the flower and soon the surrounding leaves wilt and droop. The fruiting spurs become infected and may be killed. In bad attacks the disease may spread along the whole shoot. Spores develop on the infected areas and spread the disease.

Treatment. Cut out and burn all infected parts, cutting back to sound healthy wood.

(Routine spraying with winter wash and lime sulphur also has some control.)

BROWN ROT

Different species and strains of the fungi causing Blossom Wilt, attack the fruits of apples, pears, plums and cherries and less frequently peaches, nectarines, almonds and quinces.

Symptoms. Whitish, yellow or grey pustules appear on the fruits, generally in rings. The infected fruits drop off or shrivel and remain on the trees as "mummied" fruits, to act as the source of infection in the following year. The disease also occurs among apples in store, the fruits showing the characteristic rotting or turning black.

Treatment. Collect or cut out and burn all diseased material. Examine fruit in store regularly every two or three weeks.

BULB MITE

These small round, shiny, yellowish mites often occur as a secondary pest, attacking hyacinths, lilies, narcissi and tulips which have first been damaged in some other way.

Symptoms. The mites swarm between the scales of the bulbs either in store or when growing, often causing serious rotting.

Treatment. Infested bulbs should be burned and where possible all others which may have been in contact should be fumigated in an air-tight container with paradichlorbenzene or immersed in hot-water kept at 110°F. for one hour. All bulbs must be treated carefully to avoid damage.

CABBAGE CATERPILLAR

These are the well-known larvæ of the Cabbage White butterflies and the Cabbage moth. They are found on all brassicas and are common on nasturtiums (Tropæolum).

Symptoms. The eggs are laid on the leaves, and the caterpillars not only eat the leaves but also spoil the crop with their excreta.

Treatment. Early action is essential before the caterpillars get into the hearts. The eggs and larvæ may be crushed or picked off by hand or the plants sprayed or dusted with nicotine, derris or pyrethrum. (Nicotine should not be used near harvest time.)

CABBAGE ROOT FLY

This is a serious pest of all brassicas, especially cabbage and cauliflower. The fly is ashy-grey, about $\frac{1}{4}$ inch long and like a small house fly. There are two or three generations a year.

Symptoms. Attacked plants look blue and stop growing. The leaves flag. If the plant is taken up, white, legless maggots about $\frac{1}{3}$ inch long will be found around the root or inside. The root may be partly eaten or tunnelled, or almost severed.

Treatment. Sprinkle calomel dust around the stem of each plant in a ring about 1 inch wide. Any later planted crops should be treated in this way at planting time.

CABBAGE WHITE FLY

In warm sheltered gardens a small white fly often occurs on brassica crops, the eggs and larvæ being found on the undersides of the leaves. Usually no harm is done, except when the larvæ get into the hearts.

Treatment. Spraying is rarely satisfactory as it is difficult to hit the flies. Generally a good control can be obtained by pulling off and burning the lower leaves. Stumps from an infested crop should be burned.

CANKER

The word canker is loosely used to cover any kind of wound surrounded by swollen bark or callus. It may be caused by mechanical injury when the wound usually heals naturally or by certain fungi or Woolly Aphis. Cankers due to fungi occur on cabbages and turnips and on fruit trees, principally apples and pears. The so-called canker of parsnips is a physiological disorder common on wet soils deficient in lime.

Symptoms. Small depressed areas occur in the bark and extend to form a ragged wound which often encircles the branch or twig. Whitish pustules appear followed by small, round, red bodies.

510

Treatment. As the fungus enters through wounds, any breakages in the branches and the cut surfaces made by pruning should be coated with grafting wax or white lead paint. Insects, especially Woolly Aphis, must be kept down.

Poor growing conditions, such as bad drainage, appear to favour the disease.

Where the infected branches are small they should be cut well back to healthy wood. On large branches the infected areas may be cut out with a chisel. Badly attacked trees should be grubbed. All infected material must be burned.

CAPSID BUGS

Several species of capsids, all about ⅓ inch long but varying in colour from green to reddish-brown, attack many garden plants.

Symptoms. In most cases rusty-looking pin-prick holes occur on the leaves. On apples rough scars also appear on the surface of the fruit. Frequently the growing point of a plant is damaged and poor or malformed growth follows.

Treatment. Spray or dust with nicotine, covering also the soil around the plants as the capsids are very active and usually drop off the plants when disturbed. On fruit trees winter spraying will help by controlling the egg stage.

CARROT FLY

A shiny, greenish-black fly about ⅓ inch long, with yellowish legs appears in May and again in August when the second generation occurs. It lays its eggs on or near carrots.

Symptoms. The foliage wilts and turns reddish in colour. A lifted root will show a number of small colourless maggots burrowing into the flesh.

Treatment. In badly-infested areas the crop should not be sown before the end of May. This will avoid the first generation. Seed should be sown thinly so as to avoid or reduce singling which bruises the seedlings and sets free the smell of carrots which attracts the flies. Burn any thinnings. Powdered naphthalene sprinkled along the rows at fortnightly intervals to the end of June, or frequent dusting with soot will act as repellents.

CELERY BEETLE

A small steel-blue beetle about ⅛ inch long which normally feeds on weeds may attack celery and occasionally carrots and parsnips during July and August.

Symptoms. The leaves and the stems are eaten.

Treatment. Dust with derris. (Lead arsenate may be used on young plants.)

CELERY FLY—See LEAF MINERS.

CENTIPEDES—See MILLEPEDES.

CHAFER BEETLES

There are four species. The adults vary from $\frac{1}{2}$ to 1 inch long. All have hard brownish wing-cases except the Rose Chafer which is green. The beetles feed on the leaves of many trees and shrubs and the fleshy, white, curved, brown-headed grubs feed on the roots of many plants.

Symptoms. The plant suddenly wilts and on being dug up a grub is often found. The root is often cut right through.

Treatment. The grubs should be collected whenever possible. In bad "chafer years" naphthalene should be dusted around the crops.

CHERRY SAWFLY—See SLUGWORMS.

CHOCOLATE SPOT

Occasionally this disease is serious on broad beans, if the season is wet.

Symptoms. Chocolate-coloured spots appear on the leaves and sometimes on the stems and pods. The flowers may fall.

Treatment. Top-dress with sulphate of potash and burn the haulm after harvesting.

CHRYSANTHEMUM MIDGE

A small brownish fly, about $\frac{1}{10}$ inch long, with a red abdomen, may attack chrysanthemums in greenhouses where it breeds all the year round. Occasionally in dry summers it may be found out of doors.

Symptoms. The larvæ burrow into the leaves or shoots and as they grow cause cone-shaped swellings which lead to malformation of the buds and flowers.

Treatment. Remove galls and spray every week with nicotine or BHC.

CLUB ROOT

Sometimes called Finger and Toe, this is a common and generally well-known disease, favoured by an acid condition of the soil. The cabbage family, turnips, swedes and radishes are the most important of the susceptible crops, but any Cruciferous plant is liable to attack. Many weeds such as charlock and shepherd's purse can also become infected and occasionally the disease is found on wallflowers, stocks, candytuft and others.

Symptoms. The plants look stunted and unhappy. Swellings of various shapes occur on the roots or on the stems at ground level, later becoming

512

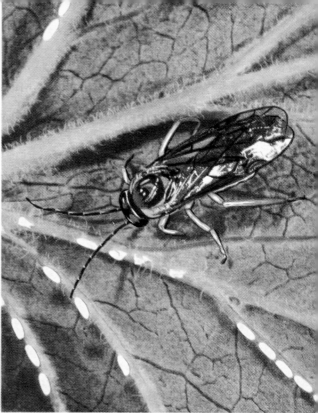

PLATE 16 *PESTS AND FRIENDS. Top left, ROSE APHIDES (PEST), Top Right, HOVER FLY (BENEFICIAL INSECT), Bottom Left, MEALY APHIS (PEST) and Bottom Right, RASPBERRY BEETLE (PEST)* *Shell Photos*

slimy as they decay. If cut through the swelling is solid and often has a marbled appearance, thus differing from the swelling caused by Gall Weevils which is hollow and usually has a maggot inside.

Treatment. The lime content of the soil must be kept up by regular dressings, and susceptible crops should be spaced as far apart as possible in the rotation. In severe cases plants should be dipped in a paste of calomel before being planted out.

CODLING MOTH

The moth is brown-grey with a coppery tip to the wings. Eggs are laid in June and July and the grub enters the fruit through the side or the eye, and burrows into the core. Apples, including the ornamental species, are most generally attacked, but pears, quince and walnut may occasionally suffer.

Symptoms. When fully fed the larva burrows its way out of the fruit which may stay on the tree or fall. It leaves a characteristic hole with no "frass" showing.

Treatment. As the larva hibernates in cracks in the bark or in rubbish such as dead leaves on the ground, general tidiness is essential. Trees with rough, moss-covered bark should be sprayed with tar oil in winter. In bad attacks lead arsenate should be sprayed on to the blossoms 14 days after petal-fall. (Note. Codling Moth should be compared with Apple Sawfly. Codling Moth occurs later and its grub has eight pairs of legs while that of the Sawfly has ten. Fruits attacked by Codling Moth do not show frass exuding from the hole in the flesh and if cut across the destroyed part will be mainly in the centre around the core.)

CORAL SPOT

The disease attacks a wide range of ornamental, forest and fruit trees and shrubs. It is particularly common on red currants, and often enters through wounds or breakage of branches.

Symptoms. Branches often wilt suddenly and die. When the wood is dead, pink to red pustules appear. These are full of spores which are later released and so spread infection.

Treatment. All wilting and dead branches should be cut out as soon as possible and burned. As the fungus can also live on dead twigs, or old stakes and posts, tidiness in the garden is essential. New stakes and posts should be treated with a preservative.

CUCKOO SPIT

The small, pale greenish-yellow larva of the Frog-hopper attacks many plants especially herbaceous plants, sucking the sap and surrounding itself with a white froth. Not usually serious.

513

Symptoms. The froth is generally seen towards the top of the shoots.
Treatment. Spray forcibly with nicotine.

CURRANT MOTHS

The Currant Clearwing and the Currant Shoot Borer are two moths which sometimes cause appreciable loss but are generally of little importance. The life histories are different but the caterpillars of both tunnel into the young shoots causing them to wilt and die.
Treatment. Cut off and burn infested shoots.

CUTWORMS OR SURFACE CATERPILLARS

This heading covers the caterpillars of several different moths. They are mostly grey to black and generally feed at night on a wide range of plants.
Symptoms. Seedlings and young plants suddenly wilt and are found to be eaten at or just below ground level.
Treatment. Collect the caterpillars to be found around any wilted plant and set baits of Paris Green and bran.

DAMPING OFF

Several different fungi are concerned and a wide range of plants in the seedling stage may be affected.
Symptoms. The fungi attack the seedlings at ground level and a sudden collapse of the stems follows.
Treatment. Good growing and general hygiene are essential. Under glass ample ventilation must be given and excessive moisture avoided. Seeds should be sown in sterilized soil or watered with Cheshunt Compound.

DEFICIENCY DISEASES

This term is used to cover a wide range of non-parasitic disorders due to the lack of any one essential plant food leading to unnatural or malformed growth. Among the most common are:

Leaf-scorch. Many trees and shrubs may show dry, yellow to reddish-brown leaves due to lack of potash.

Blotchy Ripening in tomatoes may be due to lack of potash or less commonly of nitrogen.

Brown Heart of turnips and swedes due to lack of boron may cause the roots to be tough and bitter after being cooked. Beetroot may suffer in a similar way.

Chlorosis or patchiness in the leaves may be due to lack of lime or iron.

Whiptail of cauliflowers may be due to lack of molybdenum causing the young plants to go blind and show malformed leaves.

514

Treatment. A proper system of manuring must be carried out. The trace elements, such as boron, are required only in minute quantities and are best applied in the form of good farmyard manure and organic fertilizers, e.g. hoof and horn, shoddy, blood, bonemeal, etc.

DIE-BACK

This term is used to describe various kinds of sudden die-back in the young shoots of many trees and shrubs. They may be due to poor soil or cultivation or caused by certain bacteria and fungi. The effects often resemble those of **Canker**.

Treatment. Cut out and burn affected shoots and branches.

DRY ROT OF POTATOES

The early varieties are the more susceptible and the disease is most noticeable during the storage period.

Symptoms. Infected tubers shrink and shrivel, the sunken areas showing white or pinkish pustules.

Treatment. All tubers in store should be examined regularly and infected ones removed and burned. Suspected tubers should never be used for seed as the rot is progressive and will lead to misses in the rows. Potatoes should always be handled carefully as infection easily enters through wounds.

EARTHWORMS

Earthworms are entirely beneficial. Their burrowing helps to drain and aerate the soil and they pull down large quantities of decaying vegetable matter for their food. But their casts can sometimes spoil the appearance of a lawn or interfere with games.

Treatment. Regular brushing is generally sufficient, but where large numbers are present the lawn should be dressed with a proprietary worm-killer or potassium permanganate $\frac{3}{4}$ oz. to 1 gallon of water for every square yard. Poisons such as lead arsenate or copper sulphate should be avoided as the dead worms will be poisonous to birds or poultry.

EARWIGS

Earwigs feed at night and hide during the day under leaves, in canes, boxes or rubbish. They are generally most troublesome on greenhouse plants, but also attack many plants grown out of doors.

Symptoms. The leaves show holes and eaten areas and the flowers become ragged or malformed.

Treatment. All dead leaves and rubbish should be cleaned up and the plants sprayed or dusted with DDT. Large numbers of earwigs may be trapped in pieces of sacking or crumpled paper or in plant pots loosely stuffed with straw, set up on canes.

515

EELWORMS

There are many different species and strains of eelworms and several of them cause serious damage to cultivated plants. Generally speaking, they keep to their own host-plants or groups of plants, and if in the course of rotational cropping these are not grown in the infested soil the eelworms can still exist as dormant cysts for a few years. All species are minute, the largest being just visible to the naked eye. They can live within the plant tissue or encysted in the soil, so that they are easily and quickly spread from one part of the garden to another.

Symptoms. The Stem and Bulb Eelworm causes stunted, malformed growth in a large number of herbaceous and bulbous plants. The leaves are often narrow and twisted and the stems split or wiry-looking. The Leaf Blotch Eelworm causes brown or black areas in the leaves of many greenhouses plants including ferns, and a related species causes similar and often very serious damage to Chrysanthemums which generally also show malformed flowers. The Root-knot Eelworm causes galls on the roots of many plants, particularly tomatoes, cucumbers and flowers grown in greenhouses. In bad attacks the whole root system is affected, the plant wilts and may even die. Another species attacks the buds of currants, and yet another may be extremely serious on potatoes by stunting the growth so much that little or no crop is obtained. In this case the females can often be seen as minute whitish to brownish spherical bodies on the roots or tubers.

Treatment. There is no known cure. All plants bought in should be purchased from reliable sources only. Susceptible crops should not be planted in infested soil for 3–5 years and in the vegetable garden a long rotation should be strictly followed. Greenhouse borders should be sterilized.

FLEA BEETLES

Several species of small, black or blue-black beetles about $\frac{1}{10}$ inch long, with yellowish stripes on the wing-cases, attack many plants especially the cabbage family, turnips, beetroot and several herbaceous plants. They are most destructive to seedlings.

Symptoms. The leaves show small holes as well as eaten areas. The plants look blue.

Treatment. As the beetles hibernate in rubbish, hedges, etc. a clean, tidy garden is essential. Seedlings should be sprayed or dusted with derris or DDT once a fortnight for as long as necessary.

GOOSEBERRY SAWFLY

This is a common pest which may be very destructive if not controlled in the early stages. It occasionally attacks currants also. The fly is typical

516

of many sawflies, black and yellowish in colour and $\frac{1}{3}$ inch long. The caterpillars are green at first with black spots. Later the spots disappear and small orange-coloured areas develop at both ends. There are generally three generations a year.

Symptoms. The caterpillars feed on the leaves and shoots and if unchecked may strip the whole bush of its foliage.

Treatment. Spray or dust with derris or DDT. On a small scale the caterpillars can be picked off by hand.

Note. It is important to distinguish the caterpillars of this sawfly from those of the Magpie Moth which are black, white and yellow, for although the control measures are the same, there is only one generation of Magpie Moths a year, whereas the sawflies will continue to demand attention.

GREASE BANDING—See WINTER MOTH.

GREENFLY—See APHIDES.

GREENHOUSE WHITE FLY

This white waxy-looking fly about $\frac{1}{25}$ inch long attacks many greenhouse plants. It is distinct from the Cabbage White Fly and cannot survive the winter out of doors.

Symptoms. The larvæ suck the sap causing the leaves to lose colour and look spotted. The flies fly readily when disturbed.

Treatment. Fumigate with hydrocyanic acid gas or tetrachlorethane.

GREY MOULD

Although a number of outdoor plants particularly lettuce are attacked the greatest damage is done to fruit, flowers and vegetables growing under glass.

Symptoms. A greyish velvety fungus develops and leads to decay.

Treatment. Infected material should be removed and burned. Under glass ample ventilation must be given and humidity reduced.

LACKEY MOTH

Although always present, especially in the south, this yellowish to reddish-brown moth with a wing-span of $1\frac{1}{2}$ inches, does little harm until a year comes when it assumes epidemic proportions. Most kinds of fruit trees and several kinds of forest and ornamental trees are attacked.

Symptoms. The eggs which are easily seen are laid on young shoots in the form of a bracelet made up of 100–150 eggs. When hatched, the caterpillars keep together spinning a web to form a tent in which they live. As they eat the foliage they move on, spinning another tent. The caterpillars are bluish-grey with white and orange stripes.

Treatment. The best control is to break up the "tents" and destroy the caterpillars by hand. Spraying with lead arsenate or DDT must be done early to be effective. In winter the egg-bracelets should be cut off and destroyed.

LEAF GALLS

Many different kinds of galls and swellings may often be seen on the leaves of a number of ornamental trees and shrubs. They are caused by various species of Gall-wasps, Gall-midges and Gall-mites, but only very rarely does any harm result.

Treatment. If a young and valuable tree is seriously attacked by gall-wasps or gall-midges, it should be sprayed with nicotine. If the galls are caused by gall-mites it should be sprayed with 5% lime-sulphur.

LEAF-MINERS

The larvæ of many different species of moths, weevils and flies are loosely but conveniently classed as Leaf-miners. They attack a wide range of plants, among them apples, roses, shrubs, herbaceous plants and vegetables. Chrysanthemum, cineraria, azalea, celery and beetroot are probably the most important.

Symptoms. The larvæ live on the inner tissue of the leaf between the upper and lower surfaces, making characteristic tunnels or mines as they move along.

Treatment. Weeds must be kept down since many of them can act as host plants. On a small scale the larvæ can be crushed in their mines with the finger and thumb or affected leaves can be picked off and burned. A quick-acting top-dressing can be applied to help the crop along and soot can be dusted over to repel the egg-laying adults. On a larger scale or when the attack is severe the crop should be sprayed with nicotine.

LEAF MOULD OF TOMATOES

The fungus often causes severe losses in tomatoes under glass. It is rarely seen on the outdoor crop.

Symptoms. Yellowish spots which later take on a purplish tinge, appear on the leaves in June or July. On the undersides a grey mould appears. The affected parts dry out and the leaves shrivel or die.

Treatment. The atmosphere must not get too warm or too humid. Ventilation should always be given and as soon as the disease appears must be increased. Overhead spraying must be stopped and watering reduced. The lower leaves should be stripped. If necessary a colloidal copper spray should be used at intervals of 10–14 days. At the end of the season the house should be washed down with formalin or fumigated with sulphur. Resistant varieties are obtainable.

518

LEAF ROLLER—See Slugworms and Tortrix.

LEAF SPOTS

Several different fungi attack different crops, including many herbaceous plants, but the disease is not generally serious. Celery and chrysanthemums are perhaps the most important.

Symptoms. Brown, round spots appear on the leaves and occasionally on the stems.

Treatment. With most plants good growing is generally a sufficient control. In severe attacks Bordeaux Mixture should be used. With celery the disease is carried in the seed, and care should be taken to buy from a reputable source.

LEATHER JACKETS

These are the well-known dirty-brown or greyish-black legless grubs of the Daddy Longlegs or Crane Flies. They have a tough, leathery skin, are about 1 to $1\frac{1}{2}$ inches long, and feed on the roots of a wide range of plants.

Symptoms. The plant suddenly wilts and if dug up a grub can often be found or it may have moved on to the next plant.

Treatment. General cleanliness and regular hoeing is normally sufficient. Bad attacks often follow the breaking up of old or neglected turf when baits of Paris Green or powdered naphthalene should be used.

LEOPARD MOTH

The wings are white with bluish-black spots and have a span of $2\frac{1}{2}$ inches. The moths appear in June and July and lay eggs on fruit trees, especially apples, and many ornamental and forest trees. The caterpillars are yellowish-white with black spots and grow to 2 inches long. They tunnel into the shoots and branches where they stay for 2 or 3 years.

Symptoms. The foliage turns yellow and wilts and on young trees sawdust or frass may be seen. On cutting open infested branches the tunnels may be seen.

Treatment. Cut out and burn infested branches. In severe attacks it may be necessary to grub and burn the whole tree.

MAGPIE MOTH

The caterpillars of this well-known black, white and yellow moth feed on the leaves of currants, gooseberries, laurels, apricots, nuts and other plants and if neglected may cause serious defoliation. There is one generation a year beginning in July or August when the eggs are laid.

Symptoms. The caterpillars are at first small and black. They feed till the autumn, then hibernate on the bark or dead leaves and emerge again

519

in the spring when they feed on the young growth, become much larger and black and white with a yellow stripe. They pupate generally on the tree and the moth emerges in July.

Treatment. As soon as the caterpillars are seen, spray or dust with derris or DDT. On a small scale the caterpillars may be picked off by hand.

MEALY BUG

These small, scale-like insects have a white, waxy covering, are fairly active and breed throughout the year. They occur principally in glass-houses, especially on vines, but are also found out of doors on Ribes, Ceanothus, Robinia, Laburnum and less commonly on other shrubs. They feed by sucking the sap and may occur on the roots as well as the foliage.

Treatment. Repeated spraying with nicotine is necessary. In addition glasshouses should be fumigated with hydrocyanic acid gas at the end of the season.

MILDEW

The mildews which occur on a great number of trees, shrubs and plants can be very broadly divided into two types: the Powdery mildews where the fungi live on the surface of the foliage, spoiling the appearance rather than causing serious harm, and the Downy mildews, which are more deep-seated, live within the tissues and as a rule are far more serious. Powdery mildews are found on roses, vines, apples, gooseberries, marrows, turnips, strawberries, chrysanthemums, asters, calendulas and many other plants. Downy mildews appear on brassica seedlings, lettuce, onions, spinach, vines, wallflowers, stocks, etc.

Symptoms. The Powdery mildews generally produce a whitish to greyish powdery effect on the foliage while the Downy mildews cause yellowish patches on the leaves with (generally) a greyish or purplish downy growth on the underside.

Treatment. For Powdery mildews dust with sulphur and remove any badly-infected shoots. For Downy mildews remove all infected plants and shoots and spray with Bordeaux Mixture or dust with a copper-lime dust. In both cases, avoid overcrowding and under glass give ample ventilation and reduce humidity.

MILLEPEDES

Millepedes attack the leaves of seedlings and the roots of a large number of plants and frequently eat into bulbs. They often extend the damage caused by wounds or other insects and generally set up decay. They must be distinguished from CENTIPEDES which are beneficial. (Centipedes are flat in appearance, have one pair of legs to each body segment and are

520

very active; millepedes have two pairs of legs to each segment, are more rounded and usually curl up when disturbed.)

Treatment. Regular hoeing and good cultivation is generally sufficient. In bad attacks the soil should be dressed with naphthalene or seedlings may be dusted with DDT. Large numbers may be trapped in pieces of potato or carrot buried in the soil. These baits should be marked and examined every few days.

MOSQUITOES

Mosquitoes, particularly the blood-sucking females, are a pest of the gardener and not of the plants he grows. In some gardens where there are ponds, streams or exposed water and liquid-manure tanks they can be a great nuisance. The larvæ sometimes called "wrigglers" live and feed in the water, continually rising to the surface to breathe through their tails.

Treatment. Fish in ponds will readily eat all the eggs and larvæ they can reach, and they should be helped by preventing plants from spreading over the surface of the water and providing hiding places for the pest. DDT may be sprayed on to the water *only* where there is no danger of its coming into contact with fish.

MUSHROOM FLIES

Several species of small black flies about ¼ inch long, which normally live on decaying vegetables matter, will attack mushrooms.

Symptoms. The larvæ eat into the stems and set up decay.

Treatment. Doors and ventilators should be screened with fine gauze or muslin and the beds sprayed or dusted with derris, pyrethrum or DDT. In severe attacks fumigate with hydrocyanic acid gas.

MUSHROOM MITES

Several species of mites often occur on mushroom beds, usually introduced in the manure. Slow-moving grey or white mites are the most harmful, but they have their own enemies—the more active brown mites which are therefore beneficial.

Symptoms. The mites tunnel into the stalks and caps and the mushrooms turn brown.

Treatment. Fumigation is of doubtful value. Derris or pyrethrum dust gives some control but the best method is to clean the shed and equipment thoroughly with boiling water.

MUSHROOM MOULDS

The White Plaster mould may appear as a whitish powder on the surface of the bed at spawning time and the Brown Plaster mould may occur on the compost as a white fluff which later turns brown. Both these

521

fungi rob the crop of its nutriment but neither is usually serious, and good growing is normally a sufficient control.

But there is another White mould or Mycogone which grows vigorously completely covering the mushrooms and ruining the crop. The only control is to remove and burn all infected material and when the crop is finished to disinfect the house, boxes, trays, etc. with formalin or cresylic acid.

NARCISSUS FLIES

There are three kinds: the large Narcissus Fly which confines its attacks to narcissi (which include daffodils) and two smaller ones, known as Small Bulb Flies which may also attack other bulbs and occasionally some of the root vegetables.

The Large Fly resembles a small "Bumble" bee. It lays eggs in May and June singly on or near a bulb. The larva burrows in and eats out the centre of the bulb. The Small Flies appear earlier, are more like Hover flies and lay several eggs to each bulb.

Symptoms. Bulbs which show weak or distorted growth in spring should be lifted. If soft they will probably contain the larva or chrysalis of the Large Fly or if rotten they may show the presence of the Small Flies. At the planting time the bulbs should be pressed gently; those which feel soft and springy may contain the hibernating larva of the Large Fly.

Treatment. Discard all suspicious bulbs. In bad attacks dust with BHC or DDT dusts every fortnight from end-April to end-June. Where possible suspected stocks may be given the hot-water treatment before planting, by being immersed for 1 hour in water kept at 110°F.

ONION FLY

A small grey fly with black and brown markings, resembling a house fly, may attack onions, leeks and shallots from spring onwards. The eggs are laid on the young leaves and stems. There are three generations.

Symptoms. Dirty-white maggots about $\frac{1}{3}$ inch long, burrow into the bulb. The leaves and stems turn yellow, seedlings may be killed and the bulbs begin to rot.

Treatment. Remove and burn infected plants taking care not to leave any maggots in the soil. Dust with calomel and grow the next year's crop as far away from the site as possible.

ONION SMUT

Onions, leeks, shallots and chives are attacked in the seedling stages and serious losses may occur. The disease is not general.

Symptoms. Dark, greyish stripes occur on the leaves which begin to wilt.

522

Treatment. Remove and burn infected plants. Susceptible crops should not be grown on the same site again as infection remains in the soil for many years.

PEA MOTH

A grey-brown moth about ¼ inch long may be seen fluttering over the crop from mid-June to mid-August.

Symptoms. The caterpillars eat into the pods and feed on the developing peas, causing the damage that is so well-known.

Treatment. Regular hoeing will destroy many of the larvæ which when fully-fed leave the plant to pupate in the soil. In bad areas damage can be largely avoided by sowing only early and late crops and missing out mid-season varieties. Spraying with DDT or nicotine gives partial control.

PEA WEEVIL—See BEAN WEEVIL.

PEACH LEAF CURL

Sometimes called Peach Leaf Blister, this disease is caused by a fungus which attacks peaches, nectarines, almonds and occasionally other species of Prunus.

Symptoms. The leaves become swollen, curled or malformed, look blistered and change to a reddish colour. The flowers and fruits may sometimes be affected.

Treatment. Spray with Burgundy or Bordeaux mixture in February or March as soon as the buds begin to swell.

PEAR LEAF BLISTER MITE

This may be a troublesome pest in the south of the country especially on cordons or trees trained against a wall. Apples, cotoneaster and some other trees may also be attacked. The mite is microscopic, hibernates at the base of a bud and begins to feed as the new growth develops. There are several generations a year.

Symptoms. The mite burrows into the leaf causing green or reddish blisters, which later turn brown or black. Young fruits and stalks may also be attacked.

Treatment. Lime-sulphur (5% solution) should be sprayed on just before the buds open (usually in early March). Slight attacks can be controlled by the early removal and burning of affected leaves.

PEAR MIDGE

The minute black adults, typical of "midges," lay their eggs at blossom time. The maggots burrow into the developing fruits. Mid-season varieties suffer most.

Symptoms. Attacked fruitlets have a flattened appearance. Most of them fall to the ground. If cut open they generally show the maggots inside.

Treatment. As the maggots pupate in the soil regular hoeing will destroy most of them. All infested fruits should be collected and burned. Alternatively the soil may be sprayed with tar oil wash, covering an area a little greater than the spread of the tree, or the tree may be sprayed with DDT. (Tar oil must not be applied to the tree at this time of year.)

PHYSIOLOGICAL DISORDERS

Poor conditions, lack of air or water, unsuitable temperatures in greenhouses or an abnormal climate out of doors, will produce certain well-recognized disorders in many plants. None of them is infectious.

Tomatoes seem particularly subject: irregular watering and excess of nitrogen often causes a premature Blossom Drop, and too much heat and humidity may cause a blister-like Oedema on the leaves and sometimes on the fruit. Potato tubers may show various forms of cracking or malformation, generally due to excessive moisture after a dry spell, or the flesh may show a discoloration which is probably caused by lack of humus. Many fruits may suffer from sun-scald causing discoloration of the skin or glassy patches. Apples are subject to various kinds of breakdown, particularly in store, one of the commonest being Bitter-pit which causes spongy brown spots in the flesh.

Treatment. What little can be done must be of a preventive nature and consists mainly of good and careful growing.

POTATO BLIGHT

This disease may cause very serious losses among potatoes and out-door tomatoes, especially in warm, moist summers when infection spreads rapidly. The damage done to the leaves prevents a normal crop being produced.

Symptoms. Patches appear on the leaves, generally near the edges at first. They are brown to black on top and greyish underneath. In potatoes the spores may be washed down through the soil to the tubers and cause a brownish colour on the flesh under the skin. The infected tubers may rot in store and affect sound tubers. In tomatoes the fruits shrivel, crack and rot.

Treatment. Immediately the first sign is seen the crop must be sprayed with Bordeaux or Burgundy Mixture or a proprietary copper spray. The spraying must be repeated every fortnight as necessary. Dusts may also be used (as often as once a week in a wet season). When lifting the potatoes the haulm should first be cut off and burned and only sound tubers should be put into store and none saved for seed.

POTATO SCAB

There are two forms of scab caused by different fungi, Common Scab and Corky Scab.

Symptoms. Common Scab causes the well-known rough, dry, scabby patches on the skin of potatoes. Sometimes the patches are deep and sunken, but generally they are only skin deep and are removed in peeling. The seriousness of the disease is that it spoils the appearance of the crop.

Corky Scab also causes scabby areas which later break to form a canker. It is the more serious but less common of the two.

Treatment. Common Scab is worst on dry, gravelly or overlimed soils and can be reduced by good dressings of farmyard manure or compost. Lime should never be applied to a potato crop. For Corky Scab the best remedy is to space the crop as far apart as possible in the rotation. Tubers from an infected crop should not be saved for seed.

RASPBERRY BEETLE

The beetles are about $1\frac{1}{8}$ inch long, golden-brown to greyish-brown. They attack the buds and flowers and the yellowish larvæ burrow into the fruits, causing the well-known "maggoty raspberries". Loganberries and blackberries are also attacked. Severe infestation will render the crop useless and even slight attacks will spoil the appearance of the fruit.

Symptoms. These are not generally noticed until the grubs are found inside the ripe fruit. Eradication is then impossible, but the warning is given that control measures will be essential for the following crop.

Treatment. Spray or dust with derris 10 days after flowering and again 12–14 days later.

RASPBERRY FUNGUS DISEASES

Several different fungi attack raspberries. The leaves may suffer from rust or mildew and the canes from several forms of spotting or wilting. As a rule none of these is serious and good growing, removal of infected canes, tidiness and the avoidance of overcrowding keep the crop healthy.

RASPBERRY MOTH

The moth is dark purplish-brown, small with a wing-span of $\frac{1}{4}$ inch. The eggs are laid on the flowers in June and for a time the tiny larvæ live inside the plug of the fruit but they do no harm. They leave the fruit to hibernate and the following spring crawl up the canes and enter the shoots, tunnelling inside. They are then pink to red.

Symptoms. The new shoots begin to wither and die. If cut open the caterpillars may be found.

Treatment. Cut off and burn wilted shoots and keep the bed tidy and regularly hoed.

525

RED SPIDER MITES

Three species are of importance to gardeners, the Greenhouse Red Spider which attacks a wide range of greenhouse plants including fruits like grapes and peaches, the Fruit Tree Red Spider found on fruit trees growing out of doors and the Gooseberry Red Spider which not only attacks gooseberries but also many alpine plants in the open and under glass. In hot dry summers other outdoor plants may also be attacked. The mites are small, just visible, and are usually greenish-grey to pale red, becoming more red as they mature. They generally feed on the underside. of the leaves sucking the sap and often spin a fine webbing which acts as a protection.

Symptoms. Attacked leaves lose their fresh green colour and look dry. Later they take on a rusty colour with a silvery effect and begin to fall. The mites and their webs may be seen on the undersides.

Treatment. Outdoor trees should be sprayed with a petroleum wash in winter or with lime sulphur and nicotine in spring. Greenhouses should be fumigated with azobenzene but tender-leaved plants should be sprayed with nicotine.

REVERSION

This is a serious virus disease of black currants. As infection spreads in the bush the blossoms become affected and the crop is progressively reduced. The disease is spread by the Currant Gall Mite and possibly by aphids and capsids. It can also be carried on pruning knives.

Symptoms. The leaves become smaller and narrower and the marginal teeth and main veins become fewer. A healthy leaf has 5 to 8 veins on each side of the main (middle) vein, a reverted leaf has less than 5. These symptoms are only reliable if seen during June on strong-growing shoots. They can also arise from mechanical or other damage but in such cases later growth quickly becomes normal.

Treatment. Once infected, a bush cannot be cured. The only safe course is to grub and replant with healthy stock. Cuttings should never be taken from an apparently healthy branch on a bush which also shows one or more infected branches.

RHODODENDRON BUG

The adult is about ⅛ inch long, shiny and black with netted wings. The eggs are laid in the lower surface of the leaves in late summer and the larvæ hatch in the following spring.

Symptoms. The leaves become spotted with rusty-looking spots on the underside and mottled on the upper surface.

Treatment. Nicotine should be sprayed on to the undersides of the leaves about mid-June and again 2–3 weeks later. After bad attacks

526

careful cutting back of all shoots should be done in March. These should be burned to destroy the eggs which are generally laid on the top leaves.

RHODODENDRON WHITE FLY

The small white mealy fly may be seen in June and July on the under-sides of the leaves. Eggs are laid on the leaves and the larvæ feed until the following spring.

Symptoms. The larvæ excrete honeydew which falls on to the leaves below. These become black owing to the growth of a "Sooty Mould". Where flies are suspected, shaking of the branches may dislodge the flies which at once fly upwards but quickly resettle.

Treatment. Spray or dust with nicotine in September and April, taking care to cover undersides of leaves. In bad attacks prune hard in March.

ROSE SAWFLY—See SLUGWORMS.

RUSTS

Several different species of fungi cause rusts on the foliage of a number of plants. The most important are antirrhinums, asparagus, carnations under glass, chrysanthemums, hollyhocks and mint.

Symptoms. Small brown, reddish or orange-coloured spots occur often giving a dry, rusty appearance. The spots contain the spores which may sometimes be released as a dust when the plant is shaken. Defoliation and death may follow.

Treatment. General hygiene and good, careful growing are usually a sufficient control on chrysanthemums, carnations and hollyhocks, especially if the first leaves to be attacked are removed and burned. Asparagus should be dusted with sulphur and resistant varieties of antirrhinum should be used. Infected beds of mint should be destroyed and replaced with healthy stock, although a partial control can be obtained by burning off the bed with straw in the autumn.

SAWFLIES—See SLUGWORMS.

SCALE INSECTS

There are many different species, varying in colour and shape, but all are what may be called "stationary pests". When young the larvæ move about on the host-plant, but later they develop a protective covering (which may be hard or soft) under which they live by sucking the sap from the plant. Some species attack outdoor plants including fruit trees, forest trees and ornamental trees and shrubs, the most important being apples, beech, ceanothus, cotoneaster, yew, peach, currant, ivy, holly, camellias, etc. Others are found on a wide range of greenhouse plants, particularly

527

vines, figs, ferns, orchids and palms. In numbers, scale insects can be very serious.

Symptoms. The stationary oval to round scale appears to be stuck on to the plant. Many species excrete a honeydew which falls on to other leaves and often becomes covered with a "Sooty Mould". Ants are frequently present, attracted by the honeydew.

Treatment. Tender plants should be sponged with nicotine wash. Single scales should be prised off with a pointed stick. In more serious cases nicotine should be sprayed on and deciduous trees sprayed with tar oil in winter. Greenhouses should be fumigated with hydrocyanic gas when possible.

SILVER LEAF

This disease is due to a fungus which invades the branches of trees and in some way interferes with the normal growth of the leaves by allowing air to enter between the top and bottom surfaces. This produces the characteristic silvery or leaden sheen. It is a serious disease of plums but also occurs on apples, poplars, Portugal laurel, cherries, thorns and peaches.

Symptoms. In addition to the silvering of the leaves, dead branches are usually present. On the dead wood the fruiting stage of the fungus may be seen in the form of purplish crusts several inches long or as bracket-shaped projections up to an inch wide.

Treatment. Since infection can only come from the spores in the fruiting bodies, all dead wood should be cut out and burned. This should be done early in the summer when natural healing takes place most readily. The work must be finished by 15th July (Silver Leaf Order 1923). The fruiting bodies also occur on wooden posts or stakes which should not therefore be left lying about. As the spores can only enter through wounds any broken branches should be cut clean and all pruning wounds should be covered over with white lead paint or grafting wax.

SLUGWORMS OR SAWFLIES

The name is given to a large group of Sawflies the larvæ of which resemble small slugs although they are usually white when young and become dark-green to black later, and have ten pairs of legs which is a characteristic of all sawflies. The most important species are those which attack cherries and pears, various shrubs and roses. The adult flies are generally dark in colour, about $\frac{1}{3}$ inch long, appearing in May and June and again in August when a second generation occurs.

Symptoms. The slugworms feed on the leaves, often eating the upper surface completely away. Some roll the leaves into a rough cylinder and other species, particularly the Rose Shoot-borer, burrow their way down the stem.

528

PLATE 61   Reading left to right : Apple Sucker (X), eggs of Asparagus Beetle (X) and Bean
Aphis (X).   The sign (X) indicates that the subject is magnified.   *Shell Photo and Plant Protection Ltd.*

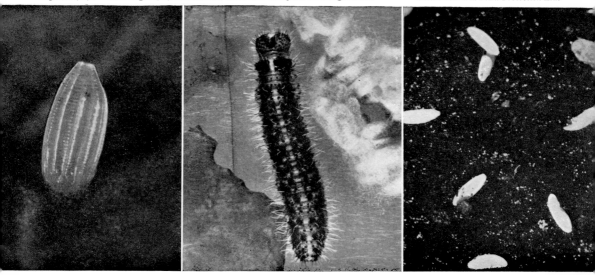

Reading left to right, *above*, egg and caterpillar of Cabbage White butterfly (X), eggs of Cabbage
Root Fly ; *below*, Cutworm (X) Flea Beetle (X), and Hover Fly (X) and egg.

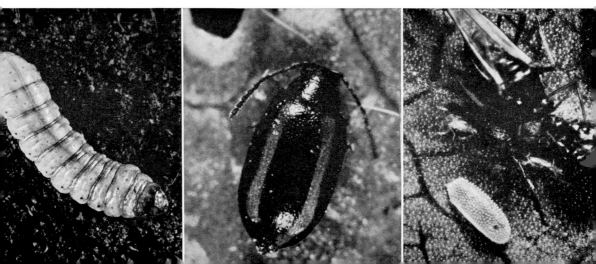

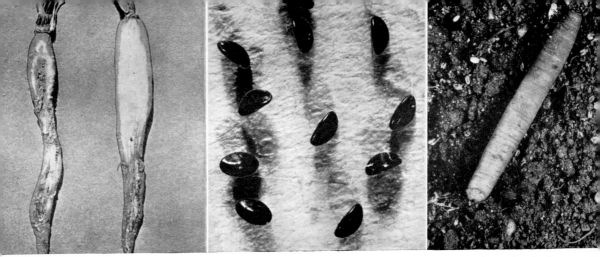

PLATE 62   *Left*, damage due to Carrot Fly, *centre and right*, eggs and larva of Leather-jacket.

Shell Photo and Plant Protection Ltd.

Reading left to right, *above*, Red Spider Mite on cucumber, Slug eggs (X) and adult on cabbage, leaf ; *below*, Raspberry Beetle (X), White Fly on cucumber and Woolly Aphis.

Treatment. Since most sawflies pupate in the soil, good and continuous cultivation helps to reduce numbers considerably. In severe attacks spraying with nicotine should be carried out. Lead arsenate may also be used except where an edible crop is being produced.

SLUGS AND SNAILS

Enormous damage is done by slugs and snails, much of it never visible. Some species feed at or above ground level, others below. Most of the feeding is done at night or on moist warm evenings and whole rows of germinating seedlings may be eaten off in a very short time. Slugs feed all the year round, snails hibernate in groups, especially in rockeries.

Treatment. Continual attention is necessary and one of the many proprietary "slug-killers" should be used or a bait can be made up at home using 1 oz. metaldehyde to 3 lbs of bran. This should be dotted about in small heaps about a foot apart.

SMALL ERMINE MOTHS

The caterpillars of several species of Ermine moths feed on the foliage of apples, hawthorn and spindle. Other fruit trees and shrubs are less commonly attacked.

Symptoms. From May to July greyish caterpillars up to $\frac{1}{2}$ inch long, with black spots, may be seen eating the leaves and living in webs spun between the leaves or twigs.

Treatment. Spray with lead arsenate. Tar oil washes may be used in winter on deciduous trees.

STORAGE ROTS

All forms of rotting which occur among fruit, vegetables, bulbs or roots in store are not necessarily serious, apart from the loss they cause. But those due to fungi and bacteria must be regarded very differently because they are generally infectious, may spread very quickly, and contaminate the store for another year.

Treatment. Stores must be kept clean and should be washed down every year with boiling water and soda. The crops in store must be regularly examined. In bad cases the store should be cleaned with formalin, but other disinfectants with characteristic odours should be avoided.

THRIPS OR THUNDER FLIES

Small black flies about $\frac{1}{15}$ inch long are often seen on many plants both out of doors and in greenhouses. As a rule, they appear to do little serious damage outside, but they act as carriers of certain virus diseases. In greenhouses they may become a serious pest of many flowering plants. They breed more or less continuously.

529

Symptoms. Thrips feed by scraping away the surface tissue and sucking the sap, causing mottled, spotted areas. In greenhouses flowers of carnations, cyclamen and many other plants may become distorted.

Treatment. Spray, or in greenhouses fumigate with nicotine.

TORTRIX MOTHS

There are a number of species which attack a wide range of plants in various ways. The larvæ appear in spring, most of them active and having the characteristic of wriggling backwards when disturbed or hanging from the leaf by a thread.

Symptoms. The larvæ feed on the leaves, shoots or buds, most of them rolling or spinning the leaves together. They are very common on oak trees. In apples the surface of the fruit is also scarred, in some herbaceous plants the flowers may be eaten, and in some shrubs the centre of the shoot may be eaten out.

Treatment. The larvæ may be crushed in the rolled leaves. In severe attacks nicotine spray or dust should be used as soon as possible (in the case of apples a few days before the blossom opens).

(See also Codling Moth and Pea Moth which belong to the Tortricidæ.)

TULIP FIRE

This can be a very serious fungus disease of tulips. It is generally worst in cold wet seasons.

Symptoms. Specks and streaks occur on the leaves and flowers and the tips of the leaves become brown and scorched.

Treatment. The bulbs should be lifted every year and all unsound ones destroyed. Tulips should not be planted in the same soil for four or five years.

TURNIP FLEA BEETLE OR TURNIP FLY—See FLEA BEETLES.

VIRUS DISEASES

This group of diseases attacks a great number of plants. All are carried in the sap and so are frequently spread by sucking insects or other means of contact. Many have been proved to be highly infectious even though no microscopically-visible organism has as yet been isolated.

Symptoms. The general symptoms are an unhappy or stunted appearance about the plant. Growth is frequently checked and there may be malformation of the foliage or the production of a bad colour. In some cases parts of the foliage may dry up and die.

The most common types are as follows:

Mosaic. Many plants are attacked, showing a mottling or spotting of the leaves. Raspberries, potatoes, dahlias, marrows, cucumbers, etc.

Leaf-roll is often found in potatoes. The lower leaves curl upwards and feel dry and papery. The plant looks stunted and spiky.

Strawberries suffer from several virus diseases which cause a yellowing of the edges of the leaves, a crinkling or the production of many small leaves and few if any flowering stems instead of normal growth.

The "breaking" of tulips is due to infection by virus.

Treatment. The greatest control is effected by keeping down insects, especially aphides, and by buying in only healthy stocks of plants from reliable sources. Seed, including seed potatoes, cuttings or any other form of propagating material should never be used from an infected crop.

WART DISEASE OF POTATOES

This disease, sometimes called Black Scab, can be very serious resulting in a crop which rots in store. Only certain varieties known as "susceptible" or "non-immune" are affected.

Symptoms. Crinkled warts appear at base of stems and on the tubers.

Treatment. Under the Wart Disease of Potatoes Order, outbreaks must be notified to the Ministry of Agriculture and Fisheries, London, S.W.1, and only immune varieties may be grown in infected soil.

WEEVILS

Weevils are a type of beetle distinguished by their snout-like heads and legless grubs. There are several important species varying from brown to black, most of them about ⅓ inch long. The adults generally hide by day and feed at night, eating the leaves of many trees, bushes and plants while the grubs live on the roots. The bark of young trees is often attacked.

The Vine Weevil may become a serious pest both out of doors and under glass, especially to alpines and plants in pots.

Symptoms. In addition to the visible damage the plants may also show a poor colour and look unhappy. The grubs may often be seen on the roots of pot-plants if the plants are knocked out of their pots.

Treatment. The adults may be trapped in small heaps of rolled leaves, pieces of sacking or corrugated paper. The grubs may be picked off the roots of pot plants. Infected plants should be repotted in fresh or sterilized soil to which DDT dust has been added (8 oz. per bushel of soil).

WATER-PLANT PESTS

Some of the plants grown in ornamental pools, particularly water lilies, may be attacked by Aphis, the larvæ of the Water Moth or Caddis Fly and the adults and larvæ of the Water Lily Beetle.

Symptoms. The Water Moth larva is a caterpillar living in a tubular case, it feeds on the submerged part of the plant. The Water Lily Beetle is brown and feeds on the leaves and petals.

531

Treatment. None of the usual sprays containing arsenic, derris or DDT can be used because of the risk of poisoning fish. Pyrethrum is reasonably safe but the best plan is to help the fish reach the insects by syringing the plant forcibly to knock the insects into the water or by submerging the whole plant for a day at intervals as required.

WILTS

Various forms of wilts occur on a number of plants grown out of doors and under glass. Many of them are due to fungi which generally cause a sudden collapse of the plant.

Treatment. In the open the cropping should be changed and in the vegetable garden a long rotation introduced. Under glass the soil should be sterilized or replaced by fresh clean soil.

WINTER MOTHS

Three different species of moths give rise to caterpillars which attack fruit-trees and many ornamental trees and shrubs. The caterpillars move with a characteristic "looping" movement.

Symptoms. The caterpillars hatch in spring and can be seen feeding on the buds and young leaves. In June they let themselves down on a silken thread to pupate in the soil.

Treatment. Since the females are wingless and crawl up the trees to lay their eggs, many can be trapped by grease bands. These should be made of grease-proof paper 6 inches wide put round the trunk as high as possible, both the top and bottom edges of the paper being tied with string. The paper should then be smeared with a proprietary brand of grease.

WIREWORMS

These are the well-known shiny, yellowish-brown grubs found in many soils, particularly when turf has been newly broken up. They are the larvæ of the Click Beetles which are brown to black, $\frac{1}{2}$ inch long and often jump with a click when disturbed. Wireworms take up to five years to reach maturity and are then about $\frac{3}{4}$ inch long. They feed voraciously on the roots of most plants and burrow into bulbs, potatoes and other roots, and occasionally into the stems of tomatoes and chrysanthemums.

Symptoms. Seedlings and young plants wilt and die and when dug up often show the grub around the roots. Larger, stronger plants generally show less visible signs of attack, and in some cases, e.g. tuberous or bulbous plants and root vegetables, the presence of wireworms may not be suspected until the roots are lifted.

Treatment. Thorough cultivation and tidiness are very important. The grubs should be collected whenever they are seen. They may also be trapped in pieces of potato or carrot put into the soil on pointed sticks or in the flower garden, controlled with BHC.

WITHER TIP—See BLOSSOM WILT.

WOOLLY APHIS—(American Blight). See APHIDES.

WOODLICE

Though living principally on decaying vegetable matter, woodlice will often attack plants especially in frames and greenhouses. They feed at night and hide during the day.

Treatment. Rubbish should always be cleared away. In bad attacks the woodlice may be trapped in potatoes or orange peel or killed with baits of Paris Green and bran.

INSECTICIDES AND FUNGICIDES

Preparation	How to Make	Principal Use
Arsenate of Lead	Mix ½ lb. lead arsenate paste *or* 4 oz. lead arsenate powder with a little water. Make up to 10 gals. stirring all the time. Add a spreader (not soft soap).	Leaf-eating caterpillars, Codling Moth and larvæ of sawflies, beetles and weevils. Must not be used on edible crops near to harvesting nor on open blossom.
BHC (Benzene hexachloride)	Buy ready for use.	General insecticide, for aphis, caterpillars, weevils, capsid, sawfly, codling moth, leaf-miners, red spider and wireworm. Must not be used on open blossom nor on vegetable root crops.
Bordeaux Mixture	Put 1 gal. water into a wooden, earthenware or china vessel, add 1 lb. of powdered copper sulphate and stir. Into another vessel put 9 gals. water, add slowly 1¼ lb. hydrated lime and stir. When dissolved add the copper sulphate solution to the lime solution. Stir and use as soon as possible. Lead arsenate, nicotine, BHC or other insecticides can be added when necessary. A spreader (not soft soap) should be used.	Downy mildews, Potato blight and scab on some varieties of apples and pears.
Burgundy Mixture	Mix as above, using 1¼ lb. washing soda instead of lime	As above.
Calomel (mercurous chloride)	Sold as a 4% powder	Root flies and Club-root.
Cheshunt Compound	Mix 1 oz. powdered copper sulphate with 5½ oz. ammonium carbonate. Dissolve 1 oz. of the mixture in a little water and make up to 2 gals. Use a wooden receptacle. Can also be bought ready for use.	To control fungi causing "damping off" of seedlings. Apply with fine rose.

533

INSECTICIDES AND FUNGICIDES—*continued.*

Preparation	How to Make	Principal Use
Colloidal copper ⎫ Colloidal sulphur ⎬ Copper-lime dust ⎭	Can be bought under various proprietary names.	General fungicide for use in place of Bordeaux or Burgundy Mixtures.
Cresylic acid	Mix 1 gal. cresylic acid with 39 gals. water. Use 4 gals per sq. yd. and dig in.	Soil insects and certain soil fungi.
DDT	Can be bought ready for using as spray, dust or smoke.	Ants, woodlice, capsids, caterpillars, carrot fly and greenhouse pests. Dangerous to fish.
Derris	Can be bought ready for using as spray or dust.	For flea-beetles and as a non-poisonous substitute for nicotine. Dangerous to fish.
Formalin	1 pint Formalin to 49 gals. water. Dig the soil and sprinkle on 3 gals. per sq. yd.	For soil insects and soil fungi.
Greenhouse Fumigants	Buy proprietary fumigants ready for use as liquids or smokes containing BHC, azobenzene, DDT, tetrachlorethane, nicotine or hydrogen cyanide.	For aphis, thrips, white fly, red spider, scale, mealy bug, leaf-miners, etc.
Lime Sulphur	Buy ready for mixing. Use at 2% before blossoming and 1% after. Arsenate of lead or nicotine may be added if desired using a spreader (not soft soap).	Apple and pear scab, also red spider and other mites.
Meta (Metaldehyde)	1 oz. Meta to 3 lb. bran. Set in small heaps 1-2 ft. apart or scattered thinly.	Slugs and snails. Cover heaps to safeguard birds and pets.
Naphthalene powder	Sprinkle on the soil 3-4 oz. per sq. yd. Rake in. (Up to 6 or 8 oz. if infestation is heavy)	Wireworms, leather-jackets, millepedes, soil caterpillars.
Nicotine	Dissolve ½ lb. soft soap in a little warm water. When cool add ¾ oz. nicotine and make up to 10 gals. with water. A proprietary spreader may be used instead of soft soap.	Aphis, capsids, thrips, leaf-miners, leaf-hoppers, scale mealy bug and small young caterpillars.
Nicotine Dust	Buy ready for use. Frequent applications necessary.	As above, also for leaf-curling insects if applied in warm weather.
Paris Green	1 oz. Paris Green to 2 lb. bran, slightly moistened.	Leatherjackets, cutworms.
	1 oz. Paris Green to 4 lb. dried blood.	Woodlice. Cover baits to safeguard birds and pets.
Pyrethrum	Buy ready for use.	As for nicotine.
Sulphur	Buy ready for use as (1) a very finely-ground powder. (2) a fumigant in greenhouses.	For Powdery mildews. As above and for Leaf Mould.
White Oil	Buy ready for using.	Mealy bug, red spider and scale.
Winter Washes	Buy proprietary brands ready for using.	For use on trees and shrubs when dormant to destroy eggs of aphis, winter moths, red spider, scale, apple sucker, etc.

CHAPTER 43

THE LEGAL SIDE OF GARDENING

By F. G. Underhay, *Barrister-at-Law*.

In connection with the garden there are certain matters of a legal nature with which most gardeners must necessarily be concerned at some time, and it is with a view to affording some assistance in dealing with such matters that the present chapter is appended.

Fences.—The word fence properly applies to a wall, drain, ditch or hedge, whether for appearance or to prevent trespass.

In the absence of evidence to the contrary, where two pieces of land are separated by a hedge and ditch, the hedge and ditch belong to the owner of the land in which the ditch is not, so that the hedge stands between the ditch and rest of the land with which both hedge and ditch go. If, however, the owner of the land in which the ditch is, has pruned the hedge and trimmed the ditch for twenty years with the knowledge and acquiescence of the adjoining owner, he will acquire a prescriptive right thereto. Where there is a ditch on both sides of the hedge, a right to the hedge can only be proved by acts of ownership. As a rule, a fence is owned by the owner of the land on which the posts stand. Trees in hedgerows generally belong to the hedge, but if it can be shown that the greater part of the roots and boughs are in the adjoining land, the tree will belong accordingly; wherever the whole of the roots are there is the ownership, and the whole of the trunk equally governs any decision. Occupiers are liable for the state of their fences, unless there is a covenant to the contrary.

Repair of Fences.—The general rule is that a person must keep his own animals from trespassing, but he is under no obligation to fence against his neighbour's unless his neighbour has acquired a prescriptive right to have such fence maintained. The mere fact, however, that a person has for more than twenty years kept up a fence between his own and the adjoining land is not, in itself, sufficient to give the owner of the latter a right to have the fence maintained; but if during that period the hedge had from time to time been repaired at the request of, or upon complaint from, the adjoining owner, it would be otherwise. If there is a prescriptive obligation to repair, the person upon whom it rests must maintain the fence in a proper condition at all times (vis major or Act of God only excepted), and is not entitled to wait until he receives notice that it is out of repair.

Stray Cattle.—If the owner of cattle turns them out upon unfenced land, he is liable for the mischief they may do upon adjoining land, upon which it is his duty to prevent them going, by fence or otherwise; but, if the land is bounded by fences belonging to adjoining land, the liability is reversed. He is entitled to rely upon the sufficiency of the fences. If his cattle get into the adjoining land through an obvious defect in the fence, the owner of the fence may be liable if they consequently come to harm. It is also the duty of the owner of the fence to restore the stray animals to their owner.

Railway fences are subjects of very great responsibility, the insufficiency of the fence being sufficiently proved by the fact of any animal having passed it. Negligence on the part of owners of animals, whereby they get on to a railway, will absolve the railway and render the owners liable for damages.

The owner of land adjoining a common may in certain circumstances be bound to maintain fences which are sufficient to keep out the ordinary commonable animals. But he is not bound in such cases to fence against animals which are of a peculiarly wandering disposition or addicted to jumping. (*See also* Nuisances and Trespass.)

Rubbish, Lumber or other Material.—Anything of this kind put against a fence so as to endanger it, may be removed by the aggrieved party, or, if the fence is destroyed, the owner of the fence can recover damages.

Fixtures.—*What are Fixtures.*—That which is attached to the soil so as to become part of the freehold, or is affixed to an original building so as to be incorporated in it, is deemed to be "a fixture". Whether a building, etc., has been so attached to the soil is a question of fact. That it rests on the ground is not, in itself, sufficient. For instance, if a greenhouse is erected upon dwarf brick walls, with a wooden course or coping upon which the house stands, the greenhouse down to and including the wooden course is not a fixture. The same applies when the wooden course itself rests upon the ground, but does not actually penetrate it. Whether an article has been so affixed to a building as to become incorporated with it is a question of fact. That it has not been so incorporated may be shown either from the way in which, or the object for which, it was affixed.

Landlord's Fixtures.—The following are landlord's fixtures, and cannot be removed by the tenant, even if he erects them:

A conservatory or greenhouse, whether attached to the house or standing in the garden, erected on and attached to a brick foundation. A boiler and pipes built into the same, also a veranda.

Articles, however, which merely adhere to the soil by their own weight, as a stone vase, a wooden summer-house, or tool-shed, or which are lightly screwed into walls, and can be removed without damaging them, such as lamp-brackets, hanging cupboards, etc., are not really *fixtures* at all, and can be removed by the tenant when he wishes.

The general rule, to which "*tenant's fixtures*" are an exception, is that fixtures are not removable. It will be noticed that they form a very considerable exception. One tenant may sometimes remove things which another could not. For instance, an ordinary householder cannot remove fruit-trees, rose-trees, shrubs, plants or roots which he has planted in his garden; but a nursery gardener may do so, on the ground that they form part of his stock-in-trade.

There is nothing, however, to prevent a landlord and tenant making a special bargain in the lease as to the tenant's right of removing fixtures at the end of the term, and any such agreement will supersede the ordinary law, so far as it is inconsistent with it.

That which is, in fact, a fixture cannot, in the absence of agreement or custom

536

to the contrary, be removed by the tenant at the end of his term of occupation, if put up either by the landlord or by a previous tenant; nor can the tenant remove it, even if put up by himself during his tenancy, unless it is within one or other of the exceptions given below. A covenant by the tenant to deliver up the demised premises and all fixtures belonging thereto will, in the absence of further explanatory words or clauses, include not only landlord's fixtures, but also any other fixtures there may be on the premises.

Fixtures Removable by Tenant.—1. Fixtures for trade purposes: thus a market gardener may remove all the plants which form his stock-in-trade, and his glasshouses. The exemption does not, however, extend to buildings of a permanent or substantial character.

2. Fixtures for agricultural purposes have been the subject of special statutes. The law relating to them is not included here.

3. Fixtures merely for the purpose of ornament or convenience. The right to remove them is not, however, absolute, but subject to the condition that they have not been affixed in such a manner as to indicate an intention that they should form part of the premises, and is dependent on their being capable of removal by the tenant without causing substantial injury to the premises. Thus as a general rule, everything that can be disengaged by drawing nails or screws (including pipes, wires, etc.), actually provided at the expense of the tenant, may be taken. But, if the fixing is by mortar or cement, the articles so fixed must generally pass to the landlord.

Where the tenant, being entitled to do so, removes a fixture, he must make good any damage done in the removal; and when a fixture has been put up by the tenant in place of something originally affixed to the premises, he must, after taking down his own fixture, replace the former article or another of a similar kind.

Time within which Right of Removal must be Exercised.—The tenant's right to remove fixtures is strictly limited to the continuance of the tenancy. After the tenancy has expired, or been terminated by forfeiture, he cannot legally remove them without the landlord's consent; but if the landlord then permits their removal, he thereby relinquishes all claim to them.

Should the landlord threaten to prevent the tenant from removing his tenant's fixtures, the latter should apply for an injunction to prevent interference. The landlord is entitled to exercise vigilance and to restrain the taking of anything that ought not to be taken. Resistance to him is an assault, or, if he exceeds his rights, he may be liable for assault as evidence may decide.

Sale on Credit of Fixtures, or anything of that kind, by an outgoing to an incoming tenant is exceedingly injudicious. The sale should always be for money down before the end of the outgoing term; for, if such property remains without being paid for, it cannot be sued upon, as it is not the incoming tenant's, but the landlord's. The tenant can ordinarily claim no compensation for any improvements he has made to the garden, or for permanent fixtures that he has erected and cannot take away on expiry of his lease.

Formation of the Garden.—A tenant has no right, without first having obtained the landlord's permission, to alter the actual layout of an established garden. He has no right to destroy trees or hedges.

537

Greenhouses, Summerhouses and Similar Buildings.—Before constructing any building backing on to a neighbour's fence or wall, which is itself higher than that fence or wall, it may be necessary to obtain permission from the Surveyor to the Local Authority and from the owner of the property. And due consideration of a neighbour's rights must be observed, as the erection of such a building is bound to affect the bed or ground on the other side of the fence or wall.

Hose and Watering.—The water supplied for household purposes and for which the tenant pays the water company's rate is not intended to be used for watering purposes in the garden. Rain water is, of course, much more satisfactory in its results, and a large water butt should be used for catching and retaining all that is available. When it is proposed to use a garden hose or sprinkler, however, the water company must be notified beforehand and the water rate adjusted in accordance with their rules and regulations.

Nuisances. I. NUISANCES AT COMMON LAW.

A private nuisance consists in the interference with another's rights. And where such is shown, in fact, to exist, it is immaterial whether the person who committed or permitted the act or omission complained of exercised care or not, and any question as to his motives is likewise irrelevant, except in the case of "reciprocal nuisances," *see* p. 539.

It must be remembered that an act which would otherwise constitute a nuisance may be justified under an Act of Parliament. Thus, if a railway company, having power to select the site for a cattle station, proceed to build it in a place where the noise from the cattle is a source of nuisance, they will not be responsible in the absence of negligence in the method of conducting their business.

Where a private nuisance exists, damages, or an injunction to prevent its continuance, or both, may be obtained by the person whose rights have been infringed, provided that a right to do that which is complained of has not been acquired by prescription. And in certain cases the person injured may himself abate the nuisance. The fact that the person who complains of the nuisance acquired his property with knowledge of the existing circumstances does not afford any defence, but in questions as to nuisance the character of the neighbourhood generally must be taken into account.

(1) NUISANCES AFFECTING A NEIGHBOUR'S PROPERTY.—Apart from statute an occupier of premises may use them as he pleases, provided that he does not interfere with the legal rights of another. The following are instances of a nuisance to property:

i. *Artificially Raising the Level of Land adjoining the Neighbour's Wall or House*, where the result is that the rain water soaks through the wall or into the house.

ii. *Causing Rain Water to Flow on to the Neighbour's Premises*.

iii. *Allowing Trees to Overhang the Adjoining Premises* constitutes a nuisance in respect to which no prescriptive right can be acquired; and if any damage is thereby caused, the owner of the trees will be responsible. Where trees overhang the adjoining premises, the occupier thereof may, even without notice to the owner of the trees, cut off the overhanging portion of the branches (or he may bring an action for damages), but in no case can a person go on to his neighbour's soil in order to remove a nuisance, except in a case of emergency, unless he has first given his neighbour notice to remove it. Overhanging trees may be cut by a neighbour as far as they overhang, whether there is injury from the overhanging or not, but cutting more than the overhanging is liable to heavy damages.

Hedges of roads, and trees that obstruct or unduly shade a road, may be lopped by any person actually inconvenienced, or by the road surveyor. By whomsoever cut, loppings belong to the owner of the tree, and must not be appropriated by the neighbour without permission. When a tree overhangs, the owner of the tree is entitled, after permission has been refused, to go upon the overhung land, either to recover loppings or to lop, and there is no trespass in law by doing either. Windfalls of fruit and fallen trees are governed by the same rule as loppings. It should be borne in mind, also, that should a person take it into his own hands to lop off the overhanging branches or fruit trees as aforesaid, he has no right to appropriate the fruit.

iv. *Allowing a Fence to Become a Source of Danger.*—An occupier of premises is likewise liable if he permits his wire fencing to become so rusted through that pieces of it fall into the grass on his neighbour's land and are swallowed by his animals with injurious consequences.

v. *Fowls.*—If fowls belonging to a neighbour damage plants in a garden, an action for damages may be brought. The fowls may be driven off or, better still, they may be captured and kept until the claim is met. The birds, however, must not be injured. They must be fed and cared for, the eggs being taken in payment (or up to double the value of food supplied is recoverable from the owner of the birds). In the same way stray dogs and cats must not be destroyed, although one is justified should a dog attempt to bite.

(2) NUISANCES AFFECTING THE NEIGHBOUR'S COMFORT OR ENJOYMENT OF HIS PREMISES.—In order to constitute any such nuisance—

The act complained of must be such as to exceed the natural and ordinary enjoyment of the occupier's property; but in considering whether such was, in fact, the case, special regard must be had to the surrounding circumstances, that is to say, to the time and place, and also the object and duration of the act complained of.

Thus, acts such as burning weeds, emptying cesspools, or making noises during repairs, although they may be a source of nuisance, must be put up with if done in the ordinary way and with reasonable care. Such acts are commonly described as "reciprocal nuisances". What is an ordinary and reasonable use of premises depends chiefly on where they are situated. But the fact that a particular nuisance existed before he acquired his property will not prevent a person from obtaining redress, even if he was previously aware of its existence. Below are specific forms of nuisances affecting the comfort of others.

Noises.—For instance, the use of noisy machinery. The ordinary habits and customs of domestic life which involve noise to the vexation of neighbours can seldom be prevented. Thus, it is extremely difficult to obtain effective redress with regard to the barking of dogs, or the crowing of cocks and the like.

Smells.—Such as that caused by rotting manure and rubbish in close proximity to residential premises.

Smoke from a chimney, whether used for trade or otherwise.

539

Obstruction of light.—In cases where a prescriptive right to such light has been acquired.

II. STATUTORY NUISANCES

It must suffice to say that there are many nuisances created by statute. For instance, under the Public Health Acts—

Any premises which are in such a state as to be—

Any pool, ditch, gutter, watercourse, privy, urinal, cesspool, drain or ashpit, which is so foul or in such a state as to be—

Any animal which is so kept as to be—

Any accumulation or deposit which is—

} a nuisance or injurious to health;

will be deemed to be nuisances liable to be dealt with summarily.

In every county or borough the County Council or Corporation, as the case may be, may make such bye-laws as they think fit for the good rule and government of the area under their jurisdiction.

Trespass.—If a person trespasses on private property, he must first be ordered off, but if he does not go the occupier, owner, or his representative, may exercise such reasonable force as may be necessary to remove him; if more than necessary force be exercised, the person resorting to it will be guilty of an assault. The trespasser may be prosecuted for assault if he offers any resistance. In respect to the trespass itself, damages can be recovered in an action, but the trespasser cannot be prosecuted unless he was trespassing in pursuit of game, or has wilfully or maliciously done any injury to property. A person found in a dwelling-house, warehouse, garage, stable, or outhouse or an enclosed yard, garden or area, for an unlawful purpose may be prosecuted. Involuntary trespass, followed by prompt withdrawal, is not actionable. (*See also* Stray Cattle, p. 535, and Fowls, p. 539).

Waste in the Garden.—In most leases there is a covenant against waste. In so far as the garden is concerned, it is waste to remove soil from the garden; to cut down fruit or timber trees. It is not waste, however, to make ditches or drains; to lop hedges or to cut down bushes (except fruit or ornamental shrubs), or trees which are not timber. "Timber" properly means trees at least twenty years old whose wood is used for building. Oak, ash and elm are considered as timber everywhere; other trees may be so by local custom. The measure of damages for breach of the covenant is the diminution in value of the reversion, i.e. the landlord's property at the end of the term.

Water Rate.—(*See* Hose and Watering.)

540

CHAPTER 44

THE GARDENER'S CALENDAR

In studying the following pages the reader should bear in mind that locality has a decided influence on the operations advocated herein. For instance, Scotland and the North are always about a fortnight behind the Midlands in cropping, while the Southern Counties are about a fortnight ahead of the Midlands. In the south-west many half-hardy plants, usually raised under glass, will grow equally well if sown outdoors in warm, sheltered situations. Readers south of the equator must take into consideration the difference in the seasons. For example, in Australia May is equivalent to November in England. This inversion is quite in favour of the Antipodes, and most of the subjects mentioned for sowing in heat in this calendar can safely be treated in the open air in Australia, and countries in similar latitudes. The forcing of vegetables, fruit, etc., is fully dealt with in our chapter on Frames and Hot-beds.

JANUARY

General Garden Work

All digging and trenching should have been completed before this. If not finished, this should be done without further delay. No work should be attempted, however, when the ground is covered with snow or muddy. Protection for growing crops must be provided where necessary. Plants against walls and on supports should be nailed up, and lawns and paths receive attention.

The Flower Garden

General Operations.—All vacant ground should be thrown up into ridges; the borders, new and old, should be trenched. Vacant ground should be constantly forked or "pointed", so that the surface is loosened and the air permitted to permeate the soil. Any alterations in the flower beds that are deemed necessary should be made. New catalogues should be obtained so that seeds may be ordered early.

Annuals.—Autumn-sown annuals in the reserve garden should be protected with mats during severe frosts.

Bedding Plants.—All ground which is to be planted later with bedding plants should be well manured.

Under Glass (Flowers).—The greenhouse should be kept clean, all dead leaves being removed from plants. Plants must be kept free from draughts, air being given from above or by means of ventilators. Pots, boxes, and soil composts should be prepared for reception of seeds and cuttings. To preserve flowers in bloom, the atmosphere must be kept moist and genial, but not wet. Water should be given regularly when necessary, especially to bulbs.

541

SEEDS TO SOW.—*Asparagus plumosus, Cannas, Freesias, Fuchsias, Gloxinias, Sweet Peas*, etc.

CUTTINGS.—*Bedding stock* to produce cuttings should be placed in heat. Cuttings of *chrysanthemums, tree carnations, heliotropes* and *verbenas* may be put in now. Place scarce varieties of *dahlias* in heat so as to secure plenty of cuttings. *Fuchsias* may now be started.

POTTING.—*Calceolaria* seedlings should be shifted into larger pots and those sown for late blooming should be pricked-off. *Hippeastrums* may be repotted and started. *Pelargoniums*, if strongly rooted, should be moved into larger pots. *Soft-wooded plants* should be repotted into larger pots for flowering.

The Vegetable Garden

General Operations.—All vegetable refuse and leaves should be collected and allowed to rot for future use. If infested with insects, it must be burned, the ashes being dug in. The hoe should be kept moving between growing crops.

SEEDS TO SOW.—*Broad Beans and Peas.* A few may be sown towards the end of this month in warm, sheltered situations. A few *cauliflowers, radishes* and other early crops may be sown on a hot-bed, or in a south border, being protected with hand-lights. *Lettuces* should be sown every fortnight. *Onions* may be sown in boxes.

PLANT.—*Potatoes* may be placed to sprout in the light in some shed free from frost. *Rhubarb* may be planted.

Under Glass (Vegetables).—Hot-beds should be made up for forcing: *asparagus, broad beans, carrots, herbs, radishes*, etc. A start can be made with forcing *cauliflowers, chicory, lettuces, rhubarb* and *seakale.*

Cucumbers may be had at any time by planting the seed in a hot-bed or under glass, about three months before the fruit is required.

SEEDS TO SOW.—*Beans* (*broad*), *beans* (*French*), *beetroot* (*Globe*), *carrots,* (stump-rooted), *aubergines, leeks, mustard and cress, onions, peas* (early), *radishes, seakale*, and *tomatoes.*

The Fruit Garden

General Operations.—The pruning of all the hardier kinds of trees should be carried out. *Apricots, cherries, figs, nectarines* and *peaches* should not be pruned this month. Trees that are to be grafted should be cut back, and the scions for grafting should be cut and heeled into the ground ready for subsequent use. The stems of old fruit trees should be lime-washed, or sprayed with caustic soda. Dead bark should be removed. It is not wise to plant trees this month.

Shrubs and Trees

General Operations.—Evergreens and deciduous shrubs may still be planted. Hedges of *beech, hawthorn* and *privet* should be pruned; also all deciduous shrubs. Cuttings of hardy deciduous shrubs may be planted in open weather and layers made of young branches. Rooted suckers should be taken from *roses, lilacs* and other shrubs for transplantation. Preparations for grafting should be made where necessary.

542

FEBRUARY

General Garden Work

All vacant ground should be weeded and trenched, and a dressing of manure and leaf-mould should be applied to vacant beds.

The Flower Garden

General Operations.—Herbaceous borders should be given a light top-dressing with manure and litter. Hoeing should be carried out whenever the weather permits. *Roses.*—Manure the rose trees well. All hardy varieties may be planted this month. Rose trees should not be pruned when planted, but after an interval of a month or six weeks. Climbing roses should be trimmed and trained.

SEEDS TO SOW.—Sow seed of *antirrhinums* (*snapdragons*), *begonias*, *lobelias*, *petunias* and *verbenas* over gentle heat.

PLANT.—*Anemones* and *ranunculuses*. Provided the weather is mild, all autumn-sown *annuals* may be transplanted. *Box edging* and other living edgings.

Under Glass (Flowers).—A night temperature of from 40° to 50° F. should be maintained. Watering should be carefully attended to. *Bedding-out plants* should be propagated now. *Dahlias* may be started in heat. *Fuchsias* should be given a little bottom heat after re-potting. *Geranium* roots which have been stored should be subjected to bottom heat and cuttings taken.

SEEDS TO SOW.—*Balsam, begonias, cannas, celosias, cobœas, cyclamens, fuchsias, thunbergias,* etc. Bedding plants such as *golden feather, lobelias, petunias,* and *pyrethrums.*

CUTTINGS.—Strike cuttings of *tree carnations* and *gardenias.*

POTTING.—Plants should be moved into larger pots as needed. *Achimenes* tubers may be potted up. Also *calceolarias* sown last August. Clumps of cannas should be divided and started in pots. *Border carnations, ferns* and *fuchsias* should be re-potted. *Hydrangeas,* and *palms,* etc., require attention.

The Vegetable Garden

General Operations.—Hoeing should be carried out whenever the weather permits. Old beds of *Brussels sprouts* and *cabbages* must be cleared off. *Pea* and *bean* sticks should be got ready as they will soon be required. *Broccoli* that has not been cut should have the leaves bent over the flower. *Leeks* should be dug up and planted close together in a cool spot. *Onions.* The ground should be well trenched for the main crop. *Peas* should be earthed up and given an occasional dusting with lime. *Potatoes.* Continue to sprout these in boxes.

SEEDS TO SOW.—*Broad beans, Brussels sprouts* (for autumn use), *cabbages* (early), *carrots, cauliflowers, mustard and cress, lettuces, onions, leeks, parsley, parsnips,* and *peas, radishes, spinach* and *turnips.*

PLANT.—*Artichokes* (globe), *garlic* and *shallots, lettuces* (winter), *early potatoes, rhubarb* and *seakale.*

Under Glass.—*Cauliflowers* and *lettuces* that have been wintering under frames or under cloches should not be coddled; the frames should only be closed when the weather is frosty. This applies to all plants in frames. *Early* *lettuces* can be pricked out on rich beds in frames. *Onions* sown in boxes last month will require thinning out. Hot-beds should be prepared under glass for *cucumbers, marrows*, etc.

SEEDS TO SOW.—*Aubergines, broad beans, beans* (French), *Brussels sprouts, capsicums, cauliflowers, celery, leeks, peas* (early), *radishes, tomatoes, turnips* and *marrows. Potatoes* for forcing may be planted.

The Fruit Garden

General Operations.—Pruning of all fruit trees should be completed this month. All trees in borders should have the ground either well mulched with manure or covered with mould and treated with liquid manure. Stocks for grafting may still be headed back this month. Scions for grafting should be taken from the parent tree, being placed in earth under a north wall. *Damsons* are best pruned this month. *Pear* and *plum* trees should be pruned. *Quince* trees are best pruned this month. *Strawberries.* New beds should be made.

Under Glass (Fruit).—The pruning, cleaning and training of all fruit trees indoors should be completed. If no bees are present, fruit trees should be fertilized by means of transferring pollen from flower to flower with a feather or camel-hair brush. Fumigation with tobacco or nicotine compound should be carried out if greenfly are present.

MARCH

General Garden Work

Ground which has been roughly dug up or left ridged through the winter should be prepared for seed sowing. The lawn should receive attention, manure being applied where the grass is thin. Grass seed may be sown, and an application of soot is useful. Where necessary, paths should be re-turfed, crazy paving being laid or repaired.

The Flower Garden

General Operations.—Vacant borders must be cleaned up, and forked over and soil for sowing biennials and perennials next month should be prepared. Superfluous dead leaves should be removed, only a few where slight protection is still desirable being left. All dead and broken shoots of *alyssum, forget-me-nots, wallflowers* and similar plants that have come through the winter must be cut away, the plants being made firm where necessary, exposed roots being covered and a top-dressing of suitable soil added if the weather is suitable. Work may now be commenced on transplanting and dividing many alpines, any thrown out by frost being firmed in again.

SEEDS TO SOW.—Sowings should be made early in the month (if dry) of *hardy annuals, clarkias, coreopsis, cosmos, delphiniums* (larkspur), *godetia, gypsophila, lavatera, lupins, nigella, poppies, sweet peas, sweet sultan*, etc., and later in the month of *alyssum, anemone, asperula, bartonia, brachycome, calendula, campanulas, China asters, gaillardias, gilia, limnanthes, mignonette, nasturtiums, nemesia, stocks, sunflowers, veronica, Virginian stocks, viscaria.*

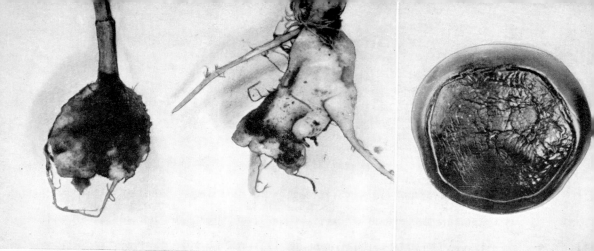

PLATE 63 *Left*, Brussels sprouts affected with Clubroot, and *right*, Blossom End Rot on tomato.

Plant Protection Ltd. and Shell Photo

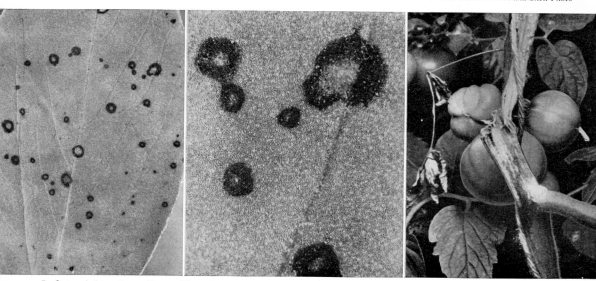

Left to right, *above*, Bean Chocolate Spot and close-up, and Botrytis of tomato stem. *Below*, Buck Eye Rot on tomato, Papery Bark Canker and Coral Spot.

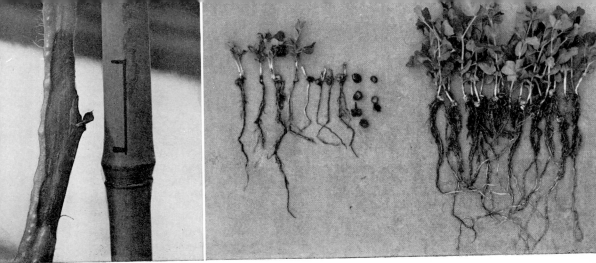

PLATE 64 *Left*, Didymella on plant stem and *right*, effect of Foot Rot on pea seedlings.

Plant Protection Ltd., and Shell Photo

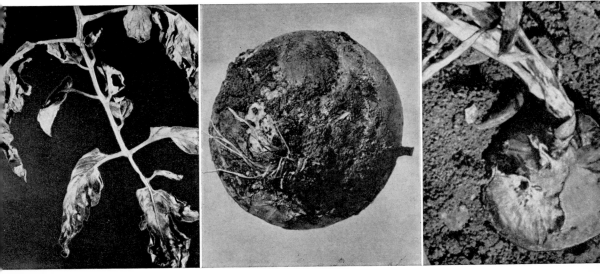

Left to right, *above*, Tomato Leaf Mould, Onion White Spot and its effects on onion. *Below*, Silver Leaf, Spotted Wilt on tomato plant and Verticilium on mushroom.

PLANT OUT.—*Bedding Plants* (protect from wind), *carnations* (layered last year), *chrysanthemums*, *dahlias* (stored through the winter), *late-flowering gladioli*, *montbretias*, *pansies* and *violas*, *ranunculus*, *roses* (if frosts are over), *summer-flowering creepers*, *sweet peas* (sown in pots). *Rock Plants*. Many of these may be propagated by means of division towards the end of the month.

PRUNING.—All creepers should be finally pruned. Old shrubs must be cut back to about 12 inches from the ground. The pruning of *roses* should be commenced (if frosts are over). *Box edging* must be trimmed, being broken up and replanted where necessary. *Hollies, laurels, bays, rhododendrons* and *conifers* may be cut back and moved.

Under Glass (Flowers).—Temperature from 45° to 50° F. by night. Growing plants should be given ample air and water. Bulbs that have lost vitality through early flowering must be discarded. *Cinerarias* that have flowered, except choice varieties, should be thrown away. Plants, if drooping, must be shaded, and, where necessary, *azaleas, camellias* and *marguerites* should be potted on. *Begonias* sown last month should be pricked off, and tubers started in heat. A start should be made with the hardening off of bedding plants.

SEEDS TO SOW.—A sowing should be made early in the month of *abronias, ageratums, antirrhinums* (*snapdragon*), *cannas, carnations, celosias* (*cockscomb*), *China asters, chrysanthemums, delphiniums, dianthus, freesias, gloxinias, heliotropes, hollyhocks, lobelias, pansies, penstemons, petunias, polyanthus, portulacas, primulas, salvias, stocks* and *verbenas*. And later on in the month: *alyssum, anagallis, anchusas, androsaces, anemones, arabis, arenaria, asparagus, asters, balsams, calceolarias, calendulas, celmisia, cinerarias, clivias, coleus blumei, draba, eryngiums, fuchsias, grevilleas, linums, nasturtiums, nemesia, nicotiana, perilla, phloxes, pyrethrums, salpiglossis, scabious, stocks* (*ten-week*), *streptocarpus, sweet peas, tagetes* (*African marigolds*), *thunbergias, zinnias,* and further sowings of those already sown earlier in the month.

CUTTINGS.—Cuttings may be taken of *abutilons, acacias, carnations* (*winter-flowering or perpetual*), *chrysanthemums* (*single late-flowering*), *fuchsias, gardenias, geraniums* and *petunias*. Rooted cuttings of *fuchsias, geraniums, heliotropes, marguerites,* etc., should be potted-on. *Dahlia roots, Marvels of Peru* and old *pelargoniums* should be placed in the warm and cuttings obtained.

POTTING.—Re-potting should be continued, plants being moved on where necessary. Pot-up *abutilons, cacti* and *ferns*.

The Vegetable Garden

General Operations.—Dug-over soil should be dug up, pulverized and made ready for seed sowing. *Winter greens* that have run to seed should be taken up, being planted close together in some odd corner. The hoe must be used freely among growing crops, and to keep the birds away the plants should be dusted with soot until they are well up. *Asparagus*. New asparagus beds should, if necessary, be made. *Mint* may be lifted, separated and replanted.

SEEDS TO SOW.—*Broad beans, broccoli, Brussels sprouts, cabbages, carrots, cauliflowers, corn salad, dwarf French beans, kale, kohl rabi, leeks, lettuces, mustard and cress, onions, parsley, parsnips, peas, radishes, rampion, seakale, shallots, spinach, swedes, tomatoes* and *turnips*.

PLANT.—*Artichokes* (*Chinese*) and *asparagus*. *Chives* should be divided. *Early peas* should be hardened off and planted out. Also *early potatoes, horseradish, rhubarb* and *seakale*.

Under Glass (Vegetables).—*Broad beans* sown in January and February should be planted out under glass. *Leeks* sown in January and February must now be pricked off.

SEEDS TO SOW.—*Asparagus, broccoli, cucumbers, dwarf French beans, leeks, lettuces, melons, mustard and cress, onions, parsley, peas, rhubarb, seakale* and *tomatoes*. Towards the end of the month sow *vegetable marrows*.

The Fruit Garden

General Operations.—Any wall fruits coming into blossom should be protected from frost and birds. The surface of the ground around the dwarf fruit trees should be hoed. This is the last month for planting until the autumn. Towards the end of the month, *apples, cherries, pears* and *plums* which were cut back in January may be grafted. The grafts should have been taken quite a month beforehand. All pruning of fruit trees, if not completed in February, should be finished early this month. New plantations of bush fruit should be made. As a general protection against insects, fruit trees should be syringed with tepid water with sulphur and soot added.

Under Glass (Fruit).—Fruit trees forced under glass must be protected against sudden changes in temperature and cold draughts. Great care must be taken in ventilating, as weather is changeable.

APRIL

General Garden Work

The hoe should be kept constantly at work destroying weeds and breaking up the surface between growing plants. If there is any sign of frost, early plants and fruit blossom still require a little protection. A keen look-out must be kept for greenfly. Slugs and snails must be searched for and destroyed. The lawn should be cut, rolled and swept and paths and walks should receive attention where necessary.

The Flower Garden

General Operations.—Preparations should be made for summer bedding and bulbs should be lifted. Staking where necessary should be seen to. *Azaleas* and tender shrubs should be protected from cold winds; also *polyanthuses*. Tender seedlings must be protected from insects and birds, all weeds being destroyed.

SEEDS TO SOW.—This is the chief month for sowing all *hardy annuals*, and towards the end of the month *half-hardy annuals* (except the tenderest) may be sown in the open. So may *biennials* and *perennials*, and all seeds intended to flower during the summer.

PLANT OUT.—*Hardy perennials* propagated by means of division and all other hardy plants.

546

THIN OUT.—*Autumn-sown hardy annuals*, and transplant *biennials*.

PRUNING.—*Roses* and many varieties of *shrubs* should be pruned.

STAKING.—Staking, where necessary, must be attended to, and creepers should be tied up and trained.

Under Glass (Flowers).—Temperature from 45° F. by night to 65° F. by day. Air should be admitted freely in mild weather and growing plants must be given plenty of water. Shade must be provided on hot days and plants requiring more space should be re-potted. All plants breaking into flower will be better for a dose of weak liquid manure. To retard the blooming of *azaleas* and similar plants, and to secure a succession, the plants should be placed on the shady side of the house. A sharp look-out for insect pests must be kept, measures to combat them being at once taken. *Aspidistras* may be divided up and re-potted. *Asters* and *stocks* should be pricked-off. *Bedding Plants.* Preparations should be made to harden-off summer-bedding plants sown in March. The tops should be pinched out to make them strong and bushy.

SEEDS TO SOW.—*Ageratum, asters, auriculas* (in shallow pans), *balsam, cinerarias, freesias, nemesia, petunias, phloxes, stocks, tree carnations* and other *half-hardy annuals* in boxes.

CUTTINGS.—Cuttings of all soft-wooded plants may now be struck. *Dahlias* and *fuchsias* may still be started in heat and cuttings obtained.

POTTING.—Re-potting should be continued where necessary. *Azaleas* should be re-potted after they have finished flowering.

The Vegetable Garden

General Operations.—The ground must be prepared for the reception of *Brussels sprouts, cauliflowers, lettuces*, etc., grown in frames. The ground should also be got ready for *runner beans*, and *celery* trenches should be dug. There is still a danger of frost and provision should be made for this. Young plants should receive protection from birds.

SEEDS TO SOW.—All kinds of herbs, salading, and vegetables may now be sown in the open.

PLANT OUT.—*Artichokes (globe)* [suckers], *artichokes (Jerusalem)* if not already done, *asparagus* (one year old), *borecole* or *kale* (six weeks old), *Brussels sprouts, cabbages, potatoes* (main crop), *rhubarb, seakale*, and *early vegetable marrows. Marjoram, mint, pennyroyal, sage, thyme*, etc., should be lifted, divided and planted out.

THIN OUT.—*Carrots, onions, parsnips*, etc., as necessary.

Under Glass (Vegetables).—SEEDS TO SOW.—*Beans (runner), cardoons, cucumbers, marrows* and *melons*.

PRICK OFF.—Main *celery* crop and *tomato* seedlings.

HARDEN OFF.—*Brussels sprouts, cauliflowers, lettuces*, etc.

The Fruit Garden

General Operations.—All grafting should be finished early this month. All trees should have been pruned. Protection to blossom on wall fruit should be continued, and syringing with quassia-chips and soft-soap solution should be carried out. Planting of fruit trees should be over, if absolutely essential to do this now, roots should be well protected from cold and heat by covering the ground with long stable manure or pebbles laid on a bed of sand. Keep the roots of wall trees moist, and attend to staking where necessary.

Apple and Pear Trees. Syringe with a summer wash to destroy apple sucker and midge. *Black Currants.* Dust or spray bushes affected with big-bud with lime and sulphur mixture every other week.

Peaches and Nectarines may be summer-pruned.

Under Glass (Fruit).—Constant vigilance must be exercised in maintaining the temperature, since the weather is changeable.

Apricots, nectarines and peaches should be fertilized by means of a feather or rabbit's tail passed from flower to flower.

MAY

General Garden Work

May is the last month during which any considerable amount of planting out should be done. The work entails much labour in thinning out seedlings, planting out, and hoeing. If the weather should turn dry, watering may have to be done, but this should be left as long as possible, as the plants will thrive better. It should not be undertaken unless absolutely essential.

The Flower Garden

General Operations.—Towards the end of the month many half hardy annuals which have been raised under glass will have to be planted out. *Bulbs* must be lifted.

SEEDS TO SOW.—*Aquilegia, asters, auriculas, Brompton stocks, cobœa, delphiniums, eccremocarpus, forget-me-nots, foxgloves, gypsophila, hardy annuals* (for succession), *night-scented stock, polyanthus* and *primrose.*

PLANT OUT.—*Abronia, antirrhinums, begonias, calceolarias, dahlias* (in pots), *hydrangeas* (in pots), *half-hardy bedding plants, scabious, violets,* etc. Spring-flowering plants such as *arabis, aubrieta, daisies* and *primroses* should be divided. Late-flowering *annuals* should be planted out.

STAKING, ETC.—All plants which require it should be staked and pegged down as planting proceeds.

THIN OUT.—All *annuals* must be thinned and transplanted where necessary.

Under Glass (Flowers).—If the greenhouse is not used very much during the summer months, it should be cleaned thoroughly at any convenient time from now onwards. Pits and frames, also, should be cleaned as they become vacant. Temperature should remain at 45° F. by night and 65° F. by day. Water must be given regularly and a moist atmosphere maintained by means of damping floors, syringing, etc. Plenty of air and shade must be given where necessary. A sharp look-out for insect pests must be kept.

Shrubs.—Wood that has borne flowers must be cut away and the bushes should be thinned out. Shrubs in the house should be hardened off for planting out.

SEEDS TO SOW.—*Achimenes, begonias, cinerarias* (in cold frame), *herbaceous calceolarias, coleuses, gloxinias, primulas,* etc.

CUTTINGS.—Cuttings of most plants may be taken now. *Azaleas, cytisuses, heaths, hydrangeas,* etc.

POTTINGS.—All plants should be repotted as it becomes necessary.

The Vegetable Garden

General Operations.—The hoe must be kept moving between rows of growing plants, and a sharp look-out for insects and pests must be maintained. *Artichokes* (*globe*). The soil should be well stirred and the shoots reduced to three. The offsets should be planted and watered copiously. *Asparagus.* When cutting asparagus all shoots should be cut off as they reach about 6 inches in height. *Herbs. Balm, mint, marjoram, savory, thyme* and other herbs may be increased by means of slips.

SEEDS TO SOW.—Seeds of all vegetables sown in March and April may still be sown for succession. *Runner beans* may be sown in quantity, and if the weather is good, *French* or *kidney beans* also. *Broccoli* and *globe beetroot* may be sown right on into July. *Herbs.* Sow *chervil* and *parsley* for winter use. *Peas* may be sown for August picking. *Saladings.* A successional sowing of *lettuces, mustard and cress, radishes,* etc., may be made.

PLANT OUT.—*Brussels sprouts,* (in well-limed land), *cauliflowers* (early sown), *celery, celeriac, kohl rabi, leeks, onions* (sown in boxes in January), *marrows* (if weather is favourable, but protect on cold nights), *potatoes* (a few late ones may still be planted), *pumpkins, savoys* and *tomatoes.*

Turnips that were sown on a hot-bed in a frame in February, also *vegetable marrows.*

Under Glass (Vegetables).—*Carrots, potatoes* and other vegetables, which have been grown in frames, will be ready for table. After replacing the old soil with fresh and re-lining, similar crops may be planted again, or the frames may be employed for raising *tomatoes* prior to planting out in the open.

Borecole or *kale* (6 weeks old) and *beans* (*runner*), that were sown last month, should be planted out.

Vegetable marrows may be planted under hand-lights.

The Fruit Garden

General Operations.—All fruit trees on dry ground will be benefited by a mulch of manure round the roots. The fruit should be thinned out to half a dozen on newly planted trees.

Apricot shoots should be pinched back. *Morello cherries* should be disbudded, also *peaches* and *nectarines.*

Raspberry suckers should be thinned out. *Strawberry* runners not required for making young plants should be cut off. Strawy litter should be placed between the plants.

Under Glass (Fruit).—In hot weather, trees should be syringed with water. *Peaches.*—If the trees were put forward in December, they will stand forcing freely—the house being kept fairly dry, but as much air as possible being given. To ripen the fruit, any leaves that may shade it should be taken off.

JUNE

General Garden Work

Hoeing and watering are both of the utmost importance. The hoe must be kept constantly at work between the rows of growing plants. Generous watering is essential. The soil must be kept as moist as possible by mulching and by stirring the surface.

The remains of all crops which have been gathered should be removed. A sharp look-out for pests should be maintained.

The Flower Garden

General Operations.—Bedding-out, if not already finished, should be completed as early as possible. *Anchusas, delphiniums, doronicums, lupins,* etc., should be cut down as the flowers fade, the roots being mulched with manure and watered regularly. The best kinds should be marked for obtaining seed. Failures must be removed, being replaced. *Carnations* (early) require disbudding and staking.

SEEDS TO SOW.—All kinds of *biennials* and *perennials* can be sown, also quick-flowering *annuals* for late-flowering.

PLANT OUT.—*Half-hardy annuals* raised in frames. Spring-flowering plants should be divided and planted out. *Begonias* may also be planted out. *Irises* which have finished flowering should be divided.

CUTTINGS.—A plot should be prepared in the reserve garden for cuttings of *rockets, sweet-williams,* and *double wallflowers* for next spring. Cuttings of *Alyssum saxatile* may be inserted under a handglass.

THIN OUT.—Seedlings of all kinds.

STAKING, ETC.—*Carnations* should be staked and tied loosely. *Dahlias* and *sweet peas* require attention.

Under Glass.—Plenty of air should be given; fumigation and syringing for insects should be attended to. The greenhouse must be shaded unless the roof is covered with creepers. Damp the floor to keep the atmosphere moist, and all faded blooms should be removed. Artificial heating should no longer be needed, unless the weather turns very damp and cold.

Azaleas and *camellias* should have a damp growing heat all the time they are making wood. Towards the end of the month, they may be stood outdoors on ashes in a semi-shaded position.

Heaths and *tender shrubs* may be hardened-off and stood outdoors.

SEEDS TO SOW.—*Calceolarias* (*herbaceous*) for next year's flowering, *cinerarias, cyclamens, primula malacoides* and *p. obconica,* also various *rock plants* for autumn planting; *aubrieta, alyssum, campanulas, candytuft* (*Iberis*), *carnations, dianthus, geraniums, linaria, saxifrages,* etc.

CUTTINGS.—Cuttings of *pelargoniums* may be taken, also root cuttings of *verbenas* in close frame.

POTTING.—All plants that require more room should be repotted. *Begonias* sown in February may be potted up. *Carnations, chrysanthemums* and *fuchsias* should be moved into their flowering pots.

CLEANING AND REPAINTING.—Now is probably the most convenient time for renovations and decorations.

550

The Vegetable Garden

General Operations.—Hoeing and watering are of the utmost importance, and pests must be guarded against. *Cauliflowers*. A little liquid manure should be given to early cauliflowers, a leaf being broken over the flower to shade it. *Lettuces*. If watered copiously, they are not so likely to run to seed. *Mushroom* beds may be made out-doors, and will bear by August. *Onions* (autumn-sown). A final top-dressing of nitrate of soda should be given. *Peas*. These should be picked off regularly. *Potatoes* may still be earthed-up. Any cleared this month may be followed by late *celery* or *winter turnips*. *Runner beans* need supports. *Seakale*. Dress with salt. *Shallots*. These should be dressed with nitrate of soda. *Vegetable marrow* plants which were planted out last month should be stopped to encourage them.

SEEDS TO SOW.—*Beans*. A last sowing of these should be made early in the month. *Cardoons, chicory* and *colewort* should also be sown. *Cucumbers* may be sown on ridges out-doors. *Endive* and *Lettuce*. Every fortnight a sowing should be made. *Mustard and cress, peas, radishes, spinach* and *swedes* may be sown. *Turnips*. The main sowing should be made.

PLANT OUT.—*Borecole* (6 weeks old), *broccoli, cardoons, cauliflowers* and *celery*. They should be planted out in wet, showery weather. *Leeks, ridge cucumbers, savoys*, for October use, should also be planted. *Tomatoes* may still be planted out. *Vegetable Marrows*. Plant these if not already out.

THIN OUT.—The main crops of *beetroots, carrots, onions*, also *parsley, salsify* and *scorzonera*.

The Fruit Garden

General Operations.—All trees require mulching. All superfluous growths on fruit trees of every kind should be thinned out and stopped. Over-vigorous shoots on young trees should be cut back. Heavily laden trees will need support. Greenfly should be attended to, insecticides being applied where necessary. *Cherry trees* should have the shoots stopped and nets arranged to save the fruit. *Currant Bushes*. Young side shoots must be pinched back. *Loganberries* may be propagated by means of layering. *Peaches* and *apricots* should be thinned if necessary. *Pear, plum*, and *cherry trees* will require disbudding. *Raspberries*. All surplus and weak canes should be pulled to ensure a good crop. *Strawberries*. These must be watered copiously, runners being layered.

JULY

General Garden Work

Hoeing, weeding and watering will be necessary throughout the month. Top-dressing round the bases of shrubs and trees and between growing crops is of great value.

The Flower Garden

General Operations.—All dead flowers should be picked off. Plants as they grow will require staking and tying. *Carnations* may be layered.

551

Chrysanthemums should have the tops pinched out. *Dahlias* should be given a mulch of manure, and staking requires attention. Flowering plants, such as *fuchsias* and *geraniums*, should be watered regularly. *Rock plants* may be propagated by means of cuttings. *Roses* should be budded.

SEEDS TO SOW.—*Perennial* and *biennial* plants for flowering the following year. *Hollyhocks* for flowering the following year may be sown. *Pansies* may be sown out-doors in boxes.

PLANT OUT.—Seedlings of all kinds. All *bedding plants* in reserve garden should be planted out. *Biennials* and *perennials* should be transplanted, and seedling *ranunculuses* should be planted out.

CUTTINGS.—Cuttings of hardy plants may be taken and placed under hand-lights, so may *rose* cuttings.

Under Glass (Flowers).—Copious watering will be required by all plants under glass. It is generally possible to give air all night without risk. A sharp look-out for pests must be kept. Plants that have finished flowering should be cut down, and bulbs should be matured and ripened. If the greenhouse has not already been thoroughly cleaned, an attempt should be made at the beginning of this month. *Carnations* that have flowered should be layered. *Carnations* in pots and *chrysanthemums* will need staking and tying. *Climbing plants* require a lot of attention. *Roses* may be pruned.

SEEDS TO SOW.—*Border carnations*, also *Brompton* and *Intermediate stocks* for winter-flowering in greenhouse. *Herbaceous calceolarias* for spring-flowering, also pinks.

PRICK OUT.—*Cinerarias* sown two months previously.

POTTING.—All those plants which need it should be repotted. *Cyclamen* should be moved into flowering pots, old plants being started in fresh soil. *Primulas* should be moved into their flowering pots. *Rhododendrons* and *azaleas* should be stood outdoors.

The Vegetable Garden

General Operations.—After the crops have been gathered, all *cabbage* stalks, *bean* stalks, and *pea* haulms should be removed. *Artichokes* (*Globe*). The head should be cut when about three parts open. *Carrots*. These should be mulched (in wet weather) with well-rotted manure and soot. *Mint and Other Sweet Herbs* should be cut for drying. *Mushroom* beds should be made in the open. *Parsley* that is running to seed should be pulled out. *Potatoes*. A final earthing-up should be given. *Runner Beans*. Sticks or strings must be provided and ample water given. *Shallots*. All loose soil covering these should be pulled away. *Tomatoes*. Tops and side shoots must be pinched off. *Marrows*. An abundance of tepid water should be given.

SEEDS TO SOW.—*Cabbages, coleworts, mustard and cress, endive, kohl rabi, lettuces, onions, parsley, radishes* (as catch crop), *spinach* (prickly for winter use), and *turnips*.

THIN OUT.—The *beetroot* crop must be kept thinned out and the hoe busy.

PLANT OUT.—*Borecole* or *kale* (6 weeks old), *broccoli, celery, colewort*, and *endive*. *Sage, savory*, etc., can be propagated by cuttings or division and planted out.

The Fruit Garden

General Operations.—Fruit on all overcrowded trees should be thinned, all unnecessary growths being removed. Water should be given generously, the surface of the ground being kept well hoed and mulched. Fruit trees may be budded when the weather is moist. Espalier and dwarf fruit trees should be trained, and ripening fruit protected from birds. Before fruit begins to ripen, *apricots, cherries, figs* and *plums* on walls should be attended to, all shoots that are not required being removed. *Apple trees* attacked by mildew must be attended to, *see* p. 520. *Cherries* and *plums* may be budded. *Loganberries* and *strawberries* may be layered.

AUGUST

General Garden Work

All dead flowers, stalks, and leaves should be removed. Watering, mulching, and hoeing constitute the chief work in the garden during the summer months.

The Flower Garden

General Operations.—Hoeing, weeding, watering and mulching, etc. *Antirrhinums.* Dead flower spikes must be cut down. *Carnations* and *pinks* should be layered. *Clematis, honeysuckle* and *wisteria* should be trained before the shoots become too long. *Dahlias.* Show plants should be disbudded, and staking and earwig traps should be seen to. *Lavender* hedges may be trimmed. *Penstemons.* Dead flower spikes must be cut down. *Roses* may still be budded. *Sweet peas* require ample water and doses of manure. All dead flowers must be picked off.

SEEDS TO SOW.—All sorts of *annuals* may be sown for spring flowering. *Antirrhinums, pansies, Iceland poppies,* and *violas.* Early in the month *intermediate stocks* should be sown; about the middle of the month *ten-week stocks.*

CUTTINGS.—Cuttings of all kinds of hardy plants and bedding plants may be struck in sandy soil. *Geraniums* should be propagated now. *Pansies and Violas.* Cuttings may still be struck. *Roses.* Cuttings of *Bourbon, China, Hybrid Perpetual and Noisette Roses* may be struck. *Saxifrages.* The offsets arising from sides of the plants should be taken off and planted in borders or pots.

PLANT.—*Amaryllis, colchicum, cyclamen, Guernsey lily* and *narcissus* in beds, borders or pots. First struck cuttings of *carnations* and *picotees* may now be planted out; some should be potted to fill vacant spaces. Seedlings of *biennials* must be pricked off and transplanted. Seedlings of *perennials* should be transplanted where crowded, and spring-flowering *perennials* should be divided and replanted. Old bulbs and bulbs in grass should be replanted.

Under Glass (Flowers).—Work should be continued as for June and July. Plants stood outdoors require constant attention; every evening they should be well syringed. *Achimenes.* As these go out of bloom, they should be placed in a frame to ripen the tubers. *Azaleas* (late-flowering). These must be re-potted and so trained that the foliage is properly drawn out before winter. *Chrysanthemums* should be disbudded. *Climbing plants* should be cut back to keep the

553

place in order. *Lilies* that have flowered require less water. *Pelargoniums.* Preparatory to cutting these down, those which have gone out of flower should be stood outdoors to ripen the wood.

SEEDS TO SOW.—All sorts of *annuals* for winter flowering. *Clarkia, cyclamen, geraniums* and *pelargoniums, schizanthus* and *stocks.*

CUTTINGS.—Cuttings of *arabis* and various other hardy rock plants may now be struck. Also *fuchsias, geraniums, heliotrope, hydrangeas* and all *half-hardy* plants.

POTTING.—*Camellias.* If these were not shifted last month, this should be done now. *Calceolarias, Chinese primroses* and *cinerarias* should be potted-off from seed boxes when large enough. *Chrysanthemums.* The potting-up should be completed. *Cyclamen* should be re-potted into flowering pots, old plants being started. *Freesias* and *Roman Hyacinths* should be potted for flowering in December. *Lachenalias* benefit by early potting. *Primulas* should be divided and be replanted in 6-inch pots.

The Vegetable Garden

General Operations.—Bean stalks and the remains of gathered crops should be removed. A row or two of French beans should be left for seed. Pests demand continual attention and must be exterminated. *Artichokes.* These must be cut down as the heads are gathered. *Globe artichokes* must not be allowed to flower. *Asparagus.* Beds must be kept clear of weeds. Unless seed is wanted, the bearing heads should be cut off. *Cucumbers* (*ridge*), *tomatoes* and *vegetable marrows* require the same attention as during July. *Mint* and *other herbs* may still be picked. *Onions* that are ripe may be harvested. *Potatoes* (early), which are being reserved for seed, should be dug up and spread in the sun. *Runner beans* should be stopped when they reach the top of sticks, the beans being picked as soon as ready. *Shallots* can be harvested in many places. *Vegetable marrows* can be cut.

EARTH UP.—*Cardoons* (towards end of month), *celery* and *leeks* need similar treatment.

SEEDS TO SOW.—*Cauliflowers* (for early summer), *colewort, corn salad, endive* (a few rows for early crop), *lettuce* (every fortnight), *onions* (for next season). *Radishes, small saladings, red cabbage* (on tilled ground) and *spinach* (for winter use), also *turnips.*

PLANT OUT.—*Broccoli, cabbages, celery* (do not earth up until November), *coleworts, endive, late greens* (in shady beds).

Under Glass (Vegetables).—SEEDS TO SOW.—*Cauliflower* (sow seed in a frame, but uncover as soon as the seed is up).

The Fruit Garden

General Operations.—Wall fruit should be protected as it ripens from wasps and birds. Earwigs and snails should be trapped. The fruit should be exposed to the sun as much as possible. Summer-pruning may be continued, and fruit trees may be budded. Bands round fruit trees should be examined, the pests being destroyed. *Apples, pears* and *plums* require thinning out if the crop is too heavy. *Apricots, peaches* and *nectarines* should be exposed to the sun as much as possible. *Cherry* trees should be washed as soon as the fruit has been gathered. *Loganberries* and *Raspberries*. Canes that have borne fruit should be cut down. *Plums* are best ripened off in a semi-dark store. *Strawberries*. All unwanted runners must be taken off, the straw litter being removed. New beds may now be planted.

SEPTEMBER

General Garden Work

Keeping the garden tidy is the principal work of the month. Dead flowers should be picked. Pea-haulms and vegetable refuse must be collected, being then covered with earth and allowed to rot. The collection and drying of certain seeds needs to be done. As ground becomes vacant, it should be dug and manured. Lawns need sweeping, and this is the best month for sowing grass and for making new lawns.

The Flower Garden

General Operations.—Peat, leaf-mould and other soils should be collected and stacked for future use. The tall-flowering plants should have plenty of support; they will need it, for heavy winds are prevalent this month. The hoe should be kept busy and weeds should be destoyed. *Climbing plants* should be cut back, being fastened up where necessary. *Dahlias* should be tied-up, disbudded, and the shoots thinned. Earwigs should be trapped and choice blooms should be protected against the sun's rays. *Hollyhocks* should be treated in the same way. *Rock plants* require attention. They should be trimmed and cut back where necessary, being propagated by means of division or by cuttings. *Roses*. Perpetual roses may still be cut back, and late briars may still be budded. *Stocks* that were budded early in the season should have the ligatures loosened; wild shoots from the stock being shortened back to about ten leaves if the bud is still dormant.

SEEDS TO SOW.—For flowering the following spring or early summer suitable hardy *annuals* should be sown. A few *antirrhinums* sown now may last through the winter. *Sweet peas* may be sown.

CUTTINGS.—Cuttings of *ageratums, antirrhinums, blue marguerites, centaureas, fuchsias, gazanias, hollyhocks, lobelias, zonal pelargoniums* (geraniums), *heliotropes, penstemons, petunias, roses*, all *bedding plants*, and many alpines can now be struck.

PLANT.—*Anemones* and *spring-flowering bulbs*, such as *crocuses, tritonia, narcissi, scillas, snowdrops*, etc., but not *tulips*. *Irises* and *hardy liliums* can also be planted.

PLANT OUT.—The transplanting of numerous early-flowering *herbaceous plants* and *shrubs* may now be carried out. *Carnations*. Rooted layers and seedlings may be planted out. *Pansies*. Early-rooted pansy cuttings may be planted out and seedlings can be pricked out in the reserve garden. Offsets of *polyanthuses* and *auriculas*, and seedlings of the former, should be planted out in reserve garden.

555

Under Glass.—Damping down should not be effected quite so often in the greenhouse. The assistance of a little heat will be needed for plants like *coleuses* and *iresines*. The plants can do with the sun now, so the shading may be washed off. Ventilation should be given freely during warm periods, water being applied carefully.

Achimenes, *begonias* and *gloxinias* should be watered until the foliage fades.

Achimenes and *gloxinias* may then be removed from pots to be stored. *Begonia* tubers should remain in the soil and should be kept frost-proof.

Climbers. Any climbers that have finished flowering should be trimmed. *Sub-tropical plants* outdoors should be brought inside now.

Tree carnations should be kept from flowering during summer. *Chrysanthemums* for winter decoration should be brought indoors. *Heaths* should be examined for mildew. *Violets* should be lifted and planted near the glass in frames, plenty of air being given. Syringing should be attended to daily.

SEEDS TO SOW.—*Clarkia, godetia* and *schizanthus.* Also *pansies* and *violas.*

CUTTINGS.—Cuttings of *bedding* and *rock plants* may now be taken. *Buddleia* and *ceanothus* cuttings should be struck in a cold frame. All cuttings taken last month should be hardened off.

POTTING.—*Calceolarias* and *cinerarias.* Suckers from old shoots should be potted-off and seedling plants should be potted-on. Hardy and half-hardy plants for room and conservatory should also be potted-up. *Chrysanthemums* should be shifted and other plants potted-on as necessary. *Pelargoniums* intended to flower the following May or June should be ready for removal to flowering-pots. As soon as they are sufficiently ripe, plants for late summer and autumn flowering should be potted-off or placed in frames.

Stocks which were sown in pans, or in reserve garden, in August, should also be potted-up.

The Vegetable Garden

General Operations.—Frequent hoeing between growing crops is still important. *Onions* should have their necks bent down. Those which are ripe should be harvested. *Potatoes* should be lifted when the haulms decay. *Tomatoes.* Leaves shading the fruit from the sun should be picked off carefully and the fruit should be thinned if necessary.

SEEDS TO SOW.—*Borecole* or *kale* (spring varieties), *cauliflowers, chervil, corn salad, mustard and cress* (for succession), *onions, radishes, spinach* and *watercress.*

PLANT OUT.—*Cabbages* (on ground vacated by onions), *coleworts, endive, kohl rabi, lettuces* (sheltered spot), *savoys, spinach* (sown towards end of July or early August), *winter greens,* etc.

EARTH UP.—*Celery* and *onions.*

Under Glass (Vegetables).—SEEDS TO SOW.—*Cauliflowers* and *lettuce* may be sown. Also *parsley* and *tomatoes* (for early spring). *Parsley* may be lifted and planted in cold frame.

Tomatoes sown in August should be potted-out singly in small pots. *Endive* and *lettuce* should be pricked out.

556

The Fruit Garden

General Operations.—All wall fruit which is now ripening should be protected. Fruit trees may still be budded; summer pruning may be continued. Trees that need root pruning should be attended to. This is a good time to buy new fruit trees. *Apples, pears* and *plums*. If the crops are too heavy, they should be thinned, and grease-bands should be applied where necessary. Early varieties of *apples* and *pears* which do not keep must be gathered, and all young shoots on *pear* trees should be stopped. *Apricots, peaches* and *nectarines* should have their future bearing shoots nailed in closely. A final thinning should be made, any leaves that shade the fruit being removed. *Cherries* require very little shortening back, but cut away cross and interior shoots in standard trees and spur back those shoots which are too close together. *Currants.* These should have all side sprays pruned away. *Gooseberries.* All shoots should be stopped and thinned. *Raspberry* canes that have fruited should be cut down and the young growths thinned out to from three to four. These should be stopped when sufficiently high. *Strawberries.* All superfluous runners should be removed; these may be replanted if new plants are wanted.

OCTOBER

General Garden Work

Leaves should be swept from lawns and paths, being heaped up in an odd corner of the garden, where they are left to decay after being covered lightly with moist earth. All vacant ground should be made ready for planting. The first frosts may make their appearance this month, hence the need for taking all tender plants indoors or otherwise protecting them. Preparation should be made for any alterations in the design of the rock garden or the flower garden, the plants being removed to the reserve garden. Gravel paths and walks should be rolled and repaired where necessary. Turf should be laid this month.

The Flower Garden

General Operations.—*China asters* and plants of a similar nature that have flowered can be lifted, put into pots, and taken indoors to bloom. *Carnations, pinks, auriculas, polyanthuses,* etc., should be placed in winter quarters. *Anemone* beds should be prepared and the tubers may be planted this month. *Bulbs.* The main planting of *tulips* should be made; practically all spring bulbs that have not been planted should be got in without delay. *Dahlia* and *hollyhock* seed should be gathered. *Dahlia* tubers must be lifted and stored. Choice *hollyhocks* should be potted up and wintered under glass. *Eranthis* (winter aconite) may be planted or propagated by division. *Gladioli* corms should be lifted and stored.

PROPAGATION.—All kinds of *herbaceous* plants may be divided.

CUTTINGS.—Cuttings of *anagallis, bouvardias, calceolarias, cerastiums, periwinkles, phloxes, ragwort, roses, salvias, various shrubs, verbenas,* etc., can now be struck.

SEEDS TO SOW.—*Sweet peas* may be sown.

557

PLANT OUT.—*Biennial* and *perennial* seedlings, *hardy spring-flowering* plants of all descriptions, also seedling *pansies*.

Under Glass (Flowers).—The nights are apt to be frosty, so the temperature of the greenhouse must be watched carefully. Air must be cautiously given and cold winds avoided. All plants before being taken into the greenhouse should be thoroughly examined and carefully cleaned. *Pelargoniums*. Great care must be exercised in watering as the leaves must be kept dry. No syringing or sprinkling is permitted. Seedlings, such as *clarkia, schizanthus* and *sweet peas*, should have their tops pinched out. *Begonia* tubers may now be stored. *Calceolarias* (shrubby). Cuttings of these may be taken. *Camellias* require attention. *Carnations* (*perpetual*) and *chrysanthemums* require disbudding.

POTTING.—*Arum lilies* should be re-potted. After *bulbs* have been potted for forcing, they should be left plunged in ashes until the shoots are ¼ inch long, when they should be removed to a cold frame, being shaded from strong light for a few days. *Hardy* and *half-hardy* plants for indoor flowering should be potted-up. Pot *roses* should be brought in from the open. Cuttings of *pansies* may be potted-up for indoor flowering.

The Vegetable Garden

General Operations.—The hoe must be kept busy between growing crops. The ground should be cleared after *beans* and *peas* and dug or trenched so that it may lie fallow during the winter. All roots to be stored must be sound. *Asparagus*. Asparagus foliage should be well-ripened before being cut down. *Beetroot* and *carrots* should be lifted when the tops fade. *Cauliflowers* grown from seed in August should be pricked out and protected with a hand-glass. *Onions* and *turnips*. Seed beds should be thinned. *Potatoes*. Any remaining potatoes should be dug and stored for winter use.

EARTH UP.—*Cardoons* (choosing dry weather), *celery* and *leeks*.

SEEDS TO SOW.—*Corn salad* and *early peas* (under a fence or on a warm south border).

PLANT OUT.—*Cabbages, endive* and *lettuces* may be transplanted to a warm border or into cold frames. *Rhubarb* may be planted. *Radishes* and *spinach* may still be sown.

Under Glass (Vegetables).—*Cauliflowers*. Cauliflower seedlings should be pricked out and placed in frames. Those sown in frames last month should be thinned. *Endive* and *lettuces* can be had until Christmas by successional pricking out. *Rhubarb* may be forced by means of lifting roots of plants two or more years old and packing them in boxes in a warm, dark place. *Mustard and cress* may be sown for succession. *Parsley* may be lifted and planted in a cold frame.

SEEDS TO SOW.—*Radishes* may be sown in a frame or on a gentle hot-bed between rows of potatoes or other crops. *Tomatoes* may now be sown.

The Fruit Garden

General Operations.—Preparations should be made for planting and towards the end of the month planting itself may be commenced. Transplanting may take place, or old trees can be lifted so that the soil may be replenished. A commencement should be made with root-pruning those trees which require it.

Grease-banding should be done at once. *Apples* and *pears* may be gathered on fine days, the fruit being handled carefully. *Apricots, cherries, currants* and *gooseberries* should be pruned this month. *Figs.* The old fruit leaves and the naked old wood should be cut away to give ample room for the new shoots. *Loganberries.* Growths which have borne fruit must be cut away to ground level. *Raspberries.* Canes which have fruited must be cut out, three or four young ones being left to the stool. New plantations may now be made. *Strawberries.* All runners should be removed from the plants.

NOVEMBER

General Garden Work

All ground as it becomes vacant should either be deeply dug or trenched, a liberal application of manure being given to all soils, with the exception of those which are very light. Very light soil should be manured in the spring. Land requiring it should be drained this month, and all alterations to the garden design should be commenced as early as possible. Paths may be remade or new ones created. All rubbish must be collected, burnt, and dug in.

The Flower Garden

General Operations.—The flower-beds should be well-manured or treated with fresh loam; the soil should be dug before the frosts appear. Herbaceous borders must be forked over, and the stalks of all plants that have done blooming should be cut down. *Carnations, picotees* and *pinks* which were layered in September or October should be potted-off and placed in their winter quarters. *Dahlias* should be taken up and stored. Seedlings that have bloomed late will be the better for being potted and kept dry through the winter. *Hollyhocks* should be propagated from the whole stools or by eyes from the flowering stems, but should not be forced. *Pansies* may be potted-off as a reserve for filling up vacancies or for making new beds in the spring. *Peonies (herbaceous).* Propagate these by means of lifting the roots and pulling the stocks apart.

CUTTINGS.—The stock of cuttings should be sorted, and those which require similar treatment during the winter should be placed together in separate frames.

PLANT OUT.—*Anemone (tubers), Canterbury bells, pansies, primroses, Sweetwilliams, violets, wallflowers,* etc., may still be planted in suitable situations. *Flags* and *English* and *Spanish irises* should be planted. *Roses* should be planted or transplanted, stocks for next season's budding being now collected and planted. *Tulip* bulbs may be planted.

Under Glass (Flowers).—The temperature should be kept at from 40° to 45° F. at night. Ventilation must be given when weather is favourable. Water is only required in moderation now. *Auriculas.* The pots should be looked over occasionally for worms, and if present, lime-water should be poured over the soil. *Calceolarias* and *cinerarias* should have any dead leaves removed, being shifted when necessary into larger pots. Late seedlings should be pricked out and potted up. *Camellias* require careful attention for the buds will be swelling. *Pansies* should be placed in the warmest part of the house. *Pelargoniums*

559

should have dead leaves removed, the shoots should be thinned out and trained, and late-blooming plants should be moved into their flowering pots.

SEEDS TO SOW.—*Cyclamen* may be sown for the following year.

POTTING.—*Azaleas, deutzias* and similar shrubs for forcing may be potted up now. Bulbs may still be potted for flowering in late spring. *Dielytras, spiræas, lilies-of-the-valley*, etc., should be potted up.

The Vegetable Garden

General Operations.—The soil should be prepared for spring sowing, and the hoe should be kept busy among growing crops. All vegetable refuse should be collected and burnt, the ashes being preserved. *Artichokes.* Some of these should be lifted and stored in sand for future use. The crowns of globe artichokes should be protected with a good mulching of leaves. *Asparagus* should be cut down, if not already done, the bed being dressed with rotten dung. *Beetroots* and *carrots* should be lifted. *Broccoli* should be heeled over early in the month. *Cauliflowers* should have the leaves tied loosely together in a point over the crown. *Celery* and *leeks* require earthing up. *Endive* should be blanched in successive lots. *Parsnips* should be covered with a little litter. *Potatoes.* The seed potatoes should be gone over carefully. *Roots.* All roots should be taken up before the end of the month. *Scorzoneras* must be left in the ground until wanted. *Spinach* will continue to grow if thinned properly.

SEEDS TO SOW.—*Beans* and *peas* can be sown.

PLANT OUT.—*Cabbages, leeks, savoys* and other late plants that will stand through the average winter.

Under Glass (Vegetables).—Vegetables in frames should not be kept in too close an atmosphere. The plants should be exposed as much as possible, being treated almost as though they were growing out-of-doors. The object of keeping *carrots, cauliflowers, endive, onions, radishes*, etc., in frames is that they stand the winter better, but they will stand in the open and, therefore, it must not be considered that they are more tender than they really are. *Rhubarb* may be lifted and forced as last month, and *seakale* may be treated in the same way towards the end of the month.

SEEDS TO SOW.—*Beans* (French) may be sown. *Lettuces, mustard and cress, radishes* and small salading may be sown any time now.

The Fruit Garden

General Operations.—During this month the greater part of the planting and transplanting of fruit trees should be carried out. When pruning dwarf trees, make up your mind as to the exact form the tree is to assume when it attains full size, and prune accordingly. The shortening of the shoots will depend largely upon this. *Cherries* should be pruned as soon as the last of the fruit has been gathered. *Currants* and *gooseberries* may be planted and pruned while the weather is favourable. *Figs* on walls should have the superfluous shoots thinned out, the points of the wood selected for bearing being pinched out. *Strawberries.* Young plantations of strawberries should have some short dung spread between the rows.

560

DECEMBER

General Garden Work

Digging and trenching should be continued; the sooner this work is completed the better. Days when the ground is not too wet must be chosen. Planting, transplanting and pruning may still be carried on, but mild days should be selected. Leaves and stems should be collected, being allowed to rot for future use.

This is the best month for repairing frames, houses, and for overhauling tools, flower-pots, seed boxes, etc.

The Flower Garden

General Operations.—This is the best month for planting climbers. Every vacant space in the reserve garden should be dug and manured. *Annuals*, or *biennials*, which are wintering in the reserve garden may need protection. *Bulbs.* Beds of *anemones* and bulbs must be sheltered in bad weather. *Carnations*, *pansies*, *pinks*, etc., should be pressed firmly into the ground after each severe frost.

Christmas roses should be protected with hand-lights. *Dahlia* roots which are in store should be examined; choice sorts may be placed in heat towards the end of the month for flowering in May. *Michaelmas daisies* should be planted. *Roses.* It is still possible to plant rose trees, but the sooner this is done the better.

Under Glass (Flowers).—The greenhouse which is used for flowers in general should be run at a minimum temperature of from 40° to 45° F., as much air as possible should be given, and occasional smokings, washings and dippings will prove beneficial. A fire may be put on in the morning with the object of expelling the damp. Plants as they come into flower may be removed to the conservatory, young plants being shifted into their blooming pots as they require it. All bad leaves should be picked off plants. The advice given last month as to watering applies with equal force this month. A start may be made with the forcing of *azaleas*, *deutzias*, *lilac* and similar shrubs. *Cacti* should be kept quite dry this month. *Chrysanthemums* and *salvias* should be cut back as they go out of flower until sufficient cuttings have been secured; then destroy the old plants. *Freesias*, *Roman hyacinths* and *narcissi* must be very gently forced. *Lilies-of-the-valley* may be potted up for succession. *Pelargoniums.* The general stock requires careful treatment this month. The latest flowering varieties should have their final shift, and all will need careful training.

A temperature of 45° F. should be maintained, the plants being kept within two or three feet of the glass to prevent their drawing. Fumigation is necessary if green-fly is present.

The Vegetable Garden

General Operations.—The ground between growing crops should be hoed on fine days. Beds of *sweet herbs* should be cleared. Any plot where *celery* has been grown can be trenched and prepared for *onions*. Sprouting trays should be got ready for *potatoes*. Stored *potatoes* and *onions* should be examined occasionally.

PROTECT.—*Celery* and *parsnips* with litter. *Endive* by means of pots covered with litter. *Lettuces* under hand-lights or cloches. If frost is severe, loose litter should be placed round the protectors. *Rhubarb* and *seakale* should be covered for forcing.

SEEDS TO SOW.—A few *beans* and *peas* of the earliest kinds.

Under Glass (Vegetables).—The treatment of plants in frames is the same during December as during November.

Seakale may be lifted and forced as last month. *Asparagus* may be forced and *tomatoes* may be sown.

SEEDS TO SOW.—*Beans* (*French*) may be sown for forcing. A few early *peas* and *radishes*, also *mustard and cress*.

The Fruit Garden

General Operations.—The pruning of fruit trees may still be continued until the end of this month, except on frosty days. The trunks of trees may be sprayed with insecticide, and if all the trees have not yet been planted, it will be better to prepare the ground only, leaving the actual planting until the spring. Large standard fruit trees need pruning only every second or third year. This should be done now if due.

Apple and *pear* trees (established) should be thinned out and pruned.

Currants and *gooseberries*, if not already pruned, should be attended to at once.

Grapes. Outdoor vines should be pruned this month. *Raspberries* should have suckers removed from stools, no pruning until March.

Under Glass (Fruit).—*Peaches.* In the *peach-house* the fruit should be started this month, according to directions given in Chapter 41, Fruit in the Greenhouse. *See* p. 498.

Strawberries. The first batch of strawberries should be introduced; plants in 48-sized pots do best for early work.

INDEX

563

INDEX

564

567

INDEX

568

INDEX

INDEX